TIME AND CHANCE

TIME AND CHANCE

GERALD FORD'S APPOINTMENT WITH HISTORY

JAMES CANNON

HarperCollinsPublishers

HarperCollins books may be purchased for educational, business, or sales promotional use. For information please write: Special Markets Department, HarperCollins Publishers, Inc., 10 East 53rd Street, New York, NY 10022.

FIRST EDITION

Designed by Joel Avirom

Library of Congress Cataloging-in-Publication Data

Cannon, James M., 1918–
    Time and chance: Gerald Ford's appointment with history / by James M. Cannon.—1st ed.
      p. cm.
    Includes bibliographical references and index.
    ISBN 0-06-016539-1
    1. Ford, Gerald R., 1913– 2. Presidents—United States—Biography. 3. Nixon, Richard M. (Richard Milhous), 1913–. 4. United States—Politics and government—1969–1974. 5. United States—Politics and government—1974–1977. 6. Watergate Affair, 1972–1974. I. Title.
E866.C36 1993
973.924′ 092—dc20   92-53362

94 95 96 97 98 ❖/HC 10 9 8 7 6 5 4 3 2 1

FOR CHERIE DAWSON CANNON

"I returned, and saw under the sun, that the race is not to the swift, nor the battle to the strong, neither yet bread to the wise, nor yet riches to men of understanding, nor yet favor to men of skill; but time and chance happeneth to them all."

Ecclesiastes 9:11

CONTENTS

PROLOGUE

In the night the rain ended, and a brisk wind blew out of Canada across Lake Michigan and the Grand Valley, clearing the sky at dawn and stripping the last leaves from the red oaks on Sherman Street. The day was filling with sunlight as the big man came through the door of the red brick schoolhouse.

He was a good six feet tall, 195 pounds, with big hands, big shoulders, and trim at the waist for a man in his late fifties. His blond hair was thinning, shading to gray, straight, and cut close. A broad forehead and square jaw dominated an open and amiable face; the deep tan and sparse wrinkles around the blue eyes showed the long afternoons outdoors. He was neatly dressed—dark gray suit, white shirt, patterned silk tie, gray overcoat—and instantly recognized.

"Jerry! Take my place," a man waiting in line insisted. "No, no," the big man answered. "You stay right there. I'll just take my turn."

It was Election Day, November 7, 1972. Gerald R. Ford, Jr., U.S. Congressman for the Fifth District of Michigan and Republican Leader of the U.S. House of Representatives, was at his polling place in Ward 3, Precinct 1, of East Grand Rapids to cast his ballot.

For Jerry Ford, it was the beginning of a momentous day in his life. Twenty-four years earlier he had first campaigned for election to the House. Twelve times the conservative Midwesterners of Grand Rapids and the surrounding counties had sent Ford to Washington to represent their concept of American patriotism and self-reliance. In return he had listened to them, answered their letters, remembered their names, and given them his industry and his best judgment. His empathy with his constituents, and their belief in his integrity, had made Jerry Ford the best-known citizen of Western Michigan.

No one who saw this affable Congressman at the polls that day would suspect that he faced a critical decision. At noon, in a quiet corner of the

Finial Restaurant atop the Union Bank Building, Ford told Walter Russell, his close friend and campaign manager: "Walt, this election is my last chance to be Speaker. If we don't gain enough seats today to control the House, I'm going to get out of politics."

Ford's friends knew that the consuming ambition of his public life was to be Speaker of the House. As a thirty-five-year-old freshman in the House two decades before, Ford had set the goal of his life—to be sovereign over that part of Congress that most directly represents the people of the nation. Thus driven, Ford worked to get ahead. He made the right friends. He planned and watched for opportunity. He gambled and won election as Minority Leader—the highest position a Republican could reach in a House owned and operated by Democrats.

In a political odyssey that was to continue for eight years, Ford campaigned for the Republican victory in the House that would make him Speaker, recruiting candidates, raising money, stirring hope, pursuing his dream. To him, 1972 was his year of opportunity: If President Nixon won by the landslide that polls predicted, his victory could bring in enough new Republicans to take control of the House.

In the afternoon Ford flew from Grand Rapids to Washington on the last flight of his long campaign to reach the summit of his career and life. To Betty Ford, waiting at their home in suburban Virginia, the sound of the key in the door was blessed. Her husband was safely home again. She kissed him with the warmth of a new bride, and he wrapped a muscular arm around her slender shoulder.

She had prepared his favorite dinner, all-American fare, steak, baked potato, and butter pecan ice cream. TV tables were set up in the family room. Betty Ford knew their life together was coming to a crossroads, and she wanted as much as he to watch the election unfold.

In San Clemente, California, at 6:59 A.M. Pacific time, a gathering of fifty schoolteachers, children, and well-wishers waited at the tidy entrance to Concordia Elementary School. When President Nixon's motorcade arrived, Election Judge Mary Stamp came out to welcome the President and Mrs. Nixon. It was arranged that Nixon would be the first voter in his precinct, and his favorite White House photographer was standing by to record the event as the President dropped his ballot in the locked steel box, waved to the crowd, and disappeared into his limousine.

On the flight back to Washington aboard *Air Force One,* the President seemed in a somber mood of contemplation. By one account, "an atmosphere of serenity" dominated the eastward passage of the President and the grandees of the Nixon Court. Henry Kissinger, Bob Haldeman, John Ehrlichman, and Robert Finch—all seemed confident of Nixon's reelection. For lunch the stewards served a Nixon favorite, enchiladas and California champagne.

As the plane neared Washington, the President invited an eminent political guest to his cabin. He was Theodore H. White, the Homer of American Presidential election campaigns. Deep in thought, Nixon spoke to White of world peace, uneasy but possible, and of his hopes to bring an honorable end to the war in Vietnam.

Yes—Nixon's words were matter of fact—he expected to be reelected by a landslide, but that would be soon forgotten. There was foreboding in his voice: More important was whether the voters "shifted allegiances" away from the Democrats and elected a Congress that would support him, or fight him. White, listening intently, sensed in Nixon's words the shadow of Watergate.

In the White House that evening the President dined early with his family, then secluded himself in the Lincoln Sitting Room. There, alone, he turned on a tape of *Victory at Sea,* listened to the stirring patriotism of Richard Rodgers's martial music, and made notes on a yellow pad for the victory speech he expected to deliver later in the evening.

Across the majesty of America that day, in hamlet and city, in schoolhouse and firehouse, some seventy-six million Americans cast their ballots to renew the Republic.

At 7:00 P.M. Walter Cronkite, as well known and trusted as any public person in the Age of Television, came on the television screen to call the results for CBS. Defining the contest, Cronkite asked: "Will the President defeat Senator George McGovern by the landslide being forecast? Will the President carry with him the five votes he needs to control the Senate? He needs thirty-nine more seats to win the House, and Republicans have a chance to do it."

The first scattered returns flashed on the screen to show the trend—Nixon leading in Florida by 2-1, in Connecticut by 60 percent, in the South by 68 percent. The Nixon victory began in the East and rolled westward across the American political landscape. He won handily every state in New England except Massachusetts, every state in the South, and every state in the Midwest. The Nixon electoral vote mounted by great leaps—95 in the first hour, then up to 150, to 210, to 254. At 8:51:40 P.M. EST Cronkite made it official: "Michigan has put Nixon over the top."

As a personal political victory, it was unmatched to that time. More

Americans voted for Nixon in 1972 than had ever before voted for any Presidential candidate. He won 61.8 percent of the popular vote, forty-nine states, and 520 of 538 electoral votes. But in a stunning show of voter independence, the same voters who endorsed Nixon switched their votes and elected a Democratic Congress to oppose him.

There had never been such a two-sided election: Nixon won, by a great majority; but his party lost. By intent or by chance, the voters had put in office a President who mistrusted the Congress, and a Congress that mistrusted the President.

It was almost midnight when President Nixon came onstage before five thousand enthusiastic Republicans gathered for the Nixon-Agnew Victory Celebration at the Shoreham Hotel. Nixon seemed subdued. He observed the amenities of gratitude but sounded a note of caution. ". . . This will be a great victory depending upon what we do with it. . . . The greater the victory the greater the responsibility."

After his sobering words, he brought Agnew to center stage. "The real test of a campaigner is to go through the fire," Nixon said. Thrusting out his jaw and wagging his lordly jowls, he paid Agnew his ultimate compliment: "He can take it. And he can dish it out too."

Together, Nixon and Agnew raised their hands high for television's obligatory shot of political victory, and a mighty roar rose from the crowd. Nixon left the stage; Agnew remained, his long face aglow with joy. He seemed assured of four more years of the best job, and the best-paying job, he had ever had in his life. So suffused with pride was Agnew by what he assumed was the President's political endorsement that he could begin to think about his own campaign for President in 1976.

In the White House, long after midnight, President Nixon sat alone in the Lincoln Sitting Room. Yellow pad in hand, this master of political calculus was already confronting the ominous numbers: The Democrats would control the House 242 to 192, and the Senate by 57 to 43. "Melancholy . . . settled over me on that victorious night," Nixon wrote. Ever a pessimist, Nixon's victory intensified his worries about Vietnam, Watergate, and a hostile Congress.

There was reason to fear: The Democrats had never liked him. They hated Nixon, as Nixon hated them. Now that he had smashed McGovern, would this new crowd of Democrats—more liberal, more anti-Nixon than the old Congress—come after him on Watergate? Since the June burglary of Democratic Headquarters, Nixon, Bob Haldeman, John Mitchell, and others had contained the issue, denied it, kept it out of the campaign. But Watergate was still being investigated by the FBI and, even worse, by the press. Too many in the Nixon campaign and in the Nixon White House were involved; too many could become witnesses. One could crack. From his days in the House and Senate, Nixon knew that a determined Congressional Committee could destroy anyone.

In their family room in Alexandria, Jerry and Betty Ford watched with pride as their good friends, Dick and Pat Nixon, appeared onscreen for the celebration of the President's overwhelming victory. But the Nixon victory made Ford's own loss all the more painful. Ford switched channels and sat quietly as Cronkite and the other network anchors reaffirmed the end of his dream to be Speaker of the House. To his wife he said: "If we can't get a majority against McGovern, with a Republican President winning virtually every state, when can we? Maybe it's time for us to get out of politics and have another life."

They were words she doubted she would ever hear. "We had given so much of our married life to politics and government service," she thought. "I had been waiting and waiting for the day when we could have a life together." But she said to her husband, as she had many times, "Jerry, I will support whatever you decide to do."

Ford reflected. He was tired of traveling, and weary of the long and draining watches on the House floor. He was frustrated; in the daily battles over laws and programs, his team almost always lost. He did not like dealing with some of Nixon's men, particularly Haldeman, John Ehrlichman, and Charles Colson. "They just seemed to think that we in Congress were their patsies." He had given the best years of his life to public service and was proud of that; but in his head and in his heart he knew it was time to leave politics.

Some sense of obligation told Ford he should stay through Nixon's second term. Then he would leave public office in January 1977, after twenty-eight years in the House, and practice law or go into business. The more he thought about such a future on that Election Night, the more his disappointment turned to optimism.

For these three men—a victorious but fearful President, an exuberant and unsuspecting Vice President, and a disappointed but resolute Congressman—November 7, 1972, was the day that turned their lives. From that day forward, events would bear Richard Nixon, Spiro Agnew, and Gerald Ford toward an appointment with history.

An American tragedy was coming; indeed, it had already begun. Within twenty-one months after the 1972 Election President Nixon and Vice President Agnew would be forced from office in disgrace; and fate or destiny or kind Providence would replace Nixon with the one man uniquely qualified to become President at a unique moment in the life of the Republic.

The enormity of President Nixon's crime after Watergate and the outcry for his impeachment obscured the qualities of his successor, then and later. As certain as Nixon's fall was the choice of Ford to be his successor. More than any other man in American public life at that moment, Gerald Ford personified what Richard Nixon was not. Ford was a man of his word. He told the truth. He could be trusted. He was honest and forthright. He was a thoughtful man, fair, forgiving, and tolerant. Everybody who knew Ford liked him; he had no enemies.

The political forces and events that put Ford in position to save the Presidency and reaffirm the legitimacy of the Federal government somehow took into account the unassailable merit of the man and his qualifications to lead the nation out of the political and Constitutional peril brought about by Watergate.

From its beginning the America democracy has had the good fortune to produce a leader, often from an unexpected quarter, whose character and actions fit the tide of history. So it was on August 9, 1974, when this good and honest man, this obscure and stolid workhorse of a Congressman from the heartland of the nation, came to the rescue of the American government. To Gerald Ford was given the responsibility to move America from untruth to truth, from darkness to light. To him came the formidable challenge to restore the integrity of the very institution of the Presidency.

This is a story of the worst and the best in American politics and public life, an account of the political crime of the century and its consequences. It is the tale of two men—Nixon and Ford—who were political contemporaries and close friends, yet as different in character as night from day.

Only one American President reached office without the vote of the people. The qualities of character that placed Ford in the Presidency run like golden threads to his childhood, leading back to a time and a place and a family that instilled in the boy the integrity, loyalty, courage, stamina, ambition, patriotism, idealism, and the habit of hard work that became part of his being. These threads of character led this young man into public life, brought him to be respected and honored by those who knew him best, and finally ordained that he become the President of the United States. And yet, Jerry Ford's own life began in shadow.

1

A BOY'S LIFE

Leslie King first struck his beautiful young bride on their honeymoon. It happened in the new and elegant Multnomah Hotel in Portland, Oregon, on September 27, 1912. The groom and his new wife, Dorothy Gardner King, were on the elevator when a man stepped in and took off his hat, as was then the custom. She nodded slightly to acknowledge the stranger's courtesy. As the newlyweds walked away from the elevator through a marble and crystal reception room, King accused her of flirting. In tears, she said she was just being polite, responding to a gentleman's good manners, as a lady should. Her denial only made him more angry.

The new husband, according to court documents filed later, "became enraged . . . and set upon her, called her vile and insulting names . . . struck and slapped her in the face and about the head." She was twenty years old, a bride of three weeks in a strange city, frightened, and far from home.

Dorothy Ayer Gardner and Leslie Lynch King had been married in a beautiful ceremony in her family church in Harvard, Illinois. Their wedding trip, a gift from his wealthy father, would take them on a luxurious journey from Illinois to the Pacific Northwest, along the Coast through California, and eastward through Denver to Omaha, where they would make their home.

After the episode at the Multnomah Hotel the two patched things up and resumed their wedding trip. Five days later, in their private room on the Pullman from San Francisco to Los Angeles, King again struck and kicked his bride. At the Lankasham Hotel in Los Angeles the next day, he created another scene, called his wife "vile and insulting names," and threatened to send her home to her parents. Again the couple made up, and took the train to Omaha, where King had promised her they would have a cottage of their own. There she learned he had deceived her: There would be no cottage for two. He moved her in to the showy, fourteen-room mansion dominated by his prosperous father and strong-willed mother.

In their first week in his parents' home, King attacked his bride again, threw her trousseau into her trunk, and ordered her out of the house. She left, took a carriage to the train station in Omaha, and rode home to her mother and father.

In Harvard, Illinois, a strait-laced small town of 3,500, Dorothy Gardner King kept her story within the family. In 1912, abuse of a wife by her husband was hushed up, told only to the family doctor or minister. Her parents wanted no gossip about their daughter.

The Gardners were among the most prominent families in Harvard. Levi Gardner, son of a Scottish immigrant and farmer, owned the leading furniture store and a thriving real estate business. He had been elected Mayor at thirty-two. His wife, Adele Augusta Ayer, was a daughter of the town's founding family. She took pride in her New England ancestry, her membership in the Daughters of the American Revolution, and in bringing up their two daughters, Tannisse and Dorothy, with the social graces. Theirs was a warm and loving home. There were books and music in the gabled, two-story roominess of the house on Church Street, set back in a neighborhood of other fine homes, shaded lawns, and genteel behavior.

For Dorothy's college education, the Gardners chose a small school in Knoxville, Illinois, that attracted young women of refinement and wealth from the Midwest and beyond. There, in the spring of 1912, Dorothy Gardner first met Leslie King, who had come from Omaha to visit his sister Marietta, a classmate and close friend of Dorothy Gardner.

Family legend has it that the attraction between Leslie King and Dorothy Gardner was mutual and instantaneous. King was infatuated by the fair and buxom brunette with a quick smile, enthusiasm for life, and uncommon energy. Dorothy, in turn, was fascinated by the tall and handsome blond with his big open face, blue eyes, strong jaw, and muscular shoulders. He was thirty, older by ten years, but that seemed unimportant. A dashing fellow, King charmed Dorothy with his tales of Western life and impressed her with his plans for the future.

The Gardners already knew a lot about the King family from Marietta, who had visited in their home. The father, Charles Henry King, had migrated from Pennsylvania to Nebraska, organized and ran a stage coach line to Wyoming, helped to expand the Burlington railroad line westward, opened supply stores and warehouses in towns along the railroad, bought ranch land, and started the first bank in Casper. At the turn of the century an Omaha newspaper estimated Charles King's net worth at ten million dollars, an extraordinary fortune for those times.

After a brief courtship of Dorothy Gardner, Leslie King went to Levi Gardner, as was the custom of the time, to ask for his daughter's hand in marriage.

What are your prospects? Gardner asked King.

King told Gardner that he had thirty-five thousand dollars cash in a bank in Omaha, earned a salary of $150 a month for managing the wool storage business that he and his father owned, and that his profits from that business and other investments brought him an income of six thousand dollars a year.

Satisfied that King could provide for his daughter in comfort, and convinced, as was Mrs. Gardner, that the two were devoted to each other and sure to find happiness, Levi Gardner gave his consent.

Their wedding, in Christ Episcopal Church on Saturday, September 7, 1912, was a significant social event in Northern Illinois. Chicago's newspapers published accounts of the wedding, and the *Harvard Herald* put the story on the front page. "The bride's gown," the *Herald* reported, "was of white satin covered with real Breton lace . . ." Marietta King, in pink satin and jeweled chiffon, stood with her close friend as maid of honor. The groom brought a large contingent from Omaha, including his parents and four groomsmen. At the reception in the Titcomb mansion, the *Herald* reported, "many Harvard people met the young Omaha man who has won one of the most popular of Harvard young ladies as his bride. . . . He is a young man of good repute and is highly regarded as a business man." After the reception the wedding party rode in a convoy of Cadillacs and Pierce-Arrows to the new brick railroad depot to see the bride and groom off as they boarded the Pullman car to Minneapolis. As Dorothy Gardner King waved good-bye to begin her new life, Levi and Adele Gardner had never seen their daughter so happy.

Only seven weeks later the bride came home to Harvard and shocked her parents with her story. Then, some days later, Leslie King showed up in Harvard at the Gardner home. In remorse for his brutishness, he pleaded with Dorothy to return with him to Omaha. On his promise of good behavior and his commitment that they would not live in his parents' home, she relented.

Back in Omaha he moved his bride into a small and depressing basement apartment. He was in debt, he revealed, and could not afford anything better. She realized that he had misled her father about his means and ability to support a wife.

More disappointments were to come. King had promised his wife that they would go to Harvard for Christmas—it was always a happy celebration in the Gardner home—but he told her he did not have the money. Her father sent her seventy-five dollars for train fare for both, but King refused to go, or to let her go. So she stayed on in Omaha and bought presents for the King family. They gave her nothing, she later told the court, and she spent Christmas Day alone in the dark apartment.

Lonely, missing the happy times with her family, Dorothy discovered during the Christmas holidays that she was pregnant with Leslie King's child.

On New Year's Day, Marietta King took her sister-in-law out of the cramped apartment to a theater matinee, and both enjoyed the outing. But when Dorothy got home, her husband was furious, called her "vile and insulting names, tore up everything in the apartment, and ordered her to leave."

Through the bitter winter and early spring of 1913 Dorothy King remained in the apartment, making the best of her new life, tolerating her husband's quick wrath and stingy ways. She was forced to go to his office each month and ask the bookkeeper for money for rent and food. Her mother came to visit, but cut her stay short when King ordered her to leave.

In June Dorothy asked her husband to allow her mother to come to Omaha for the birth of her child, and King consented. His parents were away, so they moved into the family mansion. There, at 3202 Woolworth Avenue, on Monday, July 14, 1913, the hottest day of the year in Omaha, Dorothy Gardner King gave birth to a son. He was to become the thirty-eighth President of the United States.

At the father's insistence, the child was given the name of Leslie L. King, Jr.

A day later the new father was berating his wife again.

The physician who attended her told King that for the sake of his wife's health he must stop railing at her. Concerned for the new mother and baby, the doctor assigned a nurse to stay with her at all times. King ordered his mother-in-law out of the house, but she refused to leave. King, Mrs. Gardner told the court, threatened to shoot her daughter.

Weakened by the birth of the child, and in great pain, the young mother sent a telegram to her father in a desperate cry for help. When he arrived, she told him it was impossible for her and her child to remain with King.

Gardner also talked with his son-in-law. King agreed they should separate, and added: "The sooner they leave, the better." Gardner proposed to move his daughter and grandson into an Omaha hospital. But the doctor said she was too ill for any move, and told King that he must give his wife the rest and the time necessary for her recovery.

King consented. He told his father-in-law that his wife, baby, and Mrs. Gardner could stay until "Dorothy is up and about," and able to travel to Illinois. Believing the problem resolved, Gardner returned to Harvard.

As soon as he left, King ordered his wife's nurse to leave. She refused, insisting that the doctor had ordered her to stay. A few days later King threatened his wife, son, and mother-in-law with a butcher knife. The nurse, fearing for their lives, called the police, who had to restrain King.

Again Dorothy telegraphed her father, who caught the next train to Omaha. By the time he arrived King had secured a court order that blocked the Gardners from seeing their daughter. Dorothy's parents left Omaha and waited in Council Bluffs, Iowa, across the state line.

When King was not watching, Dorothy telephoned a lawyer, who advised her to leave immediately. Afraid of what her husband might do, she did not even take time to pack. With the nurse on guard, she wrapped her sixteen-day-old baby in a blanket and fled the King mansion. Outside she found a carriage for hire and took it across the Missouri River bridge to Council Bluffs. There she joined her parents, and they all boarded the train for Chicago. It was July 30, 1913—less than eleven months after her marriage.

To avoid embarrassment to herself and to her parents, Dorothy Gardner King did not return to Harvard but moved in temporarily with her sister, Tannisse, and her husband in Oak Park, Illinois. By letter she retained an Omaha lawyer, Arthur C. Pancoast, and asked him to file for divorce. King got into court first and charged that his wife had deserted him. In her countersuit she detailed the history of his conduct from the first blow King struck on their honeymoon to his brandishing a knife over her as she lay helpless in bed with her baby. Pancoast produced her nurse, police, and other witnesses to verify her account of a violent and abusive husband. On December 19, 1913, the Omaha court found Leslie King "guilty of extreme cruelty," decreed the marriage ended, and entrusted "sole custody, care, nurture, training and rearing" of the child to the mother. King was ordered to pay his former wife three thousand dollars for back alimony, seventy-five dollars for her Victrola that he refused to send to her, and twenty-five dollars a month in child support until their son reached the age of twenty-one.

King refused to pay anything. The Court moved to seize his assets and found he had none. Deep in debt, he turned to the bottle. He sent word to his mother: "I am going to drink up every dollar I can get." Charles King fired his son from the wool firm for "inattention to business, his unauthorized overdrafts of his personal account, and increasing displeasure about his conduct."

The elder King told the court: "The trouble between Dorothy and Leslie was much against my wishes." He agreed to pay the twenty-five dollars monthly in child support.

For a proper young woman who had led a sheltered life, Dorothy Gardner King's brief marriage to Leslie King was a brutal end to innocence. Yet she came out of the experience with a resolute self-confidence and sunny optimism that remained with her all her life.

Going back to live in Harvard, however, was unacceptable in that era of propriety; so Levi and Adele Gardner left Illinois and moved to Grand Rapids, Michigan, where he had invested in real estate. There the Gardners bought a comfortable house and invited their younger daughter and baby grandson to live with them. It was the kind of city, the Gardners hoped, where Dorothy and her boy could begin a new life.

Grand Rapids, Michigan, in the first decades of the twentieth century was more than a city; it was America at its best, a community of great expectations.

A boy could grow up there with his days filled with sunshine—playing baseball, fishing in the river, swimming at the beach, and ice skating in the winter. He could get a fine education in the public schools, land a job at good pay with a future, start a business, open a store, invent a product and sell it, and become a success. He could marry a girl with the same virtues and moral values instilled in him, raise a family, and enjoy the good life.

Natural resources abounded in Western Michigan; but the people of Grand Rapids made it the community it was—a place of enterprise, self-reliance, opportunity. It began as a working man's town: Lumberjacks cut timber from the virgin forests of oak and pine and floated the logs down the Grand River. Sawyers cut and sized it into lumber; joiners and lathe operators turned it into furniture for schools, offices, and homes. As the forests were cut down, the working man learned new skills and turned to producing auto parts and machine tools.

There were also the rich: In the 1920s, Grand Rapids had a score of millionaires, and hundreds of entrepreneurs made tidy fortunes. The poor were not forgotten; they could count on the charity of churches and civic groups, and the generosity of a good neighbor.

The first outsider to envision the opportunity in this valley surrounding the swift rapids on the Grand River was Louis Campau, a thirty-five-year-old French trapper who set up a trading post in 1826. Attracted by the flat land, fertile soil, and abundant water in the region, Scottish and Irish farmers trekked from New England. After the Civil War came two great waves of emigrants. The first, from the Netherlands, injected into the mainstream of Grand Rapids' character a pronounced strain of Dutch mercantilism, thrift, and enterprise. Later, from Italy, Poland, Czechoslovakia, and Hungary, the hardy and the determined brought their strong backs, manual skills, spirit of liberty, and bright hopes.

Americans by choice, these new citizens spoke many languages, but they flew the same flag, marched in the Fourth of July parade, and together they sang the American anthem. As workers, they produced, in quality as well as quantity; and the city prospered.

In 1926, the year of the Grand Rapids Centennial, a home-grown Domesday book put the population at 169,000 and claimed with pride: "It is the forty-seventh largest city in the United States." This "Citizen's History," as the book was called, counted seven hundred manufacturing institutions— seventy of which made furniture. The city produced more school desks, church pews, wooden iceboxes, glass showcases, window sashes, and office chairs than any other city in the United States. Its good hands operated foundries and built auto bodies; its metal workers crafted products of copper, tin, brass and sheet steel. One factory in the valley produced more flypaper than any other in the nation.

A Grand Rapids man, Melville Bissell, invented the carpet sweeper, one of the first labor-saving devices for the American housewife, and built the first ones in the storeroom over his crockery store. This was a town where a man with an idea could get the backing and the money to build a factory, find the workers to make the product and the drummers to sell it. Transport was easy. The city was served by five steam and two electric railway lines; there were forty scheduled passenger trains through the terminal every day— and even daily air service to Detroit. A salesman or buyer coming to town had his choice of eight thousand hotel rooms.

The public school system ranked, according to a survey by experts from the University of Chicago, with "the best in the country." Grand Rapids was second in the nation in home ownership—more than half the population owned the houses they lived in. Frank Lloyd Wright designed two of his best residences for local merchants. The city ranked first in trees per citizen, thanks to the city forester's fifty years of assiduous plantings. Good city planning made it possible for any citizen to find a public park within half a mile of his house. Downtown there was an art gallery, four big movie houses, three impressive department stores, specialty shops of all kinds, and a new skyscraper built all the way up to twelve stories. The banks and savings associations were among the soundest in the Midwest; in Grand Rapids, people tended to save, not borrow. Tax rates were among the lowest in the state; half the money collected went to teachers and schools.

In the booming twenties the census of the city listed 134 churches, three modern hospitals, five golf courses, four flour mills, forty-nine bakeries, 196 woodcarvers, five makers of auto bodies, twenty stockbrokers, sixteen cigar makers, seventy-five auto salesman, 513 grocers, two daily newspapers, and 145 music teachers. The Civil War Veterans who held their annual convention there in 1925 pronounced Grand Rapids the most hospitable and patriotic city they had ever visited.

A glimpse of the city may be found in a 1935 novel, *Cast Down the Laurel*, written by a native, Arnold Gingrich, the founding editor of *Esquire* magazine. Of the thinly disguised Mill Center, Gingrich wrote: "Like Rome, it was built on seven hills. . . . The streets were broad and beautiful, arched from either curb with tall trees, and the white frame houses were set back overlooking smooth green lawns. It is doubtful if a city planning commission could ever find a place in which there would be less to be torn down in carrying out the scheme of the City Beautiful."

Grand Rapids, Michigan—a place from which a man can journey far and never leave. Many a man and woman who grew up there moved away in later life to escape the harsh winter of Western Michigan, but the spirit and character and values of the community abided within them. William Seidman, scion of a Grand Rapids family that created a national accounting and business management firm, went away to Dartmouth and Harvard and a career in business and public life; but he always came back. "As a place to live, as a place to grow up," Seidman said, "there was no better city in the country than Grand Rapids, Michigan."

So it was found to be by Levi and Adele Gardner, and by their young daughter and her infant son. In the fine house at 457 Lafayette Street, "Junie," as the child was called by his mother and grandparents, came out of the crib as a healthy, towheaded boy with a toothy grin and boundless energy.

At an Episcopal Church social in 1915, the first year of her new life in a new city, Dorothy Gardner King met a tall, dark-haired, and amiable bachelor. His name was Gerald R. Ford.

She found him even-tempered, courteous, and considerate. As he showed a serious interest in her, she made it a point to find out all she could about him. At twenty-four, he was just a year older than she. Born in Grand Rapids, he was only fourteen when his father was killed in a train accident. So he had to quit school to support his mother and sisters. In time he made his way up to a good job selling varnish and paint to the big furniture factories in town.

Jerry Ford worked hard, paid his bills, kept his word, went to church, voted Republican, and, so his many friends said, had a promising future. From Dorothy King's special perspective, her new beau was disciplined, gentle, self-confident, a man of his word, and respectful of a lady—everything her first husband was not. Ford had a ready smile, a booming laugh, which she heard often, and an affection for children, especially her baby boy.

For almost a year they courted; and on February 1, 1916, they were married in Grace Church, where they first met. With this second marriage, Dorothy Gardner Ford put behind her, in all ways save one, the terrible months as the wife of Leslie King. She also put behind her the two years of dependence on her parents, and devoted herself to Gerald R. Ford and to her son.

For Junie King, it was also a transformation. From the age of two, when his mother remarried, he was called Junie *Ford*, later Jerry Ford, and, in time, Gerald R. Ford, Jr. Although he was never legally adopted by his stepfather, from his earliest memory the boy and later the man looked upon Gerald R. Ford, Sr., as his father in fact as well as in name. "He was the father I grew up to believe was my father, the father I loved and learned from and respected," his stepson said. "He was my Dad."

In the memories of young Ford's childhood there is the big, black-haired, masculine presence—throwing him a football, playing catch, going fishing. "Dad, with some other men, owned a cabin on the Little South Branch of the Pere Marquette River, and he would take me there to fish, and we would walk in the woods and in the sunlight." He remembered coming home from Madison Elementary School, arriving at the rented two-family house on Madison Avenue with bruised elbows and skinned knees, to the warm comfort of his mother's arms and the attention and encouragement of "Dad."

His mother was a strict disciplinarian who recognized early that her son must learn to curb the quick temper he inherited from King. When the boy raged in anger, she reasoned with him or made faces to show him how ridiculous he looked. If reason did not work, she might twist his ear, or send him to his room to stay until he cooled off. After one episode of temper she had her son memorize Rudyard Kipling's poem "If." Remember Kipling, she said, "it will help you control that temper of yours."

Dorothy Ford's energy was renowned. She was a worker in her Episcopal parish; she was active in her garden club, her book club, her civic club, and the DAR. She collected old clothes, mended them, and delivered them, along with the bread she baked, to needy families. And she was a devoted wife and mother. By her second husband she had three sons—Tom, in 1918; Dick, in 1924; and Jim, in 1927. She provided a home, values, training, daily supervision over schoolwork, the careful examination of a report card. She imposed regular attendance at Sunday School and Church and created joyful times at Thanksgiving and Christmas. Within her own family she personified caring and discipline; she set standards and she met them herself. Strong of will, buoyant in spirit, resolute in misfortune, compassionate, kind, and certain in her beliefs in the Almighty, she imparted these qualities to her sons in great measure.

Reflecting on his happy childhood, Ford said: "I was very lucky. I was so lucky that my mother divorced my real father, who I hate to say was a bad person in many respects. She had a lot of guts to get out of that situation. When she moved to Grand Rapids and married my stepfather, that was just pure luck. We had a tremendous relationship, Dad and I. My stepfather had as much love for me, if not more, than his own three sons."

Gerald Ford, Sr., was determined that all his sons would have the education that he missed. He urged the Ford boys to excel in school, and never complained that circumstance had prevented him from completing his own education. "He never felt sorry for himself—about anything," Ford said. "He loved sports. He believed sports taught you how to live, how to compete but always by the rules, how to be part of a team, how to win, how to lose and come back to try again."

As a small businessman, Jerry Ford, Sr., believed the first principle was fair dealing, and the second, hard work. He personally guaranteed the paint he sold even if the manufacturer did not. In 1921 business was bad in Grand Rapids, and the Fords lost their house when the bank foreclosed on the mortgage. Ford came home to tell his wife and stepson: "Well, I'll just have to work harder." They rented a cheaper house at 649 Union Avenue and made friends with their working-class neighbors.

"He drilled into me the importance of honesty," Ford said. "Whatever happened, you were honest. Dad and Mother had three rules: Tell the truth, work hard, and come to dinner on time. Woe to any of us who violated those rules."

In his early school years Junie Ford began to stutter. In the first grade he discovered that he could write better with his left hand. After a brief attempt to force him to write with his right hand, his parents and teachers gave up, and the stuttering ended. From childhood on, Ford was right-handed standing up, and left-handed sitting down.

His twelfth birthday was one he always remembered: He became eligible for the Boy Scouts. He and five other boys joined Troop 15 at the Trinity Methodist Church. With three fingers raised, Ford took the Scout oath, memorized it, and never forgot it:

"On my honor I will do my best—

1) To do my duty to God and my country, and to obey the scout law;
2) To help other people at all times;
3) To keep myself physically strong, mentally awake, and morally straight."

His Scout master, Chuck Kindel, was the first Eagle Scout in Grand Rapids; with his coaching, Ford and the other Scouts in his troop moved up quickly. In three years all were Eagle Scouts. At Camp Shawondossee Ford got his first lessons in leadership, as an assistant counselor and swimming coach. As one of eight Michigan scouts selected to be a guide at Fort Mackinac one summer, Ford learned to meet and talk with people, and found he liked doing it.

When Ford was about thirteen, his mother mentioned to him, almost casually, that she had been married before, and that he had been born before she met Jerry Ford. "It didn't make a big impression on me at the time," Ford said. "I guess I didn't understand exactly what a stepfather was. Dad and I had the closest, most intimate relationship. We acted alike. We had the same interests. I thought we looked alike.

"I had never met the man she said was my father. I didn't know where he lived, couldn't have cared less about him. Because I was as happy a young man as you could find."

When Jerry Ford was in the sixth grade, his parents deliberated about where he should go to high school. As it happened, the school district lines converged on the block of Union Avenue where they lived. He could go to Central High, the establishment school for the upper middle class; Ottawa Hills, a newer school for the elite, or South High, the most diverse of the three. To South High came the children of working people, Italian-Americans, Polish-Americans, blacks, the poor youngsters who made it to high school, and a few students from enclaves of the well-to-do.

So important was the decision that the Fords turned for advice to a friend, Ralph Conger, basketball coach at Central. "You send Jerry to South," Conger said. "That's where he will learn more about living." It was the right choice: Not only did South High have the best teachers in Grand Rapids, but there Ford met a football coach who became a major influence in his life.

In the spring of 1927 Ford first tried out for a football team. On a bare dirt playground he and a hundred other eighth graders assembled in mismatched and ill-fitting uniforms. Picking teams, Coach Clifford Gettings looked at the blond and gangly Ford, five feet eight and 130 pounds, and said: "Hey, whitey, you're a center."

Ford did not even consider asking the coach why he should play center. "He saw me, and I had white hair, and he needed a center," Ford said. "That's how I became a center."

That fall Ford played first-string center on the freshman team at South High. "Coach Gettings was a stern taskmaster," he said. "I spent hours learning from him how to snap the ball back, leading a tailback a step in the direction he was going to run, putting it high and soft for a fullback coming into the line, getting it on the right hip for the punter. And then after you centered the ball, you had to be quick to block the opposing lineman who had the jump on you."

The South High freshmen played a full schedule, and Ford played every game, as center on offense and linebacker on defense. In his sophomore year, the first-string center on the South High varsity got hurt, and Ford, only fifteen, took his place. South High won the city championship, and Ford was all-city.

To his coach and to his teammates, Ford's relish for brute contact, aggressiveness, and competitive intensity made him a standout at South High. Aggressive as he was in athletics, in the schoolroom Ford came across to his classmates as an earnest and reserved boy, even shy. As a student he always had his lesson prepared. He listened more than he talked. Everyone liked him, in part because he was a football star, and in part because of his good nature and optimism about his fellow students. "Everybody has more good things about them than bad things," Ford told a high school friend. "If you accentuate the good things in dealing with a person, you can like him even though he or she had some bad qualities. If you have that attitude, you never hate anybody."

In his senior year Ford won a contest sponsored by the Majestic Theater to pick the most popular high school senior in Grand Rapids. The prize was a trip to Washington, D.C., with thirty other Midwestern youngsters for a tour of the White House, the Washington Monument, the Supreme Court, and Congress. Ford never forgot the experience of standing in the gallery of the House Chamber and seeing the House of Representatives in action. Back home he decided he wanted to be a lawyer. To get experience in public speaking he joined the school debating team, but he never did well at it.

His popularity at South High made him particularly attractive to the girls, but Ford had few dates as a youth. He had neither the money nor the time for social life. His pocket money came from mowing lawns and doing other odd jobs; his regular income came from working in a diner across the street from South High. The owner, Bill Skougis, hired the football stars as part-time help for his busy lunch trade, paying them with a free meal and two dollars a week.

One day in 1929, as Ford was making hamburgers and washing dishes at lunchtime, he looked up and saw a strange man standing near the door, watching him. For fifteen minutes the stranger stood there, saying nothing. "Can I help you?" Ford asked.

The stranger walked over and said, "Are you Leslie King?"

"No," Ford said.

"I'm your father," the man said. "You're Leslie King. I'm in town with my wife, and I would like to take you out for lunch."

Startled and hesitant, Ford said, "I'm working."

"Ask your boss if you can get off."

Ford went to see the owner. "Bill, this man wants to talk to me. He says he's my real father. Can you let me go have lunch with this person?"

Skougis looked over at the stranger and said, "Sure."

Ford took off his apron and walked outside, where a woman waited in a new Lincoln and a small girl played nearby. King introduced his wife of ten years, Margaret Atwood King, and their daughter.

At a small restaurant nearby King explained to his son that he found him by going to all the high schools in Grand Rapids and asking for Leslie King. At South High, when he was told there was no Leslie King enrolled, King asked: "Do you have a boy named Ford here?"

"Oh yes," the principal at South High said. "You mean Jerry Ford. He's at work at Skougis's across the street."

King boasted to his son that he owned vast acres of ranch land in Riverton, Wyoming, and had taken the train to Detroit to pick up a new Lincoln.

"Wouldn't you like to come out and live with us in Wyoming?" King asked.

"No," his son said. "I like it here."

As King talked, Ford studied his face, looking for some resemblance. In his mind were questions he wanted to ask: Why have you never tried to find me before? Did you come because I'm a football star and you can brag about it? Here I am, working for two dollars a week to make it through high school, and you can afford a new Lincoln—why have you never helped pay for my education?

Ford asked none of these questions. "I bit my tongue to stop myself from being impolite," he said.

As King took his son back to Skougis's diner, he said: "Can I help you financially?"

"Well, that would be nice," Ford said.

King gave his son twenty dollars.

Ford's meeting with Leslie King that day left its mark. "It was a hell of a shock for a sixteen-year-old kid," he said. "I was not frightened by him but by what I was going to tell my parents that night. And I was really terrified about that. He meant nothing to me. I had talked to him as a courtesy. I just hoped that my mother and dad would understand."

That night, after his younger brothers had gone to bed, Ford sat at the big oak dining room table to reveal what had happened. "Telling them was one of the most difficult experiences of my life," Ford said. "They did understand. They consoled me, and showed in every way that they loved me."

In his room that night he lay in the darkness thinking about the stranger who had suddenly broken into his happy life. As hard as he tried to find good in the person who claimed to be his father, he could not overcome his resentment. "Nothing could erase the image I gained of my real father that day—a carefree, well-to-do man who really didn't give a damn about the hopes and dreams of his son." He could not hold back the tears of anger. After a time he remembered a prayer from Proverbs that his Mother had taught him:

> Trust in the Lord with all thine heart; and lean not unto thine own understanding.
> In all thy ways acknowledge him, and he shall direct thy paths.

Over and over he repeated the words until at last he fell asleep.

The day that imprinted the family secret passed. Ford went back to football. In his senior year he was elected captain of the South High team that won the state championship. He was named all-state center and captain of the all-state team.

Of his all-Michigan high school center, Coach Gettings said: "Jerry was one of the hardest-working kids who ever played football for me, and totally dependable in every game. Center was one of the hardest positions. There was no quarterback underneath to hand the ball to; you had to pass the football seven or eight yards to a player in motion. I never saw Jerry make a bad pass. And on defense, he and another kid named Joe Russo made about ninety percent of the tackles."

For Ford, the football field was preparation for life. He learned to listen to coaching and perform his assigned job, that a team is greater than the individual players, and that the best performers may not get the most glory. He learned that a good attitude is infectious and can generate the extra effort that brings victory, and that defeat is inevitable—yet not an end but the first step in coming back. Ford thought of Coach Gettings as one of his greatest teachers, and there was one special lesson he remembered and followed: "You play to win. You give it everything you've got, but you always play within the rules."

The Great Depression struck America just as Jerry Ford, Jr., was thinking about college. In Grand Rapids, as in all the nation, factories closed and the best of American workers lost their jobs. For Jerry Ford, Sr., the Depression was a particularly hard blow. He bought a paint business three weeks before the stock market crashed in 1929. When his bank closed, the DuPont Corporation, knowing Ford's record for paying his debts, wired him to keep ordering supplies and to pay when he could. Rather than dismiss any of his ten employees, Jerry Ford, Sr., called them in and said: "We can pay you five dollars a week to keep you in groceries, and that's what I will pay myself. When times get better, we will make up the difference between the $5 and your regular pay, however long it takes."

Times were so hard that there seemed to be no way Jerry Ford, Jr., could get to college. The meager child support from grandfather King stopped when the old Omaha entrepreneur died a few months after losing most of his fortune in the 1929 stock market crash. When word reached Mrs. Ford that her first husband had inherited fifty thousand dollars, she asked a Nebraska court to order King to pay one hundred dollars a month so his son could attend college. She won a judgment, but the Douglas County Sheriff could not serve the order: King had moved to Wyoming, beyond the reach of the Nebraska Court, and again refused to pay anything.

Without Ford's knowledge, the principal of South High, Arthur Krause, decided to help Ford, who was not only a promising athlete but a National Honor Society student. Krause wrote Harry Kipke, coach of the Michigan football team, and invited him to Grand Rapids to talk to Ford.

Kipke did come to Grand Rapids, met Ford and his family, and took him to Ann Arbor. In that era there were no football scholarships at Michigan, but Kipke helped Ford find a job at the University hospital waiting on tables to earn his meals. Back in Grand Rapids, Ford wrote his new mentor:

June 8, 1931

Dear Mr. Kipke:

I want to thank you and Mrs. Kipke for entertaining me so wonderfully during my visit to Ann Arbor. I had a marvelous time and fully enjoyed every minute of the stay and if there is any way in which I can repay you I certainly would.

The more I see of Ann Arbor, the University, and the fellows who go there, the more I desire to attend school at Michigan. I've always wanted to be a student at the University since I was able to read about the prowess of their athletic teams and now it is almost a certainty that it will come true . . .

Sincerely yours,
Gerald Ford

A job waiting on tables was a start, but Ford had no money for tuition. Principal Krause called him in one day and said, "Jerry, tuition at Michigan is fifty dollars a semester, one hundred a year. I know your dad doesn't have that. But, you know, we have a bookstore at South High, and I think we ought to start a scholarship with the profits. I think we'll make the first award to Jerry Ford."

With that gift, and enough money saved from summer jobs to pay the rent, Ford could go to college. He and a basketball player found a third-floor back room in Ann Arbor with two army cots, a desk, and two chairs for four dollars a week. His stepfather's sister and her husband, who had no children, volunteered to send him a two-dollar check every Monday for spending money.

"Many people helped me," Ford said, "but football was my ticket to college. That's the only way I got to Michigan, and that was the luckiest break I ever had."

* * *

In mind and in spirit, Jerry Ford at eighteen was ready to leave home and home town, and go out into the world. Success—in athletics, classroom, and personal relationships—had instilled in him a quiet confidence, a readiness for any challenge. Grand Rapids as a community, and Dorothy and Gerald Ford, Sr., as parents, had put down the most solid of personal foundations.

From his mother Ford drew energy, self-discipline, and a sure and abiding sense of morality. From her and from his stepfather he learned to trust, and to be worthy of trust. Both taught, practiced, and enforced honesty, fairness, and self-reliance, a respect for learning, and the obligation of every citizen to take part in public affairs. In times of setback and misfortune, both demonstrated cheerful hope and resolution in putting things right again. Their good habits, their strong values, became those of the son in which they took such great pride and to whom they were both so devoted. When Jerry Ford left Grand Rapids to begin his new life, their values were his values. They went with him, and they remained with him.

2

LEARNING

Jerry Ford arrived at his rooming house in Ann Arbor in September 1931 with one suit, one pair of shoes, and twenty-five dollars in his wallet. He also brought along two ambitions—to make a name for himself on the football field and to do his best in the classroom to prepare for a career after college.

Like most state universities in the thirties, the University of Michigan drew from the abundance of the state's public high schools, bringing the rich, the poor, and the middle class to Ann Arbor to learn to be teachers and engineers, accountants and economists, architects, dentists, and pharmacists. By setting high educational standards and winning strong support from the Michigan legislature, a succession of university presidents built a great institution of learning. The Medical School and the Law School at Michigan were considered to be outstanding.

At that time the university had more than 25,000 undergraduate students, an excellent faculty, and an administration dedicated to education and to championship football. At a big game like Ohio State the stadium, which could seat 85,000, was packed with students, loyal alumni, and other cheering fans.

Ford pulled on his new blue-and-maize uniform for the first day of freshman football practice and found competition far more intense than at South High. The freshman team did not play other colleges; the varsity used the freshmen for practice against the next opponent. Ford was delighted: He learned from the Michigan scouts how other Big Ten teams played, and he could learn directly from Coach Kipke and the freshman coaches. Big and strong for a lineman at the time—he was six feet tall and weighed 180 pounds—Ford made first-string center on the freshman team. In spring practice he won the Morton Trophy, awarded to the first-year player showing "most improvement, best attitude, and greatest promise for the varsity."

In the classroom Ford was earning As in history, Bs in mathematics, and making friends. One day he was sitting on the steps of the Student Union when another freshman spoke to him. "I'm Dave Conklin. I was captain of the Battle Creek football team that lost to South High when you were captain. My brother is a senior in the Delta Kappa Epsilon fraternity, and he asked me to find out if you would like to be invited to a rush party for Deke." Ford did not know one fraternity from another but thanked Conklin and agreed to come to the party. He liked the clubby masculinity he observed at the Deke House, and was ready to pledge, but had no money. The Dekes gave him a job waiting on tables to earn his board. For the first time Ford began to mingle with wealthy friends; the fraternity opened new horizons. Through visits to the homes of his fraternity brothers he went for the first time to the theater in Detroit and to the opera in Chicago.

After Ford's outstanding record in freshman football, it was a terrible let-down to start his second year on the sidelines. When the 1932 season opened, Michigan had a junior at center, Chuck Bernard, an all-American. "So here I am, great prospects as a sophomore, and my competition is all-American," Ford said. For two years he was substitute center, on a Michigan team that was the undefeated national champion.

"Not playing was tough," Ford said, "but I learned a lot sitting on the bench. I learned that there was the potential always that somebody could be better than you. And Chuck was better overall. I was a better offensive center, but he was twenty-five pounds bigger and a better defensive center. Well, in those days, a coach had to choose and play one guy."

At the end of Ford's junior year, some of his admiring teammates told him they wanted to elect him captain in his senior year, but the tradition was to elect someone from the first team. Ford's competition was a classmate and close friend, Tom Austin, who played varsity tackle in their junior year. "That's fine," Ford told his friends. "That doesn't bother me. I would like to be captain. But Tom has played regularly, and I didn't. Tom has earned it."

In 1934, his senior year, Ford finally made center of the first team— which had the worst year of any Michigan team in fifty years, "In those days Harry Kipke's offense was called a punt, a pass, and a prayer," Ford said. "Well, we lost our punter. We lost our passer. All we had was a prayer, and that was not enough."

Ford played every Michigan game that year, made All-Big Ten, but missed out on being named All-American. At the end of the season the team voted Ford the most valuable player. Rarely did that honor go to a lineman.

In his last football game, Michigan lost to Northwestern. The next week Ford was invited by the Northwestern coach to play on the East team in the Shrine East-West charity game in San Francisco. "That was a great honor," Ford said. "Our team hadn't won games, so I never thought I would get that recognition." When Ford joined the other twenty-one players in Chicago on the train for San Francisco, he shook hands with Northwestern's star guard, Rip Whalen. "You know why you're here?" Whalen asked. "Because after we played Michigan I told our coach that you were the best damn center I ever played against, and that you ought to be in this East-West bowl game."

On the two-day train trip westward, four coaches of professional teams were aboard scouting the players. "None of them paid any attention to me going out," Ford said. "They were talking to all the big stars." In San Francisco, George Ackerson, the Colgate center who started the game, broke his leg two minutes later. "I was the only center left," Ford said, "so I went in and played the rest of the game, and had one of my best days ever."

On the train back to Chicago the professional coaches who had seen Ford perform on the field approached him about playing professional football. The Green Bay Packers offered him $110 a game for fourteen games; the Detroit Lions upped the offer to $200 a game. Ford thanked them but said no. "What I really wanted to do was to go to law school," Ford said, "and I thought maybe I could find some way to stay on at Michigan and do it."

But he was dead broke and one thousand dollars in debt. By his senior year Ford had moved up from washing dishes to house manager for the Dekes, but he could still not keep up with all his college bills. "My parents were having a terrible time with the paint company," Ford said. "They could not help me. So I wrote my real father in Wyoming and asked if he could help me. I never got an answer."

With his parents' permission he wrote Ralph Conger, the family friend who had first steered Ford to South High. Conger lent Ford the money so he could finish his senior year.

As graduation neared Ford went to Coach Kipke. "Coach," he said, "I want to go to law school here at Ann Arbor. Is there any chance you could put me on as an assistant coach?"

"Jerry," Kipke said, "I couldn't pay you more than one hundred dollars."

Law school at Michigan, Ford realized, was not possible. A month later Kipke telephoned. "Yale is looking for an assistant football coach," Kipke said to Ford. "Ducky Pond is in town, and I wonder if you could have lunch with Ducky and me today."

"Sure," Ford said. It could be a lucky break. Ducky Pond was the highly respected head coach at Yale; Ford had heard about him from Yale's end coach, Ivan Williamson, captain of the Michigan football team during Ford's sophomore year. At the lunch Ford discovered that Coach Pond already knew about him from Williamson, and that Kipke had strongly recommended Ford for the job at Yale. Pond invited Ford to come to New Haven for a weekend and to meet the other coaches. Ford liked what he saw, and Yale offered him $2,400 as an assistant line coach—but with a catch.

"Do you know anything about boxing?" Ford was asked.

"No, I never boxed in my life," Ford said. "But I can learn." He agreed to the terms: Coach football in the fall, boxing in the winter, football in the spring, and the whole summer off—for $2,400 a year.

"That was good money," Ford said. He could pay his debts. "And I had it in the back of my mind that if I did get to Yale, somehow I would find a way to go to Yale Law School."

It never occurred to Ford that he could not succeed as a student at Yale. He was leaving Michigan with a good academic record. Except for Cs in English composition and French, he had done well: As in history and in American government, and mostly As in fourteen economics and business administration courses. *Cum laude* he was not; a good steady student he was.

To his classmates, Ford was a rarity—a football star who also performed well as a student. The 1935 Michigan yearbook elevated Ford to its Hall of Fame with the citation: "Jerry Ford . . . because the football team chose him as their most valuable player; because he was a good student and got better grades than anyone else on the squad; because he put the DKE House back on a paying basis; because he never smokes, drinks, swears, or tells dirty stories . . . and because he's not a bit fraudulent and we can't find anything really nasty to say about him."

On graduation day in June, Ford was back in Grand Rapids, filling paint cans for the family business. Michigan mailed him his diploma, a Bachelor of Arts in Economics.

Home for the summer, Ford promptly acted to keep his promise to the Yale athletic director. He went to the Grand Rapids YMCA, signed up for a cram course in boxing, and started his lessons. He never became a good boxer, but he learned enough of the fundamentals to coach the sport at Yale.

On the threshold of his new life, Ford talked one evening to his mother and stepfather about an important matter that had long been on his mind. From infancy he had been known as Jerry Ford, Jr., but technically he was still, as his birth certificate said, Leslie King, Jr. "I wanted to take Dad's name legally," Ford said. "I was twenty-one, of age, and I could make the decision. It was my initiative, a decision on my part out of respect for him and love for him. I was about to begin my first job, and I wanted the record to be clear: So far as I was concerned, Gerald Ford *was* my father."

For his mother as well as his stepfather, it was the supreme compliment, and tears came as their son told them what he planned to do. Quietly, Ford put in his formal application to the Judge of Probate of Kent County for a change of name. On December 3, 1935, he became in law the person he had always believed himself to be, wanted to be, and made himself to be—Gerald Rudolph Ford, Jr.

Yale, in the autumn of 1935, was a superior private university for young men privileged by family connections, wealth, intellect, or all three. Well over half the new students that year had graduated from Andover, Exeter, Hotchkiss, Deerfield, and a handful of other prep schools in New England. They came to New Haven's Gothic gray to learn, to excel, and to enjoy, in the words of the school song, those "shortest, gladdest years of life."

"There was an air of luxury," said John Hersey, Class of '36 and later a Pulitzer Prize-winning author. "I was a scholarship student, and I saw with different eyes. We had, for example, waitresses in the dining hall, a menu from which you could choose your dinner, and maids to make beds and clean rooms for the boys." John Nelson, a Baltimore boy who went to Yale as a freshman in 1936, lived in Davenport College next door to a classmate who brought his string of polo ponies to Yale. "Every morning," Nelson said, "his groom would knock on his door to get his orders for the day."

Privilege there was, but learning was the foremost object at Yale. "I already knew I wanted to be a writer," Hersey said, "so I studied English literature, history, arts and letters. Yale was a challenge. I worked hard. I learned a lot. I thrived in the atmosphere. I played football because I liked the game, and did well enough to be a second-string end."

At Yale, football was one part of the splendid atmosphere, one item on the rich menu of choices—along with working on the *Yale Daily News*, discoursing after class with a favorite professor, singing with the Whiffenpoofs or the Glee Club, having a beer at Mory's, driving with the fellows up to Smith. Football was a pastime for young gentlemen at Yale, but at this game they could also excel: Larry Kelly, a Yale end, won the Heisman trophy in 1936; halfback Clinton Frank won it in 1937.

From his first days on the Yale practice field, Ford was a natural at coaching. One of his players was William Proxmire, a boxer and 150-pound end on the junior varsity football team who later became a U.S. Senator from Wisconsin. "Coach Ford was very, very conscientious," Proxmire said. "The players, for the most part anyway, were of a high order of intelligence, and they saw in Ford not only diligence, but a good mind, a first-rate mind."

"Some coaches were hotheads, always shouting, but Coach Ford was very calm and spoke to your intelligence," according to Robert A. Taft, Jr., another JV player who reached the U.S. Senate. "He taught the basics, blocking and tackling, by telling you how and showing you how."

Ford liked his new job. "I learned many things, that you had to fit in with the direction and style of your boss. You carried out your duties with the individual players; you had to show them how to play and inspire them personally to play up to the limit of their capability. And you had to be a good representative of Yale University as you traveled around to go to alumni meetings and tried to recruit good players."

For the first time in his life, Ford had extra money in his pocket, but he was as frugal as ever. He rented an inexpensive apartment, paid Ralph Conger the one thousand dollars he had borrowed to finish at Michigan, and opened a savings account in New Haven, with a specific purpose—to go to Yale Law School.

He mentioned it to the Yale athletic director. "Jerry, we're paying you twenty-four hundred dollars a year," his boss said. "You've done well, and at the end of your first year we're going to raise you to three thousand dollars. You have a full-time job. You can't go to law school."

Yale Law School also dismissed his request. An attendant in the admissions office pointed out that Yale Law accepted only one in four applicants, and politely advised Ford: "Why, 98 of the 125 freshmen entering the class are Phi Beta Kappa. Sorry."

Thus rebuffed, Ford temporarily put aside his law school plans, and began to look forward to the summer of 1936—and the first paid vacation of his life. A fellow assistant coach had spent summers as an intern forest ranger in Yellowstone National Park and suggested that Ford try for a similar appointment. Ford liked the idea—"It was better than filling paint cans." So he wrote Michigan Senator Arthur Vandenberg, a friend of his stepfather, got the job, and for seven hundred dollars bought a Ford four-door convertible for the trip.

Planning his journey, Ford decided to visit Leslie King, the stranger who had trespassed on his innocence a decade before. "Riverton, Wyoming, was on the way to Yellowstone," Ford said, "and I felt some kind of an obligation to stop by and say hello—even though he had never even answered my letter asking for help at Michigan. I must have also been thinking, 'There is bound to be some good in the person my mother first married, and I should find it.'"

Ford spent one night with Leslie King and his stepmother in Riverton. "It was a strained meeting," Ford said. "There was not much to talk about, but while I was there I could see that he had quite a bit of land, and seemed to be doing well." Neither brought up the son's letter to the father asking for one thousand dollars. Ford left the next morning.

Assigned to Yellowstone's Canyon Station, Ford spent three months in the park, directing traffic, shepherding tourists, fighting fires, and making new friends. His summer in Big Sky country instilled in him a great love of the American West and permanent respect for the National Parks system.

Driving east, Ford stopped off in Grand Rapids on his way to New Haven and talked at length to his parents about his exciting days in the West. In passing he mentioned his brief visit with Leslie King at the big ranch in Wyoming. Invigorated by his good summer, and enthusiastic about his second year of coaching at Yale, Ford drove to New Haven. On the way he again resolved to find a way to go to Yale Law School.

After her son returned to Yale, Mrs. Ford was stirred to action by the thought of King's affluence. She telephoned Ford in New Haven. "Jerry, do you know of a good lawyer who might be willing to try to collect that money that the Court ordered?"

"Yes, I do," Ford said, and recommended Bethel B. Kelley, a fellow Deke who had just graduated from Michigan Law School and was practicing in Detroit.

"My mother was bitter," Ford said. "And I mean bitter. Here was a guy who had inherited quite a lot of money from his father and never paid a dime. With her, it was a matter of principle."

Mrs. Ford retained Kelley. He reviewed the long-dormant case and in March of 1937 began legal action against King for the child support he had refused to pay after his father died. Fifteen months later a Federal Court in Wyoming ruled that King owed Mrs. Ford $6,303, plus attorney's fees. King's lawyer told the court that he could not pay it, as his "property has been wasted and almost completely exhausted [by] unwise expenditures." Mrs. Ford's lawyer offered to settle for five thousand dollars; King's lawyer offered one thousand dollars. In reply, Mrs. Ford wrote her lawyer that she would refuse to make "any concessions to Mr. King. . . . Recollecting his complete disregard for the child and his maintenance over a period of years that he was able to financially help him, I now have no sympathy for his pleas for mercy. . . . It is not my nature to be merciless or unjust, but I feel now that the boy's interests have been sacrificed too often in the past, and now a fair and just settlement should be made with no delay."

In a letter to his son, King pleaded with Ford to intercede with his mother, and hinted that if he did so, King would leave him money in his will. On the advice of his mother's lawyer, Ford replied to his father: ". . . Frankly I'm rather tired of being the go-between between you and Mother over such a disagreeable situation." He suggested a compromise at four thousand dollars. "I have taken it upon my shoulders to get Mother to agree to settle, and consequently I am believing in you as for your own honesty," Ford wrote. "If you do not do as you agree then I will feel that I have let Mother down. If you should fail me, I could hardly forgive you for Mother has put her faith in me . . ."

King still refused to pay. At Mrs. Ford's insistence, a county sheriff in Nebraska arrested King and jailed him for failure to obey the court decree. So far as her sons could remember, it was the only act of vengeance in Dorothy Gardner Ford's entire life.

King, out on bail put up by his second wife, boarded a train in Omaha for New Haven. Strangers still, both on guard, father and son agreed to resolve Mrs. Ford's claim against him. Three weeks later King broke his promise and threatened his son: ". . . We are going to fight it out. . . . You know down in the bottom of your heart your mother never spent this money on you, and I am sure, you being a *King* would not be a part of getting something for nothing. I am going to fight this to a finish and I am sure it won't be very pleasant for all concerned as the publicity in all the newspapers won't do anybody any good. Now, Jerry, be on the square with me . . ."

Reversing himself again two weeks later, King told his lawyer to pay Mrs. Ford's lawyer four thousand dollars. After deductions for attorney's fees, she received a check for $2,393 and sent it on to her son with a good-natured comment on her victory.

Dear Jerry—Have a good time! Now you know which side of the fence your bread is buttered on. Don't take it too literally . . . Love, Mama.

Ford returned the money to his mother. "I didn't need it, and she was the one who had endured what my father had done to her," Ford said. "I was just glad it was over. I never saw my father again. I never heard from him again."

Ford never wavered in his belief that somehow he would get into Yale Law School. Rebuffed by his boss and the admissions office, he decided to put his ambition to a test, and enrolled in the University of Michigan Law School in the summer of 1937. "I took two courses and got two Bs," Ford said. "That really whetted my appetite."

When he returned to New Haven in September, Ford again applied for admission to Yale Law School, and presented his grades. Two deans said no, but Professor Myres McDougal interviewed Ford and wrote: "Very mature, wise person of good judgment, good-looking, well-dressed, plenty of poise, personality excellent. Informational background not the best, but interested, mature, and serious of purpose. I see no reason for not admitting him."

Ford was admitted on a trial basis. He could take two courses during the spring of 1938. The athletic director told him that for one semester he could be a part-time law student so long as he proved he could carry his full responsibilities as a coach. "I ended up with two Bs that spring," Ford said, "and I knew I would find a way to go on."

That fall the Yale Athletic Department raised Ford's pay again, to $3,600 a year; he was head junior varsity coach, assistant line coach for the varsity, director of all scouting for Yale, and boxing coach in the winter. "But I still wanted to go to Law School," Ford said, "so I cheated a little bit. I didn't tell the Athletic Department I was going to take two courses. And I didn't tell the Law School I would continue my full-time coaching. I took two law courses, only half of the regular curriculum, and again I got two Bs. So I knew I could do both—coach and go to law school at the same time. But I must say I worked my ass off."

At the end of the 1938 football season Ford went to the athletic director. "Malcolm," Ford said, "I want to continue coaching. And I also want to go to law school. If you won't let me go to law school, I'm going to have to quit. I don't need the money. I have enough saved."

"Well, Jerry, you have handled the job," Farmer said. "We can't give you another pay increase as we had planned. But if you will do your job, you can stay on."

On his desk at the athletic office one day, Ford found a letter from a friend, a young lady in Ann Arbor. She suggested that Ford look up Phyllis Brown at Connecticut College for Women in New London. "She and I went to prep school together, and she is the most beautiful girl I ever knew," the letter said. "She loves athletics, is very active, and I think you would like her."

A couple of weeks later Ford called the girl, introduced himself, mentioned their mutual friend in Ann Arbor, and invited her to dinner. He drove the fifty miles to New London in his convertible and met Phyllis Brown.

She was a blonde and lissome beauty with merry blue-green eyes, a cascade of fine, pale-gold hair reaching to the shoulder, and a smile that filled the room with sunshine. At nineteen, she was tall, five feet eight, had the figure of a caryatid, 34-22-34, and bore herself with the poise and presence of a princess.

Miss Brown was the daughter of a department store owner in Lewiston, Maine, and an honors graduate from Abbott Academy in Andover. "I was the Eastern preppie," she said, "and everything west of Pennsylvania was the West. So I was going to meet this Westerner. I had this pseudo-sophistication—I knew how to raise my eyebrows at the right moment, and how to look a boy in the eye. So we met, Jerry and I. After one look at this 'Westerner,' I thought, 'He's a hayseed. But what a charming hayseed.'"

That night, after their first evening of getting acquainted, she said to herself, "He is a nice boy, a really nice boy. I want to see him again."

Driving back to New Haven, Ford thought, "She is as smart as she is beautiful—a really classy gal."

Well were they matched, this serious young Midwesterner and this precocious Easterner; and together they would discover a new world. "I had a great love of life, of doing things, of being part of living," Phyllis Brown said. "And then I met Jerry. He too had a lot of energy, a lot of vitality. We both simply liked to do a lot of things, so we did them together."

Half a century later, Phyllis Brown, still a woman of beauty and bearing, talked about the first great romance of her life in a voice that shimmered with love and friendship. "He was very serious," she said. "He had worked all through high school and college, playing football, waiting on tables, studying, managing the fraternity house—he had not had time to have a girl. He had not had a lot of time to play. And along comes this player of the Eastern world—me.

"I wanted him to be my playmate. I wanted him to be interested in all the things I was interested in. So we played. We played tennis. We played golf. We danced. We read books together. I was heavy into Thomas Wolfe at the time, and I read Wolfe to him. I liked to ski, so he took lessons. I wanted him to be interested in bridge, as I was; and I taught him to play. I got him interested in all these things he had never had time to do. He was a wonderful companion—such an active mind, so quick and agreeable in trying new things, so ready for any new challenge."

Ford had found a beautiful girl with a zest for living and capacity for friendship that equaled his own. "For the first time in my life," he said, "I fell deeply in love."

And so did she, in her fashion. "He had me for his girlfriend, but I was not ready to be tied," she said. "He was committed to me. I was playing the field. Scouting. I had lots of beaus, lots of young men calling and asking me out. I was a dizzy kid, a flirt. But Jerry kept hanging in there." For a young man who had never had time for playing the game of ardent suitor, it was a new kind of competition.

In the summers Ford took Phyllis to Michigan to spend a month with his family. His mother, stepfather, and brothers all thought her a splendid match for Jerry. "Phyllis was a joy to be around," Dick Ford said, "and an outstanding athlete for a girl in those days." In Michigan, Jerry and Phyllis played to a schedule—golf in the morning, sailing and tennis in the afternoon, and dancing the night away. From Michigan they would go to Maine to spend time with her family. "My parents thought Jerry was stable, conscientious—the most splendid match for me," she said. "He made a good impression because he was forthright, honest, and honorable, obviously a very solid young man. Older people saw this in him. He behaved well in any company. He was not shy but somewhat reserved, yet easy to talk with. He never embarrassed anyone, never. He never poked fun at someone else, or said or did anything unkind. I never knew anyone who didn't like him. And I think everybody assumed in Michigan and Maine that some day Phyllis would settle down and marry Jerry."

At the Dartmouth Winter Carnival in 1939, Phyllis Brown was accidentally knocked down on a ski slope by McClelland Barclay, a popular magazine cover artist. When she stood up to confront him, Barclay said calmly: "Have you ever thought of modeling?"

Until that moment she had not, but on her next trip to New York City she stopped by Barclay's studio. He sent her over to the John Robert Powers agency, and that day she became a Powers model. "It was the easiest thing in the world," she said. "I never went back to college."

To stay in the game, Ford often went to New York City—and there he found another challenging new world. Together he and Phyllis explored their Manhattan Island of wonders—the opera, the museums, the restaurants, the nightclubs. They rode on double-decker buses, saw the latest Broadway shows, and found good little inexpensive restaurants. On an evening in June of 1940 they danced in the dark at the Rainbow Room in Rockefeller Center as the city lights gleamed their magic. It was her twenty-first birthday.

As a professional model, Phyllis Brown was much in demand and making the most of it. Bradshaw Crandall painted her every month for the cover of *Cosmopolitan* Magazine. Top photographers bid for her time; she could model high fashion or show the healthy and wholesome look of the girl next door. *Look* Magazine invited her to take a boyfriend on a ski weekend in Vermont for a six-page picture story. She chose Ford. The old black-and-white photographs, in the March 12, 1940, issue of *Look*, show the two schussing down the hills above Stowe, snuggling in a horse-drawn open sleigh, joining in a songfest, dreaming by the open fire. Looking at the fading, fifty-year-old pictures, Phyllis Brown mused, "It was a golden time, before the war, before our world became so complicated. And Jerry and I were the All-American boy and the All-American girl. We could be serious, but mostly we were light-hearted, enjoying life. He was my playmate, and far more than that. He was my rock. Jerry was the person I really depended on. But he was jealous. He didn't like my flirting, and oh, he had a temper. Once, when we were at a cocktail party, Jerry got so mad at me that he put his fist right through the door at 21."

Reflecting on their years together, she said: "I offered him a whole new chapter in his life. He was interested in learning and doing and being and living. So was I. That's really all it was. Without recognizing it at the time, I probably did have a very definite influence in his life. After his mother, I was the first important woman in his life. And he was the first important man in my life, my first love affair, the first man I ever slept with—you never forget that, not ever, ever, ever.

"I believed in him," she said. "Whatever he set out to do, he made a commitment and kept it. But there was something else—Jerry had an innate awareness that was deceptive. Actually it was a cunning side. People would be talking and thinking, 'Dumb Jerry the football coach is not getting it.' But that was part of the cunning. He was listening, mulling it over and thinking it through, and then he would come up with the right answer. He was smart—not clever, not quick, but smart."

In New York City a wealthy New York business friend asked Phyllis why she wasted her time with a football coach. "Just you wait," she said. "Jerry Ford will be a great success in life. Some day he will make fifty thousand dollars a year."

* * *

Ford was twenty-six when he took his first step into politics. Patrimony and geography decreed that he would be Republican. His mother and stepfather were active Kent County Republicans, and Western Michigan was a bastion of Republican philosophy and votes.

In the spring of 1940, between his Yale law classes and coaching responsibilities, Ford began listening to Wendell Willkie on radio's popular and memorable "Information Please." He liked what he heard, and began to read every newspaper and magazine article he could find about the new star who burst on the American scene to oppose President Roosevelt. In Grand Rapids that summer, Ford spoke to his stepfather about volunteering to work with local Republicans for the Willkie cause. His stepfather suggested he talk to Frank McKay.

"I knew that Frank McKay was the big political boss who ran the Republican Party in Michigan," Ford said. "He was state treasurer. He was crooked—indicted two or three times, tried but never convicted. It was common knowledge that McKay used his influence as Michigan's treasurer to require every state agency to buy tires through his storefront office in Grand Rapids. McKay was not the kind of person Ford wanted to associate with, but he had to accept the fact that this unsavory man was the Republican power in the state and in Grand Rapids.

Ford telephoned McKay's secretary, made an appointment, went to his office, and waited to see him. And waited. "I sat in Frank McKay's office one hot summer day for four hours," Ford said. "Finally, after four hours, he gave me three minutes. He showed no interest in how I might help the party. He obviously thought I was some young whippersnapper, and ended the discussion."

Angry at the rebuff, Ford drove back East, signed up in New York City as a volunteer in the Willkie Campaign, and enlisted Phyllis Brown as well. The work at Willkie Headquarters was routine, but Ford earned a ticket to the Republican Convention. He was one of the thousands who packed Philadelphia's convention hall to chant "We Want Willkie" and help Willkie win the nomination. When he lost to President Roosevelt in November, Ford was disappointed, but talked about the experience with his cheerful spirit of finding some good in all things. "I realized that my participation did not make much difference at all to the political fate of Wendell Willkie. But it made a lot of difference to me. By participating, I learned. Not only did I learn a little about politics, but more important I learned about myself. I liked politics, everything about it."

*　　*　　*

Ford returned to Yale that September in high spirits. At last, after all the years of work and study, he had only one semester to go before he would reach his goal—a law degree. The college chapter of his life was ending. In the autumn of 1940, he coached his last Yale squad, completed the last classes, and passed the last examinations for his degree.

Ford did well at Yale. Coaching not only paid his way; on the practice field he also learned to judge the quality of men, to motivate people and be their leader. In the Law School he learned, as he put it, "the process of thinking and analysis, the application of logic to issues." His average grade for all his classes was 74.5 percent, very close to Professor McDougal's estimate when he recommended his admittance. In the Yale scoring system at the time he ranked as a solid B. He finished in the top third of the Yale Law Class of '41, which included a future Supreme Court Justice, Byron White; a future Governor of Pennsylvania, Raymond Shafer; a future Secretary of State, Cyrus Vance; and the first Director of the Peace Corps, Sargent Shriver.

Ford's class standing brought him good offers, one from a major law firm in New York and another in Philadelphia. But he had decided to go back to Grand Rapids to practice law. "I had a visceral feeling—that's where I belong, in Grand Rapids," Ford said. "In the back of my mind was the idea that I might want to run for public office, and logic told me the place for that was Grand Rapids. I had grown up there. Dad was known and respected in the community. For all that I had seen and experienced, Grand Rapids was home."

It was a bittersweet decision. For almost four years Jerry Ford and Phyllis Brown had been together for some of the happiest times of their young lives. But that chapter was also coming to an end. "Phyllis," he said, "I am going back to Grand Rapids to practice law."

She already knew. "Not for a moment did I doubt that his place was in Grand Rapids," she said. Observing his fascination with the Willkie campaign, she assumed he would go home to run for political office. "And I knew I would never be happy as a Congressman's little wife," she said. Certainly she had no intention of giving up her exciting life and successful career. "I convinced myself that it was not the end for Jerry and me," she said. "No, I thought, somehow, sometime, we'll get together again."

Ford did not. "I was very sad at the time," he said. "She was an important part of my life. But it was probably the best thing that happened to me, probably the best thing for both of us. It was a wonderful romance, but it would never have been a good marriage. Because with all her wonderful traits, with all her terrific qualities of attractiveness and ability, she had a wandering eye. It was her nature to be, well, gregarious; and somehow I sensed that would not be good for a political wife. I guess we both had more sense than to think we could make a go of marriage. We were both lucky."

Yale, Phyllis Brown, and his six years in the East brought a greater dimension to Ford's life. Reflecting on the experience, he said: "I grew up and went to school in the Middle West. I was parochial. I was provincial. Going to Yale, learning about another part of America, meeting the new challenges, the many things I learned from and with Phyllis—all of this was a great, great broadening of my understanding of the world. Not until later did I appreciate how much I benefited from the people there, how much I had learned."

FORD AND BUCHEN

In May of 1941 a sign painter carefully centered the words in black and gold on the frosted glass door of Suite 621 in the Michigan Trust Building in downtown Grand Rapids.

The newest law firm in the city was open for business. "I don't know how we had the guts to do it," Ford said. "We didn't have a client—not one client." But a client did walk in on that first day. He wanted a title search. The fee: five dollars.

Ford initiated the partnership. He and Philip Buchen had met at the Deke House in Ann Arbor, where Buchen was studying law at the University of Michigan. Amiable and tall, crippled by polio from childhood, Buchen had spent some of his early years swimming in a pool with Franklin Roosevelt at Warm Springs, Georgia. At Ann Arbor, Buchen was an honors student and an editor of the *Michigan Law Review.*

The Ford-Buchen friendship grew during the summer of 1940. Buchen was clerking in a law firm in New York City and planned to practice there. Ford talked him out of it. "Let's open our own partnership in Grand Rapids," Ford said. "It's a great city, and we will be our own bosses. I'll bring in the business, and together we'll handle the work."

Together they studied for the Michigan bar exam; together they passed on the first try. With one thousand dollars Ford had saved and one thousand dollars Buchen borrowed from his father, they could open their law office.

Soon after, as it happened, Ford learned of a citizens' group organizing to overthrow Frank McKay, the Republican political boss who had coldly dismissed his political interest the year before. One was a dentist, Dr. Willard Ver Meulen, and another was Paul Goebel, All-American at Michigan and a Grand Rapids businessman. They and four other reform-minded citizens were friends of Ford's mother and stepfather.

Ford met with Dr. Ver Meulen and Goebel. "Can I join you?"

"Jerry," Dr. Ver Meulen said, "this may not be the place for you."

"Why not?"

"The political pressure is going to be tremendous," Dr. Ver Meulen said. "You will lose clients."

"I don't have any clients," Ford said. "Count me in."

After Ford left, Goebel said to Dr. Ver Meulen: "Remember, McKay is a moral problem. Never worry about Jerry Ford, senior or junior, backing down on a moral problem."

Ford went to work with Dr. Ver Meulen, Goebel, and the others to organize the Home Front, the sole purpose of which was to throw out Boss McKay. Ford was elected president and began his first experience in what was then the essence of political success—organization. He and his fellow reformers set out to recruit a Republican candidate in each of the 142 Kent County precincts to challenge McKay's candidate. As each candidate was signed up, he was taught the rudiments of canvassing, going through the precinct block by block and house by house to identify support and opposition. Every Friday, Ford called in his Home Front team to check on their progress.

Within six months of opening his law office, Ford was as busy as he had been at Yale. In addition to organizing the Home Front, he had signed up to teach a course in business law at the University of Grand Rapids and was lending a hand to the football coach there. Occasionally he took a young lady out to dinner or a movie. Most of the time, he worked at learning and practicing law; he and Buchen had brought in as many clients as they could handle.

On Sunday, December 7, 1941, Ford spent the afternoon at the office working on a case, headed home, and on the car radio heard a news bulletin: Japanese war planes had attacked Pearl Harbor. That night, he told his mother and stepfather he was going to volunteer for the Navy, and on Monday he did.

Four months later, because of Ford's football career, the U.S. Navy called him to duty. Tom Hamilton, a star quarterback and later a coach for the U.S. Naval Academy in Annapolis, was recruiting young football coaches to put the Navy's future pilots in top physical condition. Hamilton knew Ford and brought him into the Navy's V-5 flight training program. Sworn in to the service, Ford was given Serial Number USNR 141329, commissioned an ensign, and immediately promoted to lieutenant (junior grade). At the Naval Academy he completed a month of basic training as an officer and applied for sea duty. But Hamilton sent him to the Navy's preflight school in Chapel Hill, North Carolina, to be an athletic training officer. It was not what Ford wanted, but he did his best. In his first fitness report his Commanding Officer commended him as "An outstanding officer, one of the finest in the station, and an excellent shipmate."

In the early spring of 1943, Ford got a call from Phyllis Brown, now Mrs. Robert Ricksen. She had been married some six months earlier to a handsome and fun-loving airline pilot, but she could not forget the earnest and aspiring young lawyer who shared her passion for living. While Ricksen was away on a long trip, Phyllis slipped out of New York and traveled to Chapel Hill to see Ford.

Her visit was brief. Phyllis had been there only a few hours when her mother telephoned. Unable to find her daughter in New York City, Mrs. Brown guessed where Phyllis had gone. "My father had died, suddenly, unexpectedly," Phyllis said. "So I went back to Maine. And then Jerry shipped out. And that was that."

Weeks later, after what seemed to him an unconscionably long wait for sea duty, Ford was assigned to the USS *Monterey*, a small carrier about to be launched in New Jersey and readied for combat. Built in a hurry, with a 622-foot flight deck framed and welded on top of a cruiser hull, she looked ungainly. But with her complement of 1,569 hastily trained officers and men, she could launch her forty-five aircraft in minutes. Designed as a platform for bombers, *Monterey* also carried a complement of fighter planes. For defense in battle she also had speed, well above 31 knots, and forty antiaircraft guns around her decks.

On the *Monterey*'s shakedown cruise Captain Lester Hundt made Lieutenant Ford the ship's athletic officer—he jury-rigged a basketball court on the hangar deck to keep the crew in shape—and one of ten gunnery officers. In October *Monterey* cleared the Panama Canal, stopped in San Diego to pick up a full load of SBD dive bombers, TBS torpedo bombers, and fighters, and joined Admiral William Halsey's Third Fleet in the Western Pacific, ready for action.

Her first mission: Makin. On November 19, 1943, *Monterey*'s planes struck the Japanese base in the Gilbert Islands, and for three weeks the action continued. On Christmas Day and New Year's Day the target was Kavieng, New Ireland, and her aircraft were credited with sinking a Japanese cruiser and a destroyer. As a gunnery officer, Ford's job was to stand on the fantail and direct the crews firing the 40-millimeter guns. "The Japanese planes came after us with a vengeance," Ford said. "It was every bit as much action as I had hoped to see."

To the ranks of sailors, Ford was something of a Mr. Roberts. "He was the sort of officer who looked out for his men," Seaman Second Class Ronald Smith said. "Nothing ever seemed to rattle him. One day we came under attack and I dived for cover in the hatchway. I looked up and there was Lieutenant Ford. He smiled and asked me, 'Why the hell are you in such a hurry?' "

Among his fellow officers, Ford made important friends. Captain Hundt was an avid football fan. "I cozied up to him," Ford said, "and we talked football and other sports." When an assistant navigation officer was transferred, Ford asked Captain Hundt for the job and got it. "I didn't have any idea how to take a sighting," Ford said. "But we had a great navigator who had been a former merchant marine skipper, Commander Pappy Atwood, and we had a first-class quartermaster. They taught me navigation, how to take a sighting, and with their help I learned very quickly. As a result I became the officer of the deck during General Quarters, which meant I was on the bridge with the captain, the navigator, and the air officer during combat. Couldn't have had a better place to be; I was right there where everything was going on. That gave me a whole new appreciation of operations and the fleet in combat, and of the war itself. It was good duty to be at the center of action."

In January 1944, *Monterey* launched her planes in support of the amphibious invasion of Kwajalein and Eniwetok; in February it was action against Truk, the formidable Japanese base in the Carolines. With almost no let-up, the spunky little carrier sent her aircraft into action against Palau and Hollandia, in New Guinea, against Saipan, Tinian, Guam, and the Japanese fleet in the Marianas. In the Eastern Philippine Sea her bombers were credited with sinking a Japanese carrier.

While her planes were attacking Formosa, Japanese bombers and kamikaze pilots came after all the carriers. One torpedo missed the *Monterey* and struck a cruiser, the USS *Canberra*; another hit the *Houston*. By morning they were still afloat, but the fleet was only eighty miles off Formosa, and waves of Japanese planes struck at dawn and continued to darkness. For twenty-four hours straight the antiaircraft crews on *Monterey* and the other ships stood by their guns to beat back the attackers. When the crippled cruisers were out of enemy range, *Monterey* turned about to strike at other enemy targets in the Bonins, at Wake, Yap, Luzon, Formosa, and the Ryukus. In thirteen months, ship and men earned eleven battle stars.

Monterey survived, lost aircraft and pilots, patched up its other planes, and stayed ready for battle. But after surviving the worst that Japanese airmen and submarines could send against her, she was almost lost to the peril that sailors fear most, the sea itself.

On December 17, 1944, Admiral Halsey's fleet was six hundred miles off Luzon in the East Philippine Sea when weather officers reported a "tropical disturbance" nearby. The information would prove dangerously inadequate, and *Monterey* had a green skipper. Captain Stuart Ingersoll, an aviator who had not been on a bridge in some twenty years, had taken command only months before.

As the storm approached Commander Atwood, the most experienced ship handler aboard, advised the captain to have all aircraft lashed down with half-inch steel cable. That night *Monterey* and the other ships of Halsey's fleet were struck by one of the worst typhoons the U.S. Navy ever encountered in the Pacific. The captain of the destroyer *Dewey* recorded that the ship's barometer dropped below the scales, to an estimated reading of 26.60. A Navy tanker recorded winds of 124 knots; seas may have reached 100 feet. In sight of *Monterey*, the destroyer *Monaghan* was lifted by a great wave, turned on her side and upside down, and sank. Of 250 in the crew, 244 were lost. Two other destroyers, *Spence* and *Hull*, broached and went down. The raging seas made it almost impossible to pick up survivors.

Lieutenant Ford, off the midwatch at 4:00 A.M., had just gone to sleep when the blare of General Quarters sounded before dawn.

"Waking, I thought I could smell smoke," he said. He grabbed his helmet and headed for the flight deck, which he had to cross to get to his battle station on the bridge. "I went up the passageway and out on the starboard catwalk around the ship below the flight deck. I climbed the ladder, and as I stepped on the flight deck the ship suddenly rolled about twenty-five degrees. I lost my footing, fell to the deck flat on my face, and started sliding toward the port side as if I were on a toboggan slide."

Ford skidded the full width of the flight deck, 109 feet, and was sliding feet first toward the sea. "I had enough presence of mind to spread out as I slid, and I spotted a little rim of metal that goes around the flight deck to stop tools from rolling off," he said. "I put out my feet and hit it. That broke my momentum, so instead of going over the side, I twisted my body as my feet hit the rim and I landed in the narrow catwalk just below the port edge of the flight deck."

Alone, clinging there with the sea rushing by two feet away, Ford thought of his mother's prayer from Proverbs:

Trust in the Lord with all thine heart; and lean not unto thine own under-
standing.
In all thy ways acknowledge him, and he shall direct thy paths.

After catching his breath and surveying a route, Ford climbed back up on the flight deck and ran to the bridge. From his battle station, he could see that the planes on the flight deck had been torn from their steel lashings and swept overboard. As the carrier rolled in the sea, the starboard edge of the flight deck shipped green water.

The hangar deck, jammed wing-to-wing with aircraft loaded with high-octane gasoline, was on fire. The Navy's official account of the *Monterey* ordeal stated: "The planes bounded around the hangar deck like trapped and terrified birds. . . . Showers of sparks flew as the planes crashed into each other and against the sides of the ship. In short order the surging hangar deck was a mass of shifting, whirling fires as the careening planes were ignited from their own sparks and spread flames fore and aft."

Ammunition lockers, a bulkhead away, were heating up to the danger point. Pilots and crews struggled together to drag tons of bombs and torpedoes to the side and push them overboard. Fresh air vents on the hangar deck funneled smoke from the burning gasoline into the engine and boiler rooms, forcing crews to escape or be asphyxiated; three of four boilers stopped. Without power, the seamen fighting the fires would lose pressure in their fire hoses; without power, the helmsman could not steer the ship against the storm.

On the bridge, Lieutenant Ford heard Admiral Halsey radio to Captain Ingersoll: "Abandon ship if you so order." Then came Halsey's order to nearby cruisers and destroyers: "Stand by to pick up *Monterey*'s survivors."

Ingersoll looked to Commander Atwood, who refused to abandon ship. "We'll make it," he told Ingersoll.

"Give us more time," Captain Ingersoll radioed Halsey. "I think we can solve this problem."

Commander Atwood, according to the Navy report, put "the wind and seas on his quarter, which reduced the ship's motion so the crew could put out the fires without dodging the shifting planes." After a perilous forty minutes, the fires were under control; but the ship was almost dead in the water, in danger of being taken broadside by wind and sea. Atwood sent rescue parties in gas masks into the engine rooms to bring out survivors, keep the one engine operating, and start the others. Seven hours later *Monterey* restored its full power and sailed for safe harbor at Ulithi, in the western Carolines.

She dropped anchor there with three dead, forty burned and injured, ten critically. Her planes were all damaged or lost at sea. "Battered and spent," the Navy report stated, "*Monterey* is unfit for service." She was ordered to Bremerton, Washington, to go into dry dock for repairs.

Ford applied for a transfer to another carrier in the Western Pacific, but the Navy ordered him back to the States for reassignment. On Christmas Eve 1944, he said good-bye to his skipper, his fellow officers, and the men of the *Monterey*. It was no easy parting. "I had a great feeling about my ship," he said. "I had started with her before the commissioning. I had been through battles with her. I had two skippers who treated me well. I had a friend in Pappy Atwood, who saved our ship. I made lots of good friends. I had great jobs. If you are going to be in a war, you might as well be where the action is. And that's where my ship was."

Captain Ingersoll recommended Lieutenant Ford for promotion with a glowing report on his service: "He is steady, reliable, and resourceful. . . . His unfailing good humor, pleasing personality, and natural ability as a leader made him well liked and respected by the officers and men. He is an excellent organizer, and can be relied upon for the successful conclusion of any operation which he may undertake."

On home leave, Ford spent his first days with his mother and stepfather in Grand Rapids, then flew to New York to see Phyllis Brown Ricksen. She had written him in the Pacific to let him know she was going to have a child; he wanted to see her anyway. As it turned out, too much had happened in their lives apart, and the magic was gone. "We had cocktails," Ford said, "but that was the extent of it."

His leave ended, Ford reported to his new assignment, at headquarters of the Navy Training Command in Glenview, Illinois, a suburb of Chicago. As a staff officer Ford worked with the Navy's special schools to train new young officers for action at sea and in the air and was promoted to Lieutenant Commander.

But Ford's heart was far away, in the Pacific. Again he applied for sea duty, and asked to be assigned to the *Coral Sea* or one of the other new carriers steaming westward to close the ocean ring around Japan. He was still hoping and waiting for orders back into combat when Japan surrendered on August 14, 1945.

World War II was over.

With sixteen million other young Americans, Ford had risked his life for a cause larger than himself. Few in the uniformed ranks could articulate this cause. All understood it.

Patriotism, in one word. The flag. America. To some extent the vast numbers of men and women in the Army, the Navy, and the Air Corps knew it was the cause of freedom. They were engaged in the battle to defeat the dictators, to defend America and the American way of life, to preserve liberty. In that cause they had taken part in the strange and uncivilized phenomenon of war. They had mustered their courage to overcome their fears. Many died. More were wounded. The others endured the perilous journey and survived the terrible game of kill or be killed. They had met their duty, and been tempered and transformed by the experience.

Like all who served the country in those years, Ford shared the humor and the hardship of men under fire. He, as did so many others, witnessed and demonstrated courage. They experienced the splendid mix of people who compose the American character. They saw foreign lands and foreign people, and the most discerning among them came to see the world in its singular unity. Never again would Ford and the sixteen million other men of World War II be the same.

"Before the war," Ford said, "I was a typical Midwest isolationist. I returned understanding we could never be isolated again. We were and are one world. It was clear to me, it was inevitable to me, that this country was obligated to lead in this new world. We had won the war. It was up to us to keep the peace."

Ford was not alone. He and four other future Presidents were motivated by what they had seen and experienced in World War II to commit themselves to the profession of politics, imperfect as it was, as the way to make a difference.

3

THE CHALLENGE

After his four-year odyssey across half the globe, it was Commander Ford's good fortune to have a civilian job waiting for him when he stepped off the train back in Grand Rapids. The opportunity was just what he wanted—to practice law, and with the best firm in the city.

The partnership that he and Philip Buchen started was suspended during the war when Buchen, prevented from serving in uniform because he was crippled by polio, was invited to join the firm of Butterfield, Keeney and Amberg. Buchen, upon receiving the offer, wrote Ford with two options: Either the two would resume their partnership after the war, or the firm would offer Ford a position when he returned.

In his first week back at home Ford went down to talk with Julius Amberg, a senior partner in the firm. Amberg told Ford, "We would love to have you. We can't make you a partner the first year, but I assure you it will happen."

Amberg was a brilliant man. He excelled at Harvard Law School, besting his classmate, Felix Frankfurter. During World War II Secretary of War Henry Stimson recruited Amberg as a deputy. "Amberg had a superior legal mind, the best I ever knew," Ford said. "He knew I was interested in business and economics, and said he would assign me to good cases in business, finance and mergers."

"Jerry," Amberg said, "I'm going to train you to be a good lawyer."

That was the clinching argument. Ford signed up and went to work. "I was lucky, lucky to have Julius Amberg to teach me the practice of law," Ford said.

Or was it luck? Ford was thirty-two at that time, and there had been a consistent pattern to his progress in life. People believed in him. Whether it was his earnestness, seriousness of purpose, readiness to listen, genial nature, or other qualities, there was something about him as a boy and young man that brought people to see promise and possibilities. Somehow over the years Ford had met and cultivated people who could help him, people who would train and encourage him and boost him another step along the path he had chosen. Already there was an impressive list—Scout Master Kindel, Ralph Conger, Coach Gettings, Principal Krause, Coach Kipke, Ivan Williamson, Coach Pond, Professor McDougal, Athletic Director Farmer, Phyllis Brown, Captain Hundt, Commander Atwood, Captain Ingersoll, and now Julius Amberg.

Ford was not just aware of this quality in himself; he used it. "I have always been able to develop allegiances with good people," Ford said. "I don't know how to define it, or why I have it, but I have a capability of getting people to like to work with me. I am very proud of it. I know I have had a lot of good luck. But I have always believed what my Dad used to say, 'The harder you work, the better your luck.'"

As an ambitious new lawyer at Butterfield, Keeney and Amberg, Ford arrived first in the morning and left last in the evening. Amberg, as he promised, handed Ford complicated research on corporate problems, brought him in on business transactions, taught him how to write a better brief, and coached him in delivering his arguments in court. "I was learning," Ford said, "and I found I really liked the law."

He also liked being back in Grand Rapids. His stepfather's paint business had improved, and his parents had moved to a larger house in East Grand Rapids. His brothers were out on their own, so Ford moved back in with his mother and stepfather. "I had been away from them for a long time," Ford said. "I was glad to be back home."

One day, to Ford's surprise and delight, Phyllis Brown telephoned. After reminiscing for a few minutes, she told him that she was getting a divorce and would like to see him.

"All through the war I had thought about him," she said. "My marriage hadn't worked out. I hoped Jerry was still interested in me."

Ford was more than interested; through the long months in the Pacific he had thought often of her and their wonderful years together. Her call revived all the memories, and he couldn't wait to see her. They agreed to meet at her mother's home in Maine, where she was visiting with her baby boy.

Ford bought his plane ticket and was getting ready to leave when Phyllis called again. "Jerry," she said, "I told my mother you were coming for a visit. She looked at me and said, 'I forbid you to do this. You have caused Jerry Ford enough trouble. You just call him back and tell him you have thought it over and changed your mind.'"

"Well," Ford said to her, "that's the only time you ever minded your mother." For a moment he waited, and then added, "I understand." The awkward words and pauses that followed masked the truth that neither wanted to say: It was over. Their love was a golden memory, nothing more.

Ford canceled his plane reservation. "Her mother was a person of good common sense, and her mother was right," Ford said. "It would never have worked. So, that was the finale of the romance. I put it behind me. From that point on, so far as I was concerned, she was totally out of my life."

Ford turned his attention to his law practice and to his next ambition— public office. Without being subtle about it, he began to build a political base. He signed on to raise funds for the Boy Scouts, the United Way in Grand Rapids, and the Kent County cancer drive. He agreed to serve as county disaster chairman for the American Red Cross. He joined the Kent County Farm Bureau and began meeting with farmers to learn about their problems. To find out how veterans were readjusting to civilian life, Ford joined the Furniture City Post of the American Legion, the Veterans of Foreign Wars, and the Amvets. He talked to his black classmates at South High to learn about minority problems, and became a member of the NAACP and the Urban League. These associations would, by his design, become the core of a campaign organization.

Ford's habit of working all the time began to worry his parents. His mother, who remembered Phyllis Brown with great respect and affection, thought he was still pining over the beautiful girl he lost. With the directness permitted only to mothers, Mrs. Ford asked her eldest son: "Jerry, when are you going to start dating again? Your brothers are all married and raising families. You need to find a nice girl and get married and settle down. You're not getting any younger, you know."

In August of 1947, not long after his mother's admonition, Ford was working on plans for the Kent County cancer drive with two good friends, Frank and Peg Neuman. When they finished Ford casually asked, "By the way, do you know Betty Warren?"

"Oh, sure," Peg Neuman said. "You know she's getting a divorce."

Ford did know that, and said that he had met her some weeks before at a cocktail party—"a good-looking, well-dressed young lady"—and made a point of talking to her. Now he would like to take her out.

Without hesitating, Peg Neuman got Betty Warren on the phone. "Jerry Ford wants to know if you'll come out and have a drink."

Betty Bloomer Warren remembered meeting Ford at the party, and knew he was a promising young lawyer back from the war and—as she had heard—"the town's most eligible bachelor, with a lot of girls chasing him." But she said no. As fashion coordinator for Herpolsheimer's, one of the three big department stores in the city, she had a big style show the next morning. "I'll be up late writing the continuity for that," she told Peg, "and I'm not going out with anyone while I'm waiting for my divorce."

Ford took the phone. "Let me pick you up, and we'll go out for an hour, have a beer, and you'll be refreshed when you go back to work. It'll be good for you."

Thank you, she said, but "I'm in the process of getting a divorce, and you're a lawyer, you ought to know better."

"We'll just go to some quiet little spot where nobody will see us," Ford said.

"I don't think that's quite cricket," she said.

Ford persisted, and finally she gave in. "All right," she said, "but I can only be gone twenty minutes."

When he called at her apartment to take her out, she greeted him, to his surprise, with a warm and infectious smile. She was as svelte, vivacious, and pretty as he remembered. They went to a quiet bar, and an hour later they were still talking.

"He took me home," Betty Warren said. "I went back to work. And then I began to wonder if he was ever going to call me again, because my interest was aroused."

A few days later Ford did call. Casually, cautiously, they began going out together, meeting for dinner or a movie. "He wanted a companion, and I filled the bill," she said. "He was a person of achievement, and I admired him for his community work, his involvement in civic affairs. We discovered that we both belonged to the Urban League. I found him attractive just to be with, fun to go out with on a date. That was all I was interested in at that time, because I had been so disappointed in marriage. I enjoyed the social part of going places, and you had to have a partner to do this. So our relationship started as good friends."

Ford saw in Betty Warren a personable lady with a good mind, great energy, and a plain-speaking directness—all important factors to him. Nevertheless, he said, "I had no idea that someone special had just come into my life."

Ford, committed to law practice and to a political future, did not have much time for social life. Within a year after his return from World War II, Ford decided to run for the U.S. House of Representatives. "The war got me interested in the national and international scene, in Congress," he said. "I made up my mind and that was it." His friends were skeptical; only his mother and stepfather encouraged him at first.

To win any political office in Western Michigan, Ford knew he must again confront Frank McKay. McKay was described by Jerald terHorst, the political reporter for *The Grand Rapids Press*, as "a stocky, secretive man who affected a pince-nez and a pearl stickpin, maintained a fancy automobile, but was seldom seen in public places. Lacking formal education, he spoke in short, explosive phrases, usually profane. When he did speak, however, things happened in one part of the state or another." To McKay, politics was business. He made a good living at it.

Running for Congress in Grand Rapids was a bold undertaking for a thirty-four-year-old political novice. He would have to challenge and overcome an entrenched Republican, Representative Bartel J. Jonkman, a ten-year veteran of the House with a Dutch name and a Dutch identity in a Congressional district where conservative Dutch dominated the Republican Party and the popular vote. Ford was impelled by two strong feelings of his own: Jonkman had been put in office and kept in office by McKay, and he was a politician of the past.

"Barney Jonkman had become a total isolationist," Ford said. "He was a thorn in the side of our senior senator, Arthur Vandenberg, who was converted by the war to internationalism. So here you had Senator Vandenberg trying to help President Truman with the Marshall Plan, and with the United Nations, and our own Congressman Jonkman gutting Vandenberg at home."

Ford's scanty experience in politics—as a demonstrator at the Willkie convention and his prewar months with the Home Front—did not dissuade him. "Politics is basic intuitiveness," he said. "Common sense. Knowing how to work with and sell people."

Phil Buchen suggested Ford recruit Jack Stiles, a friend of both at the University of Michigan, to be the campaign manager. Stiles had no political experience; he was a versatile young Grand Rapids businessman with aspirations to be a novelist, but he was willing to help. Together, Ford and Stiles collected the voting records of the district, applied common sense, and devised a fifteen-month plan to put Ford in office. For two amateurs, it was an impressive, and cold-blooded, political strategy.

"Jack and I looked at the election statistics for years back," Ford said. "The contest would be in the primary. No Democrat could win that district in the general election. And we came to the conclusion that Jonkman was beatable in a two-man primary, but not if he had more than one candidate against him. So we picked out three people more senior than I who were qualified and might be interested. All were friends of mine, and one by one, in a very deliberate process, I went to see them."

The first was Paul Goebel, a popular leader in civic and Republican affairs. Ford stated his case: "I think Barney Jonkman ought to be beaten. I think the Fifth District deserves better representation in Washington. I believe you are qualified, and I urge you to run. If you will agree to be the candidate, I will do everything I can to help you get elected."

"Nobody can beat Barney," Goebel replied. "He is entrenched. He has been there ten years. And if you think he ought to be beaten, why don't you run?"

Ford's next two Republican possible rivals also scoffed at anyone's chances of beating Jonkman and also suggested that Ford himself take on the incumbent. "Well," Ford said, "that was exactly what I wanted to hear them say."

After he cleared the field for his straight shot at Jonkman, Ford decided to lay low, to do nothing to alert his opponent to the coming ambush. Jonkman had taken his previous elections for granted, and Ford guessed that he would dismiss any rumor of a challenge from an unknown. "My one advantage was surprise," Ford said. "Barney seldom got back to the district. I wanted him to be overconfident."

The filing deadline for a House candidate in Michigan was almost a year away; Ford decided to wait until then to formally announce his campaign. Buchen advised him to tell nobody of his plan to run.

"Not even Betty?" Ford asked in surprise.

"Not even Betty," Buchen said.

Jerry Ford and Betty Warren were spending more and more time together, and confiding more about themselves. She explained to him why her marriage had not worked out, and he told her about his love affair with Phyllis Brown. Betty thought he was still carrying a torch for Phyllis.

In September 1947, Betty Warren's divorce was granted. She loved the freedom of being single again, and made that clear to her new beau. "We agreed not to get serious," she said.

In her twenty-nine young years, life had been serious enough. Elizabeth Bloomer was born in Chicago on April 8, 1918, the daughter of William Bloomer, a traveling salesman who sold conveyor belts to factories, and Hortense Neahr, who wrote her handsome and peripatetic husband a letter every night. Betty was the third and last child of the Bloomers. When she was two the family moved to Grand Rapids to live in a commodious frame house at 717 Fountain Street. Her father's absence left an early mark; as a girl she swore she would never marry a man who traveled.

At the age of eight she told her mother she wanted to be a dancer. She started taking lessons and, dreaming of becoming a ballerina, stayed at it through Central High School. Popular and pretty, she was still a high school freshman when she got her first job, showing dresses as a teenage model in Herpolsheimer's. Pirouetting before the mothers of her classmates, she discovered she liked being onstage.

Betty Bloomer was sixteen when her father died in a bizarre accident; he was asphyxiated under his car in his driveway, apparently while trying to repair it with the motor running. He left enough insurance to support his widow and ambitious daughter, enough to send Betty to Vermont's Bennington School of Dance for two summers. When she was twenty, her mother let her enroll at Martha Graham's studio in New York City. She loved it; she was young, on her own, and working toward her goal. To help pay her expenses she landed a job—like Phyllis Brown—with the Powers modeling agency. She posed for fashion photos, modeled hats and furs and sportswear in the garment center, and led a spartan social life. "You can't carouse and be a dancer too," Graham told her. After two years of hard training and instruction came a major disappointment: Betty Bloomer was not chosen as a main dancer for Martha Graham's major performances. Her mother drove her home.

Back in Grand Rapids she got a job at Herpolsheimer's, as assistant to the fashion coordinator. In 1942, after an exciting courtship, she married William Warren, a boy she had known since she was twelve. Exempt from military service because of diabetes, Warren was much like her father—a handsome traveling salesman who drank. After the first couple of years she knew the marriage was failing. "Even when Bill was home I wasn't happy," she said. He liked being on the road; she wanted a home. "I was ready for a house and children," but Warren preferred to spend the evening in a barroom. Thinking it through, looking at the bleak future, she realized she no longer loved her husband and decided to end the marriage.

"Dear Bill . . ." She was at home in their apartment writing him a letter telling him it was over when she got a call from his boss. Warren, he said, was in a diabetic coma in a hospital in Boston, and might not live. He did survive, and came back to Grand Rapids to live as an invalid, at his parents' home. For two years Betty Warren worked at the department store all day and came home to care for her husband at night. Then he began to get better, learned to walk again, and got his job back. "As soon as he was all right, back at work again, and could take care of himself," she wrote, "I went to a lawyer and started divorce proceedings." Her husband did not contest it. "I took a dollar in settlement," she said, "and it was finished."

To restart her life, she thought of leaving Grand Rapids to make a career in fashion. She didn't know where she wanted to go, maybe to Brazil, but of one thing she was sure: "I was so fed up with marriage that I knew I'd never consider another one." That was her state of mind when Peg Neuman called and put Jerry Ford on the phone.

Early in their friendship, Jerry Ford and Betty Warren discovered in each other qualities of trust, of loyalty, of dependability. Both liked to work hard; but when they could find the time, both liked the diversion of dinner and dancing, football games in Ann Arbor, or a quiet evening together as he puffed his pipe and read and she studied the fashion magazines.

In her he found good common sense and candor, traits he admired; in him she observed the self-reliance and indomitable spirit that her own experiences had instilled in her. She admired his sense of community service, and she liked him as a man.

"I found him physically attractive," she said. "I enjoyed his company and his friends. . . . We'd agreed not to get serious, but now I found myself wondering if I was going to ruin everything by falling in love with a man who didn't want me to love him."

He did; he just couldn't bring himself to tell her so. Ford invited her to Thanksgiving dinner with his family. "Jerry's stepfather stood as straight as an arrow," she said, "and I had the immediate impression that he lived his life that way. His mother was a handsome woman, with tremendous charisma. I could see why my mother had told me everyone liked Dorothy Ford. She seemed such a strong woman, confident and positive, just the right person to raise these four Ford boys at the table. Everyone was courteous and respectful, and I thought, 'What a wonderful family Jerry has.'"

Over the Christmas holidays of 1947 Ford went off on his own for a two-week skiing trip to Sun Valley, Idaho. As a going-away present she gave him a

Christmas stocking filled with surprises, including a pipe lighter engraved with a sentiment she felt but pondered with care before revealing: "To the light of my life." On his first day in Sun Valley, Ford said, "Suddenly it dawned on me that I missed and needed her very much." He wrote to her every night.

On New Year's Day they talked by telephone, and she mentioned that she was going to New York City the next day for Herpolsheimer's. Ford arranged for her to meet two of his favorite New York friends, Mr. and Mrs. Bradshaw Crandall.

When Betty Warren went to the Crandalls' Manhattan studio she took along Walt Jones, a longtime friend from Grand Rapids who lived in New York. After a few minutes of casual conversation, in walked Phyllis Brown. Or, as Betty wrote later, "In she slinked, Jerry's model. It hit me like a ton of bricks. She was a gorgeous blonde, skinny as a rail, and when she peeled off her mink coat and threw it on a chair, she was revealed—and I mean revealed—to be wearing a black satin dress cut down to her bottom rib." Miss Brown coolly upstaged Betty Warren from Grand Rapids and stole her escort.

Hurt and angry, Betty Warren wrote Ford that she didn't like his New York friends or him either. "I never knew why Brad did that," Ford said long after the incident, "but it almost cost me Betty."

It was not Crandall but Phyllis Brown who staged the scene. "I was such a bitch that day," she said, "but I was jealous of Jerry's new girl friend."

In January, when Jerry Ford and Betty Warren saw each other back in Grand Rapids, both realized they were in love. "The three-week separation made the difference," she said. One evening in February, as they sat side by side on the couch in her apartment, he delivered a heartfelt but cryptic proposal: "I would like to marry you, but we can't get married until next fall and I can't tell you why."

She did not ask why, or even pause. "I took him up on it instantly," she said, "before he could change his mind."

The reason was that politics came first for Ford. No personal commitment could stand in the way of his determination to win his campaign for the House of Representatives.

By spring he was sure he would face Jonkman in a one-on-one showdown in a Republican primary. He had the support of a wide and growing cadre of anti-McKay Republicans and was organizing volunteers in the precincts. "I didn't want to cause Jonkman to get active," he said, but it was time to go after blocs of key voters. "First, I had to make sure I would have the endorsements of a number of Dutch leaders. The Dutch made up sixty percent of the population of the district, and ninety percent were Republican. There were two rival groups, the Dutch Reformed Church and the Dutch Christian Reformed Church; and Jonkman was a Christian Reformed leader. I'm Irish, Scotch, and English, and have no Dutch background. Fortunately, Dr. Ver Meulen, my friend from the Home Front, got a group of Reformed leaders to be on my side. From South High I had some Christian Reformed friends. And I won the support of acquaintances I had made working with the United Way, the Red Cross, the veterans, and the farmers. So I had a broad base of leaders to go on my campaign committee before I even announced."

Ford became a formal candidate for the House in June 1948, just before the filing deadline and three months before the September primary. "Barney Jonkman just pooh-poohed my candidacy," Ford said. Then President Truman called the Eightieth Congress back into session, keeping Jonkman in Washington. Ford could campaign in the district without competition.

Ford's senior partner at the law firm, Julius Amberg, strongly opposed Jonkman and his isolationism. Amberg was a Democrat, but thought Ford highly qualified for public service and called him into his office. "Jerry," he said, "I don't know if you can beat Jonkman, but we want to help you. Why don't you come in to the office for one hour a day, and spend the rest of the time campaigning."

It was a great political gift. Without embarrassment, Ford told his boss, "I believe the people of the Fifth District are ready to vote for youth and honesty, and ready to support American leadership in preserving the peace and economic growth of the world."

In all his speeches Ford tried to be positive. He told the voters who he was and where he stood: On economic policy and government he was conservative; he believed the less government, the better; and the less taxpayer's money spent, the better. "On foreign policy, I am an internationalist," he said. "I do not believe America can live any longer in isolation." Despite the America-first tradition of Western Michigan, Ford openly and ardently championed the Marshall Plan and the United Nations.

For his campaign office Ford deliberately chose both a symbol and a site. To emphasize his World War II service, he rented a Navy surplus Quonset hut and painted it red, white, and blue; then he set it up in the parking lot of Wurzburg's downtown department store, just below the office window of his political nemesis, Frank McKay. In a couple of days, the president of the department store got a complaint from McKay.

"Get Ford off that property," McKay demanded.

The president of Wurzburg's called the company's lawyer, who happened to be Julius Amberg. Amberg sent for Ford. "Jerry, as you know, Wurzburg's is a good client of this firm, and they are getting complaints about your headquarters on their parking lot. Would you be willing to move your Quonset hut somewhere else?"

"Mr. Amberg," Ford said, "we have a contract for that space and we are not going to move that hut."

"Excellent," Amberg said. "That's exactly what I was hoping you would say."

"We would welcome a public confrontation with Frank McKay," Ford said. Both smiled. The Quonset hut stayed in Wurzburg's parking lot.

To get his name before the voters, Ford bought space on billboards. Jonkman had a reputation for being lazy, so the Ford billboards carried the slogan, "*Jerry Ford—to work for you in Congress.*"

Ford challenged Jonkman to public debates. Jonkman did not even reply. Ford pressed harder, pounding the sidewalks in every part of Grand Rapids, driving out to the small towns and farms, speaking wherever he could find someone to listen. "I would go out to the General Motors plant gate at six o'clock in the morning, and the union bosses, who hated my guts, would boo and give me a hard time," he said. "But Art Brown, my old teammate at South High, was working there, and he would always organize a counter group to cheer and applaud and show their support."

Some thirty days before the primary, Jonkman returned to Grand Rapids, expecting McKay would have the votes sewed up as usual. Ten days before the election *The Grand Rapids Press*, the larger of the two daily newspapers, endorsed Ford. Jonkman, enraged, attacked the *Press* and vilified Ford and his supporters. The *Press* retaliated by running a favorable story about Ford every day.

On primary day, Tuesday, September 14, 1948, Ford and his campaign organizers and volunteers turned out 23,632 Republican votes, to Jonkman's 14,341. For a little-known young lawyer to defeat a ten-year Republican Congressman in a solid Republican district was a major upset in Michigan, and Ford was proud. "I had gambled for my political future and won," he said. "I had won a race that, six months before, no one had given me a chance to win."

A month later, Ford and Betty Warren were married at Grace Episcopal Church in Grand Rapids. She wore sapphire blue satin and a matching picture hat; he came to the altar with shoes still muddy from campaigning on a farm that morning.

Ford had carefully selected the date, Friday, October 15, after the primary and eighteen days before the general election. Early in the campaign his political counselors, Stiles and Buchen, had persuaded him that marrying a divorcée might cost him primary votes among the moralistic Dutch. Wait, they suggested, until after the primary; the Democratic opponent will not be a serious threat in a district so strongly Republican.

The bride-to-be accepted the politics of his timetable when he revealed it to her, a month before he announced his candidacy. "I didn't know what running for Congress meant," she said. "I was very unprepared to be a political wife, but I didn't worry because I really didn't think he was going to win." Once he began campaigning openly, she became his most ardent supporter, leaving Herpolsheimer's every night to address envelopes at the Quonset hut and enlisting the store models to hand out Ford-for-Congress leaflets. "After my initial misgivings," she said, "I got carried away by the momentum of the primary battle. I wanted him to win."

At the wedding Janet Packer Ford, matron of honor, the wife of Tom, and the sister-in-law who had been around the Ford boys the longest, told the bride: "Betty, I want to warn you. Jerry's mistress will not be a woman. It will be his work."

For the new Mrs. Ford, the honeymoon was less romance than political baptism. On the afternoon of their wedding they drove to Ann Arbor, celebrated with friends until late evening, spent the night in the Allenel Hotel, and saw the Michigan-Northwestern game the next day. At dusk they drove seventy miles north to Owosso, Michigan, where New York's Governor Thomas E. Dewey—the Republican challenger to President Truman—was speaking at a political rally in his old home town. At midnight groom and bride left Owosso for Detroit, arrived at the Book-Cadillac Hotel at 3:00 A.M., spent a quiet Sunday, left for a meeting with political advisers in Ann Arbor Monday morning, and drove on to Grand Rapids. "After politicking all our wedding weekend," she said, "I was looking forward to a nice, quiet evening at home." But as they reached the edge of the city Ford said casually, "I've got a very important political meeting at 7:30. Do you suppose you could fix me a bowl of soup and a sandwich before I leave?"

"Of course, dear," she said, and did. "I knew what it was going to be like from then on," she said.

The political meeting Ford had to attend was to organize and energize the campaign workers through the final two weeks before the general election. Ford himself took nothing for granted, even though the Democratic candidate, Fred Barr, was making no more than a token effort. Barr, a friend of both Jerry and Betty Ford, even made a contribution to the Ford campaign.

On Tuesday, November 2, 1948, President Truman pulled off the political upset of the century. Not only did Truman defeat Dewey, but the Democrats also took both the House of Representatives and the Senate in a landslide.

In the Fifth District of Michigan the landslide went for Republican Jerry Ford. With his 74,191 votes in the final tally, Ford was elected to the Eighty-first Congress by 60.5 percent, a solid margin for a first political campaign. "I have to admit I was proud," Ford said. He had challenged the political boss and won.

4

A MAN OF THE HOUSE

In his best suit and with his shoes clean and shined, Representative Ford stood in the packed House chamber on Monday, January 3, 1949, to be sworn in as a member of the Eighty-first Congress. "It was a big day, a great thrill," Ford said. Looking up after taking the oath, he found the place in the gallery where he had first seen the House in session almost twenty years before, and found his bride seated high in a corner with other freshman wives. "She looked as proud as I felt," Ford said. "From that first day on, I knew I wanted the House to be my career."

A slender man with wiry black hair walked up and held out a slender hand. "I'm Dick Nixon, from California. I heard about your big win in Michigan, and I want to say hello and welcome you to the House." Ford was astonished that someone had heard of him.

For his first House office he was assigned Room 321 in the Old House office building, across the hall from a young Democrat from Massachusetts, John F. Kennedy. "Our offices were in the furthest corner, and we had a long walk to the floor of the House," Ford said. "So we spent a lot of time walking back and forth together. I didn't agree with a lot of his liberal philosophy, but I found him a smart, attractive, decent, and honorable man. I liked Jack from the first."

Having successfully challenged the Republican establishment in his Congressional District, he resolved at the beginning he would not let himself become a captive of the party establishment in the House. On his first vote Ford went against Joe Martin, the Republican Leader, and Charles Halleck, the whip, who were trying to reduce the power of the House Rules Committee. Each invited Ford in for a discussion; but the new member said no, he could not support them.

"I thought I was right, and I told them so," Ford said. Of 171 Republicans in the House, he was one of ten to vote against Martin and Halleck. The vote served a purpose: Ford wanted to show his independence, that his vote could not be taken for granted.

Soon after, Ford took another unpopular stand. Democrats were promoting a pension of $100 a month for all veterans, whether they had been wounded or even in combat. He opposed it. With some fifteen Republicans, mostly World War II veterans, he established the Chowder and Marching Society to block the automatic pension for veterans.

Chowder and Marching was Ford's first alliance in Washington. By design and by numbers, power is diffused in the House; no Member's original idea or act of legislation will bear his stamp at the end of the process. Decisions are made by alliances—within a committee, within a party, across party lines—but always in accord with the dynamics of political interests. Ford realized that politics worked in the House as it had in Grand Rapids—"You had to make allegiances to get something done."

Like all House freshmen, Ford was handed a drudge of an assignment, to be the most junior member of the minority on the Public Works Committee. He saw it as opportunity. Politics is trading; and Public Works is the marketplace. On the Public Works Committee he found out in his first House term how deals were made, how the House really worked.

One day, to Ford's surprise, President Truman invited him and other members of the committee to the White House. "Mr. Truman wanted us to approve his plan to rebuild and modernize the White House," Ford said. "He gave us a personally guided tour and showed us where Margaret's grand piano had almost fallen through the floor. But what I remembered most was when he took us in the Oval Office and I saw that little sign on his desk: 'The Buck Stops Here.' I thought, 'Well, that's a good description of a President's job.' "

Within the clubby confines of the House cloakroom, Ford found himself shunned by the more conservative Republicans within the Michigan delegation. "I had beaten one of their buddies, Barney Jonkman," Ford said.

But Earl Michener, the senior Republican from Michigan, went out of his way to help Ford. Michener, first elected in 1918, commanded respect on both sides of the aisle. To cultivate Michener, Ford would sit with him in the House chamber by the hour.

"Jerry," Michener told Ford, "you can become one of two kinds of Members in the House. You can either be a floor man, and learn how to handle debate, rules, procedures; or you can become a committee expert. If it's the latter, pick an area of your committee on which you want to be an expert. Learn more about that subject than anyone else in the House of Representatives, so that when you speak on it, people listen."

Michener put in a good word for Ford with John Taber, senior Republican on the House Appropriations Committee, and with the revered Speaker of the House, Sam Rayburn. Ford invested hours in sitting with and listening to Taber, a tight-fisted old curmudgeon from upstate New York who was admissions officer for any Republican aspiring to the Appropriations Committee. On most issues Ford was as conservative as Taber and often voted with him. Taber liked that.

From his very first day in the House, Ford kept what he called "my diary," a sketchy register of major events, routine meetings, and occasional passages of introspection. He made his notes in the five-by-eight-inch hardcover appointment books that the Ford Paint & Varnish Company gave out each year to favored customers. The sparse entries in his careful script, where all loops are closed and all i's dotted, suggest the professional and personal life of a Congressman in the fifties and sixties. Among the entries in his first weeks:

> *Move into office. Conference with Senator Vandenberg. President's State of Union Address. Session of Congress—Counting electoral votes. President's budget. Radio transcription. Call from Speaker Joe Martin. Charlie Halleck's office. Inauguration Day. Betty and I dinner at Hot Shoppe. Martha Graham dancers.*

Betty Ford had not forgotten her glory days of professional training in New York City, and seized the chance to see her idol and former teacher. Washington was exciting; and Betty Ford, like her husband, enjoyed the heady life in the Capital. She joined the Eighty-first Club of Congressional wives, where she made new friends—among them, Lady Bird Johnson, wife of a new Senator from Texas, and Muriel Humphrey, wife of a new Senator from Minnesota. Club membership entitled her to fold bandages for the Red Cross and to have tea with First Lady Bess Truman at Blair House. "It was all new and exciting," she said.

From the early years of the Republic, Washington was the Capital City where, with certain exceptions, men governed and women kept house and raised their children. Too often, the corollary effect was that men grew with responsibility and women were outdistanced. In her first year in Washington the young wife of Congressman Ford observed that danger. "I saw that I would have to grow with Jerry, or be left behind," Betty Ford said. "And I had no intention of being left behind." To find out how Congress worked she spent days on the Hill, sitting in on hearings or watching debate from the gallery. She tracked a bill to see how it worked its way through the legislative process. She watched the Supreme Court. She guided her husband's constituents around the Capitol and took a course in public speaking. On Saturday, when he worked in the office, she helped out with the mail and filing.

"Our marriage was going beautifully, and of course we were both elated when I became pregnant," she said. If it were a boy, she wanted to name him Gerald Ford, but Ford refused. He had never liked being called "Junior" or "Junie." "It can be Mike, Pat, Pete, anything," Ford said, "just so it's not a junior."

> *Ford Diary: March 3, 1950—"Alaska (statehood). For." March 7, 1950—"Hawaii (statehood). For." March 14, 1950—"Mike Ford born Doctors Hospital 6:14."*

Every day at the office there was something new, something to learn. Ford read up on President Truman's proposals to create the North Atlantic Treaty Organization to keep the peace in Europe, and voted his support. He voted for the money to build the H-bomb. When North Korea invaded South Korea, Ford publicly commended President Truman's decision to order American planes and troops in to repel the invasion. He was beginning to be recognized: the U.S. Junior Chamber of Commerce named him one of the ten outstanding young men of the year for "his vigorous and hard-hitting reform movement against well-entrenched county and state political machines."

Mornings, Ford left their one-bedroom, eighty-dollar-a-month Georgetown apartment early, often walked the three miles to Capitol Hill, unlocked the door to Room 321, read the Washington newspapers, *The New York Times,* both Grand Rapids papers, the *Press* and the *Herald,* and scanned the *Congressional Record.* He talked over the day's schedule with John Milanowski, the able young lawyer he had brought from Grand Rapids to help manage his office. "John was a tough Marine, with a good ear to listen to people and understand their feelings," Ford said. "And he got things done."

Ford struck up a friendship with Dick Nixon. "Nixon was getting a lot of publicity because of his work on the House Un-American Activities Committee investigation of Alger Hiss, and because of his performance on the Herter Committee, which went to Europe and reported back on the need and necessity for the Marshall Plan," Ford said. "I was very impressed with Dick's ability to articulate arguments on the Hiss case. He was not a spellbinding orator, but he was a very convincing speaker. He organized his remarks, he knew his subject, and he argued very logically. So my first impressions were that he was a person of considerable talent."

Ford and Nixon talked often. "One of the strongest ties of our relationship was the fact that we came from strong families that suffered adversities during the Depression," Ford said. "We respected each other because we knew the other had come up the hard way economically and politically. Both of us were strongly dedicated to certain domestic policies at home and U.S. leadership abroad. In fact, in political philosophy, we were about as close as two people could get. And Dick and I also enjoyed each other's company because we had similar outside interests in what most Americans like—football, baseball, and other athletic contests."

Every month or so Ford, Nixon, and the young and aspiring Republican warriors who organized Chowder and Marching got together with their wives for an informal dinner. Nixon, Ford observed, was either in a corner talking serious foreign policy or playing the piano for members stimulated by good spirits to sing. "Dick was not a competent piano player," Ford said, "but when he was banging out songs with the people crowded around him, he would be joyous."

Early in their friendship Ford noticed Nixon's propensity for a sudden change of mood. "One minute he was outgoing, extrovert, the next reflective, even sullen," Ford said. "My impression was that his moodiness drained a lot out of him."

During these evenings out Betty Ford and Pat Nixon became good friends. The Nixons had two baby daughters when the Fords first met them. Ford observed that Pat Nixon was "very reserved, very unemotional. Shy, I thought. She sat always in the background, but always under total self-control. Very seldom did she offer an opinion on anything; but she was interested, observing and listening, never missing anything you said about a person or an issue. She seemed to be getting it in her mind and cataloging it. What she did with it, I don't know."

In his second year in the House, Ford got an extraordinary break. The only Michigan Republican on the House Appropriations Committee gave up his seat to run for governor, and no other member from the state would give up seniority on his own committee to take the coveted position. Ford asked his friend John Taber for the slot, and Taber replied: "Jerry, if the Michigan delegation will vote for you, I want you on the committee."

Ford was at odds with his fellow Members from Michigan: He opposed a big public works project the state delegation wanted. At home with Betty, he discussed his dilemma. She reminded him of his campaign promise to vote his conscience. Yes, he said, but he wanted that seat on the Appropriations Committee. Finally she said: "Frankly, Jerry, if you're not going to vote your conscience, you're no good as a Congressman. And you might as well quit. You always say you've got to vote for what you think is right, and if that means you have to sacrifice getting on the Appropriations Committee, that's too bad."

Ford stuck to his position on the public works project, still persuaded his fellow Republicans from Michigan to support his bid, and won the seat on the Appropriations Committee. "And that," Ford said, "was the greatest break in the world—to get on one of the three best committees in the House before the end of my first term. Appropriations was where the power was, and I said to myself, 'That's going to be my specialty—how the government spends money.'"

The power of the House Committee on Appropriations is rooted in the American Revolution; it can be traced directly to the Founding Fathers' hostility to King George III's taxation without representation. At Philadelphia the Constitutional Convention wrote into Article I that only the representatives chosen directly by the people, that is, the House of Representatives— can originate a bill to tax. Standing on that Constitutional warrant, the House arrogated to itself another power—that only the body of Congress that can initiate a Federal tax can initiate a bill to spend that tax.

In 1789, in the first session of the First Congress, the first revenue bill was referred to an ad hoc Committee on Ways and Means. After the Committee was made a permanent instrument of the House in 1795, it continued to hold the authority to propose tax and spending decisions to the full House. By charter and by tradition the Committee Chairman has always wielded great power. During the Civil War Thaddeus Stevens, a Pennsylvania ironmonger, Whig-turned-Republican, and passionate abolitionist, used his authority as Chairman of Ways and Means to raise money and spend whatever was necessary for the victories of the Union armies. In 1865 the House split its power over money, with the responsibility to tax remaining with Ways and Means and the power to spend handed to a new Appropriations

Committee. Stevens, who had his choice, picked Appropriations.

From the end of the Civil War until the present time, the House has made the initial Appropriations decisions; the Senate, through its own Appropriations Committee, has been a court of appeals. When Ford was appointed to the Appropriations Committee in 1950, he became one of the nucleus of Members who make up an in-House elite with the formal title: The House Committee on Appropriations.

The name is dull. Its deliberations are tedious. Its decisions rarely make headlines because the pick-and-shovel work of Appropriations glazes the eyes of Capitol Hill reporters and their editors. But inside the House, the thirty Democrats and twenty Republicans then on Appropriations commanded particular respect. The job held the ultimate power in any government: Money.

"For me," Ford said, "it was the place to be. I began to learn how the Federal government really works." It was also the place where Ford first began to earn a reputation among the House leaders for hard work and steadiness, and for being a man who always kept his word.

Though Ford's House seat was safe in 1950, he did not take it for granted. Every recess and every long weekend, he flew or drove to Grand Rapids to visit with constituents, to see and be seen, to tour factory and farm, and to speak to veterans and businessmen and civic clubs. He never stopped campaigning, and his standing in the District was so solid that he had no opposition in the primary that year. In November he won his first reelection with 66.7 percent of the vote.

Encouraged by his success, and committed to make Washington his new home, Ford moved his family to a two-bedroom garden apartment in Alexandria, Virginia. Dick and Pat Nixon lived nearby, and recommended the parklike development as a good place to bring up young children.

With his reelection came more home-town political responsibility, and in 1951 Ford was asked to bring in a national figure to be the Lincoln Day speaker for Kent County Republicans. Ford invited Dick Nixon, just elected to the Senate from California after a campaign against Helen Gahagan Douglas that was more a back-alley brawl than a political contest. Ford calculated that Senator Nixon would draw a crowd in Grand Rapids.

"We had a big turnout," Ford said, "and after the dinner the Republican hierarchy in Kent County invited Dick and me to a private home for discussion. There were about twenty people there, and some were apprehensive about his role in the Hiss case. They were good Republicans, but concerned. For an hour and a half Nixon very articulately answered all their questions. I couldn't help but be impressed with his knowledge and his ability to speak about it."

That night Nixon stayed in the home of Ford's parents. "We had a drink and sat around late, talking about defense, international problems, the Congressional situation, the 'fifty-two election prospects, everything," Ford said. "Both of us felt that Republicans had to win the White House and Congress to reverse the spending policies of the Truman Administration. He told me how much he disliked Truman and the liberals. I told him I was for General Eisenhower and I planned to do my best to make him the candidate to lead the Republican ticket. That visit to Grand Rapids was where I first really got to know Nixon. That day and a half convinced me that he was going to play a significant role in the American political scene."

In 1951, the Republican Party was changing. After five losses in a row, Republicans wanted to win the White House, and a faction of young leaders believed they had the candidate—General Dwight D. Eisenhower, for whom the ancient Greeks might well have designed the word *charisma*.

In September of that year, Massachusetts Senator Henry Cabot Lodge met with Eisenhower in Europe and delivered a forceful argument that it would be in the national interest for him to leave NATO and become a candidate. Eisenhower agreed to think it over.

With the New Hampshire primary only weeks away, Ford and eighteen other members of the House appealed urgently to Eisenhower by letter: "An overwhelming majority of the people of the United States want you as their leader. . . . This is the surest way to preserve your efforts in Europe and to promote peace in the world." Eisenhower found it "an impressive letter," an element "in influencing me to be a candidate."

Ford joined up to challenge Senator Robert Taft and the Republican establishment because, he said, "I was convinced that if General Eisenhower were nominated he would win, and I was not comfortable with the views of Senator Taft. He was not an isolationist, but he was less of an internationalist than Eisenhower was, or I was. In addition, Taft was more liberal on some domestic policies than I was. For example, Taft was for Federal aid to education. He was for public housing. At that time I was opposed to both."

But the decision hurt Ford back in his Congressional district. In Ford's mail came rebukes from the true believers in Taft. "There was talk that the conservatives would run someone against me in the next primary," Ford said.

"I knew I had to listen, and it took a lot of explaining to people back in the district. But I had to make my own judgment about what to do. And I did."

Ford campaigned in 1952 even harder for Eisenhower after he picked Nixon for Vice President. In September, when Tom Dewey pushed Nixon to take himself off the ticket because of news stories about Nixon's "secret campaign fund," Ford wired Nixon: "I am in your corner 100 percent. Fight it to the finish just as you did the smears by the Communists when you were proving charges against Alger Hiss. . . . I will personally welcome you in Grand Rapids or any other part of Michigan." Nixon never forgot Ford's strong declaration of support.

Eisenhower brought his campaign train through Grand Rapids in the last weeks before the election. Ford, on the platform with Eisenhower, had never seen such a display of enthusiasm for a Presidential candidate. On election day Ford's early commitment to Eisenhower was validated; Ike won the Fifth District of Michigan by 64.1 percent—a victory almost equal to Ford's own 66.2 percent margin for his third term.

With the election of Eisenhower in 1952, the Republicans also won control of the Senate and the House. The new Chairman of Appropriations, John Taber, summoned Ford. "Jerry, I'm going to put you on the defense subcommittee."

It was another lucky break for Ford; of the 435 members of the House he would become one of eleven members to decide defense spending.

"There will be three groups," Taber said, "one for the Army, one for the Navy, one for the Air Force. You're a Navy man, aren't you."

"Yes," Ford said, "I spent almost four years in the Navy."

"I'm going to make you chairman of the Army panel," Taber said.

"Why, Mr. Chairman? I know more about the Navy."

"You've got too many friends in the Navy," Taber said. "All those damn admirals will be after you, and you won't resist them. But if you're with the Army, you will tell the generals to go to hell."

Ford's long hours courting Taber had paid off: For Eisenhower's first two years as president, Ford, at thirty-nine, was chairman of the Army subcommittee on Appropriations. It was the first time Ford could savor the taste of the raw power of being part of the majority in Congress.

The old-timers on the Appropriations staff could not recall a Member more devoted to his job than Ford. He relished the work. "We questioned the secretaries of Defense, State, Army, Navy, Air Force, and the heads of the Joint

Chiefs of Staff," Ford said. "We went through the documentation page by page, making them prove the need for a weapons program, requiring the best figures on costs. The eleven of us on that subcommittee knew more about the military and its programs than most admirals and generals. The brass changed, but there was almost no turnover on the committee."

Mel Laird, who served on Appropriations with Ford, said that Ford excelled at asking questions. To quiz a Defense Department witness, Ford devised his own catechism for any new weapon: "Number one, how did you decide what the costs would be? Number two, give me your schedule for the four key things—research, development, production, and deployment. Number three, give me your cost estimates in the interim." The next year, when the same witness or his successor came before the committee, Ford would bring out his notes from the previous year and ask, "This is what you told us last year where you would be. Now tell me where you are." Ford's membership in the small club that ruled Defense spending remained always bright in his memory. For him, it was the varsity, playing on the first team, and playing sixty minutes of every game. The Defense Appropriations Subcommittee room was his favorite place; he spent far more time there than in his House office or on the floor.

Except for four National Guard units, there was no military base in Ford's District. A group of Grand Rapids businessmen came to his Washington office one day, and their spokesman said: "Jerry, with all this influence you have, wouldn't it be good if we got a military base established in the Fifth District?"

"I am opposed to it," Ford said. "I have seen a number of cases where communities will get a base, and the base will bring in people and jobs, and everything is fine during a military buildup or in a war. But when the buildup ends, or the war is over, everything drops dead. In the end you have more problems than benefits."

Ford pointed out that General Motors and other firms in the district manufactured a variety of equipment and supplies for the military forces through contracts won by competitive bidding. That diversity, he believed, was better than dependence on a single military base. "I was not very popular," Ford said, "but I think in time I was proved right."

From his first term in the House Ford had publicly supported President Truman's decision to defend South Korea, and with equal fervor he supported President Eisenhower's actions to end the Korean War. In 1953 Ford decided, as the Appropriations subcommittee chairman for the Army, to see for himself what American forces and financial aid were accomplishing in the Far East.

When Congress took its August recess, Ford flew to Korea, saw the return of American prisoners of war, toured the front lines, and inspected a training camp for South Korean troops. In his diary he noted: "The R.O.K.'s in another year will have the finest army in Asia but no money to fight without our aid."

From Korea Ford flew on to Saigon. He had supported requests by Truman and Eisenhower to send military advisers and some sixty million dollars to aid the French in their fight against Ho Chi Minh and his Communist insurgents. For three days Ford inspected French forward troops and supply operations and talked with commanders and soldiers in the ranks. His conclusion: The French had neither a plan for popular government in Vietnam nor any practical strategy for winning a war against the Communists. Too much spit-and-polish military show, too little reality, he thought. The comment he set down in his diary on August 6, 1953, about the French in Vietnam was unconsciously prophetic: "Speeches. Pictures. Bally-hoo."

After a stop in Formosa to meet General and Madame Chiang Kai-shek and to confer with U.S. officials, Ford observed that the remnants of the Nationalist Chinese had neither the will nor the forces to return to the mainland. More likely, he thought, the island and its people showed the promise of becoming an economic entity and a politically separate country. In Tokyo he asked for a round of briefings on the political, military, and naval situation in the Pacific and on the mainland of Asia. From Ambassador John Moore Allison, he noted, ". . . Really got a good analysis."

Flying commercial back to the U.S., Ford stopped off in Honolulu and in San Francisco to inspect military hospitals and port facilities. In Washington he was met at the airport by Betty Ford, three-year-old Mike, and Jack, born the year before while Ford was energetically campaigning for Eisenhower. As soon as he unpacked, Ford went to the office to begin drafting his report on the trip to the Appropriations Committee.

Ford's first official mission abroad as a Congressman offers an early but telling portrait of his performance in public life. He set for himself a demanding work schedule and met it. He asked questions, and then more questions: "Does this Federal program work? Tell me how we are spending this money. Is this the best use of our funds?" He went to learn. He sought the best experts available. He listened with care, and banked his conclusions against the day he would need them.

Ford came home convinced that no country on the mainland or rim of Asia was secure from the expansionist ambitions of the USSR, Red China, or both. The trip reinforced Ford's belief that the United States had a compelling national security interest in preventing Communist expansion in Asia, and a moral obligation to assist the creation of democratic governments there. Like most World War II veterans who had been part of the American military might that defeated Japanese and German aggression, Ford believed in the postwar decades that U.S. military power was invincible. And like most, he believed that America should be prepared to use that power to advance the cause of free peoples everywhere.

Back on Capitol Hill he reported to his colleagues on the Communist threat in Asia. In particular, he told his ten fellow members of Defense Appropriations, the French were losing their War in Vietnam, and he was prepared to commit whatever American forces were necessary to stop Communist aggression in Southeast Asia.

So impressed were the Democrats on the Appropriations Committee with Ford's diligence that they handed him more responsibility when they regained control of the House in 1955. Ford flew to Europe to report on the readiness of Allied military forces and to Warsaw and Moscow to assess potential adversaries. He asked for and was granted an additional assignment—the committee overseeing U.S. foreign aid.

The authority to give away U.S. public money to foreign nations is an essential tool for every President; sometimes it takes money to persuade a needy nation to comply with some U.S. interest. For a Congressman, however, the foreign aid assignment is not only thankless but usually damaging at election time. Ford's seat was safe, and he liked his added responsibility. Every Secretary of State had to come before his committee to justify the President's need to give away money and to explain how it would be used. For Ford, it was an opportunity to find out more about the complex relationship among military spending, foreign aid, and U.S. foreign policy.

Ford's effectiveness prompted George Mahon, the West Texas Democrat who was Ford's boss on Defense Appropriations for a decade, to rely on Ford and to promote him at every opportunity. "I was impressed with his calm judgment and steady hand," Mahon said. To him, Ford not only understood national security issues, even "the intricacies of nuclear strategic capabilities"; he was never partisan on defense. "Regardless of the administration in power," Mahon said, "he works toward the accomplishment of the attainable. He is a man you can deal with."

* * *

In 1956 Representative Clarence Cannon, a crusty old-timer who was Chairman of the House Appropriations Committee, came up to Ford in the House chamber one day. "I want you to be at a certain office at 10 o'clock tomorrow morning."

"What for, Mr. Chairman?" Ford said.

"Just be there," Cannon said. He gave him the room number and told him to mention the conversation to no one.

The next day, Ford went to the room, in a remote part of the House complex, where he was met by three armed guards. "After carefully looking over my credentials, they let me in," Ford said. "Inside, I found that I was about to become a member of the Intelligence Subcommittee of Appropriations. Just the five of us—Clarence Cannon, John Taber, Dick Wigglesworth, Harry Shepherd, and myself—no staff. Allen Dulles [Director of the CIA] would bring a few of his people in for five or so days every year and we would hold hearings on the CIA budget and all related intelligence matters. No transcripts were made. None."

Ford never discussed the secret plans and proposals that he and his peers in this most privy council endorsed during his eight years of active service with the group. He would only say, "We had total access to all the CIA people and to all the other intelligence officials to ask questions. Whatever they were going to do, we knew about it."

When Ford joined the committee, the commitment had already been made to invest in U-2 photo-reconnaissance aircraft, and flights from Turkey across the USSR were beginning. In his time of service on the Committee the CIA sent arms for the Hungarian Revolution and to Laos; deposed unfriendly leaders in the Congo, Algeria, Turkey, Guatemala; built satellites to spy on any part of earth and invented devices to eavesdrop on the innermost secrets of foe and friend; organized a military invasion of Cuba that came to be known as the Bay of Pigs; and made an enormous investment in Vietnam.

Ford was admitted into the inner temple of national secrets because the Democrats in command of the House trusted him. In that day Speaker Sam Rayburn and a handful of committee chairmen ruled. The Speaker and his high command not only managed the business of legislative government with dispatch and order; they also said yes and no to all promotions. The linkage was not a coincidence.

"I was fortunate," Ford said, "that some of Speaker Rayburn's old friends on the Republican side were very kind to me." Rayburn rarely mixed with Republicans; Ford was flattered when Rayburn nodded to him in the Speaker's Lobby.

If he should ever become Speaker, Ford resolved, Sam Rayburn would be his model. "Speaker Rayburn epitomized the best in the Speakership," Ford said. "As a leader he was very strong. He was fair. He was a gentleman. He was bipartisan in the national interest. He had just the attributes that ought to be incorporated in the Speaker of the House."

After three terms and two children, Betty Ford confronted her husband one evening: "Are we ever going back to Grand Rapids? Or is Washington where we really live? You have the House, but we need a home!"

She had no doubt about his answer. "I knew that politics was in his blood, that he loved every minute of being in the House," she said. She too loved Washington, and was ready to stay, but not in their tiny, rented apartment in Alexandria, Virginia. "Jerry didn't realize that we were wall to wall in tricycles and wagons and toys," she said. "I'm sure he never noticed—he was happy at what he was doing. And he was away much of the time, while I was alone with these little kids in that little apartment." If they were going to stay in Washington, she told her husband, "We've either got to buy or build or rent a house."

"Well," Ford replied, "let's build what we want." She quickly found a new development lot they both liked at 514 Crown View Drive in Alexandria. Borrowing plans and ideas from friends who had just finished their house, they designed a two-story brick and siding suburban house, with a living room, a small den, four bedrooms, and two baths. The total cost, after they added a swimming pool and a downstairs playroom for the children, was about forty thousand dollars, which they financed with a 7 percent mortgage. In the Spring of 1955 they moved in, in time for the birth of their third son, Steven, the next year, and the birth of their daughter, Susan, in the year following.

Ford's decision to establish his family in Washington was tangible affirmation of his ambition to reach the top in the U.S. House of Representatives. His long working hours and frequent travels made it all the more important to him that he make his family comfortable in Washington. Although he had to rent part of his house in Grand Rapids to keep up the payments on the Washington home, he never lost touch with his home town. He was well aware of what could happen to a Congressman who forgot the people who sent him to Washington, so he was assiduous about keeping in touch with his constituents by letter, telephone, press release, and personal appearances. His diary logs his trips to Grand Rapids every couple of weeks; maintaining his good standing in Michigan's Fifth District was central to his ambition to be

Speaker. By his calculations, "I was young enough, and my seat was secure enough, that I could look ahead to the possibility of becoming ranking Republican on Appropriations, or even Chairman. But my great ambition was to be Speaker."

Sputnik was launched on October 4, 1957, and soon thereafter Ford was summoned to the Speaker's office. Rayburn informed Ford that he and Senate Majority Leader Lyndon B. Johnson had met with President Eisenhower to decide how to create a new Federal government agency for space. To write the necessary legislation, a bipartisan House-Senate Committee would be formed, Rayburn said, and Ford would serve on it.

For Ford, it was a welcome opportunity as well as a mark of respect. It was also his first intensive encounter with Senator Johnson of Texas. "Johnson elected himself chairman," Ford said, "and boy, did he operate."

The object was to convert the National Advisory Committee on Aeronautics and its five hundred laboratory technicians into the National Aeronautics and Space Administration. The NASA mission would be to take the country into the Age of Space. "Johnson knew exactly what he wanted," Ford said. "To get it, he didn't literally twist your arm, but the pressure of his presence and the strength of his voice and the movement of his body made it hard to say no. The way he would seek a compromise was to work on each and every person. He knew the people. He knew how far he could push, how to cajole, how to threaten.

"Any compromise that Lyndon made, he got better than fifty percent, because he was a skillful, hard working, hard-driving man in dealing with people," Ford said. "He wouldn't shout. But he would be very firm. He would be hardline, and then he would give just enough to get what he wanted. He was strong with the gavel; when he reached his goal, down came the gavel. On to the next business."

With Johnson in charge, the House and Senate not only passed the law creating the new space agency but also provided the first billions in money by his deadline—one year after *Sputnik*. To nobody's surprise, Johnson located NASA's headquarters in Texas.

"Watching Lyndon," Ford said, "I knew I was seeing a master in action."

Ford never had the slightest doubt about his choice for President in 1960. "I was committed to Nixon early, in advance, and without hesitation," Ford said. "We had talked often while he was Vice President, and I had seen him advance, not only in his political ability but in his understanding of foreign policy, of the world and the U.S. role in the world. I thought he was ready to be President and had the prospect of becoming a great President."

To work for the platform Nixon wanted, Ford ran for and won a seat as a convention delegate from the Fifth District of Michigan. Nixon, without mentioning it, put Ford's name on the short list of possible nominees for Vice President. To send up a trial balloon Nixon asked his fellow conservative and counselor Raymond Moley to promote Ford in Moley's *Newsweek* column. "Watch this Ford," Moley wrote, ". . . a conservative [who combines] the wisdom of age with the drive of youth." At Nixon's direction Moley suggested "the next Vice President should carry some of the burden of the President's domestic responsibilities since there will be demands on the Chief Executive for much traveling abroad. Ford would get on better with Congress than anyone in sight."

As the convention opened in Chicago on a sweltering July day, Ford supporters in Michigan began booming him for Vice President. But President Eisenhower came to Chicago and told Nixon he should pick former Senator Henry Cabot Lodge. The Ford campaign for Vice President was over.

Nevertheless, Ford campaigned for Nixon across the country, and in October brought Nixon to Grand Rapids for one of the most enthusiastic rallies of the year. Nixon ran well in Ford's District, but he lost the state and the election.

Two days before Nixon was to turn over the Vice Presidency to Lyndon Johnson, he brought all his old friends and allies of the Chowder and Marching Society to his Capitol office for a final session. As the drinks flowed, Nixon moved through the crowd with a smile and a handshake and a grateful word to all who had stuck by him. Observing him, Ford thought Nixon seemed downhearted, but he was sure that Nixon's political career had not ended. "I had a lot of faith in Dick," Ford said. "I said to myself, 'He'll be around.'"

5

RECOGNITION

On January 19, 1961, the day before the inauguration of John F. Kennedy as President, a major snowstorm struck Washington, bringing traffic to a standstill, marooning the famous, and leaving eight inches of powdery snow on Capitol Hill and across the city. Through the night Army troops cleared the drifts from the plaza surrounding the inaugural stands and melted the ice from Pennsylvania Avenue for the parade. At noon the next day, Congressman and Mrs. Ford, bundled in their warmest coats, sat in the bitter cold and bright sunlight outside the east front of the Capitol to see Kennedy take the oath of office as President.

"Instead of being downhearted about it, I felt good," Ford said. "I was disappointed that Dick Nixon had not won, of course; but the election was over. I knew Kennedy, and his ability, so I had no apprehension at all about the future of the country. And I was in a position in Congress where I would have some influence. Every President respects the Appropriations Committee, and I thought Kennedy would need me more than I needed him."

Ford admired oratorical skill, a talent he lacked; and he listened carefully to the soaring words and lofty promise of the new President's inaugural address. "It was," Ford said, "one of the best speeches I ever heard, or read."

As the new Congress began, and with a new President in the White House, Ford could take the measure of his political career. He had been a member of the House for twelve years, had aged from thirty-five to forty-seven, and he could expect that the Fifth District of Michigan would continue to send him back to Washington every two years—barring unforeseen events.

Healthy, vigorous, and happy, he was settled in a comfortable Virginia home, was married to a beautiful and understanding woman he loved, and had four robust children to whom he was devoted and with whom he would like to spend more time, if he could.

As senior Republican on the Defense Appropriations Subcommittee Ford spoke with authority on U.S. weapons and forces. In the argot of the day he was a hawk: He believed in building American military forces of might and reach, and in using them to stop the expansion of the Russian and the Chinese Communist empires. He was too practical a man to believe America could impose democracy on other peoples, but he never hesitated to advocate using American military power to give the citizens of another country a chance to choose their own government.

Ford's colleagues in Congress judged him to be a politician of talent and promise. "I was impressed by his diligence and inquiring mind," said Carl Elliott, an Alabama Democrat and fellow Member of the Class of '49. "Oh, he was a likable fellow. And if he didn't know the issue, he would study it and ask questions until he did." Many Democrats became Ford's friends, but none could doubt his loyalty to the Republican Party. To him there was a clear distinction between the parties. "The fundamental difference between the Republicans and Democrats on social policy is not that we don't recognize the problems of poverty, housing, and education, but in how we deal with those problems," Ford said. "Democrats believe the Federal government is the best instrument for the solution of these problems. Republicans believe these problems can best be served by state government, local government, the private sector, or a combination of the three."

In House debate Ford could be vigorously partisan; but at the end he would make a point of shaking hands and enjoying a laugh with his Democratic adversary. In negotiations, his affable nature and hearty laugh could ease the tension in the clash of philosophy and ego. He was not an initiator of programs or a creator of ideas; but he sought out policy discussion and kept his mind open to a new approach. He was an unembarrassed eclectic, picking and choosing among proposals, finding the solid middle ground, and then giving full support and credit to a colleague. He had a sure touch about what was practical and what would pass Congress. Safe in his District, secure in the hierarchy of the House, he had no need to preen on the House floor or to the press.

Ford was a workhorse, not a show horse. His fellow Members had no doubt of that, and in 1961 the American Political Science Association commended him for holding "one of the most difficult, time-consuming, and important positions in the House," that is, senior Republican on Defense Appropriations under a Democratic President. In presenting Ford its Congressional Distinguished Service Award, the Association described him: "A moderate conservative who is highly respected by his colleagues of both parties, he symbolizes the hard-working, competent legislator who eschews the more colorful, publicity seeking roles in favor of a solid record of achievement in the real work of the House: Committee work."

Ford's standing in the Washington defense and foreign policy community began to attract the attention of the international peerage of experts in the field. Invitations came in from the Bilderberg Conference, the Interparliamentary Union, the Council on Foreign Relations. Professor Henry A. Kissinger of Harvard, who had no superior in this realm of foreign policy, invited Ford up to Cambridge from time to time to address and confer with his gatherings of student intellectuals.

Ford considered Kissinger "brilliant," an assessment with which the subject was not inclined to disagree. Kissinger, in turn, was impressed with the range of Ford's knowledge of national security issues and his sure touch in practical politics. "Ford was not then articulate," Kissinger said, "but that doesn't mean he wasn't highly intelligent. This was the best selected seminar in the political science field, all graduate students; and Ford came up there and held his own marvelously."

Modest Ford was, but proud of his record—four years as part of the loyal opposition to President Truman, eight years in support of President Eisenhower. In those years the country had prospered and changed; and Ford believed he had made a small and anonymous contribution to that change— and could continue to do so. His days at the Appropriations Committee were endless and unpublicized—mornings and afternoons of listening to the factory managers of the vast Federal operation try to prove their need for more money. Diligent and stolid in his duty, Ford listened to the pleadings and toiled away over the arcane budget language and numbers. He was learning what the Federal government can do well, what it does poorly, and what it cannot do at all.

Ford had been there at the center of House power to mobilize bipartisan support for President Truman's commitment to aid the economic and social recovery of devastated Europe and defeated Japan. He was there to support building the H-bomb and the *Nautilus,* the Navy's first nuclear submarine. He was there to support Truman's war in Korea, and Truman's decision to send the first military advisers to South Vietnam. He was one of five House members all others counted on to monitor and keep the nation's intelligence secrets.

He had supported President Eisenhower's decisions to train the army of South Vietnam, to train Cuban exiles for the invasion of Castro's Cuba, to put the first U.S. satellite in orbit, to build the missiles, bombers, and submarines that formed the triangle of the Free World's deterrent against the threat of Soviet missiles. He voted to support President Eisenhower's directives to carry out the Supreme Court order to desegregate public schools, and to support the first act to protect the voting rights of blacks. Ford was a particularly strong advocate of Eisenhower's Interstate Highway System, which was already changing the social and economic design of America in ways undreamed of.

Ford entered the House as a novice; by 1961 he was a master of his trade, a worker skilled in the craft of legislative governing. At the beginning of the Kennedy administration he pledged himself to work again with a Democratic President, but at the same time he resolved to do all he could to elect more Republicans to the House. To Ford, the Kennedy mystique sweeping across Washington and bedazzling the press overlooked one significant political fact: While Kennedy had won the Presidency, barely, in 1960, the Republicans at the same time gained twenty-two seats in the House of Representatives.

The anomaly raised Ford's hopes. Midterm elections usually helped the party not in the White House. It might be possible, he thought, for the Republicans to win enough seats in 1962 to be in position to retake the House with the right Presidential candidate in 1964. "It was a long shot," Ford conceded, "but worth working for."

In his diary Ford made a singularly sad entry on January 26, 1962: "Call from Janet—Dad died." He had slipped on the ice, suffered a concussion, and died thirty-six hours later.

When Ford arrived in Grand Rapids he found his mother deep in grief but still resolute, still indomitable in spirit. Ford was deeply touched when all Grand Rapids seemed to mourn the loss. "Here was a man who never got past the eighth grade, but he was widely recognized as an outstanding citizen and good businessman, a man with an impeccable record of integrity and honesty," Ford said.

After the funeral Ford and his mother and brothers read the will. From the struggle to survive in the Depression, Gerald Ford, Sr., had brought his paint business to a degree of prosperity. In his estate were his life savings, enough to keep his widow in modest comfort for the rest of her life.

To his stepson, Gerald Ford, Sr., had given an incalculable legacy—his own good name, and the example of integrity, hard work, and fair play on which Ford built his public life. "Dad was," Ford said, "one of the truly outstanding people I ever knew in my life."

Until October of 1962, Ford and his fellow Republicans in the House expected to gain a score or more seats in the off-year elections. Campaign politics suddenly became insignificant when U.S. intelligence discovered that Khrushchev was installing Soviet nuclear missiles in Cuba, a discovery that led to the most dangerous nuclear confrontation between the United States and the USSR in the atomic age. When President Kennedy, by a combination of steely resolve and a secret bargain, induced Khrushchev to withdraw the missiles, his political popularity soared. After the danger passed, Ford—who had closely observed events through briefings of his intelligence committee—complimented Kennedy on the way he handled the crisis. "He was calm. He was firm. He was on top of it."

Relieved as he was that President Kennedy had resolved the crisis without bloodshed, Ford was dismayed at the domestic political consequences. Instead of the twenty seats they were counting on, the Republicans gained one.

Disappointed at their poor showing, frustrated by the legislative dregs handed out by the majority Democrats, a small force of young Republicans—Melvin Laird of Wisconsin, Charles Goodell of New York, Robert Griffin of Michigan, and Donald Rumsfeld, just elected to the House but not yet sworn in—came in to see Ford. "Damn it," Goodell told Ford, "we have to make a change."

Their proposition: That Ford challenge Charles Hoeven, an aging Iowan, as Chairman of the House Republican Conference. Hoeven ranked third in the Republican hierarchy of House leaders. The purpose of the Republican Conference, at least in theory, was to convert party philosophy and ideas into practical programs and campaign debating points. To the insurgents who approached Ford, Hoeven was a do-nothing leader and the conference itself was moribund.

Ford was chosen, Rumsfeld said, because "he was a workman and very well liked. The goal was to become the majority party in the House, and the question was: Is it possible to use the Republican Conference in a more creative way?"

Ford listened carefully and said, "I am interested, but before I make any commitment, I want to talk to Betty."

*   *   *

Betty Ford had flourished in Washington. Like her husband, she was challenged and transformed by life in the capital; and after fourteen years she had become her husband's most trusted political adviser.

Her role was not always easy, but she liked it, or at least some things about it. There were the good times—dinners at the White House, joining other Congressional wives at the country club, a trip to Spain and Italy. And there were the bad times, her husband's long hours and long absences, his preoccupation with his job. Often she was reminded of Janet Ford's admonition on her wedding day: Jerry Ford's mistress was work.

"I had to bring up four kids by myself," Betty Ford wrote in her own memoirs. "I couldn't say, 'Wait till your father comes home'; their father wasn't going to come home for maybe a week."

She did have help. Clara Powell, a Washingtonian then barely out of her teens, had come to work for the Fords soon after the birth of their first child. Over the years Mrs. Powell became an honorary member of the family. Calm and wise, she could cook, clean, launder, handle children and otherwise accomplish all the chores necessary to support a busy mother and Congressional wife.

To Betty Ford, it seemed that the more important her husband became in public life, the less important she became in his life. "I was resentful of Jerry's being gone so much," she said. "I was feeling terribly neglected. . . . The loneliness, the being left to yourself at night, is what makes marriages crack, makes liquor more attractive."

When Ford was at home, she and he enjoyed a drink or so before dinner, and often a nightcap as they watched the late evening news. "I wanted him to loosen up, so when he got in from work, I'd encourage him to have a beer or a martini to relax him," she said. "In my own mind, my drinking was simply convivial, and conviviality was fun. . . . Somewhere along the line, alcohol became too important in my life. . . . When Jerry was away—and as he became more important in Congress, he was often away— I'd have my five o'clock drink at a neighbor's house. Or even by myself, while talking on the phone with a neighbor. I'd have another while I was fixing dinner and then, after the kids were in bed, I'd build myself a nightcap and unwind by watching television." In time she realized she was putting a spoonful of vodka into her morning tea to give herself, as she put it, "a warm, mellow feeling."

In his preoccupation with his work and solving the problems of a vast government, Ford did not see the problem that was developing in his own home. Betty never complained, never talked to him about the daily burdens of managing a busy household or the long nights of loneliness. So when he came to her to weigh whether he should run for Republican Conference Chairman and take on even more responsibilities, she listened, inferred the obvious that he wanted to do it—and said she would support whatever decision he made.

Ford came down on the side of ambition. "By itself, the Conference chairmanship was of little importance," he said, "but these young guys wanted change, and they wanted a leader. If I defeated Charlie Hoeven, and I felt sure I could, this would be recognition. I would get a head start on the possibility of becoming Republican Leader." And that, Ford calculated, could lead to Speaker of the House.

Ford called the group into his office and agreed to challenge Hoeven. Rumsfeld, sure that Ford would agree, already had a plan ready, and handed out assignments for telephone calls and visits with Members. After six weeks of personal persuasion, and on the promise that he would generate alternative proposals to Democratic legislation, Ford and his young activists won the challenge to the Old Guard by 86–78, a margin of eight votes.

Hoeven, after he lost, said to Charles Halleck, House Minority Leader, "Charlie, you better understand, Jerry came after me. He'll be coming after you next." Halleck dismissed the possibility.

On the afternoon of November 22, 1963, Ford and his wife were driving back from a consultation about Jack's school performance when the car radio broke the news that President Kennedy had been assassinated. "I just couldn't believe it," Ford said. He raced to his House office to get more details.

A stillness came over Washington. Except for the muffled drum and the creak of caisson, the city was silent.

Ford had just arrived home for dinner two days later when he received an emergency call from a White House operator.

"Jerry," President Johnson said, "I am going to appoint a bipartisan, blue-ribbon Commission to make an authoritative and comprehensive investigation of the Kennedy assassination." Johnson listed the members—Chief Justice Earl Warren as Chairman, Allen Dulles, John McCloy, Senator Richard Russell, Senator John Sherman Cooper. "From the House, Hale Boggs is going to be one," Johnson said, "and I want you to be the other."

"Mr. President," Ford said, "I would be honored to serve, but I am overly busy on the Defense Appropriations committee and I have just taken on—"

Johnson interrupted. "Congressman, this is your national duty. You must do it."

"Well," Ford said later, "what the hell do you say? You say, 'Yes.' And I did."

Ford's selection by a Democratic President as the one Republican member of the House to serve on the Warren Commission was recognition of his standing among Democrats. Johnson chose Ford in part on the recommendation of Defense Secretary Robert McNamara, who told the new President: "I know Jerry Ford well from appearing before his committee. He is always fair and reliable. Where national security is involved, he is always nonpartisan."

For the next ten months Ford made a full commitment of time and energy to the investigation of the assassination. From the beginning he expected the work would be thankless, the findings controversial. It took a personal toll as well. "We had the responsibility to go through all the gruesome details and look at all those awful X-rays and photographs," Ford said. "It was shocking to see a friend with, literally, his brains blown out. It really hit me inside."

In his diary Ford logged all the hearings and deliberations and detailed some of the most memorable actions, including a trip that he and Chief Justice Warren made to Dallas. There they inspected the window on the sixth floor of the Texas School Book Depository where Lee Harvey Oswald, a former Marine who had once defected to Russia, stood to fire the shots that killed Kennedy and wounded then Texas Governor John Connally. Through a telescopic sight that matched Oswald's, Ford went through a simulation of the shooting. With stopwatch in hand, he and Warren followed Oswald's course from the window where he left his rifle, down the stairs, and out the front door.

For three hours Ford and Warren questioned Jack Ruby, the killer of Oswald. Ruby, Ford noted, asked that his story be verified by polygraph tests and truth serum, and Warren told Ruby it would be done. Ruby also asked that he be permitted to go to Washington and tell his story to President Johnson, but Warren demurred.

Why did he kill Oswald? Ford asked. Ruby replied, according to Ford's notes, that "he had no thought of killing Oswald until that Sunday morning," when he read a Dallas newspaper story pointing out "that Mrs. Kennedy would have to come back to Dallas to testify at the Oswald trial."

His purpose, Ruby told Warren and Ford, was to spare Jacqueline Kennedy that burden.

From Ford's perspective, the Commission did all within reason that could be done to get the facts about the Kennedy assassination. Members and six separate teams of lawyers and investigators heard every witness who had evidence, or claimed to. They looked at fingerprints, sighted the weapons, reenacted the crime, tracked down rumors, tested and retested theories.

There were differences among the Warren Commission members. At one point, Warren, Dulles, and McCloy wanted to withhold details of testimony and evidence. Russell, Boggs, and Ford insisted that it be made public, and it was—in twenty-six volumes of facts, eyewitness accounts, and supporting testimony.

To Ford, all the available evidence supported the eyewitness accounts that Oswald shot Kennedy, and no convincing facts turned up to show that anyone else was involved. The motive, Ford said, "will always be a question; but with one exception, every person who has tried or assassinated a President was mentally unbalanced."

In September of 1964, as the Commission drafted the final report, Chief Justice Warren and the other six members reached the unanimous verdict: Lee Harvey Oswald killed President Kennedy.

"The staff wanted us to say that there was no conspiracy, foreign or domestic," Ford said. "Senator Russell, Congressman Boggs, and I thought it was too strong. We finally prevailed on the Commission to change it to read, 'The Commission has found no evidence . . . of any conspiracy, domestic or foreign, to assassinate President Kennedy.' That was more accurate. To prove that a conspiracy did not exist in this case was almost impossible."

Ford never budged from his 1964 judgment that Oswald alone assassinated Kennedy. Yet, he said, "I recognized that not all questions would ever be answered."

On the day the report was made public, James Reston offered a prescient observation in *The New York Times:* "The Warren Commission . . . has tried, as a servant of history, to discover truth. But the assassination of President Kennedy was so symbolic of human irony and tragedy, and so involved in the complicated and elemental conflicts of the age, that many vital questions remain, and the philosophers, novelists and dramatists will have to take it from here. The commission has not concluded the Kennedy mystery so much as it has opened up a whole new chapter in the Kennedy legend."

*   *   *

At the 1964 Republican Convention in San Francisco Ford nominated Michigan Governor George Romney for President, even though he knew his candidate had already lost. The party's conservatives had already elected and mobilized enough delegates to nominate Senator Barry Goldwater. He won on the first ballot.

As the Fords sat with the Nixons in a VIP box for the final evening of the convention, the two men talked shop. Both agreed that as party loyalists they would campaign for the Republican ticket that fall, but neither thought Goldwater would win. Both thought they could best invest their time by campaigning to win Republican seats in the House and Senate.

A month after the Convention, the Fords were back in Washington getting ready for a two-week family vacation in a rented cottage at Bethany Beach, on the Delaware coast. Everyone was packed to go when Betty Ford woke in the night with severe pain in her neck and left arm. The next morning Ford took her to the National Orthopedic Hospital. The diagnosis: a pinched nerve. The treatment was traction and pain-killing drugs. "Go ahead and take the kids to the beach," she said. They had been counting on time with their father, and she did not want her illness to disappoint them. He did, staying for a night, leaving the children with a neighbor for the day to drive back to see her, and to stop by the office, then driving back to the beach before nightfall.

While the family was away, Betty Ford got out of bed one day, looked in a full-length mirror and saw, as she put it, "a bent old woman." To herself she said: "I am not going on this way. I am hurting, but I cannot let this be the end of the line for me. I have a long way to go, four strapping children only half raised, a great responsibility." Her doctors prescribed a series of drugs to control the pain.

With medicine, her own grit, and a demanding course in physical therapy, Betty Ford began to fight her way back to physical mobility. But her husband's twelve-hour days in the office and full schedule of out-of-town speeches made life difficult. "Yes, I did resent it," she said. "I had these four kids in this house and looked after them and saw to their school work, and I felt sorry for myself. Even to the point—while I would never voice it—it was all an inner self-pity. Because, didn't I have everything? I had a wonderful husband. A wonderful home. Four beautiful children. But internally, there was turmoil."

As a child she resented the absence of her father; with her first husband she resented the emptiness of marriage to a traveling salesman who was gone so much. Now the man she loved was away making political speeches all over the country. So often was he absent that one night she turned over in her sleep, saw him beside her, and said, "What are *you* doing here?"

Growing up, the four Ford children clearly missed their father. Michael, the oldest, who would choose the ministry, looked back on his childhood with great fondness and some regret. "My memories of growing up were pleasant," he said, "but there was a sense of feeling, well, kind of left behind in terms of my father's career. He provided very well, but we did miss his presence."

Life in the Ford family was a schedule of obligations. Ford was always there for his sons' football games, when they received an award, and on Sunday morning for church. Sometimes he took the children campaigning in Michigan. "As a child I remember admiring him for his way with people, for his care for them and their concerns," Michael said. "I could see that people looked up to him, as I did."

On Saturdays when their father was in Washington, the children were sometimes treated to a visit to his office. "Well, everyone in the car," he would say. Off they would go, and Ford would let them roam the halls of Congress, deliver mail, and go with him to get his hair cut. "It was his way of relieving Mother and giving her some time, giving her a day to be renewed," Ford's oldest son said. "He would always say, 'Be sure and write your Mom a letter,' and put us on the typewriter. We would type out our affection and special words to her, and then take them home to her."

Every year, long in advance, Ford marked off on his calendar the weeks for the family vacation; and that interlude he tried to guard against all intrusions. In the summers it might be Ottawa Beach on Lake Michigan; at Christmas it was Boyne Mountain or Vail for skiing. "Vacations were really quality time," Michael said. "There, he was one hundred ten percent concentration and attention. It was wonderful. You felt you had everything he could give you. That was just how he approached life—give it one hundred ten percent."

Ford handed along to his children the central principle he had learned from his stepfather. "You are a person of your word," he would tell them. "Rich or poor, famous or insignificant, the integrity of your word, your veracity, is a tremendous possession of great value. Keep it. Never lose it."

On November 3, 1964, President Johnson won reelection in a landslide. All through the campaign Ford could not overcome the sense of doom about Goldwater; but not once did his support waver. Twice he welcomed Goldwater to Michigan during the fall; and as a surrogate he campaigned across the country for the Republican ticket. Goldwater's loss he expected; the consequences in the House he did not. In Grand Rapids on Election Night, Ford learned that the Goldwater debacle cost the Republicans thirty-six House seats. He got so angry at the stunning loss that he got in his car and drove fourteen hours to Washington, stopping only for gas.

6

LEADER
OF THE OPPOSITION

On the morning after the Presidential Election of 1964, Ford's beloved Republican Party awoke in ruins. In the new Eighty-ninth Congress the Republican numbers in the House would be cut to 140—the lowest it had been since Alf Landon lost to Franklin Roosevelt in 1936. Looking at the wreckage, Ford could only shake his head in dismay: two Wisconsin seats lost, two lost in Pennsylvania, three in Michigan, four in Ohio, four in Iowa, four in Washington, six in New York.

To a handful of young Republican House members who had survived the Johnson landslide—Robert Griffin, Charles Goodell, and Donald Rumsfeld—something had to change. They decided to recruit a candidate to oust Charles Halleck, the sixty-four-year-old House Republican Leader. The two best prospects for defeating Halleck, they concluded, were Laird and Ford. Laird was too controversial. He had too many enemies. They settled on Ford, and for the second time in two years, Rumsfeld, Griffin, and Goodell went in to see him. "Something must be done to get new leadership in the House," Griffin said. "Halleck is too old, a bad image. He has no imagination. We are talking to two or three others, but we want to know your views. If we get behind you, would you want to do it?"

"Well," Ford said, "I agree with you that something must be done. I am interested, but I don't want to make a commitment until I think about it and talk to Betty."

For Ford, it was a critical choice: If elected House Minority Leader, he would be one big step away from becoming Speaker. But two senior Republicans on the Appropriations Committee had just been defeated, making it certain that Ford would become the ranking Republican on the Committee and second in power only to the Chairman. House rules required that Ford give up his treasured seat and great power on the Appropriations Committee if he should become Minority Leader.

Before he made up his mind, Ford did talk to his wife and to his two older sons. She knew it was what he wanted to do; as always, she said she would support his decision. Both of the boys said yes. Twelve-year-old Jack Ford added, "Go for it, Dad." Go for it Ford did, but not before an awkward session with the man he set out to defeat.

Charles Halleck, a crafty, hard-drinking House veteran from Indiana, got wind of the move to oust him and moved quickly to find out if it were true. Halleck invited the elected leaders, Whip Les Arends, Policy Chairman John Byrnes, and Ford, to lunch.

Ford, recognizing the gambit, consulted Melvin Laird, his wise and frequent adviser. Laird was a man of ambition and something of a political prodigy: He was elected to the Wisconsin State Senate at twenty-three, and to the U.S. House of Representatives at thirty. In style, Laird combined some of the best qualities of Talleyrand and a medieval alchemist. He excelled in intricate political maneuver; none exceeded him in turning dross into political gold. Close in political philosophy, Ford and Laird became allies; and Ford respected Laird's quick mind and sound judgment. On the question of challenging Halleck, Laird advised Ford: "Go for Leader. I'll go for your job. We'll both win. Here's what you say to Halleck . . ."

When Ford arrived at the Minority Leader's office for lunch the air was tense. With no attempt at subtlety, Halleck said: "I assume we are all going to run for the same offices again."

Yes, said Arends. Yes, said Byrnes. Then there was a long moment of silence.

"Charlie," Ford said, "I am not in a position to make any firm commitment. I have been approached by those who say they are going to launch a campaign to unseat you. They have talked to me. I have made no commitment to them, and they have not made one to me. In all honesty, Charlie, I cannot say that I'm going to run for the same office."

With a scowl, Halleck looked Ford in the eye and muttered an oath.

Arends later accosted Ford with a malevolent grin. "We're going to beat you badly," Arends said.

"We'll see," Ford said amiably.

Tired though he was, Halleck was still a formidable political fighter. He called on all Members in his debt, and there were many, to stand by him.

The lead switched from Halleck to Ford and back again. Halleck held the better cards—incumbency, his record of holding the party together, and all the favors he had done for his colleagues. But Ford's team of "Young Turks," as the insurgents were called, had better organization, more energy, and the message of hope. Within a week they rounded up enough votes to justify Ford's open call for revolt.

On Saturday, December 19, 1964, Ford announced his challenge to Halleck for Minority Leader. His goal, he told the press, was to lead "a fighting, forward-looking party seeking responsible and constructive solutions to national problems." At that point Ford was still short of commitments, but he gambled that he could get enough to win. "I knew the risk if I lost," Ford said. "But Charlie was tired, and I could not see anyone who would have a better chance to win than I did."

Ford had planned to spend the Christmas holidays skiing with the family in Michigan, but he left them at Boyne Mountain and flew back to Washington to join his backers—Griffin, Goodell, and Rumsfeld—in a nonstop campaign. Glen Lipscomb delivered the California delegation, the biggest single block of votes for Ford. John Anderson of Illinois, Tom Curtis of Missouri, and Al Quie of Minnesota rounded up Midwesterners. Member by Member, Ford and his campaign team won commitments. Rumsfeld kept the tally and plotted the strategy. Finally it was down to a handful on the fence, notably Kansas. Three days before Christmas, Bob Dole invited Ford to speak to the Kansas delegation, and Ford made a powerful plea for change.

On Monday, January 4, 1965, the new Congress convened, and all 140 Republicans caucused in the spacious, paneled hearing room of the House Ways and Means Committee. Senior staff assistants handed out the ballots and collected them. When the tally was complete, there were 141 ballots cast by 140 voters. "It was very embarrassing," Rumsfeld said. The Conference Chairman ordered a second ballot—and this time each Member placed his ballot in the box as his name was called. On the second ballot Ford won 73 to 67. Halleck stood and moved to make the election unanimous.

"In the end," Ford said, "Bob Dole persuaded three other Kansas Republicans to vote with him, and those four votes probably saved the day."

The first "Minority Leader" of the House of Representatives was James Madison. In drafting the Constitution Madison made no explicit provision for the job; but as a Member of the House in the First Congress he led the opposition to Alexander Hamilton's proposals to concentrate financial power in the Federal government, and became the first floor leader.

The House Speaker had by Constitutional fiat, and with gavel and mace he bossed the place. But Members, all equals in their minds, saw no need to put one above others by electing a floor leader. Thomas Jefferson took advantage of this by selecting his own leader in the House to organize support and deliver votes for a policy or program.

Egocentricity was then as rampant on Capitol Hill as it was to become in the Age of Television. For much of the first hundred years in Congress, parties were fragmented, alliances fragile, and loyalties almost nonexistent. One year, ninety-one Members of the House were candidates for Speaker.

Someone had to keep bills moving on the floor, and in the Fourth Congress the Speaker appointed the Chairman of Ways and Means to serve as the Majority Leader as well. That lasted, with some practical adjustments, until 1911, when the House rank-and-file had enough of Speaker Joseph Cannon's autocratic rule and for the first time elected a Majority Leader and a Minority Leader.

The job is what each Leader makes it. Senator Howard Baker, who invested his wealth of intellect and patience in serving as Minority Leader and Majority Leader of the Senate, liked to say, "The education of a Leader ends in the third grade, when he learns to count."

To count with accuracy, however, a Leader must know every Member's record and philosophy, strengths and weaknesses, the political cast of his constituency, and his prospects in the next election, among other things. To keep all this in his head and ready for instant retrieval, a Leader must have a superior memory. A sense of the imperfection of man helps. As does expertise in psychology, for the Leader coaches a team where each player believes he should call the signals.

Most important of all, a Leader must be someone everyone trusts. He is broker, moderator, synthesizer, the seer who can divine the middle ground that he perceives to be in the public interest. The business of legislators is the marketing of ideas; they bargain in the coin of self-interest. The Leader is the man who can bring their interests and their prices to a point of sale. He makes the deal. Day to day his objective is to neutralize conflicting views and translate them into singleness of purpose. "A leader reasons," it was once explained by Mike Mansfield, the quiet man who succeeded the overbearing Lyndon Johnson as Senate Majority Leader. "It is not that he trades. He reasons."

When the Leader represents the Majority he must try on every issue—

from declaring war to setting the hour of adjournment—to sustain that majority. In the Minority, the Leader must also keep his party united, challenge the Majority on occasion, and always be ready to defend against the Majority's rule. Howard Greene, a sage of Capitol Hill, once defined the Minority Leader's responsibility in six practical words: "He keeps the worst from happening."

In the United States Congress, preventing the worst from happening takes skill. When Ford took over as Minority Leader, he followed two men who saw it as their principal responsibility to say no to whatever the Democratic majority wanted. Ford had campaigned on a platform for change, and the change he brought was to say: Here's a better idea.

To come up with better ideas to demonstrate that the post-Goldwater Republican Party had cohesion and direction, Ford appointed a brain trust of Laird, Goodell, and John Rhodes. "We wanted to come forward with proposals that would broaden our political base," Ford said. "We wanted to begin to rebuild the party and bring younger Republicans into the House."

Popular as Ford was in the House of Representatives, to the press and therefore in the public mind he stood in the shadow of Everett McKinley Dirksen. By title Dirksen was the Minority Leader of the Senate; by reputation he was as talented an actor as ever played a role in American politics—no small distinction.

Time, in a memorable cover story on Dirksen, caught his act: "He speaks, and the words emerge in a soft, sepulchral baritone. They undulate in measured phrases, expire in breathless wisps. He fills his lungs and blows word-rings like smoke. The sentences curl upward. . . . Now he conjures moods of mirth, now of sorrow. . . . He paraphrases the Bible and church bells peal. 'Motherhood,' he whispers, and grown men weep. 'The flag,' he bugles, and everybody salutes."

To counter President Johnson's domination of the public scene, Dirksen and Halleck had staged for television and print reporters a periodic commentary on public events that came to be known as the "Ev and Charlie Show." When Ford took over, the series continued as the "Ev and Jerry Show." On television, Ford's plain and businesslike look could not match Dirksen's tousled locks of white hair and elephantine jowls. With wit, perception, and a style of oratory that amused as well as it obfuscated, Dirksen made himself the star; Ford was relegated to straight man for a masterful entertainer.

Asked one day to describe how he and Ford operated, Dirksen said: "Minority Leader Ford is the sword; I am the oilcan."

Offstage in the backrooms of politics, Dirksen was second to none. He loved to bargain, and always got something in any political deal. "I am not a moralist," Dirksen told his biographer. "I am a legislator."

Ford, when he became House Minority Leader, signed up as apprentice to the master. "Dirksen and Halleck had been close friends and allies," Ford said. "Consequently, I was apprehensive about how Ev Dirksen would treat me. So I decided I would defer to him, seek his advice, ask for his help. After all, he was my senior by a number of years. He had a national reputation, which I did not. Ev responded extremely well, and instead of being bitter because I had defeated his dear friend Charlie Halleck, he sort of brought me to his bosom."

Working with Dirksen, Ford came to have even greater respect for his keen mind and negotiating skills. "I found Everett Dirksen to be one of the most competent political figures I ever met," Ford said. "He was the last of the Titans on the Hill."

The other Titan of the Hill had moved to the White House. Dirksen and Johnson had become friends and sometime allies when they served in the House; in the Senate the two concocted and put across many a deal—most of them, such as civil rights, in the public interest. After Johnson became President the two continued to talk daily. So close were Dirksen and Johnson that it fell to Ford to be the leader of the constructive opposition to the President.

Ford liked Johnson and enjoyed being in his gargantuan presence. "I'll never forget one time," Ford said. "He invited me to opening day of the baseball season in Washington, and Ev Dirksen and I sat with LBJ in the Presidential box. The President ate five hot dogs. He had a tremendous hand, and he put that huge hand around that hot dog and just devoured it—not one, not two, but five hot dogs."

Ford thought President Johnson was driven to show that he, a Southerner, could get social legislation through Congress that Kennedy, a Northern liberal, had not been able to pass. Compelled to prove that he was the more effective President, Johnson "moved too fast on a whole raft of broad-based social legislation—the Poverty Program, the Job Corps, a number of Civil Rights proposals, Federal Aid to Education," Ford said. "He put the pressure on his two-to-one majorities in the House and Senate to enact legislative programs hook, line, and sinker without thorough hearings and debate. We passed some very loose legislation. Congress gave the bureaucracy too much control. So some of the well-intentioned programs fell flat on their face, the Poverty Program being in many aspects the best example."

Outnumbered and outmaneuvered, Ford could only grit his teeth and watch it happen. "Frankly," he said, "I got very disgusted with the performance of that Eighty-ninth Congress; it was a disgrace. They were not independent. They were tools of the White House."

On the War in Vietnam, Ford differed strongly with the Johnson Administration—not on the fact that the United States had entered the war but that President Johnson himself was not doing enough to win it. Twelve years earlier, Ford had returned from Vietnam and Korea convinced that the United States should use its military power to block Communist expansion in Asia; nothing since had changed his mind. Consequently, Ford believed that President Johnson should not only prosecute the war but pay for it. "President Johnson believed we could have guns and butter without a tax increase," Ford said. "I was convinced then that he was planting the seeds for inflation and economic distress."

In 1965, not long after he became Minority Leader, Ford told President Johnson in a White House meeting: "We went in Vietnam to win, and militarily we must do what we have to do to win." It was a deliberate act by Ford; he wanted to tell the President face-to-face where he stood on Vietnam before he carried his arguments into a public forum.

Johnson struck back. Annoyed at Ford's criticisms of his conduct of the war, he told reporters at the LBJ Ranch in Texas that Ford had leaked a false report about his refusal to call up military reserves for the Vietnam War; Johnson went on to say that "the Leader's carelessness was endangering the lives of our troops in Vietnam."

When Ford read Johnson's accusation on the front pages of the *The Washington Post* the next morning, he was shocked. "The story was false," Ford said, "and I had to conclude that Johnson was deliberately questioning my integrity." He had no way to refute Johnson's charge—until he received a letter from Sam Shaffer, the indefatigable Capitol Hill reporter for *Newsweek* who knew the traits of both Ford and Johnson. Shaffer had attended Ford's luncheon for Capitol reporters, where Johnson said the leak occurred. He wrote Ford: "The subject of Vietnam never even came up. The President's allegation is untrue." Ford, with Shaffer's permission, handed out copies of the letter at his next press conference.

Some time later Johnson called the Congressional Leaders to the White House to discuss whether he should order the withdrawal of all American dependents from Vietnam. "Mr. President," Ford said, "I think the presence of U.S. dependents inhibits our capability to carry out military missions. Their presence indicates to the enemy that we don't take this conflict seriously. I strongly urge you to take the dependents out. I believe you should move forward with a military plan and win the war."

Johnson said he could not risk military action that would provoke the People's Republic of China to become more directly involved, as they had in Korea. Nor, he added, could he make any military move that might encourage the Soviet Union to increase their military aid to North Vietnam—or take aggressive action elsewhere in the world.

In a one-on-one meeting with the President at another time, Ford urged Johnson to bomb Hanoi with everything short of nuclear weapons and to move enough U.S. forces into Cambodia to stop the use of sanctuaries. "Use our full non-nuclear capability," Ford told the President. "I will support you publicly if you make that decision." If the Vietnam War drags on, Ford said to Johnson, "I don't believe that Congress or the public will continue to support it."

The war went on. Day by day, the body count of Communist soldiers and the body count of American soldiers went up, with no end in prospect.

When she was eight years old, Susan Ford came into her mother's room one evening and found her so racked with sobs that she ran to get Clara Powell. Ms. Powell calmed Mrs. Ford and telephoned Ford, who was out on the *Sequoia* with President Johnson and other Congressional leaders discussing the Vietnam War.

Ford, brought ashore, raced home. Mrs. Ford's doctor was there when he arrived. While the Fords and the doctor were talking, Mrs. Powell took Susan and Steven, then nine, into another room and told them that their mother was very sick and would need to go to a psychiatrist.

"The collapse had been a long time building," Mrs. Ford wrote. "I'd felt as though I were doing everything for everyone else, and I was not getting any attention at all." She began seeing a psychiatrist twice a week. "I could tell him all the problems I couldn't talk to anybody else about—my back hurts, there's dope in the schools, Jerry's away. . . . Up until then, I'd thought I should be strong enough to shoulder my own burdens, not carry them to somebody else."

Mrs. Ford responded well to the therapy. "The doctor taught me that I had to take time out to do some things for myself," she said. "He told me to believe that I was important, and that if I went to pieces I wouldn't be of much value to Jerry or the children."

From her perspective, she said, "I'd lost my feeling of self-worth, and that's what sent me for help. I think a lot of women go through this. Their husbands have fascinating jobs, their children start to turn into independent people, and the women begin to feel useless, empty. After I went into therapy, Jerry and I talked it over, and we came to the conclusion that my mental state had a lot to do with my physical illness."

The case of a man putting ambition before family is not rare in Washington. Democracy is intended to attract men and women of high purpose and even higher ambition. All highly successful politicians, Republican and Democratic, conservative and liberal, rich and poor, have one common denominator—stamina. Physical stamina. And many are self-driven, as Ford was, by the Calvinist teaching that the Lord blesses a long day's work; in fact, He expects it.

In Jerry Ford's case, he was driven not only by the ambition to win Republican control of the House and become Speaker but by an even more commanding sense of duty. He, like many others who dedicate themselves to public life, was caught in the conviction that he had been awarded this responsible position in the American democracy for a purpose, and it was his first duty to serve the country. "Every good Congressman is driven by the work ethic," it was once observed by former Representative Jack Marsh, a philosopher as wise about human nature as about politics. "He tells himself, 'I've got this big job. I've got to work at it. I must serve the country.' The reward is you get to go make a speech at the firehouse in Altoona."

Ford's family, like others, took great pride in his leadership in public life and his accomplishments; but they paid a price for Dad's journeys to Altoona and Great Falls and Little Falls and all the other places on the itinerary of his crusade.

From the beginning of their life together Betty Ford never had any doubt about her priorities. "No matter what circumstances there were," she said, "there was never at any time in our marriage—and he and I have talked about this—that separation or divorce ever surfaced. We were in love. We had difficulties. We would get mad at each other. But we were in love and we were committed. No thought of changing that would ever cross our minds. My first commitment was and is to my marriage and to my family. The most successful thing in my life is our marriage and our four children. Even though I am a feminist, I would always put first my marriage and my family."

On September 15, 1965, Ford met Richard Nixon for breakfast at the Mayflower Hotel in downtown Washington. Friendship, plus the strong commitment each had to rebuilding the Republican Party, continued to bring Ford and Nixon together from time to time. Nixon, after losing his campaign for Governor of California in 1962, had moved to New York City to practice law—and plot his political comeback. They discussed Vietnam and the rising anger across the land against Johnson's conduct of the War. Region by region, Ford and Nixon evaluated the chances to convert dissent against Johnson into Republican gains in 1966. By the end of their talk Ford and Nixon were political partners in the business of regaining House seats lost in 1964—Ford to build the numbers that could make him Speaker, Nixon to restore his standing in the party, and to lay the political foundation for another campaign for President.

Campaigning for Republican House and Senate candidates would be political capital in the bank for Nixon. "This was the job I increasingly saw as my own," Nixon wrote. "It was pragmatism more than altruism that led me to take it on, because I believed that whoever did would gain a significant advantage in the race for the 1968 Presidential nomination. . . . I did not reveal to my family or anyone else that this was what I had in mind." But Ford knew. He left their breakfast that morning certain that Nixon would run for President in 1968, and equally certain that he would support him.

In Ford's first term as Minority Leader the Republicans did come forward with alternatives to Johnson's Great Society—Federal Revenue Sharing, an economic growth plan, expansion of voting rights protection to all states. But some House Republicans who elected Ford to change the party's image faulted him for not moving fast enough. "You had to kick him in the ass usually to get him to do anything," Laird said. "You had to keep prodding him to meet with the newspaper people to tell them about our alternatives, to sell our programs. If I set up these luncheons with reporters, he would do them—and do a great job." Ford was reluctant to court the press. He liked reporters, but he did not initiate any press interview that might suggest he was looking for personal publicity. With Laird, that was never a problem.

Symbiosis of a high order marked the Ford-Laird association. Ford benefited from Laird's drive and inventiveness; Laird made use of the trust and confidence Ford inspired on both sides of the aisle. "Mel's got a very quick mind," Ford said. "He has a long-range view of what's going to happen, and knows what he wants to do. And he's a prodigious worker. He can be abrasive at times, and is always scheming. He doesn't scheme for any sinister reason; he just likes to keep the pot boiling. Mel is an idea man. He is a pusher, and I respond to that kind of challenge, so it was a good combination. We respected one another. We confided in one another." Ford never made any serious move in the House or thereafter without consulting his friend and partner, Mel Laird.

In creativity and foresight Laird was a rarity in Congress. "I like to plan things for two, three, or four years in advance," Laird said. "I think it's important in politics to always have a game plan in mind as to how things are going to move. Now, some people refer to that as scheming. I really think it's planning." As to his friend Ford, Laird said: "Jerry doesn't catch on as rapidly as he should to the political significance of an event or an issue. It takes him a while to get to understand the issue. Once he understands it, there's no problem—but it does take him time."

Looking ahead to 1968, Laird convinced Ford that he needed to boost the quality of his staff by adding a senior press counselor. Laird had just the man—Robert T. Hartmann. Ford accepted Laird's recommendation, and hired Hartmann.

Grumpy, stocky, broad of face and beam, Hartmann was constructed like the forward gun turret on a battleship, and at first meeting seemed about as friendly. But his abilities surpassed his forbidding manner. As a former Washington Bureau Chief for the *Los Angeles Times*, he had covered Capitol Hill, the White House, politics in Europe, and wars in the Middle East. To Ford, it was even more important that "Bob was an out-and-out Republican news man. There was never any doubt about where he stood."

In personality, Hartmann and Ford could not have been more different. Ford trusted almost everyone; Hartmann suspected almost everyone. Hartmann was as cantankerous as Ford was genial. Yet many qualities they shared. Both loved political life and thrived on its daily excitement; both held to a conservative Republican view of the national interest.

Hartmann began as a newspaperman in an earlier age, when the paper's star reporter kept a bottle of whiskey in the drawer, wore his snap-brim hat at his desk, and arrived in the office just before deadline to pound out his front-page story. Into this penurious but engaging profession Hartmann entered as a copy boy on the *Los Angeles Times* in 1939. A bright young graduate of Stanford, and a hard worker, Hartmann moved up through the police beat and was doing well when World War II interrupted his career. He signed up for the Navy, became an officer, and spent four years in the Pacific, mostly under Admiral William F. Halsey and Admiral Chester Nimitz.

The *Los Angeles Times*, in those days, was owned and dominated by Harry Chandler; and he used his paper to glorify Los Angeles, make money, and elect California Republicans to high office. Hartmann, one of the *Times*'s most talented political reporters, was back from the Pacific and writing politics when Chandler decided to support a thirty-three-year-old Whittier lawyer, Richard Nixon, for the House of Representatives. "We discovered Nixon," Hartmann said. "It was a hopeless little district for a Republican, but Nixon had been in the Navy and we called him a war hero. He won, narrowly."

After Nixon became Vice President, Chandler sent Hartmann to Washington to be chief of the *Times* bureau. "I saw a lot of Vice President Nixon," Hartmann said. "We were his home-town paper." Over time Hartmann broadened his circle of Republican friends. Among his neighbors, and news sources, were three rising Republican Congressmen—Mel Laird, Glen Lipscomb, and John Rhodes.

Getting to know his new boss, Hartmann said, "I found Ford was not inarticulate. He was very intelligent, but almost tone-deaf to a felicitous combination of words. And he did not see that words are for the purpose of making things happen." To Hartmann's surprise, Ford, unlike most politicians, "knew his strengths and did not mind confessing his own shortcomings. He was better at talking specifics than concepts. His memory for the substance of issues and bills was extraordinary, and he was masterful with budget figures. He was not tongue-tied at a press conference. He could say what he meant. But to get the flow of words right so that anyone would remember what he said, he had to work at it, all the time. And he was ready to do that."

Ford hired Hartmann as press adviser but quickly came to rely on him for political advice and speechwriting. In time Ford discovered that Hartmann could put on paper the beliefs and words that he on his own found it hard to articulate. "He understood my feelings, and he could express them," Ford said.

Hartmann had a good ear for the spoken word, and he listened to Ford in debate, in the office, on the telephone, on the stump. He was not a literary stylist; had he been, it would have been lost on Ford. Hartmann scorned the elegant apposition of a Ted Sorensen and the imaginative alliteration of a William Safire. When he sat down at the typewriter, Hartmann was looking for the everyday words and common-sense logic that were so natural to Ford. Of Hartmann's contributions, Ford said: "His speeches were the best ones I gave."

In 1966 Ford campaigned to the limits of his House schedule and physical endurance. In some two hundred speeches for House candidates, he attacked Johnson's rubber-stamp Congress, Johnson's Vietnam War, and Johnson's foundering Great Society. To an audience in Ohio, Ford said: "Congress now is a pawn in the hands of the White House, and fifty percent of the members are puppets who dance when the President pulls the strings." Ford rebuked Johnson, in public and often, for not using the Air Force more effectively to bomb North Vietnam. Before a militant American Legion audience Ford asked: "Why are we pulling our best punches in Vietnam? Why?"

Nixon, on his parallel campaign track, was making such a good case for electing Republicans that the House Republican Campaign Committee, with Ford's encouragement, gave Nixon a half hour of prime time on the NBC network to turn out the Republican vote.

On Election Day in 1966 both Ford and Nixon were rewarded. The Republicans picked up three Senate seats, six governors, and—best of all—forty-seven seats in the House.

In the new Congress, Minority Leader Ford would have 187 Republicans in his ranks, the most in a decade, and only thirty-one seats short of a majority. Buoyed with success and optimism, he convinced himself that if the Republicans nominated Nixon for President in 1968, they could win a majority of the House and he could become Speaker.

Back in Washington after the 1966 election, Ford collided head-on with the raw anger of Lyndon Johnson. "The President was furious with me," Ford said, "not only because of Democratic losses in the House but also because I had attacked his policies."

Johnson set out to diminish Ford, and succeeded. "Dumb," Johnson called Ford. "Jerry played football too many times without a helmet," he would gleefully tell confidants. His favorite jibe, in the less scatological version: "Jerry can't walk and chew gum at the same time."

In Washington, there is no cut like a wisecrack, no weapon so effective as laughter. The nation's capital is a Court of Gossip, and the peers and courtiers of the political community and the national press relish and swiftly pass along a derogatory joke or comment about anyone in power. Wise-cracks, quips, the graphic cruelty of a Herblock cartoon—all forms of scathing humor create a mindset. Johnson's charges that Ford was a dolt and a stumblebum stuck.

Ford heard all the stories. So did his friends, and they insisted he strike back in a personal attack on Johnson. Ford said no, partly because revenge was not in his character, partly because he understood that Johnson was already wounded, stung to wrath by the poison of popular criticism of the War in Vietnam. "I never retaliated," Ford said. "I knew he was wrong. I just made up my mind I was not going to let it bother me."

At the President's regular bipartisan leadership meetings in the Cabinet Room, Ford and Johnson discussed their policy differences face to face. "He could be tough," Ford said, "but I don't think he was mean. He believed in hard-hitting politics, and if that meant hitting the Republican Leader in the House, he could do that. But I don't think it was petty meanness; it was political toughness."

In her last years Jerry Ford's mother would often say, "I want to drop dead with my boots on." She did exactly that. On September 17, 1967, Dorothy Gardner Ford died in her pew in Grace Church on Sunday morning just before the service was to begin.

Ford had gone out early that morning to play in a golf tournament at Burning Tree. When he returned to Crown View Drive, Betty Ford told him the bad news.

At her death Mrs. Gerald R. Ford, Sr., was seventy-five, her vigor diminished by illness, her spirit as indomitable as ever. She not only survived two heart attacks, diabetes, a splenectomy, and a double mastectomy; each time she resumed her busy schedule of volunteer work at the hospital and with her garden and book clubs. At the end she was still on the go. After her death her oldest son checked her calendar; she was booked for the next month.

At the funeral service, Michael Ford, seventeen, sat with his parents. "It was the first time I saw my father cry," he said. "It was very hard for me. I cried more for him than I cried for her death, because I knew he was in pain."

On August 5, 1968, the Republican National Convention opened in Miami Beach. It was the first of four days of tribal rites that conclude with a war dance around the feet of the party's nominee for President.

By long tradition the Republican Leader of the House leads the rites, so on opening day Jerry Ford, in a brand new blue suit he had bought for the occasion, gaveled the delegates to order. For Ford, center stage on national television was a rare experience, and he reveled in it.

As Chairman, he had to be officially neutral in the battle between Richard Nixon, Governor Nelson Rockefeller of New York, and Governor Ronald Reagan of California, the three aspiring to the office. But it was Nixon, in Ford's view, who had done more than anyone else to revive the party's spirit after '64. It was Nixon, he believed, who had earned the nomination, and who was best qualified to be President. "I was a Nixon man even before the 1968 campaign began," Ford said. "No equivocation. No question. He knew that, and so did everybody else."

Nixon, as expected, won on the first ballot, and invited Ford to the midnight conference to discuss the Vice Presidential nomination. The senior leaders of the Republican Party, fewer than a dozen, were there at the table, with Dirksen in the place of honor on Nixon's right and Ford on Nixon's left.

"Jerry," Nixon said, turning to face Ford, "I know you've thought about being VP in the past. Would you take it now?"

"Dick," Ford replied, "I am totally dedicated to being Speaker of the House. As you know, we picked up forty-seven seats at the last election, and now we have one hundred eighty-seven Members. If we do well in this election, and I believe we will, we can get the necessary two hundred eighteen we need to have a Majority."

"Who are you in favor of?" Nixon asked.

"I strongly recommend John Lindsay," Ford said. "He is very able and he speaks very well." Ford thought it would be a great ticket, a California conservative and a New York moderate. Bob Wilson, a California Congressman and friend of Nixon, seconded the Lindsay proposal. "But you could sense that the idea of Lindsay wasn't going very far," Ford said. "Apparently there was some enmity between Nixon and Lindsay."

At the time Ford assumed that Nixon was making him a serious offer of the Vice Presidential nomination. "Later," Ford said, "I learned that the decision for Agnew had already been made. But when the question was asked of me I thought it was an open situation."

The Nixon-Agnew ticket left Miami with a solid lead over the Democratic ticket headed by Vice President Hubert Humphrey and Senator Edmund Muskie. That lead vanished during the campaign, but Nixon held on to a precarious plurality. When all the 1968 votes were counted, Nixon had 43.4 percent of the popular vote, only .7 percent more than Humphrey. But thirty-two states gave Nixon 301 electoral votes—thirty-one more than he needed to win.

So thin was Nixon's victory that he delivered little help to Ford's candidates for the House. Republicans picked up only five seats, a big disappointment to Ford. He was still twenty-six votes away from becoming Speaker. Ford was disappointed, but immediately began looking ahead to the next elections. "I was confident that with Nixon in the White House we would build a good Republican record by nineteen seventy-two," Ford said. "I believed we would have a good chance to win the House with his reelection."

Two weeks before the end of Lyndon Johnson's Presidency, a White House assistant called Ford to say the President would like to see him. No reason was given.

Johnson welcomed Ford to the Oval Office and the two of them sat by the fireplace facing each other. Johnson began by talking about the campaign and why the Democrats lost. "Nixon ran the better race," Johnson said. "He was smart—he picked Agnew, from a border state. The Democrats were stupid. My liberal friends thought it was a great coup to pick Muskie. Just take a good look at it: Muskie came from a state with four electoral votes."

Ford listened as the President rambled on about his eagerness to get back to his Texas home on the Pedernales River. "He loved the ranch," Ford said. "I saw how much he loved it in the way he talked about getting away from all the pressures and the turmoil and the sadness. He was sad that his overwhelming election in 1964 had not given him all the satisfaction that he wanted. He was sad that the war was dragging on.

"But he was very proud, and rightfully, of his civil rights program and his voting rights legislation. He did more in the liberal area of legislation—civil rights, Federal aid to education, housing, the whole raft of programs that liberals in the Democratic Party had been trying to get for years—more than any other President. He got them through Congress, and he didn't understand the liberals' lack of gratitude. He couldn't understand why they never brought him in their circle of friends. And oh, he resented it."

"Mr. President," Ford said, "you have changed the direction of this country domestically. Whether I always agreed with you or not, you have changed the course of the country."

Johnson listened briefly, then continued his monologue. After almost an hour President Johnson said: "Jerry, you and I have had a lot of head-to-head confrontations. I've been pretty tough on you, and you've been a little rough on me at times. But I never doubted your integrity."

"Mr. President," Ford said, "I never doubted your integrity. I didn't like some of the things you said about me, and obviously you didn't like some of the things I said about you. But I never questioned your loyalty or your patriotism."

Johnson leaned forward, brought his face within inches of Ford's, and said: "I never doubted yours."

The two men stood, and the President placed his long arm around Ford's shoulders, walked him to the door, and said gravely: "When I leave here I want you to know we are friends and we always will be."

Riding back to the Hill, Ford was touched, moved, by the personal farewell of a man he admired as a great public servant.

7

⚜

FROM TRIUMPH
TO TRAGEDY

On Monday, January 20, 1969, for the sixth time, Congressman and Mrs. Gerald R. Ford took their seats on the East Front of the Capitol to attend the inauguration of a President. Their friends Dick and Pat Nixon had come a long way in the twenty years since they first met. Observing the ceremony and listening to the inaugural address, Ford felt the country stood on the threshold of a historic new era of national progress.

"I had tremendous faith in Dick Nixon's ability," Ford said. "I had great respect for his intelligence, his knowledge of the issues, his understanding of how politics works. I was very optimistic. I thought Nixon would be a great President."

A week later Ford, with the partisan leaders of Congress, went to their first meeting with the new President. After the turmoil of Lyndon Johnson's latter years in the White House, Ford thought he was seeing the beginning of a new accord between the White House and Congress. The meeting over, President Nixon climbed into his limousine and went up to Capitol Hill for what *The Washington Post* described as "a rousing welcome in the well of the House." Speaker John McCormack warmly received the new President, recessed the House so that Nixon could personally greet each Member, and hosted a luncheon for the new President in the Speaker's private dining room.

In a move to give Members something tangible to remember him by,

Nixon took the occasion to endorse a major pay raise for Congress—from $30,000 a year to $42,500. The gesture was effective; but of his plans for dealing with domestic and international issues, Nixon said nothing.

Ford waited for Nixon's direction. "As Minority Leader under a Democratic Administration, my responsibility had been to propose Republican alternatives," Ford said. Now his responsibility was reversed. "My job was to push Nixon's programs through the House. Ev Dirksen had to do the same thing on the Senate floor." Both waited for proposals to push. And waited.

Ford and Dirksen expected that Nixon would be different from his predecessor, but the difference went far beyond their expectations. With Johnson, there was no mistaking what he wanted, and there was no mistaking that if necessary Johnson would run over Congress to get it.

"Incredibly," Ford said, "Ev and I had trouble finding anyone on the White House staff dealing with policy who was interested in consulting with us on domestic legislative priorities."

In truth, in those first weeks in office Nixon did not know what he wanted. For him, as for most new U.S. presidents, the campaign to get elected had consumed all the time and all the energy of the candidate and his team. Only after he won did Nixon seriously examine how he might deal with the War in Vietnam and a lengthening list of insoluble domestic problems.

In New York City during the Nixon transition, Osborn Elliott, the editor of *Newsweek,* went to the Hotel Pierre for a brief visit with the President-elect. Bryce Harlow, the elfin wise man who had come up from Washington to assist Nixon in the transition, welcomed him.

"Bryce," Elliott asked, "now that the election is over, what great objectives will Mr. Nixon want to accomplish as President?"

With a twinkle in his eye, Harlow looked at the editor in mock astonishment. "Are you kidding?" he said. "When Dick Nixon was finally elected as President, he attained eighty percent of all his goals in life. He has no idea of what he will do after he is sworn in."

Ford's talks with Nixon during the first year of the Nixon Presidency were as direct and candid as they had always been. But Ford saw less of Nixon, his friend, than he had seen of Johnson, his adversary. It was apparent to Ford, as to other Republicans in Congress, that their new President was focusing on the War in Vietnam and on foreign policy. Only a month after he took office Nixon flew off to Europe for a week to consult with Allied leaders; Capitol Hill noted that the new President might better have spent that time conferring with the Leaders of the U.S. Congress.

Ford became convinced that Nixon was making a mistake in neglecting Congress. Nixon, in turn, thought it was futile for him to try to win over the Democratic majorities. Both were right.

It was part of Nixon's plan to propose a series of domestic programs; but he began his Presidency in fear and foreboding of the Democrats who controlled Congress. "[I] could not overcome the reality that I was still the first President in 120 years to begin his term with both houses of Congress controlled by the opposition party," Nixon wrote. "Washington is a city run primarily by Democrats and liberals, dominated by like-minded newspapers and other media." Neither Ford nor Dirksen was yet aware of it, but they were part of the Congress that Nixon detested.

Nixon's attitude was reflected in his staff. Ford, who could get along with almost everyone, actively disliked Bob Haldeman and John Ehrlichman. "They were obnoxious when it came to their dealings with the Congress," Ford said.

Ford asked Ehrlichman to come to the Hill only once. "We had a hot issue where we had to get the White House Domestic Council, which Ehrlichman headed, on the same wavelength with Republicans in Congress. So I got all the Senate and House Republican leadership and members involved to my office, and Ehrlichman came with two of his people. Everyone was trying to find an answer, but John Ehrlichman sat over in a corner in a big chair, obviously bored to death. He was silent, totally disdainful of the serious effort we were making to work out an accommodation. I'm not sure he didn't sleep; he had his hands over his eyes. I was disgusted."

Ehrlichman, in turn, disdained Ford, along with the rest of Congress. He found Ford "slow to grasp the substantive information" in Nixon's proposals but accurate in judging Congressional reaction. Ford, Ehrlichman wrote, "instinctively knew the mood and tempo of the House, because he was just like most of them."

Ford worked well with most of the Nixon Cabinet, but he had reservations about Attorney General John Mitchell. At an embassy dinner soon after Nixon took office, Ford was seated next to Martha Mitchell. "She was arrogant and impolite," he said, and openly disdainful of Congress. When she told Ford that the President and the Cabinet would run the government as they wished—"Make no mistake about that"—Ford wondered if she were reflecting her husband's attitudes.

Any time he was in the White House, Ford made a point of seeing Kissinger. The two continued to trade—Kissinger's strategic wisdom for Ford's political counsel. It was through Kissinger that Ford first got to know

General Alexander Haig, the deputy to Kissinger at the National Security Council. When Kissinger had a particularly sensitive foreign policy development he wanted Ford to know about right away, he would send Haig up to brief the House Leader. Ford liked Haig and thought highly of his talents and his military record.

In H-230, Ford's office off the House floor in the Capitol, the door was always open to two men Ford regarded as among the best ever to represent a President. Bryce Harlow, Ford said, was "a man of total integrity. He understood the Hill. He knew the subject he wanted to talk about. With his great sense of humor went a deep understanding of people. A man of unbelievable good judgment—Bryce just had that infinite wisdom when it came to judgment."

Younger but no less able in Ford's view was Bill Timmons—"a very bright practical person, trained on the Hill by [Senator] Bill Brock. Timmons and I were ideologically in the same spectrum, and I liked him on a very personal basis, always trusted him. Bill's a pro. He did a great job for Nixon, and under the toughest of circumstances."

In his first twenty years in Congress, Ford rarely made a major error of politics or judgment. His actions were so steady and his views so predictable that reporters found him dull. It was Ford's nature to avoid discord in public; and even in the most strenuous debates, he never made a personal attack on a Democrat. That is, he did not until the spring of 1970.

At that time, for reasons he could never adequately explain in public or to his closest friends, Ford tried to impeach one of the most popular Democrats in high office—Supreme Court Justice William O. Douglas.

The idea had come to Ford a year earlier, after another Supreme Court Justice, Abe Fortas, was forced to resign when *Life* Magazine exposed payments of twenty thousand dollars yearly to Fortas from a foundation set up by Louis Wolfson, who was serving time in a Federal prison for violating securities laws. The controversy over Fortas revived an earlier *Los Angeles Times* report: For almost ten years Justice Douglas had been paid twelve thousand dollars a year by Alvin Parvin, who had business connections to organized crime. The bad publicity about the payments caused Justice Douglas to resign from Parvin's foundation; but he stayed on the Supreme Court.

Ford believed that Parvin's payments to Douglas were certainly inappropriate, probably illegal, and should be investigated. He assigned Hartmann to recruit a team of part-time investigators, but they came up with nothing to justify impeachment charges. The Justice Department found no conflict of interest case against Douglas. Ford, frustrated, summoned Richard Helms, Director of the CIA, to ask if there were something sinister about Douglas's vacation walking tours in the USSR. Helms told Ford the CIA had no evidence that Douglas had ties to Communists. Nevertheless, Ford had made up his mind that Douglas was unfit to remain on the Court. His stubbornness got the better of his judgment, and he let it be known that he would put the issue before the House.

On the evening of April 15, 1970, before a sizable audience on the House floor and in the galleries, Ford did not press his best argument—that Douglas had accepted fees for legal work despite a Federal law barring Federal judges to practice law. Nor did he lay out a good case that Douglas had a conflict of interest by representing a man with ties to criminals.

Instead, quite out of character, he attacked Douglas personally—"fractious behavior as the first sign of senility" . . . "his writings in a pornographic magazine with a portfolio of obscene photographs on one side of it and a literary admonition to get a gun and start shooting at the first white face you see on the other" . . . "He does not give a tinker's damn what we think of him and his behavior on the Bench" . . . "He is unfit and should be removed."

Instantly, Douglas's large and powerful following in Washington launched a counterattack. Liberals of all faiths revered Douglas and considered Ford's accusation an impertinence and an outrage. In the House some forty Democrats signed a statement charging that Ford was attacking the "integrity and independence" of the Supreme Court.

Ford did have substantial support in the House; fifty-nine Republicans and fifty-two conservative Democrats cosponsored his resolution calling for a special bipartisan House committee to find out whether there were grounds for impeachment. But the Democrats had public sentiment behind them, and they had the votes. Speaker McCormack turned the issue over to the House Judiciary Committee, controlled almost two-to-one by liberal Democrats. The Committee held no hearings and called no witnesses; the Democratic majority simply voted to exonerate Douglas.

Ford was soundly beaten, in the House of Representatives and in public opinion. "I got a terrible press," Ford said later. Indeed he did. *New Republic* Columnist John Osborne wrote that Ford's attempt to have Douglas impeached was "the shoddiest enterprise on his record."

Ford was shaken by the unseemly Douglas episode. He was convinced, he said, "there were questionable things that Douglas did." But his failed attempt damaged Ford's reputation for leadership and fairness; and consequently, he said, "It was a mistake."

In 1970, Ford campaigned every week for House members and some weeks he campaigned every day. Never had he traveled so far or so often for his colleagues; and in the last weeks of his own campaign, he made forty-six public appearances in Grand Rapids and the smaller communities of his District. As usual, he was reelected with almost two-thirds of the vote. In the House races, the Republicans lost twelve seats. In the Ninety-second Congress Ford would have 180 Republicans—thirty-eight seats short of a majority. But in his optimistic view, a gain of thirty-eight seats would be within reach in 1972.

After all the campaign traveling, Ford took his family to Vail, Colorado, for a long holiday. Skiing was the Ford family sport; and in June 1970 they had pooled their savings and borrowed enough to buy a three-bedroom condominium for $59,700 in downtown Vail. Christmas of 1970 was to be their first family holiday and vacation in the new house. Mrs. Ford and thirteen-year-old Susan flew out early to get everything ready. For almost two weeks the Fords were together, with the days devoted to long runs down the mountains and the evenings to the warmth of a close family. Years later, Susan said, "It was the best of times."

On January 4, 1971, after a full day on the ski slope, Ford propped up his feet in the evening to watch a prime-time interview of President Nixon on his first two years in office. Four of TV's best—John Chancellor, Eric Sevareid, Howard K. Smith, and Nancy Dickerson—questioned Nixon on Vietnam, the economy, Cuba, the Middle East, U.S.-Soviet relations, his goals as President, his health, his outlook, his disappointments.

Nixon had not always performed well on television, but this time his responses came across as knowledgeable and candid. "I thought he did a great job, one of his best," Ford said. He called Nixon to congratulate him.

The President thanked Ford, and suggested it was time for them to talk politics and the future. "Jerry," the President said, "why don't you and Betty come out and see us?"

"Well," Ford said, "we are here with the children in Vail, but after they go back to school we could come by."

"I'll have my people contact you," Nixon said.

A White House plane arrived in Colorado for the Fords and flew them to Newport Beach. From there a White House helicopter picked them up and landed them at the Nixon compound in San Clemente. When Ford climbed aboard and saw the other guests—Bob and Delores Hope, Henry Kissinger, and Arnold Palmer—he realized his meeting with Nixon would be social, not business. "Nixon gave us a tour of La Casa Pacifica and the grounds," Ford said, "and Pat showed the gals around the house. It was a delightful evening. Seldom in all the years that I'd known the President had I seen him so relaxed."

Back in Washington for the opening of the Ninety-second Congress, Ford started his campaign to win the House of Representatives in 1972 and become Speaker. For years he had been preaching to his fellow Republicans the lesson that worked so well for him in Michigan's Fifth Congressional District: "Build a good record. Campaign on that record."

President Nixon, after a slow start, was beginning to build a domestic record. As the House Republican Leader, Ford commended the goals in Nixon's 1971 State of the Union—welfare reform, improving the environment, broadening health care, and giving more responsibility and more Federal funds to state and local government. When Nixon sent up a major proposal to reform the welfare system, Ford organized a bipartisan coalition to support it. The Nixon Family Assistance Plan would provide training and enough money to working poor and unemployed to lift themselves out of poverty. Twice the plan passed the House, "thanks in large part to the leadership of Jerry Ford with help from Wilbur Mills," Nixon said. Twice the Democrats in the Senate voted it down.

When two powerful Democrats in the Senate, Muskie and Henry Jackson, reached a jurisdictional impasse on environmental bills, Nixon decided to proceed on his own. Using his Presidential authority to reorganize the Executive Department, he created the Environmental Protection Agency, the National Oceanic and Atmospheric Administration, and the Federal Energy Administration; consolidated the Peace Corps and Vista into Action; and restructured his budget bureau into the Office of Management and Budget, to emphasize the Executive responsibility for management as well as spending.

As part of his new Federalism, Nixon sent Congress an initiative welcomed in every state capital and at the grass roots of every village and city—Federal Revenue Sharing. It was not a new idea; President Andrew Jackson distributed Federal surplus to the states in 1836. In modern times it was a Republican Congressman, Mel Laird, who first introduced a bill to share Federal taxes with state governments. Ford strongly supported Laird and the Revenue Sharing concept. It exemplified good Republican philosophy: Each of the three tiers of the American government—Federal, state, and local—should concentrate on what it does best.

In brief, the idea was that Washington was best at such responsibilities as national defense, foreign policy, and raising taxes; states were best at building highways and funding universities; and cities were best at running the police department, planting trees in the neighborhood park, and hiring good teachers for the public schools.

All through the 1960s many Republicans and Democrats paid homage to Revenue Sharing with press releases. But it was the Republicans in Congress and in the state houses who persuaded Nixon to put it on his agenda in 1971. At the urging of Ford and Senate Minority Leader Hugh Scott, and after an ardent political pitch in the Oval Office by Governor Nelson Rockefeller of New York and Vice President Agnew, Nixon agreed to commit five billion dollars yearly "to be used as the States and localities see fit."

Before Nixon went public with the proposal, Ford had already accepted the toughest assignment: To get the bill through the House, whose Members preferred to spend Federal money themselves rather than send it to the local mayor. For eighteen months, Ford held his Republican supporters together and worked with Democratic allies in the House and a broad coalition of governors, mayors, and county executives to expand that support. In time the coalition even converted Wilbur Mills, Chairman of Ways and Means, from leading the opposition to leading the support for passing Revenue Sharing. In June of 1972 Ford's bipartisan Revenue Sharing coalition won, 223–185, after a long and hard-fought battle. Ford was proud of this victory for a major Republican initiative; he looked on it as a good example of what he could accomplish if he should become Speaker.

On Saturday, June 17, 1972, Ford was in Michigan for a typically busy weekend—speaking to the Veterans of Foreign Wars in Grand Rapids, attending a Republican State Convention and speaking at a Wolverine Boys State assembly in Lansing. On his car radio on Sunday morning he heard a news report that five burglars had been caught in the act of breaking into Democratic National Committee Headquarters in Washington, evidently to bug the office of the Chairman.

"Who could be so stupid?" Ford thought. "What was there to gain from breaking into the Democrats' National Headquarters? Who would do such a thing? And why? It's incomprehensible."

Back in Washington on Monday morning, Ford read on the front page of *The Washington Post* that James W. McCord, one of the five Watergate burglars, was on the payroll of the Nixon reelection committee as a security operative. As it happened, Ford was meeting that morning in his Capitol office with John O. Marsh, a friend, former Democratic Congressman from Virginia, and lawyer in downtown Washington.

"Jack," Ford said, "do you suppose anyone in the White House might have been involved in this Watergate burglary?"

"Jerry," Marsh said, "I know this fellow McCord, and I know he works closely with John Mitchell."

Marsh explained that, by chance, his law office was in the same building as the Nixon campaign offices—the Olmstead building at 1701 Pennsylvania Avenue, NW, diagonally across from the Executive Office Building that is part of the White House complex. Marsh was on the eleventh floor. Mitchell, Chairman of the Committee to Reelect the President, and his campaign staff were on lower floors. As Marsh told the story to Ford, James McCord had come to Marsh's office and introduced himself as director of security for the Nixon campaign. McCord told Marsh he was opening a new campaign office on the eleventh floor for Martha Mitchell, the wife of the chairman. McCord explained that Mrs. Mitchell was spending so much time in the campaign offices that her husband decided to give her an office of her own, separate from the campaign offices. As a courtesy, Marsh permitted McCord to use the telephone and copier in his law office until equipment could be installed in the new office for Mrs. Mitchell.

After describing how he happened to know McCord, Marsh said to Ford: "When I saw McCord's picture in the *Post* this morning, not only was I surprised, but it immediately raised a question in my mind as to who else might be involved. In light of McCord's position, and who he works for, it seems to me that someone at a very high level was bound to have had some knowledge or association with this break-in at the Watergate."

Ford was silent for a long moment. The Dick Nixon he knew was far too experienced a politician to have been involved in such a silly stunt. Maybe some amateur campaign workers were involved; and if that was the case, Ford was confident that Nixon could simply get rid of them and go on with the business of governing and winning his reelection. In a firm voice, he said to Marsh: "If there was anyone in the White House involved, Nixon ought to fire them, and I don't care how high it would go. If he does that, it will be the end of it."

By coincidence, Ford was scheduled to meet that day with Mitchell. Ford, along with Senate Republican Leader Hugh Scott and the chairmen of the Republican House and Senate campaigns, had set up the meeting with Mitchell and his deputy, Jeb Magruder, to coordinate the campaigns for Congress and the reelection of President Nixon.

Ford walked into Mitchell's private office early, by design. Before the others arrived, Ford said: "John, did you or the Nixon Campaign Committee have anything to do with the break-in at the Democratic National Headquarters?"

Mitchell looked Ford in the eye and said: "Absolutely not!"

Ford took Mitchell at his word.

On the weekend that Watergate began, President Nixon was in the Bahamas and Florida. He flew down on Friday afternoon, after a White House ceremony to award, posthumously, the Presidential Medal of Freedom to John Paul Vann, an extraordinary American soldier and leader in the Vietnam War. In Grand Cay, 120 miles off the Florida Coast, the President rested, walked, swam, and read.

Early Sunday morning he flew to Key Biscayne. In his memoirs Nixon states that he first learned of Watergate when he went into the kitchen of his condominium to get a cup of coffee and saw *The Miami Herald* on the counter. A headline on the front page caught his attention:

MIAMIANS HELD IN D.C. TRY
TO BUG DEMO HEADQUARTERS

Nixon read the story, which stated that Cuban exiles working for the CIA were caught in the burglary, but did not suggest that any Republican might be involved. "It sounded preposterous," Nixon wrote. "I dismissed it as some sort of prank."

Nevertheless, Nixon was so alarmed that he telephoned his "political point man" Charles Colson to demand an explanation. Talking to Colson, Nixon got so mad that he threw an ashtray across his Key Biscayne living room.

Nixon's fright, that Colson had bungled, distracted him from another political scheme: To dump Spiro T. Agnew from the 1972 Republican ticket and replace him with John Connally.

Nixon had developed a political crush on the vainglorious and capable Democrat from Texas, and he was contriving to convert Connally into a Republican and make him the next President. From Key Biscayne he telephoned Connally, traveling the world on a Presidential mission, and found him in Canberra, Australia. Aglow with pleasure after his thirty-minute conversation, Nixon told Haldeman to invite Connally to meet him in San Clemente. There Nixon planned to talk with Connally again about the Vice Presidential nomination.

Although Nixon was worried about Watergate, he instructed the White House press secretary, Ron Ziegler, to dismiss the incident as "a third-rate burglary."

From the beginning, the Watergate break-in was an enigma. Early on the morning of Saturday June 17, 1972, a building guard in the Watergate office building in the Foggy Bottom neighborhood of northwest Washington noticed tape on a door lock. He suspected burglary, and called the police. At 2:30 A.M. three plainclothes officers for the District of Columbia walked the back stairs to the sixth floor and discovered the door had been pried open. Suddenly, they burst into the headquarters of the Democratic National Committee with guns drawn. "Don't shoot," one man said, with his hands in the air. Five men were arrested.

All wore business suits and rubber gloves. Some carried cameras and film; others had tools to pick locks and plant listening devices in walls and telephones. Together they had $2,300 in cash, mostly in hundred-dollar bills with the serial numbers in sequence. Their leader, who first told police he was Edward Martin, was later identified as James W. McCord, Jr., a former agent for the CIA and the FBI who was security chief for the Committee to Reelect the President, known by the acronym CRP, or, in journalese, "Creep." The other four burglars, all involved with the CIA in anti-Castro activities, were Bernard Barker, Virgilio Gonzalez, Eugenio Martinez, and Frank Sturgis. They were hired hands on call to do the CIA's less tasteful work, pick a lock, bug a phone, train a guerrilla.

In the pockets of two of the burglars police found the name and phone number of Howard Hunt. Police traced the number; it was in the Nixon White House.

Under questioning the burglars told police that they worked for Hunt, a former CIA agent and White House consultant, and G. Gordon Liddy, a lawyer and, like McCord, a former FBI agent. Liddy was legal counsel for the Nixon campaign finance committee. The story they told was that they had broken into the Democratic headquarters to replace a telephone bug that had stopped working. Bugging a telephone is a Federal crime, so the D.C. police called in the FBI.

This, obviously, was no ordinary crime. An FBI officer on watch that Saturday morning alerted Henry Petersen, Assistant Attorney General for the Criminal Division, and a nonpartisan workhorse at the Department of Justice since the Truman Administration. Petersen thought it prudent to notify the Attorney General, Richard Kleindienst, who, only seven days earlier, had moved up from deputy to take over the Justice Department when John Mitchell became chairman of the Nixon campaign for reelection.

Petersen caught Kleindienst at home, just before he left for a golf match, and told his boss what he knew—that there had been a break-in at Democratic National Headquarters, and five men were arrested. Certainly it was a puzzling incident, they agreed; possibly it was a serious crime.

Kleindienst, as he had planned, went on to Burning Tree, Washington's golf course for the powerful and the elite. As he was having lunch in the club dining room, he saw two men vigorously motioning to him from an archway across the room. One was Liddy, whom he knew as an erratic and flamboyant former assistant to John Ehrlichman; the other was Powell Moore, a drawling Georgian whom Mitchell had taken from Justice to be Nixon's campaign press secretary. Kleindienst left his table to see what they wanted.

"Where can we talk in private?" Liddy asked.

Kleindienst took them into a club locker room.

Liddy said quickly: "John Mitchell sent me from Los Angeles to inform you that some of the persons who were arrested last night at the Watergate Hotel might be employed by either the White House or the Committee to Reelect the President, and he wants you to get them out of jail at once!"

"What in the hell are you talking about, Liddy?" Kleindienst said. "John Mitchell knows how to find me. I don't believe he gave you any such instructions."

Kleindienst picked up a nearby phone and called Petersen: "Henry, I don't know what this is all about, but those persons arrested last night are to be treated just like anyone else."

Turning angrily to Liddy, Kleindienst told him to leave the club immediately or he would have him arrested.

Liddy had not talked to John Mitchell but to Magruder. Mitchell and Magruder were in California to talk with Governor Ronald Reagan about his role in Nixon's reelection campaign. Liddy had telephoned Magruder early in the morning with the bad news about the arrest of the campaign team. Magruder, upon hearing that campaign workers were caught in the act, called Bob Reisner, a junior staffer at campaign headquarters, and asked him to remove tell-tale documents from the Nixon reelection committee files.

Magruder told Mitchell that the five men in prison included McCord, Mitchell's own campaign security chief. Mitchell was stunned. Twice he had turned down Liddy's expensive and dubious schemes to spy on Democrats and to disrupt their Presidential convention. How, he asked Magruder, did this happen?

* * *

At 5:00 P.M., John Ehrlichman was called at home: A Secret Service agent had picked up the police report that one of the Watergate burglars was carrying Howard Hunt's White House phone number, and wanted to alert Ehrlichman.

Ehrlichman knew that Hunt had worked for Charles Colson, and might still be. He telephoned Colson, who insisted that Hunt no longer worked for him. Ehrlichman was skeptical, and put in a call to alert Haldeman.

Washington, no stranger to political shenanigans and chicanery, had never had a political burglary before. It was news, maybe big news; and one newspaper, *The Washington Post*, was already on top of the story. Alfred Lewis, the *Post*'s tenured police reporter, telephoned the first account of the burglary to the rewrite desk a few hours after the five men were jailed. Two young *Post* reporters, Bob Woodward and Carl Bernstein, were assigned to investigate the incident; and on Sunday, June 18, the *Post* printed on the front page the first Watergate story:

5 HELD IN PLOT TO BUG
DEMOCRATS' OFFICE HERE
BY ALFRED E. LEWIS

> Five men, one of whom said he is a former employee of the Central Intelligence Agency, were arrested at 2:30 A.M. yesterday in what authorities described as an elaborate plot to bug the offices of the Democratic National Committee here.

This first *Post* story about Watergate hit the Associated Press A-wire on Saturday night and by Sunday morning reached across the country and around the world.

To anyone who believed he knew something about politics—which is to say, almost everyone in Washington—the notion of breaking into a party headquarters was bizarre, even laughable: What, of value, could anyone expect to find, or hear, in a party chairman's office? Consequently, when the press rounded up the usual political opinions, the reaction was disbelief. In upstate New York, where he was campaigning for the Democratic Presidential nomination, Senator George McGovern told the political reporters traveling with him that he doubted the Republican Party or its leaders were involved. In Washington, scholarly Mike Mansfield, the Democratic Majority Leader of the Senate, shook his head and said, No, he did not believe the Republican Party had anything to do with the burglary.

The Democrats were wrong. On Monday, June 19, *The Washington Post*—in a front page story by Woodward and Bernstein—reported that one of the five men arrested at Watergate "is the salaried security coordinator for President Nixon's reelection committee."

Mitchell, responding for the Nixon campaign, told reporters he was "surprised and dismayed" at McCord's arrest. "There is no place in our campaign, or in the electoral process, for this type of activity," Mitchell said emphatically, "and we will not permit it or condone it."

The identification of a Nixon campaign worker as one of the burglars outraged the Democrats. Larry O'Brien, the Democratic chairman whose office had been entered, told the press this "bugging incident . . . raised the highest questions about the integrity of the political process." O'Brien and Joe Califano, counsel for the Democratic National Committee, filed a million-dollar lawsuit against the Nixon campaign.

The Chairman of the Republican National Committee, Bob Dole, issued a public condemnation: "We deplore action of this kind in and out of politics." Dole, who had mentioned to close friends that there were too many amateurs running the Nixon reelection campaign, suspected the worst.

President Nixon learned more about his campaign's role in Watergate aboard *Air Force One,* on his flight back to Washington Monday night. Haldeman came in to his private cabin to report that Mitchell had called with "disturbing news"—confirmation that the Nixon campaign staff was involved in the burglary.

The President replied that he hoped no White House people were involved. However, as a preemptive stroke against bad publicity, Nixon also told Haldeman: ". . . Get somebody on the PR side who will get out some of the negatives" on the Democrats.

Back in the White House on Tuesday morning, June 20, the President picked up *The Washington Post* and read on the front page:

WHITE HOUSE CONSULTANT
TIED TO BUGGING FIGURE

A consultant to White House Special Counsel Charles W. Colson is listed in the address books of two of the five men arrested in an attempt to bug the Democratic National Headquarters.

The story went on to point out that Howard Hunt had, until a month before the burglary, worked in the White House for Colson.

"The mention of Colson's name gave me a start," Nixon wrote. ". . . Colson was a member of my inner circle of aides and advisers, and if he was drawn in, it was a whole new situation. I had always valued his hardball instincts. Now I wondered if he might have gone too far."

Nixon called in Haldeman to find out more. Did Mitchell know about the break-in beforehand?

No, Haldeman said. Mitchell, they agreed, was too smart for that.

Did Haldeman know any more about the reason for the break-in? Nixon asked.

The five men went in to fix a telephone tap that was not working, Haldeman said. They also believed they could find important papers about Democratic contributors and Chairman O'Brien's finances, Haldeman continued, and they planned to photograph the documents.

Did Colson know in advance about the break-in? Nixon asked.

Haldeman said that he and others, including Colson, knew that the committee was looking for intelligence about the Democrats, but he said he did not believe that Colson had specific knowledge of Watergate before it happened.

Nixon said he was worried about Colson.

"Why?" Haldeman asked.

"I can't stand an FBI interrogation of Colson," Nixon said.

"Chuck tells me he's clean," Haldeman replied.

"Colson can talk about the President, if he cracks," Nixon said. He told Haldeman that he had ordered Colson to dig up the dirt about a financial deal between O'Brien and the billionaire financier Howard Hughes. Nixon hated O'Brien. "After the Kent State tragedy, he virtually accused me of killing the four students," Nixon said. Nixon also had an old score to settle with Hughes. When he was Vice President, Nixon's sleaze of a brother, Donald, borrowed $205,000 from Hughes to start a business. When Donald's venture failed and he couldn't pay the debt, the story of his finagling with the notorious Howard Hughes became a major political embarrassment for Nixon in two campaigns—for president in 1960 and for Governor of California in 1962. Nixon never healed from any political wound. In early 1972, when Ehrlichman came in one day to show him an IRS "sensitive case" report connecting O'Brien and Hughes in a complicated mineral lease deal, Nixon saw the chance for revenge. He told Ehrlichman to speed up the IRS audit and get the O'Brien-Hughes story out before the election. But George Shultz, then Secretary of the Treasury, told Ehrlichman: "Look, we don't intervene with the IRS audits. This will take its normal course." Thwarted, once again, by one of his own Cabinet appointees, Nixon turned to his nether agent, Colson, to find out something to discredit O'Brien.

"Colson told me he was going to get the information I wanted one way or the other," Nixon said to Haldeman. "Colson called [Magruder] and got the whole operation started. Right from the Goddamn White House."

Haldeman suggested he get Colson in and talk with him.

Nixon said he had already "talked to Chuck. . . . He says he's innocent." But Nixon was suspicious, and went on to say that he thought Colson "had known specifically that the Watergate bugging project was under way."

How did Howard Hunt, the consultant to Colson, get involved? Nixon asked.

Hunt was across the street in a motel room, actually observing the burglars in O'Brien's office, Haldeman said.

How did the police find out about Hunt? Nixon wanted to know.

Hunt's name was in the address books of two of the Cubans, Haldeman said, and one of the Cubans had a $6.90 check signed by Hunt and payable to Hunt's country club. Hunt, Haldeman added, was hiding from the FBI, but Colson knew how to get in touch with him.

The Cuban and CIA connections intrigued the President and Haldeman. Four of the burglars were Cuban exiles; all five—and Hunt and McCord—had links to the CIA.

"Whatever the case," Nixon wrote, "I saw that a Cuban explanation for the break-in would have two advantages for us. It would protect us from the political impact of the disclosure of the CRP's involvement, and it would undercut the Democrats by calling attention to . . . McGovern's naive policy toward Castro."

Nixon called Colson in that afternoon to find out how much Colson knew about the break-in, and to assess whether Colson might crack under FBI questioning.

Colson had earned his standing with the President because he, like Nixon, relished getting the dirt on political enemies and using it. In Colson, Nixon found a man so ambitious to become a Presidential favorite that he would, as Ehrlichman put it, "take on the rough chores others wouldn't do."

From the beginning of Nixon's political career, it was his way to attack and try to destroy the character of his opponent. In his first race for Congress he accused Jerry Voorhis of being supported by Communists. In his campaign for the Senate in 1950 Nixon defeated Helen Gahagan Douglas with a "pink sheet" slanted to show she was un-American.

In the summer of 1969, only a few months after he became President, Nixon ordered John Ehrlichman, then White House Counsel, to hire a private investigator to find out what really happened at Chappaquiddick when Senator Ted Kennedy and a young woman went off the bridge and she was drowned. "Don't let up on this for a minute," the President told Ehrlichman. Nixon was disappointed that Ehrlichman's investigator turned up nothing that had not been in the newspapers.

In the second year of his Presidency, Nixon told Haldeman and Ehrlichman to "get tough, and to get information about what the other side [is] doing. . . . We should come up with the kind of imaginative dirty tricks that our Democratic opponents used against us." Nixon ordered that Senator Edmund Muskie be followed, and told his staff to check the files of the IRS and the FBI to look for damaging information about well-known Democrats.

But Haldeman and Ehrlichman did not show enough enthusiasm for this "intelligence gathering," as Nixon called it. "Increasingly," Nixon wrote, "I turned to Chuck Colson to act as my political point man. . . . His instinct for the political jugular and his ability to get things done made him a lightning rod for my own frustrations at the timidity of most Republicans."

Colson deliberately appealed to the dark half of Nixon, fed him tidbits of juicy gossip, carried out his palace intrigues, and served as a kind of grim court jester for this monarch without a sense of humor. In time Colson became alter ego to the lesser Nixon: consequently, the President had reason to be alarmed when the FBI linked the Watergate burglars to Hunt, and then linked Hunt to Colson.

When Colson walked into the Oval Office on that third day after the Watergate burglary, Nixon said: "Hi. Now I hope everybody is not going to get in a tizzy about the, uh, Democratic Committee."

"Pick up that goddamn *Washington Post* and see that guilt by association," Colson replied, referring to the *Post* story that morning about his close connection to Howard Hunt.

The President and Colson discussed whether the burglars might talk, and whether McCord, or Hunt, might take the blame for the crime. In a rambling attempt to reassure Colson, Nixon suggested that tapping the Democratic National Committee was justified. "A lot of people think you oughta wiretap," Nixon said. "They probably figure they're doing it to us, which they are." For more than an hour the two men talked, hopeful that the Watergate incident would blow over, but fearful of what O'Brien's lawyers might discover if "our people," as Nixon described them, were called to testify. In particular, Nixon told Colson, "I don't think you should testify. . . . Just stonewall it."

Colson thought they should give the public the line that the break-in was a Cuban-American move to connect McGovern to Castro.

That's the plan, Nixon said. As Colson was leaving, the President told him not to worry. "It's gonna be forgotten after a while."

That evening Nixon telephoned John Mitchell, who apologized for not doing a better job of policing the Nixon campaign staff. Nixon thought Mitchell sounded "completely tired and worn out," and tried to reassure him.

Late that night Nixon came up with what he thought was such a great idea that he telephoned Haldeman at home. If the press would buy the Cuban explanation, Nixon said, he would call his friend Bebe Rebozo in Miami and get him to persuade Cuban leaders there to start a campaign to raise bail money for the Cubans in the D.C. jail. We could, Nixon told Haldeman, "make a big media issue out of it. . . . We might even make Watergate work in our favor."

The antics of President Nixon and his staff in reacting to Watergate seem as curious in retrospect as the Watergate break-in itself. It was to be expected that the first priority for the President and his political advisers would be to prevent damage to the Nixon campaign for reelection. Usually, in American campaign politics, the solution for a campaign worker's mistake is to fire the culprit, make a grudging apology to the opponent, and stir up something else for the press to write about.

In the first days after the Watergate burglary the President could simply have denounced the attempt to bug Democratic headquarters and ordered Mitchell to dismiss every campaign worker who had a part in it. But that was not Nixon's way. He never even considered that solution, or so he said. "I had been in politics too long, and seen everything from dirty tricks to vote fraud," he wrote. "I could not muster much moral outrage over a political bugging."

And so, in that spirit, President Nixon's part in the cover-up began. Instead of dismissing the "preposterous" actions of his campaign workers, Nixon intervened in their defense. By that act he consciously and irretrievably embraced the campaign's folly.

Yet his intervention followed no concept or plan; step by step, day by day, it just happened. The first round of White House lies about Watergate made all the other lies almost inevitable.

To shield Nixon and his actions there came together around him, more by proximity than design, a five-man ring of conspiracy—Haldeman, Ehrlichman, Mitchell, Colson, and John Dean, a clever young White House counsel and protégé of Mitchell and Ehrlichman. Each in his own way set out to prevent political damage to the President; together they put up a wall around him—and around themselves—to conceal their plots and actions not only from the press and the public but from their own White House colleagues.

Their strategy, if it can be called that, was to silence the burglars, stop the FBI investigation, deny in public what they were busily doing in private, and hope the incident would soon blow over.

Within this inner circle, Bob Haldeman, who spent the most time with Nixon, reported on the progress of the cover-up and carried out Nixon's instructions. John Ehrlichman, aggressive, sardonic, the most cerebral and calculating of the group, designed countermeasures. Chuck Colson carried messages to and from the campaign agents in jail and their lawyers. John Mitchell, the oldest and most experienced member of the team, calmed the nervous and the guilty at campaign headquarters, and tried to focus his campaign workers on the election in November.

Dean, only thirty-three, made the cover-up team by conning Acting FBI Director Pat Gray and Assistant Attorney General Henry Petersen into informing him regularly on what the Watergate witnesses were telling FBI agents and prosecutors. In effect, Dean had an open line into enemy headquarters.

During the first four days after Watergate, the actions of Nixon and his collaborators moved from antic to absurd to criminal. After Haldeman heard from Mitchell that Liddy had masterminded the break-in, Ehrlichman suggested that Liddy be persuaded to confess that he was responsible for Watergate, accept the blame, and take the punishment. Nixon liked Ehrlichman's proposal. Taking a rap, the President said to Haldeman, is done quite often. But Nixon said he could not agree to Ehrlichman's plan if Liddy might implicate Mitchell. Nobody could guarantee what Liddy might do, Haldeman said. To those who knew him well, Liddy was looked upon as a political geek. He once boasted of forcing himself to eat a rat to test his will, and he would hold his forearm over a flame to demonstrate his mastery over pain. Mitchell, Haldeman told the President, considered Liddy unstable.

Furthermore, Haldeman said, he was no longer certain that Mitchell had not been involved in Watergate; just that day Mitchell had told him that someone should shut down the FBI investigation.

The Democrats, Nixon said angrily to Haldeman, have been bugging people for years, and "*they* never got caught." Maybe, the President suggested, we should plant a bug in the White House and find it ourselves and blame it on the Democrats.

Thursday, the fifth day after the break-in, brought Nixon good news: Dean had learned from the FBI's latest status report on the investigation that the FBI did not know how Hunt, Colson's associate, was involved. More important, the FBI had not been able to find the link between the hundred-dollar bills the burglars carried and Nixon campaign money. The Cuban connection, Haldeman said, was the story the White House was trying to sell to the FBI and the press.

Getting ready for a White House press conference, his first since Watergate hit the front pages and the network news, Nixon told Haldeman that reporters would certainly ask if there was White House involvement. Reporters would be suspicious of him, Nixon said, and if he qualified his answer in any way, the press would perceive that as guilt. So Nixon proposed to respond with a flat no.

Ziegler agreed. He had no reason to say otherwise. To keep the press in the dark, the conspirators were keeping Ziegler in the dark.

As Nixon predicted, one reporter asked if he had investigated whether there was a link between the bugging and the White House. Nixon replied, on live television before millions of Americans, "The White House has had no involvement whatever in this particular incident."

8

BETRAYED

*J*une 23, 1972. At 8:00 A.M., Jerry Ford and House Majority Leader Hale Boggs met with President Nixon for a highly visible sendoff for an official mission to the People's Republic of China. It was only four months after Nixon had accomplished his momentous initiative to reopen American relations with Red China.

Ford and Boggs and their wives were making the journey in response to an invitation from the government of Communist China, a visit that President Nixon had suggested to Chinese leaders. He wanted all the senior leaders of Congress to meet the Chinese leaders, and they in turn wanted to establish better relations with the highest-ranking American officials.

Briefing Ford and Boggs on the Chinese leaders and reflecting on his dramatic success with Red China put Nixon in good spirits. He talked at length about Mao Tse-tung and Chou En-lai, sharing his experiences on his history-making trip, and offering pointers on how to deal with the old revolutionaries running the vast country.

"The President was knowledgeable, told us what to expect, what to look out for," Ford said. "His breakthrough to China was his major achievement, and he was justifiably proud of what he had accomplished. He was riding high, at his pinnacle."

Ford and Boggs left the White House at 9:30 A.M. for the drive to Andrews Air Force Base.

Within an hour, Nixon and Haldeman took an action that would in time force Nixon from the White House and make Ford President.

At 10:04 A.M. Haldeman came in to the Oval Office with bad news. "We're back in the problem area," Haldeman said. The FBI, he warned President Nixon, had traced the hundred-dollar bills in the pockets of the Watergate burglars to the Nixon reelection committee.

Nixon and Haldeman were alone. There was a proposed solution, Haldeman said quietly, suggested by Mitchell and supported by Dean. The idea, as Haldeman described it, was for the Deputy Director of the CIA, Vernon Walters, "to call Pat Gray [Acting FBI Director] and just say, 'Stay to hell out of this—this is, ah, business here we don't want you to go any further on it.' That's not an unusual development, and, ah, that would take care of it."

"What about Pat Gray?" the President asked, wondering if Gray would call off the investigation.

"Pat does want to," Haldeman said. "He doesn't know how to, and he doesn't have any basis for doing it. Given this, he will then have the basis."

"Yeah," Nixon said.

The scenario, Haldeman said, would be for Walters to "call [Gray] in and say, 'We've got the signal from across the river to put the hold on this.' And that will fit rather well because the FBI agents who are working the case, at this point, feel that's what it is."

"They've traced the money?" Nixon asked. "Who'd they trace it to?"

"Well, they've traced it to a name," Haldeman said, "but they haven't gotten to the guy yet."

"Would it be somebody here?" Nixon asked.

"Ken Dahlberg," Haldeman said.

"Who the hell is Ken Dahlberg?" the President asked.

"He gave twenty-five thousand dollars in Minnesota," Haldeman said, and "the check went directly to this guy Barker."

"It isn't from the Committee, though, from Stans?" the President said hopefully. Maurice Stans was Finance Chairman of the Committee to Reelect the President.

"Yeah. It is," Haldeman said. "It's directly traceable and there's some more through some Texas people that went to the Mexican bank which can also be traced. . . . They'll get their names today."

Nixon suggested the donors say "they were approached by the Cubans. That's what Dahlberg has to say, the Texans too . . ."

"Well, if they will," Haldeman said. "But then we're relying on more and more people all the time. That's the problem, and they'll stop if we take this other route."

"All right," the President said.

"And you seem to think the thing to do is get them to stop," Haldeman said.

"Right, fine," the President said.

"They say the only way to do that is from White House instructions," Haldeman said. "And it's got to be to Helms and to—ah, what's his name—Walters."

"Walters," the President said.

"And the proposal would be that Ehrlichman and I call them and say, ah—"

"All right, fine," the President interrupted. "How do you call him in—I mean you just—well, we protected Helms from one hell of a lot of things."

"That's what Ehrlichman says," Haldeman said.

"Of course, this Hunt, that will uncover a lot of things," Nixon said. "We just feel that it would be very detrimental to have this thing go any further. This involves these Cubans, Hunt, and a lot of hanky-panky that we have nothing to do with ourselves. Well, what the hell, did Mitchell know about this?"

"I think so," Haldeman said. "I don't think he knew the details, but I think he knew."

"Well," the President asked, "who was the asshole who did? Is it Liddy? Is that the fellow? He must be a little nuts!"

"He is," Haldeman said.

"I mean, he just isn't well screwed on, is he?" the President said. "Is that the problem?"

"No, but he was under pressure, apparently, to get more information, and as he got more pressure, he pushed the people harder to move harder."

"Pressure from Mitchell?" the President asked.

"Apparently."

"All right, fine," the President said. "We won't second-guess Mitchell and the rest. Thank God it wasn't Colson."

"The FBI interviewed Colson yesterday," Haldeman said. "And after their interrogation of Colson yesterday, they concluded it was not the White House, but are now convinced it is a CIA thing, so the CIA turnoff would—"

The President interrupted. "Well . . . I'm not going to get that involved."

"No, sir," said Haldeman. "We don't want you to."

"You call them in," the President said.

"Good deal," said Haldeman.

"Play it tough," the President said. "That's the way they play it, and that's the way we are going to play it."

"Okay," Haldeman said.

Nixon went over the game plan again with Haldeman: "When you get the [CIA] people in, say, 'Look, the problem is that this will open the whole, the whole Bay of Pigs thing, and the President just feels that—' Without going into the details—don't, don't lie to them to the extent to say there is no involvement, but just say this is a comedy of errors. Without getting into it, the President believes that it is going to open the whole Bay of Pigs thing again. . . . They should call the FBI in and [say] don't go any further into this case, period!"

Nixon's threat about reopening "the Bay of Pigs thing" was a code phrase for the CIA attempts to assassinate Fidel Castro after the CIA's 1961 failure in the Bay of Pigs landings.

After a pause, Nixon said: "Well, can you get it done?"

"I think so," Haldeman said.

At 1:04 P.M., with CIA Director Richard Helms and Walters on the way to the White House, Nixon again brought Haldeman into the Oval Office to go over the plan. "Just say," Nixon said, with more fervor than logic, the involvement of Cuban CIA workers in the Watergate break-in "would make the CIA look bad. . . . It is likely to blow the whole Bay of Pigs thing, which we think would be very unfortunate—both for the CIA, and for the country, at this time, and for American foreign policy. Just tell him to lay off."

"Yep. That's the basis to do it on," Haldeman said. "Just leave it at that."

Haldeman went to Ehrlichman's office on the second floor of the West wing, directly above the Oval Office, to wait for Helms and Walters.

As they sat down and Haldeman began to lay out the plan, Helms interrupted, and said he had already talked to Gray at the FBI and told him the CIA was not involved in any way in Watergate.

Well, Haldeman said, "The President asked me to tell you this entire affair may be connected to the Bay of Pigs, and if it opens up, the Bay of Pigs may be blown."

Helms reacted angrily. His voice rising, he said: "The Bay of Pigs had nothing to do with this. I have no concern about the Bay of Pigs."

Haldeman waited for Helms to calm down. "I'm just following my instructions, Dick," Haldeman said. "This is what the President told me to relay to you."

Suddenly, to the surprise of Haldeman and Ehrlichman, Helms agreed that Walters should talk with Gray. Helms told Walters to remind Gray "of the agreement between the FBI and the CIA that if they run into or expose one another's 'assets' [agents], they will not interfere with each other."

At 2:20 P.M. Haldeman walked across West Executive Avenue to Nixon's private office, Room 175 of the Old Executive Office Building.

"No problem," Haldeman said. "Walters is going to make a call to Gray. That's the way we put it, and that's the way it was left."

Nixon assumed the problem was fixed. "As far as I was concerned," he wrote, "this was the end of our worries about Watergate."

On Sunday, June 25, 1972, the sleek white Boeing 707 bearing the Congressional delegation arrived in Beijing in the late afternoon, in time for Ford, Boggs, their wives, and their aides to have dinner in the Great Hall of the People. For two days they combined business and pleasure, listening to briefings from U.S. diplomats and a U.N. delegation, touring museums and a Jeep plant, and observing a demonstration of surgery under acupuncture.

With an air of good-natured mystery, the Chinese told them that nothing was scheduled for their third evening, but something might develop. At 8:30 P.M. word came that Premier Chou En-lai was inviting the visiting American leaders to dinner in a private chamber of the Great Hall.

The Chinese Premier greeted them warmly. "He had sharp, steely eyes, short black hair, a little gray," Ford said. "He was alert, quick, and healthy. It was amazing to me that Chou En-lai had gone on the Long March under the most horrendously adverse conditions, and could live that long and look that healthy."

The Premier arranged his guests in a semicircle. "He sat in the middle, Hale Boggs on his right, and I on his left, then our wives and some staff members," Ford said. "We had tea, Chinese hors d'oeuvres, a chat, and then went into dinner, at a number of small tables. The dinner was delicious, beautifully served. About midnight Chou En-lai very graciously turned to Lindy Boggs and Betty and said, through his interpreter, how nice it was to have had them for dinner and he knew how tired they were and that they had a long day the next day. Of course, Lindy and Betty were being excused, but it was so properly, discreetly done."

The Premier then took Ford and Boggs into a nearby conference room, and got down to business. "He launched into a tough diatribe against the role of the United States in the Pacific, blaming us for Vietnam, Korea, and other troubles," Ford said. From their briefings Boggs and Ford knew to expect that, and responded by defining American interests and intentions in the Pacific.

"Chou En-lai was very pleasant in conversation, but always probing," Ford said. "He was very well informed about domestic as well as foreign policies of the United States. He talked with Hale about pollution in New Orleans, in Hale's Congressional District. He asked why we were not strengthening NATO, and vehemently opposed McGovern's proposed thirty billion dollar cut in U.S. defense spending. He wanted the United States to be a power in the Pacific as a buffer against the Soviet Union; in everything he was anti-Soviet."

Both Congressmen pressed the Premier for assistance in releasing American prisoners of war in Vietnam, but Chou En-lai made no commitment. When Ford raised a question about whether China might restore good relations with the USSR, Chou En-lai did not wait for the interpreter but said, in perfect English: "Never! Never!"

The discussion ended at 3:00 A.M. "I never had a more interesting political discussion," Ford said. "Chou En-lai was one of the most able intellectual political figures I ever met—imposing in his intelligence and his knowledge, and fluent in discussing issues."

After two weeks in China, Ford flew home, landed at Andrews Air Force Base, went to his office, and telephoned President Nixon to report on his trip.

Two days later Ford took advantage of the Congressional recess during the Democratic National Convention and entered Bethesda Naval Hospital for surgery on the left knee—first injured playing football during his junior year at South High. He was still recuperating there when President Nixon telephoned, on Ford's fifty-ninth birthday, to wish him well.

Nixon called Ford from California, where he had gone to escape Washington heat and Watergate headlines, and to prepare himself for renomination and the election campaign.

To Nixon's dismay, his worries over Watergate had not ended with Haldeman's June 23 instructions to Helms and Walters. Some ten days later, Haldeman told Nixon that Walters made the call to Gray, but it didn't work. Why not? Nixon asked. Because Gray was under pressure from the U.S. Attorney to press the Watergate investigation and determine who was behind it, Haldeman said. In that case, Nixon told Haldeman, Walters should ask Attorney General Kleindienst to limit the U.S. Attorney's investigation.

Haldeman countered by suggesting to the President that the best way to deal with Watergate was to put the blame directly on John Mitchell, the man in charge of the campaign.

"I won't do that to him," Nixon said. "To hell with it. I'd rather lose the election."

Was there, Nixon asked, any way to get the campaign workers who were involved to plead guilty and get it over with? Haldeman had no answer but came in later to tell Nixon that Liddy had agreed to take sole responsibility for the break-in.

Who will take care of Liddy's family? Nixon asked.

Haldeman said there was money for that. And, he ventured, if Liddy should receive a long sentence, he could be paroled or pardoned after the election. The President agreed.

Whatever you do, Nixon told Haldeman, move quickly and cut our losses. "Get the damn thing done."

But "the damn thing" continued. The President was badly shaken when Mitchell resigned as campaign chairman—because of his wife, Mitchell said.

To those who knew Martha Mitchell, it seemed the least risky course. She loved attention, in a drawing room or in the press, and spent most of her time getting it. But she was as smart as she was irrepressible. When she sensed that Watergate was damaging the man she loved, she telephoned reporters and said she had told her husband to leave politics or she would reveal the whole Watergate story. Martha Mitchell did not know the whole story, but she was fully capable of inventing one and getting it in print.

To Mitchell, she was becoming more burden than beloved. In despair Mitchell had told Haldeman one day, "You and the President don't realize how much time I have to spend keeping her on an even keel—or how much it's affected my ability to run the campaign."

Nixon, in sadness, accepted the loss of his campaign manager. "I considered John Mitchell to be one of my few close personal friends," Nixon wrote. "I believed that I owed my election as President in 1968 largely to his strength as a counselor and his skill as a manager."

When Nixon invited Mitchell to his hideaway for a private luncheon, he was shocked. Mitchell's hand was shaking so much that he couldn't eat his soup, Nixon said.

With something less than chivalry, Nixon blamed Martha Mitchell for Watergate in his diary: "We have had a slip-up due to the fact that Mitchell was so obsessed with the problems he had with Martha. . . . Without Martha, I am sure that the Watergate thing would never have happened."

From California, Nixon telephoned Gray to congratulate him on the FBI's handling of an airline hijacking. Gray thanked the President and brought up Watergate. He told Nixon that Walters had told him that very morning that "the CIA had no interest in the matter and that pursuing the investigation would not be an embarrassment to the CIA." Gray added that he and Walters suspected that a senior official in the White House, whose identity they did not yet know, might be trying to obstruct the FBI investigation.

Nixon was alarmed. "I was suddenly confronted with the one thing I had wanted most to avoid: White House involvement in Watergate," Nixon said. "I told Gray emphatically to go ahead with his full investigation."

Frightened that Gray and Walters had perceived the truth, Nixon reversed his June 23 decision. In his diary he noted: "We have to live with this one and hope to bring it to a conclusion without too much rubbing off on the presidency before the election. . . . As I emphasized to Ehrlichman and Haldeman, we must do nothing to indicate to Pat Gray or the CIA that the White House is trying to suppress the investigation."

Nixon, in a walk with Ehrlichman on the beach at San Clemente, suggested that Magruder, as Liddy's supervisor, take the blame for the Watergate break-in. There could be clemency for the guilty after the election, Nixon suggested, but no commitment should be made before then. Ehrlichman said he had been thinking about Gray's phone conversation with the President, and concluded that the FBI suspected that Colson "was responsible for Watergate and was trying to put [the President] on the spot in order to protect himself."

In mid-July, in his Pacific retreat, Nixon sat up late watching the Democratic National Convention. To his experienced political eye, it was "a political shambles" with feminists and homosexuals and other radical activists displacing the traditional party leaders who could deliver winning blocs of votes. He was delighted that the Convention chairman let McGovern's militants of the "new politics" squander all the prime television time. It was almost 3:00 A.M. Eastern time before the nominee even reached the Convention stage for his acceptance speech.

When McGovern finished, Nixon called Haldeman: "Well, they nominated the wrong man." Until the last day Nixon thought that the Democrats would turn to Ted Kennedy, the opponent Nixon feared most.

"The election was decided the day McGovern was nominated," Nixon told historian Theodore White. "McGovern did to his party what Goldwater did."

To provide a dramatic opening to his own campaign, Nixon planned a surprise: A day or so after the Democratic Convention, he would announce John Connally as his new running mate and heir apparent.

Mitchell had warned Nixon a month or so earlier that any attempt to dump Agnew would offend the Vice President's conservative supporters and thereby damage Nixon's own chances for reelection. But Nixon had not given up the idea, and Connally arrived in San Clemente ostensibly to report on his global Presidential mission.

For three hours Nixon and Connally talked Presidential politics. Connally turned down Nixon's offer of the Vice Presidency. It was not a job he wanted, he said, and he doubted that the leaders and workers of the Republican Party would accept a former Democrat so readily.

Nixon had to admit it was a good point; Mitchell had told him the same thing. But Nixon still thought Connally was the most qualified man in the country to be the next President, and proposed an alternative plan: Connally would head a nationwide Democrats for Nixon movement in 1972. After Nixon's reelection, Connally would become a Republican; and Nixon would use the political power of the White House to make Connally the Republican nominee in 1976 and to elect him as the next President.

At his next press conference Nixon told reporters that he and Connally had discussed the Vice Presidency. "Secretary Connally, whose political judgment I respect very much, strongly urged that Vice President Agnew be continued on the ticket," Nixon said.

Connally made his commitment to the reelection of Nixon. "I will not support [the Democratic ticket] for the first time in my life," Connally said. He had agreed, he added, to become the national chairman of Democrats for Nixon.

For Connally's first big assignment, Nixon asked him to handle his fellow Democrat, Governor George Wallace. "Go down there and see him, and let me know what he wants," Nixon said.

Connally reported back that Wallace had decided not to run as a third party candidate, and wanted Nixon to "beat the hell" out of McGovern. Connally, after his talk with Wallace, boasted to Colson: "We might well say that this was the day the election was won."

Still, there loomed the specter of Watergate. After Nixon returned to Washington in late July, he asked Ehrlichman for a status report. Ehrlichman, in his crisp way, briefed the President: Magruder was being interrogated. Dean had reported that Magruder was weak and unstable, and might crack. Magruder could implicate others, specifically Mitchell and Haldeman. Dean had suggested that Magruder accept the responsibility for the break-in and stop the damage there, but Magruder would not agree.

Well, Nixon told Ehrlichman, there might be a pardon for Magruder, and others, but it would have to be after the election.

Colson came in later to advise Nixon that Hunt, whose date with the grand jury was imminent, would not talk. Nixon was pleased, and told Colson that Hunt might come under a general postelection pardon he was contemplating, for political crimes committed by Republicans and Democrats.

Haldeman brought Nixon still another report: Magruder was almost sure to be indicted.

Magruder, Nixon insisted, must "draw the line on anything that might involve Mitchell." Make sure, Nixon added, that Magruder is given money for lawyers and tipped off to the pardon possibility.

Haldeman had more bad news: He had just learned from the Justice Department that Federal prosecutors were investigating Ehrlichman.

Nixon was shocked. In a single afternoon, Ehrlichman had told him Haldeman might be implicated, and now Haldeman was telling him that Ehrlichman might be prosecuted.

From opening day, on August 21, 1972, in Miami Beach, the Republican National Convention of 1972 was a cross between the coronation of the Queen of England and the pounding redundance of a late-night television commercial. Ford, in presiding over the major evening sessions, followed the minute-by-minute script approved by Haldeman and enforced by young men in blue suits with neatly knotted ties and walkie-talkies up their sleeves.

Everything was scheduled and organized not for the delegates in the hall but for middle America, to convey a sense of order at home and the promise of peace in the world. The Republicans arrived united in the cause of four more years for President Nixon. From the CBS booth overlooking the convention floor, commentator Eric Sevareid intoned: "This is the convention of good feelings . . . contented, pleased with itself."

The Republicans had good reason to be pleased—McGovern had proved himself in the five weeks between conventions to be the most inept Presidential nominee of modern history. He bungled his Vice Presidential choice. He broke promises to the people who were trying to organize and assist his campaign. He reneged on commitments to labor leaders. He authorized secret negotiations with Hanoi, then denied he had done so.

To political reporters, McGovern came across as an amiable and well-meaning guy who couldn't say no and was in over his head. The more the voters found out about McGovern, the lower he sank in the polls. On the eve of the Republican convention President Nixon was ahead 57 percent to 34 percent, an unprecedented margin.

All factions and philosophies of the Republican party had been brought together for the renomination of Nixon. On the right stood Governor Ronald Reagan, making a rousing keynote address, and Senator Barry Goldwater, stirring the hearts and voices of the patriots to new decibels of acclaim.

To bring in the moderates, Nixon had chosen Governor Nelson Rockefeller of New York to nominate him. In 1972, as in 1964 and 1968, the moderates and liberals in the party could still command about one-third of the party votes. Nixon wanted them too, wanted all Republicans. Rockefeller was reluctant to make so visible a personal endorsement of Nixon when John Mitchell first telephoned him; he put aside his misgivings when he thought about how many Federal grants were pending that could benefit the people of New York State. Then he eased his discomfort by crafting a speech that praised Nixon's record in office, but not his character.

Haldeman, missing no detail in the convention arrangements, had a functionary advise Mrs. Rockefeller that her seat in the VIP section would be needed as soon as her husband left the podium.

On the third night of the convention, on schedule at 10:26 P.M. in the East, prime time in all continental U.S. time zones, Nixon came to center stage to speak to the nation. "I ask everyone listening to me tonight—Democrats, Republicans, and independents—to join our majority . . ."

Nixon's words followed his deliberate decision to make his reelection campaign a personal contest and to diminish party loyalties. Months earlier Haldeman had persuaded Peter Dailey, a friend and New York City advertising executive, to take charge of the November Group, which would handle all television and written material for the campaign. Dailey explained the strategy: "Anything we do that makes their crossover decision to Nixon difficult is wrong—like trying to get a Republican Congress. This is not a campaign of Republicans against Democrats. It's Richard Nixon against George McGovern. If we harden them on party lines—that could go wrong."

Two weeks after the Republican convention the Gallup Poll gave Nixon 64 percent and McGovern only 30 percent. Watergate was simply not a campaign problem. A poll taken by Robert Teeter in September found that 70 percent of those polled were aware of Watergate, but only 6 percent thought that Richard Nixon had anything to do with it. Americans still believed Richard Nixon; Americans trusted their President.

Riding high, President Nixon held his first postconvention press conference back in the White House. Anticipating a Watergate question, the President had his answer ready: The White House counsel, John Dean, had conducted a full investigation, and in Nixon's words: "I can say categorically that his investigation indicates that no one in the White House staff, no one in this administration, presently employed, was involved in this very bizarre incident."

On September 15, 1972, three months after Watergate and less than two months before the election, a Federal grand jury handed down the first indictments. Hunt, former consultant to Colson, Liddy, former assistant to Ehrlichman, McCord, Jr., former director of security for the Nixon reelection campaign, and four former CIA employees—Sturgis, Barker, Gonzalez, and Martinez—were charged with breaking and entering the Watergate offices, stealing documents, and planting listening devices.

Inside the White House, Nixon was elated. Attorney General Kleindienst had already briefed him and the Cabinet: No one in the White House, and only McCord at the campaign committee, would be named in the indictments.

Late that afternoon, after the news hit the press wires, Nixon met with Haldeman and Dean in the Oval Office. Dean assured the President that Watergate would be contained through November 7, Election Day. "Three months ago I would have had trouble predicting there would be a day when this would be forgotten, but I think I can say that fifty-four days from now nothing is going to come crashing down to our surprise," Dean said.

Nixon complimented Dean: "The way you have handled all this seems to me has been very skillful, putting your fingers in the leaks that have sprung here and sprung there. The Grand Jury is dismissed now?"

"That is correct," Dean said. "They have let them go so there will be no continued investigation prompted by the Grand Jury's inquiry."

Like the battle-scarred old warrior he was, Nixon reassured his lieutenants: "We are all in it together. This is a war. We take a few shots and it will be over. We will give them a few shots and it will be over. Don't worry. I wouldn't want to be on the other side right now. Would you?"

"Along that line," Dean replied, "I have begun to keep notes on a lot of people who are emerging as less than our friends, because this will be over some day, and we shouldn't forget the way some of them treated us."

"I want the most comprehensive notes on all those who tried to do us in," the President said. "They are asking for it, and they are going to get it."

Dean mentioned that the Chairman of the House Banking Committee, Wright Patman, was trying to get his committee to investigate whether the campaign was laundering money through foreign banks. "Whether we can be successful in turning that off or not, I don't know. . . . Jerry Ford is not really taking an active interest in this matter that is developing, so Stans is going to see Jerry Ford and try to brief him and explain to him the problems he has." Stans and Ford had been friends since Stans was President Eisenhower's budget director.

"What about Ford?" Nixon asked. If anybody can talk to Patman, John Connally could do it, the President said. Both were from Texas. "But if Ford can get the minority members . . . Jerry should talk to Widnall. (William B. Widnall of New Jersey was a senior Republican on the Banking Committee.) After all, if we ever win the House, Jerry will be Speaker, and he could tell [Widnall] if he did not get off—he will not be Chairman, ever."

"That would be very helpful . . ." Dean said. "If Jerry could get a little action on this."

"Damn it, Jerry should," Haldeman said. "That is exactly the thing he was talking about, that the reason [Congress is] staying is so that they can run investigations."

"The point is," Nixon said, "they ought to raise hell about these hearings . . ."

"That is the last forum where we have the least problem right now," Dean said. "Kennedy has already said he may call hearings of the Administrative Practices sub-committee. . . . [But] we just take one thing at a time."

"You really can't sit and worry about it all the time," the President said. "The worst may happen but it may not. So you just try to button it up as well as you can and hope for the best, and remember basically the damn business is unfortunately trying to cut our losses."

"It has been kept away from the White House and of course completely from the President," Haldeman said. "The only tie to the White House is the Colson effort they keep trying to pull in."

To stop the Patman investigation, Nixon told Ehrlichman to get Ford to organize opposition with the help of Garry Brown, a Michigan Republican and member of Patman's Committee. "They ought to get off their ass," Nixon said. "No use to let Patman have a free ride here."

A more diplomatic version of Nixon's message did reach Ford, but he had already met with Republican members of Patman's Committee. They were sure that Patman, who had a record of using Committee power for partisan purposes, wanted to go on a campaign fishing expedition. At the request of Brown and other Committee Republicans, Ford wrote all fifteen Republicans on the Banking Committee to warn against any House investigation motivated by politics; he urged each Republican "to be present at the Committee meeting to assure that the investigative resolution is appropriately drawn." As it turned out, fourteen Republicans and six Democrats defeated Patman's request for subpoena power to investigate Nixon campaign money practices. With that, the Patman investigation collapsed.

Try as they did, the Democrats could not generate any popular support in making Watergate a campaign issue. Near the end of the campaign, Senator Sam Ervin of North Carolina publicly declared that President Nixon owed the nation an explanation of Watergate and insisted he clear it up before the election. Nixon ignored Ervin.

In his campaign for Speaker of the House, Ford barnstormed the country for Republican candidates from the end of the Republican Convention through October. The polls forecast a Republican landslide, big enough—Ford hoped—to bring in the thirty-eight House seats he needed to win the House. "I believed it was possible," Ford said. "We had a good record, good candidates. And with a big Nixon win, I thought we could make it."

To Ford and to other Republicans, the closing weeks of the Presidential Campaign seemed too good to believe. McGovern floundered outside the mainstream of the electorate. Some Democrats openly opposed him; many more quietly decided either to support Nixon or not vote at all. While former President Lyndon Johnson publicly supported the Democratic ticket, he privately sent campaign advice through Billy Graham to Nixon: "Ignore McGovern, and get out with the people. But stay above the campaign, like I did with Goldwater. . . . The McGovern people are going to defeat themselves."

Nixon was running on his record. His opening to China, summit with Soviet Premier Leonid Brezhnev, and progress in strategic arms limitations put him in a commanding position on handling foreign policy. There was other good news for Nixon: U.S. troops were coming back from Vietnam; casualties were down. Kissinger declared, "Peace is at hand."

The U.S. had made a deal to sell $750 million of grain to the Soviet Union, a boon to the Midwest. The space shuttle was being built—more jobs in aerospace. The Alaska pipeline, finally acted on by Congress, promised cheap new energy. The economy was looking up.

Ford had to fit his campaign travels into the long-running sessions of the House, which continued into October. One priority Republican proposal, Revenue Sharing, was still in question. On October 13, 1972, the Senate—in great part because of the efforts of Minority Leader Hugh Scott, Senator Howard H. Baker, Jr., who had first been elected on the issue, and Finance Chairman Russell Long—passed the final bill. One more day and it would have been too late; Congress adjourned and went home.

To make the most of the bipartisan victory for a Republican initiative, White House advance men staged the signing ceremony at Philadelphia's Independence Hall. On a sunny October day President Nixon signed the bill and stood by the Liberty Bell to hand out keepsake pens to an impressive gathering of Democrats and Republicans, congressmen, senators, governors, mayors, county executives, village selectmen, and others who stood to benefit.

For Ford and his fellow Republicans, who had initiated and built the coalition that passed Revenue Sharing in the House, it was a major party victory. For Nixon the Presidential candidate, Revenue Sharing was a bank night bonanza—money, big Federal money, handed out to every precinct in America, in a good cause, two weeks before Election Day.

One more time Jerry Ford had delivered for Dick Nixon.

Ford did not attend the Philadelphia ceremony; it conflicted with a campaign schedule that took him to aid Republican House candidates in Illinois, Ohio, Wyoming, Nevada, and New Mexico; to Dallas, Grand Rapids, New York City, Columbus, Kankakee, Provo, and Altoona. As he traveled, Ford was becoming more and more exasperated at how little help his candidates for Congress were getting from the White House or the President's reelection committee. "The Nixon campaign in 'seventy-two was oriented to Nixon's reelection, in terms of money and campaign effort," Ford said. "It was like trying to get blood out of a turnip to convince the campaign powers that controlled the money that five thousand dollars here or twenty thousand dollars there in a House or Senate race might have made the difference."

When the 1972 campaign ended, the Nixon reelection committee had millions of dollars left over; but Nixon never considered sharing the wealth of his campaign contributions with his party's candidates for the House. His tracking polls showed he typically ran ten points ahead of incumbent Republican House members, so he would not tie himself to them. "The moment I do that," he said, "I pull myself down to their level. . . . Part of our problem is that we have a lot of lousy candidates. The good ones will go up with me; the bad ones will go down."

As Election Day neared, the prospects of peace in Vietnam lengthened Nixon's lead over McGovern. Inside the White House, the President worried. The Grand Jury continued to question his campaign aides.

And *The Washington Post,* Nixon was convinced, was trying to wreck his campaign. One *Post* story in October said that the President's appointments secretary, Dwight Chapin, had hired a friend, Donald Segretti, to sabotage the Democratic campaign. With less than two weeks to go before the election, the *Post* reported that Haldeman, Nixon's Chief of Staff, had a secret fund in the White House to finance "spying and sabotage."

In his diary Nixon noted: "Haldeman spoke rather darkly of the fact that there was a clique in the White House that were out to get him. I trust he is not getting a persecution complex." That evening the President called Haldeman and tried to reassure him. The priority, Nixon said, is to take the heat and keep the campaign on balance in the last two weeks before the election.

On election eve, the President took a long walk on the beach at San Clemente and reflected on his political successes—"the Peking trip, the Moscow trip," and a winning campaign for reelection. "The only sour note," he wrote in his diary, "is Watergate."

A discordant note it was, in a campaign that was otherwise well orchestrated. In the election year of his first term President Nixon could point to a record of peace and prosperity. He did bring about an accord with China; he did manage to make the USSR seem less threatening. At home, inflation was down. Real income was improving by 4 percent yearly. In the politically crucial July-September quarter of 1972 the Gross National Product was rising at 6.3 percent. Social Security payments were up. Draft calls were down.

But Americans vote not for statistics but for a man. Or against the other man. In that respect Nixon was lucky in 1972. For the first time in his three races for President, he drew an inept opponent.

McGovern was a high-minded but uncertain man. Richard Dougherty, the journalist, novelist, and idealist who joined the McGovern cause as press secretary, compared McGovern to a character from nineteenth-century fiction: "Mostly a creature out of Tolstoy: a Levin, I'd think, full of dreams for the betterment of society; at one time awash with affection for the common man and at another irritated by his ignorance and cupidity; full of love of country and yet impatient with it for failing to meet his own lofty standards of Christian decency."

In the end the choice for President in 1972 was between a leader and a dreamer. The outcome was more a defeat of McGovern than landslide for Nixon, more doubt about the one than endorsement of the other.

Many Americans chose neither; almost half of those old enough to vote stayed home, the lowest percentage of turnout since 1948. Of Democrats who did go to the polls, 37 percent voted for Nixon. In his last *The Making of the President,* Theodore White wrote: "It was not what the voters thought of

Richard Nixon, but what they thought of George McGovern."

The Nixon strategy for a personal victory worked—through Election Day. But his calculated decision to distance himself from Republican candidates must bear some of the burden for his party's defeat in the Congressional elections.

The Nixon popular mandate made no visible impression on Democrats in Congress; by winning 242 seats in the House and holding 56 seats in the Senate, the Democrats there claimed their own mandate. So the split decision by the voters in 1972 guaranteed a collision of the two Washington powers.

For President Nixon, the coming confrontation was more dangerous because his overwhelming victory so angered so many Democrats that they were determined to use their power in Congress to retaliate. And Watergate was there waiting to be used against Nixon.

By the intervention of President Nixon, Watergate had been contained, masked, denied, and covered up for four months and twenty days until America had voted. Nixon knew that by containing Watergate he had invited his own destruction. For all of his political life Nixon had been both blessed and cursed with an unusual capacity to envision the political future. On the night of his grandest electoral victory Nixon knew that the reckoning with Watergate had only been postponed.

9

THE BURDEN OF GUILT

Two days after the 1972 election, Jerry and Betty Ford flew to Jamaica for a ten-day vacation at Tryall, a beautiful resort on the outskirts of Montego Bay. Since his election-night decision to retire from the House, Ford had begun to look ahead to a new life and a new career.

With the Fords at Tryall were three of their favorite couples—Bill and Peggy Whyte, Rod and Annabel Markley, and Congressman John and Mary Lou Jarman, of Oklahoma. Whyte was the Washington Vice President of U.S. Steel, and Markley held the same position with Ford Motor Co.

Out on the Tryall golf course, Ford confided his plans to leave politics and go into private life. Whyte and Markley were considering early retirement to form a partnership to lobby for major corporate clients; Ford asked whether, when he left Congress in 1977, he might join their firm.

To Whyte, the reason for Ford's interest in business was plain. "It was money as much as anything," Whyte said. "Jerry never had any money." For all of their years in Congress, the Fords had lived from paycheck to paycheck. Their two oldest boys were in college, and Steve and Susan would be ready in a few years.

Ford had not yet decided whether to go into business with Whyte and Markley, or practice law again, or look for another opportunity. "But," he said, "I did know that after one more campaign and one more term in the House, Betty and I would have a new life."

While Ford was golfing in Jamaica and looking forward to a prosperous new life, the world of Richard Nixon was beginning to break apart.

On the morning after his remarkable political victory, he fired everyone on the White House staff and in the Cabinet. It was not an impulse; for much of his first term Nixon had brooded about the ineffectiveness of his own appointees. In the last weeks of the campaign he told Haldeman: "We're going to have a house cleaning. It's time for a new team. . . . We didn't do it when we came in before, but now we have a mandate. And one of the mandates is to do the cleaning up that we didn't do in 'sixty-eight.'"

The President raged against his own Cabinet: "Mitchell was captured by the bureaucracy. . . . Rogers was totally captured [at State]. . . . Mel Laird, he didn't change anybody. . . . The people who ran the Pentagon before are still running the goddam Pentagon. . . . HEW, the whole damn bunch. . . . Let's remember the VA—clean those bastards out. . . . Take that Park Service, they've been screwing us for four years. Rog Morton won't get rid of that son-of-a-bitch. But he's got to go."

Anger and revenge often drove Nixon. At Camp David on the Saturday after the election he told Haldeman he wanted the IRS to investigate "all major Democratic contributors and all backers" of newly elected Democratic senators. He considered appointing William Casey as IRS Commissioner to make certain the Democrats were punished.

Suddenly, six days after the election, the ghost of Watergate reappeared in the White House. Howard Hunt telephoned Colson at his White House office to deliver a message from himself and the others in jail since the Watergate break-in. Now that the election is over, Hunt asked, where is our payment for keeping quiet?

Colson taped the conversation—"for my own protection," he explained later. "The reason I called you," Hunt said to Colson, was "because commitments that were made to all of us at the onset have not been kept. . . . We've set a deadline now for close of business on the twenty-fifth of November for the . . . liquidation of . . . promises from July and August. . . . We can understand some hesitancy prior to the election, but there doesn't seem to be any [need] of that now."

Colson handed the tape over to Dean. When Dean heard Hunt's message, "the bottom of my stomach fell out," he said. Dean took a White House car to Camp David to play the tape for Haldeman and Ehrlichman. They suggested he get the money for Hunt and the others from Mitchell. Dean flew to New York City and presented Hunt's demand to Mitchell. He stared at Dean, shook his head, and walked out.

Two days later, in a discussion with Haldeman at Camp David, Nixon said abruptly: "Colson's got to go." Haldeman, taken by surprise, started to say something in Colson's defense, but Nixon interrupted. "I've already decided this," he said curtly. "I don't want to keep anyone . . . who may be hit with some of the Watergate fallout in the future. I just don't know what might come up—and it's much better for Chuck to leave now, when all the changes are being made, and appear to be doing it on his own initiative, than for him to be forced to leave under a cloud at some future time."

Getting Colson to resign would have to be done carefully, Nixon said; they could not risk making an enemy of him. To start the process, Nixon instructed Haldeman about how to approach Colson: "Say, 'I'm doing this without the President's knowledge, but there is an inevitable problem with the Hunt trial, and the President can't let you go under fire. We can't be sure what will come out. And on the positive side you're headed outside now, and will have a continuing relation with the President, in the Clark Clifford role. The problem is your position inside will erode with the election over. The President needs you on the outside where you're free to set up a campaign firm as well as a law firm. You could do the poll brokering. *Now* is the time to pick up the clients—law and PR, and we just don't have the job inside. The President is determined to get politics out of the White House. You've got to go in to the President and say you've thought it through, you've reached the conclusion, and this is what you should do. Be a big man.'"

Dutifully, Haldeman did talk to Colson, but Colson refused to accept a Presidential dismissal through Haldeman. Colson went in to see Nixon and pleaded that he be allowed to stay. To persuade him to quit, Nixon promised him he would have a visible and continuing friendship with the White House that would help his law business. Colson agreed to resign in December.

Nixon's first postelection move against Vice President Agnew came on November 14, 1972, one week after the election. The President gave the orders to Haldeman in Aspen Cottage, at Camp David. "We have a tough thing to do here," Nixon warned. "Tell him, 'We must cut, including your staff.' Collapse his councils and other assignments. Shift his Office of Intergovernmental Relations to Community Development. We need to keep leverage over him, so don't break it off now. But we do *not* want to further his interests. We don't want him to have the appearance of heir apparent, but we also don't want to appear to push him down. Pitch the Bicentennial Commission as a great opportunity for him. Agnew is not the ideal choice for that, but he may be the best of a bad lot."

Nixon's move against Agnew was part of his strategy to name his successor. Connally, he told Haldeman, is "the only possibility for 'seventy-six.

He can have a Cabinet job if he wants it." With his customary deference to the palace favorite, Nixon told Haldeman to set up a meeting with Connally "at his convenience" so they could discuss their joint political plans.

Proceeding with his plan, Nixon invited Agnew to Key Biscayne to talk about his role in the second term. Flying down to Florida to meet with the President, Agnew thought: "As a Vice President who worked hard and contributed to our reelection by a huge majority, I will receive some praise this time. I will get a very important assignment."

The President greeted Agnew but sat in silence as Ehrlichman delivered the message: "We think you ought to spend most of your time working on the Bicentennial."

"The Bicentennial?" Agnew was shocked. The very idea, Agnew said, "made me shudder." He could hardly believe his relegation to a job he felt so unimportant.

"Gentlemen," Agnew said, "I look upon the Bicentennial as a loser, because everybody has his own ideas about it and nobody can be the head of it without making a million enemies. A potential Presidential candidate doesn't want to make any enemies."

The mention of his ambitions for 1976 was the wrong thing for Agnew to say to Nixon.

Early in December, Mrs. Howard Hunt was killed in a plane crash in Chicago. Investigators discovered she had been carrying ten thousand dollars in cash, in hundred-dollar bills, to aid the family of one of the Watergate burglars in jail.

Colson went in to see Nixon, and said he was worried that the death of Hunt's wife might cause Hunt to break his silence and talk to prosecutors. The President told Colson Mrs. Hunt's death would make it easier for him to grant clemency after his trial. "Hunt's is a simple case," the President said. "I mean, after all, the man's wife was killed; he's got one child that has—"

"Brain damage from an automobile accident," Colson said.

"That's right!" Nixon said. "We'll build that son-of-a-bitch up like nobody's business. We'll have [William] Buckley write a column and say, you know, that he should have clemency, if you've given eighteen years of service. That's what we'll do." Colson relayed the clemency message to Hunt.

On opening day of the new Congress, the House Republican Conference elected Ford to be the Minority Leader of the House for the fifth time. Hartmann and two other Ford staffers knew that it would be Ford's last run for Leader. Ford had told them of his own plans, and suggested they think about getting other jobs.

A couple of days later Ford rode to the White House with the freshmen Congressmen to meet the President. It was the first time Ford had seen Nixon since his reelection. The President was as friendly as ever, but there was no opportunity for serious talk.

To Ford, the President looked edgy, drawn. Well, Ford thought, Nixon has a lot on his mind—negotiations to end the Vietnam War, the Watergate trial, and plans for his second term.

Only a few days after the opening of the Ninety-third Congress, Thomas P. O'Neill, who had been elected House Majority Leader after Hale Boggs died in an airplane accident, went in to see Speaker Carl Albert.

"We better start getting ready," O'Neill said. "This guy is going to be impeached before we're through."

Albert told O'Neill there was no evidence to support the impeachment of President Nixon.

"Maybe not," O'Neill said. "I'm only telling you what I can hear and see, and what I know. . . . It's got me worried."

O'Neill had been suspicious about the Nixon campaign operations for months. When some of O'Neill's regular Massachusetts contributors to Democratic campaigns had declined to send their checks, he had asked them why. The answer, O'Neill said, was that businessmen had been warned they might lose government contracts or have trouble with the IRS if they gave to Democrats. "What really scared me was that all of this funny business and intimidation was being carried out before an election that the Republicans couldn't lose even if they tried," O'Neill said.

O'Neill also mentioned to Peter Rodino, the new chairman of the House Judiciary Committee, the possibility that Watergate might lead to impeaching Nixon. Shaking his head, Rodino said: "Tip, you're not a lawyer. You're only going on intuition."

At the White House, Nixon observed "the first signs of finger-pointing." One day Haldeman told Nixon that Colson may have known about Watergate in advance. Three days later Colson came in and told Nixon that Haldeman and Ehrlichman may have been involved in planning the Watergate break-in. In addition, Colson said ominously, the plan to collect negative information on the Democrats had been discussed in Attorney General

Mitchell's office at the Justice Department before he left to become campaign manager.

On January 8, 1973, six months and two weeks after the Watergate break-in, the trial of the seven Watergate defendants began. John J. Sirica, Chief Judge of the U.S. District Court in Washington, had assigned himself to the trial. He knew it would be a contentious case, and believed the presence of a Republican judge would eliminate accusations of political partisanship.

Sirica was first appointed to the Federal bench by President Eisenhower, on the recommendation of William Rogers, then deputy Attorney General. Although others in the Justice Department thought Sirica marginally qualified as a legal scholar, Rogers argued that Sirica was a strong and conscientious trial lawyer.

In his two decades on the bench Judge Sirica had earned the nickname "Maximum John" for the tough sentences he handed down. The son of an Italian immigrant, a barber, Sirica had worked his way through Georgetown University Law School as a boxing coach. For a time he boxed professionally as a welterweight; Jack Dempsey was best man at his wedding.

As a good Republican Sirica had supported Willkie, Dewey, and Eisenhower; but in his judicial robe, he belonged to no party. "Hell, yes, I'm a Republican," he once told a reporter. "But when I get on the bench, politics is out. Then it's my duty to search for the truth."

Getting at the truth was Sirica's mission in any trial. If he thought the prosecutor was insufficiently aggressive in bringing out all the facts, Sirica would take over the questioning himself.

From the very beginning of the Watergate trial, Judge Sirica found the chief prosecutor, Earl Silbert, too soft in questioning witnesses. From the bench, Sirica personally asked the witnesses the tough questions: Who planned the bugging? What were they after? Where did they get the money they carried?

Three days into the trial Hunt pleaded guilty and was freed on bail. Colson was worried; he thought Hunt may have made a secret deal with the prosecutor.

On January 15, 1973, five days before President Nixon was to be inaugurated for a second term, the four Cubans arrested at the Watergate pleaded guilty. "I was relieved," Nixon said. "I thought this would spare us the difficulties of a noisy public trial and all the distraction that would produce at such a critical time." Later he saw the danger. In his diary Nixon noted: "Obviously the judge is going to throw the book at them and this will present quite a problem when it comes to a pardon."

While the trial of Liddy and McCord continued, the tight ring of Nixon's inner defense was weakening: Colson came in to tell the President that he was worried that Hunt, facing a long prison sentence, might confess, and in his confession implicate Haldeman and Ehrlichman. Haldeman advised Nixon that *The New York Times* was working on a story that would show the campaign intelligence chain ran from Liddy to Colson to Mitchell.

Inside the White House there was no surprise when the Watergate jury handed down its verdict—Liddy and McCord guilty of burglary, wiretapping, and conspiracy. But what Judge Sirica said after the verdict made the guilty all the more dangerous to the White House. Sirica told the Court, the press, and most importantly the men just convicted that many questions about Watergate were still unanswered.

It would be up to a Senate investigating committee to uncover the rest of the Watergate story, Sirica told the Court. By postponing sentencing, Judge Sirica deliberately put pressure on the Watergate burglars to tell the whole truth about Watergate or face long prison terms.

Even before the new Congress convened, Democrats in the Senate were demanding a special committee to investigate Watergate. Republicans joined in—some to clear the party's once good name, others out of conviction that, whatever Nixon's campaign workers had done, the President himself had no part in it. On February 7, 1973, the Senate voted 77–0 to create the Senate Select Committee on Presidential Campaign Activities. Its purpose was to find out if Nixon's campaign managers had broken Federal laws, violated campaign ethics, or both.

As created, the committee could also have investigated the Democratic Presidential campaign of George McGovern; but McGovern performed so poorly and his campaign failed so miserably that the only conceivable McGovern crime was egregious incompetence.

To chair the Select Committee, which quickly and permanently became the "Senate Watergate Committee," the leaders of the Senate chose a wise, folksy, gabby, and aging Democratic Senator, Sam Ervin of North Carolina, and a shrewd, quick-witted, youthful Republican Senator, Howard H. Baker, Jr., of Tennessee.

Senator Baker, a considerate and careful man, and a friend of President Nixon, thought it prudent to see Nixon and reassure him about the inquiry and hearings. "I am your friend," Baker said to the President in a personal visit, "and I don't think this committee can do anything to you. I know a lot of things go on around a President that he doesn't know about, and it looks like that was the situation in this case."

Nixon listened but said nothing reassuring. "I went away feeling queasy about the whole situation," Baker said.

Senator Baker had good reason to feel queasy; Nixon was so concerned about the Senate investigation that he told his staff to organize a counteroffensive. On March 13, 1973, Nixon summoned Dean to his office for a status report.

"Apparently you haven't been able to do anything on my project of getting on the offensive," Nixon said.

"But I have, sir, to the contrary," Dean said.

"Have you kicked a few butts around?" Nixon asked.

Dean said that a White House aide was drafting a message from Senator Goldwater to Senator Ervin on the theme: Why not investigate the dirty tricks against President Nixon?

"Good!" Nixon said, and asked if anyone was investigating questionable contributions to the McGovern Campaign. "Do you need any IRS stuff?"

"We have a couple of sources over there that I can go to," Dean said. He explained that he went around the Commissioner of the IRS. "We can get right in and get what we need."

The two talked on for an hour, with Nixon's curiosity reaching deeply into the details of Watergate. What were campaign workers telling prosecutors? he asked. Who was leaking what to the press? He asked Dean to explain how campaign money ended up in the Miami bank account of Bernard Barker, one of the burglars who pleaded guilty.

There were checks from Mexico, Dean said. American political candidates are legally barred from accepting foreign contributions, Dean explained, so Liddy gave the Mexican checks to Barker to cash.

Probing and listening, Nixon wanted to know which campaign witnesses were scared, and how well each was preparing himself to testify. Dean mentioned that he, Haldeman, Ehrlichman, and Colson would also be called to testify.

"None will be witnesses," Nixon said.

"They won't be witnesses?" Dean was surprised.

"Hell no," Nixon said. "They will make statements. That will be the line which I think we have to get across to Ziegler in all his briefings where he is constantly saying we will provide information. . . . We will not furnish it in a formal session. That would be a breakdown of [executive] privilege. Period. Do you agree with that?"

"I agree. I agree." Dean said the White House witnesses could respond with sworn answers to written questions from the Senate Committee and thereby avoid "cross-examination."

"That's right!" Nixon said.

Shifting back to the trial of the burglars, Nixon asked: "Well, what about the sentencing? When the hell is he going to sentence?"

"No one knows what in the world Sirica is doing," Dean said.

"When will the Ervin thing be hitting the fan?" Nixon asked.

"About the first of May."

"Well, it must be a big show," Nixon said, because the Senate Committee will be trying to find out: "Is there a higher-up? Let's face it, I think they are really after Haldeman."

"Haldeman and Mitchell," Dean said.

"Colson is not a big enough name for them," Nixon said. "They are after Haldeman and after Mitchell. . . . Where do you see Colson coming into it? . . . He sure as hell knows Hunt. That we know. Was very close to him."

"Chuck has told me that he had no knowledge, specific knowledge, of the Watergate before it occurred," Dean said.

The President complained that all the campaign intelligence operations had produced "poor pickings." Haldeman and Colson had briefed him regularly during the campaign, he said, "but they never had a thing to report. What was the matter? Did they never get anything out of the damn thing?"

"I don't think they ever got anything, sir," Dean said.

"A dry hole?"

"That's right," Dean replied.

Nixon cursed. "Who the hell was gathering intelligence?"

"That was Liddy and his outfit," Dean said.

"Apart from Watergate?" Nixon asked.

"That's right," Dean said. "Well, you see Watergate was part of intelligence gathering, and this was their first thing . . ."

"That was such a stupid thing!" Nixon said. He thought for a moment and asked: "Is it too late to go the hang-out road?"

"Yes," Dean said, pointing out that any one witness could create problems for others. "So there are dangers, Mr. President. . . . There is a reason for not everyone going up and testifying."

"I see," Nixon said. "Oh, no, no, no! I didn't mean to have everyone go up and testify. . . . I mean put the story out, the PR people. Here is the story, the true story about Watergate."

"They would never believe it," Dean said, explaining that the press and

Congress would never buy the story that rogue campaign workers invented and executed Watergate without White House involvement.

Over the next few days, John Dean began to brood about his own guilt in the continuing cover-up of Watergate. He said that he often sat alone behind the closed door of his White House office thinking of "all the weak spots in the cover-up," convincing himself he would eventually be caught and sent to prison, wondering if he could escape, disappear, hide in Central America. He saw himself as "a meek, favor-currying staff man," no match for the big guys—Haldeman, Ehrlichman, Mitchell—playing the deadly game of trying to get each other to "fall on the sword" to save the President.

Fearful that he might end up taking the blame for Watergate, Dean asked the President for an appointment so that he could, as he told his wife, "tell him the cover-up couldn't go on."

At 10:12 A.M., on March 21, 1973, Dean, nervous but determined, met alone with the President in the Oval Office.

"Well, sit down, sit down," Nixon said hospitably. "What is the Dean summary of the day about?"

Dean, very serious, had selected the words for a dramatic opening. "We have a cancer within, close to the Presidency, that is growing," Dean said, "growing daily . . . growing geometrically." The problem "compounds itself," Dean said, because "one, we are being blackmailed, and two, people are going to start perjuring themselves very quickly . . . to protect other people in the line. And there is no assurance—"

"That that won't bust?" Nixon interrupted.

"That that won't bust," Dean said. "So let me give you the sort of basic facts, talking first about the Watergate. . . . First of all on the Watergate: how did it all start, where did it start? Okay. It started with an instruction to me from Bob Haldeman to see if we couldn't set up a perfectly legitimate campaign intelligence operation over at the Reelection Committee. Not being in this business, I turned to somebody who had been in this business, Jack Caulfield."

Caulfield, Dean explained, was a former New York City policeman and Nixon security officer. Dean told Caulfield to come up with a plan—"a normal infiltration, buying information from secretaries, and all that sort of thing." Dean took Caulfield's plan to Mitchell and Ehrlichman; they rejected it as too cautious and suggested Dean recruit someone more aggressive.

"That is when I came up with Gordon Liddy," Dean said. "They needed a lawyer. Gordon had an intelligence background from his FBI service. . . . He had done some extremely sensitive things. . . . while he had been at the White House, and he had apparently done them well—going out into Ellsberg's doctor's office."

In June, 1971, Daniel Ellsberg, a senior foreign policy adviser in the Defense Department, leaked to *The New York Times* some 7,000 pages of classified documents on the conduct of the War in Vietnam during the Kennedy and Johnson administrations. The publication of the secret documents, which became known as the Pentagon Papers, outraged Nixon, Kissinger, and others in the White House. They considered Ellsberg's actions certainly reprehensible and probably illegal, and they wanted him punished. Two Ehrlichman aides, Egil Krogh and David Young, were assigned to find about Ellsberg's associates and motives. Some three months after the *Times* published the Pentagon Papers, Krogh and Young authorized Liddy and Hunt to break into the Beverly Hills office of Ellsberg's psychiatrist. It was this operation that brought Liddy to the attention of Nixon's senior staff.

"I took Liddy over to meet Mitchell," Dean said, continuing his report to Nixon, and Mitchell hired him to plan campaign intelligence. In January of 1972 Dean met with Mitchell and Magruder in the Attorney General's office to hear Liddy present his plan.

"Liddy," Dean said, "laid out a million-dollar plan that was the most incredible thing I have ever laid my eyes on, all in codes, and involved black-bag operations, kidnapping, providing prostitutes to weaken the opposition, bugging, mugging teams. It was just an incredible Liddy thing."

"Tell me this," Nixon said. "Did Mitchell go along?"

"No, no, not at all," Dean said. "Mitchell just sat there puffing [his pipe] and laughing. . . . And so Liddy was told to go back to the drawing board and come up with something realistic. So there was a second meeting. . . . They were discussing again bugging, kidnapping, and the like." At that point, Dean said he told the group that such actions were illegal and should not even be discussed in the office of the Attorney General.

Later, Dean said, he advised Haldeman of Liddy's proposals and warned that any such intelligence operation would be "a growing disaster." Haldeman agreed. "I thought at that point that the thing was turned off," Dean said.

Then Liddy came up with a third plan, Dean said, but couldn't get it approved by Mitchell or Magruder. "So Liddy and Hunt apparently came to see Chuck Colson, and Chuck Colson picked up the telephone and called Magruder and said, 'You all either fish or cut bait. This is absurd to have these guys over there and not using them. If you are not going to use them, I may use them.'"

"When was this?" Nixon asked.

"This was apparently in February of 'seventy-two," Dean said.

"Did Colson know what they were talking about?" Nixon asked.

"I can only assume, because of his close relationship with Hunt, that he had a damn good idea," Dean replied. "He would probably deny it today, and probably get away with denying it . . . unless Hunt blows on him."

"But then Hunt isn't enough," Nixon said. "It takes two [to convict], doesn't it?"

"Probably. Probably. But Liddy was there also and if Liddy were to blow—"

Nixon interrupted: "Then you have a problem . . . as to the criminal liability in the White House." Had Colson talked to Haldeman about the third Liddy proposal?

"No, I don't think so," Dean said. "But here is the next thing that comes in the chain." Gordon Strachan, Dean said, was apparently getting information from the first bug planted at Democratic headquarters and giving it to Haldeman, his boss. "At one point, Bob even gave instructions" to shift targets, from Senator Muskie to Senator McGovern.

"They had never bugged Muskie, though, did they?" Nixon said.

"No, they hadn't," Dean said, "but they had infiltrated it by a secretary . . . and a chauffeur. There is nothing illegal about that."

Dean turned from explaining what had actually happened to what witnesses were testifying. "I don't know if Mitchell has perjured himself in the Grand Jury or not. . . . I know that Magruder has perjured himself in the Grand Jury. I know that [Herbert] Porter [a Magruder deputy] has perjured himself in the Grand Jury."

Dean said both "set up their scenario" before testifying before the Grand Jury, and that he had cleared it. Their story, in Dean's words: "Liddy had come over as counsel and we knew he had these capacities to do legitimate intelligence. We had no idea what he was doing. He was given an authorization of two hundred and fifty thousand dollars to collect information. . . . We had no knowledge that he was going to bug the DNC."

"The point is, that is not true," Nixon said.

"That's right."

"Magruder did know it was going to take place?" Nixon asked.

"Magruder gave the instructions to be back in the DNC," Dean said.

"He did?" Nixon said.

"Yes."

"You know that?" Nixon asked.

"Yes," Dean said.

"I see. Okay," the President said.

The White House was drawn into Watergate after the break-in, Dean said. Hunt, McCord and the other burglars "started making demands" for money—money for their lawyers and their families. To pay their demands, Dean said, Mitchell, Haldeman, Ehrlichman, and he himself had all become involved.

"And that," Dean said, "is an obstruction of justice."

"You were taking care of witnesses," Nixon said. "How did Bob get in it?"

Dean replied that he asked Haldeman to provide cash from a $350,000 campaign fund in his White House safe to meet the demands from the Watergate burglars. "We decided there was no price too high to pay [not] to let this thing blow up in front of the election."

"I think we should be able to handle that issue pretty well," Nixon said. "Maybe some lawsuits."

"I think we can too," Dean said. "Here is what is happening right now. . . . One, this is going to be a continual blackmail operation by Hunt and Liddy and the Cubans. . . . McCord wanted to talk about commutation. . . . And as you know, Colson has talked directly to Hunt about commutation. . . . They are the very sort of things that the Senate is going to be looking most for. I don't think they can find them, frankly."

"Pretty hard," Nixon said.

"The blackmail is continuing," Dean said. "Hunt now is demanding another seventy-two thousand dollars for his own personal expenses; another fifty thousand dollars to pay attorney's fees. . . . He wanted it as of the close of business yesterday. . . . Hunt has now made a direct threat against Ehrlichman. . . . He says, 'I will bring John Ehrlichman down to his knees and put him in jail. I have done enough seamy things for he and Krogh, they'll never survive it.' "

"Was he talking about Ellsberg?" Nixon asked.

"Ellsberg, and apparently some other things," Dean said. "The Cubans that were used in the Watergate were also the same Cubans that Hunt and Liddy used for this California Ellsberg thing, for the break-in out there."

Paying blackmail, Dean told the President, "will compound the obstruction of justice situation. It will cost money. It is dangerous. . . . There is a real problem in raising money."

"How much money do you need?" Nixon asked.

"I would say these people are going to cost a million dollars over the next two years," Dean said.

"We could get that," the President said. "You could get a million dollars. You could get it in cash. I know where it could be gotten. It is not easy, but it could be done. But the question is, who the hell would handle it?"

"Well," Dean said, "I think that is something that Mitchell ought to be charged with."

"I would think so too," Nixon said. Reviewing the risks, he added: "Your major guy to keep under control is Hunt? . . . Does he know a lot?"

"He could sink Chuck Colson," Dean said. "Apparently he is quite distressed with Colson. He thinks Colson has abandoned him."

Nixon paused at the mention of Colson, then said: "Just looking at the immediate problem, don't you think you have to handle Hunt's financial situation damn soon?"

"I talked with Mitchell about that last night and—"

Nixon interrupted: "It seems to me we have to keep the cap on the bottle that much, or we don't have any options."

"That's right," Dean said.

"Either that," Nixon said, "or it all blows right now."

A growing concern, Dean said, is that "everybody is now starting to watch after their behind," and the suspects on the White House staff were all retaining lawyers to defend themselves.

"They are scared," Nixon said.

"We were able to hold it for a long time," Dean said, but now he felt that he himself could go to jail.

"Oh, hell no!" the President said. "What would you go to jail for?"

"The obstruction of justice," Dean said.

"Well, I don't know," Nixon said. "I feel it could be cut off at the pass, maybe, the obstruction of justice."

Dean suggested that Henry Petersen, head of the Criminal Division at Justice, might advise them on how to minimize the damage to all the White House people involved.

"Petersen doesn't know, does he?" Nixon asked.

"No," Dean said. "I know he doesn't now."

"Talking about your obstruction of justice, I don't see it," Nixon said.

"Well, I have been a conduit for information on taking care of people out there who are guilty of crimes," Dean said.

"Oh, you mean like the blackmailers?" Nixon said.

"The blackmailers. Right."

"Well," the President said, "let me put it frankly: I wonder if that doesn't have to be continued. Let me put it this way: Let us suppose that you get the million bucks, and you get the proper way to handle it. You could hold that side?"

Dean agreed.

"It would seem to me that would be worthwhile," Nixon said.

He buzzed the intercom for Haldeman, brought him in, and told him he wanted Haldeman and Dean to meet with Ehrlichman and Mitchell to coordinate their testimony about Watergate. Don't include Colson, Nixon added, because he "talks too much."

Nixon told Haldeman that Hunt was threatening to expose Ehrlichman on the Ellsberg break-in.

"What's he planning on?" Haldeman asked. "Money?"

"It's about a hundred twenty thousand dollars. That's what, Bob," Nixon said. "That would be easy. It is not easy to deliver, but it is easy to get." Paying blackmail is a risk, Nixon said. "First, it is going to require approximately a million dollars to take care of the jackasses who are in jail. That can be arranged. . . . But you realize that after we are gone, and assuming we can expend this money, then they are going to crack and it would be an unseemly story. . . . And the second thing is, we are not going to be able to deliver on any of a clemency thing. You know Colson has gone around on this clemency thing with Hunt and the rest?"

Dean said Colson had told Hunt he would be out of jail by Christmas.

"That is your fatal flaw in Chuck," Haldeman said. "He is an operator in expediency, and he will pay at the time and where he is to accomplish whatever he is there to do. . . . I would believe he has made that commitment if Hunt says he has."

"The only thing we could do with [Hunt] would be to parole him," Nixon said.

But Judge Sirica could sentence Hunt "in a way that makes parole even impossible," Dean said.

"Now, let me tell you," the President said, "we could get the money. There is no problem in that. We can't provide the clemency."

Haldeman was skeptical about the money, and pointed out that nobody in the White House could be asking for money to keep the burglars quiet. "The problem with the blackmailing," Haldeman said, was not that you "need twenty thousand dollars or a hundred thousand dollars today. But what do you need tomorrow, or next year, or five years from now?" Haldeman said that much of the $350,000 of campaign money in his White House safe was used to keep the Watergate burglars quiet. "That's what we had to have to get us through November seventh," he said.

In desperation Nixon tried to think of other options, but soon gave up. "To hell with it!" he said. "For your immediate things you have no choice but to come up with the hundred twenty thousand dollars or whatever it is. Right?"

"That's right," Dean said.

"Would you agree that that's the prime thing that you damn well better get done?" Nixon said.

"Obviously," Dean said, and Hunt "ought to be given some signal" that the money will be paid.

"For Christ's sake," the President said. "Get it."

Two days later, Judge Sirica destroyed all the White House plans. In his courtroom Sirica passed sentence on the Watergate burglars, and, in an adroit judicial maneuver, broke the bonds of silence among the conspirators.

By design Sirica imposed the stiffest sentence—six years to twenty years—on Liddy, who had boasted that he would never testify about Watergate.

For Hunt and the four Cubans, who had pleaded guilty and remained silent up to that point, Judge Sirica provided an incentive to become cooperative witnesses. He issued a provisional sentence that would keep them in jail, worrying, for five months before he decided on a final sentence that might be as much as forty years.

To McCord, who had taken the first step to becoming a key witness for the prosecution, Judge Sirica awarded a measure of freedom and at the same time dropped a bombshell on Nixon: He made public a letter that McCord had written him from prison two days before.

In the letter McCord lamented his own dilemma: If he continued to refuse to talk, he must "expect a much more severe sentence." If he told the truth, "members of my family have expressed fear for my life." But he had decided, he said, to write to Judge Sirica "in the interests of justice."

"There was political pressure applied to the defendants to plead guilty and remain silent," McCord revealed in his letter.

"Perjury occurred during the trial in matters highly material to the very structure, orientation and impact of the government's case, and to the motivation and intent of the defendants.

"Others involved in the Watergate operation were not identified during the trial, when they could have been by those testifying.

"The Watergate operation was not a CIA operation. . . . I know for a fact that it was not."

Sirica freed McCord on bail and postponed passing sentence for three months—long enough to see whether McCord would tell the rest of the Watergate story when he testified before the Senate Watergate Committee.

With this judicial maneuver, Sirica turned McCord, and McCord cracked the Watergate case.

With the cover-up blown by McCord, the ring of conspirators in the White House—Haldeman, Ehrlichman, Colson, Mitchell and Dean—came apart.

Dean was first to turn on the others. Before he went before the Grand Jury, Dean had his lawyer meet with Federal prosecutors to discuss whether Dean might exchange testimony for leniency. Dean informed Haldeman that he was exploring a plea bargain.

Haldeman immediately informed Nixon, and suggested Dean might even testify against the President to get immunity for himself. Nixon was alarmed, and suspected that Dean had lured him into talking about blackmail and pardons to enrich the testimony he could deliver to prosecutors.

Dean's attempt to make a deal with prosecutors frightened other witnesses into conspiring against each other. Magruder threatened to go back before the Grand Jury and bring down Mitchell and Dean.

Ehrlichman learned that he and Haldeman were targets of the prosecutors; he proposed to Nixon that Mitchell voluntarily and publicly accept the moral and legal responsibility for Watergate. Haldeman supported that idea, and said a Mitchell confession might satisfy the press and end the investigation. Nixon, after agonizing about it, agreed, but said Ehrlichman should suggest the idea to Mitchell. Ehrlichman talked to Mitchell; but Mitchell refused to take the fall for the break-in or the cover-up.

Nixon, ready to sacrifice anyone to save himself, suggested to Ehrlichman that Haldeman and Dean go on leaves of absence. Ehrlichman said no; Dean was more dangerous outside the White House than in.

After the Sunday church service in the White House on April 15, Attorney General Kleindienst went in to see the President to notify him, officially, that Haldeman and Ehrlichman were targets of the prosecution, on the basis of evidence given to the prosecutors by Dean.

Nixon was appalled. He could not bring himself to believe that the two men closest to him might be indicted. Recognizing that, Kleindienst brought in Henry Petersen to convince the President. Petersen advised Nixon that the indictment of Haldeman and Ehrlichman was not yet certain, but that he felt both should resign.

No, Nixon said, he would not fire them without proof of their guilt.

For Nixon, it was a long Sunday. Early that evening he met with Haldeman and Ehrlichman and told them of the Attorney General's warning that they could be indicted. Both Kleindienst and Petersen recommended that they resign, Nixon said. Neither Haldeman nor Ehrlichman agreed.

Then Dean telephoned and asked to see the President. The two had not talked since Dean had traded his knowledge of White House crimes to save himself. In Nixon's office that evening, Dean said that both Haldeman and Ehrlichman were guilty of obstruction of justice. Nixon thought Dean seemed "almost cocky." He assumed that Dean, in his deal with prosecutors to escape prison, had given enough evidence against Haldeman and Ehrlichman to convict them—and possibly to impeach the President.

With the conspiracy of silence collapsing around him, Nixon decided he must make a public statement in his own defense. He told the press: "On March 21, as a result of serious charges which came to my attention, I began intensive new inquiries into this whole matter." He promised to suspend anyone on his staff who was indicted and fire anyone convicted. In a show of resolve, he added: "I condemn any attempts to cover up in this case, no matter who is involved."

Out of public view, indecision and fear immobilized Nixon. He realized that Haldeman and Ehrlichman would have to leave the White House, but he could not muster the nerve to tell them. "I was faced with having to fire my friends for things that I myself was part of, things that I could not accept as morally or legally wrong, no matter how much that opened me to charges of cynicism and amorality," Nixon wrote. "I was selfish enough about my own survival to want them to leave; but I was not so ruthless as to be able to confront easily the idea of hurting people I cared about so deeply."

What to do? Nixon said he was "governed by contradictory impulses: I tried to persuade them to go—while I insisted that I could not offer up my friends as sacrifices. I said that we had to do the right thing no matter how painful it was—while I cast about for any possible way to avert the damage, even if it took us to the edge of the law."

On Capitol Hill, Jerry Ford was beset by reporters asking for his comments on Watergate. Every day he heard almost the same questions: "Do you think White House aides should be required to testify before the Senate Watergate Committee?" "Was Nixon involved in Watergate?" "Is Nixon part of the cover-up?"

Ford dodged the questions as best he could. He did not believe that President Nixon had anything to do with Watergate, but he was suspicious about some of the people at the White House and at the Nixon campaign. Privately he believed that the quickest and best way to end Watergate would be to have the Nixon staff go before the grand jury or the Senate Watergate Committee and fully disclose the facts. But Ford did not say so publicly because he did not want to put himself at odds with the President's position on executive privilege. Finally Ford decided to go public on his differences with the White House—but not on Capitol Hill.

In a speech to a Republican gathering in the small town of St. Johns, Michigan, Ford said: "The way to clear up Watergate is for John Mitchell, Bob Haldeman, John Dean, and any others who have publicly said they are not involved in, and had no information on Watergate, [to] go before the Senate Committee, take an oath, and deny it publicly. They say they're innocent. They say they were not involved. Say it under oath."

Ford might as well have made the speech on the White House steps. His statement hit the UPI wire that night, and the White House staff read it the next morning. A few days later Nixon invited Ford to the Oval Office for a private visit.

Talking one on one, Nixon assured Ford that he had nothing to do with the Watergate break-in, and blamed all the charges on Democratic partisan politics. The President also told Ford that he had been so preoccupied with foreign policy, and especially the initiatives to China and negotiations with Russia, that "these inconsequential political things escaped my attention."

Ford believed his old friend. "You have to believe the President, and I did believe him," Ford said. "He had never lied to me."

In public, Nixon tried to show he was fully engaged in running the government. He met with the Prime Minister of Italy and staged a Cabinet session to discuss energy and the economy. But except for ceremonies, Nixon was spending almost all of his time in dealing with Watergate.

Nixon asked Pat Buchanan, a gifted speechwriter whose political judgment he trusted, to appraise his situation. Buchanan, in a memo, told Nixon that he had two choices: To clean up the White House himself, as Eisenhower had done; or to cover up for his people, as Harding had done.

If Haldeman and Ehrlichman should be called before the grand jury, Buchanan added, they should resign.

On April 20, 1973, John Mitchell said, in a *New York Times* interview, that he had rejected Liddy's plan to bug Democratic Headquarters. Nixon read the story and concluded that Mitchell was implying that Colson subsequently authorized Liddy's plan. After seeing the Mitchell story, Nixon called for *Air Force One* and flew to Florida. "I needed time to think," he wrote.

Key Biscayne gave Nixon no escape; Dean's testimony to the prosecutors continued to leak. Dean had, according to *The Washington Post*, delivered White House documents to support his charges about the bugging and the cover-up. *The New York Times* reported that Dean had arranged more than $175,000 in payoffs to defendants. On his way to church on Easter Sunday, Nixon saw someone holding a placard: "Is the President honest?"

On Monday, Nixon met with Chappie Rose, a former law partner in New York City. Nixon had asked Rose to fly down to Florida to help find a way out of the situation. Rose listened to the roster of Nixon aides facing indictments and observed, quoting Gladstone: "The first essential for a Prime Minister is to be a good butcher."

But Nixon could not bring himself to be the butcher. He agreed that Haldeman and Ehrlichman had to go, but said he couldn't tell them. Ziegler, a Haldeman protégé, was given the dread assignment. In his meeting with Ziegler, Haldeman first said he would resign; but then his lawyer told him it would weaken his case. When Nixon returned to Washington, Haldeman came in to tell Nixon he was unwilling to resign.

When Ziegler delivered Nixon's message about resigning to Ehrlichman, he thought, "The Presidency is in some lot of trouble . . . if Ron Ziegler has become Lord Chamberlain."

Ehrlichman went in to see Nixon to say bluntly that he would not resign, and added: "From what I've been told by you, it sounds to me like the talks with Dean could result in the President's impeachment."

It was the first time anyone said directly to President Nixon that he might be impeached.

Two days later *The New York Times* reported that Dean had indeed told prosecutors that President Nixon himself took part in the cover-up of the Watergate burglary.

On Saturday, April 28, Ehrlichman telephoned Nixon late at night. Courteous and direct, as always, Ehrlichman said that the President should recognize his own responsibility for the crimes being investigated. Nixon concluded that Ehrlichman was politely suggesting he should resign as President.

Across the continent, in Palm Springs, California, Jerry Ford was enjoying his annual spring golf vacation. A friend happened to mention that John Connally was playing in a golf tournament nearby. Ford had been planning to get together with Connally, so he called him up and suggested they meet for breakfast. Connally agreed, and they met the next morning.

As they talked, each expressed his sympathy for their mutual friend, Richard Nixon. Both suspected that Nixon's campaign staff was responsible for Watergate. Nixon, they agreed, was much too smart a political operator to get involved with anything like a political burglary.

Ford turned to his reason for the meeting. "John," he said, "there's something I want you to know, and I'd like you to keep it in confidence. Betty and I have made a decision that I am going to retire from the House after one more term. I won't be running in 1976. If you are going to be a candidate for the Republican nomination for President in 1976, it's very likely I would be willing to help in any way I could. I'll be a free agent, and I think you would be a good candidate. I'm not ready yet to make a firm commitment, but I wanted you to know that I may be in a position to be helpful."

Connally thanked Ford and said, "Jerry, it's much too early for me to make a decision, but I appreciate your interest. If I do decide to run, I will certainly contact you. And I'm grateful, very grateful." When they finished breakfast and stood up to go, both promised to keep in touch.

Sunday, April 29, 1973, was a day of epiphany for Richard Nixon. He had journeyed to Camp David to find a path out of his greatest crisis, and in his retreat on the mountaintop Nixon saw the reality of what had happened and what was to come.

He was caught in Watergate. He knew it. To survive, he would have to continue to lie about it. To survive, he would have to fight, fight the hardest political battle of his life. And fight he would, on and on and on, because he hated his enemies and persecutors, and the more Nixon hated, the more he fought. Yet, on that Sunday, Richard Nixon realized that his Presidency was over.

To prepare for that day, Nixon had turned to the friend who had counseled him throughout his political life, William P. Rogers. Nixon and Rogers first met in Navy training at Quonset, Rhode Island, during World War II. Both grew up poor, worked their way through college and law school, and fought in the Pacific. At twenty-four, Rogers was the youngest lawyer on the staff of New York District Attorney Thomas E. Dewey.

The friendship of Rogers and Nixon deepened on Capitol Hill: In 1948, Congressman Nixon became concerned that he may have made a mistake in believing Whittaker Chambers's accusation that Alger Hiss was a Communist agent, and asked Rogers, then Counsel for a Senate investigating committee, to assess the conflicts in testimony. Rogers studied the transcripts and told Nixon: You should believe Chambers. In 1952, Rogers worked with New York Governor Thomas Dewey to put Senator Nixon on the ticket with Eisenhower.

Nixon knew he could count on Rogers in a crisis. During the 1952 Presidential Campaign, when newspapers broke the story that Nixon kept a secret fund of contributions to pay his political expenses, four Nixon friends stood by him—Bob Finch, Jerry Ford, Murray Chotiner, and Bill Rogers. Nixon, in fact, asked Rogers to explain the "Secret Fund" to his mother. Nixon could not bring himself to talk to her about it. Rogers convinced Hannah Milhous Nixon that her son had done nothing wrong.

Rogers was a man of quiet wisdom, independence, and principle; when called on, he served as Nixon's conscience. An excellent lawyer, he had been Attorney General under Eisenhower and Nixon's first Secretary of State.

Now, in this crisis of '73, President Nixon asked for Rogers's counsel: What should he do about Bob Haldeman and John Ehrlichman?

Rogers, after reviewing the evidence against Haldeman and Ehrlichman, gave the President his judgment: Both were likely to be indicted, tried, and convicted. In the President's interest, and in the public interest, Rogers said, Haldeman and Ehrlichman should be asked to resign.

Nixon agreed it had to be done, and asked Rogers to tell Haldeman and Ehrlichman they should resign.

"Mr. President," Rogers said, "they would not accept it from me. They must hear it directly from you."

Nixon slowly nodded his head and said yes, he knew he had to do it himself. But he asked Rogers to be at Camp David to help him through the ordeal. When Rogers arrived late on Saturday, they agreed that Nixon would talk first to Haldeman, then to Ehrlichman, while Rogers would wait in a separate cabin and be available if the President needed him.

Early on that Sunday morning the President telephoned Haldeman. "It's got to be a resignation," Nixon said, and asked him to come up to Camp David and bring Ehrlichman.

Haldeman was having coffee with his wife, Jo, in their Georgetown house when Nixon called. When he put down the phone, she asked: "What did he say, Bob?" Haldeman decided not to tell her until he talked to the President. "I'll know for sure after I see him," he said.

Haldeman telephoned Ehrlichman. "Voice of doom," he said. "We go to Camp David today."

In the helicopter over Maryland, Haldeman told Ehrlichman: "It's resignation, John, not leave of absence."

Ehrlichman swore.

When they landed Ziegler met them. "Let's take a walk," Ziegler said, drawing Haldeman aside. "The President's taking it so hard. He's just totally broken, Bob."

Haldeman went first to see the President. Distraught and abject, Nixon confessed that he himself was most to blame for Watergate, and professed that asking for Bob's resignation was the hardest decision he had ever made.

"Last night," Nixon confided in a low voice, "I knelt down and . . . prayed that I wouldn't wake up in the morning. I just couldn't face going on."

Haldeman thought the President was looking for sympathy, inviting pity, as he often did, and told the President not to indulge himself but to go ahead and deal with the problems.

"I told him again that I disagreed with his decision because I didn't think it would do him any good," Haldeman said. "The press wouldn't stop going after him, the Congressional hearings wouldn't stop just because he had gotten rid of us." However, Haldeman said, if that was the President's decision, he would—as he always had—abide by it.

When Ehrlichman arrived at the President's lodge to be told that he must resign, Nixon, trying to be solicitous, asked what he might do to help.

"Only one thing," Ehrlichman said bitterly. "Explain this to my children."

Nixon's sacrifice of Haldeman and Ehrlichman was as irrational as it was dangerous; either could testify to his guilt. In fact, as Ehrlichman protested his resignation in his face-to-face confrontation, he coldly reminded the President: "I have done nothing . . . without your implied or direct approval."

For Nixon, talking to Haldeman and Ehrlichman was even worse than he feared. Ordering the political execution of his two most trusted men left the President a broken man.

"I felt as if I had cut off one arm and then the other," Nixon wrote. "The amputation may have been necessary for even a chance at survival, but what I had to do left me so anguished and saddened that from that day on the Presidency lost all joy for me."

On that Sunday afternoon Nixon first revealed his secret fear: He would not finish his second term.

There at Camp David, from the living room of Aspen Lodge, Nixon looked across the cool green hills of Maryland in the darkening light as he waited for Haldeman and Ehrlichman to return with their formal letters of resignation. With the President was Ron Ziegler, who was becoming the one person to hear Nixon's confessions and keep his secrets. Deep in thought, the President said quietly:

"It's all over, Ron. Do you know that?"

"No, sir," Ziegler replied.

"Well, it is," Nixon said. "It's all over."

When Haldeman and Ehrlichman brought in their forced confessions, Nixon sent for Rogers to join them to review the letters. When Rogers arrived he saw that Nixon, Haldeman, and Ehrlichman—all three—were crying.

Later that afternoon Nixon first said aloud that he might resign. Working on a draft of his first address to the nation about Watergate, the President suddenly turned to Ray Price, the White House wordsmith with the ability to find and articulate the best side of Nixon's nature.

"Ray, you are the most honest, cool, objective man I know," Nixon said. "If you feel I should resign, I am ready to do so. You won't have to tell me. You should just put it in the next draft."

Price was startled. "It was unsettling to have the President tell you he was thinking about resigning," Price said. "I was very concerned about his state of mind."

For six years Price had traveled the world with Nixon, and written for Nixon and listened to Nixon; he had seen Nixon up in spirit and down in disappointment, but he had never seen him like this. Responding carefully, feeling his way with words, Price avoided a direct answer and tried to move the discussion away from Nixon's sense of doom. "I began to talk to him about why he should not resign. I led him back into the world affairs field, and reminded him of all the things that were unfinished in his Presidency, and all the things he could finish. Finally I got the President back up and focusing again."

Minutes later Price found Ziegler and described the depressed mood of "the patient," as they sometimes referred to Nixon. "Ron and I were consulting back and forth during that weekend not only about what would be in the speech—but Ron was concerned, as I was, about what condition the President would be in to deliver it," Price said. He decided not to mention that the President had used the word "resign"—not to Ziegler, not to anyone.

Nixon asked Rogers to stay for dinner, but they found little to talk about. Rogers thought the President seemed sad, down in spirit, but resolute. "His instinct for survival was evident, unmistakable," Rogers said. "It was clear to me that he would not give up, that he would fight on."

Later that evening, alone in his study, Nixon engaged in a debate with himself—to tell the truth or to lie. "People were waiting for a yes or no answer to the question of whether I was also involved in Watergate," Nixon wrote. "If I had given the true answer, I would have had to say that without fully realizing the implications of my actions I had become deeply entangled in the complicated mesh of decisions . . . that comprised the Watergate cover-up."

As he ended his soliloquy that April evening, Nixon's own dark political instincts won the debate. "I felt that if in this speech I admitted any vulnerabilities, my opponents would savage me with them. I decided to answer no to the question of whether I was involved in Watergate. I hoped that, after the agony of the past weeks, a firm statement of my innocence, accompanied by the symbolic cleansing of the administration with the departure of Haldeman, Ehrlichman and Dean . . . would convince people that the various Watergate probes could and should be brought to a quick conclusion. . . . I could not have made a more disastrous miscalculation."

On the next day the White House press office announced the resignations of Haldeman, Ehrlichman, Dean, and Kleindienst.

To restore the reputation of the Justice Department, Nixon asked Elliot Richardson, a Bostonian regarded in official Washington as a man of unasailable rectitude, to leave as Secretary of Defense and become Attorney General. Before he accepted, Richardson asked for, and Nixon granted, full authority over the Watergate investigation.

"You must pursue this investigation even if it leads to the President," Nixon said. "I'm innocent. You've got to believe I'm innocent. If you don't, don't take the job. The important thing is the Presidency. If need be, save the Presidency from the President."

Richardson, carefully taking notes during their discussion, was convinced that Nixon was indeed innocent or he would not have granted such complete control over the investigation.

That evening the President delivered to the American people, on national television, the travesty of the truth that he had consciously chosen as his course of action.

In that address Nixon said he "immediately ordered an investigation" after he first learned of Watergate. He told the nation that he had tried to find out whether "members of my administration were in any way involved. I received repeated assurances that they were not. . . . Until March of this year, I remained convinced that the charges of involvement by members of the White House staff were false. . . . I was determined that we should get to the bottom of the matter, and that the truth should be fully brought out—no matter who was involved. . . . I will not place the blame on subordinates."

Only a desperate man could have told such a lie, or then made this public commitment in announcing the appointment of Richardson: "I have given him absolute authority to make all decisions bearing upon the prosecution of the Watergate case . . . to pursue this case wherever it leads."

Ford, at home in Virginia listening to the speech, was certain that Nixon was right to rid himself of Haldeman, Ehrlichman, and Dean. Ford trusted none of the three, and suspected one or all might somehow have been involved in Watergate. Talking to reporters, Ford said: "The resignations were a necessary first step by the White House in clearing the air on the Watergate Affair."

Ford commended the appointment of Richardson; under the new Attorney General, he said, "All of the facts will come to light and all of those involved will be exposed."

Ford was still convinced that the President was a victim of whatever had happened, and said so: "I have the greatest confidence in the President, and I am absolutely positive he had nothing to do with this mess."

Looking ahead, Ford's greatest concern was that Watergate would damage Republican candidates for the House in the 1974 elections. "If so," he said, "it would be most tragic and undeserved. No Republican Member of Congress was in any way involved in the Watergate affair."

10

THE REGENCY

Early in the morning a rain shower swept across downtown Washington, and a brisk northwest wind scattered petals of dogwood blossoms in ivory and gold on the south lawn of the White House. The Western sky cleared, then darkened again; a storm was coming. The President left the Mansion, walked through the colonnade past the Rose Garden to the West Wing, and, by the official White House log of Thursday, May 3, 1973, arrived in the Oval Office at 8:22 A.M.

After the ritual National Security briefing from Henry Kissinger—the Lebanese Army was fighting Palestinian guerrillas in Beirut; U.S. Phantom jets had bombed Communist positions in Cambodia again—Nixon met with David Bruce, his new emissary to China, and telephoned Secretary of State Rogers. He then met for thirty-one minutes with Ron Ziegler, his closest confidant now that Haldeman was gone.

Nixon's longtime friend and new White House counsel, Leonard Garment, came in to brief him on legal developments on Watergate. That done, Nixon walked across West Executive Avenue and up the wide granite steps to the dark comfort of his den in the baroque Executive Office Building. There, in his refuge from the people and problems that flowed endlessly through the Oval Office, the President sat in his old brown chair and propped his feet on the ottoman. Writing with an old-fashioned fountain pen on a yellow pad, he began setting down his thoughts and ideas, working until it was time for him to see his most important visitor of the day.

Shortly after noon Nixon returned to the Oval Office. At 12:18 P.M.,

Steve Bull, the Presidential assistant for appointments, opened the door and announced: "Mr. President, General Haig."

General Alexander M. Haig, Jr., marched in—tall, erect, in a tailored Army uniform with four silver stars gleaming on each shoulder. The President stood up to greet his impressive visitor. A quick handshake, and the General sat in the chair to Nixon's right and faced him across the carved mahogany desk.

"Al," Nixon said, "I know I am asking you to make a great sacrifice."

"Mr. President," Haig said quietly, as he looked the President right in the eye, "you know that I am always ready to serve you and the country."

The words had the air of a patriotic minuet but were spoken in sincerity. There was a crisp respect between the two men. Neither liked small talk, and as Haig said, "We were not backslappers." The two moved to the business at hand. Haig knew why he had been summoned: The President wanted him to take Haldeman's place as White House Chief of Staff.

Nixon could not manage the Presidency without a deputy, as he discovered within twenty-four hours after he forced Haldeman out. His first and only choice was Haig. The President trusted few people; Haig, who had been Kissinger's Deputy Assistant for National Security Affairs in Nixon's first term, was one of those few. The President liked strength and confidence in a man; Haig had demonstrated both. Haig knew Nixon's White House and how it worked; he had left only four months earlier, when the President appointed him Vice Chief of Staff of the Army. In his new job at the Pentagon Haig was deeply involved in rebuilding the Army after the lessons of Vietnam, and in defining the Army's mission in national security.

Nixon described Haig as "steady, intelligent and tough. What he might have lacked in political experience and organizational finesse he made up for in sheer force of personality. He also had the enormous stamina that the job required. He knew how to drive people, and he knew how to inspire them. Equally important to me, he understood Kissinger."

Before Haig came into his office that afternoon, Nixon knew he would accept the job. One of Nixon's quirks was that he would not offer a Presidential appointment until he was sure the candidate for the job would say yes. So the President had asked Haldeman—with whom Nixon talked every day or so after he fired him—to sound Haig out. Haldeman tracked Haig down through the White House switchboard, and found him in Fort Benning, Georgia, having dinner with fellow officers.

"Al," Haldeman said, "the President wants you to be his new chief of staff in the White House."

"Bob," Haig said, "I prefer not to do it. I am totally engrossed in the Army again, and I want to finish my career as a military man." In addition, Haig told Haldeman, "I don't think it would be good for the President. He should think twice about having any military man in so powerful an office in the White House."

Haldeman went back to the Oval Office and told the President of Haig's reluctance. Nixon immediately dismissed Haig's objections. Haldeman telephoned Haig again, with the President sitting nearby.

"Al," Haldeman said, "I am with the President, and he wants you to do this."

"Bob," Haig said, "you must give me time to tell Abe first. I'll see him tomorrow morning, and then I'll come in to see the President." Haig flew to Washington the next morning and told General Creighton Abrams, who was awaiting Senate confirmation as Army Chief of Staff, about the summons from the Commander in Chief. Abrams agreed Haig must accept the assignment. Then Haig went directly to see the President.

Nixon clearly set forth his priorities: He did not want Haig to try to handle Watergate; he and his lawyers would manage that problem.

"Amen, brother," Haig thought, as the President talked. Whatever the Watergate problem was, Haig was relieved that he need not become involved. "I thought that was possible," Haig said, "because I didn't know anything about Watergate."

The President was specific and emphatic: He wanted Haig to run the White House staff and operations, to organize the information that he as President would need to make decisions and take action.

Haig listened carefully. Going back to the White House, he had already calculated, could end his chance to ever reach his ambition to become Chairman of the Joint Chiefs of Staff. But Haig recognized duty: The Commander in Chief was ordering him on a mission.

To counter the loss of his military career there would be the power and the challenge of managing, in the President's name, the government of the country. Bold by nature, Haig was ready to take charge. He was confident that he could not only handle the White House staff and operations; he could also take part in directing American foreign policy and preserving national security at the highest level.

Haig did not discount the danger of Watergate. It was a major problem, obviously; it had just cost Haldeman his job and reputation. But Haig accepted President Nixon's word that he and his lawyers could handle it. At the end of their discussion, the President said: "Al, it will be good to have you back."

"Mr. President, I look forward to being back."

General Haig said he would report for duty in the White House the next day, and stood up. They shook hands. The meeting ended. It had taken six minutes.

President Nixon, buoyed and relieved, left the White House within the hour for a long weekend in Key Biscayne, Florida. Soon after *Air Force One* took off, the thunderstorm that had threatened all day broke across the city, and Washington was struck by high winds, rolling thunder, and jagged arcs of lightning.

The next day, Haig took command. In full military uniform, he set up head-quarters in the sun-filled, spacious office in the Southwest corner of the West Wing, the office that has been handed along from one Chief of Staff to another since Eisenhower's time. This office, only forty-five hurried steps from the President's door, is recognized by the Washington peerage—a court of some eight hundred Cabinet dukes, Congressional earls, fief holders of bureaucracies, high-priced lords of the bar, media barons and knights—as second in rank only to the Oval Office itself.

Ambition had brought Al Haig to his new command—ambition and struggle, courage in battle, and a talent for the brassy competition of military politics. In eight years Haig climbed over his West Point classmates from the obscurity of a staff colonel standing watch in Lyndon Johnson's Pentagon to four-star general. Yet nothing in the forty-eight years of Alexander Haig's life could have prepared him to be all that he had to be—Acting President of the United States, watchman over the Constitutional process, the seneschal who forced Vice President Agnew out of office, and the man who maneuvered the resignation of President Nixon so that Vice President Ford could take over to preserve the Presidency.

Haig was Warwick, Metternich, Brutus. He came to preserve the reign he found it necessary to end. His was the hand that changed power in the American democracy. Haig did not know it, could not know it when he became Chief of Staff; but he was to become regent of the Government of the United States.

To some who at close range saw it all happen, Haig was a villain. To others he was a hero. In truth he was both.

Early in life Haig learned to deal with the unexpected. Born to upper-middle-class status in a Mainline suburb of Philadelphia, Alex—as his Scotch-Irish father and Irish Catholic mother called him—was the second of three children in a prospering family in the prospering Twenties. "My father was a very promising young attorney in Philadelphia, making money hand over fist, and spending it faster than he made it. And suddenly he died," Haig said. It was 1935, in the hard times of the Depression. Alex was ten.

The Haigs lost everything. A wealthy uncle helped the proud mother keep up appearances. Alex, when not in parochial school, worked where a boy could—running a newspaper route, doing chores for the local post office, delivering messages. In his teens he decided he wanted to go to West Point; but on his first try, he was turned down. His grades were too low. So he went to work, part of the time as a dapper floorwalker at John Wanamaker's department store, and saved enough money to pay tuition and room at Notre Dame. He earned his meals by working in the student cafeteria, learned to study, and brought up his grades.

In 1944 he finally made it to West Point, in part because of his good grades at Notre Dame, and in part because an uncle persuaded a Philadelphia Congressman to give young Haig an alternate appointment. From his first days as a cadet Haig had problems at West Point, in conduct and in the classroom. "I was a youngster without a father, and I chafed under the discipline. I had a great bent for enjoying myself, and I raised a lot of hell. On the soft sciences—arts and letters, history, English, psychology, the social sciences—I did very well. I did not like bridges and engineering, and I was lackluster at it."

As punishment for sneaking out to a bar after taps one night, Haig's leave was canceled for the summer before his senior year. A tough old colonel who had lost a leg at Hurtgen Forest put him to work training cadets in the field. "It was the first time I got to organize things, to run things," he said, "and it began to generate in me a very keen interest in organizing and managing military affairs." In the 1947 yearbook a prescient classmate described Cadet Haig: "Strong convictions and even stronger ambitions."

Haig graduated without distinction—number 214 in a class of 310. In his defense, Haig says, "That was substantially better than Eisenhower, and far better than George Patton." Like Eisenhower, Patton, and other mediocrities of the West Point classrooms, Haig was assigned to a less brainy branch of the Army. In Haig's case, it was to tanks for training, and then to his first command—as a platoon leader in the First Cavalry Division in Tokyo.

In Japan, life was easy for occupation troops. There, as had been the practice before Pearl Harbor, the American Army in peacetime used contact sports to arouse the competitive spirit of officers and men. The Supreme Commander, General Douglas MacArthur, liked football; so, naturally, every officer liked football. Haig played quarterback for the First Cavalry, the home-town team in Tokyo. "You got well known if you played," Haig said. He was transferred from troop duty to be an aide to Major General Edward Almond, Chief of Staff to MacArthur.

Serving in the palace of the American Caesar opened a new world of military prestige and power to First Lieutenant Haig. "That was like drinking at the fire hose," he said. "I had daily exposure to MacArthur; and General Almond had both the military side and the civil side." Haig saw MacArthur and his general staff for what they really were: the government of Japan. "I was always interested in politics," Haig said, and he watched as "a Constitution was developed for Japan, under MacArthur, which was a mirror image of the most progressive American conceptions."

To Haig, the MacArthur government dealt skillfully with the Communist threat in Japan. "This wasn't test tube stuff, this was formed in the vortex of a political situation." Serving under MacArthur advanced "my great interest in national security policy, foreign policy, the Soviet problem." At General Headquarters, Haig also learned about politics and the use of power, and he glimpsed the comforts and perquisites of high military office.

At a concert one evening Lieutenant Haig met Patricia Antoinette Fox, the blonde daughter of Major General Alonzo P. Fox, MacArthur's Chief of Staff for the occupation. Haig and Pat Fox were married in Tokyo on May 24, 1950—five weeks before the Korean War began.

As an aide to General Almond, Haig landed at Inchon with X Corps, fought across the Han River to liberate Seoul, then crossed the Korean peninsula to Hungnam to take part in the U.S. drive to the border of China. With Almond, who had bragged to his subordinates that he would not stop until he reached the Yalu River, Haig went to the very border of Red China on November 21, 1950. "I didn't like it," Haig said, "because at that very time hundreds of thousands of Chinese were in Almond's rear. We knew the Chinese were there, but MacArthur's GHQ would not accept it."

Days later, hours later in some sectors along the Korea front, American troops were surrounded, fighting desperately in bitter cold to escape the Chinese trap. On Christmas Eve of 1950, six months after the Korean War began, Captain Haig and the other survivors of Almond's X Corps escaped by ship to Pusan, to regroup after their Dunkirk, and to get ready to fight again.

Haig, dizzy with hepatitis contracted from drinking from polluted streams, was hospitalized and sent back to Japan. The experience of Korea left its mark. "I saw the Korean War both from the battlefield and the strategic point of view," Haig said. He observed the connection between military power and politics; he witnessed at close hand the great MacArthur in victory and in defeat. He saw, in person, the two imperial Communist powers, the Soviet Union and Red China, using surrogates to drain or defeat America's random attempts toward international peace and self-determination. Out of this experience Haig refined and set his own ambition, to make his contribution in the international affairs of his country and the world.

Shipped back to the States, Haig returned to West Point as a tactical training officer. The teacher continued to learn; on his own initiative Haig drove three times a week to Columbia University to take graduate courses in business administration. The Army, as part of its design for prospective generals, assigned Haig to troop duty in Europe, then to logistics, and promoted him. Back in Washington, Major Haig earned a Masters in International Relations at Georgetown University and served in the Pentagon on the Berlin and NATO desk.

There, in 1961, Lieutenant Colonel Haig was first noticed by Dr. Fritz Kraemer, a monocled refugee from Germany and a master at spotting talent. During World War II, Dr. Kraemer, then an adviser to the U.S. Army on the German army, delivered an indoctrination briefing to a company of infantrymen; and a curly-headed, nineteen-year-old private by the name of Henry A. Kissinger wrote him a letter complimenting him on the speech. Kraemer came by to look up Private Kissinger in a maneuver area. "I had been taken out of a college program and sent to the Infantry, and I felt extremely sorry for myself," Kissinger said.

"Just stick with this," Kraemer told him. "In due course, if the opportunity presents itself, I may do something." A few months later the division commander came by the company. "I was doing latrine duty," Kissinger said, "and that meant I had to keep the situation map in the company dayroom."

"Soldier, come over here," the general said to the private. "Explain that map to me."

"I did," Kissinger said.

When Private Kissinger completed his strategic analysis of the situation, the general asked: "What are you doing in the Infantry? Do you know Fritz Kraemer?"

"Yes," Kissinger said. "I met him once."

"Take this soldier's name," the general said to an aide.

A short time later, Kissinger was transferred to G-2, the intelligence section.

After the war, Kraemer and Kissinger continued to work together; and for decades after, Kraemer kept his eye on the military's brightest and best, and pushed them along.

During the Cuban missile crisis Haig was assigned—at Kraemer's suggestion—to monitor the military situation for Army Secretary Cyrus Vance and his general counsel, Joseph Califano. When President Kennedy sent the first U.S. forces into Vietnam, Haig was assigned to monitor the situation for Defense Secretary Robert McNamara. "I was an eyewitness to the beginning of our involvement in Vietnam," Haig said. "I disagreed with the way we were fighting the war there, and said so." He asked to be assigned to Vietnam, but was turned down. After a year at the Army War College, Haig threatened to resign unless he was sent to Vietnam. "I was determined to go," he said. "Why? That's where the action was. And I had a tremendous ego involvement in Vietnam because I had told them it was so badly managed. I wanted to see it firsthand."

After six months as operations officer of the First Infantry Division, Haig finally won a command, the First Battalion of the Twenty-sixth Infantry Regiment at a hot crossroads north of Saigon that came under regular attack from the Vietcong. Wounded once, near the eye when a Vietcong prisoner blew himself up with a grenade, shot down twice in helicopters, Haig was awarded the Distinguished Service Cross for leading his troops in combat near An Loc. For his leadership on the battlefield he was promoted to brigade commander. In 1967, he returned to West Point, as a Colonel, to be deputy commandant.

After the 1968 election President-elect Nixon asked Kissinger to become his National Security Adviser, and Kissinger was searching for the most able military assistant he could find.

"The military kept giving me names of intellectual military people," Kissinger said. "I didn't need an intellectual. I had plenty of experience with intellectuals. I didn't need systems analysis; I could hire that. I wanted a combat officer who was also very smart. I wanted somebody who had been in the field, somebody who had seen combat in Vietnam, who could tell me what the combat people thought, who could tell me how it would look from a combat point of view, because the first job of the military assistant was liaison to the Pentagon."

Fritz Kraemer, at Haig's suggestion, called Kissinger to recommend Haig. McNamara also telephoned Kissinger about Haig. Kissinger looked at Haig's record, was impressed by his combat experience, and sent for him. Kissinger's opening words, as Haig remembers them: "I don't want any goddam overeducated sophisticated armchair army officer. What is your view of Vietnam?"

Haig told Kissinger, and the two talked for an hour. "My views were close to his," Haig said.

Kissinger gave Haig the job.

In the Nixon White House, Henry Kissinger brought together the most highly qualified staff ever to serve on the National Security Council. It was a combination of experience, expertise, scholarship, intellect, and stamina. Kissinger—demanding, difficult, overbearing—drove each man and woman in his office without mercy or gratitude, drove each to excel beyond what any one of them thought he or she could accomplish. As Kissinger's deputy, Haig managed the bruised egos, the intelligence pouring in from all over the world, the documents, and the papers Kissinger was preparing for the President.

"The staff, I hired," Kissinger said. "Haig managed it. He was superb."

First to arrive in the early morning, Haig was also the last to leave at night. "If you see the lights burning late in the West Wing," Nixon once said, "it is Al Haig doing Henry's work." By dedication to his job, by loyalty to Kissinger and to Nixon, and by his capacity to deliver on assignments, Haig made himself indispensable—and therefore powerful.

The President sent Haig to Vietnam as his personal emissary a dozen times, sought his advice, trusted his judgment. Kissinger made demands on Haig that were sometimes outrageous, but Haig endured. He was tireless, disciplined in temper, and learned how to disagree with Kissinger without provoking a tirade. "Henry's world view and my world view were incredibly similar," Haig said. "And it was not because one brainwashed the other, but we both came to the task with a convergence of view. We seldom clashed intellectually. We clashed in other ways."

In time Kissinger began to feel threatened by President Nixon's private meetings with Haig; when Haig left the NSC to go back to the Pentagon, Kissinger was relieved. But then Haldeman was forced to resign.

Kissinger was ambivalent about Haig's return to the White House in the powerful position of Chief of Staff. But he recognized that Haig was the only choice. "It had to be somebody Nixon had confidence in," Kissinger said. "It had to be somebody who had a lot of administrative experience. It had to be somebody who knew the personalities. It had to be somebody who was quite ruthless. And it had to be somebody who knew me, so that we could coordinate the foreign and domestic side. If this were a class in political science, I could find calmer people than Haig. Sure, there were personalities who were less abrasive; but if they were less abrasive, they would not have met the other tests."

Nixon needed Haig; that Kissinger knew. But Kissinger worried that Haig might try to reduce his own influence and access to Nixon. Haig, sensing this, made no effort to reassure his former boss.

Haig, in the Army tradition of an officer taking over a new military command, surveyed the perimeter of his responsibility and assessed the state of his forces. His first finding was a command not up to strength. "We had over ninety vacancies—Cabinet and sub-Cabinet positions, White House staff, independent agencies," he said. "Recruiting to fill these vacancies was the first order of business. With Watergate, that was a tough job."

Watergate had changed everything. When Haig left the White House only four months earlier, Watergate seemed no more than an annoyance, a political accusation. Now he could see that Watergate dominated the White House: It consumed the President's time, drained his energy, and occupied his thoughts.

Haig got a glimpse of events to come when Leonard Garment, Nixon's new counsel, came in to brief him on the most pressing legal concerns: A Federal grand jury preparing to indict Mitchell and Stans; guidelines for Nixon aides who might need to claim executive privilege in testifying before the Senate and the Federal grand jury; a second-hand report of Dean's statements to the Watergate prosecutor; an account of Colson's interrogation by the FBI.

In Haig's military mind, he was going into battle with too little information. But there was no way he could get the facts about the break-in or the events that followed. Except for the President, everyone in the inner ring of the cover-up conspiracy—Haldeman, Ehrlichman, Mitchell, Colson and Dean—was gone. By that time Nixon would talk to nobody about what they, and he, had done. "There was no way we could get a handle on the case," Garment said. "Everything was confusing, conflicting. And, I thought, threatening to the President." But when Garment tried to find out exactly what the threat was, he came to a wall of silence.

Haig heard so many contradictions and discrepancies in the stories that he realized Watergate was even more confusing eleven months after the event than it was when it happened. He quickly realized Watergate could jeopardize his own career and reputation. Just as quickly, he decided he must look to his own defense, protect his own flanks and rear.

Haig telephoned Fred Buzhardt, a longtime friend and fellow West Point graduate who was Counsel for the Defense Department, and asked him to come over to the White House to help, at least temporarily. "It was one of the wise things I did," Haig said. "I decided I would never touch a thing about Watergate unless I had a lawyer's opinion on whether it was appropriate or not appropriate."

On Haig's second day as Chief of Staff, Nixon called him from Florida and suggested he fly down. On Monday, their first working day in Key Biscayne, Nixon and Haig met for most of the day to discuss White House operations, Congressional relations, foreign policy, Vietnam—and Watergate.

The President assured Haig that Watergate was "just partisan politics," and "a PR problem." Haig accepted Nixon's word that he had no involvement with Watergate before or after it happened. To Haig, Nixon's denial rang true: The Richard Nixon that Haig had worked with for four years was much too smart to be involved in a pointless and bungled political burglary.

Haig also saw that the Watergate problem had been badly managed by Haldeman, by the White House lawyers, by the White House press office, and by Nixon himself. By the time Haig flew back to Washington, he realized that his new command was to defend the President, and the Presidency.

Nixon was wrong when he said he and his lawyers could handle Watergate; of that Haig was certain. Watergate, Haig realized, was the principal concern of Nixon and much of the White House staff. "I rapidly learned that it would have been impossible to stay out of it," Haig said.

Nixon withheld the facts from the man he put in charge of his defense. Nixon did not tell Haig that he had conspired to obstruct justice and silence witnesses with money and promises of pardons, or that he had lied to the American people about it. Nixon did not tell Haig the truth about Watergate—that he was no victim of overzealous campaign workers; that in reality he, the President of the United States, was the godfather of the cover-up.

Nor did Nixon reveal to Haig the secrets of Camp David—that in despair he had confided to Ziegler that Watergate would end his Presidency, that he asked Price whether he should resign.

Haig's arrival, his cheerful confidence and brisk style, revived the spirits of the President and the survivors on his staff. "Al brought a military élan to the place; his presence invigorated all of us," Garment said.

At Haig's urging, the President took a step to lift the morale of the weary White House troops enduring the Watergate siege. Haig persuaded Nixon to bring in twenty-one top White House aides for a pep talk. For thirteen minutes, a long time for Nixon, the President talked to the senior staff. He asked them to join him in regaining the momentum of the first term, to press forward with the Nixon program for executive reorganization, to advance the Nixon plan for a new international order in the world.

As Minority Leader of the House, Ford observed that the President was not making decisions on serious bills and other issues before Congress. He sensed the reason for the disarray in the White House; he had seen first-hand how much Nixon depended on Haldeman and Ehrlichman. Although Ford admired Haig as a soldier and respected his foreign policy expertise, he worried that Haig lacked political experience and judgment.

The troubles of the White House prompted other senior Republicans to push Ford to do something, "to get some reliable people to go down there and straighten out the White House staff," as Ford put it. He talked to Mel Laird and Bryce Harlow, and strongly urged them to return to the White House and help the President pull himself and the Republican Party out of a desperate situation. Appealing to their patriotism, Ford said to Laird and Harlow: "It is in the best interests of the United States that the President have the kind of expertise and assistance you can offer. Frankly, if you don't do this, we may have a catastrophe in the second term of this Administration."

Laird shook his head and said: "Jerry, I'm not happy about going down there and working in that jungle." Laird was doing well in business; it would be a major sacrifice to cancel the projects he had just started.

Laird and Harlow came under added pressure from Senate Republican Leader Hugh Scott, and from Speaker Carl Albert and Senate Democratic Leader Mike Mansfield. All insisted it was in the country's interest that integrity and confidence be restored in the White House. Finally Laird and Harlow agreed to go—"The government was at a standstill," Laird said—but only if the President personally convinced them that he had nothing to do with Watergate.

Face to face, Nixon assured them that he was innocent, Laird said, so he and Harlow agreed to return to the White House and help the President for six months or so.

"It was not the best relationship I've ever had in working in the White House," Laird said. "Nixon felt he was forced to take us. And I didn't really find out until I got over there that the only thing the President was concerned about was Watergate. There were decisions being made in foreign policy, but I have to give Henry Kissinger credit for that. Henry really had a free hand; he would do things in the name of Nixon, and Nixon wouldn't challenge him."

Four weeks after he rejoined the White House, Laird said, "I became aware that I had not been told the truth. But I could not walk out that fast. I had agreed to go over and help out for six months to a year." He felt he should honor his commitment not just to the President but also to the Congressional leaders who were depending on him and Harlow.

On May 10, 1973, the President announced that John Connally was joining the White House staff as an unpaid special adviser. Ten days earlier Connally had switched from Democrat to Republican; and to the outsider, it looked as though Connally had boarded a sinking ship of state.

In fact, the Connally switch was part of a Nixon plot. A month or so earlier, Haldeman had told Nixon that Federal prosecutors were investigating Vice President Agnew. Nixon confided to Connally that Agnew might be forced to resign. If that happened, Nixon could appoint Connally to replace Agnew as Vice President and thereby put him in a commanding position to win the Republican nomination for President in 1976. To make the scheme work, Nixon told Connally he must first become a Republican. So he did.

In the spring and summer of 1973, the Washington press corps discovered gold in Watergate. Never had there been such a mother lode of hard news, startling confessions, and leaks from "sources" motivated by ego, revenge, or both—all the great things that make newsmongering the exciting life that it is. Benjamin Bradlee, the audacious managing editor at *The Washington Post,* would never forget it. "Every day I went to the office with a bucket, and by press time it was full."

In May *The Washington Post* won a Pulitzer Prize for breaking and pursuing the Watergate story. There was no question about it: The *Post* was first to dig out the connections between the crime and the Nixon campaign, and the most persistent in keeping the scandal before the public until Judge Sirica got the burglars to talk.

Day by day Watergate turned into a compelling national drama. As it did, Washington reporters performed like a Greek chorus: With note pad and microphone they explained the action onstage, commented on the players, hailed the heroes, jeered the villains, and congratulated themselves on their own performances.

As the Senate Watergate Committee prepared for hearings in May, the curtain opened for the beginning of a tragedy. CIA Deputy Director Vernon Walters was subpoenaed by another Senate Committee and told to bring the memorandum he wrote after he and Helms met with Haldeman and Ehrlichman in the White House on June 23, 1972—the day that Nixon and Haldeman asked the CIA to tell the FBI to back off the Watergate investigation. Walters, a friend of Nixon for some twenty years, showed his notes to the President before he turned them over to the Committee. "The minute we saw them," Nixon wrote, "we knew we had a problem."

At the insistence of Democrats in Congress, Attorney General Richardson appointed an independent Special Prosecutor to conduct the Watergate investigation. The appointment was an obvious threat to Nixon, but he was powerless to stop it. To convince Richardson to take the job, Nixon promised him complete authority over the Watergate investigation. To win confirmation in the Senate, Richardson promised to appoint Archibald Cox, a Harvard law professor and former Solicitor General for both President Kennedy and President Johnson, as the Special Prosecutor. To make sure he could prosecute without restraint by anyone, Cox exacted from Richardson the promise that he would have full and unquestioned authority to call any witness, review any documents, see any evidence, investigate any suspect, and prosecute anyone involved in Watergate. Cox could be removed, under Richardson's commitment, only for "extraordinary improprieties on his part."

In his own view, Cox would be reporting only to his own conscience and judgment. His appointment empowered him, in his mind and on the Senate record, to investigate any person connected with Watergate. "Even if that trail should lead to the Oval Office?" asked Senator Robert Byrd. "Wherever that trail may lead," Cox promised.

To counter the daily barrage of bad publicity, the President attempted a media counteroffensive. With Nixon setting the theme, Haig, Price, and Ziegler brought out a four-thousand-word Presidential statement conceding that his 1972 campaign leaders had engaged in unethical and illegal actions. But the President specifically and categorically denied his own involvement:

> I took no part in, nor was I aware of, any . . . efforts that may have been made to cover up Watergate.
>
> At no time did I authorize any offer of Executive clemency for the Watergate defendants, nor did I know of any such offer.
>
> I did not know, until the time of my own investigation, of any efforts to provide the Watergate defendants with funds.
>
> At no time did I attempt, or did I authorize others to attempt, to implicate the CIA in the Watergate matter.

All these main points in the Presidential statement were false, but only Nixon knew that. Nixon even insisted he wanted a thorough investigation;

and he commended Richardson for appointing Cox. "In this effort he has my full support," Nixon said.

Neither the press nor the public believed Nixon. Garment was jeered in the White House press room when he tried to answer reporters' questions about the President's statement. *The Wall Street Journal* concluded, after reviewing Nixon's latest sophistry, "The President is acting like a man with something to hide."

The latest Gallup Poll found that 93 percent of Americans had heard enough about Watergate to have an opinion: One third of the public believed Nixon knew about Watergate before it happened, and another third said he did not know about the break-in beforehand but tried to cover it up after he found out about it.

The worse his plight became, the more Nixon secluded himself. Often he sat brooding, like Raskolnikov, about his crimes. Late one evening, after a splendid and stirring White House dinner for the prisoners of war who had returned from Vietnam, he went alone to the Lincoln Sitting Room and sat before the fire, thinking with pride, "I had played a role in bringing these men back home." Then he was reminded of Watergate. "The contrast between the splendid lift of this night and the dreary daily drain of Watergate suddenly struck me with an almost physical force," he wrote. Tricia and Julie joined him to share their joy of the occasion. After they talked briefly, their father suddenly said: "Do you think I should resign?"

"Don't even think of it!" Tricia said. In her diary she wrote: "He had done nothing wrong. There was no reason to resign."

On Sunday, June 3, the President looked at the front page of *The Washington Post* and *The New York Times*. Dean, the *Post* reported, told Federal prosecutors and Senate investigators that he discussed the Watergate cover-up with the President at least thirty-five times. Further on in the story, Nixon read that Dean had also told prosecutors about his discussion with Nixon about raising one million dollars. A sense of dread came over Nixon. "I asked Haig whether I shouldn't resign."

Absolutely not, Haig replied. Haig proposed a solution. As Chief of Staff he knew that Nixon had installed a taping system to record his conversations in the Oval Office, in his EOB office, and on his telephones. Haig urged Nixon to listen to the tapes of his talks with Dean that would exonerate him. Nixon agreed, and Haig arranged for the President to begin listening in his EOB office the next day.

Steve Bull, Nixon's personal aide, threaded the first tape into the machine and showed the President how to work the buttons. Following Bull's instructions, Nixon put on earphones and turned on the tape. Voices rose and faded. Pushing the "play" and "rewind" buttons, Nixon listened all day to his talks with Dean. Some segments would be hard to explain, Nixon realized, but he was overjoyed about one part of the tape. He thought that conversation suggested he did not know about the cover-up before March 21, 1973.

The President was so relieved that he called in Haig and Ziegler to share the good news. But he would not let them listen to the tape.

On a day off from their House duties, Jerry Ford and Tip O'Neill played in the annual Democratic-Republican Golf Tournament at Andrews Air Force Base. Riding along in a golf cart, Ford confided to O'Neill that he had decided to retire from the House. "I promised Betty I'd quit after one more term," Ford said. "I've got it figured that my pension is worth about twenty-six thousand dollars a year. But you've got to get us a pay raise. You're the Majority Leader, and you're the only one who can do it. Naturally, I'll do what I can to help you."

"What do you have in mind?" O'Neill asked.

"Well, I'd like to get my pension up to thirty thousand dollars," Ford said. "Then I can go back to Grand Rapids. I want to practice law three days a week and play golf the other four. I figure I can make around twenty-five thousand dollars in my practice, and together with the pension I'll have a good living. Betty and I will take a vacation in the winter, and I'll be living the life of a gentleman."

O'Neill was not surprised at Ford's decision to leave the House; he was familiar with, but not sympathetic to, Ford's long years of frustration at being in the minority. As for the pay raise, O'Neill said, "Let me think about it."

Day after day in the White House, Haig heard a grim litany of woe for President Nixon. Special Prosecutor Cox told reporters he might subpoena Nixon to testify before the Watergate Grand Jury. Dean was scheduled to begin his testimony before the Senate Watergate Committee on June 18—the day Leonid Brezhnev would arrive in Washington for a Summit Conference. Reluctantly, and at the request of the White House, Chairman Ervin postponed Dean's appearance for a week. On the day Brezhnev arrived, Cox told a news conference that he was examining the legal question of whether he could indict the President before he had been impeached by the House of Representatives.

For the week of Brezhnev's visit, Nixon had a respite from his troubles. He welcomed Brezhnev to the Oval Office, honored him with a state dinner, took him to Camp David and to California. The two talked peace, arms limitations, and the balance of nuclear power. On the day Brezhnev left, the President turned with regret back to Watergate. It was a year and a week after the break-in.

On Monday, June 25, 1973, Nixon's stone wall of defense—that he knew nothing of Watergate or the cover-up—was breached. In the marbled grandeur of the Caucus Room of the Old Senate Office Building, John Dean took the witness stand before the Watergate Committee. Through live network television coverage, Dean also became the first White House witness to tell the American people about Watergate.

Owlish and imperturbable, Dean testified under oath to President Nixon's detailed and specific actions to cover up the Watergate break-in. Under questioning from Senators, some of it hostile, Dean stuck to his story, displaying an extraordinary ability to remember his conversations with the President and to retrieve his memories on the stand under the bright lights and high stress, and at the risk of perjury.

A powerful witness Dean was, but there was something about him that did not ring true—he was too slick, too glib. It was obvious that he had involved himself deeply in the cover-up, then stopped and turned against the President in a transparent effort to save himself—no matter how much it cost Nixon or anyone else.

At the noon break on the fourth day of his testimony, Senator Howard Baker, the Watergate Committee's co-chairman, and his press secretary, Ron McMahan, walked to the Senators' dining room in the Dirksen Building to discuss the course of the hearings. Baker, a Tennessee trial lawyer with a gift for sensing what a jury might be wondering, told McMahan that he was concerned that the questioning by the Senators tended to wander, sometimes into irrelevance. "We need to focus on the main issue," Baker said. He thought he had come up with the right question to ask Dean, and every other White House witness. When the hearing resumed that afternoon and it was Baker's turn to speak, he took the microphone and put his question to Dean:

"What did the President know, and when did he know it?"

The question went to the heart of the Watergate investigation. Baker reflected the darkest suspicions of prosecutors and press, and the doubts of people all over America. Baker asked the right question, but it would be another fourteen months before the question was answered.

Friday, the thirteenth of July, 1973, was a blistering hot day in Washington. In a small, overcrowded office in the Dirksen Building, Senate Watergate Committee investigators were questioning Alexander Butterfield, a retired Air Force colonel who handled White House communications and records. Butterfield had been asked to talk to Senate investigators in the hope that his records might help answer the question: Who was telling the truth—John Dean or Richard Nixon?

As a witness, Butterfield was earnest and cooperative; but he attended no Watergate meetings with Dean or the President. Butterfield was more of a functionary; he knew the President's files, records, procedures, and schedules.

Don Sanders, a former FBI agent serving as deputy counsel for the committee Republicans, thought Dean might be lying about his talks with Nixon and was searching for some way to prove it. Sanders asked Butterfield: How could the White House provide such detailed accounts of when and where Dean and Nixon had talked?

From the President's log, Butterfield said. He explained that the log is a compendium of information collected from the White House telephone operators, who list all calls to and from the President; from the Secret Service and the secretaries who record names and times of everyone who sees the President; and from White House staff members who prepare memos for the President before an important meeting and summarize it afterward.

Sanders reminded Butterfield of that part of Dean's testimony where Dean said he thought Nixon might be taping their conversation.

"Is it possible Dean knew what he was talking about?" Sanders asked Butterfield.

There was a long and significant pause before Butterfield said quietly: "There is tape in each of the President's offices. It is kept by the Secret Service, and only four other men know about it. Dean had no way of knowing about it. He was just guessing."

"Taping?" Sanders asked. Then he thought: Taping in the White House? Taping the President's highly confidential and often classified conversations? If there were tapes, they could prove who was telling the truth, President Nixon, or John Dean.

Sanders found a private telephone, and reached Fred Thompson, chief counsel for the Republicans on the Watergate committee, at a Capitol Hill bar talking to two reporters. Sanders told Thompson about the tapes.

Thompson immediately telephoned Baker, who was not particularly surprised. Make sure, Baker advised Thompson, that you call Buzhardt down at the White House and let him know that the existence of the tapes is no longer secret.

Ervin and Baker decided to bring Butterfield before the Committee on Monday.

The President was in Bethesda Naval Hospital on that Friday, taken there the night before with a 102-degree fever brought on by viral pneumonia, according to a White House announcement. Haig did not call Nixon immediately, but waited until Monday morning to let him know that Butterfield had disclosed the secret of the White House taping system, and would testify about it within hours.

Nixon was shocked; he alone knew what was on the tapes. He immediately summoned his close advisers to the hospital room and asked them whether he should destroy the tapes. Buzhardt gave his legal opinion that the tapes were Nixon's personal property and he could destroy them. Garment insisted the tapes were evidence; he opposed any move to destroy them. Haig argued that whatever the legal situation, history would find the President guilty if he destroyed the tapes. Vice President Agnew stopped in briefly, and gave a strong political opinion: The Nixon tapes would be an irresistible attraction to Democrats; the President must destroy them.

Nixon telephoned Haldeman to get his view. Keep them, Haldeman said, they are your best defense. In his hospital bed Nixon first concluded he should destroy the tapes, then decided they were his "best insurance against the unforeseeable future."

Anticipating that the Senate, Court, or Special Prosecutor would subpoena the tapes, Nixon's lawyers—Garment, Buzhardt, and Charles Alan Wright, a Constitutional scholar and new member of the defense team—met with Nixon at the hospital. Garment, who had known Nixon longest, spoke for all three, suggesting that they begin reviewing the tapes to organize the evidence for the President's defense.

"No," the President said. "Never." When the lawyers tried to press their point, Nixon angrily shut off the discussion. "No, no, no!"

Soon after, as expected, the President received a formal letter of request from Senator Ervin that copies of the White House tapes be turned over to the Senate Watergate Committee. Nixon refused. Complying would jeopardize "the fundamental Constitutional role of the Presidency," Nixon said. "This I must and shall resist."

Haig said that he had never seen Nixon so emphatic, so determined. "It makes you wonder what must be on those tapes," Haig said. Do you suppose, he asked a colleague, that it is the Constitution he's worried about, or does he have something to hide?

High summer reigned over Washington. As temperatures soared into the nineties, the great Constitutional battle between the President and the Congress began. On Monday, July 23, 1973, Senate Watergate Committee Chairman Ervin read Nixon's letter of refusal and called the other six members of the Senate Watergate committee into executive session. There, after a stormy three-hour session, the seven Senators voted unanimously to subpoena specific Nixon tapes and documents they considered essential to their investigation of the Watergate crime.

Frustrated and overwrought, Ervin charged that Watergate was "the greatest tragedy this country has ever suffered, [worse than] the Civil War." With deep regret in his voice, Senator Baker said, "I am unhappy that it is necessary for us to come to the brink of a Constitutional confrontation . . . between the Congress and the White House."

Before the day was over, Senate lawyers delivered two subpoenas for the tapes to White House lawyers Buzhardt and Garment. Within the hour Special Prosecutor Cox sent over a third subpoena for tapes.

Haig informed the President. He said no.

Nixon was bitter. He told Haig that he was not only under attack from the Democratic Congress, but the Special Prosecutor appointed by his own Attorney General had joined the opposition. Hoping to avoid an open confrontation, Haig asked Richardson to come to the White House to discuss Cox's actions. When they met, Haig warned Richardson that if Cox continued to go after the President, Cox might have to be fired. Richardson listened to Haig's lecture, and finally said quietly: "Al, there is a more immediate problem." Haig looked at him, and waited. Richardson said the United States Attorney in Baltimore had evidence that Vice President Agnew had solicited and accepted cash bribes, before and since he became Vice President. Richardson told Haig he must meet with the President to inform him officially of the investigation of Agnew.

"It was one of the greatest shocks of my life," Haig said, but he was not totally surprised. Agnew had complained to him that Federal prosecutors in Maryland were conducting an investigation that might be politically damaging. Haig knew that Richardson would not ask to see the President unless he were certain of a strong case against Agnew. So Haig promptly reported Richardson's information about Agnew to the President.

Nixon told Haig he already knew about Agnew's problem.

11

OUTCAST

An American President, whatever he says in public, wants his Vice President to be marginally qualified, to curb his competitive instincts, to contain any ideas he might have on public issues, and to be available when needed but never in the way.

In 1968, just before Richard Nixon won the Republican nomination for President, he asked Rogers Morton for his opinion of Maryland Governor Spiro T. Agnew as a candidate for Vice President. Potentially good, Morton said, and went on to describe Agnew: A moderate Republican with a good law-and-order record who would appeal to Middle America; lazy, but could deliver on the speechmaking chores expected of a Vice President.

Nixon chose Ted Agnew. At first Agnew himself did not believe it. Several weeks before, Nixon had thanked Agnew for his support and asked if he might want to be in a Nixon Cabinet. No, Agnew said, he was not sure he was qualified for the Cabinet; but he would like at some time to be considered for appointment as a Federal judge.

As Agnew was surprised, so also were the delegates to the Republican Convention in Miami Beach: "Ted *who?*"

Ted Agnew was the son of Theodore Spiro Anagnostopoulos, who emigrated to America from Greece and started selling from a pushcart. Young Agnew worked his way through the University of Baltimore Law School and got into politics. Through a combination of his own ambition and factional fighting among Democrats, Agnew was elected Baltimore County Executive and then Governor. After the Nixon-Agnew ticket was elected in 1968, Nixon announced he would assign Agnew important responsibilities, and gave him an office in the West Wing of the White House.

As usual, the promise of a meaningful role for the Vice President was not kept. As Eisenhower treated Nixon, Nixon treated Agnew. From the first days of the Nixon Presidency the real players were Kissinger, Haldeman, Ehrlichman, Mitchell—but not Agnew. Except at Cabinet meetings, Agnew rarely saw the President. In his bitter memoir Agnew said, "I was never allowed to come close enough to participate with him in any decision."

So near, so far. Agnew sat in his office only steps away from the Oval Office, hoping that Nixon would ask for his advice. Nixon ignored him. At one Cabinet meeting in 1969 Agnew offered his own opinion on an issue. The President just looked at him. Later, Haldeman came around to tell the Vice President, "The President does not like you to take an opposite view at a Cabinet meeting."

Agnew was given some good assignments. He greeted the governors and mayors who came to Washington and found the President too busy to see them. He delivered the party speeches. And his uninhibited speaking style made him a natural to become Nixon's heir to the low road. White House speechwriters found in Agnew an open outlet for their best slasher words: "nattering nabobs of negativism" and "hopeless, hysterical hypochondriacs of history." With good humor and tongue in cheek, Agnew delivered them; they were well within the Maryland political tradition of strained alliteration. By attacking the media, Agnew created a new Agnew, and ended his neuter status. In his first year in office, Agnew became the new champion of the Republican hard right.

Agnew relished the press attention. He liked the foreign trips, winging around the world in his own *Air Force Two,* reviewing the troops at the airport, hearing the siren song of the police escort. "He never met a dictator he didn't like," said Mike Dunn, his friend, counselor, and military assistant. Dunn, a Major General out of Harvard ROTC, worked out the plans for Agnew's official visits with the Shah of Iran, Franco, Chiang Kai-shek, Haile Selasse, Mobutu, Marcos, and the sheiks of Araby. Invariably, the Vice President talked law and order with them; and chiefs of state looked on Ted and Judy Agnew as Very Important People, to be banqueted, gifted, treated as royals. And then Agnew would come home, to be ignored.

Discouraged and frustrated, Agnew considered going in to see Nixon to tell him that he wanted to leave after the first term—until he heard rumors that Nixon might dump him in 1972 for John Connally. Stubborn and scrappy by nature, Agnew was no man to be pushed, not even by the President. He encouraged his conservative supporters around the country to put pressure on John Mitchell, Nixon's campaign manager.

Mitchell warned Nixon that any attempt to dump Agnew in 1972 could damage his own reelection. Nixon, nevertheless, was dead set on making Connally Vice President in 1972 and the Republican nominee for President in 1976. To Agnew's rescue came Barry Goldwater, the godhead of the conservative Republican movement. Agnew must be renominated, Goldwater decreed. "Agnew's popularity equals that of the President."

Two days later Nixon called Agnew in and told him he would be on the ticket again. It was one week after Connally had declined Nixon's offer of the Vice Presidential nomination.

After the 1972 reelection, Nixon immediately resumed his plotting to nominate and elect John Connally as the next President. Yet he wanted to avoid an open break with Agnew. Right after the inaugural for their second term, Nixon handed Agnew just the kind of assignment he relished: a mission to the Far East, to meet with the leaders of Thailand, Malaysia, Singapore, Indonesia, Laos, Vietnam, Cambodia, and the Philippines. Agnew was to convey the assurance of President Nixon that despite the peace pact with North Vietnam, the U.S. would still continue its military and economic aid.

Returning from Asia in February, *Air Force Two* landed in California so that Agnew could report to the President on his mission. While Agnew was waiting to see Nixon in Newport Beach, he took an urgent telephone call from George White, his longtime friend and first law partner in Maryland. White said he must see Agnew immediately, about a matter too important to discuss on the telephone. Fine, Agnew said, fly out here to California.

White was a man of calm and confidence; but in Agnew's hotel room in California he was distraught and nervous, and his report almost disjointed. The message was blunt: Federal prosecutors in Baltimore were investigating charges that Agnew had taken bribes.

White, with the scraps of information he had, tried to explain. George Beall, the U.S. Attorney for Maryland, was working with the Baltimore office of the IRS in a sweeping investigation of charges that Maryland public officials had been paid kickbacks by contractors and engineers on public contracts. One of the men subpoenaed in the investigation, Lester Matz, was a substantial contributor to Agnew's campaigns. Another man being questioned was Jerome B. Wolff, who not only handled public works contracts for Agnew in Baltimore County and Annapolis but had been a senior aide to the Vice President in the White House.

White told Agnew that Matz, and then Wolff, had come separately to tell him that he must persuade Agnew to stop the Federal investigation or, White said, "They will say they made kickback payments to you."

Agnew was outraged. The charges were untrue, he told White, and he would not be blackmailed.

From California Agnew telephoned Attorney General Richard Kleindienst to complain that his political enemies in the state were using the U.S. Attorney in Baltimore to try to embarrass him. Kleindienst tried to reassure Agnew. He knew about the investigation; and Beall had told him that Agnew was not a target. Federal prosecutors were investigating Dale Anderson, the incumbent Baltimore County Executive, and a Democrat, Kleindienst said.

Just to make sure, however, Kleindienst telephoned Beall. Again Beall assured Kleindienst that there was no evidence against Agnew; furthermore, he said, the statute of limitations had run out on anything that took place while Agnew was Baltimore County Executive.

After his call from Kleindienst, Beall summarized the conversation with his three top assistants supervising the investigation—Barnet Skolnik, Russell T. Baker, Jr., and Ronald Liebman. Beall mentioned that the Vice President was quite concerned about the possibility of political embarrassment.

Casually, Baker said: Agnew is "acting like a guilty man." The others chuckled. In a calm, matter-of-fact voice, Baker said: "We're going to get Agnew."

George Beall, the chief Federal prosecutor in Baltimore, was thirty-five years old, the son of a former U.S. Senator, and the brother of Senator J. Glenn Beall, Jr. When he was sworn in as U.S. Attorney in 1970, Beall resolved to continue a long tradition of prosecuting political corruption in Maryland. His predecessors had convicted, among others, two Congressmen, one U.S. Senator, and the Speaker of the Maryland Assembly.

In a conversation with Robert Browne, head of the IRS intelligence division in Baltimore, Beall learned of reports that bribery of public officials was a common practice in Baltimore County. The prime suspect, according to the IRS, was Dale Anderson, the Baltimore County Executive and a Democrat. Beall called a Federal grand jury and began issuing subpoenas to contractors and consultants who were hired by the county.

Two of those subpoenas were served on Agnew's friends, Lester Matz and Jerry Wolff.

A few days after Agnew returned to Washington from California, Agnew tried to stop the investigation. He told Kleindienst that his political enemies were trying to smear him. Agnew asked Senator Beall to talk to his brother, but Beall replied: "George is very independent. He doesn't like me to talk to him about anything going on in the U.S. Attorney's office." Agnew also asked Haldeman to intercede with Senator Beall. Haldeman made no commitment, but reported Agnew's request to Nixon.

Nixon told Haldeman to tell Agnew that the Watergate problem made help impossible. In fact, Nixon said, any effort by anyone in the White House to influence the Maryland investigation would create another cover-up.

Agnew appealed to John Mitchell for help in calling off the investigation. Mitchell—even though he was preoccupied with preparations for his own defense—spoke to Nixon about it. Nixon said he could do nothing.

Finally Agnew went in to see the President, and Nixon tried to reassure him. "Don't worry about it," he said. "There's not going to be any problem." Agnew came away thinking the President was distracted and that he did not take the Maryland investigation seriously. Agnew decided to hire a lawyer, and asked Charles Colson, by then out of the White House and in private practice in Washington, to recommend a good lawyer. On Colson's recommendation, Agnew retained Judah Best.

To assess the case, Best went to Baltimore to talk to Beall, who assured him Agnew was not a target of the investigation. Best so advised Agnew, but Agnew didn't believe it. White kept calling to warn him that Matz and Wolff, and now another friend, Bud Hammerman, were going to implicate Agnew if he did not stop the investigation.

On May 18, 1973, Matz and Wolff carried out their threat. Their counsel, Joseph Kaplan, went in to see Assistant U.S. Attorney Russell Baker and told him that his clients had evidence that would incriminate the Vice President. Baker, suspecting a trap, pointed out that the statute of limitations had already run out on anything that Agnew might have done as Baltimore County Executive. Kaplan coolly replied that his clients did indeed have evidence of payoffs to Agnew going back that far, but they also had evidence of payoffs to Agnew when he was Governor—and when he was Vice President.

Baker immediately reported to Beall; it was the first direct charge against Agnew. Beall knew he should inform the new Attorney General, but Richardson had not yet been confirmed by the Senate. After Richardson was sworn in on May 25, Beall waited a few days, drove to Washington, walked in to the Attorney General's office, and asked to see Richardson. What about? the secretary asked. "I'm sorry," Beall said. "I can only tell you that it is a most important matter." Kleindienst, he added, might have mentioned it to Richardson. The secretary would not let him in to see Richardson.

Finally, some ten days later, Beall did see Richardson and advised him of the evidence against Agnew. Richardson listened, doodled, and made notes. "In his brahmin fashion, Mr. Richardson leaned back in his chair, looked at the ceiling, reflected, and uttered an expletive that seemed utterly out of character," Beall said. "I had never met the man before."

After the meeting Richardson called Kleindienst and asked what he knew about the investigation of the Vice President. Kleindienst apologetically said he had not had a chance to mention it. But Richardson did hear from the White House. Fred Buzhardt telephoned to say they were getting complaints about the tough tactics practiced by the U.S. Attorney in Baltimore. Richardson was blunt: "If anyone in the White House has a complaint about the operations of the Justice Department, tell him to call me."

In Baltimore, all through June, the testimony of witnesses and the documents confirmed the evidence against Agnew. It was so strong, Beall concluded, that it was imperative that he show the evidence to Richardson. On July 3, Beall took his three-man team to the Justice Department. In the middle of his presentation, a secretary handed Richardson a note and he left the room.

It was a telephone call from Haig, who was in California with Nixon. The President, Haig said, read a story in *The Los Angeles Times* that morning stating that Special Prosecutor Cox planned to investigate Nixon's purchase of his $1.5 million home in San Clemente. What was Cox doing? The President wanted to know, Haig said. Richardson promised to find out and went back into the meeting with Beall.

As Beall and his assistants talked through the evidence, Richardson was thinking: What does it mean for the country? Reflecting aloud to his visitors, he asked: How would a trial of Agnew affect the Administration's capacity to govern? Under the Constitution, could a Vice President be required to appear before a grand jury? Should he inform the President? If Agnew is guilty, would it not be best that he resign?

Ending the session, Richardson emphasized that the enormity of the problem required the greatest caution. "Make no move until you conduct further investigation," he told Beall. "Be sure you have solid evidence."

Alone in his office, Richardson felt ill. "It was," he said, "like a kick in the stomach." He went home and slumped in a chair. "It was as bleak a day as I'd ever had."

In a week the Baltimore prosecutors were back with more evidence—"evidence so damning that I had to inform President Nixon," Richardson said.

Richardson rode over to the West Wing to tell Haig that he must see the President to inform him officially of the charges against the Vice President.

In the Oval Office Richardson formally advised the President that his Vice President was almost sure to be indicted, on as many as forty specific charges of taking kickbacks and bribes. There was even testimony that Agnew had taken bribes in his White House office. The witnesses were credible, Richardson said, and the documents irrefutable.

"Those Maryland politicians," Nixon said. "They're all like that."

Nixon told Richardson to have Henry Petersen review the evidence. In addition, Nixon said, Richardson should see Agnew in person and summarize the charges against him.

In the solitude of his office back at Justice, Richardson made a decision. As Attorney General of Massachusetts, he had learned that "a prosecutor sometimes has to make the judgment that in the public interest it is necessary to get all the facts out and on the public record, and then decline to prosecute because of greater considerations."

What was the public interest here? he asked himself. As Attorney General, he knew enough about the evidence against President Nixon to know that impeachment was possible. He had seen enough evidence against Vice President Agnew to believe he was guilty and could be convicted of bribery. The President himself might not survive; and to Richardson, the risk of having a felon next in line to succeed Nixon was unacceptable.

On his own Richardson made the judgment that it would be in the national interest to persuade, or force, Agnew to resign—forthwith. To accomplish that, Richardson said to an aide, "We must quickly complete the investigation of Agnew and put before the Court all the evidence we have. But the larger purpose is to get the Vice President out of office, get him to resign. There is no purpose in sending Agnew to jail; there is a compelling need to move him out of the line of succession to the Presidency, and without delay."

That afternoon Richardson went to the EOB and into Agnew's office. "Normally a prosecutor does not go to see the person accused," he said to himself. "However, since the accused is the Vice President of the United States, I will do it."

To Agnew, Richardson seemed "even more stiff and starchy" than usual. Richardson opened the conversation by saying, "I am here because the President asked me to come. I would not have been here otherwise."

Agnew, with three defense lawyers at his side, did the talking. He was outraged by the charges, and said that Beall and his staff were politically motivated. He complained that the prosecutors were disrespectful: In the documents they referred to him as "Agnew" instead of "The Vice President" or "Vice President Agnew."

Richardson spoke with care, providing enough detail to convince Agnew of the seriousness of the charges, but holding back on evidence that would tip his lawyers to ways to fashion Agnew's defense. Richardson did name some of the witnesses who would testify that they paid Agnew to receive contracts from the state.

"The whole thing is a fabrication," Agnew replied in anger. Every Governor of Maryland awards contracts, he said, and some would naturally go to qualified architects and engineers who were friends and contributors to his campaigns.

One of his lawyers, Judah Best, broke in to say that Beall and his prosecutors were openly threatening potential witnesses against the Vice President. Best said Agnew's associates were being told: "Talk, or you will be indicted."

Richardson, knowing that Agnew did not like or trust him, made his final point: "The President has directed me to have Henry Petersen evaluate the charges."

As soon as the Attorney General left, Agnew called Haig and insisted that he must talk to the President that day, to "tell him my side of the story." Haig said he would call him back. Agnew waited. Late in the afternoon he learned that the President had flown to Camp David. Still he waited in his office, expecting to be called and invited to see Nixon at Camp David. About 9:00 P.M. Art Sohmer, Agnew's Chief of Staff, told him that *The Wall Street Journal* would break the story of the criminal investigation of the Vice President the next morning.

"There is something else," Sohmer said. "We are not going to Camp David. The President is sending Bryce Harlow here to see you, tonight."

Agnew felt better. He liked Harlow; he planned to ask Harlow to help him in his campaign for President in 1976. Fifteen minutes later Harlow arrived, with Haig.

"When am I going to see the President?" Agnew asked.

The President, Harlow explained, was so shocked by the charges against the Vice President that he had gone to his mountain retreat to consider this new threat to the survival of his Presidency. Haig said the President had sent the two of them to speak in his behalf. To Agnew, Haig was rambling about "legitimacy of government," "uncontrollable circumstances," "the ability to carry out the responsibilities of the Constitutional office."

Harlow was more direct. "This is a national crisis," he said quietly. "Congress will undoubtedly act. You will be impeached."

"What are you here to tell me?" Agnew asked.

"We think you should resign," Haig said.

"Resign?" Agnew was in a fury. "Without even a chance to talk to the President?"

"Yes," Haig replied. "Resign immediately. This case is so serious there is no other way it can be resolved."

"Did the President send you down here to say that?" Agnew asked.

"We are not here on our own," Haig said. "We have been with the President all evening at Camp David, thoroughly discussing the matter. We came here to tell you that you should resign, tonight."

"You mean the President wants me to resign right now?"

"Yes," Haig said.

Agnew told them he would not accept the President's message through an intermediary. "I'm not going to resign," Agnew said firmly. "I'm not going to do anything until I see the President."

Haig and Harlow left.

On the first Saturday in August, Jerry Ford, Mel Laird, and a group of some twenty Members from the House flew to Groton, Connecticut, for the ceremonial laying of the keel of the *Glennard Lipscomb*, a nuclear submarine. Lipscomb, a Congressman from California until his death two years earlier, had been a close friend of Ford and Laird, and an ardent supporter of the U.S. Navy.

On the return flight, Laird sat next to Ford, and the two talked about Nixon and his problems, the disaster of Watergate, and the rumors that Agnew was also being investigated. "You think things are bad now," Laird said. "They're going to get worse."

Laird would not say any more about Agnew, but Ford surmised that the Vice President was facing indictment on criminal charges.

On August 7, *The Wall Street Journal* broke the Agnew story: "A New Watergate? Spiro Agnew Is Target of a Criminal Inquiry; Extortion Is Alleged. Bribery and Tax Fraud Also Alleged; Vice President Retains Criminal Lawyers." That same day Nixon agreed to see Agnew. Hoping for some expression of support, Agnew walked to Nixon's hideaway in the EOB. The

President greeted him warmly, began with irrelevant small talk, and generalized about what Richardson had told him about the Agnew charges.

Agnew listened. A Vice President does not interrupt the President. Before going in, Agnew had made up his mind to confront Nixon with this question: "Were Haig and Harlow speaking for you when they demanded my resignation?" As the monologue ran on, Agnew lost his nerve. When Nixon stopped talking, Agnew lamely complained that witnesses were being promised immunity to testify against him, and that the Baltimore prosecutors were motivated by politics.

"Can you function effectively as Vice President?" Nixon asked.

Absolutely yes, Agnew said, and went on to point out that all the witnesses against him faced income tax prosecution, and all were bargaining with the prosecutors to save themselves by implicating the Vice President. When Agnew complained about Richardson, Nixon said, "I've had my problems with him too." The President assured Agnew that Petersen would review all the evidence, form his own legal opinion of the case, and report back directly to him.

Agnew told the President that he wanted to hold a press conference the next day to defend himself. Nixon advised him not to make any statement he might regret later. Agnew left. The President had not mentioned resignation, so, Agnew said to himself, "I felt there was no need for me to bring up the subject."

At his press conference the next day Agnew said the accusations against him were "false and scurrilous and malicious." Are you denying the charges? a reporter asked. "I am denying them outright and I am labeling them . . . as damned lies." Did you ever take money from contractors? "Absolutely not," Agnew said. Buzhardt listened to a speaker wired into the press room and went in to tell Nixon that Agnew's denials were inexplicable in light of the evidence he had seen.

At the Justice Department, Petersen intensified his review of the case against Agnew. Determined to be thorough, Petersen had the FBI use lie detectors with key witnesses to find out if they were telling the truth. They passed. Petersen studied all the documentary evidence and interviewed witnesses himself. In the end he concluded: There was no doubt about Agnew's guilt; the case was solid. He advised Richardson that Beall should take the case to the grand jury and ask for an indictment. If they delayed, Petersen said, they all risked being publicly accused of a second cover-up.

* * *

In late August, Governor Nelson Rockefeller decided to quietly explore the idea of a campaign to be appointed Vice President in case Agnew should resign. Until that time, Rockefeller had never had any interest in being Vice President; but Watergate created a unique situation, and Rockefeller made a new assessment: Taking Agnew's place would make him President if Nixon should resign—and if not, the Vice Presidency would put Rockefeller in the lead position for the Republican Presidential nomination in 1976.

Kissinger, a close friend, advised Rockefeller that he should not campaign for Agnew's job. Kissinger said Nixon had already made his choice—John Connally.

On Labor Day weekend Agnew came in to see the President in the Oval Office, and changed his story: He was being unjustly accused because he and his family had used campaign funds for travel and other expenses necessary for his public appearances. "I could see," Nixon noted, "that he was no longer as sure" a jury would find him innocent.

Nixon talked to Haig, and Haig turned the screw. With Buzhardt, Haig went to Agnew's office. They were there at the President's request, Buzhardt said, to advise the Vice President that Petersen and other Justice Department lawyers believed the evidence strong enough to convict the Vice President and send him to jail.

"I am *not* guilty," Agnew told them, and said he would take his case to the House of Representatives. With all the press accusations he would never get a fair trial in the courts, Agnew said, so he would take the risk of being impeached.

The President is opposed to that, Haig said. Furthermore, he added, "you could face both impeachment and indictment, the worst of both worlds. You should resign at once, Mr. Vice President."

"No!" Agnew said. "I refuse."

That night Haig and Buzhardt again went to see Agnew and his lawyers. Buzhardt began detailing the testimony that would be used against him in Court. At one point the argument became so acrimonious that Agnew left the room.

While he was gone, Best said: "What's the deal? What will you give me if he resigns? Let's cut out the bullshit and work something out." At the minimum, Best said, there must be an absolute guarantee that if Agnew should resign, he would not be prosecuted.

Later, alone with Agnew, Best told him what he had proposed. "Well," Agnew said wearily, "let's explore what terms we can get." Buzhardt made an offer: Jobs for his staff, an office for his transition, and Secret Service protection for six months.

Once he began bargaining, Agnew knew he must tell Judy, his wife. At home that evening, he told her the bad news. She fainted.

On September 13, John Connally met with President Nixon just before he set out on a campaign tour of the Republican Party he had just joined. Connally and Nixon had decided that the trip to win over party leaders would prepare the way for Nixon to nominate Connally as Vice President when Agnew resigned.

Just before Connally began the tour, Hal Bruno, senior political reporter for *Newsweek,* asked Connally: If Agnew resigns and Nixon offers you the Vice Presidency, will you take it?

"Yes," Connally said without hesitation, then added: "But only on my terms. That is, I would have the meaningful assignment of taking charge of the entire economic scene. Then I would ride into the 'seventy-six Convention as the Vice President who saved the economy."

A few days later, Agnew went to see Nixon. Agnew, Nixon observed, no longer "protested his complete innocence. Now he asked what I thought he should do, and talked poignantly about the problems of going away and starting a new life." That decision, Nixon told him, is one that only you can make. Agnew insisted he must put his case before the House, contending that he, like the President, was protected by the Constitution from being tried unless he had been impeached.

On September 15, Harlow and Garment went to Capitol Hill to see Minority Leader Ford and Minority Whip Les Arends. Harlow asked Ford if he, as Republican Leader, could arrange for Agnew to meet with Speaker Albert and other House Democrats on the impeachment question. Ford reluctantly accepted the assignment. To guard against any impropriety, Ford told Harlow and Garment that Agnew should put in writing a formal request for the meeting with Speaker Albert.

Two days later, Agnew told Best he would not plead guilty to any criminal charges but would consider a nolo contendere plea to one charge of underpaying his income tax. Richardson again insisted that Agnew must plead guilty to a felony. Agnew sent his lawyers back with his reply: No. Never.

On September 19, Haig went to Agnew's office to notify him officially that the Justice Department would proceed immediately to ask the grand jury for an indictment. When that happens, Haig said, "The President will call for your resignation."

Agnew was not sure that Haig was speaking for the President or for himself. "I want to talk to the President," Agnew said to Haig. "I insist upon seeing him now."

When he saw Nixon the next day, Agnew said that Richardson was trying to force him to admit to crimes he had not committed, and he wanted to fight on. "Will you support me?" Agnew asked.

Nixon was slow to answer. "You must do what is best for you and your family," he said.

Agnew proposed a deal: "I would be willing to resign and plead nolo contendere to a tax misdemeanor to end this whole miserable business."

As soon as Agnew left, Nixon sent word to Richardson that Agnew might negotiate but that the terms must not be unduly harsh.

Talks resumed. "No jail," Agnew's lawyers insisted. Richardson was not ready to make that commitment.

On Friday, September 21, Buzhardt reported to Nixon that he thought Best and Richardson were close to agreement. Agnew had agreed to consider the terms over the weekend and let them know on Monday. "I think it is just about over," Buzhardt told the President.

On Saturday morning two leaks to the press killed the deal. *The Washington Post* reported that Agnew was plea bargaining. CBS reporter Fred Graham broadcast that Petersen had given colleagues in the Justice Department his opinion of the case against Agnew: "We've got the evidence. We've got it cold."

Irate, and feeling betrayed, Agnew charged that the prosecutors were leaking reports to weaken his position. Break off negotiations, he told his lawyers.

Three days later, Agnew told Nixon that he would take his case to the House.

Ford, at Harlow's request, arranged a meeting for Agnew in Speaker Albert's office. Ford was accompanied by Arends; Albert had summoned O'Neill and Peter Rodino, Chairman of the House Judiciary Committee.

When all were seated, Ford opened the discussion cautiously: "The Vice President wanted to consult with you. You have agreed, and now I'm going to let him carry the ball."

Calmly, in a matter-of-fact voice, Agnew explained his predicament: The press, some in Congress, and some in the Nixon White House were trying to force him out of office on false charges. His lawyers advised him that a Vice President must be impeached before he could be charged with a crime. He had come to the House leadership, he said, to ask that the House inquire into the charges against him and determine whether he should be impeached.

Albert and the Democratic leaders, who would make the decision, listened to Agnew but made no commitment. When Agnew left, O'Neill told the Speaker: "I don't like Agnew's idea. His case is already in the courts, and that's where it belongs." Rodino also opposed any move by the House to become involved in the Agnew investigation. Ford told Albert in confidence that he opposed Agnew's attempt to divert the charges against him. Soon after the meeting ended, Richardson telephoned Albert to let him know, before the House reached any decision, that the evidence against Agnew was going to the grand jury that day. Richardson said he expected that Agnew would be indicted.

On the following day, Speaker Albert announced that the House would not intervene in the Agnew case.

For Agnew, the options were shrinking; but he was still full of fight. Scheduled to speak to the National Federation of Republican Women in California on September 29, Agnew looked over the routine prepared remarks as he flew west on *Air Force Two*. Suddenly he threw the draft aside, and decided he would tell these Republicans, and anyone else who wanted to listen, exactly how he felt. All the anger, frustration, disappointment, betrayal—he would let it all out.

Winging the speech, Agnew delivered a ringing denial of all the accusations against him. He charged that he was the victim of witnesses who told lies to the prosecutors to save their own skins. He accused the Justice Department of using him to regain its reputation after bungling the Watergate investigation. The audience loved it. They jumped to their feet to cheer, and roared their delight at his promise: "I will not resign if indicted." Over the noise he shouted again: "I will not resign if indicted."

Stirred by these ardent Republicans, believing he had found support at last, Agnew resolved to "carry my fight all the way to final victory or defeat. . . . I dare the Justice Department to do its worst—take the case to the grand jury, try to get an indictment, and then try to take me to trial."

To Haig, the Agnew speech was outrageous. The charges of Justice Department bungling of the Watergate investigation seemed to strike at Nixon himself. Haig called the President at Camp David to let him know that Agnew had launched a counterattack.

Nixon was concerned but preoccupied. He was there on the mountain listening to White House tapes with Rose Mary Woods. She had served as Nixon's loyal and confidential secretary since "the boss," as she called him, was in Congress. Over the years of total devotion to his personal and political advancement, she had become not just close to the Nixon family, but almost one of them. Woods was one person Nixon was sure he could always trust, and so the two of them had gone to Camp David to find out whether the White House tapes that were being subpoenaed by Judge Sirica would exonerate him or convict him.

With Nixon committed to saving himself, and events making it less and less certain that the President could survive, Haig knew that he and he alone must force the Vice President to resign. Haig summoned General Mike Dunn, the Vice President's national security assistant and Haig's comrade from the battlefields of Korea and Vietnam.

As soon as Dunn walked in, he was forcibly struck by the gravity of Haig's words and manner. Haig quickly got to the point: "The President needs your help, Mike." He told Dunn the evidence against the Vice President was incontrovertible. The prosecutors, he said, have "an ironclad case for conviction."

"What do you want the Vice President to do?" Dunn asked.

"Resign," Haig said, and added that if Agnew admitted guilt on the tax charge, there would be no further prosecution. "He can go like a gentleman, and there will be no durance vile, and we will set it up so that it goes easily for him.

"Or," and Haig paused, "he can stand and fight and it will be no holds barred. And there will be no safety net." Once he is indicted, Haig said, "it can and will get nasty and dirty."

Dunn said the Vice President told him he was not guilty, and he accepted Agnew's word. "Should I leave the Vice President's staff?"

"No, the President needs you there," Haig said. "We need someone close to the Vice President to give him this message: 'Guilt will be the verdict in court.'"

For an hour Haig went over with Dunn the evidence against Agnew, the burden of Watergate, the plight of the President, the need to preserve the Constitutional process, the danger of having the man next in line of Presidential succession on trial.

Haig had one final message that he wanted Dunn to give to Agnew. He told Dunn to take this warning "from General Haig" in exactly these words:

"The President has a lot of power—don't forget that."

When Haig ended, General Dunn promised to do his best, as both a friend of the Vice President and as an Army officer ordered to carry out a mission for the Commander in Chief.

Dunn hurried back to see Agnew, who was about to leave to make a speech in Chicago. Both suspected that Agnew's office was bugged, so Dunn suggested they talk in the corridor. For half an hour Agnew and Dunn—the Vice President and his national security adviser—walked around and around the second-floor corridor of the EOB, talking quietly.

Dunn relayed General Haig's explicit warning: "The President has a lot of power—don't forget that." Agnew listened in silence. "They are tough cookies," Dunn said. "Their minds are made up. You want it easy, or you want it hard. You've got a family to think about. You've got yourself to think about. You make the decision, but I would encourage you to decide very soon. The time is running out of the glass. The last few sands are on their way down."

"I've got to think about it," Agnew told Dunn, as they paced the corridor. "I've got to think about it. It is a tough decision. I do not want to resign. But I've got a family, a lot of considerations."

"I could tell that he was very shaken by what I was telling him," Dunn said. "I was his friend; he knew that. And I remained his friend. Haig was being the bad cop, and he played that role with aplomb and even relish. I was the good cop. I was also being a good soldier; the President needed this done."

When the Vice President left to take his plane to Chicago, he couldn't shake Haig's threatening words: ". . . Nasty and dirty. . . . The President has a lot of power—don't forget that."

"His remark sent a chill through my body," Agnew wrote. He thought about secret sessions of the National Security Council he had attended, and the sinister methods of the CIA. "I feared for my life," Agnew said. "If a decision had been made to eliminate me—through an automobile accident, a fake suicide, or whatever—the order would not have been traced back to the White House any more than the 'get Castro' orders were ever traced to their source." Agnew had no doubt that if necessary, Haig could arrange to have him killed.

Haig's warning convinced Agnew that he must resign. "There was one thing and only one thing that brought me back to the bargaining table with the prosecutors: Mr. Nixon's threat, relayed by Haig, that things would 'get nasty and dirty' unless I resigned at once." Agnew sent his lawyers back to negotiate with the prosecutors.

With Agnew almost ready to make his deal and resign, President Nixon called in Bryce Harlow and Mel Laird to tell them that he intended to nominate Connally as Vice President. Nixon wanted Harlow and Laird to help him get Connally confirmed in the House and Senate.

"Mr. President," Laird said, "we cannot get Connally confirmed. It will be a disaster."

"Well, I disagree with you," the President said. "Connally is the best qualified, and he is my choice."

Laird and Harlow agreed Connally was qualified. But they both pointed out, as forcefully as they dared, that the nomination of Connally would exacerbate the antagonism over Watergate that already threatened the President with impeachment.

Nixon was unmoved; he wanted Connally.

"Mr. President," Harlow said, "look at it from John Connally's future. If he is rejected by Congress in the confirmation process, it would end his political career."

"We cannot help," Laird said flatly. "It is an impossible assignment."

The President was adamant.

"Would you talk to the leaders of the Senate and House, both parties, before you make your decision?" Laird said. "We'll get them in here to talk to you."

Nixon agreed, but first he sent Laird, Harlow, and other White House assistants to Capitol Hill to assess the prospects for the confirmation of Connally.

Tom Korologos, Nixon's best emissary to the Senate, went up to talk to Senator Robert Byrd, the Deputy Majority Leader and a partisan Democrat who would either be a strong ally or fearful opponent. He caught up with him by the Ohio Clock, the baronial ornament that stands in the privileged lobby just south of the Senate Chamber.

Could John Connally be confirmed by the Senate for Vice President? Korologos asked him.

Byrd waved his arm toward the polished mahogany doors leading directly to the Senate floor, and said: "Tom, tell my friend Dick Nixon that if he sends Connally's name to the Senate, blood will be running out from under that Senate door."

The message to Nixon from the House of Representatives, delivered from Speaker Albert through Harlow, was less vivid but no less firm. "Bryce," Albert said, "the Democrats in the House don't think much of Connally changing his colors. The House will not confirm Connally, and you can tell the President that."

If the House could make the choice, Albert told Harlow, it would be Jerry Ford.

Confronted by the reality that Connally could not be confirmed in either the House or the Senate, Nixon finally conceded. "I had Haig call Connally again and tell him that, while he still remained my first choice, I was very seriously concerned whether he could survive a confirmation battle."

Connally, who had opened an office in the Mayflower Hotel to await his nomination, told Haig he understood. Connally said he had been told by Democratic friends that he could not be confirmed.

On Saturday, October 6, the eve of Yom Kippur, the most holy Day of Atonement in the Jewish calendar, Egypt and Syria attacked Israel on two fronts. The invasion was encouraged and armed by the USSR, and the United States was backing Israel with ammunition and planes. In the heat of the battle, the United States and the USSR risked a direct confrontation.

The crisis in the Middle East made it all the more imperative that Agnew resign, Richardson decided. On Sunday morning, the day after the Yom Kippur invasion began, Richardson met with Beall and his Baltimore team to work out the final details of the deal for Agnew's resignation.

Beall's prosecutors insisted that Agnew must go to trial or at least plead guilty to a felony. With war threatening, Richardson said, a long trial of the Vice President was unthinkable. The first priority, Richardson said, "is to get that guy out of here!"

Finally the two sides agreed, and met secretly with Federal Judge Walter Hoffman in a Virginia motel to review the deal: Vice President Agnew agreed to resign and plead nolo contendere to the felony charge that he had not paid taxes. The Attorney General would file with the Court a detailed account of all the charges against Agnew. In a statement to the Court Richardson would then say the public interest was best served not by prosecuting the Vice President but by his resignation.

For three days the prosecutors worked day and night to prepare a forty-page document detailing the evidence that Agnew was guilty of bribery and extortion. Among the charges:

- Agnew, as Governor of Maryland, arranged for Bud Hammerman to solicit cash payments from engineering firms to which Agnew awarded state contracts, with Agnew deciding the split—50 percent for himself, 25 percent for Hammerman, and 25 percent for Wolff, the roads commissioner. Wolff provided detailed records of the dates, amounts and sources of the money he received under the scheme.
- Allen Green, head of an engineering firm, agreed to make regular payments to Governor Agnew for state contracts, and delivered envelopes containing two thousand dollars to three thousand dollars to Agnew six to nine times a year. Green continued to pay Agnew after he became Vice President—eight thousand dollars a year in 1969 and 1970; six thousand dollars a year in 1971 and 1972. Green's last payment was "during the Christmas season in December of 1972." They were discontinued only after Green learned of the U.S. Attorney's investigation.
- Matz gave twenty thousand dollars in cash in a manila envelope to Agnew in the Governor's office for contracts to his engineering firm. After Agnew became Vice President, Matz paid him in cash in the Vice President's EOB office—one payment of ten thousand dollars, one of five thousand dollars, one of two thousand, five hundred dollars.

Altogether, the payments to Agnew totaled more than one hundred thousand dollars, and were made over the span of six years. Vice President Agnew accepted the last envelope of cash in his office in the White House.

In his statement to the Court, Richardson put on the public record the balance of interests he considered in making his historic bargain: Sworn evidence justified "an indictment charging bribery and extortion against the Vice President," Richardson said, but the prolonged trial of the man next in line to the Presidency could have "disastrous consequences to vital interests of the United States."

Agnew claimed he was innocent of all the charges except the one he did not contest, but conceded that his indictment, trial, and possible impeachment "would seriously prejudice the national interest."

Judge Hoffman, in accepting Agnew's plea and Richardson's bargain, said it was time to bring an end "to this tragic event in history."

The resignation took effect at 2:05 P.M. on October 10, 1973. At that moment an attorney for Agnew presented to Secretary of State Kissinger in the White House a document that stated:

Dear Mr. Secretary:

   I hereby resign the office of Vice President of the United States, effective immediately.

Sincerely,

Spiro T. Agnew

   Secretary Kissinger handed Agnew's resignation to an assistant to make copies, which are in the National Archives. The original disappeared. It has never been found.

On his final full day as Vice President, Agnew met for the last time with President Nixon in the Oval Office. As Agnew said good-bye, tears filled his eyes, and Nixon gave him a pat on the back in sympathy. Agnew felt the President's hand on his back and thought—"incongruously," he put it—that Nixon was pushing him out the door.

12

THE CHOICE

On the morning of October 10, 1973, Jerry Ford was in his Capitol Office getting ready for the opening of the House session when General Haig called from the White House. The President would like to see him, Haig said.

Ford walked down the stairs to the carriage entrance and got into his black Lincoln sedan. His driver, Dick Frazier, pulled out into the traffic on Independence Avenue for the two-and-a-half-mile drive to the Southwest gate of the White House. It was a beautiful October day, sunny, in the 60s; and the oaks and elms on Capitol Hill were beginning to turn into the russet and gold of a Potomac autumn.

During his ten-minute ride, Ford wondered why the President wanted to see him, and guessed that Nixon probably wanted to update him on the Yom Kippur War or talk about a particular bill pending in the House. As he entered the West Wing, a White House aide advised him the President would meet him in his hideaway in the EOB, and escorted Ford across West Executive Avenue to Room 175. When Ford walked into Nixon's private office, he found him in a sport coat, tie, and slacks, sitting in a comfortable chair with his feet propped on an ottoman, and smoking a pipe.

"Mr. President," Ford said, "seldom if ever have I seen you smoke a pipe."

"Well, Jerry," Nixon said, "I do it when I'm alone, or want to relax, or I'm talking to someone like you—an old friend."

Ford took the other big chair in the office and lit his own pipe, and the two men began to talk. Nixon asked about Betty and the Ford children; Ford asked about Pat Nixon and their daughters. "He was completely relaxed, probably the most relaxed of any time I saw him while he was President," Ford said.

Then the President got to the point. "Jerry, we've got a serious problem. The Vice President is in serious difficulty."

Ford nodded, and listened, puffing at his pipe. Nixon said that Agnew, as Baltimore County executive, had taken cash payments from contractors doing business with the county, and had continued the practice as Governor of Maryland. Worse than that, Nixon said, he had learned from Attorney General Richardson that Agnew had accepted cash payments in the Vice President's office in the very building in which Nixon and Ford were talking. Richardson, the President continued, had worked out a plea bargain with Agnew, his lawyers, and the Court: If Agnew would resign, he would not be prosecuted. Ford continued to smoke his pipe, listening, and asking a question every now and then. He thought to himself that someone had been derelict in not investigating Agnew's finances before he was nominated in 1968, and before he was renominated in 1972. But Ford did not mention his thoughts.

The longer Nixon talked about Agnew and his troubles, the more puzzled Ford became. Why, he wondered, is the President taking so much of his time to tell me about this? Ford got up once to leave, but Nixon waved him back to the chair. Perhaps Nixon was just lonely, needed to tell his troubles to somebody, and was easing his burden in a comfortable and candid talk with an old political friend and ally.

The President was still talking when Ford got a message about an upcoming vote in the House, and Nixon let him go. As Ford rode back to the Capitol, he remained puzzled about why Nixon would spend all that time talking to him about Agnew. When Frazier pulled into the carriage entrance, Ford walked onto the House floor and took his seat in the Minority Leader's chair.

Moments later, a fellow Republican from Michigan, Elford Cederberg, dashed from the Republican cloak room and clapped Ford on the back. "Have you heard?"

"What?" Ford said.

"Agnew resigned," Cederberg said.

Suddenly Ford understood—Nixon was considering him for Vice President and had been making a fresh judgment of his old friend, measuring Ford's political and personal loyalty.

* * *

Joe Waggoner, the leader of Southern conservative Democrats in the House, was in his office when he heard that Agnew had resigned. Waggoner walked immediately to the House floor to find Ford. "Jerry," he said, "how would you like to be Vice President?" Ford stroked his chin for a moment and said, "Well, Joe, it would be a good way to end my political career."

"I'm going to call the President and tell him what I think he ought to do," Waggoner said. Ford paused, looked Waggoner in the eye, and said: "Go ahead."

As soon as Agnew resigned, the President called in the leaders of Congress, as he had promised Laird and Harlow. Senate Minority Leader Hugh Scott and House Minority Leader Ford were first to meet with Nixon. He told them he had already studied the Twenty-fifth Amendment and would move promptly to nominate a Vice President.

For Ford, his second visit with Nixon in a few hours was particularly interesting. In Scott's presence, nothing was said of their earlier discussion. Ford guessed he might be on a list of possibilities for Vice President; but even if he were, he did not expect to be chosen. He believed that Nixon would judge him to be a greater asset in the House.

The President told Ford and Scott that he wanted to poll all Republicans in the House and Senate, and asked them to have each Member submit three names, ranked in order, for the nomination. Nixon said he would also ask George Bush, Chairman of the Republican National Committee, to collect recommendations from all members of the RNC.

All these secret recommendations, Nixon said, explaining the rules for his political game, were to be delivered personally by Ford, Scott, and Bush no later than 6:00 P.M. the next day to Rose Mary Woods at the White House. Woods would personally deliver them to the President.

An hour after Ford and Scott left the Oval Office, Speaker Carl Albert and Senate Majority Leader Mike Mansfield were ushered in. As Laird and Harlow had insisted, Nixon had invited the Democratic Leaders in to get their views on the best candidates for Vice President.

The three men had much in common. All three had served together in the House of Representatives a quarter of a century earlier. Each knew the character, strengths, weaknesses, and passions of the others. In political philosophy they differed strongly; in their dedication to public life and to the profession of politics, they were joined. Each of the three had reached the pinnacle of his ambition from hard beginnings.

Mansfield, the oldest, was seventy. Laconic and wise, Mansfield was as slender and angular as a billboard cowboy. His sharp eyes and aquiline face suggested the visage of a golden eagle. First elected to the Senate in 1952, Mansfield's cool judgment and legislative skill so impressed the Senate mules—Richard Russell, Lister Hill, James Eastland, Harry Byrd, and John Stennis—that they selected him for the path to leadership. When Lyndon Johnson was elected Majority Leader in 1955, he wanted to choose his own deputy; but the collective of higher powers in the Senate said, in effect: No, Lyndon, you need a balance wheel, and we have decided on Mansfield. When Johnson became Vice President, Mansfield became the Senate Majority Leader by acclamation.

Speaker Albert, like Majority Leader Mansfield, never sought power in Congress, but gained it by impressing others with his own dedication and integrity. "A little giant," his classmates had described him in his high school yearbook, and Albert was proud of the nickname. He was broad of beam and stood only five feet two, but he towered over other men in the House of Representatives by combining an amiable disposition, a scholarly mind, the mastery of procedure, and a storehouse of knowledge about how members voted and why.

Albert first came to the House in 1947, in the freshman class that included John Kennedy and Richard Nixon. Albert's diligence in studying the process and getting to know the Members impressed Sam Rayburn, whose Texas district sprawled along the Red River just south of Albert's. Rayburn brought Albert into his daily whiskey-and-branch-water gathering, and placed him on the House leadership track; fifty-seven years after he decided as a boy to be a Congressman, Carl Albert was elected Speaker of the House.

Ambition, determination, and chance brought Nixon, Albert, and Mansfield to command great power in the American democracy. An uncommon event—the resignation of the Vice President—brought them to the Oval Office of the White House to make the choice that changed history.

The President quickly got down to the business at hand. "The Vice President has resigned, and under the Twenty-fifth Amendment it is my responsibility to nominate a Vice President," Nixon said. He paused and turned to the Speaker.

"Carl, are you interested in it?" the President asked.

Albert assumed the question was rhetorical: Either the President was just trying to be gracious, or he was testing Albert's feelings about being next in line of succession to the Presidency.

"No, Mr. President," Albert said. "Not at all. I came to Washington to be a Congressman."

"Well," Nixon said, "is there somebody who you think would be a good choice?"

"No," Albert said, "that's your job, Mr. President."

Mansfield spoke up. "I do. I can name two persons that I think you should consider. One is Senator John Sherman Cooper, and the other is your former Secretary of State, Bill Rogers. Either one of those would be qualified."

Albert thought, "Mike is very opinionated on some things, and those two persons are close to his thinking, especially on Vietnam." So Albert decided to name his own choice.

"Well," Albert said, "if Mike is going to make a suggestion, I'm going to make a suggestion."

"Who is that?" the President asked. "Jerry Ford?"

"Yes, sir, Jerry Ford," Albert said. "I can tell you something, Mr. President. He would be the easiest man that I know of to confirm in the House of Representatives. There won't be any question in my mind but that he would be confirmed. And it would not be a long, drawn-out matter either."

The President looked at Mansfield. "I think Ford would be a good choice," Mansfield said, "but the decision is yours, Mr. President."

Or was it? The President had asked for their advice; once given, once the two Democratic leaders identified the one man who could be confirmed in both the House and the Senate, Nixon was in no position to nominate anyone else.

"We gave Nixon no choice but Ford," Albert said after the meeting. "Congress made Jerry Ford President."

After Albert and Mansfield left the Oval Office, Laird and Harlow went in to see the President.

"How do you know Ford would accept?" Nixon asked.

"I will sound him out and let you know," Laird said. "But I am sure he would. I know we can get Ford through both the House and Senate, and, Mr. President, we need to get this over with."

Nixon looked at Harlow. "Mr. President, I agree with Mel. We need to get this over with."

After his second trip to the White House that day, Ford rushed back to the House to vote for a bill he strongly supported, Home Rule for Washington.

Back in his Capitol office, he talked over the Agnew resignation with Hartmann. "It's really sad about Agnew," Ford said. "Why do these guys think they can get away with it? He could have made twice that much honestly— well, legally anyhow—practicing law. I just wonder how much more of this the country can take."

At home in Alexandria, Ford sat down for a quiet drink with his wife and talked over the day's events. "Poor Judy," Betty Ford said, referring to Mrs. Agnew. Mrs. Ford did not know her well, but the wives of men in public life are bonded by common ties of neglect; each knows she takes second place to the mistress of politics.

As the Fords watched the late news together, Laird telephoned. After the briefest of courtesies, he said: "Jerry, if you were asked, would you accept the Vice Presidential nomination?"

In the afternoon Ford had guessed his name might be on a list to be considered; Laird's call required a serious answer.

"Mel," Ford said, "let me talk to Betty, and I'll call you back."

"Let me talk to Betty." For the twenty, five years of their marriage, Jerry Ford had been saying those five words before he made any major political decision. He respected her mind, trusted her instincts, and believed her conscience infallible. She had opinions and expressed them; but once his decision was made, she supported him. Her loyalty was total.

Ford wondered if he would even like the job. "I don't know if I want to leave the action of being Republican leader in the House for a job that is largely ceremonial and has no impact on legislation," he said to his wife. "Would I be happy working at such a slow pace?"

"I don't know how it would affect the children," Mrs. Ford said. Mike, 23 and the oldest, was in Gordon Conwell Seminary; Jack, 21, was studying forestry at Utah State; Steve, 17, was in his senior year of public high school; and Susan, 16, was at Holton Arms. Not one, they agreed, would like being watched by the Secret Service.

On the other hand, the President and the Republican Party that Ford had served so loyally would be according him a high honor. "Since I'm not ever going to be Speaker, it would be a nice cap for my career," Ford said.

"Well, Jerry," she said, "it would be an honor, and recognition of your long service to the party and the country." Both agreed that serving as Vice President for the balance of the Nixon term would fit very well with Ford's plans to retire from politics in January 1977.

The decisive element for Ford was that the President was asking him to consider it, and Ford had never turned down a major assignment from any

President, Republican or Democratic. After two hours of weighing the pros and cons, Ford and his wife agreed—first, that the President was not likely to ask him, and second, that if he should, Ford would accept.

Late that night, Ford telephoned Laird. "Mel," Ford said, "Betty and I have talked about it and agreed that if I am asked, I will accept. I'll do whatever the President wants me to do, but I am not going to do anything to stimulate a campaign. I'm not promoting myself. Betty and I have already made plans for our future. As you know, I'm getting out of politics in January of 'seventy-seven anyway; and we are happy with what we have already decided to do."

"I understand," Laird said. "I don't know what's going to happen. I just wanted to check."

Laird called President Nixon. "I talked to Jerry, and he talked to Betty, and Jerry will accept," Laird told Nixon. "You should also know that Jerry promised Betty he will get out of politics in January nineteen seventy-seven."

When Laird put down the phone, he was sure that Nixon would nominate Ford.

On the next morning the President invited the Democratic and Republican leaders of Congress to meet with him to discuss the procedures for the nomination and confirmation of a new Vice President. In front of all the other leaders from the Hill, the President said casually, "I'd like to be in the shape with the American public that Jerry Ford is."

Ford thought it was just Presidential small talk, and not significant.

President Nixon had not asked the American people for their suggestions, but they sent their own nominees anyway: Mamie Eisenhower suggested William Rogers. John Wayne telegraphed from California: ". . . the most untarnished and honorable American in politics . . . Ronald Reagan." Henry Salvatori, a member of Reagan's kitchen cabinet, telephoned his message: "Governor Rockefeller would serve the country's best interests." Frank Fitzsimmons, head of the Teamsters, wired: "John Connally."

In the first quick count of telegrams that reached the White House, Barry Goldwater got 293 votes, Ronald Reagan 106, John Connally 45, Nelson Rockefeller 31, and Howard Baker 23.

As instructed by the President, Scott, Ford, and Bush marched down to the White House and gave the ballots they had collected to Rose Mary Woods. The Senate, as usual, had no consensus. Rockefeller got six votes,

Goldwater five, Connally four, and Reagan four. Bob Dole, aware that no secret keeps in Washington, covered his flanks by sending in eight names that he took care to list alphabetically—Ann Armstrong, Ed Brooke, Connally, Goldwater, Reagan, Rockefeller, Rogers, and Don Rumsfeld.

In the House of Representatives, it was Ford by a landslide. From liberal Pete McCloskey to conservative John Rousselot, California was for Ford. The New Yorkers—Jack Kemp, Barber Conable, Frank Horton, Henry Smith, Bob McEwen, Ben Gilman, Ham Fish, Don Mitchell, Carleton King—chose Ford. Michigan was unanimous for Ford. He was the first choice of the other big Republican delegations from Illinois, Pennsylvania, Ohio, New Jersey, and Indiana. Except for Texas, which voted for Connally, Bush, or Ann Armstrong, the South chose Ford. He led in the Northeast, the West—William Armstrong of Colorado wrote in longhand one word to the President: "Ford." Ford himself recommended, in order, Connally, Laird, Rockefeller, and Reagan.

George Bush tallied his poll of 142 members of the Republican National Committee and sent the results to Nixon: Rockefeller, 30 votes; Connally, 27 votes; Goldwater, 22 votes; Reagan, 17 votes; Bush, 15 votes; Ford, 4 votes.

In her "eyes only" memo to the President, Rose Mary Woods summarized the choices and—unaware that Nixon had already decided that Connally could not be confirmed—included "a few comments" in opposition to Connally. Senator Robert Taft, Jr., said he "would find great difficulty in supporting Connally." Conservative Senator James Buckley warned that "on both the Democratic and Republican side there will be disposition to probe maliciously and extensively into the special interest affiliations of John Connally. [It] could be disastrous." A Democrat on the Watergate Committee, Senator Dan Inouye, warned Nixon: It "would be a major error to nominate John Connally—not because he is disqualified but because many on the Democratic side would be determined to destroy Connally."

The President's own staff offered their choices: Ray Price, the craftsman of Nixon's most thoughtful speeches, made the case for William Rogers. "He's a symbol of integrity and decency . . . a firm supporter of your foreign policies . . . a man of genuine stature . . . his loyalty to you has been proven."

Patrick Buchanan, the President's conservative theoretician, put the arguments for Ford in one crisp page:

A) First, he is a strong, tough individual, if not brilliant, whose foreign and defense policy views mirror those of the President.
B) Secondly, he has the capacity, the integrity, to be a good President, should something happen.

C) His choice would unite the GOP, not divide it as would the selection of Rockefeller, Reagan or JBC . . .

D) Ford . . . could work the Republican vein on behalf of the President . . .

E) The choice of Ford would not disserve the constituency that chose the President last fall; it would be consistent with the national mandate given last November.

To make his choice, Nixon isolated himself on the mountaintop at Camp David. In his study at Aspen Lodge, he wrote down four criteria: The man must be qualified to be President, a close supporter of his own domestic and foreign policies, loyal, and confirmable by Congress. Then Nixon read through the polls and comments and concluded that first place was a tie between Rockefeller and Reagan. Connally was third, Ford was fourth. "Ford, however, was first choice among members of Congress," Nixon said, "and they were the ones who would have to approve the man I nominated."

The decisive factor in Nixon's calculations was getting his choice confirmed by Congress. "Ford," he said, "met all four of the criteria I had established but was without question the front-runner when it came to the key qualification of confirmability. . . . In view of my own weak political position at that time, confirmability had to be a major consideration in my decision.

"Personal factors enter into such a decision," Nixon said. "I knew all of the final four personally and had great respect for each one of them, but I had known Jerry Ford longer and better than any of the rest. We had served in Congress together. I had often campaigned for him in his district. In 1962 when ABC invited Alger Hiss to appear on a special entitled, 'The Political Obituary of Richard Nixon,' Jerry Ford appeared on my behalf. One factor which particularly demonstrated to me that he had outstanding leadership qualifications was the indispensable role he played in getting support for our controversial family assistance program, which passed the House but then, unfortunately, was rejected by the Senate."

On Nixon's political scorecard, Ford ended up with the most points. "No one of these incidents was the decisive factor which led to my selection of Jerry Ford for Vice President," Nixon said, "but taken together what they added up to was that he was my oldest and closest friend of the four finalists, that he shared my views on domestic as well as foreign policy issues, that he was willing to step up to making tough decisions on unpopular issues, and that he above all could be counted upon to be a team player. Some of the others among the final four met most of these tests, but Ford's confirmability gave him an edge which the others could not match and was the decisive factor in my final decision."

In Nixon's mind, he was naming the man likely to be the next President. The noose of Watergate was closing. Congress had already turned against him. The American people were turning against him. His popular support, according to Gallup, had dropped to 27 percent and was still going down; two thirds of the public believed that their President was somehow involved in the Watergate crime.

"By the time I selected Ford," Nixon said, "my approval rating had sharply declined and while I was still determined to fight as hard as possible to serve out the balance of my term, I felt that as a political realist there was at least a fifty percent chance that Ford might become President."

Thus Nixon acknowledged his dread of the consequences of Watergate ten months before he was forced to resign.

At Camp David, in the stillness of that sunny October morning in 1973, the oaks and shagbark hickories were changing to crimson and gold as President Nixon prepared to return to the White House. His decision was made, but he wanted one commitment from Ford. The President's helicopter put him back on the White House lawn at 8:31 A.M. Nixon went directly to the Oval Office, told Haig he wanted to see Ford and Scott, and directed Ziegler to arrange for television coverage for his announcement at 9:00 P.M. that evening.

Haig telephoned Ford and asked him to see the President at 11:00 A.M. "Hugh Scott was coming too, so we assumed it was some legislative problem to discuss," Ford said. "But when we got there, Haig took Scott in first and asked me to wait. This was unusual."

To Scott, the President said, "I cannot select you for Vice President because you are my Leader in the Senate, and because [Pennsylvania] Governor Shapp would appoint a Democrat to your seat."

After they talked for a few minutes, Scott asked: "Does this apply to Jerry Ford?" The President hesitated. Scott was renowned for the accuracy of the notes he took at White House meetings, and for his willingness to share those notes with favorite reporters.

"Yes," Nixon said to Scott.

Scott left, and Ford came in alone. After a brief comment about the tragedy of Agnew, Nixon said: "I'm going to nominate you for Vice President. I believe you can be confirmed. You and I have been friends for a long time, and I feel very comfortable with your voting record and your leadership. But there is one thing I want you to know. Come 'seventy-six, I am going to campaign to nominate John Connally to be President."

"Mr. President, that's no problem for me," Ford said. "I have no further political ambitions. Betty and I decided some time ago that I would run one more time in nineteen hundred and seventy-four, and then quit. I made a firm commitment to Betty to be out of politics come January nineteen hundred and seventy-seven. And as a matter of fact, I think John Connally would be a first-class candidate. I told him, oh, four or five months ago, when he was in Palm Springs for a golf tournament, that I thought he would make a good candidate for President, and if he decided to run, I might be willing to help him."

Ford had spoken the magic words; he too would support Connally in 1976.

The President appeared to be delighted; Ford had confirmed what Laird had said, that he would retire from politics in 1976. In minutes the President and his nominee had reached an understanding: Nixon and Ford would support Connally for President in 1976.

Nixon went on to say that he wanted Ford, after his confirmation, to focus on domestic affairs, energy problems, and Republican politics; and he was counting on him to help in dealing with Congress.

"That sounds fine to me," Ford said.

They talked on for almost forty minutes, until Nixon summoned Haig to discuss the arrangements for the announcement that evening. Nixon concluded by telling Ford to say nothing to anyone, not even to Betty, and that he would call them at home that evening to give them both the good news.

As Ford stood to leave, the President called in his official photographer, Ollie Atkins. Beaming with pride, Nixon said: "Come on in, Ollie. Take the picture and make history."

Riding back to the Capitol, Ford reflected on Nixon's zeal to put Connally in the White House. "I don't know what Nixon's reaction would have been if I had said, 'Well, Mr. President, if I am Vice President, I would want to be a candidate for President.' I don't know whether he would have changed his mind."

By the time Ford reached his office, Scott had already told his fellow Senators and the press, "It is not going to be Jerry Ford." Scott's speculation hit the UPI wire. Ford said nothing to his staff or to his wife. But he closed his office door, picked up a desk pen, and began writing his acceptance speech. He finished in fifteen minutes, folded the two pages, and put them in the inside pocket of his coat.

He shared his secret with no one; but when he arrived home at 6:30 P.M., unusually early for him, Betty suspected something was up.

"Do you know who the President is going to nominate?" she asked.

"The only thing I know," he said, suppressing a smile, "is that the President is going to telephone his choice soon."

At 7:00 P.M. the unlisted phone in the Fords' bedroom rang. Susan Ford answered it. "Dad, the White House is calling."

Ford bounded upstairs, took the receiver, and heard Haig say, "The President wants to talk to you."

"Jerry," the President said, "I want you to be the Vice President, and I think Betty ought to hear what I'm telling you."

Ford told the President that his unlisted number had no extension, and asked: "Can you hang up and call back on the other number?"

A few moments of silence, and the other phone rang. This time Betty Ford also heard the President say, "Jerry, I want you to be the Vice President."

"I didn't know whether to say thank you or not," Mrs. Ford said. As soon as they got off the phone with Nixon, Ford told Betty of his commitment to the President that morning, that he would finish out the Vice President's term and retire from politics on January 20, 1977.

Two hours later the President put on a show in the East Room of the White House for an overflow crowd—the Cabinet, the leaders and committee powers of Congress, White House staff—and for live, prime-time network television. In his nominating speech, Nixon began with the kind of bloviating usually heard only on the convention platform: "We face great dangers, but also . . . very great opportunities. . . . more Americans have better jobs at higher wages . . ." The reason for the occasion, Agnew's felony and forced resignation, was not mentioned; but Nixon struck a glancing blow at the Watergate investigation: "It is vital that we turn away from the obsessions of the past and turn to the great challenges of the future."

Like an old-time convention orator, Nixon said his nominee "is a man who has served for twenty-five years in the House of Representatives with great distinction." All eyes turned to Jerry Ford, and the room burst into applause. "Ladies and gentlemen," the President admonished, pretending to be stern, "please don't be premature. There are several here who have served twenty-five years in the House."

The President picked up the text again: "He is a man also who has been unwavering in his support of the policies that brought peace with honor for

America in Vietnam. . . . And above all, he is a man who, if the responsibilities of the great office I hold should fall upon him . . . we could all say, the leadership of America is in good hands. Our distinguished guests and my fellow Americans, I proudly present to you . . . Congressman Gerald Ford of Michigan."

The enthusiasm of the response in the East Room was convincing; for this Congressional audience, Ford was manifestly the right choice.

Ford came to the stage, took his speech from his coat pocket, and for a moment seemed unable to speak. Finally, he found his voice:

"Mr. President, I am deeply honored and I am extremely grateful and I am terribly humble. But I pledge to you, and I pledge to my colleagues in the Congress, and I pledge to the American people, that to the best of my ability—if confirmed by my colleagues in the Congress—that I will do my utmost to the best of my ability to serve this country well and to perform those duties that will be my new assignment as effectively and as efficiently and with as much accomplishment as possible . . .

"It seems to me that we want, in America, a united America. I hope I have some assets that might be helpful in working with the Congress in doing what I can throughout our country to make America a united America. I pledge to you my full efforts, and I pledge the same to my colleagues and to the American people. Thank you very much."

The words were standard-model Ford—dutiful, modest, redundant, promising only what he could deliver: "The best of my ability."

At a White House reception to honor the nominee, Nixon's Secretary of Housing and Urban Development, the cheerfully voluble James Lynn, struck up a conversation with House Minority Leader O'Neill. "Tip," Lynn said, "what do you think of this? History is being made. The Twenty-fifth Amendment is being enacted for the first time. I bet we'll never see another night like this one."

"No," O'Neill said, "not for another eight months."

Lynn was shocked, and thought O'Neill was just displaying his Democratic partisanship.

After their evening in the spotlight, the Vice President–designate and Mrs. Ford left for their home in Alexandria, under guard by the Secret Service for the first time. On the way Ford reflected on the curious nature of the occasion, and on Nixon's failure to mention why he had to nominate a new Vice President. "The ceremony was oddly exuberant," he said to Betty. "It had all the trappings and the hoopla of a political convention."

To Ford, it did not seem right to celebrate another man's tragedy. He had defeated political opponents, in Michigan and in the House; but he had never before been promoted because another man was destroyed. At home he found a message from Agnew, who had telephoned to congratulate him and wish him well.

Ford called Agnew to thank him. To Agnew, Ford said: "I want you to know how sorry I am that events worked out this way."

13

IMPEACH!

On Saturday, the first day of his new life, the Vice President-to-be rose before dawn as usual, took his morning swim, and went to his office in the Capitol. The House and Senate were in special session to receive his nomination; Capitol newspaper and telephone reporters were waiting, en masse, for his first press conference since the nomination.

Ford was relaxed, matter-of-fact. He promised a full disclosure of his assets, tax returns, everything. Asked about future Presidential ambitions, he replied: "Let me say, as emphatically and as strongly as I can, I have no intention of being a candidate for any office, President, Vice President, or anything else, in nineteen hundred and seventy-six."

When Ford walked onto the House floor, members rose for a spontaneous ovation; it was both friendship for the man and pride of the clan. For the first time since Roosevelt picked Speaker John Nance Garner in 1932, a Member of the House had been nominated for Vice President.

To open the morning session, House Chaplain Edward Latch, reflecting the higher thoughts of his fold, quoted from a poem by Josiah Gilbert Holland:

> *God give us men! A time like this demands*
> *Strong minds, great hearts, true faith, and ready hands;*
> *Men whom the lust of office does not kill;*
> *Men whom the spoils of office cannot buy;*
> *Men who possess opinions and a will;*
> *Men who have honor, men who will not lie.*

The chaplain ended his prayer: "God bless Jerry Ford. Amen."

At 10:05 Speaker Albert recognized Ronald Geisler, a White House messenger, standing at the rear of the House chamber. He walked halfway down the aisle, bowed once to the Speaker, and said: "I am directed by the President of the United States to deliver to the House of Representatives a message in writing."

The House clerk, standing at the dais, read the unprecedented text:

To the Congress of the United States:

Pursuant to the provisions of Section 2 of the 25th Amendment of the Constitution of the United States, I hereby nominate Gerald R. Ford of Michigan to be Vice President of the United States.

> Richard Nixon
> The White House
> Oct. 13, 1973.

Again the House Members stood and applauded as their colleague, pleased but calm about his overnight fame, sat at the Leader's desk on the Republican side of the Chamber. Peter Rodino, the chairman of the House Judiciary Committee that would investigate his qualifications and consider the nomination, came over to shake Ford's hand.

A House page came up to Ford: Haig was calling. The President wanted his new partner to come down to the White House for a photo opportunity and a national security briefing from Secretary of State Kissinger.

Ford obliged. At the White House the forced jollity with the President for the cameras was over quickly. Ford listened intently as Kissinger reported on Israel's war against Egypt and Syria, and the delivery of U.S. aid to Israel.

After the high-strategy session, Ford returned directly to the simpler life of being the Congressman from the Fifth District of Michigan. As he had for twenty-five years, Ford flew to Grand Rapids and drove twenty miles north to march in the annual Cedar Springs Red Flannel Day. This was a rite of October in the bustling village of 1,800 souls that boasted of being the world center for manufacturing red flannel underwear and nightgowns.

Cedar Springs, Michigan, was "Our Town," middle class, middle income, middle America, Congressman Ford's kind of community. It was the America that works hard, values thrift and enterprise, goes to church, supports the public schools, and pays its bills. Leading the parade came the high school band; Ford walked all five blocks of the town's main street, greeting old friends by their first names, and moved almost to tears by the earnest warmth of their blessings.

In an interview for his hometown newspaper, *The Grand Rapids Press,* Ford said he had accepted the Vice Presidency as the capstone of his political career. Again he said: "I have no intention of running for any political office in 1976." He said he was ready to be tested under the terms of the Twenty-fifth Amendment, which he had supported after the Kennedy assassination. He told a reporter that the House and Senate should undertake a rigorous examination of his character as a man and his qualifications for Vice President. "I really think to protect themselves and for my own benefit, they ought to make sure my record is one that they approve," Ford said. "I wouldn't want a cursory examination."

There is irony in the first day of the Nixon-Ford partnership: Ford was free in the friendly crowd of his beloved Michigan homeland, prepared to open his record to the most critical examination by his peers and the public. Nixon was imprisoned and alone, bound by the tapes of his own creation, hiding in fear with the evidence of his guilt, and beset by an international crisis—War in the Middle East.

After Kissinger's briefing, Nixon returned to his highest priority—defending himself against Watergate. Twenty-four hours earlier the U.S. Circuit Court of Appeals had ruled 5-2 (the majority all Democratic appointees, the minority Republican) that the President must surrender to Judge Sirica the tapes of nine Presidential conversations about Watergate.

Nixon had refused to permit even his own lawyers to hear the tapes, and for good reason. He had listened, and heard enough to know that the tapes showed he ordered the cover-up. The tapes were evidence against himself: There was own voice, telling Haldeman to use the CIA to stop the FBI investigation, at another point telling Dean to buy the silence of witnesses.

The tapes, Nixon knew, would end his Presidency. It was too late to destroy them. It would be fatal to permit Garment or Buzhardt to hear them; they could be obligated to report the new evidence to the Court. Nixon had no choice but to keep the tapes under his personal control in the White House, to fight as long and as hard as he could to prevent Judge Sirica or anyone else from hearing them.

Buzhardt, who had begun to suspect what might be on the tapes, laid out the options for Nixon: He could reject the Circuit Court decision, try to negotiate through his attorneys with Cox, withdraw the matter from any further Court consideration on the basis of separation of powers, or fire Cox. All options were dangerous, Buzhardt advised Nixon, but firing Cox was clearly the "most dangerous."

Buzhardt, in his six months as Haig's lawyer, had also taken over as chief legal counsel to Nixon on Watergate. Nixon liked and trusted the quiet, stooped, and doleful Buzhardt. He was a prodigious worker, and Nixon had him deal with Ervin and Sirica on the tapes, and with Agnew on the plea bargain. To other Nixon staff members, Buzhardt was a self-contained, consummate White House operative. "Fred," Jerry Jones said, "sought the shadows and left no tracks."

On the mountain at Camp David, the October sun warmed the winding pathways through the woods and clearings. Inside Aspen Lodge, Nixon was at work, jotting notes on a yellow pad, trying to decide what to do about the Court order to give up the tapes. Beyond the legal problem, immense as it was, Nixon saw the peril of public opinion turning against him. For a discussion with Haig and Ziegler, he noted: "We must not kid ourselves. . . . Both Gallup and Harris show our support going down from 38 [in August] to 32, and in Harris the number [in favor] of resignation rising to 31, with 56 opposed. Aren't we in a losing battle with the media despite the personal efforts I have made . . . ? Are we facing the fact that the public attitudes may have hardened to the point that we can't change them?"

A refusal to comply with the Court order and give up the White House tapes would cost him further in public support, Nixon thought, and for that he blamed his newest arch-enemy, Cox. If Nixon accepted the Court of Appeals order and delivered the nine tapes, it would only encourage Cox to subpoena more tapes, and ever more tapes. "Firing him seemed to be the only way to rid the administration of the partisan viper we had planted in our bosom," Nixon noted.

Out of this impulse to attack, Nixon wrote out a two-part plan: First, he would have Richardson dismiss Cox and put the Watergate investigation in the hands of the Justice Department. That would stop any future subpoenas for more tapes. Second, Nixon would not defy the Court order but circumvent it. He would agree to provide summaries, not transcripts, of the nine tapes that Judge Sirica and the Court of Appeals had ordered him to give up.

In this new Nixon scenario, a trusted few in the White House would listen to the tapes, draft summaries, and submit them for review and verification to Senator John Stennis, an aging conservative Democrat and former Mississippi judge who commanded wide respect on Capitol Hill.

On Sunday morning Nixon flew from Camp David to Washington and invited Stennis to his White House worship service to sound him out. Stennis, not realizing that Nixon was using him to conceal evidence from the Court, agreed to be part of Nixon's plan.

Speaker Albert had assured President Nixon that Jerry Ford would be promptly confirmed. But Albert had spoken too quickly. On the first day of House business after the Ford nomination was received, Albert faced a new problem. A faction of House Democrats saw in Nixon's weakness and Agnew's resignation an opportunity to seize the Presidency.

"Get off your goddamned ass, and we can take this Presidency." In the language of the New York City hard-hats and shopkeepers she represented in the House, Bella Abzug confronted Albert in his office just off the House floor. Abzug, a talented lawyer who entered any room with the subtlety of a subway train, towered over the five-foot-two-inch Speaker and outweighed him by thirty-five pounds. Punching Albert in the chest to emphasize her points, Abzug said: "Why in the hell are you going to let those bastards keep this? We can get control and keep control."

Abzug, and a score or more other Democrats of the aggressive left, were plotting a coup: The House would refuse to confirm Ford as Vice President and impeach Nixon. Then Speaker Albert, as next in line of Presidential succession, would become President Albert—and the Democrats would get control of the White House and all the power of the Federal government.

Using *The New York Times* op-ed page to advance her cause, Abzug argued: "Under the Succession Act of 1947, we already have an elected official designated to replace the President in the absence of a Vice President. The Speaker of the House is just as well qualified to stand around and wait as is House Minority Leader Ford. . . . Does anyone seriously think that the American people would select Gerald Ford as their President, if they had a choice?"

Turning the Twenty-fifth Amendment on its head, Abzug said, "Only after the House Judiciary Committee [decides] whether a bill of impeachment should be returned against the President would it be proper for the committee to take up the question of who shall be Vice President."

Delay of Ford's confirmation was the strategy. Joseph Moakley, a Massachusetts Democrat, and ten colleagues petitioned the House to take no action on Ford until Nixon released his tapes to Judge Sirica. Jerome Waldie, a far-left California Democrat and member of the Judiciary Committee, argued for postponing action on Ford until the Supreme Court ruled on the tapes.

Speaker Albert did not like being Nixon's potential successor. Every political and social move of his busy life was shadowed by Secret Service agents, and he wanted nothing more than to extricate himself from being next in line for Presidential succession.

"I didn't even give a thought to trying to get the job," Albert said. "I knew what I would do if something should happen to President Nixon, but I gave no thought to trying to become President. I knew the House as a whole would not be party to any Democratic attempt to take over the government, as some wanted. The Republicans had been elected to the White House, and so far as I was concerned, that was the way it was going to be."

The vehemence of the stop-the-confirmation faction reached Congressman Peter Rodino as well. As chairman of the Judiciary Committee, Rodino would manage Ford's confirmation—and his committee would also handle any resolution to impeach the President. "There was pressure, heavy pressure, to get me to delay the confirmation so that if we went ahead with impeaching Nixon there would be a vacancy, and the Democratic Speaker would take over," Rodino said. He talked with Albert about the machinations that could turn into a Constitutional coup. "Taking over the Presidency was the furthest thing from the Speaker's mind," Rodino said. "He wanted no part of that at all."

Albert told Rodino to push his committee for quick action on Ford. "Move," Albert told Rodino. "Move as fast as you can. Proceed in a proper way, but move as fast as you can."

Abzug and the takeover faction of Democrats insisted that the issue be brought before the full party caucus of the House. In their closed session, Rodino took the podium to appeal to the better nature of the majority of Democrats: "How wrong it would be for us to go down the road that some are advocating," he said to his fellow Democrats. "We must not stand in the way of the Constitutional process. The responsible thing for us to do is to proceed with the confirmation."

Rodino won the argument, but at a price. He agreed to delay the start of confirmation hearings until the full-field investigation by the Federal Bureau of Investigation of Gerald Ford was complete. This would keep Albert next in line to the Presidency for at least another month.

As Albert and Rodino maneuvered to put down the Abzug rebellion, a new crisis began at the opposite end of Pennsylvania Avenue. On Monday morning President Nixon told Haig to order Attorney General Richardson to fire Special Prosecutor Cox. Haig could have been forthright in approaching Richardson; instead, for reasons never explained, Haig deceived Richardson. To lure him to the White House, he telephoned and said that the President needed the Attorney General's help with the Middle East crisis. Could Richardson come to the White House right away? When Richardson arrived, Haig told him that the President was not available; he would meet with Haig and Buzhardt.

Haig opened the discussion by briefing Richardson on the confrontation between the United States and the USSR in the Middle East war. "I'm ready to go, Al," Richardson said. "Shall I go home and pack my bag?"

No, Haig said, you can best help with the Middle East situation by resolving the President's legal problems with Judge Sirica and Cox over the Watergate tapes. The President had a new plan, Haig said. He would submit to Judge Sirica not the subpoenaed tapes but his own edited transcripts of the tapes. And the President wanted Richardson to dismiss Cox. With Cox gone, Buzhardt added gratuitously, the case would be moot; there would be no special prosecutor to subpoena more tapes.

To Richardson, the summons to the White House was so false, and the ruse to deal with the subpoenas so clumsy, that he was deeply offended. Moreover, Richardson said, if the President fires Cox, "I will have to resign." In words chosen with great care, he pointed out that he had committed to the Senate that Cox would be removed from office only "for extraordinary improprieties." There had been none, Richardson said, thus there was no just reason to dismiss Cox. With that, Richardson returned to his office.

Nixon, who had not found the courage to face his Attorney General and order him to fire Cox, was alarmed when Haig told him of Richardson's reaction. "Richardson's resignation was something we wanted to avoid at all costs," Nixon said. He told Haig to try to persuade Richardson to sell Cox on the Stennis plan, but Cox must agree to subpoena no more tapes.

Richardson did try to persuade Cox "to go along" with the Stennis proposal; but Cox refused, in writing. In a memorandum to Richardson, Cox said he could not accept the President's limits on his right to hear and present to the Court any White House tapes that might be evidence to Watergate crimes.

Richardson recalled Nixon's public promise to him five months earlier— "absolute authority to make all decisions bearing upon the prosecution of the Watergate case . . . to pursue this case wherever it leads." The President's promise was not being kept. At home that evening, Richardson picked up a yellow legal pad and wrote at the top: "Why I Must Resign." As he put on paper a brief of the elements of his decision, Richardson noted, "I am in fact loyal to the President, and I am by temperament a team player." But, he concluded, he was no longer "as independent as I should be" to serve as Attorney General.

On Friday Richardson went to the White House to deliver his resignation to the President, but Haig intercepted him. Maybe, Haig said, the White House should go ahead with the Stennis plan, and that—Haig added hopefully—would incite Cox to resign. Thus Richardson would be spared from firing Cox. Again Richardson talked with Cox, then telephoned Haig to say that Cox would not resign.

Nixon, upon learning of Cox's position, concluded that further negotiations were useless. He told Haig to have the White House press office issue a Nixon statement announcing the Stennis plan and ordering Cox to ask for no more tapes, documents, or White House memoranda.

Cox immediately called reporters to his office and responded: "I cannot be a party to such an agreement." Would he resign? a reporter asked. "No," Cox said. "Hell, no!"

Later, in a press conference on Saturday afternoon, Cox reiterated his refusal to accept the Presidential order. "It is my duty as special prosecutor," he said, to tell the Court that the President is not complying with the Court order. In fact, Cox said, he might ask the Court to hold the President "guilty of contempt" if he continued to refuse to turn over the nine subpoenaed tapes.

To Nixon, Cox's defiance was an unacceptable challenge. "I thought that Cox had deliberately exceeded his authority," Nixon wrote. "I felt that he was trying to get me personally, and I wanted him out."

Haig telephoned Richardson with the President's order: Fire Cox.

"I can't do that," Richardson said, and asked to see the President immediately to offer his resignation.

An hour later Haig called Richardson and asked him to come to the White House. Haig brought him up to date on the Middle East crisis, and told him of Kissinger's meetings with Brezhnev in Moscow to try to end the crisis. Haig cautioned Richardson that his resignation might signal to the Russians a weakness within the Nixon government, and asked him to delay his resignation until the crisis was over.

Richardson said he could not. Haig took him in to the Oval Office. "It was an emotional meeting," Nixon wrote. "I told him how serious I thought the next days were going to be with respect to the situation in the Mideast, and I repeated Haig's arguments in a personal appeal to him to delay his resignation in order not to trigger a domestic crisis at such a critical time for us abroad."

Richardson was moved. "The hardest part was having to refuse his urgent appeal to delay my resignation until the Middle East crisis had abated," Richardson said. But he had been promised independence when he accepted the responsibility of Attorney General, Richardson said, and he had assured the Senate, before he was confirmed, that he and Cox would be independent in investigating and prosecuting Watergate. If he could not keep that commitment, Richardson said to Nixon, "I feel that I have no choice but to go forward with this."

Nixon responded angrily: "Be it on your head. I am sorry that you feel that you have to act on the basis of a purely personal commitment rather than the national interest."

"I am acting on the basis of the national interest as I see it," Richardson said firmly.

"Your perception of the national interest is so different from mine," Nixon replied.

Richardson left the Oval Office and returned to his Justice Department office to tell his staff.

Haig telephoned William Ruckleshaus, Deputy Attorney General, and told him he was giving an order from the President: Fire Cox.

With the Middle East in crisis, Ruckleshaus replied, why not wait a week?

"No," Haig said. "Your Commander in Chief has given you an order. You have no alternative."

"Other than to resign," Ruckleshaus replied.

If Ruckleshaus felt that way, Haig suggested, he could fire Cox and resign a week later.

"If you really are determined to get rid of Cox," Ruckleshaus said, "I think Bork may be your man."

Haig asked Ruckleshaus to put Solicitor General Robert Bork on the phone. Bork, as third ranking officer of the Justice Department, agreed to take over as Acting Attorney General and fire Cox. Haig sent Garment and Buzhardt over in a White House car to bring Bork to the White House. In the Oval Office the President signed an order appointing Bork Acting Attorney General, and Bork signed a two paragraph letter dismissing Cox as Special Prosecutor.

At 8:25 P.M. on Saturday, October 20, Ziegler called in the White House press corps and delivered four bulletins: Cox was fired. Richardson resigned. Ruckleshaus, at Nixon's insistence, was not allowed to resign but dismissed. The office of the Special Prosecutor was abolished.

Within the hour FBI agents entered the offices of Cox and his staff to stop them if they tried to remove any files. Henry Ruth, deputy to Cox, told the press the FBI would not even let him take out a letter from his wife.

The story hit the wires, broke open the front pages of Sunday newspapers, and interrupted broadcasts. NBC correspondent John Chancellor was just sitting down for dinner in New York City. "I heard the news and rushed off to NBC, unbidden and unfed," Chancellor said. "The newsroom at Thirty Rock was filling up with volunteers when I arrived—and around ten that evening, to our surprise, wives began to arrive with sandwiches and coffee for hungry husbands. The firing of Cox had touched a nerve."

In an NBC news special that evening, Chancellor solemnly told his audience: "The country tonight is in the midst of what may be the most serious Constitutional crisis in its history."

To the Washington press corps, the firing of Cox, the resignation of Richardson, and the dismissal of Ruckleshaus became the "Saturday Night Massacre." But the real victim of the massacre was President Nixon himself. By law, by precedent, and by Supreme Court rulings, every President has the power to dismiss an appointee without warning or explanation. But on that Saturday night, Nixon's legal right was not the point.

In the newsrooms that shape American public opinion, Nixon's strike against the Department of Justice seemed infamous and menacing, worse than Watergate itself. To reporters, Watergate was a mystery, an intriguing detective story. But this was murder on Constitution Avenue, with Dick Nixon the bad guy in the black hat shooting the good guys in the back.

In damage to President Nixon, the decapitation of the Justice Department was a disaster.

Inside the White House, Nixon ordered an immediate survey to assess the reaction of Congress to the Massacre. He was worried that a majority of the House might be ready to vote to impeach him. He was less concerned about the Senate; he did not believe that two thirds of the Senate was ready to convict him. But he could not be sure of that either.

To find out, Bill Timmons, Nixon's chief of Congressional Relations, put his entire staff to work on Sunday, calling members in their districts and home states through the long Columbus Day weekend. By Monday Timmons had a report ready for Haig and the President. "There is not sufficient support in the House to impeach the President or in the Senate to convict him," Timmons wrote in a confidential memorandum. Of forty-six Republican and Democratic senators Timmons and his team reached, thirty-six supported the President, and ten opposed him. Of the seventy-two members of the House they canvassed, sixty-two stood with the President and ten were opposed. But Timmons added a significant caution: "The public is in shock and the media in the states are extremely critical of the President. These are influencing members of Congress."

The Timmons memorandum was the first White House count of votes on impeachment.

House Majority Leader Tip O'Neill spent all day Sunday and Monday taking calls from his fellow Democrats. "All we talked about was impeachment," O'Neill said. The chairman of the House Republican Conference, John Anderson, listened to his colleagues and his Democratic friends and predicted, "Impeachment resolutions are going to be raining down like hailstones."

Asked by the press for his view on why Nixon had taken such drastic action against Cox, Richardson, and Ruckleshaus, Senator Robert Byrd, deputy leader of the Senate Democrats, said there was "no way to avoid the assumption" that the President was trying to conceal evidence on the tapes.

When Ford heard the news of the firings, he was appalled at what Nixon had done, and baffled by why he did it. "I assumed the President was innocent," Ford said. "He had told me so. I assumed no documents would prove otherwise. But if he was innocent, then he would have no problem in furnishing the documents, and it was dumb politically not to do so. I felt he should have turned over the documents rather than precipitate a crisis like he did."

Haig telephoned Ford to explain what had happened. Nixon, Haig said, was angry and resentful, and blamed Richardson and Ruckleshaus for letting him down during an international crisis. Ford told Haig that he was concerned that the incident would turn public opinion, and Congress, against the President. Haig replied that Cox had to be fired to sustain the principle of Executive Privilege and protect the confidentiality of Presidential papers.

Privately Ford began to wonder if Nixon had some other reason to withhold the tapes. "If Nixon were not innocent, if he knew the documents that Cox wanted would tighten the noose, I could see why he wanted to fire Cox."

But in public Ford felt compelled to defend Nixon. He told reporters: "The President had no other choice. Mr. Cox refused to accept the compromise issue."

The resignation of Richardson and the firing of Cox and Ruckleshaus escalated from news bulletin to national crisis. Twelve House members attending a North Atlantic Assembly meeting in Ankara left in midsession to fly home, stopping only for fuel. Western Union lines into Washington were jammed. The Capitol switchboard called in extra telephone operators to deal with angry constituents. Within days, three million Americans telephoned, wired, or wrote their Representatives in protest; Capitol Hill had never before experienced such a popular outcry.

Speaker Albert could see the storm coming, could see that he would face the most demanding test of his public life. "To that point I carefully had kept the House clear of any investigation of the President," Albert said. But after the Massacre at Justice, Albert saw Nixon in a new light. Nixon fired Cox, Albert reasoned, "to conceal evidence." If that were true, Albert thought, "impeachment was a possibility. Its consideration was the House's duty. How to manage it responsibly required the Speaker's decision."

Albert would need an ally to guarantee a deliberate and orderly process; by an irony of circumstance, Albert would turn for support to the Republican Leader of the House, Gerald Ford. The two men—one next in line to succeed the President and the other the nominee to become next in line—conferred in Albert's office to make certain that the House would not vote in anger to impeach the President. The House must act, there was no escaping that; but it fell to Albert and Ford to see that Members acted not in haste but with judgment and a minimum of partisanship. Thus Albert and Ford sought to keep in office a President one or the other might succeed.

"I knew there was wild opposition to what Nixon had done, regardless of his legal right to do it," Albert said. "I knew Nixon was in trouble. If someone could find a way to bring impeachment to a vote on the House floor that first day, it might pass." Albert and Ford agreed—first, that they would use their power as Leaders to block any vote by the full House on impeachment; second, that the Speaker would reject the proposal by some Democrats that he appoint an anti-Nixon committee to consider impeachment; and third, that Ford and his Republicans would vote with all the Democrats that the Speaker could muster to put all impeachment resolutions in the hands of Rodino and his Judiciary Committee. "Whatever the committee decision," Albert said, "no one could claim it had been rigged."

Ford left the Speaker's office, met with the Republican leaders of the House, and got their agreement on the procedure.

By 10:00 A.M. Albert was ready. On Tuesday morning, October 23, 1973, as he stepped to the rostrum to gavel the House of Representatives into session, a score of members were waiting in line to introduce Resolutions of Impeachment of the President of the United States.

All day long they spoke, in anger, rage, sorrow, bitterness, and conviction. Clarence Long of Maryland said his district had voted three to one for Nixon as President; now his telephone calls were five to one for impeachment. Donald Riegle, of Michigan, said: "The President . . . has disgraced his country and himself." Herman Badillo, of New York, said, "It is ironic that the man who campaigned [for law and order] has now become the nation's number one lawbreaker and obstructor of justice." The issue, said Lloyd Meeds of Washington, is "whether the Nation should continue under a President who believes himself above the law." Ken Hechler, of West Virginia, said, "Entirely too much emphasis has been placed on 'the tapes,' when the fundamental issue is whether the President is obstructing justice." Louis Stokes, of Cleveland, Ohio, expressed what many believed: "This country is in mortal danger." Jonathan Bingham, of New York City, put it simply: "The President has given us no alternative but to go ahead with impeachment proceedings." Margaret Heckler, a Massachusetts Republican, used a variation of the Nixon 1972 campaign slogan: "Now, more than ever, we need . . . to get to the bottom of these crimes." Her Democratic colleague, Patsy Mink of Hawaii, spoke in sorrow: "President Nixon has broken the people's trust both in him and in the office of the Presidency."

Thomas "Lud" Ashley, of Ohio, whose great-grandfather introduced the impeachment bill against President Andrew Johnson, took the floor to say, "That resolution of impeachment failed, as it should have, because it was introduced by my great-grandfather for purely partisan reasons." But today, Ashley said, President Nixon "has given us no alternative."

In his office near the House floor, Albert listened to the speeches. "We in the House must examine the President," he wrote, "and the American people will examine the House of Representatives." Convinced that the will of the House was to go forward toward impeachment, Albert walked onto the floor, took the Speaker's Chair, and announced that he was directing Chairman Rodino and the House Judiciary Committee to begin a formal inquiry into grounds for the impeachment of President Nixon.

"I did not put it to a vote," the Speaker said. "I did not ask for advice. But I knew that no decision I could ever make would be more significant for my country."

Speaker Albert's decision shattered the last legal barrier against disclosure of the Nixon tapes. Under the Constitution, the House may claim the absolute right to examine any evidence against any Federal official under investigation for impeachment, including the President of the United States.

*　　*　　*

Isolated in the White House, Nixon realized his mistake. "Although I had been prepared for a major and adverse reaction to Cox's firing," Nixon wrote, "I was taken by surprise by the ferocious intensity of the reaction that actually occurred. For the first time I recognized the depth of the impact Watergate had been having on America. . . . My actions were the result of serious miscalculation." Of all the miscalculations Nixon made to cover up Watergate, none had greater consequences than the Saturday Night Massacre.

To the President's dismay, Acting Attorney General Robert Bork took the position that a new Special Prosecutor must be appointed to continue the investigation of Watergate crimes. Public opinion backed up Bork, and Nixon was forced to yield. And with popular feeling so strongly against him, Nixon could not risk the gambit of sending the Court his own edited transcripts of the tapes. On Tuesday, October 23, Nixon sent his lawyer into Judge Sirica's Court to announce that the President would abide by the Appeals Court ruling and turn over the nine tapes to Sirica.

In the end Nixon lost his battle with Cox, lost the tapes, and lost the confidence of the American people. With the Saturday Night Massacre, Nixon made it certain that the House would act to impeach him.

But first, Albert and the Democratic leaders in Congress decided, they must confirm Ford as Vice President.

14

PASSAGE

To be confirmed as Vice President under the new Twenty-fifth Amendment, Gerald Ford bared his life. Not only was he willing to cooperate with the Congressional investigation of his personal history and public career; he welcomed it. "I have no apprehension about anything they might find," Ford said. "I want them to see that I am as clean as a whistle." He called in Bob Hartmann and other close advisers. "Hold nothing back," Ford told them. "Anything they want, if we have it, give it to them. I don't want any papers from the files destroyed, or hidden, or doctored up. We are not going to cover up anything, and we are not going to stonewall."

With that, he opened an unlocked drawer of his desk in his Capitol office, pulled out his check stubs for ten years, his income tax returns, copies of the reports he had filed every two years on campaign contributions and expenditures, and tossed them on the desk. "This will do for a start," Ford said. "Anything looks funny, ask me about it."

To assist the investigators, Ford told his lawyer, his accountant, his banker, his doctor, his peers in the House, his personal friends, and his brothers to put everything on the record. He asked every public official who had ever dealt with him, in his Congressional District and throughout the state of Michigan, to make those dealings public. Ford directed every department and agency of the Federal government in Washington to reveal everything he had ever asked anyone to do for a constituent. He authorized full investigations by the Federal Bureau of Investigation, by the Internal Revenue Service, and by investigators for the House and Senate Committees that would examine his fitness to be Vice President.

And thorough the investigation of Ford was. The FBI assigned 350 agents to the job. They questioned his childhood friends, his parents' friends, his teachers in elementary school and in Sunday school. Federal agents examined Ford's record in the Boy Scouts, talked to his football coaches, his teammates, and members of the teams he played against. They interviewed his college classmates, his fraternity brothers, his professors at Yale Law School. They searched out Navy officers and seamen who had served with Ford in the Pacific during World War II. They talked to the supporters and opponents of his political campaigns, looking for any skulduggery or dirty politics.

Ford authorized an FBI examination of his bank accounts, one managed for House members by the Sergeant at Arms and the other at the National Bank of Washington. He opened to scrutiny the personal bank accounts of his two children still at home, Steve, 17, and Susan, 16.

Seventy FBI agents went to Grand Rapids to conduct interviews, and right away Ford's old friends began calling his office to let him know the questions they were asking. To all his callers Ford said: "Tell them the truth. Give them everything."

The IRS audited Ford's tax returns for the previous seven years, and matched the figures with every check he had written during that time. Then the Joint Congressional Committee for Internal Revenue Taxation reviewed the IRS audits.

The IRS found one mistake: Ford had deducted as a business expense two suits he had bought to spruce up his appearance for the 1972 Republican National Convention. IRS disallowed the deduction and Ford sent the IRS a check for $435.77.

The staff of the Library of Congress searched through twenty-five years of the *Congressional Record* to find every speech, comment, and vote by Ford, and to establish from that record Ford's political philosophy. Thousands of votes and speeches by Ford in the House showed a clear, consistent, and predictable public man. Dr. Joseph Gorman, the Library of Congress historian who organized the study, opened the 144-page summary with a telling observation about Ford—his position on Federal budget policy: "From the earliest days of his Congressional career, Congressman Ford can be placed with the reasonably balanced budget school of fiscal policy. Virtually without deviation, he has favored reducing spending and balancing the budget. He has resisted increasing the share of the public sector at the expense of the private and frequently has advocated cutting taxes within the structures of a balanced budget." Gorman had expressed the central theme of Ford's political career. In addition, the Library staff went through twenty-five years of *The New York*

Times and *The Grand Rapids Press* and copied every story that mentioned Ford from his first day in Congress.

House and Senate staff investigators combed through the financial records of every one of Ford's thirteen campaigns for the House, looking for any improper or illegal political contribution or expenditure. They looked at his medical records, talked to his doctors, and matched the medical deductions on his tax returns. His doctors reported the nominee to be in excellent physical condition for a man of sixty, or even fewer years.

Other Congressional investigators tracked down every Federal government contract of more than fifty thousand dollars awarded in Ford's district during his twenty-five years of public service to see if any could be connected to political or personal gain. They found none. They talked to the Grand Rapids police, the Kent County Sheriff and the Michigan state police; Ford had no police record. They talked to the Grand Rapids Bar Association, the Michigan Bar Association, and the American Bar Association. There were no complaints. They talked to members of the Warren Commission; his colleagues there commended Ford for his diligence and judgment. They searched the financial records of his stepfather's paint business; everything was in order.

Ford had served briefly on two corporate boards in Grand Rapids, Old Kent Bank and Rospatch; the FBI inspected the records of the companies and found nothing improper; Ford had attended every board meeting for which he had been paid.

Ford wrote George Bush, chairman of the Republican National Committee, and asked him to turn over to the FBI any records of his travel and work for the party that the FBI might want to inspect.

The FBI looked at his House payroll accounts to see if there had been any evidence of kickbacks or other improprieties; there were none. They read every weekly newsletter he had written to constituents, and checked, month by month, the allowance and expenditure of his House printing account. Everything was certified to be in order.

No American politician's public career and personal life had ever been scrutinized so fully. When the Congressional investigation ended, the FBI had interviewed more than one thousand persons about Ford and produced a report of 1,700 single-spaced pages. The FBI summary and the reports of the IRS, House, and Senate investigations were all turned over to Senator Howard Cannon, Chairman of the Senate Rules Committee, and Representative Rodino, Chairman of the House Judiciary Committee.

*   *   *

Cannon and Rodino and their committees had been selected by the bipartisan leaders of the Senate and House to consider all the facts, question Ford and other witnesses in public session, and vote a recommendation on whether Ford should be confirmed. Like Ford, Cannon and Rodino knew they carried a responsibility: This first use of the Twenty-fifth Amendment would set a strong precedent.

How Ford conducted himself as the nominee for Vice President, and how Congress managed his confirmation, would be scrutinized by a future President, a future Congress, and a future Supreme Court if the time should ever come when the Court would have to decide a controversy over Presidential succession.

Ford, Cannon, and Rodino also shared an unspoken but common purpose—to establish in the public mind a contrast: the openness of Ford and the Congressional process versus the secretive business going on at the Nixon White House.

A week before he was to testify before the Senate Rules Committee, Ford wrote Chairman Cannon to say, in essence, I've sent you everything, but let me know if you need anything else. "I am as anxious as any Member of the 93rd Congress to establish a sound precedent under the 25th Amendment to the Constitution," Ford wrote to Cannon. "Although this is a novel experience for me, and certainly unprecedented in history, I hope, as you do, that it will result in a greater public confidence in government."

The Senate took up Ford's nomination first, in part because the Senate was experienced in confirming Presidential appointments, but in greater part because some members of the House Judiciary Committee were determined to delay the hearings.

The most vociferous proponents of impeaching Nixon, a Committee faction that included Jerome Waldie, Elizabeth Holtzman, Charles Rangel, John Seiberling, John Conyers, Jr., and Robert Drinan, were also the most passionate advocates of delaying the confirmation of Ford. Every day or so they roughed up the Committee staff chief, Jerome Zeifman—a common practice when members of the House and Senate hesitate to criticize their Chairman—with demands that Zeifman try harder to find a way to block Ford's nomination.

"You should be chasing every nickel and dime in Ford's income tax records until you find something wrong," one Committee member told Zeifman. "You know that 95 percent of Americans cannot survive an intense tax audit, and you have got to find something on Ford."

"How did Ford buy that condo in Vail?" another asked Zeifman. "Who lent him the money? There's got to be something in that transaction we can question."

"Let's subpoena all the tapes of conversations between Nixon and Ford," a third Committee member suggested. "There must be something there we can use to get Ford."

In the House Dining Room one morning a group of the "fire eaters," as Zeifman called them, confronted Jack Brooks, the third ranking Democrat on the Committee. They asked Brooks to join their cause, or at least help them. Brooks, a plain-speaking Texan, fixed his colleagues with a cold, raptorial eye. "What you guys are trying to do," he said, "is half-assed, candy-ass foolish politics." Brooks, as acerbic a partisan as any Democrat alive, wanted to impeach Nixon as soon as possible. "Let's do what's right by the Lord," Brooks said. "We will confirm Ford. Now, as to Nixon: The son of a bitch committed high crimes and misdemeanors. Let's impeach the son of a bitch as soon as possible. But we will confirm Ford first. I've got to look my grandchildren in the eye and tell them I did what was right."

One morning in late October Speaker Albert brought Rodino and Zeifman into his office. "How is it going?" Albert asked.

Rodino briefed Albert on the progress of the investigation, and Zeifman said some members were still plotting to delay and ultimately block Ford's confirmation. "They are hell bent to find something on Ford, to nail him," Zeifman said, "and the longer it goes, the more furious they become."

"Well," Albert replied, "God forbid that Nixon should drop dead, or be impeached before we confirm Ford. Neither I nor any other Democrat who came into the Presidency in that way would be able to govern."

Outside the U.S. Senate, along the curving pathways and shaded lawns of the campuslike park east of the Capitol, the oaks and tulip poplars were crowned in bronze and ocher, and the nip of autumn was in the air. Inside, in Room 1202 of the Dirksen Senate Office Building, cameras and the umbilical cords of television seemed to be everywhere. With merry eyes and a quick smile, Betty Ford—beaming with pride—sat in the front row with Mrs. Roberta Hartmann, the wife of Ford's principal staff counselor.

At 10:05 A.M. on November 1, 1973, Congressman Gerald R. Ford took the witness chair before the Senate Committee on Rules and Administration and was sworn in. The nine Senators on the Committee dais looked as solemn as the witness.

They were all there, Chairman Howard Cannon said, to judge the qualifications of Ford to be Vice President. "But," he added, "if history is to instruct us, this committee should view its obligations as no less important than the selection of a potential President of the United States."

A stocky, rumpled, sixty-one-year-old former prosecutor from Las Vegas, Cannon had grown up on a Utah cattle ranch managed by his English father. He worked his way through the University of Arizona law school, learned to fly, and narrowly escaped capture by the German Army when his C-47 was shot down after he dropped paratroopers during the Allied invasion of Europe.

Cannon was in his first year as chairman of Senate Rules—the committee responsible for everything from assigning office space to Federal elections and Presidential succession, which was the premise for the committee's claim to the confirmation of a Vice President.

In his opening statement, Chairman Cannon took note of the fact that some of his fellow Democrats proposed "that the nomination of Mr. Ford be made hostage to the domestic political warfare currently under way," a euphemism for Nixon's three-front war against the courts, the prosecutors, and Congress. "We see no merit—but only danger—in such an approach," Cannon said.

Directing the Committee's attention to the confirmation of Ford, Cannon fixed the parameters: He should not be judged on his political philosophy or voting record. "The President has exercised his option to choose a man whose philosophy and politics are virtually identical to his own," he said. But the Committee must examine "his morals, his integrity, his financial history, and possible conflicts of interest. . . . This is the first time in the history of our country that any nominee for either of its two top posts has been subjected to such an exhaustive investigation."

Speaking slowly and deliberately, Cannon continued: "It is for the members of this committee to establish a precedent—a solid, Constitutional precedent—by pursuing an orderly, logical, thorough, and honest inquiry into the nominee's qualifications. . . . It behooves us to conduct these hearings as painstakingly, as fairly, and as honestly as is humanly possible so that the results will be accepted as just and honorable."

In the witness chair Ford waited. He had put on his best blue suit, and set it off with a silk foulard in a blue and white geometric pattern. His burly frame at ease, his eyes locked on each Senator who spoke, Ford listened carefully.

Thousands of hours Ford had himself spent questioning witnesses, so he knew the rules: Be attentive. Be respectful, and just a shade deferential. Never interrupt a Member of the House or Senate when he is speaking, whether he is making sense, rambling, or just showing off for the audience or the cameras. Focus hard on the question when it is asked. Make sure you understand it. Answer it briefly, courteously—and very carefully. If you differ, say so; but make it polite and brief. Never argue with a Senator or Congressman; you are certain to lose. You can stand on a principle, and you may be right; but never forget that the Member of Congress holds the power, for he has the vote.

In his opening remarks Ford said that in preparing for confirmation he had asked himself: What are my qualifications to be Vice President? What would I do in the job if I am confirmed? "My answer is that I believe I can be a ready conciliator and calm communicator between the White House and Capitol Hill," Ford said. Only one year earlier, he pointed out, the voters of the country simultaneously reelected President Nixon by a landslide and chose a Democratic House and Senate. By that split mandate, Ford suggested, the country expected its President and its Congress to work together.

Events had divided them, Ford said, and he wanted to help bridge the gulf that separated Congress and the President. "I believe I can do this, not because I know much about the Vice Presidency, but because I know both the Congress of the United States and the President of the United States as well and as intimately as anybody who has known both for a quarter century."

He recognized the gravity of President Nixon's conflict with Congress, and he understood Congress's mistrust of Nixon, but he saw himself as close to both. "I count most of the Members of the Senate and of the House as my friends," he said, but he also made it clear that he was loyal to Nixon. "The President of the United States has been my friend from the time he was a second-termer from California in the House, and took time to make a freshman from Michigan very welcome.

"He has always been truthful to me, as have my good friends in the Congress. I have never misled them when they might have wanted to hear something gentler than the truth. And if I change jobs, that is the way I intend to continue.

"Truth is the glue on the bond that holds government together, and not only government, but civilization itself. So gentlemen, I readily promise to answer your questions truthfully. I know you will not pull any punches. . . . Through my testimony, it is my intention to replace misunderstanding with understanding, and to substitute truths for untruth."

The words, carefully thought through and crafted beforehand, were meant to show that Ford was and would be his own man, that he was and would be different from President Nixon.

In his opening questions, Chairman Cannon emphasized that Congress, in considering Ford, was acting in place of the seventy-six million Americans who had voted in the 1972 Presidential election. With the House Judiciary Committee already considering the impeachment of President Nixon, Ford could become President, Cannon suggested. Yet, Cannon said, Ford's own philosophy and Congressional district were too conservative for him properly to represent all the American people.

Well, Ford replied, "I must differ with the interpretation of the political attitudes of the Fifth Congressional District in Michigan. It is, in my mind, a moderate electorate, and my own views are not as conservative as might have been in that regard. I consider myself a moderate, certainly on domestic affairs, conservative on fiscal affairs, but a very dyed-in-the-wool internationalist in foreign policy."

Ford conceded that he had never campaigned for national office, but added, in good humor, that he thought himself close enough to the mainstream that if he had, "I might have done at least fairly well." For the record, however, he wanted the committee and the country to know that he had "no intention of seeking any public office in nineteen seventy-six."

If everything goes well for three years, Senator Allen asked, "Do you think you might be subject to a draft?"

"Well," Ford said, "the answer is still 'no.' I have no intention to run, and I can foresee no circumstances where I would change my mind. I have no intention of seeking public office in nineteen seventy-six."

Next to question Ford was Senator Robert Byrd. The two had served together in the House, and Ford was ready for what he was sure would be Byrd's tough questions.

For Bob Byrd, the Senate was the pinnacle of life. By grit and tenacity he had struggled upward. An orphan in the grime of West Virginia's coal fields, Byrd worked his way through school, entered politics, and was elected to the House of Representatives. Driven to succeed, he put himself through Georgetown University Law School at night while serving in the House, and then moved to the calm and courtesies of the Senate. There he mastered the rules and process, built his support senator by senator, and waited for the chance to challenge the charming but dissolute Edward Kennedy for Deputy Minority Leader.

Byrd won. As an ally he was strong; in opposition he could be deadly. No Member came to a Senate session or a Senate hearing better prepared; none was better at interrogating a witness.

"On April 4, 1963," Byrd said to Ford, "you delivered a speech in the

House of Representatives on executive privilege." Reading from the *Congressional Record,* Byrd cited a statement that Ford made after President Kennedy's fiasco at the Bay of Pigs: "Executive privilege is most often used in opposition to the public interest."

Byrd looked at the witness: "Mr. Ford, the shoe is on the other foot now. Would you say that this statement still represents your thinking on this subject?"

"Yes, I would, Senator Byrd."

"Now, Mr. Ford, do you feel that executive privilege should be invoked by a Chief Executive, any Chief Executive, to avoid release of evidence when allegations of criminal conduct have been made with respect to the Presidential office itself?"

Byrd's reference to Nixon was obvious. Choosing his words carefully, Ford replied: "The judgment has to be based on what is in the best interest of the country. We certainly do not want any person who is a criminal to go free because of the refusal of any documents . . ."

"Is it your opinion," Byrd asked, "that withholding of information which may go to the commission of serious crimes is justified under any circumstances when ordered by a President?"

"At the moment, I cannot foresee any."

"Would not the concealment of such information constitute an obstruction of justice?" Byrd asked.

"In the normal context," Ford said, "I would say yes."

Would a President ever be justified in disobeying a court order? Byrd asked.

"I would strongly say," Ford replied, "any person, including the President, where a determination has been made by the highest court of the land, ought to obey a court order."

If Ford should become President, Byrd asked, would he ever withhold documents that a court had ordered him to hand over?

Months earlier, Ford replied, he had said publicly that President Nixon should turn over the Watergate documents and tapes to the court and to the Senate Watergate Committee. "I have qualified it by saying that, in my opinion, there were serious legal and constitutional questions involved, but if I had to weigh those two, the political public impact on the one hand, and the legal and constitutional issues on the other, I think my judgment would be to make them available."

Turning to Nixon's firing of Special Prosecutor Archibald Cox, Byrd asked Ford if he would support a Court-appointed Special Prosecutor.

"I firmly believe that there ought to be a Special Prosecutor in the Department of Justice," Ford said. "A Special Prosecutor under the sole discretion and supervision of Judge Sirica . . . would raise serious matters of separation of powers and therefore I do not favor that."

How, Byrd asked, would Ford protect a Special Prosecutor from being summarily dismissed if he got too close to evidence of a White House crime?

"I don't think you really can do it by law," Ford said. "I think you have to have faith in the man who appointed him, faith in the person who is appointed, and an understanding of good faith between the Congress and the Chief Executive."

Following the Byrd line of questioning, Senator Claiborne Pell asked: "Under what circumstances do you think the President—if you were President—would be permitted not to be truthful, to lie to the American people?"

"I do not think a President under any circumstances that I can envision ought to lie to the American people," Ford said.

"Should the House Judiciary Committee press on with this inquiry into impeachment?" Senator Mark Hatfield asked.

"I think that is the way to clear the air," Ford said.

"You feel," Hatfield said, "they should proceed with diligence and due haste?"

"I do," Ford said.

"You think that would clear the air?"

"I think it would be very helpful in clearing the air," Ford said. "I do not believe there are grounds—but that is a personal judgment—but I think it would be very helpful in the minds of the American people if they knew that such an inquiry was being conducted."

How would Ford define an impeachable offense? Senator Pell asked. Pell read from the *Congressional Record:* "An impeachable offense is whatever a majority of the House of Representatives considers it to be at a given moment in history." It was a statement by Ford during the House debate on his resolution to impeach Justice Douglas.

Is that still your view? Pell asked.

"Yes," Ford said, "I am still of that opinion . . . I think it is what any Congress decides at any given moment."

If Ford were to be confirmed as Vice President, Senator Hatfield wanted to know, would he express his views freely and frankly to the President, and make his differences known?

"I have always felt that I could speak very directly to the President, whether I agreed or disagreed with him," Ford said. As an example, Ford cited a vote on Vietnam four months earlier. The House, he explained, was debating a bill that would set a cutoff date for U.S. troops in Vietnam. As Republican Leader of the House, Ford had privately told Nixon and House Republicans that a cutoff date must be accepted. During the debate, Ford testified, he left the House floor to consult with the President on the telephone. "I went back in the cloakroom and talked to him. I said, 'Mr President, number one, I think you ought to accept it. Number two, it is going to happen anyhow, and number three, I think it is the best thing for the country to end this slaughter.' He agreed, and I think I had some impact on his decision."

In principle, Ford said, "As long as you have your full opportunity to have an input into the decisionmaking process, if you lose, you should not go out and deliberately undercut that policy. I have learned a long time ago, Senator, after a decision is made, after a play has been called, you do not go out and tackle your own quarterback . . ."

Hatfield asked Ford what he saw as his role with the American people.

"To calm the waters," Ford replied.

"Can I infer," Hatfield asked, "that your decision not to be a candidate in 1976 gives you greater freedom, greater flexibility to play this peacemaker role as you envision it?"

"It certainly does," Ford said. "Nobody can accuse me of seeking personal political aggrandizement."

Would Ford, like other Vice Presidents, campaign hard for members of his party?

Yes, Ford said, but not by attacking Democrats. In campaigning for Republican candidates for the House, he pointed out: "I never go into a Democratic district and speak unkindly about an incumbent. I always . . . speak affirmatively about my party and my President."

Was it true that he would rather be Speaker of the House than President of the United States?

"I do not have any hesitancy to reaffirm that," Ford said. "I really dedicated my life, up until now, to trying to qualify for and be equipped to be the Speaker; but the fates of political life have denied me that, so here I am."

During the Senate hearings, Ford authorized the committee to release to the press his income tax returns to the IRS and his net worth statement. At the time of his nomination as Vice President, Gerald and Betty Ford had $1,281 in bank accounts. He had a $9,031 investment in the Ford family paint company, and Mrs. Ford had $3,240 in shares of Central Telephone of Illinois she had inherited, plus $1,299 in a mutual fund in her name. The cash value of their life insurance was $8,500, and he had $49,400 in the Congressional retirement system. They valued their principal home in Alexandria, Virginia, at $70,000, their ski lodge in Colorado at $65,000, the Grand Rapids house they rented out at $25,000, and their one-fourth interest in a Michigan cabin at $2,000. They figured their furniture in their three houses was worth $19,600 and their cars $6,725. All told, they put their net worth at $261,078. They had accomplished this on an annual salary that ranged from $12,500 in Ford's first year to $42,500 in 1973—plus $10,000 to $15,000 a year Ford earned by making speeches.

Senator Williams asked how it was that the Fords had no mortgage on any one of their real estate properties.

Ford said it was his practice to borrow only for "immediate cash obligations," such as paying his taxes. He had taken out a mortgage in 1950 to buy his Grand Rapids house and paid it off in 1964. When he built his Alexandria house in 1955, he financed part of it and paid off the mortgage in 1966 with money Mrs. Ford inherited from her stepfather.

Ford said his family had pooled their resources and paid $59,700 in cash for the Vail condominium in 1970. He and Mrs. Ford used $7,734 in savings and borrowed $6,845 on the equity in their life insurance policies. He got an advance of $19,600 from the House Sergeant at Arms against his salary, sold their share of a Michigan ski property for $3,500, and put in a $13,604 inheritance from his parents. The four Ford children, each an avid skier, put up the $8,442 balance by borrowing on their insurance policies.

Ford's willingness to open the details of his financial affairs surprised the press and brought compliments from the committee. Of the witness, Chairman Cannon said: "I have been impressed by his candid and complete disclosures, his spirit of cooperation, and his willingness to lay bare all information relative to his public and private life."

The Senate Committee did question Ford about bad marks that Congressional investigators had turned up on Ford's record. One awkward incident cost Ford credibility and cast doubt on his capacity to make judgments about people. Ten days or so before the hearings began, Columnist Jack Anderson published in his syndicated column a shocking accusation: An impecunious New York lobbyist and publicity seeker, Robert Winter-Berger, had given an affidavit to an Anderson assistant stating that he lent Ford about $15,000 between 1966 and 1969 to pay for Mrs. Ford's hospital bills, and that the money had never been repaid.

Winter-Berger also said that he had persuaded Ford to see Dr. Arnold Hutschnecker, a New York physician who also dealt with psychological and emotional problems. In American politics, at least in that decade, elected officials were not allowed to visit psychiatrists. Only the year before another nominee for Vice President, Senator Thomas Eagleton, had been dropped from the Democratic ticket by George McGovern after a newspaper reported that Eagleton had been treated by a psychiatrist. When the Anderson column about Ford came out, the huntsmen of the press rode off in pursuit of another Eagleton story.

Ford and his confirmation team recognized that they must confront the Winter-Berger charge immediately, get all the facts, and make them public. By prearrangement, Senator Robert Griffin, third-ranking Republican on the Rules Committee, and Ford's close friend and colleague on the Michigan Congressional delegation, brought up the accusations on the first day of hearings.

"Congressman Ford," Griffin asked, "are you now or have you ever been under psychiatric care?"

"I am disgustingly sane," Ford replied. "I have never had to go to any psychiatrist or any other person in the medical field related to psychology for any treatment period."

Griffin asked Ford to respond to "published allegations concerning a visit you apparently made to a doctor's office."

"The fact is," Ford replied, "I never visited Dr. Hutschnecker for any treatment. I visited his office once in New York City for approximately fifteen minutes at the request of a man named Mr. Winter-Berger. I had a pleasant conversation with Dr. Hutschnecker. As I recollect, he gave me a lecture on leadership. Well, that was interesting. I was trying to be a leader for the Republicans at that time."

Griffin read out other charges in Winter-Berger's affidavit: "Between 1966 and September of 1969, I personally loaned Gerald Ford in the neighborhood of $15,000. The money was delivered to Ford in cash to cover the illness and hospitalization of his wife. . . . The money was never repaid. I never asked for repayment and it was never offered. At other times he complained that he was short of money. The loans were made in amounts of $50 to about $250."

"What are your comments on that?" Griffin asked Ford.

"I am glad you asked that question," Ford said, "because I want to, at this time, categorically, unqualifiably, and unreservedly say that is a lie."

Ford did know Winter-Berger and said so. The story, as Ford explained it, was that two friends he had known since high school, Peter Boter and his sister, Mrs. Alice Boter Weston, wrote to say they wanted him to meet "a disgruntled Democrat who wanted to help Republicans." Ms. Weston brought the man, Robert Winter-Berger, to Ford's Congressional office.

Some time after the visit, Winter-Berger attended a Kent County Republican dinner in Grand Rapids where Ford spoke, and contributed $500 to the Kent County Republican Finance Committee. Then he began visiting Ford's office, pleading with Ford's secretaries for appointments, waiting in the corridor off the House floor to intercept Ford on the way to his office.

Courtesy is a habit in responsible public officials; their staff assistants are taught to be patient and gracious with even the most obstreperous and unworthy supplicants insisting on "just a few minutes with the boss." Neither Ford nor anyone on his staff wanted to offend this friend of Ford's friend, even when he became a nuisance.

Winter-Berger kept badgering Ford to see Dr. Hutschnecker, who, Winter-Berger told Ford, "had an interest in political leaders and their efforts to do a better job."

Trying to explain to the committee, Ford said: "It finally got to be such a persistent request, and such a pain, to be frank, that I said, on this occasion, while I am going to be in New York to make a speech, between the end of the speech and the flight back to Washington, I would stop to see Dr. Hutschnecker for a very limited period of time, just to get the request out of the way."

In time, Ford said, Winter-Berger began coming around less often. Then Ford learned that the Justice Department was investigating the man. "When I heard that," Ford said, "I told my staff, 'No longer will he be permitted in the office.'"

Of the whole Winter-Berger affair, Ford said: "I think it shows how any one of us, certainly including myself, can be duped." Ford refused to criticize the Boters, his friends of forty years, for getting him involved with Winter-Berger. He told the committee: "I believed and I still believe that they were acting in good faith and that they likewise were duped."

To verify Ford's testimony, the committee questioned Dr. Hutschnecker, who gave the committee a sworn statement confirming Ford's account and affirming that Ford had never been his patient. Winter-Berger was also called as a witness, and the committee found his sworn testimony so contradictory that they voted to send it to the Justice Department to determine whether Winter-Berger should be indicted for perjury.

Out of Ford's past also came a question related to Watergate, brought out by Senator James Allen. "Would you comment on newspaper stories that you helped Mr. Gordon Liddy, convicted in the Watergate break-in, get a job in the Treasury Department four years ago, and were responsible for him being brought to Washington?"

"Here are the facts," Ford said. "In nineteen sixty-eight, in my capacity as Minority Leader, I traveled that year, as I have in the past and subsequently, around the country trying to help the Republican candidates. I went up to Dutchess County, in New York State. We had Ham Fish, Jr., running for that House seat. In a very controversial primary, Mr. Liddy and Mr. Fish battled it out, and Mr. Fish won."

After he lost the Republican primary, Ford continued, Liddy said he would run on the Conservative Party ballot line, "and the local people up there said if Mr. Liddy does that and campaigns, it means the Democrats will win." Fish and his supporters wanted Ford to ask Liddy to forgo an active campaign, which he did. Liddy, in turn, wanted a job in Washington, and Ford said that if Nixon won, he would put in a good word for him.

"Well," Ford said, "Mr. Fish won. Mr. Nixon won. Some time in the spring of nineteen sixty-nine, the Dutchess County political figures came down to see me [and] asked me if I would make a phone call over to the Treasury Department, endorsing their request for a job for Mr. Liddy."

Ford had seen Liddy's résumé, and was favorably impressed. Liddy had been an FBI agent and an assistant county prosecutor, and Ford was advised that Liddy had a good record as a lawyer. "I did call over there," Ford said. He talked to Eugene Rossides, an Assistant Secretary of the Treasury and also a New Yorker. "If you can help out I would appreciate it," Ford told Rossides. "That is all I did. He got the job. What happened to him afterwards, I have no responsibility for."

It was an extraordinary chain of events: Ford, in trying to elect more Republicans to the House, had helped the political rogue who planned the Watergate crime that imperiled President Nixon. The committee accepted Ford's word and explanation—it was a chance occurrence of politics.

On the second full day of the Vice Presidential hearings, the Committee examined Ford on his knowledge of international affairs and U.S. foreign policy. The perception in the Capital's foreign policy community, an arcane and incestuous guild that admitted few elected officials, was that Ford was uninformed. Ford's views on foreign policy were considered particularly significant because at least four of the five Democrats on the committee expected him to become President. They thought it imperative that his experience and views, or the lack of them, be placed on the public record.

Ford was fully aware that in the salons of Georgetown he was thought to be inexperienced and uniformed about national security and foreign policy.

He wanted to show that his responsibilities in the House had put him in the position to discuss national security with four Presidents—Eisenhower, Kennedy, Johnson, and Nixon—and with all their secretaries of State and Defense, and their intelligence chiefs. These were not casual talks; for twelve years he had questioned them on spending for U.S. weapons and forces, on the necessities of foreign aid, on where and how much could be spent for intelligence.

Ford had never tried to impress anyone with his knowledge of international affairs; it was not his nature to boast. But now in this public forum, he was eager to set the record straight. Senator Hugh Scott, knowing this, tossed an easy question to begin the discussion. "You have had a wide familiarity with the evolution of American foreign policy," Scott said. "For how many years would you state that your experience has covered?"

"I was uniquely fortunate when I first came to Congress," Ford said, "because our senior Senator at that time from Michigan was the late Senator Arthur Vandenberg. He was a close personal friend of my father, and when I came here in nineteen forty-nine as a freshman, Senator Vandenberg and his wife sort of took my wife and myself under their wing . . . Senator Vandenberg really had a tremendous impact on my attitude in relationship to foreign policy." Before World War II, Ford explained, he—like Vandenberg—was an isolationist. "But during the war and as a result of our international experiences, Senator Vandenberg made a great transition from isolationism to internationalism. I in a very much more minor capacity also saw the light."

Scott asked Ford whether he knew any foreign leaders. Ford answered that he and then House Majority Leader Hale Boggs spent two weeks in China in the summer of 1972 to discuss trade, international security, and people-to-people exchanges in education, sports, and the arts. On that trip, Ford said, he had spent a lot of time with Chou En-lai and other leaders. He went on to enumerate his meetings with the leaders of the Soviet Union, Japan, and France. As a member of the Inter-Parliamentary Union, Ford added, he had met with his world counterparts in Warsaw, Belgrade, and Brussels.

Senator Pell, a former foreign service officer, asked how Ford might deal with dictators. "We are talking to you as a potential President, not in your capacity as Vice President," Pell said. Would you put "more pressure . . . on human rights, the question of torture, the question of restraint from immigration?"

Ford said that he felt strongly about U.S. efforts to get the USSR to permit Soviet Jews to emigrate to Israel. In general, Ford said, he believed that the United States should use trade and the U.S. consumer market as an incentive to promote human rights and reforms to benefit people. "There comes a point, however, where you just can't tell another country they have to do it, but we can certainly try."

If you became President, Pell asked, "would it be your intention to keep Dr. Kissinger as Secretary of State?"

"I think," Ford said carefully, "he is a superb Secretary of State."

"You may one day become the Chief Executive of the United States," Senator Byrd said. "Do you favor any kind of exploratory review of current United States policy toward Cuba?"

"I certainly think we ought to have a continuing exploratory review of our policy with Cuba," Ford said. "If a policy is not working, or it can be improved, certainly the top strategists in the Department of State and the Office of the President ought to be working on how we can make the policy more effective."

Has NATO outlived its usefulness, Byrd asked, and what changes should be made in U.S. military commitments to NATO?

The NATO allies should carry a larger part of the military costs, Ford replied, but "I do not think at this stage we should unilaterally withdraw [part] of our contribution in troops. We are in the process of troop negotiations with the Soviet Union . . . and I would rather have a mutual reduction, rather than a unilateral." Support of NATO, Ford emphasized, had been a bipartisan commitment since President Truman sent General Eisenhower to Europe in 1951 to organize NATO.

Should the United States, Byrd asked, "enter into a firm treaty with the State of Israel to guarantee Israel its independence in the case of external attack from a foreign border?"

"I do not think the United States should enter into such an agreement," Ford said.

"Do you think a closer dialogue with the Arab states might be to the advantage of the United States?" Byrd asked.

Yes, Ford said, and commended Secretary of State Kissinger for his continuing efforts to accomplish that.

"If you were to become President," Byrd asked, would you "counsel with, and seek the advice and consent of the Senate and the Senate Foreign Relations Committee" on major international issues?

"There has to be that relationship," Ford said. "Yes, sir."

Byrd reminded Ford that when they were both in the House and John Foster Dulles was Secretary of State, they both supported U.S. participation in SEATO. Now, Byrd asked: "How do you feel about continued U.S. participation in SEATO?"

"Well," Ford said, "the situation is considerably different today. . . . In the first place our changed relationships with the Chinese People's Republic. So I would strongly urge a review of that arrangement to see if it ought to be enlarged, revised, or reduced."

What would you do about Communist China's claim that Taiwan is part of the People's Republic?

"I would handle the matter as it is being currently handled," Ford said. Recognizing the sensitivity in Taiwan and on the mainland, and trying to be diplomatic, Ford pointed out that neither side was trying to force the issue at that time, but it "will have to eventually be resolved as the world moves down the road."

Turning the hearing to a domestic controversy, Senator Allen, a conservative Democrat from Alabama, asked: What is your position on a Constitutional amendment to ban busing in the public schools?

"Senator Allen," Ford said, "if the Federal courts persist in trying to have forced busing to achieve racial balance in public schools, and if there is no other way in which we can remedy that situation, I would favor that amendment." Some Federal courts, Ford added, "used a little common sense and judgment and recognized good faith efforts." Vigorously bringing his hand down on the witness table, he added: "[I] believe in integration, but do not believe that forced busing to achieve racial balance is the way to improve education."

"You would favor the neighborhood schools?" Allen asked.

"I certainly believe in the neighborhood school concept," Ford said. "I believe in compensatory education, helping schools . . . in the more disadvantaged areas, putting more money in there with more teachers, better facilities—that we make a major effort in those areas to upgrade the educational opportunities. . . . Forced busing has . . . caused more trouble and more tension wherever it has happened than almost anything else in our society of late."

"Should we not have a uniform rule [on desegregation of public schools] throughout the nation?" Allen asked.

"No question about that," Ford said. "You really cannot differentiate between de facto and de jure segregation. They all ought to be treated in the same way, whether in Detroit, or Birmingham, or Los Angeles."

Senator Hatfield set about to explore Ford's concept of the Presidency. "How would you describe Presidential leadership . . . the basic characteristics of leadership?"

Instantly wary, Ford paused. He recognized that the wrong response could suggest he had designs on Nixon's job. "I have been concentrating on the Vice Presidency," Ford replied, "so I have not given as much thought, and should not, to the other. So what I say here is strictly what comes to my mind."

Choosing his words with care, Ford said: "A President must have policies, domestic and foreign, that bring support from the people who elected him. Therefore, it is performance on the job, achieving peace around the world, to the degree that our country can effect it, achieving a kind of equity and prosperity at home domestically—those policies are really what a President has to work on and effectuate and implement. To me that is the most important role of a President."

"Would you not also agree," Hatfield asked, that a President "can be right on the basics and the policies, and still not have the confidence and faith and trust of the people?"

"Yes," Ford said. "I served here when some Presidents were not very popular." The best example was Truman, Ford said. "But he stuck doggedly to decisions he had made, and in retrospect the decisions were right, and today I feel, and I think most Americans feel, that he was a first-class President. . . . Is it not more important that the decision be right . . . than to rely on what Gallup says for August and what Gallup says for September? I think so."

What, Hatfield asked, are "some of the personal characteristics that are important to Presidential leadership?"

"I think the President has to be a person of great truth," Ford said, "and the American people have to believe that he is truthful. I believe that a President has to be a man of thought, and not impetuous, and the people have to have a faith that he is thoughtful. . . . I believe that a President has to exemplify by his personal life the standards—morally, ethically, and otherwise—by which most Americans live their lives."

Can a President admit mistakes? Hatfield asked.

"Oh, sure," Ford said. "The American people realize that Presidents, like the rest of us, can and do make mistakes. They hope that are not too frequent, however."

Hatfield pointed out that *Time* magazine and other publications were calling for Nixon's resignation, and asked: "What counsel would you give to the President to change this situation?"

"To the degree that the President can," Ford said, "I think the immediate problem is clearing up the various aspects of the so-called Watergate affair. My own personal feeling is that the President had no participation in its planning or execution, or any knowledge of it. I think the public wants him in any and every way that he can, by documentation or otherwise, to clear it up. I think it will be, and that will be a very great help, because I just know that he had no participation in it."

In some kind of an "open forum"? Hatfield asked.

"Well, I have not thought of the format," Ford said. "But whatever the doubts are, I think they have to be cleared up, by whatever documentation the President or others might have. I believe he is completely innocent, and I think there must be certain documentation to prove that . . ."

"Can Richard Nixon save his Presidency?" Hatfield asked.

"I think so," Ford said. "It is going to take a lot of help from a lot of people, but I think his ability, I hope his capacity to communicate . . . will permit him to finish the office with a fine record. And I think that he can, not because I am a Republican, not because I was nominated by him, but because I want it to be for the good of the American people."

Is that, Hatfield said, "what you are going to devote your time and your interest to doing?"

"To the extent that I can," Ford said. "The maximum."

Chairman Cannon wanted to know Ford's attitude toward the press. "Now recently," he said, "President Nixon made a broadside attack on the media, and blamed them for much of the trouble in town. Do you share the President's blanket condemnation?"

"No, I do not," Ford said.

"Has not the media in fact played a major role in digging out the true facts surrounding the Watergate scandal?" Cannon asked.

"Yes," Ford said. "They were a most significant contributor to the exposure of the Watergate situation."

"What do you see as the role of the free press in our system of free democracy?"

"I think the role, Mr. Chairman, is to dig out the facts and to print the facts," Ford said. "But I hasten to add that they also have corresponding responsibility to make sure that what they print are the facts, and furthermore, that in the course of their writing about the facts, they maintain a factual approach. . . . In the editorial page, of course, that is different. In the headlines, and on the front page, I think we ought to have the facts, period."

"Now," Cannon said, "a memorandum . . . by Robert H. Bork, as Solicitor General, asserted that the President of the United States is immune from criminal prosecution. . . . First, do you believe that a President is immune from prosecution for a crime, so long as he holds office?"

"That is my understanding," Ford said. "Under the Constitution, before a President can be charged and convicted of a crime, he must be impeached and convicted under the impeachment clause."

"Do you believe that a President can legally prevent or terminate any criminal investigation or prosecution involving the President?" Senator Cannon asked.

"I do not think he should," Ford said. "I hope there will never be a President who will take such action."

"If," Cannon asked, "a President resigned his office before his term expired, would his successor have the power to prevent or to terminate any investigation or criminal prosecution charges against the former President?"

"Would he have the authority?" Ford asked, making sure he heard the question right.

"Yes," Cannon said. "Would he have the power?"

"I do not think the public would stand for it," Ford said.

"Whether he has the technical authority or not, I cannot give you a categorical answer. The Attorney General, in my opinion, with the help and support of the American people, would be the controlling factor."

Again Cannon asked: "Do you believe that any President or Vice President of the United States should claim absolute immunity from prosecution while in office?"

"Well, as I said a moment ago," Ford replied, "as I understand the Constitution, a President has to be impeached and convicted before he can be prosecuted. But once he has been impeached and convicted by the Congress, then he is not immune under any circumstances to criminal prosecution."

Not in that exchange, or at any other time during the Senate hearings, did Cannon or any other member of the committee ask Ford if he might pardon Nixon. In fact, the transcript does not show the word "pardon" was ever used by anyone.

After his two full days on the stand, Ford's questioning by the Senate ended. In effect, the Senate hearings took the place of a political campaign. Instead of a nominee for Vice President making a prepared speech in an auditorium, this candidate was required to give thoughtful answers to serious questions about how he would reach important policy decisions. Instead of being questioned by political reporters, Ford was interrogated by working politicians elected to operate the government. In the process, Ford gave the American people an opportunity to judge his worth—even though they could not vote for or against him.

By questioning Ford and other witnesses, the nine Senators on the Rules Committee—five Democrats, four Republicans—produced more relevant information about a public official than had ever been known about any person in or out of American public office. In the end the Committee members judged Ford to be honest, knowledgeable, and capable. He showed little charisma but a lot of common sense. With his stolid earnestness went a sense of calm; he seemed to be a man with a steady hand. He conserved the taxpayers' money as earnestly as he did his own. He knew more about economics and foreign policy that even his friends suspected. His judgment was good—reliable, but not infallible. He had made mistakes and could easily admit them. He was loyal; he stood by his friend President Nixon. At the same time he could and did insist on moving ahead on the resolution to impeach Nixon; he was convinced the evidence was not there and was confident that the House inquiry would find Nixon innocent.

After Ford's testimony, the Committee brought in Senator Birch Bayh, the author of the Twenty-fifth Amendment and the chief organizer, eight years earlier, of the successful campaign to pass it. In concept, Bayh explained, the framers established two principles: First, the nominee for Vice President should be "a member of the President's own party and thus . . . compatible in temperament and view with the President." Second, "we felt that a confirmation by both the Senate and the House would tend to create public confidence in the selection. . . . We felt, I think appropriately so, as I look back on it, that we in the Congress were able to represent the people, all of the people in our country, in what can accurately be called a Congressional election of this new Vice President."

The singular act of including the House in the act of confirming a Presidential nominee, Bayh said, made it imperative that the President "choose a person of national stature [who might] succeed to the very office of the Presidency itself."

The decision by Congress, Bayh said, should rest on this question: "Is this nominee qualified not just to be Vice President, but is he fully qualified to assume the most powerful job in the world, that of the President of the United States . . . ? In this case, we are acting as a surrogate electoral body for the people."

On November 20 the committee met to vote on Ford's confirmation. Senator Byrd, as Deputy Minority Leader of the Senate, claimed the right to make the motion to approve Ford. Senator Marlow Cook, as ranking Republican on the committee, seconded it. The nine members of the committee found Ford qualified and voted unanimously to confirm Gerald Ford as Vice President. A week later the Senate voted ninety-two to three in favor of confirmation.

Ten days after the firing of Archibald Cox as Special Prosecutor, Nixon picked Leon Jaworski for the job, on the recommendation of John Connally. Jaworski was a Texan, a conservative Democrat, former President of the American Bar Association, and a friend of Connally—who assured Nixon that Jaworski was no Cox but had great respect for the Presidency.

Conally was so reassuring about Jaworski that Nixon boasted to Colson, "We have a good understanding. It will be a good working relationship."

But when Haig called Jaworski on behalf of Nixon, he found Jaworski reluctant. The dismissal of Cox was proof that an appointee of Nixon would not have full freedom to investigate and prosecute the Watergate crimes. But Haig knew that if he could not recruit Jaworski, the Democrats in Congress might appoint a Special Prosecutor on their own.

To persuade Jaworski to accept the appointment, Haig offered a new guarantee of independence: a Presidential commitment for full independence, backed up by a panel of eight members of Congress—the bipartisan leaders of the House and Senate, and the bipartisan leaders of the House and Senate Judiciary committees.

Jaworski, still wary, warned Haig: "I feel that every person criminally involved [in Watergate] should be prosecuted. If I take this job, I'm going to work this way."

"That's just what we want," Haig said.

Jaworski accepted on that basis, and Haig said the White House would announce the appointment the next day. "Remember," Haig added, "the key words in any news conference are that you've got the right to take the President to Court."

"I'll remember," Jaworski said.

While Ford testified before the Senate Committee, President Nixon flew to Key Biscayne, Florida—"to think and get some rest," he said.

In Washington, his troubles compounded. White House Counsel Buzhardt appeared before Judge Sirica to say, with considerable embarrassment, that the White House staff could not find two of the nine subpoenaed tapes that Nixon had agreed to turn over to the Court. As best he could, Buzhardt tried to convince Judge Sirica that the two tapes had never existed.

After his humiliating experience, Buzhardt returned to the White House and talked to Nixon's co-counsel, Leonard Garment. Each discovered the other had begun to wonder whether Nixon was guilty.

As experienced lawyers, they doubted that Nixon's actions were those of an innocent man. Each was caught in the bind that a good lawyer fears most—trying to defend a client who may not be telling him the truth. Nixon had refused, flatly and vehemently, to permit either Buzhardt or Garment to listen to the tapes or see any transcript. Talking it over, Buzhardt and Garment realized they both suspected that President Nixon was covering up a crime from his own lawyers.

Together they decided to go to the President, confront him with the evidence they had gleaned from testimony before the Court and the Senate Watergate Committee, and advise him to resign. To prepare for the trip, Garment summarized on paper the specific charges—that Nixon knew of the burglary of Daniel Ellsberg's psychiatrist, that he attempted to get the CIA to stop the FBI investigation of Watergate, and that he ordered payments to the Watergate burglars to keep them from testifying.

On Saturday morning, Buzhardt and Garment flew to Key Biscayne. That night they confronted Haig and Ziegler in Key Biscayne. Garment said that the President had concealed evidence from them and lied about his own involvement in the attempt to cover up Watergate. To back up his statement, Garment detailed the charges.

Garment also told Haig and Ziegler that the President even proposed to manufacture evidence. Recounting the story, Garment said that Nixon claimed he had made a dictabelt recording after a sensitive discussion with John Dean. But when the Dictabelt was subpoenaed, the President could not find it. Well, the President pointed out, he still had his notes, and asked: "Why can't we make a new Dictabelt?"

That in itself was a felony, Garment said, and serious enough to implicate the four of them in obstruction of justice.

Haig asked Garment for his recommendation.

The President should resign, Garment said.

Ziegler reddened with anger, and strongly objected.

Haig was shocked. "We don't even have a Vice President," he said.

A resignation, Garment replied, could take effect after Ford is confirmed.

Garment asked that he and Buzhardt be permitted to go in person to make their case to the President.

Absolutely not, Haig said. As chief of staff he would tell the President why the two had come to Key Biscayne, but he knew what Nixon would say: He would never resign.

Haig did tell Nixon about the meeting, and Nixon said he sympathized with Garment and Buzhardt. "They had been . . . regularly undermined by events and now by me," Nixon said. But he would not talk to them. The two White House lawyers returned to Washington without seeing their client.

A few nights later Nixon concluded a televised address on the energy crisis by saying, "Tonight I would like to give my answer to those who have suggested that I resign. I have no intention whatever of walking away from the job I was elected to do."

Nixon also decided to tell his side of the Watergate story to all those in Congress who might support him. In nine two-hour sessions, Nixon met with almost three hundred Members. Among them was Representative John Anderson, a wise and promising young Republican leader who had written the President to propose that he appear voluntarily before a Joint Session of Congress for, say, four hours, and answer any and all questions about Watergate.

No, Nixon told Anderson and the group, he would not do that. "If I gave a speech and said, 'I didn't do it,' the Democrats would say, 'The son of a bitch is lying'; and the Republicans would say, 'Ho hum, he is probably lying but he is our son of a bitch.'"

As part of his effort to stop the defections of Republicans, Nixon asked George Bush, Chairman of the Republican National Committee, to bring in for a White House breakfast the twenty-one top party leaders who made up the Republican Coordinating Committee. Nixon insisted to the party group that he was not involved in the Watergate burglary or cover-up. Bush urged Nixon to release the tapes and documents that would prove his innocence, adding: "Nothing less than a full disclosure on Watergate, including the tapes, will restore your credibility in the party."

All through November Nixon repeated a curious pattern: He kept promising what would be disastrous to deliver. In mid-month Nixon flew to Orlando to address a convention of his tormentors—the media, the four hundred managing editors of the Associated Press newspapers. There he promised to make public all the relevant tapes and facts about Watergate, and to pay the back taxes he owed. He also revealed his earnings as a lawyer in his eight years out of office, and his net worth, about seven hundred thousand dollars.

In words unseemly of any President, "People have got to know whether or not their President is a crook," Nixon said. "Well, I am not a crook. I have earned everything I have got."

Four days later, disaster struck Nixon again. Haig came in to tell him that part of the tape of a key conversation he had with Bob Haldeman on June 20, 1972—three days after Watergate—was missing. This was one of the nine tapes the President had promised to surrender to Judge Sirica, Haig said, and evidently eighteen and a half minutes had been erased.

Buzhardt, weary but resolute, had no choice: He went into Judge Sirica's Court and admitted the new problem. For a firsthand explanation, Sirica summoned Rose Mary Woods, the person Nixon trusted to transcribe the tapes. On the witness stand Ms. Woods said she might have accidentally pressed the wrong button and caused part of the gap, but she was sure she had not erased all eighteen and a half minutes. Electronic experts estimated the erase button had been pushed at least five times to eliminate all that section of tape. Haig, reaching into metaphysics, suggested "sinister forces" caused the gap.

John Mitchell, who continued to talk by telephone with the President as he prepared for his own trial for perjury, could only shake his head in dismay at Nixon's stumbling efforts to defend his Presidency. To *Newsweek* reporter Hal Bruno, a friend and former neighbor, Mitchell said with grim finality: "This has been a political disaster."

Of the three main buildings that provide offices for the 435 Members of the House of Representatives, the Rayburn Building is the least representative of the American character, or of Sam Rayburn. It is showy on the outside, and cold white marble on the inside.

On the second floor of Rayburn is Room 2141, the hearing room of the House Judiciary Committee. On the morning of November 15, 1973, all thirty-eight Members of the Judiciary Committee met there to begin the process of considering a nominee for Vice President. When Ford walked into the Committee hearing room on the first day, he was warmly welcomed—but not by all Members. Chairman Rodino made it clear that Members had a larger responsibility than passing judgment on a colleague. "All of us on this committee know Gerald Ford," Rodino said. "But Mr. Ford knows, and the American people will know, that this affords the nominee no privilege or advantage before this committee."

As Rodino began to swear in Ford as the witness, one Member objected. "Mr. Chairman, a point of order," Representative John Conyers said. ". . . My participation in these hearings is conditioned on the record showing my continuous and strenuous objections to the convening of these hearings before our acting upon resolutions before this committee to impeach the President of the United States."

Impeach now: That was the intent of Conyers. And he was supported by almost half of the twenty-one Democrats on the Judiciary Committee. But the Democratic powers in the House—Speaker Albert, Majority Leader O'Neill, Rodino, and others—had already made the decision to confirm Ford first, and they could command enough votes to make that happen. Rodino overruled Conyers's point of order and directed Ford to begin his testimony.

Ford knew that he must find a way to affirm his loyalty to President Nixon and at the same time assert his own independence. Ford's way was to take this issue head-on. "Of course I support the President," Ford said. "He is my friend of a quarter-century. His political philosophy is very close to my own. He is the head of my party and the Constitutional Chief Executive of the Nation. He was chosen quite emphatically by the people a year ago as I, if confirmed as Vice President, will not have been.

"Not only have I usually supported President Nixon in the House, I also supported Presidents Truman and Eisenhower and Kennedy and Johnson, whenever the national interest was at stake. As a Member of the House, I have voiced my support of Presidents publicly when I thought they were right and my criticisms publicly when I thought they were wrong. . . . Those of you who know me know that I am my own man."

But what did Ford know about Watergate? That was the question asked by Representative George Danielson, a California Democrat. "I want to ask you very specifically," Danielson said, "did you or have you at any time on or after June 17, 1972—that is the day of Watergate—have you spoken with President Nixon in person or on the telephone regarding the burglary of the national headquarters of the Democratic Party?"

"I cannot remember whether it was one or more, but we have discussed the burglary of the Democratic Party," Ford replied, "and we both agreed it was a stupid, naive operation that no intelligent person with any judgment would authorize or undertake."

"Have you," Danielson continued, "spoken with former Attorney General Mitchell about this subject, by telephone or in person?"

"About four days after the burglary," Ford replied, "I and three or four other Republicans were meeting with Mr. Mitchell and . . . I asked Mr. Mitchell if he knew something about the inquiry and he looked me in the eye and said he did not. Based on that assurance I made a number of comments subsequently that he did not know anything about it."

Had Ford ever talked with anyone about raising funds for the defendants?

"I did not," Ford said.

"We must ask the questions that are on the public's mind," Danielson said, and continued: Did Ford know about the White House tapes?

"I frankly did not know they existed," Ford said. "I was as caught by surprise as I think everybody else was."

Did Ford know anything about the White House plumbers' operation, or the burglary of Daniel Ellsberg's psychiatrist?

"I did not," Ford said.

Where did Ford stand on impeaching Nixon?

"I am for this committee continuing the investigation as to the charges of impeachment," Ford said. "The more expeditiously you conduct the investigation the better, because, as I have said several times here, I don't think on the basis of the information I know there are grounds for impeachment."

In the eyes of the Committee's liberal Democrats, Ford had two marks against him—loyalty to Nixon, and his attempt to impeach Justice Douglas.

Ford stood his ground on Douglas: "The facts are, and the committee found it to be the truth, that Justice Douglas did receive $350 for writing an article in a magazine published by Mr. Ralph Ginzburg; and on two occasions, while Mr. Ginzburg had court cases before the Supreme Court, Justice Douglas did not disqualify himself. On both occasions he voted for Mr. Ginzburg, one in the case involving Senator Goldwater, and the other involving the criminal proceeding in the distribution or mailing of the magazine *Eros*.

"Now, my point, and I still think it is a valid one, a member of the Supreme Court, if he has been paid by a litigant who is before this court at the highest level, should disqualify himself rather than vote on the matter before the Court. And unfortunately, and I think regrettably, Justice Douglas did it twice. He did not disqualify himself. I am glad to report in subsequent . . . cases, not identical, but somewhat similar circumstances, that Justice Douglas did disqualify himself and I applaud him for it."

Badgered by insinuating questions from Waldie, a disputatious liberal who was using the hearings to promote his campaign for Governor of California, Ford lost his temper. In response to one of Waldie's sarcastic interruptions Ford pointed out that Justice Douglas's article had been printed in a Ginzburg publication next to five pages of photographs of nudes in pornographic poses—and to prove his point Ford took a copy of the magazine from his briefing book, and waved the nude photos before the Committee.

"Mr. Ford," Waldie admonished, "do you think that is very good taste to display those before the television cameras?"

"Well," Ford said, "I am displaying them before the committee to point out—"

"I think it is a lamentable breach," Waldie said.

Chairman Rodino, offended at Ford's display of nude pictures before a hearing by his Committee, cut them both off.

In contrast to the Democrats, the seventeen Republicans on the Judiciary Committee were unanimous for Ford. They complimented his record, his character, his unfailing fairness as a party leader.

From the FBI report Representative Tom Railsback quoted the flattering comments of Senate Democrats—Hubert Humphrey ("trustworthy"), George McGovern ("unquestionable integrity"). Into the record went the observation of Leonard Woodcock, President of the United Auto Workers: "He has the capacity to bring a torn country together." Ford's election opponent in 1972, Jean McKee, told the FBI: "Mr. Ford is a straightshooter, clean, and would restore confidence in the Government."

For two weeks the hearings continued, with Conyers, Waldie, and other Democrats searching for some reason to stop the confirmation. Twice Ford was called back to explain points of concern. Patiently he went over all the points that had already been covered.

Rodino, with the backing of Speaker Albert, finally set a deadline; and on November 29, 1973, the committee met for the vote. Just before going to the Committee room, Rodino telephoned Ford: "Jerry, you have the votes for the Committee to report out your nomination; but I want you to know that I am not going to support you."

"Peter," Ford replied, "I understand. Don't you be concerned about that at all."

Ford, aware that Rodino's Congressional district had a large black electorate, guessed that Rodino's position had to do with his next campaign. "That was not the reason," Rodino said. "I was a liberal. I believed that Justice Douglas was a great jurist. And there was something about Ford showing those nude pictures to the television cameras that just did not sit well with me. So I made sure that Jerry had the votes for the nomination to go to the floor, and then I called to tell him my position."

Rodino's Committee count was correct: seventeen Republicans and twelve Democrats voted to confirm Ford. On December 6, 1973, Speaker Albert brought the nomination to the floor. After little debate, the House of Representatives voted 387 to 35 to confirm Ford as Vice President.

Haig insisted that Ford be sworn in at the White House. Speaker Albert said no, that Ford should take the oath in the House of Representatives, where he had served for twenty-four years and eleven months. Albert was determined to make a point for history: Under the Twenty-fifth Amendment, it was the President who made the nomination; but it was 535 Members of the House and Senate, representing the American voters, who had taken the Constitutional role of the Electoral College and, in effect, elected Ford Vice President.

President Nixon agreed to come to the House floor for the swearing-in ceremony, but Timmons picked up word that the Democrats in the House planned to give Ford more applause. That was no problem, Ford said; he and the President would come in together and share the applause.

With Betty holding a Bible given them by their oldest son, and Chief Justice Warren Burger conducting the ceremony, Ford took the oath of office as Vice President of the United States at 6:10 P.M., December 6, 1973.

At the swearing-in of Vice President Ford, the political balance in Washington instantly shifted. Earlier, President Nixon's protection against impeachment was an absolute if unwritten political reality: Congress, and popular opinion, could not accept the idea of Agnew as President. Better the Nixon they knew, with all his flaws, than the ranting charlatan they perceived Agnew to be.

Nixon, in an aside to Kissinger, had cynically observed that by putting Ford into the Vice Presidency he had taken out new insurance against impeachment. It was one more miscalculation. On the day after Ford became Vice President, Republican Chairman Bush told *Newsweek*'s Hal Bruno: "I don't think Ford increases chances of impeachment; but he sure increases talk about it, and that may be just as bad."

15

THE NARROW PATH

In his new job Vice President Ford found himself a happy man. His landslide of an endorsement by Democrats and Republicans in Congress was looked upon as a special election he won on his own. His victory on Capitol Hill clearly distanced him from Nixon. Overnight, Ford became the new magnet of Washington's attention.

For him, the gift of the Vice Presidency was also a gift of time; no longer was he bound by a legislative schedule concocted by Democrats. A gift of time, and of access to the vast Executive storehouse of information. As Vice President, Ford found himself with unlimited opportunity to do what he liked best: Examine and study the mammoth, creaking engine of the Federal government and look for ways to improve it.

In his first days in his new office on the second floor of the EOB, he called for briefings on three favorite subjects—Budget, Defense, and the Republican Party. Roy Ash, director of Office of Management and Budget, and his deputy, Fred Malek, reported on the newest budget estimates—$300 billion in fiscal 1975, with a projected deficit of six billion dollars, and a $330 billion budget for fiscal 1976. Ford was dismayed at how fast the Federal government was growing.

Ford stopped off at the Pentagon for breakfast one morning and a briefing from Secretary of Defense James Schlesinger, who thought the meeting would be a courtesy call. Ford had risen even earlier than usual that morning and written out twelve specific questions about arms and military planning. When the breakfast ended, Ford concluded that Schlesinger was "very bright, and a prodigious worker," but showed poor judgment in dealing with Congress.

On Capitol Hill Ford joined the forty-three Republican senators for their regular Tuesday lunch to discuss Senate business and politics. Afterward he brought RNC Chairman Bush around to the Vice President's ceremonial office just off the Senate floor for a frank political talk.

Ford and Bush were allies as well as friends; each saw in the other a man he could trust as well as a party leader. In 1966, still in his first term as House Minority Leader, Ford had flown to Houston to meet Bush, then the young leader of Harris County Republicans. If Bush won a seat in the House, Ford promised that he would do his best to place him on the House Ways and Means Committee, the guardian of the oil depletion allowance that kept Texas rich. Bush did win. Ford kept his word. It was not easy to place a freshman Republican in so prized a position; but Ford spent the political capital necessary to make it happen.

In the House, Ford and Bush found much in common—Yale, Navy service in the Pacific, love of outdoor sports, loyalty to the Republican Party, and a deep commitment to public life.

In this first meeting between Ford as Vice President and Bush as Republican Chairman, Bush told Ford that President Nixon's hold on the party was slipping. In the off-year New Jersey elections, Bush said, the twin scandals over Agnew and Watergate defeated thirteen Republican incumbents in the State Senate and twenty-five in the Assembly. Private polls taken for the RNC showed the 1974 Congressional elections could be a disaster for Republicans. Ford agreed the outlook was bad at that moment, but told Bush he was sure that Nixon was not involved in Watergate. "When the facts all come out," he said to Bush, "I believe the President will be cleared."

For the Christmas holiday Ford and his family packed their skis and presents into *Air Force Two* and took off for Colorado. He and Betty wanted this Christmas to be their best yet. "It was our last private Christmas, the last one where we could just be ourselves," Susan Ford said.

Gathered around a roaring fire in their three-bedroom condo in downtown Vail, they watched the snow fall, drift through the tall firs, and deepen on the runs of the mountain slopes. Life was good. Ford was a happy husband and father, and proud of his success in public life. With his confirmation as Vice President, he felt that all the years of hard work in the House had been recognized; no public man in the country's history had been so endorsed by his peers in Congress. With all the cheer of the Christmas season and all the optimism in his nature, Ford was looking ahead to more good times with his family after he retired as Vice President.

President Nixon went to Camp David for the weekend before Christmas of 1973. Sitting in his study on Sunday, he looked out at the bare trees framed against the clear blue December sky, and wrote in his journal: "Last Christmas here?"

All through the holidays he brooded over whether his Presidency was nearing the end. After a quiet Christmas dinner with the family in the White House, Nixon left the next day for the seclusion of San Clemente. Except for telephone calls to the stalwarts he was counting on for help in Congress—Ford, Scott, Griffin, Goldwater, Rhodes, Michel—Nixon kept to himself until the late afternoon of the last day of 1973. At 4:35 P.M. Haig brought in James D. St. Clair, a highly respected Boston lawyer Colson had suggested to Nixon to head his defense against impeachment.

After he and Nixon talked for an hour, St. Clair concluded the President had a good case. He agreed to defend Nixon against all Watergate charges.

That night Nixon remained alone in his study to see in the New Year. At 1:15 A.M. he picked up a yellow pad to pen another soliloquy for his memoirs: "The basic question is: Do I fight all out or do I now begin the long process to prepare for a change, meaning, in effect, resignation."

Resignation—he couldn't get it out of his mind. He had first mentioned it to Ray Price at Camp David nine months earlier. He had talked about it with his daughters Tricia and Julie, with Haig and Ziegler. "But the idea was anathema to me," Nixon wrote; resignation would be surrender to hated political enemies. "The answer—fight." In the stillness beside the Pacific he wrote on and on to persuade himself: "Fight because if I am forced to resign the press will become a much too dominant force in the nation, not only in this administration but for years to come. Fight because resignation would set a precedent and result in a permanent and very destructive change in our whole constitutional system. Fight because resignation could lead to a collapse of our foreign policy initiatives."

In Washington, the Capitol was almost empty. Congress was out of session, away for the holidays, listening to the woes and wisdom of the voters back home. But the Senate Watergate Committee was busy; their lawyers delivered to the White House three subpoenas covering more than four hundred of the President's tapes and documents. The House was beginning to move: Judiciary Committee Chairman Rodino announced a deadline—April, 1974—for the committee to make its judgment on whether there were grounds for impeaching the President.

To start the New Year the White House announced that James St. Clair would take over from Buzhardt as head of the legal team defending Nixon against Watergate. Buzhardt remained on the team as White House Counsel. Both would be needed: Judge Sirica ruled that five of the President's tapes turned over to him did in fact relate to Watergate, and sent them on to Special Prosecutor Jaworski. The IRS announced that its auditors would reexamine Nixon's income tax returns for his Presidential years.

Nixon rejected the Senate Watergate Committee subpoenas for White House tapes and documents. Turning over the Presidential papers, he wrote to Chairman Ervin, "would unquestionably destroy any vestige of confidentiality of Presidential communications."

The seeds of rebellion were germinating among Republican leaders. In a "Confidential and eyes only" letter to General Haig, Bush reported increasing criticism in the party because Nixon would not make public the tapes that would prove his innocence. "We must get the promised information out right away," Bush wrote Haig. "If it is not released each Congressman and Senator will have a justifiable reason to try to put distance between himself and the White House. There will be a *major* outcry. . . . The press will play this Republican outcry for all it is worth."

The Republican Party was already divided, Bush said. "There is strong support for the President, but there is a non-vocal group of considerable size that feels the President will have to resign 'unless things are cleared up.' "

Hugh Scott, Republican Leader of the Senate, wrote a letter to the *Philadelphia Bulletin* insisting that the President make public the documentary evidence of his innocence, and "the sooner the better." Bryce Harlow went in to see the President alone and warned, "You are on your way to impeachment."

Goldwater, whose opinion was critical to Nixon's survival, told *The Christian Science Monitor* that the American public no longer believed their President. In an interview with Godfrey Sperling, Goldwater said, "I don't think it's Watergate, frankly, as much as it's just a question in people's minds of just how honest is this man. I hate to think of the old adage, 'Would you buy a used car from Dick Nixon?'—but that's what people are asking around the country."

It was significant, Goldwater said, that Nixon's best political advisers,

Mel Laird and Bryce Harlow, were leaving. "Now I can't believe that Nixon would listen to General Haig on political matters when General Haig doesn't know anything about political matters," Goldwater said. "I just can't believe he would listen to Ziegler. That, in my opinion, would be disastrous. . . . Ziegler doesn't understand politics."

Sperling, always a fair reporter, got in touch with Pat Buchanan to offer Haig equal space in the *Monitor* for a response. To Buchanan, Haig said curtly: "I don't need combat with Barry or more press."

At Haig's suggestion, President and Mrs. Nixon invited Senator and Mrs. Goldwater to a private dinner in the White House. Later Goldwater told Sperling that it was purely social; Watergate was not mentioned. And, Goldwater said, "I am still sticking to everything I said in the interview."

Vice President Ford, in his first major television appearance after he was sworn in, offended his new boss. Observing the confrontation between the President and the Senate over four hundred tapes and documents, Ford concluded the Senate demand was excessive. But to him common sense made it obvious that Nixon could not deny the Senate evidence of illegal actions by anyone in the White House. Hoping to be—as he had testified in his confirmation hearings—a conciliator between Congress and the President, Ford suggested on "Meet the Press," "There may be—and I underline may be— some area of compromise."

What Ford did not know was that he was undermining the President's last line of defense. A quick response came from the White House press office: The Vice President was speaking for himself. "White House Disowns Ford's View on Tapes," ran the headline over Lou Cannon's story in *The Washington Post*. After that, Ford said, "There was a chill in my relations."

Ford learned a lesson. He resolved to stay out of Nixon's battles with Congress and the courts—as best he could. "It was," he said, "one tough job to maintain support for a President under siege, with conditions deteriorating virtually every day, and at the same time trying to maintain my own personal integrity. Because the deeper the Nixon White House got into trouble, the more easily it could have been for me to get engulfed in that swamp.

"And yet I didn't want to appear disloyal. And of course I was always under scrutiny. If I said anything the wrong way, people would say, 'You're just trying to become President.' So it was a very narrow path. And not a very pleasant one."

Life became more unpleasant as Nixon's aides set out to put Ford and his staff in their place. It has been suggested that some secret potion served in the White House mess causes members of every President's staff to disdain every incumbent Vice President, whoever he is. In the Nixon White House, the staff contempt for Ford was only slightly less than it had been for Agnew. Haig sent a junior assistant, Bruce Kehrli, and a functionary, Dewey Clower, to tell Hartmann, Ford's Chief of Staff, how the new Vice President should conduct himself. Our objective, Kehrli proudly told Hartmann, "is to make Jerry Ford part of the White House staff."

Hartmann was incensed, and said so to Ford. "Simmer down, Bob," the Vice President said, and assured him everything would work out.

Hartmann was unconvinced. "My differences with Haig and the White House staff were basically simple," Hartmann said. "Al Haig was working in the interests of Richard Nixon, and those were not necessarily the interests of Gerald Ford. To me they were out to screw us and use us in every way they could. It was my duty to be wary, and the Vice President seemed to me to be so unwary. He is not without guile, but he is not instinctively suspicious. And his antennae for spotting a self-server do not always work."

Haig, in turn, disdained Hartmann. He told Nixon and others in the West Wing that Hartmann constantly leaked stories to the press and was a heavy drinker. "The Secret Service reported to me that Bob would get drunk in the office, take off his clothes, and chase his secretary around the desk," Haig said.

The charge was not true, but it reflected Haig's antagonism toward Ford's closest adviser. Hartmann received one Haig message that was even more ominous. Haig told Commander Howard Kerr, Ford's naval aide: "If that fellow Hartmann keeps getting in my way, he's going to find himself on a slab."

Haig usually ignored Hartmann and dealt directly with the Vice President. He would telephone and say, "Jerry, the President would like you to fill in for him . . ." In a flagrant attempt to capture and use Ford, Haig tried to impose watch officers on his Vice Presidential staff and suggested that Nixon's staff write Ford's speeches—as they had Agnew's. Ford agreed.

In mid-January, Haig asked Ford to substitute for Nixon in speaking to the American Farm Bureau Federation in Atlantic City and sent Ford the speech, which had been drafted for Nixon with the standard Nixon defense— "a few extreme partisans . . . bent on stretching out the ordeal of Watergate for their own purposes."

Ford made the speech, using Nixon's words, and was then embarrassed that he had said in public things he did not believe. He was already angry with himself about it when, on the flight back to Washington, he was informed that Federal investigators had discovered that the infamous eighteen-and-a half-minute gap in the one critical Nixon tape was the result of five separate, deliberate erasures.

Ford suddenly realized he was being used by Haig and by Nixon—just as Hartmann had been trying to tell him. Back in his EOB office Ford called in Hartmann. "My credibility will erode overnight," Ford said. "Get whatever help you need, but from now on, you're in charge of speeches."

Congress returned to Washington and on Monday, January 21, 1974, Ford took the Vice President's chair for the first time in the Cabinet Room, as Nixon met with the bipartisan leaders of the House and Senate. Foreign policy was discussed. Domestic issues were raised. But Watergate, the main subject on all minds, was not mentioned. After the meeting Nixon took Ford into the Oval Office. There Watergate was mentioned.

With Haig taking notes, the President began talking, expounding on world affairs, reminiscing about politics, insisting on his innocence. "The President said there was material that would clear him of any involvement in the Watergate mess and he volunteered to show me some of it," Ford said. "He also claimed that he had absolutely nothing to do with the eighteen-and-a-half-minute erasure on the tape." Ford thought it would be unwise for him to look at any evidence and replied, not entirely in candor, that his confidence in the President made it unnecessary for him to listen to White House tapes or examine documents.

The meeting went on and on. Nixon "began to ramble, about the political history of our time, and the things we had done together in Congress years before," Ford said. "It was embarrassing. I had a lot of appointments on my agenda that day. I knew that he had work to do and I felt I ought to leave. But you just don't get up and walk out on the President while he is talking. I kept looking at my watch, but he didn't seem to notice, and he continued to give me his impressions of world affairs and his reactions to what was happening on Capitol Hill."

As the President talked, Ford realized that Nixon was possessed by the fear that his foreign policy triumphs would be overwhelmed by the disaster of Watergate. "He needed me as an escape valve," Ford said. "He was a prisoner in the Oval Office."

Ford never put a direct question to Nixon about Watergate. He knew what to ask—"Mr. President, did you know about the Watergate break-in?" "Were you involved in the cover-up?"—but thought it inappropriate. "If I had asked those questions as House Republican Leader, that would have been asking, 'Mr. President, are you guilty?' And if I had asked him after I became Vice President, then it might seem that I was suggesting that I ought to be President."

Ford fought the suspicion that Nixon might be guilty. "I knew it would be a catastrophe for the country to have a President impeached, or forced to resign," Ford said. "Because of what it would do the country, I honestly did not want to be President."

Time and events changed Ford's belief in Nixon's innocence. There was no one thing that shattered Ford's illusion but rather a migration of judgments. The journey took him, during the first months of his Vice Presidency, from absolute faith in Nixon's word to quiet concern, from concern to doubt, from doubt to suspicion, and, finally, to use his own word, "denial." The idea that he might become President came not as a sudden revelation but as a feeling that crept into his consciousness like a dark shadow.

As it did, Ford's ingrained sense of public duty kept telling him: Be prepared.

Quietly and unobtrusively he accelerated the pace of his learning. At least once a week Secretary of State Kissinger or National Security Council Deputy Brent Scowcroft walked across West Executive Avenue to spend an hour briefing Ford on world developments and crises. "I was being brought up to date," Ford said. "Maybe I was overconfident, but because of my experience on the committees of Defense Appropriations and Foreign Aid, and because I had, as Republican Leader, attended meetings with Kennedy, Johnson, and Nixon whenever we had a foreign policy crisis, I thought I was pretty well informed. But Henry and Brent kept me up to date."

To find out what was going on in the Executive departments, Ford met with every Cabinet member for a status report and question-and-answer session. He listened to Atomic Energy Commissioner Dixie Lee Ray on nuclear weapons and the practical problems of nuclear power. He spent quiet hours with OMB deputies Paul O'Neill and Frank Zarb, two men who could tell him what was really happening in the labyrinths of the vast Federal bureaucracy. He invited Arthur Burns, Chairman of the Federal Reserve, to his office; puffing on their pipes, Ford and Burns talked long and often about fiscal and economic issues. "I had no problem talking economics with Ford," Burns said. "He had a better grasp of economics than any other President I served."

Ford opened the big mahogany door of his EOB office to the diplomats who needed to meet him and cable home their appraisals of the man who might become President. Lord Cromer of the United Kingdom paid him a formal visit. Ambassador Dobrynin, representing the Soviet Union, invited the Vice President and Mrs. Ford to a quiet dinner for superpower talk. The French Ambassador, Jacques Kosciusko-Morizet, made his official call. Helmut Kohl, leader of the German opposition, stopped in to discuss Europe. Ford strode across Pennsylvania Avenue to Blair House to meet with King Hussein and discuss the Middle East.

Since Nixon had isolated himself, Ford became the man to see for visiting Republicans. California Governor Ronald Reagan dropped in for a half hour, as did Governor Bob Ray of Iowa. Governor Meldrim Thompson of New Hampshire paid his respects, as did Jake Garn, then Mayor of Salt Lake City, and Richard Lugar, Mayor of Indianapolis.

Ford opened his door to the press to show them he was different from Nixon. In one short span Ford was interviewed by Marquis Childs, Rowland Evans, Charles Bartlett, Aldo Beckman, and Marvin Arrowsmith; by Juan Cameron of *Fortune* Magazine, by *The Economist*, and by Tom DeFrank for a *Newsweek* cover story. *Time* editors had a private dinner with him.

At every opportunity Ford rode up to Capitol Hill. He was allowed to keep a small office near the House floor where members—Democratic and Republican—could drop in for private talks. As he had for years, he met every week in a brief prayer session with House friends—John Rhodes, Mel Laird, and Al Quie. He presided over the Senate on appropriate occasions and made a practice of joining Republican Senators for their Tuesday policy lunches. He called on Speaker Albert, and had a long visit with his friend and mentor, George Mahon, chairman of the House Appropriations Committee. His political base was Congress; Ford was determined to keep it solid.

As part of his plan to be prepared for whatever was coming, Ford decided he must strengthen his own staff. At first he depended on Hartmann, press secretary Paul Miltich, appointments secretary Mildred Leonard, and a handful of assistants he brought from the Hill. He saw no need to recruit new people. "In the first place," Ford said, "I didn't expect to be in the political arena after I was Vice President. So why bring in a person for two years?"

Prudence prompted him to change his mind. One day Ford called in Hartmann. "Bob, we better think about bringing in a couple more good people to work with us," Ford said. "But I want to avoid former Members of Congress. My position has changed, and a former Member may not understand that it is different now."

"Where do you want to begin?" Hartmann asked.

"I want a national security adviser—not someone in uniform, but someone who has military and foreign policy knowledge, and who understands that I spent some years on Appropriations in that area myself," Ford said. "And he ought to be able to work with Congress."

"Well," Hartmann said, "would you want to make an exception to your no-former-Members rule and consider Jack Marsh for that job?"

Ford thought for a moment. Marsh, a former Democratic Congressman, met all of Ford's qualifications, and was then at the Pentagon as Assistant Secretary of Defense for Legislative Affairs.

"Jack would be excellent," Ford said. "Would you get Jack in here?"

Marsh, when he got the call from Hartmann, thought that Ford wanted to discuss defense legislation. Trim, erect, and amiable, Marsh walked into the Vice President's office in the EOB and held out his hand. Ford grasped it warmly and said: "Jack, I want you to come to work for me."

Marsh broke into a big smile. Without hesitation he said calmly: "The answer is yes, Jerry. Just let me tell Schlesinger and I'll be here."

Like Ford, John O. Marsh, Jr., had a strong sense of public duty. A Virginian by ancestry, birth, and conviction, Marsh was trained and schooled in the Jeffersonian ideal—the "natural aristocracy [of] virtue and talents."

Marsh was the gifted only child of Nell Wayland Marsh, a schoolteacher from Staunton who drilled him in English and history, and a father forced to leave medical school when he became ill with tuberculosis. During the Depression the parents barely made ends meet in the Shenandoah Valley where they lived, but both mother and father instilled in their son the high-minded honor and sense of duty that they themselves lived and taught.

After high school, Marsh enlisted in the U.S. Army. In 1945, while still eighteen, he was commissioned a second lieutenant at the Infantry Officer Candidate School in Fort Benning, Georgia—days before the first atomic bomb was dropped on Hiroshima.

After a year with the U.S. occupation forces in Germany, Marsh returned to Virginia to study Law at Washington and Lee under the G.I. Bill of Rights. As a country lawyer in Strasburg, Virginia, Marsh became active in community affairs. He organized an effort to bring a boat builder, textile plants, and other new job makers into the valley. He served on the Shenandoah County school board that built three modern high schools. As an active member of the Jaycees, Marsh initiated and organized a campaign to plant Liberty Trees throughout the country as living reminders of the American heritage of freedom. In 1959 the Liberty Tree campaign was selected as the outstanding Jaycees project in the nation.

When the Democratic Congressman for the District became ill in 1962,

Marsh ran for the seat and, with the support of Harry Byrd's powerful political organization, won. Young—he was thirty-six—and idealistic, Representative Marsh set out to make his mark. The first bill he introduced was a resolution to commemorate the Bicentennial of the American Revolution. He got it passed, President Johnson signed it, and Speaker McCormack appointed Marsh to the Commission to plan the celebration.

A fellow Member of the House Class of 1963, Don Rumsfeld, first encouraged Marsh to get to know Ford. "Jerry Ford's friendliness reached across the aisle," Marsh said. On many issues, such as a strong national defense, Marsh found that he, as a conservative Democrat, and Ford, as an internationalist Republican, usually stood together and voted together.

Marsh, like Ford, supported President Johnson on the Vietnam War. While much of the country demonstrated against Vietnam, Marsh mobilized Jaycees in his district to declare popular support of the American cause. He organized churches to collect food, clothing and medicine for shipment to the troops. On the premise that a Congressman should do more than make speeches about the War, Marsh—a paratrooper and Major in the National Guard—volunteered to serve a month of active duty in Vietnam. In combat gear, Marsh spent December in the Vietnam highlands. One night he shared a foxhole with a promising young officer he had come to know in the Pentagon, Lieutenant Colonel Alexander Haig, who commanded a battalion in the Iron Triangle. "Al and I, and George Joulwan, his operations officer, spent the night jumping in and out of foxholes, trying to keep our tails from getting shot off," Marsh said.

On the floor of the House his speeches were reasoned and his actions independent. When a House faction moved, at the beginning of the Ninetieth Congress, to refuse to seat black Representative Adam Clayton Powell because of conduct unbecoming a Member, Marsh argued that such an action violated the Constitution. Only the people of a Congressional District decide who shall represent them, he contended. At the end of a bitter debate the House refused to seat Powell; Marsh was the only Southerner in the House to vote to grant Powell the seat to which his Harlem constituency had elected him. *The Richmond Times-Dispatch* commended his action: "Everyone should admire the cool independence and devotion to principle with which John O. Marsh, Jr., confronted this crucial issue, and cast his vote as his conscience dictated, despite a contrary clamor from many of his constituents."

On Veterans Day in 1969 Marsh was the only Democratic congressman who would speak at a Support-the-Forces rally President Nixon sponsored at the Washington Monument. Near the end of his fourth term, Marsh broke with the Democratic Party hierarchy in Virginia on a matter of principle and decided not to run for reelection. He began a law practice in Washington, in an office at 1701 Pennsylvania Avenue, where, by chance, the Nixon reelection campaign offices opened a year later. When the Democrats nominated Senator McGovern in 1972, Marsh signed up with Democrats for Nixon. After his reelection, President Nixon personally appointed Marsh to be the senior Defense official dealing with Congress on military legislation.

In the Office of the Vice President, Marsh and Hartmann became senior partners. Hartmann was closer to Ford, and the more experienced with the press; but his gifts did not include human relations. "People tended to underestimate Bob because they overreacted to his personality," Marsh said. Marsh, with no known enemies, provided an effective balance to Hartmann's irascible nature. In political maneuvering, Hartmann was blunt and direct, Marsh adroit and persuasive. Marsh also had friends in the White House, notably President Nixon and Haig.

Both Marsh and Hartmann could see the storm coming. Each believed Nixon would be forced from office, and that Ford would become President, almost certainly in some form of political upheaval. To Hartmann, it was political intuition. Marsh saw legal evidence linking Nixon with one or more crimes. He had observed the close working connection between James McCord and John Mitchell. John Lehman, a friend of Marsh in Nixon's NSC, had also confided that the Ellsberg break-in had been authorized by John Ehrlichman, the President's counsel. To Marsh, the details of Watergate and the Ellsberg burglary, when laid out before the liberal majority of the House Judiciary Committee, would almost certainly lead to Nixon's impeachment.

Yet, despite their belief that a Ford Presidency was inevitable, neither Hartmann nor Marsh would even mention it to Ford or to anyone else. Gossip in the Vice President's office could leak and produce a tragic result. "There was no 'lean and hungry look' in our part of the EOB," Marsh said. No office speculation was permitted. "If Hartmann or I heard of any talk on this very sensitive issue, we squelched it," Marsh said. He and Hartmann knew they must protect the integrity and openness that had brought Ford into the Vice Presidency—qualities that would be vital to the legitimacy of government when Ford become President.

In his hideaway in the same wing of the EOB, Nixon contemplated the prospect of impeachment not as a legal proceeding but as one more political battle. It is not surprising; Nixon's life was politics, not the law. As the House Judiciary Committee began its proceedings, Nixon spent much of his time counting votes. "I was about to embark on the campaign of my life," he wrote. Bemoaning the loss of support among Republicans in Congress, he confessed, "It was largely my own fault. Too many who had tried to defend me in the past had been burned."

Sitting alone with his fears, Nixon studied the list of the thirty-eight members of the House Judiciary Committee—twenty-one Democrats, seventeen Republicans. Going through the roster, Nixon wrote off eighteen Democrats as partisan liberals. The other three Democrats were Southern conservatives—James Mann of South Carolina, Walter Flowers of Alabama, and Ray Thornton of Arkansas. "My only hope would be either to hold every Republican and pick up two of the Southern Democrats, or to hold sixteen Republicans and win all three of the Southerners," he wrote. But all his calculations could fall against the "enemy within: the tapes. . . . The ones I had already reviewed were bad enough; now what might be on the others haunted us all."

In a private memo to Haig, Timmons wrote: "There is speculation on Capitol Hill that Tip O'Neill is pulling the strings behind the House Judiciary Committee and that the Democrats' strategy is to force a confrontation quickly on the President's tapes and papers, contempt citation and impeachment." O'Neill, Timmons noted, had made an off-the-record prediction in Massachusetts that Nixon would be forced to resign by early summer.

White House Counselor Anne Armstrong sent Haig and Timmons a private count of the Texas House delegation: Eleven of twenty Democrats were ready to vote for impeachment.

On March 18, 1974, Senator James Buckley of New York issued a public call that Nixon resign for the good of the country. It was a heavy blow to Nixon's hope of survival. Not only did Jim Buckley represent the vigorously intellectual family that best articulated the doctrine of the Conservative movement in America; but in four years in the Senate Buckley had earned his colleagues' respect as a singular example of reason, courage, and unshakable independence.

In addressing the crisis, Buckley put his case in an essay blending history, politics, and logic. From its origin in "a trivial and foolish incident," Buckley wrote, "Watergate has expanded on a scale that has plunged our country into what historians call 'a crisis of the regime' . . . a disorder, a trauma, involving every tissue of the nation, conspicuously including its moral and spiritual dimensions." The Constitutional process of impeachment would not "bring an end to our national agony," Buckley said, but make "the ruler of the mightiest nation on earth ... the prisoner in the dock."

There was but one way out of the crisis, Buckley said to the President: "I believe that your voluntary resignation at this particular time would represent an extraordinary act of courage and patriotism and personal sacrifice on your part, and that it would be seen as such by your countrymen and by future historians."

Nixon, in a press conference in Houston the next day, delivered a cold response to Buckley's letter. The Watergate charges were false, he said. "It also takes courage to stand and fight for what you believe is right, and that is what I intend to do."

Two days later Nixon asked House Republican Leader John Rhodes to the Oval Office to get his advice on a request from the House Judiciary Committee that he surrender forty more White House tapes. Would House Republicans support him if he refused to turn over the tapes?

No, Rhodes answered. The President's standing in the House was so low that Members would not risk voting against any reasonable Judiciary effort to get evidence for impeachment. Rhodes warned Nixon: If he rejected a House subpoena for evidence for its impeachment investigation, Republicans would join Democrats in voting the President in contempt of Congress—and that itself would be grounds for impeachment.

After dinner that night Nixon, alone in the Lincoln Sitting Room, reflected on his dilemma. At 2:00 A.M. the next morning, he picked up his yellow pad. "Lowest day," he wrote. "Contempt equals impeachment."

A few days later Nixon, through Haig, asked Ford to come in to the Oval Office for a one-on-one talk. Haig had suggested to the President that he thank Ford for his public statements of support and suggest delicately that Ford stop traveling so much and stay in town to lobby Republicans in the House to commit to vote against impeachment.

Nixon did thank Ford for his public support but stopped short of asking him to lobby for votes against impeachment. While the two were together the conversation turned to politics. In a special election to fill Ford's House seat, the Fifth District of Michigan had just elected a Democrat for the first time since 1910. Nixon asked Ford: "Why did it happen?"

Ford, believing it would be improper to mislead the President, said simply: "Watergate."

* * *

RIGHT
Dorothy Gardner King with her
firstborn son, Leslie King, Jr.,
a few months after she fled from
the husband who threatened their
lives. (*Gerald R. Ford Library*)

BELOW, LEFT
Gerald Ford at three in Grand
Rapids. With the remarriage of his
mother, "Junior" King has become
"Junior" Ford.
(*Gerald R. Ford Library*)

BELOW, RIGHT
In Peter Pan collar and all ready
for Sunday school, Junior Ford at
six or seven years old.
(*Gerald R. Ford Library*)

Gerald Ford, Sr., in 1927 with his stepson and sons, Tom (*left*),
Dick (*right*), and Jim (*on his lap*). (*Gerald R. Ford Library*)

Eagle Scout Jerry Ford raises the flag with the
Guard of Honor at Michigan's Mackinac Island State Park.
(*Gerald R. Ford Library*)

Phyllis Brown, Ford's all-American Girl and the first love of his life. To a hard-working Yale coach and law student, she brought learning and sophistication, good times and youthful passion. (*The collection of Phyllis Brown Phillips*)

The class that excelled: Ford is eighth from left in the back row of this 1940 photo of the Yale Law School fraternity. In this same row, Sargent Shriver, first Director of the Peace Corps and Democratic nominee for Vice President, is fifth from right; and Supreme Court Justice Potter Stewart is second from right. In the fourth row, Secretary of State Cyrus Vance is at the left end, Pennsylvania Governor Raymond Shafer is eighth from right, and Supreme Court Justice Byron White is seventh from right. In the second row, Colorado Senator Peter Dominick is eighth from left and FAA Administrator Najeeb Halaby is second from right. In the front row, author Walter Lord is at the left end, Pennsylvania Governor William Scranton is fourth from the right end, and Stanley Resor is third from the right end. (*Gerald R. Ford Library*)

RIGHT
Ford and his mentor, Representative John Taber of New York. Ford courted the old curmudgeon and got the Appropriations Committee seat he wanted. (*Gerald R. Ford Library*)

LEFT
Friends and allies: Ford and new Senator Richard Nixon discuss plans for Nixon's Lincoln Day visit to Grand Rapids in February 1951. "That visit," Ford said, "was where I first really got to know Nixon." (*Gerald R. Ford Library*)

BELOW
During the Korean War, Ford inspects the Oppama Ordnance Depot. (*Gerald R. Ford Library*)

RIGHT

Congressional wife: Betty Ford holds her husband's coat, and Michael his briefcase. Her view: "Wall-to-wall playpens and tricycles." (*Gerald R. Ford Library*)

BELOW

Ford (*standing, second from right*) and Vice President Nixon at a gathering of the influential Chowder and Marching Club to celebrate Nixon's forty-fourth birthday. (*Gerald R. Ford Library*)

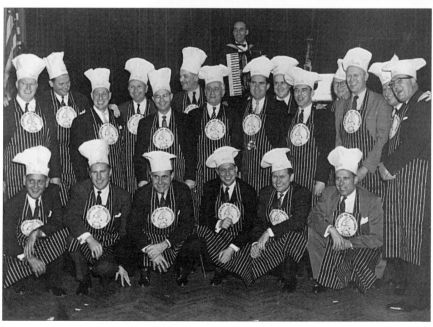

≡

As Michigan's favorite son in 1960, Ford arrived at the Republican National Convention ambitious to be Nixon's running mate. Nixon encouraged him; but Eisenhower dictated the choice: Lodge. (*Gerald R. Ford Library*)

≡

Betty Ford, with Michael, Jack, Steve, and Susan. "I had to bring up four kids by myself. I was feeling terribly neglected. The loneliness makes marriages crack, makes liquor more attractive." (*Gerald R. Ford Library*)

Power baseball: House Minority
Leader Ford, House Whip Leslie
Arends, President Johnson, Vice
President Humphrey, Speaker John
McCormack, Senate Majority Leader
Mike Mansfield. In the row behind
them, Senate Minority Leader Everett
Dirksen, White House aide Lawrence
O'Brien, and House Majority Leader
Carl Albert, at Opening Day of the
1965 baseball season.
(*Gerald R. Ford Library*)

CENTER

Exit: Eight days after their landslide
reelection, Nixon shows Agnew to the
door at Camp David and begins his
inside campaign to end Agnew's
political career.
(*The Nixon Presidential Papers*)

LEFT

Heir apparent. Nixon and John Connally in
Aspen House at Camp David on November 16,
1972. Nixon offered Connally any Cabinet job
he wanted and the 1976 Republican nomination
for President.
(*The Nixon Presidential Papers*)

ABOVE

Nixon and Ford reach an understanding in the Oval Office on October 12, 1973: Ford would serve out the balance of Agnew's term as Vice President and support John Connally to succeed Nixon in 1976. (*The Nixon Presidential Papers*)

LEFT

On the eve of the Saturday Night Massacre, Nixon and Haig walk the South Lawn of the White House to plan the dismissal of Special Prosecutor Archibald Cox. (*The Nixon Presidential Papers*)

≡

Standing before the House Speaker's rostrum he could never never attain, Ford takes the oath of office as Vice President on December 6, 1973. (*The Nixon Presidential Papers*)

History is manifest in this tableau: Two months earlier Speaker Albert, on the podium at left, had imposed Congress' choice on Nixon. Seven months later, Chief Justice Warren Burger, administering the oath, wrote the Court judgment that forced President Nixon, at right, to reveal the evidence that forced him to resign. Weeks after Nixon was forced from office, Senator James O. Eastland, President ProTem of the Senate, intervened with Special Prosecutor Leon Jaworski to stop the indictment of Nixon.

≡

BELOW
Grim of face, determined to be resolute, Nixon waves a final farewell to the White House that consumed him. (*George Tames*)

"I will resign as President." As soon as the White House photographer finished taking this last photograph of Nixon and Ford in the Oval Office, Nixon tells Ford he will resign the next day. The Presidential desk is already bare.
(*The Nixon Presidential Papers*)

Pain and sadness, for Julie Nixon and David Eisenhower, Betty and Gerald Ford. The President-to-be waves a solemn goodbye to his fallen friend.
(*George Tames*)

TOP

Knowing that his Presidency would stand or fall on his testimony, Ford tells a House Judiciary why he pardoned Nixon. "There was no deal, period, under no circumstances."
(*Gerald R. Ford Library*)

CENTER

Ford and Soviet General Secretary Leonid Brezhnev. At Ford's first summit, in Vladivostok: soccer, football, and nuclear missiles.
(*Gerald R. Ford Library*)

BOTTOM

End in Vietnam: Ford, Vice President Rockefeller, and Secretary of State Kissinger get the word that the last Americans in Saigon are lifted, under fire, from the roof of the U.S. Embassy. "It was the saddest hour of my time in the White House."
(*Gerald R. Ford Library*)

To stay in shape in the White House, Ford keeps his daily regimen: fifty push-ups and twenty miles on the stationary bicycle. (*George Tames*)

Ford gives Republican National Chairman George Bush a new job: Heading the U.S. Mission to the People's Republic of China. (*Gerald R. Ford Library*)

Presidential debate. Ford and Jimmy Carter debate foreign policy in San Francisco; by mistakenly declaring Poland free of Russian domination, Ford lost the debate—and credibility. (*White House photos by David Kennerly*)

Election night, 1976: The impending defeat is reflected in the expressions of Ford and his campaign sidekick, Joe Garagiola.
(*White House photos by David Kennerly*)

Instead of curbing his public appearances, in the spring of 1974 Ford expanded them. In his quiet way he made a deliberate decision to travel throughout America and declare his independence, at least to the extent that he could. "He deliberately fled Washington, very deliberately," Hartmann said. "He just told me to accept every invitation he possibly could. His travel itinerary became almost continuous. He was not being devious. On the other hand he was nobody's fool. I am sure the thought crossed his mind that he was a lot safer out on the road than he was in his office. The best way to show he was not Nixon's boy was to go out in the country and express thoughts that were vaguely at variance. He didn't want to seem to be sitting around waiting for the phone to ring so Nixon could ask his advice about something."

For the Vice President's travels, Haig assigned him a noisy and dented prop-driven Air Force Convair, far less swift and comfortable than the four-engine Boeing jets used by President Nixon, Kissinger, and Haig himself.

Ford welcomed his second-hand wings. With his own plane he could travel whenever and wherever he chose to go. He flew to Michigan for Gerald R. Ford Day, to Ohio for a Touchdown Club dinner, to Kentucky, Chicago, and Cincinnati to make political speeches, to Omaha for a briefing by the chiefs of intelligence and operations at the Strategic Air Command, to New York City to receive an American-Israel Friendship Award and to lunch with the editors of *The New York Times.*

In flight, Ford's seat in the rear of *Air Force Two* was his office. He walked aboard carrying his own briefcase and a bundle of newspapers and magazines. First the newspapers came out, and he went through *The Washington Post, The New York Times, The Grand Rapids Press, The Wall Street Journal,* the *Los Angeles Times,* and any local newspaper he picked up. Then he would take out the news magazines—*Time, Newsweek,* and *U.S. News & World Report*—tear out all the postcard advertisements stapled through the bindings, and proceed to read each magazine. When he finished the news magazines, he would open his briefcase, read reports and memoranda, and sign any correspondence that had been drafted for his signature. There was no small talk to him or around him; and his traveling companions knew never to ask him a question until the ritual of his work was over. After a trip, when he got back to the office, he emptied the briefcase, refilled it with new material to read, and took it on the next trip. On average, he was reading five hours a day.

By late March, on swings through Phoenix, Denver, New York City, Miami, Tampa, Boston, and Philadelphia, Ford was trying out new lines: "I am my own man" and "I shall remain my own man." The audience cheered. He broke an earlier rule and began answering "what-if" questions. Henry Brandon of the *London Times* asked in an interview, "If you became President what would you do to make sure that such a scandal is not repeated?"

"We ought not to employ and tolerate people who have that kind of mentality," Ford said, and he would turn the campaign over to the Republican National Committee, which has "the professionals who would not have done such an idiotic thing as the break-in . . ."

The press spotted the dynamics. Marjorie Hunter, who covered the Vice President for *The New York Times,* observed that as Ford distanced himself from Nixon, his audiences were becoming bigger and friendlier. "The Vice President has all but abandoned earlier efforts to improve the President's image," Hunter wrote. "The man has changed, too. He appears more sure of himself. He frequently tosses away prepared speeches and speaks whatever happens to be on his mind. He breaks into a smile when confronted with even the toughest, most politically embarrassing questions at news conferences." On a night flight from Cincinnati to Washington, Ford explained his objective to Hunter: "I'm doing everything I can to put the party back together."

The Republican Party recognized that. Massachusetts Governor Francis Sargent called publicly for Nixon to step down so Ford could become President. Clare Booth Luce telephoned Anne Armstrong at the White House to say that in Chicago she had seen Ford on Kupcinet's television show: "He was utterly splendid. Quiet, dignified, humorous, forceful, and never fudged on an answer."

In taking the Vice Presidency on the road, Ford was trying to help the Republican Party and put distance between himself and Nixon's White House. "Nixon couldn't campaign for anybody," he said. "So I had the principal responsibility to hold seats, especially House seats. It was not easy, because there wasn't a hell of a lot to talk about. My friends in the House were still my friends, and when I was in Washington I felt very comfortable going up to Capitol Hill—more comfortable than going to the White House.

"The White House entourage of Haig and the others, well, they treated me and my staff like we were just sort of necessary evils. We didn't mind. We just went out and did our own thing."

By the end of March Ford was publicly attacking Watergate and the Nixon amateurs who caused it. To a Chicago gathering of a thousand Republicans from the Midwest, he proclaimed, "Never again must Americans allow an arrogant, elite guard of political adolescents" to direct a Republican Presidential campaign. The crowd loved it, interrupted with cheers and applause, and gave him a standing ovation as he concluded. From Chicago Ford flew on to Clearwater, Florida, to deliver the same fighting words to a rally of nine hundred Republicans. Again he left on a high wave of enthusiasm and applause.

On the flight back to Washington that night, John Osborne, columnist for *The New Republic,* asked if he might talk with Ford for a few minutes.

"Sure, sit down," Ford said. Ford liked and trusted Osborne; and after his splendid day, he felt like talking. Osborne said he was interested in whether Ford had thought much about what he would do if he should become President.

Ford began with his standard litany: He did not expect to become President and did not want to be President. But, he told Osborne, he did recognize that it could happen. If it should, Ford went on, Kissinger, "a superb Secretary of State," would remain on the job. They had already talked about it, he said. As for the other members of the Cabinet, he would want to keep Peter Brennan at Labor, Rogers Morton at Interior, and Jim Lynn at Housing and Urban Development. He would not keep Schlesinger at Defense; he was a brilliant intellectual but incapable of dealing with Congress.

For White House staff, Ford said he would try to persuade Melvin Laird and Bryce Harlow to return. Both were superb. Ford would take with him his own senior Vice Presidential staff, and might keep Haig, "a great manager" who was holding the Nixon White House together. But Ford was not sure that Haig and Hartmann could work together, and thought Haig might want to return to the Army. As for Ron Ziegler, Nixon's press secretary, he would be out.

Of Nixon, Ford said, he rambled on in meetings, reminisced, wasted everyone's time. Nixon, he told Osborne, had some kind of a "change of personality" over the last year.

When the Osborne story came out the next week, the White House retaliated. Pat Buchanan publicly warned against the impeachment of Nixon; Ford, he said, "lacks Nixon's foreign policy skills."

Nixon himself still assumed that Ford provided insurance against impeachment. In the Oval Office talking to Governor Nelson Rockefeller of New York one day, Nixon put his hands on the arms of his chair and said with sarcasm: "Can you imagine Jerry Ford sitting in this chair?"

Rockefeller mentioned the disdainful Nixon comment to Senator Jack Javits, and it was published in *Newsweek.* Ford was incensed and went in to ask the President if the story was true. Nixon denied it, and told Haig to telephone Rockefeller and ask him to deny it also. Rockefeller did as asked.

Outside the White House, the cherry blossoms bloomed and vanished with the soft rains during that warm and splendid Spring of 1974 in Washington. Inside, President Nixon could see the closing of the ring.

On April 11, for the first time in history, the House Judiciary Committee subpoenaed a President to provide evidence that might lead to his impeachment. By a vote of 33-3, a margin that shocked the White House, the Committee demanded that Nixon turn over the tapes and related documents of forty conversations he had with Haldeman, Ehrlichman, Dean, and others about Watergate. Committee Chairman Rodino gave the President two weeks to comply, or be in contempt of Congress.

The Watergate Special Prosecutor was also ready to force Nixon to give up the White House tapes for the impending trial of Mitchell, Haldeman, and the others indicted for Watergate. From his first day on the job some four months earlier Jaworski had realized the hard evidence of the Watergate crimes was in Nixon's hands, so he wrote the President to ask for certain tapes. When he received nothing, Jaworski went to Court. Judge Sirica, at Jaworski's request, subpoenaed the tapes of sixty-four Nixon conversations about Watergate.

At that point Nixon feared the House more than the Court. In the hope of closing off the continuing demands for tapes, Nixon announced he would not only turn over forty-two transcripts to the House Judiciary Committee but also make the tapes public. On April 30 the White House press office released a 1,308-page document of transcripts of Nixon conversations. Even though many vulgarities were deleted, a stunned public learned for the first time of Nixon's habit of speaking in foul-mouthed cynicism. Almost lost in the commotion over "expletive deleted" was the announcement by the President's senior defense lawyer, James St. Clair, that Nixon would refuse to hand over to Special Prosecutor Jaworski the tapes and documents that Judge Sirica had subpoenaed.

On Monday, May 6, Nixon first heard the tapes of his June 23, 1972, conversations with Haldeman, he wrote in his memoirs. There in his EOB hideaway that day he listened to himself telling Haldeman to ask CIA Deputy Vernon Walters to stop the FBI investigation of Watergate. That tape, Nixon immediately realized, would prove that he had lied about those meetings. "I had indicated in all my public statements that the sole motive for calling in the CIA had been national security," he wrote. "But there was no doubt now that we had been talking about political implications that morning." Nixon had long acted as though he were guilty; when he listened to the June 23 tape, he knew he was guilty.

Nixon deliberately did not tell his lawyers—St. Clair, Buzhardt, and Garment—that he had found this evidence against himself. Nor would he permit them or anyone else to hear this incriminating tape. He ordered it locked in the vault.

For two days Nixon pondered what he should do with this damning evidence. The only way to conceal the tape of his June 23 conversations with Haldeman, he concluded, was to conceal all the tapes—whatever the cost. So he made that decision. He told Buzhardt and St. Clair that he would deliver no more White House tapes—not to Rodino's Committee, not to Sirica's Court, not to Prosecutor Jaworski. "Perhaps," Nixon said to Ziegler, "this is Armageddon."

By openly defying the Court and Congress, Nixon did in fact provoke the final battle. The next day, May 9, the House Judiciary Committee opened hearings on Nixon's impeachment. John Rhodes, the Republican Leader on whom Nixon was counting to manage his defense in the House, said publicly that Nixon should consider resigning.

As the House moved toward impeaching Nixon, Special Prosecutor Jaworski asked the Supreme Court to rule on whether the President could legally refuse to comply with his subpoena. After considering the Constitutional questions for a week, Chief Justice Warren Burger himself decided that the Supreme Court would hear the case, titled, appropriately, *United States* v. *Nixon*.

By late Spring of 1974, Ford was expanding his national campaign to establish his identity and credibility. His travels took him to Ohio, Colorado, and Michigan; to Kansas for Bob Dole; to New York City to lunch with the Associated Press and have dinner with Hearst editors; to the Greenbrier Hotel in West Virginia to talk to bankers; to Washington to address the Republican National Committee. He made the commencement address at the University of Michigan, spoke to the Economic Club of New York City, flew through the Midwest and the South, on to Hawaii, then returned to Washington long enough to lay a Memorial Day wreath at the Tomb of the Unknown Soldier. After a Cabinet meeting he was off to Charlotte, Birmingham, and a stirring speech to the Republican convention in New Hampshire.

In every corner of America Ford heard the same words—"Nixon is finished." To himself he calculated "the odds were fifty-fifty that Nixon would have to step down eventually. Yet I couldn't afford to mention it to anyone—not my family, not my staff, and certainly not the press."

Late in May, Ford went in alone to tell the President that he could no longer support his refusal to supply documents to the House Judiciary Committee. As politely as he could, Ford warned Nixon that if he continued the legal confrontation, he would lose in the Committee and in the House.

"I know you and others would do it differently," Nixon said, "but we think we're right and we're going to continue to do it this way."

Not long after his meeting with Nixon, Ford dutifully told a Republican audience in Columbus, "The preponderance of the evidence is that [Nixon] is innocent of any involvement in any cover-up." Minutes later he learned that a Federal Grand Jury in Washington had included Nixon as an unindicted co-conspirator in the cover-up. Stung again, embarrassed again, Ford was furious. "I was in an impossible situation," he said. "I couldn't abandon Nixon, because that would make it appear that I was trying to position myself to become President. Nor could I get too close to him, because if I did I'd risk being sucked into the whirlpool myself."

Ford decided the only thing he could do was zigzag—to be inconsistent in his comments. One day the tilt would be favorable: Nixon is innocent of an impeachable offense, he would say. The next day he would tilt against him: "Nixon was wrong to refuse to turn over relevant Watergate documents and tapes to the House Judiciary Committee." But he always felt he had to be slightly more loyal than independent. "I was determined to make sure Nixon could never say that I undercut him," Ford said.

Embattled in his own capital, Nixon turned abroad in one last attempt to save himself. Kissinger had made enough progress in resolving the Arab-Israeli conflict to justify a personal journey by Nixon to Egypt, Syria, Saudi Arabia, Jordan, and Israel. Nixon pressed Kissinger to arrange the trip to provide him the opportunity to flee his troubles at least for a brief time and to devote his dwindling energies and reputation to the true love of his life, foreign affairs.

For ten days in June the great white Presidential jet, with the American flag on its side, lifted Nixon from capital to capital. The Arabs and Israelis pledged specific actions to resolve differences; and by any reasonable measure, Nixon's "Journey for Peace" was a major success. Kissinger, Nixon's companion in statecraft, wrote later that only President Nixon "could have imposed the complex and tough policy that got us this far . . ." When Nixon's helicopter landed on the South Lawn of the White House, Vice President

Ford was there to lead the homecoming. Quoting from Matthew's version of the Beatitudes, Ford said: "Blessed is the peacemaker."

Peacemaking was not enough. On June 20, the day after Nixon's return, Jaworski renewed the attack. In a brief he filed with the Supreme Court, Jaworski stated that the White House tapes were necessary to the prosecution of Haldeman, Ehrlichman, and the others—and that the President himself was part of a conspiracy to obstruct justice.

To get a fresh reading on the likelihood of his impeachment, Nixon telephoned Joe Waggoner, a pro-Nixon Democrat from Louisiana. Canny and persuasive, Waggoner often led a coalition of Democrats to support Nixon on major issues; and he was recognized as one of the best vote counters in the House. He told Nixon that he could deliver seventy Democratic votes against impeachment. For a moment Nixon's hopes soared—with that many Democrats and the 150 Republicans in Timmons's vote counts, Nixon calculated he could escape impeachment. But Waggoner warned Nixon: "The only thing that would change these votes would be that you could be held in contempt of the Supreme Court, for any reason."

Nixon knew he was about to be caught. If he disclosed the evidence on the tapes, the House might impeach him for obstructing justice. If he refused a Supreme Court order to turn over the tapes, the House might impeach him for contempt of the Court. His only remaining hope, Nixon realized, was the Supreme Court. In his diary he wrote, "After my call with Joe Waggoner . . . I realized that we are really looking at about thirty days in which the climactic decision with regard to whether we are able to stay in office."

With the Watergate sword hanging over his head, Nixon prepared to leave again, after only five days in Washington, for Summit III in Moscow. Never had an American President set off on a major diplomatic enterprise with so little prospect of success. The USSR was intransigent. Nixon's own Defense Secretary, James Schlesinger, was collaborating with Democrats in the Senate to undercut the President's disarmament options. This 1974 mission to Moscow, Kissinger wrote, was "an encounter doomed to irrelevance."

Moreover, the President was ill, and had been for weeks. A painful blood clot in his left leg, diagnosed as phlebitis, compelled the White House physician, Dr. William Lukash, to plead with the President to postpone the trip. Nixon refused, and ordered that his illness and pain be kept secret from the press and his Russian hosts.

In long days of meetings with Brezhnev, Nixon discussed detente, the reduction of nuclear weapons, and European security, and signed agreements on energy, the environment, and arms that were useful but brought little public recognition. Kissinger considered the Summit a success after all, and observed: "Nixon was at his best; he managed to overcome the agony more and more devouring him for one last exhibition of his conceptual prowess." It was Nixon's last foreign trip as President.

In an attempt to shore up his support in the Senate, Nixon invited his favorite conservative Democratic Senators to the Cabinet Room to tell them his side of the Watergate story. Among his guests were both Mississippi Senators, James Eastland, 70, seated at Nixon's right, and John Stennis, 73, at Nixon's left. Nixon talked about old times and Southern college football before he got around to the purpose of the meeting. "Now I want to brief you on this Watergate—" he said, but Eastland interrupted.

"Mr. President, we don't need to hear any explanations. We don't even want to talk about Watergate. We're witcha. Everybody in this room's witcha."

Nixon thanked him, rambled on about other subjects, and again said: "We've got to talk about this Watergate situation—"

Again Eastland interrupted, "We don't want to hear about Watergate."

Nixon tried for the third time: "To get back to Watergate—"

When Eastland started to break in again, Stennis reached over in front of Nixon and clamped his hand on Eastland's forearm. "Jim! Jim!" Stennis said in exasperation. "Shut up and let the boy speak."

On the first Monday after the July 4 holiday, eight black-robed members of the United States Supreme Court filed into the imposing marble chamber to hear the case *United States* v. *Richard Nixon.* His words echoing off the coffered ceiling, Special Prosecutor Jaworski argued that not even a President had the Constitutional right to withhold evidence of a crime. Nixon's St. Clair contended that every President must preserve the right to private communication with his counselors. "The President is not above the law," St. Clair said. "Nor does he contend that he is. What he does contend is that as President the law can be applied to him in only one way, and that is by impeachment."

The opinion of the Court was never in doubt. On the very next day Chief Justice Warren Burger called the seven other participating justices into his conference room to consider the case. All agreed that President Nixon must surrender the tapes to Sirica's Court and Jaworski, but the justices' reasons differed. Chief Justice Burger assigned himself to write the opinion, and the process of drafting and rewriting and compromising took almost two weeks.

On July 12 the President again left Washington, this time to seclude himself in his walled haven in San Clemente. As it happened, Vice President Ford was campaigning nearby for California Republicans, and went to see Nixon. The President tried to discuss the problems of the economy, but Ford thought he seemed distracted. "It was clear to me that he wasn't as strong either mentally or physically as he had been before," Ford said. "I had a growing sense of his frustration, his resentment, and his lack of a calm, deliberate approach to the problems of government. His resolve to stay and fight seemed to be weakening."

The next week Timmons telephoned Nixon to deliver an ominous report: O'Neill, Rodino, and other House Democratic leaders were pressing the few wavering Democrats on Judiciary to vote to impeach. To hold the Southern conservatives on a floor vote, Timmons pointed out, the President must hold at least two on the Committee. "We think we have Walter Flowers, maybe more," Timmons told the President.

Weighing the dangers, Nixon noted in his diary: "If Timmons' more pessimistic views prevail, the battle for the balance of the year [will be] in the Senate." The House vote, he calculated, would be "very damn close" even before the Supreme Court decides.

On Tuesday, July 23, Representative Lawrence Hogan, a conservative Republican from Maryland on the Judiciary Committee, announced that he would vote for impeachment. It was a severe shock to Nixon. He and Timmons had assumed Hogan was a sure vote, and the announcement "dealt us a very bad blow," Nixon said.

Timmons telephoned with more bad news. "Mr. President," Timmons said, "we have lost all three Southern Democrats on the Committee."

"I was stunned," Nixon wrote. "I had been prepared to lose one and had steeled myself for losing two. But losing all three meant certain defeat on the House floor. It meant impeachment." Nixon called Haig in. We must, Nixon said, do something to get at least one of the Southerners back.

Haig suggested that the President telephone Alabama Governor George Wallace and ask him to talk to Flowers. Nixon agreed, called Wallace, and said, "George, I'm just calling to ask if you're still with me."

"No, Mr. President, I'm afraid I'm not."

Wallace added that he was praying for the President but believed it would be improper for him to ask Flowers to change his vote.

The conversation ended. Nixon put the phone down, turned to Haig and said: "Well, Al, there goes the Presidency."

* * *

In hope or in despair, Nixon telephoned Waggoner for another assessment of his prospects in the House. With the loss of the three Southerners on Judiciary, Waggoner replied, he could hold no more than thirty-five votes on the floor. In a gentle voice Waggoner said quietly: "Mr. President, unless something changes, I'm afraid you are going to lose in the House."

Sitting alone in his San Clemente study that night, Nixon wrote: "My options have been reduced to only two: resign or be impeached . . . 12:01 A.M. Lowest point in the Presidency, and Supreme Court still to come."

Eight hours later the Court acted. On Wednesday, July 24, 1974, Chief Justice Burger delivered the unanimous decision from the lofty bench of the Supreme Court Chamber. In brief the Court said that neither Nixon nor any other President may use Executive Privilege to withhold evidence of a crime. The Court upheld Judge Sirica's order to Nixon: Deliver the sixty-four White House tapes under subpoena to Special Prosecutor Jaworski.

In San Clemente, the decision was a staggering blow to Nixon. Of the four sitting Justices he had appointed, one—Rehnquist—recused himself. But surely, Nixon hoped, Burger, Blackmun, and Powell might support his claim that the Constitutional separation of powers gave him the right to protect confidential White House discussions.

Angry, feeling persecuted, and fearful of the consequences of the unanimous ruling against him, Nixon said he would refuse to carry out the Court decision. Haig and St. Clair talked him out of it. They persuaded him that refusal to give the tapes to Jaworski would cost him his remaining support in Congress and make impeachment certain.

But Nixon knew that complying with the Supreme Court order would make impeachment just as certain. He, unlike the others, had heard the evidence on the June 23, 1972, tape.

Now that he must give up that tape, Nixon realized it was urgent that he have his lawyers tell him whether his conversation with Haldeman that day was as incriminating as he thought it was. In his office he grabbed the phone from Haig, who was talking to Buzhardt. "There might be a problem with the June 23 tape, Fred," Nixon said. "Get right on it and get back to Al."

Across the continent in his White House office, Buzhardt listened to the tape, carefully inscribing on a yellow legal pad the ominous words. Through the earphones he heard the voice of President Nixon conspiring with Haldeman to use the CIA to stop the FBI investigation of the Watergate break-in. Again and again Buzhardt played the tape, transcribing in longhand, checking and rechecking this first written account of the June 23 tape. There was no mistaking the voices, no mistaking the import of the evidence.

To Buzhardt, it was a clear case of obstructing justice. He realized that Nixon had lied to him and to St. Clair, and they in turn had misled the House Judiciary Committee and a Federal Court.

Buzhardt telephoned Haig. "Well, we've found the smoking pistol."

"Are you sure?" Haig asked.

"Yes, it's the ball game," Buzhardt said, and recounted how Nixon told Haldeman to tell the CIA to stop the FBI investigation.

"What do you think we ought to do?" Haig asked.

"The President ought to think about his options," Buzhardt said. He could refuse the Supreme Court order and resign, or turn over the tapes.

Haig delivered Buzhardt's opinion to Nixon, and Nixon asked that he have Buzhardt listen again. Buzhardt did so, called back, and told Haig for the second time that he was certain that the tape was evidence of a Nixon crime.

With Haig and St. Clair on the telephone, Buzhardt offered a new idea: The entire Watergate problem—the trials of Mitchell and the others, the tapes, compliance with the Supreme Court order, impeachment—could be "mooted" if Nixon would pardon all the Watergate defendants, pardon himself, and then resign.

Buzhardt told Haig and St. Clair he had already researched the legal precedents supporting a President's Constitutional power to pardon. He had found Supreme Court decisions upholding a President's authority to pardon a person even before he had been indicted or tried.

Nixon told Haig he would consider Buzhardt's sweeping proposal, even though he regarded it as "drastic."

After a two-hour debate with Haig, St. Clair, and Ziegler, Nixon finally accepted their counsel that he not only accept the Court order but also make an immediate public statement saying so. Grudgingly he accepted their draft of a Nixon statement: "I have instructed Mr. St. Clair to take whatever measures are necessary to comply with that decision in all respects."

That night the House Judiciary Committee began debating on live television the Articles of Impeachment of President Richard Nixon. In his study beside the Pacific, Nixon watched his own trial on live television. "My supporters were eloquent—but they were fighting a losing battle," he wrote. "And now, like slow-fused dynamite waiting to explode, was the June 23 tape."

On the morning of the Supreme Court decision, by the luck of the schedule that he followed so faithfully, Ford had his weekly prayer session with

Rhodes, Laird, and Quie in the House Prayer Room in the Capitol. It was a solemn time: All four prayed for the country, and asked that the Vice President be given strength and guidance in the days ahead.

From the Hill, Ford went to *The Washington Post* building for an off-the-record lunch with *Post* Board Chairman Katharine Graham and her editors. Asked if Nixon would comply with the Supreme Court order, Ford said he did not know.

In California Nixon was still going through the motions of the Presidency. Two days after the Supreme Court decision, Kissinger brought Hans-Dietrich Genscher, Foreign Minister of West Germany, to San Clemente. "I was shocked by the ravages just a week had wrought on Nixon's appearance," Kissinger wrote. "His coloring was pallid. Though he seemed composed, it clearly took every ounce of his energy to conduct a serious conversation."

Later in the day Kissinger and Haig talked for the first time about the possibility of a Nixon resignation. Together, in Haig's small office next to Nixon's in San Clemente, the two coworkers and rivals reached a common judgment: Nixon could not survive, and for the country's sake he should resign as soon as possible. Impeachment in the House and trial by the Senate should be avoided at all cost, they concluded, but they could not push him to leave. Kissinger said, and Haig agreed, that Nixon would resign only if his own judgment of the national interest dictated that course.

On Saturday, July 27, the House Judiciary Committee voted 27-11 (all twenty-one Democrats and six Republicans) for Article I of impeachment, charging obstruction of justice. Nixon heard the news from Ziegler when he returned to his San Clemente compound after a swim in the Pacific.

That night Nixon and his family had a quiet dinner at Casa Pacifica; they were returning to Washington the next day. Later Nixon sat alone in his study, writing in his diary. "And so we will be back on Monday. [St. Clair and Haig] will listen to the tapes, and my guess is that they might well come to me and say, 'We just don't think this is manageable.' . . . Then I have a hard call—that call being as to whether I decide to bite the bullet on resignation or whether I continue to fight it through the House and wait until the House vote and then resign on the basis that I can't put the country through the months that would be involved in an impeachment trial." With a grim look ahead at life after the Presidency, Nixon wondered how he could pay his personal expenses, whether he could sell a book or his Presidential papers.

* * *

Haig, back in his West Wing office on Monday morning, told Pat McKee, a trusted secretary he had inherited from Haldeman, to transcribe the June 23 tape. Carefully she threaded the tape and put on the earphones. "I heard the voices—the President's and Haldeman's," she said, "and when they came to the part about how they would get the FBI to stop the Watergate investigation, I felt a chill. I shivered. I knew it was over."

McKee took the transcript in to Haig and showed him the condemning passages. "Good God!" Haig said.

"After reading this document," Haig wrote, "I knew that the clock had stopped in Richard Nixon's White House." From that moment on, Haig was convinced beyond doubt "that Nixon's words on this tape would establish his guilt in the public mind and also in his trial before the Senate, and that he could not possibly survive its release."

Once Haig joined in Buzhardt's judgment that all hope of saving the Nixon Presidency was lost, they waited for the third man. St. Clair returned from a long weekend in Cape Cod and read the June 23 transcript for the first time. "Fatal," he said to Haig. Not only was it a clear-cut case of obstruction of justice by President Nixon, St. Clair said, but any delay in turning the evidence over to Judge Sirica and Jaworski could bring criminal charges against Haig, Buzhardt, and St. Clair himself for withholding evidence.

On Nixon's first day back in Washington, the House Judiciary Committee voted 28-10 for Article II of impeachment, charging Nixon violated his oath of office by abusing Presidential power. "He has, acting personally, and through his subordinates, endeavored to" use the IRS, the FBI, and the CIA against his political adversaries, the Article stated.

Across the Capitol Rotunda to the North the Senate voted to establish rules for the trial of the President. Senate Majority Leader Mike Mansfield said that in view of its historical importance, the Senate trial of Nixon would be televised.

As chance would have it, on that same day a Federal court in downtown Washington indicted John Connally—the man Nixon wanted to be his successor as President—for perjury and accepting a bribe.

Alone in the EOB, Nixon telephoned John Mitchell, his friend and senior partner in law and politics. Even though Mitchell was facing trial himself, he was the man Nixon turned to as the shrewdest of counselors. Nixon told Mitchell about the incriminating evidence on the June 23 tape about to be released, and said he faced the hard choice of resigning, or fighting impeachment in the House and conviction in the Senate. He asked for Mitchell's recommendations about what he should do.

As so often he had, Mitchell gave Nixon advice that was brief and blunt. Dick, he said, make the best deal you can and resign.

Urging immediate action, Mitchell told Nixon that if he could get a deal that would protect him from future prosecution, he should resign from the Presidency as quickly as possible.

Nixon knew that his best protection from future prosecution would be a preemptive pardon. He was familiar with Presidential pardons; he had granted 863 of them.

Nixon summoned Buzhardt, his counsel. It was time to work out a plea bargain.

Buzhardt reviewed a President's power to grant a preemptive pardon. He had personally looked up the precedents. The Supreme Court, he said, had specifically ruled that a President can block the indictment and trial of any person by pardoning him before charges were brought.

As the President, Nixon could pardon himself, as Buzhardt had suggested only days earlier when the Supreme Court decided against Nixon on the tapes.

Nixon indicated he would not pardon himself but raised a question: If he should resign, could Ford, as the new President, pardon him?

Buzhardt replied that such a course would be legal.

The question was: Would Ford agree to a pardon in advance?

Nixon knew Ford well. He knew that Ford would not respond to an appeal to his own ambition—Nixon had seen nothing in Ford's actions to suggest he was conniving to be President—but Ford might agree to pardon Nixon if he were convinced a Nixon resignation would be in the national interest.

The matter was highly sensitive: Nixon decided he should not and would not talk directly to Ford about it. Any approach to Ford about agreeing to grant a pardon would have to be done in total secrecy, by someone he and Ford would trust. Only Haig had the standing to speak for the President to the Vice President; and Haig could be trusted.

Nixon decided that he could use his client-lawyer relationship with Buzhardt to define the terms of a deal with Ford, and that Haig should present those terms to Ford.

Nixon would not talk directly to Haig about it; each should be able to deny he had ever discussed it with the other. Buzhardt, as the President's counsel, would relay the Nixon proposal to Haig: Nixon would resign if Ford agreed in advance to pardon him.

Haig would not question that Buzhardt was speaking for Nixon on this bold stroke of a plan. It was typically Nixon—combining the national interest with his own. And Ford would not question that Haig was speaking with authority.

However, since Haig was not a lawyer, Ford would be skeptical of Haig's legal knowledge of a President's pardon authority. So Buzhardt should put in writing the legal information that Ford would need to consider the proposal.

To carry out Nixon's plan, Buzhardt wrote out on a yellow legal pad two pages for Haig to give to Ford. The first set forth a lawyerly, half-page summary of the President's power to pardon a person before indictment or trial. The second, also in Buzhardt's handwriting, was the draft of a Ford pardon for Nixon.

The first was intended to convince Ford that he could pardon Nixon; the second would show Ford that a Presidential pardon was technically simple: He could do it quickly, and without any need to discuss it with anyone. The information was right there; all Ford would have to do is fill in the date on the pardon form, insert the name of Richard Nixon, and sign it.

At mid-morning on Wednesday, July 31, Nixon asked Haig to come to his EOB office. Until then, Nixon had not asked Haig for his opinion on the damage the June 23 tape would cause when delivered to Judge Sirica, and Special Prosecutor Jaworski, and made public. "Mr. President, I just don't see how we can survive this one," Haig said. ". . . This tape will deal a fatal blow to public opinion, to your supporters on the Hill, and to the party. The Cabinet won't hold; the Republican Party won't hold; your own staff won't hold. Once this tape gets out, it's over."

As soon as he returned to the West Wing, Haig telephoned Kissinger at the State Department to say he was coming to see him immediately. Kissinger waited, wondering. Haig strode in, closed the door, and told Kissinger about the evidence on the June 23 tape. It was the judgment of St. Clair and Buzhardt that this tape was the smoking gun that would impeach and convict Nixon, Haig said. The two men agreed that it would be tragic for the country if Nixon insisted on going through the impeachment process in the House and trial by the Senate. Kissinger believed that Haig was uniquely positioned to "ease Nixon's decision to resign."

Vice President Ford, traveling in California and Nevada, was unaware of the new and fatal evidence against Nixon. After a night flight from San Diego, Vice President Ford arrived at his Alexandria home at 4:50 A.M., Wednesday,

July 31. Up early, as usual, Ford hosted a ceremony in his EOB conference room for General John C. Meyer, a longtime friend retiring from the Air Force, and left again for a benefit golf tournament in Worcester, Massachusetts. He had been asked to play by his close and jovial friend, House Majority Leader Tip O'Neill. Ford enjoyed beating O'Neill at golf, and invited him and other House leaders to go up in his plane.

As soon as they were airborne, Les Arends, the Republican whip, took Ford aside. "Jesus, Jerry, do you have any idea how serious this thing is? Tip's been counting votes, and he says Nixon has no more than forty votes in the House and twenty-four in the Senate."

"Oh, Tip doesn't know what he's talking about," Ford said.

"Come on, Jerry," Arends said. "There's nobody who can count better than Tip."

Playing in the Pleasant Valley Golf Classic outside Worcester that day, Ford avoided talking to O'Neill about anything more serious than their golf game. The two were jolly and relaxed, old friends bantering on the tee and posing for a press photographer with their arms around each other. It did not strike home to Ford during that pleasant outing that his best friend among the Democrats was totally committed to forcing Nixon from office and thereby making him, Jerry Ford, President.

When Ford arrived home late that evening, there was a message for him. Haig wanted to see him the next morning.

16

PROPOSITION

On the morning of Thursday, August 1, 1974, Nixon arrived in his office unusually early and immediately asked Haig to come in. "I have decided to resign," Nixon said. His voice was firm and matter-of-fact, and his manner composed. He told Haig he was ready to accept the judgment of his lawyers that his own words on the June 23 tape could not be explained. He would not force the country to go through the ordeal of impeachment.

Nixon laid out his plan—to take his family to Camp David to tell them of his decision, to resign on Monday night, to remain in Washington for two weeks, and then to go to San Clemente.

Haig said he would of course carry out whatever plan the President made. "But I wonder if waiting until Monday is the best choice open to you," Haig said. "The tape is going to be delivered to Judge Sirica today." Once that is done, Haig pointed out, the new evidence will quickly leak to the press and generate a new public outcry about Watergate. "It might be better to resign tomorrow night and leave town immediately," Haig said.

Nixon said he would think about it. In the meantime, he told Haig to have Ray Price begin work on a resignation speech for Monday night. "Tell Ray I will admit mistakes," Nixon said, "but I will not grovel."

Nixon also told Haig to advise Vice President Ford that he should be prepared to take over the Presidency sometime in the next few days. "Tell Jerry I am thinking of resigning, without indicating when," Nixon said. "And impress on him the need for absolute secrecy. This is a decision I must make for and by myself—right up to the end." In particular, Nixon warned Haig, he did not want a delegation of Republican leaders or Congressmen asking for his resignation. "I've resisted political pressure all my life," Nixon said, "and if I get it now I may change my mind."

Ford had arrived in his office before 8 o'clock that morning, and had just finished reading the daily intelligence summary when Haig called to say he must see the Vice President as soon as possible. "It's urgent," Haig said.

"Come over now," Ford said. He handed the classified documents back to David Peterson, the CIA liaison officer to the White House, and told Hartmann that Haig needed to see him immediately.

Hartmann, suspicious of Haig, suggested that Marsh or he, or both, be present. "You might want to have a witness to who said what," Hartmann said.

"Okay, Bob, you sit in," Ford said.

At 9:05 A.M. when Haig hurried in to the Vice President's office, Ford thought he seemed anxious and burdened, but in control.

Haig glowered at Hartmann but realized he was not going to leave. Haig did not trust Hartmann, so he decided to warn Ford that new evidence had been found but hold off on saying any more until he could see Ford alone.

"I want to alert you that things are deteriorating," Haig said. "The whole ball game may be over. You'd better start thinking about a change in your life. I can't tell you what's going to happen, but I have to tell you what I know." One tape that would be turned over to Judge Sirica would be "very damaging" to Nixon's defense.

"How bad is it?" Ford asked.

Haig said he had not seen the evidence himself, but "White House lawyers" who had heard the tape were convinced that it eliminated any chance Nixon may have had to avoid being impeached.

To make the situation even more threatening, Haig said, St. Clair now realized that he had misrepresented the facts in his arguments before the Court and the House Judiciary Committee. Consequently, St. Clair insisted that the true facts be disclosed promptly to the Court, the Judiciary Committee, and the public.

"How is the President holding up?" Ford asked.

The President, Haig said, keeps changing his mind. One hour he is determined to fight impeachment in the House and then fight conviction in the Senate, Haig said; the next he may talk of resignation. Haig stressed that he could not judge what the President might eventually decide.

For forty-five minutes Haig talked. Ford said little, Hartmann nothing. Ford mentioned that he would be traveling during the next few days, and asked Haig to keep in touch. When Haig left, Ford swore Hartmann to secrecy about what had been said.

Haig returned to his West Wing office, his mission unfinished because Hartmann was there. Nixon had given him specific instructions: "Tell Ford to be ready. Tell him I want absolute secrecy. Tell him what's coming. But don't tell him when."

Haig knew he must see Ford again, as soon as possible, and with no one else present. But first Haig wanted to get his lawyer's advice on what he could and should say to the Vice President about any arrangements or understandings for the transfer of Presidential power. He sent for Buzhardt.

Buzhardt came in to Haig's office well prepared. He advised Haig that he could inform the Vice President that the President, in addition to resignation or impeachment, had a range of other options. Nixon could step aside under the Twenty-fifth Amendment during the impeachment and Senate trial, Buzhardt said. He could simply delay making any decision in the hope that something would turn up to save him. He might try to get by with a censure vote introduced by a Nixon ally. Such an effort would probably fail, Buzhardt said, but the idea was worth mentioning. Or, he continued, Nixon could pardon himself and resign.

Could a President do that, Haig asked. Yes, Buzhardt said, he had carefully researched the issue. Another option, Buzhardt said, was the one he had suggested a week earlier—that Nixon pardon Mitchell, Haldeman, Ehrlichman, and all the others involved in Watergate, and then resign.

There was still another option, Buzhardt said, and went on to explain to Haig the Nixon idea: The President could resign and be pardoned by his successor. Haig asked: If Ford became President, could he pardon Nixon even before he had been charged or indicted? Yes, Buzhardt said, in his judgment the Supreme Court had confirmed that a President had that power.

To guide Haig in his discussion with Ford, Buzhardt handed Haig the two documents he had written out on a yellow legal pad—a half-page legal summary of a President's authority to pardon a person not yet charged with a crime, and the proper form for a Presidential pardon of Nixon.

Haig took the two documents from Buzhardt and put in a call for Ford.

As Haig was discussing Nixon's options in the West Wing, Ford left the EOB with Hartmann and Marsh for his Capitol office, to meet with Israeli Foreign Minister Yigal Allon and Ambassador Simcha Dinitz. En route, in the back of the black Lincoln limousine, there was silence. To Hartmann, it was clear that Ford had decided to say nothing to Marsh about the Haig meeting.

Minutes after Ford walked into the Vice President's office just off the Senate floor, Haig called. After a brief, cryptic conversation, Ford hung up the phone, and said to Hartmann and Marsh: "Al wants to see me this afternoon, alone. I will meet him at three-thirty, in the EOB."

Hartmann started to suggest someone else be present, but Ford interrupted. "Never mind," he said firmly. "I'll fill you in."

Alone in his EOB office waiting for Haig, Ford wondered where events were headed. Ahead he could envision only tragedy for his friend, and tragedy for the country. "I had come to think Nixon had lost touch with reality," Ford said. "It was obvious that he could longer govern." Ford thought of the accomplishments of Nixon's first term as President, and how Watergate had destroyed it all.

A tap on the door at 3:30 P.M., and Haig came in. Ford stood, shook Haig's hand, and motioned for him to sit on the couch to his right. Ford sat in an armchair on Haig's left. As Ford studied Haig's face and bearing, he thought, "Al looks even more beaten and harassed than when he was here this morning."

Speaking deliberately, and looking Ford right in the eye, Haig said: "Are you ready, Mr. Vice President, to assume the Presidency in a short period of time?"

"If it happens, Al, I am prepared," Ford said.

There was a quiet chill in Haig's voice as he continued. Since their morning meeting, he said, he had read the transcript of a tape that clearly showed President Nixon was guilty of a crime. The tape was evidence that Nixon knew about Watergate six days after it happened, Haig said, and it showed that he not only authorized the cover-up but was part of it. When the transcript becomes public in a few days, Haig said, it will provide the evidence that will force Nixon to resign or face certain impeachment in the House and conviction in the Senate.

Ford was silent. He had dreaded this moment. Even though he had anticipated what Haig might say, the reality that he would become President struck Ford with terrible force. He waited and said nothing.

Haig proceeded as Nixon had asked: He told Ford that Nixon was "thinking of resigning," possibly within a few days. But Haig emphasized, as Nixon had instructed him, that a decision to resign was one that the President would make for and by himself—"right up to the end." To guide Ford in his own actions, Haig said: "Under no circumstances can you assume he's going to resign until he tells you. As close as I am to the President and the situation, I don't know."

Haig asked Ford to assess Nixon's situation on the Hill. "My assessment is that if he fights this through, he will be impeached in the House and the odds are overwhelming that he will be convicted in the Senate," Ford said. "With these additional tapes that are to be made available, there will be a groundswell of a demand for resignation."

Haig reiterated that he did not know what Nixon might decide to do; but "White House lawyers," as he described them, had made a list of various courses of action Nixon might consider in his situation. From memory, Haig talked through the options Buzhardt had proposed—Nixon could step aside temporarily under the Twenty-fifth Amendment, put off making any decision, try for a censure vote, pardon himself and resign, or pardon all the Watergate defendants, pardon himself, and resign. Then Haig described a sixth option. As Ford remembered it: "Finally, Haig said that according to some on Nixon's White House staff, Nixon could agree to leave in return for an agreement that the new President—Gerald Ford—would pardon him."

Haig handed Ford the two sheets of paper in Buzhardt's handwriting—one describing a President's power to pardon, the other the proper legal form Ford could use in granting Nixon the pardon.

In discussing the options, Haig emphasized that he was not a lawyer and had no part in drawing up the proposals but had been instructed to present them to Ford. Then, after disclaiming any position of his own, Haig asked Ford if he had any recommendation as to what Nixon should do.

Ford had no doubt about how he should respond to the first five options; all were choices open to Nixon. "Al," Ford said, "I don't think it would be proper for me to make any recommendations at all. I am an interested party."

But the last proposal was a course of action that only he could take if he should become President—and he had a question about that. "What is the extent of a President's pardon power?" Ford asked.

"It's my understanding from a White House lawyer that a President does have authority to grant a pardon even before criminal action has been taken against an individual," Haig replied, referring to Buzhardt's summary of the law and precedents.

Haig did not identify the "White House lawyer" who had written the two documents. Ford assumed it was St. Clair, the senior and better known lawyer who had titular responsibility for Nixon's defense against impeachment.

Ford listened, his thoughts in conflict. Haig was informing him of new evidence of Nixon's guilt, and advising that he should prepare to become President. "But I just didn't think it was in the country's interest to have a President thrown out of office, even for good reasons," Ford said.

Haig was also telling him that Nixon was ready to resign, possibly the next day, if he were assured that Ford would pardon him. But Ford had resolved months earlier, in the first days of his Vice Presidency, to avoid any action that might suggest, as he put it, "I was making a grab at being President." Now Haig was proposing he join an effort to persuade Nixon to resign. "I was shocked by the smoking gun revelation," Ford said. "I listened to the six options, but I did not urge Haig to do anything to get Nixon to resign. That was *his* choice."

Deliberating as Haig talked, Ford made a judgment: He wanted a legal opinion on the new evidence against Nixon, and he wanted to avoid any immediate reply to Haig's proposal of a pardon.

"Al," Ford said, "I will need some time to think about this. I want to talk to St. Clair. I want to talk to my wife before giving any response."

He would, he added, give Haig an answer.

Haig left the Buzhardt papers with Ford and stood up to leave. Ford folded the yellow pages and put them in his pocket. Looking gravely at each other, the two men shook hands. Suddenly, impulsively, each put his arm around the other's shoulder. "We've got to keep in contact," Haig said. "Things could break so fast that we have to be accessible to each other."

It was 4:20 P.M.; Ford and Haig had talked alone for fifty minutes.

As Ford sat back down, the full impact of Haig's message struck him. "I am about to become President," he thought. "It's going to happen."

The new evidence made it certain that Nixon would be impeached or forced to resign—and he would take Nixon's place.

Ford was not at all apprehensive about the job itself. In his quarter century in Washington he had observed five Presidents at close range and had no doubt he could handle it. He had neither tried nor expected to be President, but he was ready—if necessary—to take on the responsibility. And now it was only hours or days before he would do so.

Ford was also angry that Nixon, a friend he trusted, had lied to him. "The hurt was very deep," Ford said. "I wanted time to think, and I wanted to be alone."

He was slumped in the chair, gripping the arms and staring rigidly into space when, moments later, Marsh walked in.

Marsh took one look at Ford and thought, "He looks like a man thunderstruck." In a quiet voice Marsh said that Mrs. Ford was waiting outside for him to go with her to look at the house being readied for the Vice President. Ford nodded, and said nothing. Marsh backed out of the room.

Through another door Hartmann came from his private office next to the Vice President and interrupted Ford's reflections. "His face was grim," Hartmann wrote. "He looked as if a two-hundred-pound blocker had just hit him in the stomach."

Ford motioned Hartmann to a seat. "What I am going to tell you must not go any further than this room," Ford said. He told Hartmann about the new evidence of Nixon's guilt, that resignation was imminent or impeachment certain, and described the options Haig had listed.

When Ford reached the final option—that Nixon would resign if Ford would agree to pardon him—Hartmann burst out: "Jesus! What did you tell him?"

"I didn't tell him anything," Ford said. "I told him I needed time to think about it."

"You what?" Hartmann was almost shouting. "That's almost the worst answer Haig could take back to the White House. You told Haig you are willing to entertain the idea of a pardon if he resigns—that's probably all Haig and Nixon want to know."

"But Bob," Ford said defensively, "Al wasn't suggesting that. It was just one of the ideas that he said were being kicked around by people at the White House."

"But Haig didn't discuss this delicate matter without Nixon's knowing about it," Hartmann said. "And he mentioned the pardon option, and you sat there listening to him. Well, silence implies assent. He probably went back to the White House and told Nixon that he'd mentioned the idea and that you weren't uncomfortable with it. It was extremely improper for him to bring the subject up. I think you should have taken Haig by the scruff of the neck and the seat of the pants and thrown him the hell out of the office. And then you should have called an immediate press conference and told the world why!"

"Bob"—Ford's voice was rising now—"you're overreacting, making a mountain out of a molehill."

"Well," Hartmann said, "I think you ought to get Jack Marsh's judgment on this."

Ford looked at his watch. "All right, I'll talk to Jack, but I don't have time now." He had promised his wife he would go with her to look at Admiral's House, the rambling manor house that Congress had taken away from the Chief of Naval Operations and renovated to be the Vice President's residence. The Fords planned to move there in late summer, and Betty was working with the Navy and an interior decorator to get it ready.

Ford realized, after what Haig had just told him, it was ridiculous to go look at the house. But a sudden cancellation would prompt questions from Commander Kerr, the naval aide waiting to accompany the Fords, and from the Navy officers awaiting them at the house. "That," Ford thought, "I don't need."

Hartmann returned to his own office, closed the door, and told his secretary to hold all telephone calls. "I desperately needed to talk to somebody," he said. "If the Vice President were even contemplating a prior pledge to pardon Nixon, he would have to be dissuaded as quickly as possible." Hartmann knew he would need help, and made a short list of Ford's closest and wisest friends. When he crossed off those who couldn't keep a secret, he was left with Betty Ford, Jack Marsh, and Bryce Harlow.

Hartmann asked Marsh to come to his office. "Jack, you know that Al Haig was in there alone with him half the afternoon," Hartmann said. "I can't tell you what went on, or even hint at it, but I am scared witless he might make a terrible mistake. I made him promise he would tell you, himself, what he just told me—before he does anything. That's all I can say, except he'll be coming back here, so don't go away."

After wasting a precious hour inspecting a house he knew he would never occupy, Ford returned to the EOB and went into his private bathroom to shower and change into evening clothes. As he was putting on his jacket, Hartmann reminded him about talking to Marsh.

Ford said he wanted to talk to St. Clair the first thing the next morning.

"Jack is standing by, and I think you ought to talk to him before this goes any further," Hartmann said.

Annoyed at Hartmann's persistence, Ford said he did not have time, that he was already late.

Hartmann was certain that Ford still did not comprehend the political and ethical jeopardy of discussing the pardon with Haig. "Boss," Hartmann said, "you just can't get involved with this thing in any way. Whatever the President decides, whatever Haig and his lawyers tell him, the Vice President must not have any part of it. And you ought not even be thinking about pardons. Nobody has any power to pardon anybody except the President, and you're not President yet."

"Al says it could happen within a week," Ford said, shaking his head in sadness. He picked up his briefcase and started for the door.

Hartmann was almost frantic. "I know you're rushed, but I've been waiting all day to say this: You are going to be President. But you won't be able to run the country if you have anything at all to do with the way Nixon leaves office. You can't advocate resignation any more than you can advocate impeachment. . . . You didn't ask to be Vice President. You can't let anybody ever say you lifted one finger to make yourself President, or the job won't be worth having. I think this is terribly important."

"Well, I'm going to sleep on it," Ford said. "I want to talk to Betty. And I told Al to send St. Clair over first thing in the morning." Suddenly Ford turned to smile at Hartmann. "Thanks, Bob. I'll talk to Jack then, too."

After he left Ford's office, Haig met with Nixon for more than an hour and returned to his West Wing office about 6:45 P.M. Waiting for him there was the impeachment defense team—Timmons, Dean Burch, Buchanan, Price, Buzhardt, Jerry Jones, David Gergen, a few others.

Using an organization chart on an easel, Haig said the defense of the President would require "total mobilization" of the White House staff. Pointing to his battle map, Haig said there would be a "strategy group" at the top, a "working group" to feed intelligence to the top command, and three task forces—one to defend against each of the three Articles of Impeachment.

Timmons, the senior Nixon assistant who dealt face-to-face with Congressmen, raised a point: To plan an effective defense with the President's supporters in the House, Timmons said, "We need to read the transcripts of the tapes going to Judge Sirica on Monday."

No, Haig said, the President had not authorized that. Timmons protested vigorously, arguing that it would be devastating to dump another nasty surprise on the President's Republican supporters.

"There are problems," Haig said.

"Why can't we be trusted to know what they are?" Timmons demanded. "At least let Pat Buchanan read the transcripts."

No, Haig repeated, the President said no. Haig told them to do their best with the information they had, and adjourned the meeting.

When all had left, Haig sent for Price. "We need a resignation speech," Haig said. "The mobilization meeting was largely for cover." Haig said he,

Buzhardt, and St. Clair had read the June 23 transcript, and it showed that Nixon was part of the cover-up from the very beginning.

Brisk and efficient as always, Haig outlined the situation and assigned Price his mission: The transcripts will go public Monday. The President might resign that day. He has been given options to consider. If he does resign, you will draft the resignation speech. Your draft will have to explain the transcripts and state why he is resigning.

Walking back to his office in the EOB, Price thought about his grim assignment. A cerebral student of men and events, Price reflected on the dual nature of the Richard Nixon he had come to know since he signed on as a speechwriter eight years earlier. He admired the President Nixon of high aspirations and great ability in world affairs, but Price also knew that Nixon had a dark side, and somewhere within the darker instincts of Nixon's nature there lay the motive for this crime.

Nixon left the White House late in the afternoon to have dinner with his friend Bebe Rebozo on the *Sequoia*. As the Presidential yacht cruised on the Potomac, Nixon told Rebozo of the evidence on the June 23 tape. "I have decided that I should resign," Nixon said. He asked Rebozo to help him convince the family that resignation was the only course left.

That night the Vice President and Mrs. Ford were guests of honor at an elegant dinner hosted by the *Washington Star*'s society-and-gossip columnist Betty Beale and her husband, George Graber. Among the guests were other reporters—ABC's Barbara Walters and *New York Times* Washington Bureau Chief Clifton Daniel. The Vice President chatted amiably through the evening. Not one reporter present, Ford said, asked him anything that touched on what was about to happen at the White House.

After the dinner, Ford and his wife sat down with a bourbon and water in the family room of their home. He told her about the two meetings with Haig during the day, about the new evidence against Nixon, and what it all meant. "Either we will go to the White House next week," he said, "or we'll be dangling for six months while the impeachment process takes place in the House and a trial goes through the Senate."

Betty Ford's first thought was for the Nixons; in her daily prayers she had been fervently asking that President Nixon could remain in office. Her second thought was about the Ford children, and how living in the White House might affect them.

Ford told her about the options Haig described, and she read the yellow pages of notes Haig had given Ford. Shocked, she realized that Haig had told her husband "that Nixon would resign if he would pardon him." Her immediate reaction was that her husband should not assume the Presidency as part of any deal. She turned to Ford: "You can't do that, Jerry."

But Ford pointed out the irreparable damage to the country if Nixon put himself through the process of impeachment in the House and then a long and humiliating trial by the Senate. For an hour they discussed Ford's dilemma, and the terrible crisis of state. Finally Ford said: "This just has to stop. It's tearing the country to pieces." Betty agreed with that, and said he must do whatever he thought was right. As always, she pledged to him her support for whatever decision he made.

Sometime after 1 A.M. Ford said to his wife: "I am going to go ahead and get this over with." He picked up the telephone in the family room and called Haig.

"Al," Ford said, "I've talked with Betty, and we're prepared, but we can't get involved in the White House decision-making process. You should do whatever you decide to do; its all right with me."

"I understand," Haig said. "I'll be in touch with you tomorrow."

Earlier in the evening Haig had been with Nixon in the EOB reviewing the President's resignation plans; but he gave no hint that Nixon had decided to announce his resignation in four days. Instead, Haig told Ford: "Nothing had changed. The situation is as fluid as ever."

Ford put down the phone. Somehow, he felt, it would soon be over. He told Betty that they and their three sons and daughter must prepare themselves for a change in their lives beyond anything they had imagined. Their words solemn but resolute, he and Betty talked about the responsibilities that would fall on him and on her. The way ahead would not be easy, they agreed; but belief and confidence ran deep within both. Somehow, they knew, they could make that momentous change and meet their new responsibilities.

In the darkness of their bedroom, Jerry and Betty Ford held hands and prayed aloud, each saying words that came to them:

"God, give us strength, give us wisdom, give us guidance as the possibility of a new life confronts us.

"We promise to do our very best, whatever may take place.

"You have sustained us in the past.

"We have faith in Your guiding hand in the difficult and challenging days ahead.

"In Jesus' name we pray."

Ford concluded with the prayer that had been his favorite since childhood: *"Trust in the Lord with all thine heart; and lean not unto thine own understanding. In all thy ways acknowledge Him, and He shall direct thy paths."*

Ford slept well and rose even earlier than usual to be ready for whatever the day might bring. It was Friday, August 2, 1974. "I wanted to see St. Clair as quickly as possible," Ford said, and he was waiting in his EOB office when St. Clair came in promptly at 8:00 A.M.

As soon as they sat down, Ford asked: "Is the new evidence enough, in your best judgment, to impeach and convict the President?"

St. Clair began by making it clear that he had learned only four days earlier of the evidence on the June 23 tapes. St. Clair was shocked, he said, not only by the evidence but also by Nixon's decision to withhold this crucial information from his own lawyers. "Until I found out about those tapes," St. Clair said, "I was absolutely convinced that the President was not guilty of an impeachable offense, and I was preparing my defense based on that belief."

"What's your assessment now?" Ford asked.

"Probably the same as yours," St. Clair said. "Unquestionably, this will lead the House to impeach the President. It will lead the Senate to convict him. The question now is: What does he do? Resign, or fight it through?"

"Do you know of any other new or damaging evidence besides what's on the June 23 tapes?" Ford asked.

"No," St. Clair said.

Ford moved on to his critical second concern: Haig's options. Ford reviewed the options that Haig had proposed on the afternoon before, concluding with the proposal that Nixon could resign and Ford could pardon him.

St. Clair listened quietly. "I was not the source of any White House legal opinion about a President's power to issue pardons," St. Clair said.

Ford was surprised at St. Clair's quick move to distance himself from Haig's proposal for a pardon by Ford. If the "White House lawyers" mentioned by Haig did not include Nixon's chief defense counsel, Ford wondered who had written the legal summary of a President's pardon authority and the draft form of a pardon for Nixon.

As soon as his meeting with St. Clair ended, Ford brought in Marsh and summarized all that happened during his two discussions with Haig. Marsh looked at the two pardon notes that Haig had left with Ford and immediately recognized Buzhardt's handwriting; he had worked closely with Buzhardt at the Pentagon.

Marsh read the documents carefully. The first was a clear, well-written summary of a President's right to pardon a person before indictment or trial. It was a good lawyer's brief, Marsh thought, just the kind of thorough job one could expect of Buzhardt. The second, Marsh saw, was the correct form for a Presidential pardon. Everything was on the page except the date, the name of the person to be pardoned, and a Presidential signature.

To himself Marsh thought: Nixon and Buzhardt, with Haig as their agent, had anticipated that Ford would not know his power to pardon, or how to frame the language of a pardon, so they would just do it for him. They were taking no chances that Ford would need to go elsewhere to find out what he could do and how to do it; they had it all arranged in a do-it-yourself pardon kit.

"I realized right away that Haig jeopardized the Vice President the moment he spoke the word *pardon*," Marsh said. Suddenly it was clear why Haig insisted on meeting Ford alone; he wanted no witness.

To Ford, Marsh spoke directly. "I am in strong agreement with Bob. You can't be involved in anything that might at some point sound like some kind of deal,"

"Haig was not suggesting a deal," Ford said firmly. "These options hadn't even originated with him. . . . I said nothing to signal approval or disapproval of any of them."

In some exasperation Ford added, "Betty and I talked it over last night. We feel we are ready. This just has to stop; it's tearing the country to pieces. I decided to go ahead and get it over with, so I called Al Haig and told him they should do whatever they decide to do; it's all right with me."

Marsh asked quietly: "During your conversation with Al last night, what was said about a pardon?"

"Nothing that I can recall," Ford said.

Marsh became even more concerned. "Then Haig might conclude, on the basis of your earlier talk, that a future pardon was still a viable option as an inducement to get Nixon to resign," Marsh said.

"Of course not," Ford snapped. "Haig knows better than that. There was no commitment, just conversation—and in strict confidence."

Ford's benign view of Haig's proposal alarmed Marsh and Hartmann. They knew that Nixon would use anybody to save himself. To Marsh and Hartmann, there was no doubt that Nixon was taking advantage of his long friendship with Ford, that Nixon was counting on Ford's good and trusting nature to escape prosecution.

Marsh, in his gentle way, was adamant that the pardon proposal by Haig must be rejected. "If you don't believe Bob and me," Marsh said to Ford, "talk to someone else whose advice you value."

"Well, who?" Ford said.

Marsh suggested Bryce Harlow.

Ford thought it over and told Hartmann to get Harlow to come in as soon as possible.

Harlow, Ford said, "has more common sense and political perception than anyone I know."

While Hartmann was arranging for Harlow to come to Ford's office in the EOB, Ford left for Capitol Hill to meet Senate Majority Leader Mike Mansfield and Minority Leader Hugh Scott. Mansfield had asked for the meeting to discuss the procedures the Senate would follow in Nixon's trial if the House should impeach him. They met Ford in his Capitol office. Ford could not tell them of the new evidence against Nixon; nor did he mention that Nixon might be close to resignation. Even in private conversation with two men he trusted so completely, Ford masked his knowledge and discussed in earnest the Senate trial that he believed would never take place.

The three men noted for the record that under the Constitution a Vice President, though he serves as President of the Senate, does not preside at the trial of a President because he is a party at interest. Ford said he would absent himself from the Senate chamber during any preliminary discussions about a Nixon trial. Mansfield and Scott agreed that was proper. Mansfield said that he, as Majority Leader of the Senate, accepted the obligation to preserve the rights of the accused President and would see that the fairness of process guaranteed by the Constitution would be upheld.

After Mansfield left, Scott told Ford that he and Goldwater had completed a fresh count of the Senate. Nixon had thirty-six votes, but eleven were soft. To escape conviction, he would need thirty-four.

Ford was silent. Scott waited, then said, "I know you can't react, Jerry, and that you have to support the President." The emotion of the moment made it difficult for either to speak. "You're all we've got now," Scott said, his voice trembling, "and I mean the country."

Ford's next visitor was Senator Robert Griffin, in for a quick lunch and to give Ford new information. With his spectacles and quiet manner, Griffin gave the impression of a small-town lawyer in Traverse City, Michigan—which he had been before he served five terms in the House and then moved on to the Senate. There, as Republican deputy leader, he had been strong and effective in support of Nixon. In the White House, Timmons and Nixon were counting on Griffin's feisty skills in floor debate if impeachment should reach the Senate.

Now, for the first time, Griffin told Ford he had come to doubt Nixon's innocence. He had seen some House Judiciary evidence against Nixon; he had not yet told Timmons, but could no longer defend Nixon. "Jerry," Griffin said, "you might think about toning down your public statements supporting Nixon."

Ford listened, but he was uncomfortable. With Griffin, as with Mansfield and Scott, he could not say anything about the new evidence against Nixon. To Griffin's suggestion, Ford said: "Well, I'll think about it."

After returning to his EOB office, Ford met for almost an hour with James Reston, the sage of *The New York Times*. Ford did not even hint of the forthcoming revelations about Nixon, and the article Reston wrote concentrated on Ford himself: "He is the same open, unspoiled character. He is calm and fatalistic about his place in the current drama, as if he were an accidental player in some large inevitable script beyond his control. . . . But as President Nixon's troubles have deepened and Mr. Ford's responsibilities have increased, the Vice President has become more canny."

While Ford was talking with Reston, Representative Charles Wiggins drove his brown Mazda 240Z through the Southwest Gate of the White House and parked alongside the West Wing. Wiggins, a stocky, graying Republican of forty-six, represented a part of California's Orange County that was once in Nixon's Congressional District. Though other Republicans were more senior on the Judiciary Committee, Wiggins's intellect and ability had made him the day-to-day leader of Nixon's defense in Committee deliberations. Wiggins commanded the respect of Democrats and Republicans alike for his legal acumen, integrity, and forensic skills. He never consulted anyone in the White House about Nixon's case; to him that would have been improper. But he had seen no evidence that Nixon was personally involved in a crime, so he personally argued against and voted against all three Articles of Impeachment.

As he waited in the ground floor of the West Wing for the security guard to clear him, Wiggins wondered why Haig had telephoned and asked him to come to the White House. In Haig's office a few minutes later, it became brutally clear. Haig and St. Clair told him that new and damaging evidence on a tape would be turned over to the Court on Monday, and the President wanted Wiggins to read the transcript of the tape and advise the Nixon lawyers on how it might affect his defense in the House.

Sitting at the conference table in Haig's spacious corner office, Wiggins read through the transcript, then went back to the key pages and studied them. "Here it is," Wiggins thought, "Nixon giving the go-ahead to Haldeman's suggestion that he and Ehrlichman use the CIA to stop the FBI investigation. Here it is—a direct involvement by President Nixon, a classic effort on his part to obstruct justice, clear evidence that he is impeachable."

Wiggins turned to Haig and St. Clair and told them there was no question: The transcript held the evidence of obstruction of justice that made Nixon "vulnerable to a legitimate impeachment."

"What are the consequences?" St. Clair asked.

"The Presidency of Richard Nixon has effectively been destroyed," Wiggins said. "It is a fatal blow. He should resign. I recommend to you both that you urge the President to resign."

"Do you want to talk to the President?" Haig asked.

Wiggins thought for a moment. He considered the House Judiciary Committee to be in a quasi-judicial role; a personal discussion with the President would almost certainly be misunderstood. "No," Wiggins said to Haig. "I would not have anything to say to him other than what I have told you."

Deeply concerned that the President and White House lawyers had been withholding evidence, Wiggins asked what was to be done with the transcript. "The full text will be released on Monday," Haig said.

"I will respect that over the weekend," Wiggins said. "But if you do not release it on Monday, then I will report to my committee what has occurred here today."

As soon as Wiggins left the White House, Haig went to Nixon's office and reported on Wiggins's reaction. As Nixon got the message: "Wiggins said impeachment in the House and conviction in the Senate were now no longer in doubt. Unless I planned to withhold the tape from the Court by pleading the Fifth Amendment, I should get ready to resign right away. Like St. Clair, he felt that unless he reported the existence of the tape, he would himself become party to an obstruction of justice."

Wiggins confirmed Nixon's worst fears about the House reaction to the transcript. In despair, Nixon decided the time had come to show the fatal evidence to his family—so they could see why he had to resign.

Wiggins's verdict on the June 23 transcript was a turning point for Haig; he decided it was time to inform Nixon's other strong defenders. Haig telephoned John Rhodes and Hugh Scott to ask them to examine the evidence, but neither Scott nor Rhodes would come to the White House. Each was suspicious; each thought he would somehow be used by Nixon, Haig, or both.

Desperate for support in persuading Nixon to accept reality and resign, Haig telephoned Griffin and caught him just as he was leaving to catch a plane to Michigan. Griffin would not change his plans, so Haig told Griffin over the phone that new evidence on the tapes had convinced the White House lawyers that Nixon had full knowledge of the Watergate cover-up from the beginning.

Griffin, Haig suggested, could help in two ways—by giving Nixon an accurate evaluation of how many votes this new evidence would cost Nixon in the Senate and by encouraging him to resign. On his flight to Michigan, Griffin began drafting a letter to Nixon that would urge him to step down.

Ford, at the end of his interview with Reston, closed the door of his office in the EOB. He needed time, time alone to think through and make the most important political decision of his life: Should he agree to pardon President Nixon to get him to resign?

Which course was in the best interests of the country: To say no, and thereby so arouse the warrior spirit in Nixon's nature that he would fight on, carry the battle and his vengeance to the house and Senate and dare them to bring down an elected President—whatever the consequences to himself and the American government? Or should Ford say yes to the pardon, and bring a swift end to a President who could no longer govern.

For almost twenty-four hours, ever since Haig had proposed the deal, Ford had asked himself, over and over: What is the right thing to do?

Ford had a quality rare in politicians: He could come close to separating his own political gain from what he believed to be the national interest. He was not ambitious to be President. He had resolved, when he first became the Vice President, that he would do nothing to undermine Nixon and put himself in the White House. Now, eight months later, and having just been officially informed that Nixon had committed the high crime of obstructing justice, Ford still held to the personal conviction that he should take no step to influence Nixon to resign. Ford was personally and morally opposed to making himself President over Nixon's political body.

On the other hand, Ford had privately concluded at least two or three weeks earlier that Nixon could no longer govern and should resign for the good of the country. Ford saw that Haig, by his words and actions of the previous afternoon, had also convinced himself that Nixon could not survive and should resign. Haig's opinion weighed heavily on Ford. As Chief of Staff,

Haig was unquestionably loyal to Nixon; but Ford had never doubted that Haig was first an American prepared to sacrifice his career or his life for his country. It was no small act for an officer of Haig's merit to propose that a Vice President take action to displace a President. And Haig had made a point of emphasizing that Nixon might decide to fight on, whatever the consequences to himself and the country, unless he could expect a pardon.

A bargain in the public interest did not offend Ford; he had spent twenty-five years in Congress. At the moment when Haig suggested the pardon, Ford realized that his best course was neither to accept Haig's proposal, nor to reject it. As an old hand in political negotiation, Ford knew that sometimes the best answer is not to answer at all. In response to Haig, Ford said, "I acted as I always had when a big issue was presented to me: I would say, 'Well, I want to think about it.' Then I would listen to the pros and cons, and decide."

Ford was sobered by the strong reaction of Hartmann, his political counselor, and Marsh, his conscience. He respected their judgment. He understood that their first priority was to protect him. Ford was not as naive as Hartmann and Marsh supposed; his first concern was his own responsibility to act in this situation. And what he saw most clearly was the instability of the United States government and the imperative to get Nixon out of office to restore not just stability but the legitimacy of the American democracy. If his agreement to a pardon should be necessary to accomplish that and end a national crisis, Ford could accept that political reality—even though he realized the cost to his personal reputation would be high.

What was the right thing to do? Ford was still pondering the question when, at 3:30 P.M., Bryce Harlow arrived. In that meeting, Ford said, "I told Bryce everything I knew"—the full story of Haig's two visits on the previous day, the options Haig discussed, including the proposal of a Nixon resignation if promised a pardon, and Ford's midnight phone call to Haig. "Bryce listened, his expression betraying no emotion at all," Ford said. "Only after I finished did he let me know in no uncertain terms that he agreed with Bob and Jack."

Harlow's advice was explicit, and Hartmann made notes.

"Mr. Vice President," Harlow said to Ford, "I cannot for a moment believe that all this was Al Haig's own idea, or that the matters he discussed originated with 'the White House staff.' It is inconceivable that he was not carrying out a mission for the President, with precise instructions, and that it is the President who wants to hear your recommendations and test your reaction to the pardon question.

"But the President knows that he must be able to swear under oath that he never discussed this with you and that you must be able to swear that you never discussed it with him. Therefore, he sends Haig, and therefore I would not advise you to try to clarify the matter with the President himself. That would only make matters worse, if that's possible.

"Bob and Jack are absolutely right, however, that there is grave danger here of compromising your future independence, because there is bound to be suspicion and bitterness when you take the place of the man who nominated you. You are going to be President for nearly three and hopefully seven years. Whether Nixon resigns or is convicted, the probability is that the question of a pardon will come before you sometime before you leave office.

"There must not be any cause for anyone to cry 'deal' if you have to make that decision, or any mystery about your position now that you know what Haig and St. Clair have told you. But the most urgent thing, Mr. Vice President, is to tell Al Haig, straight out and unequivocally, that whatever discussions you and he had yesterday and last night were purely hypothetical and conversational, that you will in no manner, affirmatively or negatively, advise him or the President as to his future course, and nothing you may have said is to be represented to the President, or to anyone else, to the contrary."

All during Harlow's forceful declamation, Hartmann observed, Ford "sat back with his hands clasped in front of his lips, impassively, as he did when concentrating."

Harlow's reasoning brought Ford around. When Harlow finished, Ford realized that, important as it was to get Nixon out of office, a deal to bring that about would imperil his own Presidency and ability to govern. Harlow brought Ford to see that the national interest would not be served by replacing one flawed Presidency with another.

"All right," Ford said, "I'll call Al now." But first he wrote out what he would say. With his text before him, Ford got Haig on the telephone and—with Hartmann and Harlow as witnesses—read his statement to Haig: "I want you to understand that I have no intention of recommending what the President should do about resigning or not resigning, and that nothing we talked about yesterday afternoon should be given any consideration in whatever decision the President may wish to make."

"You're absolutely right," Haig said. When he hung up the phone, Haig guessed what had happened. Ford's staff had insisted that he tell Haig: "No deal."

"That's what I wanted Nixon and Haig to know," Ford said.

*   *   *

Ford destroyed Buzhardt's handwritten notes suggesting the pardon. "I didn't want to have them around," Ford said.

In the Washington bureau of *Newsweek,* two blocks west of the White House, Hal Bruno telephoned John Mitchell. With the magazine deadline close, Bruno was calling for guidance to his editors in New York about what might happen.

Mitchell had talked with Nixon, and told Bruno: "The President does understand the dimension of the problem. They miscounted the Supreme Court. They miscounted the Judiciary Committee. Now, for the first time, they are counting accurately, and it is too late in the game."

"What's going to happen next?" Bruno asked.

Mitchell said that Nixon's resignation could come within a week or ten days—"if the deal can be forged. The only thing that could stand in the way is the President being neurotic or crazy enough to let everything fall in on him."

17

REVERSAL

After Ford turned down the deal for a pardon, Nixon reversed his decision to resign. Late on Friday night, August 2, Nixon telephoned Haig at home and said he had changed his mind. "Let them impeach me," Nixon told Haig. "We'll fight it out to the end."

His new plan was to release the new transcripts on Monday afternoon and discuss them in a television address to the nation that night.

Haig sent for Price. Stop work on the resignation speech, Haig said, relaying new instructions: Nixon wanted a speech explaining the June 23 transcript and emphasizing a President's duty to go through the Constitutional process of impeachment and trial.

Price, dismayed at Nixon's reversal of course, told Haig he would carry out Nixon's instructions; but Price insisted that Haig pass on to the President a strong dissent. "There is no way for the President to survive," Price said, "and the only way for him to leave with dignity is to leave now, rather than fight it out and be clawed to shreds."

At 7:50 A.M. on Saturday, August 3, the Vice President's limousine arrived at Andrews Air Force Base and stopped near the steps of the aging Convair bearing the imposing designation *Air Force Two*. With his battered old briefcase, an armful of newspapers, and a warm greeting for his Air Force crew, Ford walked aboard. This three-day trip to Mississippi and Louisiana had long been on his schedule; he, Hartmann, and Marsh decided a sudden cancellation would generate too many speculative news stories.

Ford's plane was often half empty; but on that day it was packed with extra Secret Service agents and a full load of curious reporters. The first stop was Starkville, Mississippi, where Ford spoke for Ben Hilbun, the Republican candidate for the House. While Ford was at the podium, Hartmann took an urgent telephone call from Senator Bob Griffin. Griffin, traveling in Michigan, told Hartmann he had drafted a letter to Nixon calling for his immediate resignation and wanted to clear it with Ford.

On the next leg of the trip, Hartmann briefed Ford on what he saw as "Griffin's ultimatum." Griffin, Ford knew, did not make snap judgments; and Griffin's decision to call publicly for Nixon's resignation could signal that Nixon had already lost the votes necessary to save him in the Senate.

When he landed in Jackson, Mississippi, Ford got Griffin on the phone and listened as he read his draft. Griffin's first point was that Nixon should resign; his second that he must obey any Senate subpoena for the tapes. Griffin had heard, he carefully said to Ford, that another damaging tape had been discovered. Ford felt awkward; his pledge of secrecy still prevented him from telling Griffin that his letter to Nixon was pointless—the tapes would be public in two days. "Bob," Ford said, "do what you think is right."

As Ford waited to go to the platform to campaign for Thad Cochran, a new Member in the House, Cochran mentioned a personal political concern to Ford: If he voted to impeach the President, it would almost certainly cost him his seat. But Cochran said he thought the evidence against Nixon was very strong.

"Thad," the Vice President said, putting his hand on Cochran's shoulder, "you may not ever have to cast that vote."

In Hattiesburg, at an airport rally for Representative Trent Lott, a reporter asked Ford if he were "soft-pedaling" his support of Nixon. "My views today are just as strong as they were two days ago," Ford replied. "I still believe the President is innocent of any impeachable offense."

Hartmann winced. Ford had never learned how to lie and did not do it well when he tried. Away from the crowd, Hartmann suggested to Ford that if he were asked again, he qualify the statement at least slightly. "I had to say that," Ford said. "Had I said otherwise, the whole house of cards might collapse."

In midmorning on Saturday, Julie Nixon Eisenhower asked Pat Buchanan to come to the residence. To the Nixon daughters, Buchanan was almost like family, loyal, devoted, as much of a Nixon believer as they.

Julie and Tricia, their husbands, and Bebe Rebozo were having coffee in the solarium when Buchanan joined them. Buchanan dreaded what was coming, having to tell them that Nixon should resign. Julie Nixon began by saying the family was united against a resignation, and that her father was bitter about staff defections. Buchanan listened and finally spoke quietly: "If the President decides to fight this out in the Senate, I'll be with him. . . . [But] there comes a time when you have to say, 'It's finished, it's over.' Nothing would be served by dredging it down through the Senate—not for any of us." Julie and Tricia still opposed their father's resignation.

On impulse, Buchanan and Rebozo walked over to Nixon's hideaway in the EOB and asked that the President be told they were there. Nixon would not see them.

In the early afternoon Nixon received Griffin's letter demanding that he provide tapes to the Senate and calling for his resignation. Griffin had dictated it from Michigan to his press secretary, and directed him to deliver it to the White House for Nixon's immediate attention.

As soon as Nixon read the letter, he summoned Haig. Infuriated, Nixon said: "Pompous little jackass. Who the hell does he think he is?" Nixon suspected that Ford, through his friend Griffin, might be trying to pressure him into resigning. He told Haig that any pressure or threat only made him more determined to fight on, and he had decided to fight on through the Senate.

Haig did not tell Nixon that the day before he had encouraged Griffin to push for resignation, but said that Griffin might be part of a group, including Hartmann, trying to force the President from office.

In the late afternoon, Nixon suddenly decided to take his family to Camp David. Even on the mountaintop it was hot and humid, and they all had a swim. Sitting out on the terrace, Nixon thought: "It is easy to see why Franklin Roosevelt named this place Shangri-la." It was to be the last weekend the Nixons spent at Camp David.

Sunday morning brought more bad news for Nixon: He would lose his Presidential pension and all other Federal allowances and protection if he were impeached. In *The New York Times,* R. W. Apple, Jr., reported that the Government Accounting Office had examined the Presidential pension law and concluded that Nixon would receive his pension if he should resign from office, but not if he were impeached and convicted.

At noon on that Sunday a line of thunderstorms swept through Washington and away to the east, and the clearing sky permitted a Presidential helicopter to lift off its pad at the Pentagon, bound for Camp David. On board were Haig, Ziegler, Buchanan, Price, St. Clair, and—by the specific invitation of the President—three wives, Pat Haig, Shelley Buchanan, and Billie St. Clair.

When the helicopter landed, Haig went directly to Aspen House to see Nixon, and brought back his latest decision. Nixon would not make a speech after all but issue a written statement to accompany the new transcripts to be handed out in the White House press room the next day.

Price finished a draft statement, and the team worked on a revision. Haig took it to Nixon, who had made his own notes on what should be included. Nixon's idea was to minimize his order to Haldeman to have the CIA block the FBI investigation, and to emphasize that Nixon had, some time after, told FBI Director Gray to press the investigation.

Haig read Nixon's notes and said, "It's no use, Mr. President."

Haig explained that Nixon's own lawyers were insisting on a statement that made it clear that the June 23 evidence had been withheld from them, and consequently "they had based their case before the Judiciary Committee on a premise that proved false." St. Clair and Buzhardt were worried, for good reasons, about their own reputations.

"The hell with it," Nixon said to Haig. "It really doesn't matter. Let them put out anything they want. My decision has already been made."

On Sunday, August 4, 1974, Vice President Ford teed off at a golf course in New Orleans shortly after 8:00 A.M. It was a sweltering morning, but Ford played the full course and played well. His concentration was good, his score in the usual high 80s.

Back at his hotel he watched the news on television and went out in the afternoon to tour a hospital for crippled children. That evening he was the guest of honor at a small, quiet dinner arranged by Congressman David Treen at the Ponchartrain. After dinner Ford called his wife. "I was concerned about how she was feeling and what the children were doing," he said. "Then, too, I wanted her impressions of the news. . . . She had a good ear and a remarkable sensitivity for the nuances of what was happening."

"Everything is quiet," Betty Ford said. She had heard that Nixon and a few trusted aides had gone to Camp David to plan their strategy, but she didn't know anything more.

That morning's *Washington Post,* she added, carried an article headlined "A Capitol in Agony."

*   *   *

At 9:15 on Monday morning, August 5, 1974, Vice President Ford stepped up to the microphones at the Marriott Hotel in New Orleans to address the national convention of the Disabled American Veterans. As the thunderous applause began to subside, the National Commander, John Soave, said over the loudspeaker: "Thank you, Mr. President."

Laughter swept the room as Soave, who happened to be from Michigan, tried to correct his slip. It was an awkward moment for Ford. "That was the first time anyone called me 'Mr. President,'" Ford said.

While Ford was speaking, Hartmann telephoned Marsh, on watch back in the Vice President's office. Marsh suggested that Hartmann advise Ford that the little support Nixon still had in Congress was eroding fast. "If Jerry is going to make a statement separating his future actions from the President, he should think about doing it soon," Marsh said. "There may not be much time left."

"I've tried, Jack," Hartmann said. "But you know, maybe he *wants* to be the next to the last to leave the sinking ship. He's an old Navy man, and that's the Executive Officer's role." Hartmann asked Marsh to draft for Ford a statement of independence.

By midafternoon Ford was back in his EOB office. Marsh briefed the Vice President and Hartmann on developments, then telephoned Haig to advise him that Ford had returned. Haig hurried over to the EOB. "He looked more haggard than before," Ford observed. "I had never seen a man so physically and emotionally drained."

Despite his fatigue, Haig delivered a crisp report to the Vice President: The White House will release the tape transcripts in the late afternoon. Nixon keeps changing his mind on whether to resign or fight. The family insists he hang on for the good of the country; but the White House lawyers and staff who have seen the transcript are convinced he should resign for the good of the country. How it will come out, Haig said, "I don't know myself. It could go either way."

Neither Ford nor Haig mentioned the pardon.

After Haig left, Ford realized how deeply Nixon's indecision was affecting his own state of mind. "No longer was there the slightest doubt in my mind as to the outcome of the struggle," Ford said. "Nixon was finished. The only question now was when he would realize this and what he would do about it. I was tired. I hadn't seen Betty or the children for several days." Ford went home, took a long swim, and had a drink on the patio with Mrs. Ford. Steve and Susan were home, and they planned a quiet dinner together.

Hartmann telephoned to say that the White House had just released the new Nixon transcripts, and suggested he send a copy out to Ford's house. "No," Ford said, "I'll read it in the newspapers in the morning."

On that Monday, Haig launched the political equivalent of a military envelopment. The harder Nixon tried to escape the inevitable consequences of Watergate, the more Haig was determined to surround the President with the reality that he had lost almost all support. By this strategy, Haig planned to force Nixon's surrender to resignation.

As a first step, Haig began putting the evidence of Nixon's guilt in the hands of those leading his defense. Haig brought in George Bush and told him of the evidence to be made public that afternoon. Bush had suspected that Nixon was holding something back; but the June 23 transcript was worse than Bush had calculated. His own duty, he felt, was to hold the party together.

Bush, Buzhardt, and Dean Burch, a senior adviser to Nixon and former National Chairman, rode out to House Republican Leader John Rhodes's house. They waited in the living room as Rhodes read the transcript. "This is incredible," he said when he finished. "There's no chance in the world he won't be impeached." He told his visitors that he himself would vote to impeach Nixon on the evidence in the transcript. Rhodes was angry. For the sake of the country, he said, the House should act swiftly and force a quick Senate vote.

From Rhodes's house, Buzhardt and Burch went to the Capitol and joined St. Clair and Timmons in the Republican Whip's office just outside the House floor. There they showed the transcript to the ten Republicans on the House Judiciary Committee who had stood by Nixon and voted against all the Articles of Impeachment. After they read it, all decided to vote to impeach the President.

On the Senate side of the Capitol, St. Clair, Buzhardt, and Timmons went to the back room of Minority Leader Scott's office and handed out copies of the Nixon transcripts to Scott, Griffin, John Tower, Bill Brock, and Norris Cotton—all of whom had been Nixon supporters in the Senate. Their verdict was unanimous: The President must resign.

Dean Burch took copies of the transcript and Nixon's public statement of explanation to Senator Goldwater's office. Goldwater read both and was appalled. Nixon's statement, he said, was "as duplicitous as the man himself."

At 4:00 P.M. the White House press office released the transcript of the June 23 tape and a thousand-word statement by Nixon attempting to justify his actions in the Watergate cover-up. In it Nixon neither admitted guilt nor claimed complete innocence, but said: "I am firmly convinced that the record, in its entirety, does not justify the extreme step of impeachment and removal of a President."

An hour later the President and his family left for a dinner cruise down the Potomac on the *Sequoia*. His reason: "I did not want them to have to endure the ordeal of watching the evening news broadcasts." After dinner he went alone to a small cabin and lay down in the darkness. Washington, he thought, was being "whipped into a frenzy of excitement by the revelation of the June 23 tape. By now everyone would be scrambling for position, and few, if any, would want to be found standing with me."

After a time, Nixon's curiosity prompted him to call Haig to find out about the press reaction to the transcripts and his public explanation of the June 23 tape. The reaction was worse than expected, Haig said, and a new count indicated the Senate was lost. Nixon refused to believe him. He would not resign, Nixon told Haig, and instructed Haig to call a Cabinet meeting for the next morning so he could make that clear.

The Fords had just finished dinner when Major George Joulwan, Haig's deputy, telephoned to notify the Vice President that Nixon had scheduled a Cabinet meeting for Tuesday morning. As he hung up the phone, Ford said to himself, Nixon is probably going to tell the Cabinet he has decided to resign.

Later, in the family room, Ford told his wife that he was going to tell the President, face to face at the Cabinet meeting, that he would no longer support him.

"I was surprised he had gone along with it as long as he had," Betty Ford said. "He is a loyal person, but I worried for fear he was damaging his own image."

Early on Tuesday morning, August 6, 1974, Senator Barry Goldwater was becoming more and more angry. Driving from his Washington apartment to his Senate office, he kept thinking about the damage Richard Nixon was doing to the country, to the Presidency, and to the Republican Party. Goldwater did not like Nixon and he did not trust Nixon. He was no man to hide a strong opinion, about Nixon or anyone else, and his legendary ire had been rising since Burch showed him Nixon's transparently false explanation of the Watergate cover-up.

Goldwater was still seething when, minutes after he reached his office,

George Bush telephoned to say that the President had called an emergency Cabinet meeting. Both Goldwater and Bush agreed that impeachment in the House was certain. And, Goldwater added, "I don't think he'll get fifteen votes in the Senate."

"How can we impress the seriousness of this on the President?" Bush asked.

"I don't have the answer for that," Goldwater said.

But he did. When he ended his conversation with Bush, Goldwater telephoned Burch at the White House and said: "My head count shows that the President has no more than fifteen or sixteen senators with him, not enough to block a two-thirds vote for conviction. And he might have as few as a dozen." Birch went to Haig's office to relay the message.

By 7:00 A.M. Jack Marsh was in the Vice President's office making final changes to the talking points Ford would use at the Cabinet meeting. Ford reviewed the draft with Marsh and Hartmann and put the two pages in his pocket.

When Hartmann arrived with Ford at the Cabinet Room, they found that Haig had taken Hartmann's name off the list of invitees. "Just follow me in and sit down," Ford said.

When Nixon walked in, head down, the Cabinet members stood silently. It was the first time that Nixon had not been applauded when he entered. As all sat down at the long table, shaped like an nineteenth-century coffin, the room was silent.

"The tension around the table was unbelievable," Ford said. "I was nervous, and so, I think, was everyone else. Yet Nixon appeared not to notice." Ford, directly across the table from the President and less than five feet away, observed him intently.

"I would like to discuss the most important issue confronting the nation, and confronting us internationally too—inflation," the President began.

"My God!" Ford thought, as Nixon rambled on about inflation. "The more I listened, the more apprehensive I became. He looked tired and drawn. He was talking about something that was totally irrelevant to the circumstances that confronted him and the nation as well. I thought it was a ludicrous attempt to avoid the hard decisions he had to make."

Suddenly the President shifted to Watergate and the June 23 tape. National security was his motive in directing Haldeman to have the CIA stop the FBI investigation, Nixon said. But Nixon's remarks were in direct contradiction to his own words—which his Cabinet Members had read in *The Washington Post* and *The New York Times* that morning. In his monologue to the Cabinet, Nixon seemed to have lost touch with reality. "I thought it was proper to make the tapes available now, before the House votes on impeachment," Nixon said—ignoring the fact that everyone in the Cabinet Room knew that the Supreme Court had forced him to surrender the tapes. At no time was there any "intentional breach of the law" or "obstruction of justice," he said. "I am convinced there is no evidence of an impeachable offense." He had considered resignation, he said, but rejected it. "I will accept whatever verdict the Senate hands down."

Ford, with mounting anxiety, was waiting for his chance to speak—to assert his independence or lose the chance forever. "Mr. President," Ford said, "with your indulgence, I have something to say."

Nixon looked up, surprised. "Well, Jerry, go ahead."

The faces at the table turned toward Ford.

Without looking at the notes in his pocket, Ford began. "Everyone here recognizes the difficult position I'm in," Ford said. "No one regrets more than I do this whole tragic episode. I have deep personal sympathy for you, Mr. President, and your fine family. But I wish to emphasize that had I known what has been discussed in reference to Watergate in the last twenty-four hours, I would not have made a number of the statements I made either as Minority Leader or as Vice President.

"I came to a decision yesterday and you may be aware that I informed the press that because of commitments to Congress and the public, I'll have no further comment on the issue because I'm a party in interest. I'm sure there will be impeachment in the House. I can't predict the Senate outcome. I will make no comment concerning this. You have given us the finest foreign policy this country has ever had. A super job, and the people appreciate it. Let me assure you that I expect to continue to support the Administration's foreign policy and the fight against inflation."

Nixon, Ford thought, "seemed taken aback by what I had to say."

But Nixon coolly replied: "I think your position is exactly correct."

Hartmann, listening carefully, thought Ford had fallen short of "his own Declaration of Independence."

After Ford's statement, Nixon began talking about the economy again, and mentioned a proposal for a domestic summit of business and labor leaders to address inflation.

Attorney General William Saxbe interrupted. "Mr. President, I don't think we ought to have a summit conference," Saxbe said. "We ought to be sure you have the ability to govern."

"We were all stunned," Ford said. "There was a long silence."

"Bill," Nixon said coldly, "I have the ability just as I have had for the last five and a half years."

George Bush spoke up. The Republican Party is in a shambles, Bush said, and the midterm Congressional elections will be disastrous. Watergate must be brought to an end, Bush said.

Nixon brushed Bush's comments aside.

Kissinger, as senior member of the Cabinet, stepped in. With all the solemnity of voice and manner that he could command, Kissinger said: "We are here to do the nation's business. This is a very difficult time for our country. Our duty is to show confidence. We must demonstrate that the country can go through its Constitutional processes. For the sake of foreign policy we must act with assurance and total unity."

The confrontation ended, and all stood as Nixon left his last Cabinet meeting. "It was cruel," Kissinger wrote. "And it was necessary. For Nixon's own appointees to turn on him was not the best way to end a Presidency. Yet he had left them no other choice. . . . It was vintage Nixon. Fearing individual rejection, he had assembled the largest possible forum; hoping for a vote of confidence, he sought to confront them with a fait accompli and thereby triggered their near-rebellion."

Kissinger left the Cabinet Room and went in to see Nixon in the Oval Office. As they talked, Nixon told Kissinger, "Henry, I want you to know how much I appreciate your support and handling of foreign policy over these last months."

Nixon, as he remembered it, then told Kissinger, "I feel that I have to resign."

Kissinger remembered the conversation differently: He said that he proposed that Nixon end his Presidency. "I owed it to him to say that his best service to the country now would be to resign," Kissinger wrote. "An impeachment trial would preoccupy him for months, obsess the nation, and paralyze our foreign policy. . . . In my view, he should leave in a manner that appeared as an act of his choice . . . He said he appreciated what I said. He would take it seriously. He would be in touch."

When Kissinger left, he did not believe that Nixon had reached a decision about resignation.

From the Cabinet meeting Ford went directly to the Capitol to attend the Senate Republican Policy lunch. The room was packed, and Ford had barely reached his seat at the center of the U-shaped table when Senator Tower asked him, "Can you tell us what's going on at the White House?"

"Well, the President believes he is not guilty of an impeachable offense," Ford said. "He concedes the House battle is lost, and that the situation has to be resolved in the Senate."

Blunt as usual, Senator Goldwater spoke up. "I've been defending Richard Nixon for years. . . . We can't support this any longer. He has lied to us, and we can be lied to only so many times. I am sick and tired of it. The best thing Dick Nixon could do for the country and for the party is to get the hell out of the White House—the sooner the better. As far as I am concerned, he can get out this afternoon."

Goldwater had barely finished speaking when a page from the Republican cloakroom handed him a note: The White House is calling. Across the corridor in the Senate Republican cloakroom, Goldwater picked up the phone.

"General Haig is calling, Senator," the White House operator said. Goldwater heard Haig's voice, and then a second click. A self-taught electronics expert, Goldwater assumed that Nixon was listening on an extension.

"Barry," Haig said, "how many votes does the President have in the Senate?"

"No more than a dozen," Goldwater snapped. "It's all over. It's finished. Al, Dick Nixon has lied to me for the very last time. And to a hell of a lot of others in the House and Senate. We're sick to death of it all."

When Goldwater returned to the Senators' meeting, Ford was trying to respond to hostile questions about the President. Senator Jack Javits said Ford should tell Nixon what the Republican Senators were saying. Senator Brock asked Ford, "What more can we Senators do to transmit our feelings to the President?"

"I can't be a conduit either way," Ford said. "I can't pass along any information."

Senator Norris Cotton stood up. "I have great sympathy for Richard Nixon," he said. "We entered Congress and were sworn in on the same day, and we've been friends ever since. But . . . the good of the nation, the people and the Constitution are involved. It's no use to sit here and merely talk to each other. . . . There must be some way that we as Republican Senators can officially warn the President that the decision he has apparently made can only lead into more serious difficulty for the country and himself."

As Cotton and Senator James McClure discussed sending a delegation of Republican Senators to talk to Nixon, Ford interrupted. "I don't think I should be part of this discussion any more," the Vice President said. "I'd like to excuse myself." As Ford walked from the room, the Senators applauded him.

As the Secret Service drove Ford westward along Pennsylvania Avenue toward the White House complex, he realized he had just witnessed the proof of his earlier conclusion: Nixon was finished.

The verdict was inescapable: Now that they had read the June 23 transcript, the Republican members of the Senate were certain to vote to convict the President. As soon as Ford reached his EOB office he called in Hartmann.

"Bob," Ford said, "I think you'd better start thinking about what I should say after the swearing-in. I don't want anything fancy, but think about it."

"How much time do we have?" Hartmann asked.

"Two or three days—maybe less," Ford said. "It will probably all be over in seventy-two hours."

After the Cabinet meeting and his talk with Kissinger, Nixon was alone in the Oval Office for forty-five minutes. At 1:30 P.M. he summoned Timmons.

Grabbing his jacket, Timmons quickly called Korologos. "Latest count in the Senate, Tom—the boss just sent for me."

"My guess is we're down to six or seven," Korologos said. "Here's who I think they are: Bennett, Cotton, Curtis, Hruska, Stennis, Allen, Eastland."

When Timmons walked into the Oval Office, Nixon looked up and said quietly: "Bill, where do we stand in the Senate?"

"Mr. President," Timmons said, "we can count on only seven members of the Senate." Sitting there at the President's desk, Timmons and Nixon went over the Senate roster, Nixon shaking his head as he called off the names of defecting friends once so strong and loyal. All that remained was the meager list of the still faithful: Four Republicans, Wallace Bennett, Norris Cotton, Carl Curtis, and Roman Hruska; and three Democrats, James Allen, John Stennis, and James Eastland.

In less than twenty-four hours after the June 23 transcript was released, Nixon had lost at least twenty-seven Senate votes. He had lost any hope of survival.

"Senator Goldwater has been designated by the Republicans to bring down his assessment of the situation in the Senate to you," Timmons said.

There was a long moment of silence. "Bill," the President said, "set a meeting up with Goldwater for tomorrow afternoon. And Scott and Rhodes should come too."

18

DELIVERANCE

In midafternoon of Tuesday, August 6, 1974, President Nixon made his final decision to resign. He cites no single reason in his memoirs, no last act of persuasion. So complex a man was Nixon that it is doubtful he ever made any vital decision for a simple, obvious reason. Several elements played some part:

On that day, Nixon first knew the Senate was lost. Goldwater said so. Timmons, in three discussions with Nixon that afternoon, said so. Thirty-four votes in the Senate had been Nixon's final hope of survival; and until that afternoon, he could persuade himself there was hope.

At the Cabinet meeting that morning Nixon saw that his own appointees were lost, grimly waiting for him to get out. Saxbe had all but said, "In the Name of God, go!" Henry Kissinger, the only Cabinet member who really commanded Nixon's respect, told him resignation would best preserve the foreign policy successes of which they were both so proud. And on that day Nixon knew his support in the Republican Party was lost—Chairman Bush had told him so.

The June 23 tape broke Nixon. Once that transcript became public, Nixon knew he could not escape the anger rising throughout the land in reaction to his bald misuse of office to cover up the Watergate break-in. He had promised his daughters he would wait for the reaction to the June 23 tapes; and it had come: Guilty.

Nixon had known long before what the verdict would be; no public man of his times had keener extrasensory political perception. He knew that once his dark secret became known, the American public that had honored him with a landslide reelection twenty months earlier would be lost beyond retrieval.

And that happened. When the self-incriminating words of the President of the United States could be heard on television and read in newspapers, the guilt that Nixon knew privately became the guilt that all America knew. In the public mind, the man no longer deserved to be President.

Political reality left Nixon one option. For sixteen months of anguish, since the April Sunday when he first spoke of it at Camp David, he had considered resignation. He had momentarily tilted toward it, rejected it, debated it with his family and staff favorites, and finally come back to it in agony.

He put it off, again and again, convincing himself that the country needed him. He lived with the knowledge of his guilt in covering up the Watergate crime. But he hid the evidence from his closest and most loyal advisers, hid it from the lawyers who tried their best to defend him, from his Congressional supporters who wanted to believe in him and did believe in him—and from his own suffering family. To all, he lied.

Not once but repeatedly, not casually but systematically, Nixon lied about Watergate.

Nixon made the final decision of his Presidency alone, in the private place he had selected for the making of great decisions—Room 175 of the Old Executive Office Building. The first to know was Rose Mary Woods, the person who had served him longest and most loyally.

At about 3:30 P.M., Nixon called Woods to say he needed her help in convincing his family that the June 23 tape had cost him so much support that he could no longer govern and therefore he must resign.

While Woods went about her sad mission, Nixon picked up a yellow pad, wrote "Resignation Speech" at the top, and filled several pages for Ray Price to use in drafting his final address. Among the notes: "situation reached a point where it was clear I [do] not retain the necessary support to conduct the business of government . . . [understand] the motivations and considerations of those who [are] no longer able to stand with me and that I would be eternally grateful to those who had."

When Nixon finished he sent for Haig and Ziegler. "Things are moving very fast now," he said, "so I think it should be sooner than later. I have decided on Thursday night. I will do it with no rancor and no loss of dignity. I will do it gracefully."

To these two men, if never to the American people, Nixon could admit the truth. "Well," he said, "I screwed it up good, real good, didn't I?" The three men walked down the long steps of the EOB, across West Executive Avenue, through the White House, past the Rose Garden, and into the first floor of the residence. At the elevator, Nixon said: "It's settled then. It will be Thursday night."

As the President drafted notes for his resignation speech, Ford worked in his office only one curved staircase and a few doors away. But neither sought out the other. Nixon was not yet ready to reveal his final decision to Ford; and Ford, having resolved to show his independence, was determined to keep his distance.

After directing Hartmann to start on an inaugural speech, Ford concentrated on his schedule. He met a delegation from the Japanese Diet, held a press interview with Vermont C. Royster, editor of *The Wall Street Journal*, and met with a group of homebuilders worried about the economy.

RNC Chairman Bush came in to discuss a political fund-raiser in Los Angeles, where Ford was to be the main speaker. "George, you may want to get a backup speaker," Ford said. "I may need to be here this weekend."

Haig called Ford late in the day. Nixon had just told Haig of the decision to resign in two days, but Haig withheld that information from Ford. "I can't tell you what's going to happen," Haig said to Ford. "One moment I think there will be a resignation, the next I get the feeling that he's going to fight it through."

Ford was also circumspect; he did not tell Haig that he was preparing to assume the Presidency and had already told Hartmann to write his inaugural speech.

At dinner at their home that evening, the Fords were joined by Philip Buchen, Ford's first law partner. Ford and Buchen had remained close friends over the years; and Ford, after he became Vice President, had asked Buchen to come to Washington part-time to assist with a study commission on privacy. Over a drink before dinner, Ford said, "Phil, I want you to keep this confidential, but I think all this will be over in seventy-two hours or less."

Buchen was not surprised. He told Ford he had long expected that he would become President. With some pride Buchen revealed that for the past three months he had been meeting with a group to make plans for a Ford Presidency.

Ford was astonished. He asked who was in the group.

Buchen named four young associates he had met during his commission work—Clay Whitehead, Jonathan Moore, Brian Lamb, and Larry Lynn. Ford knew none of them. Buchen said he had kept their discussions secret because he was sure if Ford knew what was afoot, he would have stopped them.

"It was a dangerous and questionable undertaking," Ford thought. "If Nixon or any of his supporters found out, it would have been construed as an act of disloyalty on my part, and the results could have been disastrous."

But Ford did not criticize Buchen. Instead, he said, "Phil, I think we need some people of more stature and experience."

"Tell me who I can call on," Buchen said.

Ford gave him a quick list. Three were former House Members, Senator Griffin, Interior Secretary Rogers Morton, and Governor William Scranton of Pennsylvania; and one was an incumbent, Representative John Byrnes of Wisconsin. "And be sure to include Bryce Harlow and Bill Whyte," Ford said. Betty Ford got her address book and gave Buchen their phone numbers.

Certain that Ford would need a new White House press secretary, Buchen suggested Jerald terHorst, a Grand Rapids native who had moved to Washington and become bureau chief for *The Detroit News*. Ford knew ter-Horst well, liked him, and agreed.

Dinner over, Buchen called a cab to take him to the University Club, where he was staying. "I need to go and get on the phone," Buchen said. "I'll see if we can get these people together tomorrow night." As he started to go down the front steps, he turned to look at Ford—remembering the aspiring young lawyer from Grand Rapids and seeing the man now poised to become President. "Jerry," Buchen said, "I'm proud of you."

At 3:00 A.M. Wednesday, August 7, 1974, the alarm went off in Bob Hartmann's house in Bethesda, Maryland. As he made coffee, Hartmann realized that the next hours would present the biggest challenge of his life: to write Ford's inaugural speech. Themes and ideas began to emerge, and he jotted some down—"take charge," "legitimacy of his succession," "make an asset of his nonelection and no-debts to anyone," "set a course for the nation," "comity with Congress," "reassurance on foreign policy," "compassion for Nixon but distance."

Suddenly Hartmann knew he had the right phrase: "My fellow Americans, our long national nightmare is over." For four hours he sweated at his typewriter—composing, revising, changing, making it sound the way Ford talked. Satisfied with his first draft, he headed for the EOB.

At his home in Alexandria, Ford woke early, swam his laps in the backyard pool, and was en route to Capitol Hill for a Chowder and Marching

Society breakfast when the Secret Service relayed a message that Haig needed to see him right away. Ford told his driver to head for the EOB.

Haig had an urgent reason to divert Ford from going to the Hill: he had heard that Chowder and Marching members had called the meeting as part of a plot to demand Nixon's resignation. If that happened and Ford was there, Nixon would be convinced that Ford had joined a faction trying to force him out. Haig's information turned out to be wrong, but he was taking no chances.

In the EOB, Haig spoke to Ford with unusual formality: "Mr. Vice President, I think it's time for you to prepare to assume the office of President." Haig said that Nixon was considering a plan to announce his decision on Thursday night and resign at noon on Friday. But Haig added a cautious note: "The President has not made a final decision yet. But I believe he is about to accept the fact that he will have to resign."

When Haig left, Ford called in Hartmann and Marsh to give them Haig's latest report. "The President is going on television, probably tomorrow evening," Ford said. "It appears now that he will resign. But he's still President, and he could change his mind. If he resigns, it will probably be Friday, effective at noon. That's when I'll be sworn in."

"Where?" Hartmann asked.

"They're talking about the Oval Office," Ford said.

Both Hartmann and Marsh protested. Marsh pointed out that the small size of the Oval Office would rule out all but a handful of Administration and Congressional officials and Ford friends who should be there for Ford's inaugural.

"But they want just a small ceremony," Ford said.

"The hell with what *they* want," Hartmann said. "It's what do *you* want. *You* are going to be the President."

Ford accepted their recommendation that the ceremony should be in the East Room of the White House.

"Who do you want to swear you in?" Hartmann asked.

"I understand the Chief Justice is in Europe," Ford said, "but Buchen's group is working on that."

"Buchen's group?" Hartmann asked in astonishment.

Ford told them that Buchen had organized a secret transition group three months earlier. Hartmann was furious. "I have been telling reporters for months, given my word, that nobody on this staff was doing anything to plan to take over the White House—"

"Bob," Ford broke in, "Phil didn't tell me what he was doing until last night."

Even now, Ford said, they must avoid any action that could be perceived by Nixon as pressure for resignation. The wrong move by anyone working on Ford's behalf might provoke Nixon to change his mind.

To guard against that, Ford said, he wanted Marsh to take charge of his transition into the Presidency. Marsh was to oversee Buchen's group, arrange the inaugural and invite the guests, and do everything necessary to bring about an orderly change in government.

High on the priority list, they agreed, was a new press secretary for the Ford White House. Ford mentioned Buchen's suggestion—Jerald terHorst. "Jerry would be great," Hartmann said. Marsh did not know terHorst.

At 11:15 A.M., Ford left the EOB for Capitol Hill, and the Wednesday prayer session with Rhodes, Laird, and Quie. "The pattern was always the same," Ford said. "One of us started out with a simple prayer. Then we went around the room in no predetermined sequence. When the last person had finished, we said the Lord's Prayer in unison." On that Wednesday, Ford said, "the prayers the others offered were all in my behalf as the potential President. And mine were for their support—and God's—in meeting the new challenges I would face."

At 10:00 A.M., when Nixon reached the Oval Office, he found Ray Price's draft of his resignation speech on his desk. Nixon took it to his EOB office to review; but first he had to deal with another issue: pardon requests from two men whose loyalty had overcome their judgment.

A day earlier, Haldeman had called Haig to ask that he give Nixon two messages: One, Haldeman strongly opposed resignation. Two, if Nixon should decide to resign, his last act should be to pardon all the Watergate defendants. That, Haldeman suggested ominously to Haig, would be "in the President's interest."

Rose Mary Woods told Nixon that John Ehrlichman, in a telephone call to Julie Nixon Eisenhower, had made a similar request for a pardon. Haig, aware that both men were awaiting trial and could testify on the stand about Nixon's involvement in Watergate, thought the two calls contained a threat of blackmail.

Nixon telephoned Haldeman. "I felt that I owed it to him to listen to his eleventh-hour plea," Nixon wrote. "He urged me to take more time and think [resignation] through again, but if I had made up my mind, he would like me to consider issuing a blanket pardon for all the Watergate defendants. I could not help but feel and share the despair that he must be feeling. I had hoped that after the 1974 election I would be in a position to grant pardons, but I had never foreseen all that would happen. I did not give him an answer."

Tricia called her father; she and Ed Cox wanted to see him. "We still wanted to caution him to be sure resignation was the only step to take," she said. Soon after, Cox and David Eisenhower came in to propose that he wait a few more days, at least. Nixon told them that impeachment in the House and a trial in the Senate would make it impossible for a President to govern.

Even so, Cox argued, "you would be a lot stronger and more credible than Ford." Furthermore, Cox said, the resignation would not end the President's troubles. He said he knew some of the young attorneys in the Special Prosecutor's office. "They are smart and ruthless; they hate you. They will harass you and hound you in civil and criminal actions across this country for the rest of your life if you resign."

Talking with Cox and Eisenhower, Nixon compared his plight to Greek drama, and said: "The tragedy [must] be seen through until the end as fate would have it."

Bill Timmons was in his office in the West Wing of the White House when he got a call from Robert McClory, a Republican Member of the House Judiciary. McClory asked Timmons to deliver to Nixon an important message from Chairman Rodino. McClory said Rodino had called him aside and asked him to inform Nixon that the Judiciary Committee had "absolutely no interest in pursuing any kind of criminal action against the President should he elect to resign." Timmons was dubious, but passed the message on to Nixon.

Alone in his hideaway, Nixon worked on his resignation speech through the afternoon. At 5:00 P.M. Steve Bull called to say that Senator Goldwater, Senate Republican Leader Scott, and House Republican Leader Rhodes had arrived outside the Oval Office for their appointment with the President.

Nixon walked down the long granite steps outside his office, crossed West Executive Avenue, and went to the Oval Office to hear the verdict of this political jury.

Goldwater, Scott, and Rhodes dreaded telling the President he had lost Congress, but they were convinced it was necessary. Bull opened the door to the Oval Office, and the three men from Capitol Hill walked in.

Nixon stood, greeted each with a handshake, and invited them to sit down. All three faced the President across his desk—Goldwater in the center, Scott on the left, Rhodes on the right.

Putting up a front, Nixon pushed back his chair, put his feet up on the desk, and asked: "How do things look?"

"Nixon acted as though he had just made a hole in one," Goldwater said. "He talked about old friends, old political wars, days gone by. I wondered how long it would take him to get to the point of why we were there. Slowly his voice took on a different tone, a hard tone."

Nixon talked of having campaigned for some Republicans who had now turned against him. "I will remember them," he said, with a thrust of his jaw. Then he began to speak more slowly, and it was as though he were alone, listening to the sound of his own voice, remembering.

"Suddenly, sharply, Nixon ended his soliloquy," Goldwater said. "He snapped at Rhodes that the situation—meaning impeachment—in the House was not good. Before Rhodes could answer, Nixon abruptly clumped his feet on the floor, wheeled his chair around, and faced Scott. Scott turned to me, saying I would be the spokesman for the group. For a split second, Nixon stopped. He had not planned it this way—Goldwater face to face. He stared at me, then said, 'Okay, Barry, go ahead.'

"This is no time to mince words," Goldwater said, looking directly at Nixon. "Things are bad."

"Less than half a dozen votes?" Nixon asked sarcastically, his eyes narrowing at Goldwater. Goldwater was certain then that Nixon had been listening in on the telephone call Haig made to Goldwater the previous day.

"Ten at most," Goldwater said. "Maybe less. Some aren't firm."

Nixon turned to Scott, quietly puffing on an unlit pipe.

"Maybe fifteen," Scott said. "It's pretty grim." To back up his count, Scott called off the names of Senators who were longtime supporters of Nixon and now committed to vote for his conviction.

"Involuntarily," Nixon wrote, "I winced at the names of men I had worked to help elect, men who were my friends."

Nixon turned to Rhodes.

"Mr. President," Rhodes said evenly, "I don't think you'll do any better in the House."

"Do I have any options?" Nixon asked Rhodes.

Rhodes hesitated, thinking about the throng of reporters waiting to confront them on the White House grounds. "I want to tell the people outside that we didn't discuss any options," he said.

"Never mind," Nixon said curtly. "It's my decision."

They had not raised the question, but Nixon professed that he was "not interested in a pardon or amnesty." In a firm voice he said, "I will make the decision that is in the best interests of the country. I am going to be all right."

Nixon stood to end the meeting, and said: "I just want to thank you for coming up to tell me."

The three emissaries from Capitol Hill walked down the corridor of the West Wing to brief Haig on the meeting. "We told Haig there had been no demands and no deals," Goldwater said. "And in our conversation with President Nixon, there was no demand, no deal of any kind. No deal was necessary. No deal was possible.

"Nixon didn't have the votes to make a deal."

With the White House press, Goldwater, Scott, and Rhodes stuck to their story: They had not given Nixon a count of his supporters. The President had not made a decision but would act in the nation's best interests.

"I intensely disliked not laying it on the line," Goldwater said, "but if I had [told the press] Nixon was certain to lose in both houses, there was no telling how he would have reacted."

Back in his Senate office, Goldwater telephoned Benjamin Bradlee, managing editor of *The Washington Post*. "I have talked to Nixon," Goldwater said, "and he may resign, and that would be in the best interest of the country. But if he is pushed, especially by the press and especially by your paper, he will get mad and he may change his mind. So if you love your country, lay off for a day and let him resign."

Bradlee looked at the lead Lou Cannon and Carroll Kirkpatrick had written for the front page the next morning: "President Nixon was reported yesterday to be nearing a decision to resign, but there was no official confirmation from the White House. Three White House sources said that the question now was only one of timing . . ."

Bradlee let the story stand.

In the Senate Republican cloakroom, Goldwater warned his colleagues to say nothing about Nixon. "Just everybody be quiet now," Goldwater said. "Don't go out and tell the press that he ought to resign, or anything else. I believe he is going to resign, but not if we start trying to force him to do it."

Alone in the Oval Office after hearing the verdict from his own leaders in Congress, the President decided to reaffirm to his family his decision to resign, and end their appeals to postpone it. "I called Rose and asked her to tell the family that a final check of my dwindling support in Congress had confirmed that I had to resign," Nixon wrote. "I asked her to tell them that Goldwater, Stennis, Scott, and Rhodes were all going to be voting for impeachment. My decision was irrevocable, and I asked her to suggest that we not talk about it any more when I went over for dinner."

The next priority, Nixon thought, was how to preserve his foreign policy. How could he make sure that the five years of his Presidential initiatives and actions in foreign policy would not be lost? He asked Haig to call Henry and get him over.

At 5:58 P.M., Kissinger was at the State Department when an assistant told him Haig was on the telephone—"urgent."

"Can you come over to the White House right away?" Haig asked.

Kissinger dropped the phone and left. "It was the only time I ever saw HAK run," said Chris Vick, Kissinger's assistant. As she put Kissinger's phone back in the cradle, Vick thought of the rumors around the White House that Nixon might take his life and wondered: "Has the President killed himself?"

The Secretary of State's black limousine raced the eight blocks to the White House and Kissinger hurried to the President's office.

"When I entered the Oval Office, I found Nixon alone with his back to the room, gazing at the Rose Garden through the bay windows," Kissinger wrote. "Nixon turned when he heard me. He seemed very composed, almost at ease. He had decided to resign, he said. The Republican leaders had reinforced his instinct that there was not enough support left in the Congress to justify a struggle. The country needed some repose. He could save our foreign policy only by avoiding a Constitutional crisis. . . . The effort seemed to drain him and I feared for his composure."

Nixon told Kissinger of his plan to speak to the nation on Thursday and resign on Friday. There would be a need, Nixon said, to notify all foreign governments of the change, and to send special messages to the Soviet Union, China, and the Middle East countries.

"Every nation would need assurance that my departure from the scene would not mean a change in America's foreign policy," Nixon wrote. "They would have little knowledge of Jerry Ford, so I wanted to let them know how strongly he had supported my foreign policy while he was in the House of Representatives and as Vice President, and how they could count on him to continue that policy as President."

Nixon told Kissinger that he must remain as Secretary of State for President Ford. "The whole world will need reassurance that my leaving won't change our policies. You can give them that reassurance, and Jerry will need your help. Just as there is no question but that I must go, there really is no question but that you must stay."

Ford accelerated his briefings. Brent Scowcroft, deputy at NSC, brought him up to date on national security issues. Fred Malek, deputy at OMB, brought in the latest figures on budget outlays and deficit projections.

Ford also invested time in interviews with three reporters for whom he had particular respect—Alan Otten of *The Wall Street Journal,* Paul Martin of *U.S. News & World Report,* and Marjorie Hunter of *The New York Times.* The Secretary of the Navy, William Middendorf, and the Chief of Naval Operations, Admiral James Holloway, made a courtesy call, and Admiral Holloway presented a painting of the USS *Monterey,* the carrier Ford had served aboard in the Pacific during World War II.

Hartmann and Marsh came in to deliver a progress report on plans for the transition. Marsh had learned from Haig that President Nixon would invite Ford to the Oval Office on Thursday morning to officially inform the Vice President that he would assume the Presidency at noon on Friday.

In the late afternoon Ford closed his door to study and read aloud the inaugural speech that Hartmann had prepared. "Bob had done a great job," Ford said. "He always waited until the last minute—it almost drove me crazy. But he always came through."

Ford was particularly pleased at the words that set the theme—"just a little straight talk among friends."

"Bob has that great capability of picking a sentence or a phrase for a speech where it sounds like me, a sentence that I can do well," Ford said.

He was less certain about "Truth is the glue that holds government together." At first he decided to "knock it out of the speech. I thought it was corny, not in the mood of an acceptance speech. And Bob fought like a tiger to keep it in, and finally I capitulated. He was absolutely right."

Tears came to Ford's eyes as he read, "I am indebted to no man, and only to one woman, my dear wife." Hartmann, Ford thought, "understands my feelings perfectly."

The suggestion for a kind word about the anguish of President Nixon came from Ford. "I insisted that something be in there that would show my concern for the Nixons, and Bob agreed. He brought in the line, 'May our former president, who brought peace to millions, find it for himself.' It was just right. It was what I wanted to say."

*   *   *

That evening, after dinner with his family, Nixon called Kissinger and asked him to come over to the residence. In the Lincoln Sitting Room they talked for an hour about their good times together, the trips to China, to the USSR, Europe, the Middle East. "For some reason the agony and the loss of what was about to happen became most acute for me during that conversation," Nixon wrote. Nixon opened a bottle of brandy, and the two comrades in arms and politics, fame and infamy, attempted a farewell toast. As they put their glasses aside, Nixon asked Kissinger to pray with him, and the two men knelt in silence.

At 9:50 A.M., on Thursday, August 8, 1974, Vice President Ford, Marsh, Colonel Jack Walker, the Vice President's Army aide, and a squad of Secret Service agents walked across Pennsylvania Avenue to Blair House. Ford was there at the request of President Nixon to present the Congressional Medal of Honor to the families of seven military men killed in Vietnam.

Ford was always deeply moved by patriotic ceremony, and this one, under the circumstances, was even more difficult. "I tell you, it was tough," he said. "We carried it out, but my mind was not totally occupied with the awards, important as they were. I was thinking of other things down the line."

As soon as the Secret Service reported to Haig that Ford was back to his office, Haig telephoned Ford. "The President wants to see you," he said. "I think you know what he's going to say."

Haig spoke, Ford said, "in a quiet voice, a solemn tone. It was as though Al were telling me, 'Well, Mr. Vice President, the decision has been made. You come on over; he wants to talk to you, tell you himself.' I felt that Al was relieved that a decision had been made."

Two Secret Service agents jumped up to accompany Ford as he immediately headed out the door. They walked the hundred feet to the elevator, rode to the ground floor, headed out the archway, crossed West Executive Avenue, angled northeast to the West Wing, and walked briskly upstairs. Ford stopped momentarily by Haig's office.

Haig stood and shook hands with Ford. Together they walked to the President's reception room outside the Oval Office. There Haig stopped. "The President wants to see you alone, Mr. Vice President."

Ford sat on the couch, waiting. Moments later, Nixon told Steve Bull on the intercom he was ready. Bull opened the door into the Oval Office and announced: "Mr. President, the Vice President is here to see you."

The President was seated but stood as soon as Ford walked in. As they shook hands, their eyes met.

"Sit down," Nixon said, motioning to the chair on his right.

"He looked very solemn," Ford said. "He sat upright. I was looking directly at him. He was obviously tense, taut, under great strain. He was not emotional, ever. He was calm and collected, but at the same time you could feel the emotion beneath the surface. And yet, he tried to make it a pleasant, congenial atmosphere as we talked. He came right to the point."

"I have made the decision to resign," Nixon told Ford in a firm and deliberate voice. "It's in the best interest of the country. I won't go into the arguments pro and con. I've made my decision."

For a moment Nixon paused, then said simply: "Jerry, I know you'll do a good job."

"Mr. President," Ford said, "you know that I am saddened by this circumstance. You know I would have wanted it to be otherwise, but I am ready to do the job and I think I am fully qualified to do it."

"I know you are too," Nixon said.

"That was all," Ford said, "and that part didn't take long. It was obviously very, very hard for him. But once he had told me it was a fait accompli, it was like a burden had been lifted from him."

It was Nixon's habit in the Oval Office, Ford had observed, to roll "that big chair" away from the Presidential desk and lean back to affect a closeness and put a visitor at ease. Now Nixon did so; and with feet propped up, he began a general tutorial on governing, and on foreign policy in particular.

"He relaxed, and it was a much more informal, low-keyed conversation," Ford said. "Once that first ten minutes was over, he had a totally different demeanor. He gave me suggestions and advice. It was like a person who had the burdens of the world taken off his shoulders, and he was offering a good friend the best advice that he could give for the job that I was about to assume.

"He talked very pragmatically about problems that we were facing in the domestic economy. He took some time to talk about foreign policy, and the important responsibilities Secretary Kissinger had.

"He talked about SALT II; about Brezhnev, said that he was tough and bright, but could be flexible, and how he dealt with him; about the importance of NATO. He hoped I would continue a strong policy in Vietnam, maintain our military strength, and keep working for peace in the Middle East. He emphasized the role that Kissinger could play."

"Henry is a genius," Nixon said, "but you do not have to accept everything that he recommends. He can be invaluable, and he will be very loyal, but you cannot let him have a totally free hand."

"He talked about the economy," Ford said. "It was inevitable because the economy was really beginning to hurt—and hurt not only in the inflation, which was horrendous, but there were some ominous signs in the economy generally as far as a slowdown. He emphasized that I should work with Federal Reserve Chairman Arthur Burns, and explained why I should avoid wage and price controls."

Ford was listening, concentrating. Nixon offered a general comment on his Cabinet and White House staff—"good people"—and suggested Ford might keep some of them. Except for Kissinger, he mentioned none by name.

Nixon emphasized to Ford the importance of choosing a highly qualified Vice President. "There are many good people," Nixon said, "and it's your choice. I won't be talking to you about it again, but you want somebody who will add stature to the Administration, who will generate national as well as international confidence."

"He thought Nelson Rockefeller would be a very good man," Ford said, "but identified no one else."

To Ford, "It was a very high-level discussion. He showed no vindictiveness toward anybody. He did ninety percent of the talking but made no complaint against the Democrats in Congress or the press." Watergate was not mentioned once, Ford said, nor was a possible pardon.

Nixon, intent to the last on being master of his public appearances, concluded the extraordinary session with Ford by detailing the plan for his departure. He and his family would go to the East Room to say good-bye to the staff and Cabinet, then move directly out through the diplomatic entrance to the helicopter.

From the diplomatic entrance, Nixon said, they would walk to the helicopter, and leave the White House for Andrews Air Force Base. From Andrews they would fly in *Air Force One* for San Clemente.

Nixon suggested that the Vice President and Mrs. Ford meet the Nixons in the diplomatic entrance and walk to the helicopter with them. Ford agreed.

"Where will you be sworn in?" the President asked.

"Well," Ford said, "I decided not to go to the Capitol because some up there might try to turn the occasion into some kind of celebration."

"I'll be gone before noon," Nixon said. "If you like, you could be sworn in here in the White House, as Truman was."

Ford said he had decided to be inaugurated in the East Room.

Finally, there was no more to be said. It was eleven minutes after noon. They had been talking for seventy minutes. Nixon stood, walked around his desk, and joined Ford as they headed to the side door of the Oval Office.

"He put his arm around me as we walked to the door, and we walked out on this little porch," Ford said. For a few moments the two old friends lingered there on the covered walkway outside the Oval Office.

"Thank you for your loyal support over these painful weeks and months," Nixon said. "You will have my prayers in the days and years ahead."

No historic phrases were exchanged. "I couldn't be very elegant with words because the emotion was too great," Ford said. "The words just didn't come out easily. I'm sure I said, 'I'll see you tomorrow. Give Pat and the family my best.' And I'm sure he said, 'Well, you and Betty will enjoy living in the mansion. We'll see you tomorrow.' Those were the words between two friends at a critical moment not only in each of our lives but in our country's history. It was a dramatic moment—just the two of us there."

The President left Ford on the porch and walked back into the Oval Office.

Ford walked quickly away, along the porch and across the south lawn. He did not look back. Forty yards away his limousine waited, and he headed straight for it, not looking at the Secret Service agents waiting there. "I just looked right at that car, and wanted them to open the door and get in it and get out of this terribly dramatic circumstance. I really just wanted to be alone."

19

TRANSITION

In distance, Ford's ride through the south lawn of the White House to the archway of the EOB was less than two blocks. In time, the trip took less than a minute. But it was long enough for Ford to recover full command of his emotions.

The uncertainty had ended. Through all that had happened in those terrible eight days of August, and despite Ford's conviction that Nixon had no practical choice except resignation, Ford did not really believe that Richard Nixon would surrender the Presidency until Nixon himself told him so. Once Nixon said face to face he had decided to resign, Ford's anxiety over what Nixon might do turned into confidence about what he, Gerald Ford, was ready to do.

By the time Ford reached his office, he was beginning to feel a sense of release and resolve. Now he could get to work to bring about a calm and orderly transfer of executive power.

His first action was to telephone Kissinger. "I thought it urgent to tell him right away how I felt about him," Ford said.

"Henry," the Vice President said, in the loud voice he habitually uses on the telephone, "I need you. The country needs you. I want you to stay. I'll do everything I can to work with you."

"Sir," Kissinger replied, "it is my job to get along with you, and not yours to get along with me."

With less than twenty-four hours to get ready, Ford brought in Hartmann, Marsh, and Buchen to go over actions to be taken and decisions to be made before the swearing-in. Ford reaffirmed his decision to hold his inaugural in the East Room of the White House and told Marsh to find some way to get Chief Justice Warren Burger there to administer the oath of office.

"That was of great importance to Ford," Marsh said. "He wanted the dignity and imprimatur that only the Chief Justice would bring to the occasion." Marsh had Burger's itinerary—he was traveling in the Netherlands—and got him on the telephone for the Vice President.

"Mr. Chief Justice," Ford said, "I guess you've heard the news. I hate to interrupt your trip, but I would like it very much if you could be here for the swearing-in."

"Oh, I *want* to be there," Burger said immediately. "I've *got* to be there."

Marsh, who had already arranged an Air Force plane, got on the phone and told the Chief Justice the time and place where he would be picked up and flown nonstop to Washington.

To Ford it was critical that the list of guests be put together by his most practiced hand at treating political egos; so he entrusted that responsibility to Marsh. Since only 275 guests could be accommodated in the East Room, Marsh developed a rational concept for invitations: First, the Ford family. Second, the Cabinet and top White House staff. Third, the bipartisan leaders of Congress, the chairmen and ranking members of Congressional committees, all his House colleagues of his Class of '48, and all the Michigan Congressional delegation.

The Washington diplomatic corps made the list; each would need to cable his foreign minister about the momentous transfer of American political power. And there were special guests: Richard Frazier, Ford's House driver; Ms. Clara Powell, the Ford family's close friend and maid; and Representative Lindy Boggs, the widow of his friend, House Majority Leader Hale Boggs. "I just knew Ford would want former Speaker John McCormack there, so I mentioned it," Marsh said. "Good idea, Jack," Ford said. Marsh sent a plane for McCormack.

Everyone had to be invited by telephone, and the calls from the White House switchboard continued into the middle of the night.

Ford personally called Hugh Scott to invite him to the ceremony. "As you know, Hugh, things have come to pass," he said. "Our relationship has been excellent, and I expect it to continue. . . . Accessibility and openness will be the hallmarks of my Administration."

He called Tip O'Neill. "Tip, I want you at my swearing-in."

"Are wives invited, Jerry? The reason I'm asking is that I've already told Millie to pack and get down here."

"Wives were not invited," Ford said, "but they are now."

O'Neill read a statement he was about to make, saying that Congress would cooperate with Ford, but Ford must cooperate with Congress.

"That's fine, Tip," Ford said. "And I want to say I'll be relying on you for your advice and assistance."

After a brief silence O'Neill said: "Christ, Jerry, isn't this a wonderful country? Here we can talk like this and you and I can be friends, and eighteen months from now I'll be going around the country kicking your ass in."

"That's a hell of a way to speak to the next President of the United States," Ford said. They both laughed.

Ford asked Hartmann to bring in his "acceptance speech," as he kept calling it; he wanted to go over it with Hartmann one more time.

"Just one thing troubles me," Ford said, "and that's this line 'Our long national nightmare is over.' Isn't that a little hard on Dick? Could we soften that?"

"No, no, no!" Hartmann said. "Don't you see, that's your whole speech. That's what you have to proclaim to the whole country—to the whole world. That's what everybody *needs* to hear, *wants* to hear, has *got* to hear you say. It's like FDR saying 'All we have to fear is fear itself.' Maybe it isn't quite true, but saying it will make it come true. *You* have to turn the country around.

"Junk all the rest of the speech if you want to, but not that. That is going to be the headline in every paper, the lead in every story. This hasn't been a nightmare just for Nixon and his family. It's been a nightmare for everybody—for you, for me, for Nixon's enemies as well as his friends. Don't you think it's been a nightmare for Carl Albert, for Peter Rodino? Most Americans voted for Nixon less than two years ago. Hasn't it been a nightmare for them? This has been a *national* nightmare, and it's got to be stopped. You're the only one who can."

Never had Hartmann been so insistent. "I was ready to beg, get down on my knees, put my life on the line for that sentence," he said.

Ford looked at the line again, and after a long pause said: "Okay, Bob. I guess you're right. I hadn't thought about it that way."

He paused again and looked at Hartmann. "And thank you," Ford said. "You did a wonderful job. I don't know how you did it."

Ford put the speech back in his coat pocket and decided to work on his delivery by rehearsing it with Betty that night.

In midafternoon Kissinger arrived in Ford's office for what Ford described as "a thorough briefing on the world situation. We were still having plenty of trouble in Vietnam and Cambodia. We talked about the desirability of continuing the plans for the meeting with Brezhnev in Vladivostok. Henry urged me, as soon as I was sworn in the next day or in the next several days, to meet with the Ambassadors from the NATO countries, from Africa, Latin America, the Middle East, the Far East. I agreed, and told him to set them up to begin the following afternoon.

"We talked about the two hats that he had—Secretary of State and National Security Adviser. I said to him that at that time I didn't want to make any change in that situation. I think it's worked well, and let's keep it that way."

At the White House in the afternoon, Haig returned from a rendezvous at his home in Virginia with Leon Jaworski, the Watergate Special Prosecutor.

Haig had called Jaworski the day before to suggest the meeting. Jaworski agreed, on the condition that no deal on the prosecution would be made or even discussed.

After Mrs. Haig served Haig and Jaworski tea and coffee in the living room, she disappeared. In Jaworski's account of the meeting, he spoke first: "I think we should have a clear understanding, Al, that we're not going to reach any kind of agreements about the President at this meeting."

"I know that," Haig said. "That's not why I wanted to meet. The President is going to resign tonight, if you haven't guessed."

Jaworski nodded, and waited.

"Now," Haig continued, Nixon is "going to be taking his tapes and papers with him, Leon. There's no hanky-panky involved. Your office will have access to them if you need them. He's going to San Clemente tomorrow and the tapes and papers will be shipped out later. . . . The President and I both felt we owed it to you to let you know what's going to happen."

Jaworski warned Haig that all material must be available to the Special Prosecutor's office for the trials of Mitchell, Haldeman, Ehrlichman, and other Watergate defendants.

Haig told Jaworski that Haldeman and Ehrlichman had asked for a Presidential pardon but that Nixon had decided he would pardon none of the Watergate defendants. "Another thing, Leon . . . under no circumstances is the President going to testify in that cover-up trial or any other proceeding," Haig said. "If necessary, he'll take the Fifth Amendment."

Gratuitously, Haig added, "I don't mind telling you that I haven't the slightest doubt that the tapes were screwed with." Jaworski assumed Haig was suggesting that Nixon was responsible for the eighteen-and-a-half-minute gap.

"Are you going to stay on and help Ford?" Jaworski asked.

"Yes, but I don't know how long. Certainly a number of weeks."

Jaworski asked if President Nixon's supporters in Congress were "going to pass a resolution that would, in effect, tell me not to move against him."

"Oh yes!" Haig said. "I think it will be passed within a day or two. With no difficulty."

President Nixon spent most of the last afternoon of his Presidency alone, in his favorite brown chair in EOB Room 175, his daytime sanctuary. Buzhardt interrupted his reverie to show him a written request for a pardon that had just come in from Haldeman.

Nixon looked it over. Haldeman had drafted a statement announcing pardons for the Watergate defendants and a Vietnam amnesty in the hope that Nixon would insert it in his resignation speech. "It was a painful decision not to grant his request, but tying their pardon to the granting of amnesty to Vietnam draft dodgers was unthinkable," Nixon wrote. "And to grant a blanket pardon to all those involved in Watergate would have raised the issue to hysterical political levels."

While Nixon was still talking to Buzhardt, Haig came in to report on his secret meeting with Jaworski.

Haig said there was no bargaining; he had informed Jaworski of the President's decision to resign, and Jaworski agreed that it was the right decision. Haig said it was his impression that Nixon had "nothing to fear" from the Special Prosecutor.

"Considering the way his office has acted in the past," Nixon said, "I have little reason to feel assured."

After the eventful day, Vice President Ford left his office to go home for dinner and to be with Betty Ford to watch the President's resignation speech on television. They sat beside each other in the family room with their two youngest children.

"Steve and Susan were saddened, and they were also somewhat awestricken by the obvious changes in their lives that were going to take place the next day," Ford said. "Betty and I didn't say much; we were so engrossed, so preoccupied by just watching it. A lot was going through my mind, and hers—how was this going to affect each of our lives, and our joint lives?"

As he listened to Nixon, Ford reacted with disdain when Nixon said, "I no longer have a strong enough political base in the Congress to justify continuing."

Shaking his head, Ford thought Nixon was unable to admit his own blame for Watergate. "The fact that he was predicating his departure and resignation on the circumstance that he had lost the base in Congress, it shocked me," Ford said. "It would have had a better ring and a better response from the American people if he had been more forthcoming, more contrite, and asked for forgiveness. I don't think any of those things were reflected."

At the end of the speech Ford stepped outside into the summer drizzle and told reporters staked out on his lawn: "This is one of the most difficult and very saddest periods, and one of the saddest incidents I've ever witnessed. Let me say that I think the President has made one of the greatest personal sacrifices for the country, and one of the finest personal decisions on behalf of all of us."

Though he was not yet President, Ford had made a Presidential decision; and he announced it: "I have asked Henry Kissinger, as Secretary of State, to stay on, and to be the Secretary of State under the new Administration. . . . He and I will be working together in the pursuit of peace in the future as we have achieved it in the past."

In the hope that he could take the first step toward restoring the comity long absent between the White House and Congress, Ford made a solemn commitment to work with Democrats and Republicans on Capitol Hill to bring about "what's good for America and good for the world."

Later, as always when he was at home, Jerry and Betty Ford sat together to watch the eleven o'clock news. Their conversation covered the practical— what they should wear the next day—and the extraordinary—when they should plan to move into the White House.

Of that remarkable day, Thursday, August 8, 1974, Ford said, "after being told by President Nixon that he was resigning the Presidency and I would be sworn in the next day, I had very mixed feelings.

"I was inwardly deeply saddened that a longtime, personal friend, whom I had campaigned for in nineteen sixty, nineteen sixty-eight, and nineteen seventy-two, and whom I admired greatly as a superb foreign policy Commander in Chief, would resign the Presidency. Betty and I, since early nineteen forty-nine, had had such a wonderful relationship with the Nixons. To have such a tragedy happen to good friends was extremely difficult to understand and accept.

"On the other hand, it was a tremendous relief to have the festering crisis resolved. For the previous nine months I had been sitting on a time bomb with a blowup likely to take place at any time as new, damaging evidence kept surfacing.

". . . Betty and I had never wanted President Nixon to leave the White House until his second term expired in January, nineteen seventy-seven; but we were not at all comfortable with probable developments for the next two and a half years when there would likely be the impeachment process under way.

"The night of August eighth, in our home, was surprisingly uneventful. Betty and I . . . had a quiet feeling of confidence that we were prepared to handle our new responsibilities and challenges. . . . We retired early. Before sleeping we held hands and offered my prayer from Proverbs—'Trust in the Lord with all thine heart . . .'"

President Nixon finished his resignation speech and left the Oval Office for the last time. Kissinger was waiting in the corridor. "Mr. President," he said, "after most of your major speeches in this office we have walked together back to your house. I would be honored to walk with you again tonight."

Past the Rose Garden they slowly made their way, Kissinger talking in a low voice, trying to reassure the President about his place in history. At the doorway into the residence, Kissinger stopped. Julie Nixon Eisenhower was waiting there for her father, and she walked with him to the elevator.

Upstairs, the Nixon family met the President with tears and trembling embraces. Outside the White House, on Pennsylvania Avenue and in Lafayette Park, a large crowd shouted and waved placards. Mrs. Nixon, believing they were supporters, suggested the President listen to them.

But Nixon had already heard the noise of the demonstrators. "I assumed they were against me," Nixon said.

They were. They were chanting "Jail to the Chief."

After the family went to bed, Nixon went to the Lincoln Sitting Room and sat alone. At 1:30 A.M. his manservant, Manolo Sanchez, came in to ask if he could do anything else for the President.

"Yes," Nixon said. "Turn out all the lights in the residence. Tonight is a time for darkness."

Soon after daybreak on Friday, August 9, 1974, Ford woke in his suburban home and thought about the day to come. "I had slept well," Ford said, "and this reflected my confidence that I was prepared to do the job."

His sorrow over what was happening to the Nixons was mixed with relief that the waiting was over. Gerald Ford was ready to take command. In his mind, twenty-five years in Congress and nine years as a House Leader had given him the training and experience to be an effective President.

Promptly at 8:00 A.M., Phil Buchen and Congressman John Byrnes arrived. Over coffee in the family room, Buchen handed Ford a four-page memorandum of recommendations for the transition. In the Vice President's limousine on the way to the EOB, Buchen and Byrnes sat quietly as Ford read the memo.

"This group recommends strongly that you need a temporary operational group interposed between you and the old White House staff. . . . We share your view that there should be no Chief of Staff, especially at the outset. However, there should be someone who could rapidly and efficiently organize the new staff organization, but who will not be perceived or be eager to be Chief of Staff."

Ford, on the previous afternoon, had sent for Donald Rumsfeld, U.S. Ambassador to NATO, to come back for a few weeks to manage the transition.

Ford read on: ". . . You should have a series of meetings the first few days to assert your personal direction and control over the executive branch of the government," with Congressional Leaders, key White House staff, Cabinet, Governors, and the Washington diplomatic corps. Ford had already told Marsh that his first priority was to meet with the Leaders of the House and Senate. Marsh had made the arrangements.

On one issue, continuity versus change, the advice of Buchen's team was emphatic: "You must walk a delicate line between compassion and consideration for the former President's staff and the rapid assertion of your personal control over the executive branch. . . . Al Haig has done yeoman service for his country. You should meet with him personally as soon as possible and prevail upon him to help you and your transition team, thus completing the holding-together he has done for so long. He also will be needed for liaison with Mr. Nixon and his family. However, he should not be expected, asked, or be given the option to become *your* Chief of Staff."

Ford was ambivalent about Haig. He knew, far better than anyone else, that Haig had held the White House together for months; but Ford had no intention of yielding to Haig the degree of Presidential authority that Nixon had given him.

As the limousine pulled up into the arch under the EOB, Ford paused thoughtfully, then looked at Buchen and Byrnes. "Thanks for a fine job," he said.

Like a condemned man, President Nixon chose for his last breakfast in the White House his favorite—corned beef hash and poached eggs, to be served in the Lincoln Sitting Room. He was there making notes for his farewell to the staff when he heard a knock on the door, and Haig came in.

"This is something that will have to be done, Mr. President, and I thought you would rather do it now."

Haig handed him a letter, on White House stationery, addressed to the Secretary of State: "I hereby resign the Office of President of the United States."

President Nixon signed it.

By that act, Richard Milhous Nixon legally ended his Presidency. In his own mind, or so he said at the time, it had ended on the mountaintop at Camp David fifteen months earlier when, weighing his own complicity in the Watergate cover-up, he had the apocalyptic vision that his Presidency was over. It was then that he first spoke of resigning, then that he began to agonize over his own guilt in the Watergate crime and to dread the political gallows.

For the people of America, a vast number of whom had voted for Nixon and believed in him as their President, the final act in the drama of the Nixon Presidency was played out in the East Room of the White House on the morning he left.

At 9:32 A.M. the President, with his family arrayed at his side, stood at the podium behind the Presidential seal to say good-bye to his Cabinet, senior advisers, and the rank and file of loyal workers who served them all. He was there also to say good-bye—through the immediacy and intimacy of television—to the larger world beyond the East Room, to all the Nixon believers and haters in the sphere of his tumultuous political life.

Television is theater; its electronic alchemy puts the drama of history right in front of us when it happens and keeps it alive. The video of Nixon's White House farewell is vivid, dire, and unforgettable:

On the TV screen there Nixon is again, still President, on stage, the camera moving in so close that it becomes merciless. There is Pat Nixon, stoic and impassive; Tricia Nixon Cox, masking her feelings like her mother; Julie Nixon Eisenhower, her face as mobile and expressive as her father's. Ed Cox is solemn. David Eisenhower smiles when Nixon does; somehow it seems incongruous. Nixon is sweating, understandable in the circumstances and under the searing heat of the lights. He sweats at the temples, on his memorable nose and jowls, on the upper lip and jutting jaw. With the knuckle of his right forefinger he quickly wipes it away.

The applause is long; Nixon lets it run. He weeps. He forces a smile. He struggles. He sniffs. When he begins to speak, he shows the real Nixon—no speechwriter would have done this. He rambles. He reminisces. He dissembles. His earnest effort at humor becomes an anxious cry from the soul. He tries to be strong, but his voice betrays him. The eyes of his wife and daughters dart anxiously toward him each time he pauses for long moments to regain his composure.

He does not say good-bye, but—"Au revoir. We'll see you again." The upbeat words are unexpected; there is strong applause.

He commends the people who have served him and now pack the elegant room of gold and white. He pays tribute to the White House itself, "This is the best House . . . this house has a great heart, and that heart comes from those who serve."

In his disjointed phrases he sketches a self-portrait: "Sure we've done some things wrong . . . the top man always takes the responsibility, and I've never ducked it . . . mistakes yes, but for personal gain, never; you did what you believed in, sometimes right, sometimes wrong, and I only wish that I were a wealthy man, at the present time I've got to find a way to pay my taxes; and if I were I would like to recompense you for the sacrifices that all of you have made to serve the government . . . far more important than money, it's the cause bigger than yourself, it's the cause of making this the greatest nation in the world, the leader of the world . . . with our leadership it will know peace, it will know plenty . . . most important, we must be strong here, strong in our hearts, strong in our souls, strong in our belief, and strong in our willingness to sacrifice."

He pauses, and after a few moments, a far look comes to his eyes, and he seems to be talking not to the sad faces before him but to himself. "I remember my old man." He shakes his jowls. "I think that they would have called him sort of a little man, a common man. He didn't consider himself that way. You know what he was? He was a streetcar motorman at first, and then he was a farmer, and then he had a lemon ranch—it was the poorest lemon ranch in California, I can assure you—he sold it before they found oil on it." He smiles and draws a ripple of nervous laughter. "And then he was a grocer, but he was a great man—" He pauses, for long moments. "—because he did his job . . . and every job counts. Up to the hilt. Regardless of what happened."

Now Nixon's visible anguish makes it difficult for him to continue. Anxiously he clears his throat to regain his voice; his glazed eyes and sentimental words suggest his thoughts are moving on a stream of distant memory.

"Nobody will ever write a book probably about my mother. . . . My mother was a saint—" There is another pause to regain his composure. "—and I think of her, two boys dying of tuberculosis, nursing four others in order that she could take care of my older brother for three years in Arizona, and seeing each of them die, and when they died, it was like one of her own. Yes, she would have no books written about her—" Tears well in his eyes. "—but she was a saint . . ."

The words and memories of his mother seem to suffuse him with pathos. To end it, Nixon says brusquely: "Now, however, we look to the future." But he plunges back into emotion by reading the moving words Theodore Roosevelt wrote, in his twenties, when his young bride died: "Her life had been always in the sunshine, there had never come to her a single great sorrow . . . bright and sunny temperament and her saintly unselfishness. Fair, pure and joyous as a maiden, loving, tender and happy as a young wife, when she had just become a mother and her life seemed to be just begun, and the years seemed so bright before her, and by a strange terrible fate, death came near, and when my heart's dearest died, the light went from my life forever."

Nixon reaches the lesson of his farewell: "That was T.R. He thought the light had gone from his life forever but he went on and he not only became President but as an ex-President, he served his country, always in the arena. Tempestuous, strong, sometimes wrong, sometimes right, but he was a *man.*

"And as I leave, let me say, that's an example I think all of us should remember. . . . We think that when we suffer a defeat that all is ended. We think, as T.R. says, 'the light has left his life forever.' Not true. It's only a beginning, always . . .

"The greatness comes, and you are really tested, when you take some knocks, some disappointments, when sadness comes. Because only if you have been in the deepest valley can you ever know how magnificent it is to be on the highest mountain . . ."

To close his farewell address, Nixon dispenses advice that, had he followed it, might have kept him in office: "Always remember, others may hate you, but those who hate you don't win unless you hate them, and then you destroy yourself."

With a resolute wave to these stricken friends, President Nixon and his family leave the podium. The U.S. Marine Band strikes up a sprightly march and breaks the somber mood.

Vice President and Mrs. Ford are waiting downstairs in the Diplomatic Reception Room when President Nixon and his family join them. Tears come with the handshakes; these are old friends, close friends. After a few moments the President glances at his wrist watch: time to go. He leads the way out. Across the red carpet rolled out for the occasion, they walk four abreast— President Nixon on the left, Mrs. Nixon, Mrs. Ford, Vice President Ford—to the stair of the waiting helicopter.

"Not many words were said," Ford recalls. "I think we all tried to be nonemotional. We put on the strongest, bravest front. We wished them good health and happiness. We tried to be warm and friendly and cordial as good friends should be, and not to break up in a very emotional circumstance."

As the helicopter lifts President Nixon away from the White House for the last time, Vice President and Mrs. Ford wave good-bye. Holding hands, they walk back into the White House. To reassure his wife, Ford says quietly: "We can do it."

Henry Kissinger observes the departure of President Nixon from the South Portico of the White House, which overlooks the patch of green lawn where the scene takes place. Watching the Vice President, Kissinger thinks of the burden of responsibility that Ford will bear, beginning at noon. "No one had taken over the Presidency in more challenging circumstances," Kissinger wrote. "And the prayer that had eluded me two nights earlier came to me as I watched Gerald Ford enter the White House: For the sake of all of us, that fate would be kind to this good man, that his heart would be stout, and that America under his leadership would find again its faith."

At 11:35 A.M. General Alexander Haig delivers President Nixon's letter of resignation to Secretary of State Henry Kissinger in his White House office.

At 11:45 A.M., John O. Marsh, Assistant to the Vice President, enters Vice President Ford's office in the Old Executive Office Building.

"It's time to go over," Marsh says.

Ford nods and stands.

"Jerry," Marsh says, "this is the last time I can ever call you by that name. From now on, it will be 'Mr. President.'"

Ford is moved, unable to speak. They shake hands and walk together to the East Room of the White House. It is the same room where President Nixon said farewell; but two hours later the gloom has lifted. Guests are chatting quietly, cordially. At Ford's request, the band does not play "Hail to the Chief" when he enters.

As the clock reaches noon, Chief Justice Warren Burger walks to the podium. "Mr. Vice President, are you prepared to take the oath as President?"

"I am, sir," Ford says firmly.

Mrs. Ford holds the Bible, opened to Ford's favorite prayer in Proverbs 3. At 12:03 P.M. on August 9, 1974, Gerald R. Ford takes the oath of office that makes him the thirty-eighth President of the United States.

As he stands to be sworn, the main thing he is determined to do is "to appear strong, confident, assured."

The new President begins his remarks in a firm and deliberate voice and reads rapidly. He purposely does not pause to invite applause for any of his lines. He knows this speech is important, but he has decided he will get the ceremonies over with as expeditiously as possible.

"The oath that I have taken is the same oath that was taken by George Washington and by every President under the Constitution. But I assume the Presidency under extraordinary circumstances never before experienced by Americans. This is an hour of history that troubles our minds and hurts our hearts.

"Therefore, I feel it is my first duty to make an unprecedented compact with my countrymen. Not an inaugural address, not a fireside chat, not a campaign speech—just a little straight talk among friends. . . . I am acutely aware that you have not elected me as your President by your ballots, and so I ask you to confirm me as your President with your prayers . . .

"If you have not chosen me by secret ballot, neither have I gained office by any secret promises. I have not campaigned either for the Presidency or the Vice Presidency. I have not subscribed to any partisan platform. I am indebted to no man, and only to one woman—my dear wife—as I begin this difficult job." At the reference to Betty, his voice almost breaks, but he regains control.

"I have not sought this enormous responsibility, but I will not shirk it. Those who nominated me and confirmed me as Vice President were my friends and are my friends. They were of both parties, elected by all the people and acting under the Constitution in their name. It is only fitting then that I should pledge to them and to you that I will be the President of all the people."

Ford promises to work closely with Congress "on the priority business of the Nation" and pledges to cooperate with all nations in "an uninterrupted and sincere search for peace."

With a pause for emphasis, Ford says: "My fellow Americans, our long national nightmare is over.

"Our Constitution works; our great Republic is a government of laws and not of men. Here the people rule. But there is a higher Power, by whatever name we honor Him, who ordains not only righteousness but love, not only justice but mercy.

"As we bind up the internal wounds of Watergate, more painful and more poisonous than those of foreign wars, let us restore the golden rule to our political process, and let brotherly love purge our hearts of suspicion and of hate.

"In the beginning, I asked you to pray for me. Before closing, I ask again your prayers, for Richard Nixon and for his family. May our former President, who brought peace to millions, find it for himself. May God bless and comfort his wonderful wife and daughters, whose love and loyalty will forever be a shining legacy to all who bear the burdens of the White House."

For the first time Ford must stop speaking; the thought of his old friend airborne into exile causes his voice to break. Mrs. Ford looks at him in anxiety; she shares his feeling about the Nixons, and knew this would be a hard line for him to deliver. To himself Ford says: "I am not going to permit myself to become emotional. It is of maximum importance that the country see somebody who is strong and who is not breaking down in this ceremony."

Ford's voice comes back to normal as he continues: "I can only guess at those burdens, although I have witnessed at close hand the tragedies that befell three Presidents and the lesser trials of others.

"With all the strength and all the good sense I have gained from life, with all the confidence my family, my friends, and my dedicated staff impart to me, and with the good will of countless Americans I have encountered in recent visits to forty states, I now solemnly reaffirm my promise I made to you last December 6: to uphold the Constitution, to do what is right as God gives me to see the right, and to do the very best I can for America.

"God helping me, I will not let you down. Thank you."

Applause fills the East Room, and the Marine Band strikes up "America the Beautiful." On television the voiceover of ABC Commentator Howard K. Smith describes Ford's eight-minute address as "a perfect little gem of an acceptance speech." Edmund Morris, Pulitzer Prize–winning biographer of Theodore Roosevelt, remembers "the simple, unstudied eloquence of Ford's 'inaugural address'—one sentence that both healed and joined. After the self-consciously pretty prose of JFK, the gross vulgarisms of LBJ, and those floods of inarticulate monologue tape-recorded by the Nixon White House, here was a man who restored common speech to Presidential rhetoric." For the witnesses to this morning of history in the East Room, there is a change of spirit. As he stands to join in the swelling applause for the new President, Paul O'Neill, Deputy Director of OMB, observes: "People are smiling. It's been a long time since I've seen anyone smile in the White House."

And so the long nightmare of Watergate ends, twenty-five months and twenty-two days after it began. At least in that hour it seems to be over.

America awakens to find a new President, a new voice, a new face on the television set in the living room. At their first look the people around the country can see that this new President is no charismatic Roosevelt or Eisenhower or Kennedy. In fact, after Lyndon Johnson's five years of body counts in Vietnam and bloody demonstrations in the cities; and after five years of Richard Nixon's summits in Red China and in Russia, and after the national outrage over Watergate, the new man seems plain.

Gerald Ford is plain. He is a workhorse in the American democracy. Never did he think he might be President. He comes to the office with no agenda, no manifesto for a time of greatness. He is the President because it is his Constitutional responsibility—no other reason. For him the country is calling him to duty; and duty, as he sees it, is to serve out the time remaining in his predecessor's term, "to do the very best I can for America."

20

THE LEGACY
AND THE PARDON

As soon as he stepped off the inaugural dais, Ford went to work. From the East Room he walked directly down the corridor to the Red Room to meet with the ten elected Leaders of the House and Senate. To Ford, nothing had a higher priority than restoring good will between the White House and Congress.

When the new President entered the Red Room, voices were hushed, the mood solemn. Everyone seemed traumatized. Ford spoke quietly to Speaker Albert and Senate Majority Leader Mike Mansfield. "How soon," he asked, "will it be possible for me to speak to a joint session of Congress?"

"Well, Mr. President," Albert said, suddenly realizing that he would no longer call his old friend "Jerry," "how soon do you want to come?"

The earliest possibility was Monday night, three days later; and after a brief discussion among Albert, Mansfield, and Ford, it was settled. Other Congressmen joined the gathering, and within fifteen minutes the somber occasion transformed itself into a celebration. Tensions dropped. People laughed. "I guess we all realized a great burden had been lifted from all our shoulders," Speaker Albert said.

Haig did not attend. Asked why, Haig said curtly: "I don't dance on a dead man's grave."

From the comradeship of the Red Room Ford went down one floor, walked through the shaded colonnade beside the Rose Garden, and made a quick right turn into the White House Press Room. There were smiles, he was pleased to see, on the faces of most of the White House correspondents.

"We will have one of yours as my Press Secretary, Jerry terHorst," the new President said. Ford, on the previous afternoon, had offered the job to terHorst and he had accepted immediately.

In this first meeting with the press as President, Ford invited "the kind of rapport and friendship which we had in the past." To the reporters he promised: "We will have an open, we will have a candid Administration."

From the press room Ford walked briskly to the Oval Office where Betty, their children, his three half-brothers, and their families had gathered. Nixon's desk was still there, empty and cleared of all papers.

As all arranged themselves for a family portrait by the White House photographer, the Ford family felt more resolution than reunion. "Those were dark days," Michael Ford said. He was worried about his father. He felt that the problems of the economy, Vietnam, and the Watergate crisis could mean his father was walking into a no-win situation. Nevertheless, he said, "I believed my father was the man to bring our country back to a place of honor."

As Ford was visiting with his family, General Haig interrupted and took the new President across the White House corridor to the Roosevelt Room. Haig had decided who President Nixon would and would not see; assuming his authority would continue, Haig decided that a first priority for President Ford would be to meet with the holdover senior staff, nominally Nixon's, but actually reporting to Haig.

When Ford walked into the Roosevelt Room, ten senior assistants to Nixon were seated around the conference table. There was a chair for Ford, one for Haig, none for Hartmann or Marsh. Haig had not invited anyone from Ford's Vice Presidential staff, but Hartmann and Marsh came on their own and stood in the back.

To guide the new President in what he should say to the Nixon loyalists, Haig had given Ford a memo that was in part homage to Nixon and in part the first strong move by Haig to retain his authority as Acting President:

The main purposes of this meeting are to:
(1) Reassure the staff of your respect, your need for their help, and your regard for President Nixon.
(2) Inform the staff of the role the Transition Team will play for the next few weeks and their relation to it.

We suggest that this be a fairly short meeting covering the following general points:

1. The stress on the staff in these last few days and indeed the last year.
2. How important it is that they stayed in Mr. Nixon's service.
3. The special and heroic role of Al Haig.
4. Your personal need for the staff to remain intact and in place for a time to help you and the Transition Team.
5. The Team members will be in touch with them and General Haig will be actively involved in the Transition Team's efforts.

DO NOTS—At this time, do not commit yourself to dealing directly with anyone but Al Haig.

DO—Ask each staff member to be alert to problems and to make suggestions to Al Haig or to Transition Team members.

Haig looked on Ford's transition team as a temporary nuisance. It was Haig's plan to put Ford's transition team in a position subordinate to the White House Chief of Staff, and—as soon as practical—terminate its existence.

Ford, in talking to Nixon's men, did not go as far as Haig suggested in his memorandum of talking points. But Ford did say that Haig "has unselfishly agreed to stay on." And, by appealing so ardently for the help of Nixon's former aides, Ford left the impression that Haig would continue as White House Chief of Staff and that little would change from the old Nixon White House.

Marsh was surprised. Hartmann was outraged. Both observed that Ford's transition team had made a point of emphasizing that Haig should not remain as Chief of Staff.

But Ford could not bring himself to dismiss Haig or even diminish his station. Part of it was personal. Ford's respect for Haig had become even higher during Nixon's last days in office; Ford believed that he and the country owed Haig a great debt. And part of Ford's reason for keeping Haig in place was Ford's conviction that his responsibility was to continue Nixon's policies and programs—and Haig was the best person to manage that continuity.

As it happened, Ford's initial dependence on Haig matched Haig's determination to hold on to the vast power he had accumulated under Nixon. Haig doubted that Ford wanted to be President, and questioned whether Ford was up to the task. "Jerry needs me more than he realizes," Haig said, "and I can run his White House with the back of my hand."

At 1:05 P.M., twenty-five miles west of the White House, Donald Rumsfeld, U.S. Ambassador to NATO, landed at Dulles Airport. He and Joyce Rumsfeld had been driving along the French Riviera after a ten-day cruise in the Mediterranean when she picked up the *International Herald-Tribune* and read that Nixon might resign.

From a phone booth in the South of France, Rumsfeld telephoned his office in Brussels; his secretary told him she had just received a message from the Vice President: Come to Washington immediately. In Nice, Rumsfeld boarded a plane for Dulles, where he was met by his protégé and former assistant, Richard Cheney, and a White House car. The driver handed Rumsfeld a sealed envelope.

It was a letter from Ford, asking Rumsfeld to head the team to manage the transition into the new Ford Administration. Rumsfeld, as Ford's letter instructed him, headed directly for the White House.

From his meeting with Nixon's senior staff, Ford left the Roosevelt Room to stride twenty paces down the corridor to the Cabinet Room for a discussion of the worsening economic situation he had just inherited.

At Ford's direction, Haig and William Seidman brought together Nixon's economic advisers and Arthur Burns, Chairman of the Federal Reserve System and a longtime friend of Ford. In a vigorous and open discussion Ford put three basic questions: Where do we stand? What is the state of the economy? What are the prospects for the future?

Sitting for the first time in the President's chair in the Cabinet room, Ford listened to the views of each man and set forth a new economic policy. "A reduction in Federal spending is an absolute requirement. I am determined to veto any excessive spending bill, any excessive appropriation bill, sent down here to the White House from Capitol Hill."

Ford asked Seidman to have the ad hoc economic policy group put in writing an analysis of the main causes of inflation and unemployment and give him their recommendations on how to attack these problems and increase industrial production.

At 2:21 P.M. Ford went back down the corridor to the Roosevelt Room. There, waiting with Secretary of State Kissinger, were thirteen ambassadors from the NATO nations, the first of fifty-seven foreign emissaries the President saw in his first hours in office.

"My concern was to get President Ford established as a serious leader—right away," Kissinger said. "Nobody knew anything about him, and it was necessary to establish the concept of continuity in foreign policy."

Every ambassador to Washington was under pressure to cable his government an immediate evaluation of the new American leader; Ford and Kissinger knew that and decided the previous afternoon to provide every senior diplomat an opportunity to meet the new President on his first day in office.

Briefing Ford before the meetings, Kissinger suggested two priorities: "We must reassure our Allies that there will be no serious change in our foreign policy, and we must tell [USSR Ambassador] Dobrynin that under no circumstances should the Soviet Union seek to take advantage of this period of change in the American Presidency."

Even as he was meeting with the ambassadors, streams of cables were going out from Ford to the leader of every nation with whom the United States had diplomatic relations. Kissinger, Scowcroft, and the NSC staff had worked most of the night to prepare individual cables with a common theme: The United States has a new President; the transfer of power came about in a democratic way; President Ford is firmly in command; American foreign policy will continue.

In his personal message to Soviet Premier Leonid Brezhnev, Ford made a point of inviting Brezhnev to visit the United States.

While Ford was meeting with diplomats, his new press secretary, Jerald terHorst, was finding out that his journalistic friends were no longer so friendly. As terHorst held his first press conference, White House reporters seemed more interested in the former President than the new.

"Did former President Nixon sign a pardon for himself prior to leaving office?" a reporter asked.

TerHorst did not know.

Will the Nixon tapes and documents under subpoena be handed over?

"This question will have to be answered by the President's legal office," terHorst said.

"Does President Ford have any views on a grant of immunity to former President Nixon?"

In Ford's hearings before his confirmation for Vice President, terHorst said, he opposed immunity for Nixon.

"What has happened to President Nixon's tapes? Did he take them with him or are they still in the White House?"

"Those tapes are still in the White House," terHorst said, in the custody of Buzhardt and St. Clair.

As the press conference was ending some twenty minutes later, terHorst told the reporters that he had just been advised that Nixon did not sign a pardon or any form of immunity for himself or anyone else before he left office.

A reporter asked terHorst to find out if Ford's position was still that he did not favor granting Nixon immunity from prosecution.

"Yes, I can assure you of that," terHorst said.

The reporter asked again: "He is not in favor of immunity?"

"I can assure you of that," terHorst said.

At 5:40 P.M. President Ford strode into the Cabinet Room to meet with his new transition team. Buchen's group had been advisory; to get his Presidency organized, Ford picked four House veterans he liked and trusted. He put Rumsfeld in charge; "Rummy" was a hard worker, an excellent organizer, and totally loyal. To work with the Cabinet, Ford chose Interior Secretary Rogers Morton, a canny politician and close confidant. To recruit new people, Ford brought in Governor William Scranton of Pennsylvania. Ford and Scranton had been friends and political allies since Yale. For the fourth member of his transition team Ford chose Marsh, and gave him a dual responsibility: To represent Ford on Capitol Hill, and to link the Vice Presidential staff with the White House staff.

Ford went into this first meeting of his transition team with no clear idea of what he wanted the team to do. Nor did he know how to organize the White House. He had told Buchen he wanted no strong chief of staff like Haldeman or Haig; but he had no plan to move Haig out or change the way Haig operated.

Ford's idea of a White House staff system was to have six or seven senior and coequal assistants come in to see him every day to discuss issues and work out decisions. As House Minority Leader he ran his office and made decisions that way, and he saw no reason he couldn't do that in the White House.

In Ford's rambling, twenty-minute discussion of the transition, Haig took advantage of the obvious lack of any advance planning and suggested that Cabinet members continue to report to him. Ford did not contest it.

During the meeting Rumsfeld listened, said little, and made notes. He concluded that Ford's first priority should be "to move from an illegitimate government in the minds of the American people to a legitimate government." Since Ford had already decided to keep Kissinger, the Nixon Cabinet, Haig, and the Nixon White House staff, it would be difficult to convince the American public that the Nixon government had changed much. Rumsfeld, as a veteran of the White House and a master of organization, also felt that

Ford's "spokes-of-the-wheel" staff operation would not work. But that was the President's decision, and he would respect it.

After the meeting Rumsfeld went in to report to Ford. He said that he and the other three members of his team would assist Haig and his staff in adjusting White House operations to Ford's way of working, complete their work, and go out of business in a month. Ford, enormously relieved that he had summoned Rumsfeld, agreed.

General Haig was waiting for President Ford when he arrived at the Oval Office at 8:30 on Saturday morning. From the moment the new President had been sworn in, Haig's authority was in doubt. He had come to resolve it.

In a bold move to usurp power, Haig handed Ford a ten-page document on White House operations. Its premise was that Ford would not know how to be President, and that Haig should continue as Acting President to guide and direct decisions in the name of the new President. Haig, in instructing Staff Secretary Jerry Jones to draft the memo, had told Jones: "We have to rescue Ford from his own inexperience."

The memorandum described how the Nixon White House staff worked, explained why it worked well, and predicted that Ford's spokes-of-the-wheel concept would fail. To make his point, Haig told Ford that he would remain as White House Chief of Staff only on his terms. "I have certain authorities as Chief of Staff," Haig said, "and one of these authorities is hiring and firing. And the first guy to go will be Hartmann."

Ford was shocked at Haig's audacity but said nothing. Haig, he thought, still seemed to be under great stress.

"Think about it," Haig said. "And I'll see you in two days."

As Haig rose to leave, Ford said, "Al, Bob Hartmann is someone I will handle."

Ford decided that Haig must go.

An hour later, in a deliberate change from the formality of Nixon's Cabinet sessions, Ford walked into the Cabinet Room and went around the table to shake hands and greet every Member by name. After everyone was seated, Ford said: "I do not want and will not accept any resignations at this point. We need continuity and stability. I am looking forward to working with each and every one of you."

Ford did foresee changes in the Cabinet and the White House staff. But he had never fired anyone, and initially he hesitated about turning out any of Nixon's appointees. Consequently, by putting his priority not on change but on continuity, Ford confused his own staff, the Nixon holdovers, and the public.

After his informal exchange with the Cabinet, Ford walked back to the Oval Office and took Kissinger in with him. It was their first meeting alone after Ford became President.

"Henry," Ford said, "during my confirmation as Vice President I made a commitment to the Senate that I would not be a candidate for President in 1976. I believe my role as President will be enhanced if I make a public announcement to that effect. I believe I will strengthen myself in the Congress, and in the country, by making it clear that the decisions I make as President have no relation to my political future because I have no intention of being a candidate."

Kissinger was astonished but maintained his equanimity. He paused a moment to deliberate and said, very slowly, "Mr. President, in my judgment that would be a mistake. A very serious mistake, especially as it relates to foreign policy. It would mean that for more than two years foreign governments—both Allies and adversaries—would know they were dealing with a lame-duck President, and therefore our foreign policy initiatives would be in a stalemate."

The idea was pure Ford: The best of intentions, but a measure of naivete. Something—ingenuousness, an innate trust that people would take him at his word, a career in Congressional politics that left blind spots about aspects of Presidential politics—sometimes prevented him from gauging the consequences of a well-motivated act.

Kissinger's argument struck Ford forcefully. He did not decide at that moment that he would be a candidate in 1976, but he was persuaded by Kissinger that he should not volunteer to the American public that he was a lame duck.

From his discussion with Kissinger, Ford went immediately into the Cabinet Room to meet with his National Security Council. He faced his first national security decision: Should he authorize the CIA to go forward with a significant intelligence operation that could provoke a confrontation with the USSR?

Ford had known about the operation from the beginning. In 1968 a Soviet submarine sank in the Pacific Ocean in seventeen thousand feet of water. The CIA proposed to build a special vessel to recover the sub and bring it to the United States. If the mission were successful, it would be a major intelligence prize—detailed information about Soviet nuclear missiles,

Soviet naval war plans, systems of command and communication, metallur-gical and shipbuilding techniques. While he was still in the House, Ford had helped the CIA get the three-hundred-million-dollar House appropriation to build a special vessel, the *Glomar Explorer,* to recover the Soviet sub.

Only days before Ford became President, the *Glomar Explorer* was on station. The crew was ready to drop huge claws to pick up the Soviet subma-rine and lift it into the open bottom of the CIA ship. Then the hull would be closed and *Glomar Explorer* would haul its find back to the United States.

But an armed Russian trawler was circling the American ship and taking photographs with an enormous telephoto lens, and Russian sailors might attempt to board the CIA ship as soon as it recovered the Soviet submarine. *Glomar Explorer* was unarmed, as part of its cover. No U.S. Navy ship was close enough to aid.

Ford questioned CIA Director William Colby to assess the chances of success and the risk of Soviet armed intervention; and he asked General George Brown, Chairman of the Joint Chiefs of Staff, how quickly the U.S. Navy could get a warship to aid the CIA ship, if necessary. After listening to Colby, Brown, and other NSC officials, Ford gave the order to go ahead with the mission. By the CIA's account, the Soviet submarine broke into pieces as it was being lifted, but it is known that significant weapons, parts, codes and other information were brought to the United States.

At dusk on Saturday, Benton Becker was working in Ford's Vice Presidential suite in the EOB when he noticed military trucks lined up on West Executive Avenue, outside the basement entrance to the West Wing of the White House. As he watched, Becker saw men carting sealed boxes and file cabinets from the White House and loading them into Air Force trucks. When he went outside to find out what was happening, he learned that the trucks were taking Nixon's papers to Andrews Air Force Base to be airlifted to Nixon's office in San Clemente.

Becker was a self-assured Miami lawyer who from time to time con-tributed his legal services to Ford. He had assisted Hartmann and Buchen in preparing for Ford's confirmation as Vice President. There in the EOB as a volunteer to help Buchen with the transition, Becker had no authority from Ford or Buchen or anyone else to stop the Air Force. But he did. On the premise that there might be evidence in the boxes, Becker asked the officer in charge, "Who authorized this shipment?"

"I answer to General Haig," the officer said.

Becker tried to find Haig, Hartmann, Buchen, or someone in authority, but everyone was gone. So he persuaded Secret Service agents on duty that no documents should be removed without the permission of the new President. An agent went outside in the dark and told the Air Force men to unload their trucks and leave empty.

Watergate was not over. On Monday, Ford's fourth day as President, the White House press corps confronted terHorst about Haig's attempt to spirit away the Nixon tapes and documents. At the midday briefing, terHorst was hit with twenty-two questions about Nixon and the Saturday night incident. "Jerry, was Nixon blocked from taking the tapes out of the storage here?" one reporter asked. TerHorst did not know; nobody had told him about it. Where are the tapes? Does Nixon own them? Did Haig talk to Attorney General Saxbe about them? Had Nixon called Ford about his tapes and papers? TerHorst said he would have to find out the answers.

An hour after reporters asked terHorst about the tapes, Fred Buzhardt, who still held the title of White House Counsel and reported to Haig, telephoned Jerry Jones, the senior aide Haig had entrusted with the Nixon tapes.

"Jerry," Buzhardt said, "go box all the tapes."

Jones left his Staff Secretary's office in the basement, walked over to the locked room in the EOB where the tapes were kept, and let himself in the door.

"I was by myself," Jones recalls. "It was hotter than hell—an August afternoon in an office that had no air-conditioning. As I put the tapes into cardboard boxes, I made an inventory for each box. For hours I was there, and I was just finishing up when Fred came in. I looked at him. He was ashen."

"Jerry," Buzhardt said, "we just can't do this. If we let these tapes out of here, all hell is going to break loose. You and I may go to jail."

"What do you want me to do, Fred?"

"Lock them back up," Buzhardt said.

As they talked, an Air Force officer with a truck waited outside the EOB to take the boxes away for the flight to Nixon in California.

"It was close," Jones said. "In ten more minutes, had Fred not come in to reverse himself, the Nixon tapes would have been in the truck and gone."

At 8:45 on Monday evening, Ford arrived in the Presidential limousine at the carriage entrance on the House side of the U.S. Capitol. He could barely control his emotions; for the first time as President, he was coming back to the place that had been his life. From the entrance President Ford was escorted along the nineteenth-century baroque corridor and up one flight of stairs to the Speaker's Office. The corridor was packed with Capitol policemen, pages, employees, and others Ford had known for years. He was deeply touched; tears came to his eyes.

In the Speaker's Office Ford went around the room and shook hands with friends from the best years of his life—Carl Albert, Mike Mansfield, Tip O'Neill, Hugh Scott, John Rhodes. As he walked into the House Chamber, he touched off a jubilee of cheers and applause from Members and guests on the floor and in the galleries. The ovation, joyous and enthusiastic, continued long after he reached the rostrum. As he stood there he looked up to the gallery to find Mrs. Ford and their children. For a moment, in his mind's eye he could see Betty there as a bride, a quarter of a century earlier. In front of him he looked down to find Chief Justice Burger and the justices, the Cabinet—plus Haig, Marsh, and Hartmann—on his right, the diplomatic corps in its own gallery.

Finally the crowd was quiet, and Ford could begin, with a directness he felt: "My fellow Americans, we have a lot of work to do. My former colleagues, you and I have a lot of work to do. Let's get on with it. . . . My motto toward the Congress is communication, conciliation, compromise, and cooperation. . . . I do not want a honeymoon with you. I want a good marriage. . . . I want problem solving which requires my best efforts and also your best efforts. . . . Now I ask you to join with me in getting this country revved up and moving."

In this first talk President Ford wanted both to reassure and to warn. As to U.S. foreign policy, he said, "There will be no change of course, no relaxation of vigilance . . . as the watch changes." At home, he continued, "My instinctive judgment is that the state of the Union is excellent. But the state of our economy is not so good. . . . Inflation is domestic enemy number one." He cited other urgent domestic needs: ". . . To bring the Federal budget into balance . . . quality education . . . better health care financing. . . . We must not let last winter's energy crisis happen again."

In a peroration that spoke to the past and the future, Ford said, "Frequently, along the tortuous road of recent months from this chamber to the President's House, I protested that I was my own man. Now I realize that I was wrong. I am your man, for it was your carefully weighed confirmation that changed my occupation. The truth is I am the people's man, for you acted in their name, and I accepted and began my new and solemn trust with a promise to serve all the people and do the best that I can for America."

It was a good speech, and Ford delivered it well. Hedley Donovan, the editor-in-chief of *Time,* watched from the press gallery. "This was perhaps the most moving presidential speech I have ever heard," he wrote.

When President Ford stepped off the podium and found himself surrounded by the warmth of his political comrades, he knew he had done well. "I tried to project a calmness, and a steady hand," he said. "A President asserts leadership by communicating with the public and the Congress what the problems are. He has to go to the people with one hand and pull Congress with the other. He can't get Congress to move unless he has the people with him."

Most of all, Ford wanted this speech to change the national subject. For almost two years, official Washington had been in thrall to Watergate and Nixon. As the new President, Ford intended to lead Congress and the country out of its preoccupation with the tragic events that forced Nixon from office and immobilized the American government.

The message Ford intended to deliver to Congress was: Forget Dick Nixon. Let's get back to work.

Aware of the nature if not the dimension of the domestic and international problems he inherited, Ford was nevertheless optimistic. At the beginning of his Presidency he hoped that he could swiftly put an end to Watergate and persuade Congress and the public to work together to end the crises he inherited. But that was hope, not reality. No sooner had Nixon been forced out than official Washington became transfixed with the new question: Will Richard Nixon, now that he is a private citizen, be prosecuted?

Powerful voices said yes. The American Bar Association, through president Chesterfield Smith, affirmed its stand: Equal justice required that Nixon be indicted and tried. Senate Majority Leader Mansfield and House Majority Leader O'Neill opposed any move by Congress to stop an indictment. Governor Nelson Rockefeller, of New York, was one of the few willing to state publicly: "Let him go—he's suffered enough."

The only man who could decide whether to prosecute Nixon or let him go was Special Prosecutor Jaworski, and he was still weighing whether to go to the Federal grand jury with evidence of crimes by Nixon. On the night of Nixon's resignation speech Jaworski stated emphatically to the press that he had made no deal with Haig or anyone else on whether to prosecute Nixon.

In California, Nixon waited in fear. Of his first full day back in San Clemente, he wrote: "The blows began to fall again. The Special Prosecutor, Leon Jaworski, had been delighted when Al Haig informed him of my decision to resign. He thought it would be in the best interests of the country. Haig reported to me that based on his conversation, he did not believe we would continue to suffer harassment by the Special Prosecutor. He had not reckoned on Jaworski's staff. Far from being satisfied by the resignation, their appetites for finishing the injured victim were whetted."

A few days later, Jaworski received a call from Senator James Eastland, chairman of the Senate Judiciary Committee. A conservative Democrat from Mississippi, Eastland had the broad countenance of a Delta bullfrog, the outlook of an antebellum plantation owner, and the power to prevent the appointment of any Federal judge in America. He was a longtime friend of Nixon and a strong supporter of Jaworski. Eastland invited Jaworski to come to his Senate office.

When Jaworski arrived, Eastland spent little time with pleasantries, but came to the point.

Nixon had called him from San Clemente, Eastland said. "He was crying. He said, 'Jim, don't let Jaworski put me in that trial with Haldeman and Ehrlichman. I can't take any more.'"

Eastland shook his head. There was pity in his voice. "He's in bad shape, Leon."

Jaworski understood. But he insisted there was not the slightest intimation that Eastland was trying to twist his arm.

The actions and words of Nixon in his first days of exile were those of a man who feels betrayed. What Haig had actually told Nixon about his talk with Jaworski, or what Haig had conveyed to Nixon after his pardon proposal to Vice President Ford, are known only to Haig and Nixon. But Nixon's tearful attempt to get Eastland to intervene with Jaworski to stop an indictment suggests that Nixon, once he resigned, knew he could expect neither leniency nor a pardon. Events strongly suggest that Haig misled Nixon to encourage his resignation. Exaggeration in the national interest is not unknown in Washington affairs; done well, it can pass for statesmanship.

Nixon, as usual, was not wrong about who was out to get him. At the Washington offices of the Special Prosecution Force, thousands of letters and telegrams appealed to Jaworski: Indict Nixon. Jaworski asked each senior lawyer on his staff to give him an opinion on whether he should prosecute. Without exception, they recommended indictment.

To these lawyers, the evidence against Nixon was so compelling that it would be a travesty against the justice system not to try Nixon for his crimes. The

June 23 tape caught Nixon in the act of obstructing justice, and Jaworski's lawyers turned up more offenses—illegal tax deductions, using the IRS to punish political enemies. If convicted, Nixon could be sentenced to prison for thirty to sixty years.

But Jaworski, a stickler for fairness, faced a dilemma. He knew the grand jury would indict Nixon, but how could Nixon be guaranteed his Constitutional right to a fair trial? Popular opinion judged Nixon guilty and demanded his trial, but the same popular opinion would make it impossible for Nixon to get a fair trial. Where, Jaworski asked himself, could he find a community of adult Americans who had not seen on television, or read about, the criminal charges against Richard Nixon? "To the media," Jaworski said, "Nixon had, for all practical purposes, admitted guilt with his resignation."

In a compelling argument to indict Nixon, George Frampton, one of Jaworski's senior prosecutors, dismissed the idea that Nixon "has suffered enough and a concomitant feeling that the country must get on to other things." That, he said, is "a political decision" for Congress or President Ford.

With remarkable prescience, Frampton wrote that unless prosecuted, "Mr. Nixon . . . will continue to be supported in lavish style with a pension and subsidies at taxpayers' expense until his death. . . . The prospect of Mr. Nixon publishing his memoirs (and thereby adding several million dollars to his net worth) should remind us that unlike his aides who are convicted of crimes, Mr. Nixon will have the 'last say' about his own role in Watergate if he is not prosecuted. . . . Mr. Nixon in his writing and speaking will . . . argue that only the political hysteria of the times brought about his downfall."

Jaworski's deputy, Henry Ruth, concluded in a detailed summary of the charges against Nixon that "indictment of an ex-President" meant "travail and submerged disgust" for the Special Prosecutor, but "in institutional and justice terms, appears absolutely necessary." Only the political system should intervene to stop an indictment, Ruth wrote to Jaworski. "One can make a strong argument for leniency, and if President Ford is so inclined, I think he ought to do it early rather than late. For this reason, if you decide to recommend indictment, I think it fair and proper to notify . . . the White House sufficiently in advance so that pardon action could be taken before indictment."

Jaworski decided to take his time. "I knew in my own mind that if an indictment were returned and the court asked me if I believed Nixon could receive a prompt, fair trial as guaranteed by the Constitution, I would have to answer, as an officer of the court, in the negative," Jaworski said. "If the question were then asked as to how long it would be before Nixon could be afforded his Constitutional rights, I would have to say in fairness that I did not know."

As Jaworski was caught in a dilemma, so was President Ford. While he was trying to get on with the business of governing, Ford found he was spending more and more time dealing with Nixon problems—Nixon's tapes and documents, Nixon's sizable staff in California and who was going to pay for them—and contending with the Nixon loyalists still in the White House.

Haig, in easing the way for the resignation, had promised Nixon that he would send all his papers to San Clemente, some thirteen thousand cubic feet of files at the National Archives and more locked away in the EOB. To block that shipment, Democrats in both the House and Senate introduced bills to impound all of Nixon's White House files. "The tapes and documents must be produced," Representative Jonathan Bingham of New York City said on the House floor. "The full story of Watergate is not known."

The press would not let up either. Maxine Cheshire, an acerbic columnist for *The Washington Post*, telephoned the White House press office to ask: "How do we know Julie is not packing evidence in there with Pat Nixon's dresses?"

Haig was no man to be stopped by Congress or the press. He had made his promise to Nixon to deliver the papers and tapes; he intended to keep it. Exercising his power as Chief of Staff, Haig had St. Clair and Buzhardt, still on duty in Ford's White House, cite publicly the legal precedents that Nixon's papers were his own property.

"The hell with the precedents," Hartmann said to Ford. He, Marsh, and Buchen pointed out to Ford that he was responsible to protect any evidence that might be subpoenaed by the courts or the Special Prosecutor—particularly if that evidence incriminated Nixon.

At the least, Buchen suggested, the President should get an authoritative legal opinion on whether Nixon had the right to claim his papers and tapes.

Ford, angry that St. Clair's opinion on Nixon's ownership had not been cleared with him, summoned Attorney General William Saxbe. "Bill," the President said. "Who owns these documents? I need you to give me an official opinion before we do anything."

Saxbe delivered the Justice Department opinion: Nixon owned the tapes and papers. Buchen, Hartmann, and Becker stood by in the Oval Office as Ford read the opinion. When he finished, Ford asked each for his views. "If those records are put on an airplane and sent to Richard Nixon," Becker replied, "history will view that as the final act of cover-up in the Watergate affair."

"I think you're right," the President said, and told Buchen to draft an order stating that only the Nixons' personal clothing could be shipped from the White House.

Ford also realized he had waited too long to have his own lawyers. Without consulting anyone, he told terHorst to announce that Buchen would take over immediately as White House Counsel. St. Clair and Buzhardt were given no choice but to offer their resignations. An outraged Haig railed at ter-Horst for not clearing with him Ford's appointment of Buchen.

Ford went further. He removed Haig from any responsibility for dealing with Nixon. From that point on, Ford said, Buchen would have custody of Nixon's papers and tapes, and Marsh would be the liaison officer with Nixon and his staff on other matters.

In the privacy of his paneled White House office, once the place of power, Haig knew that his supremacy in the White House was over. But he was not yet ready to leave. To Jerry Jones, one of his most trusted aides, Haig said, "I have lost the battle. But I will stay long enough to get Nixon the pardon."

Ford, in his first days in the White House, deliberately set out to create a contrast with Nixon's isolation, to see people and to be seen. So much energy was displayed that it seemed as though Ford was campaigning for the job he already held. To the Oval Office he brought in George Meany, President of the AFL-CIO; he brought in mayors and governors. He signed a bill permitting Americans to buy and sell gold for the first time since 1934. He telephoned his former House colleague, Charles Rangel of New York City, and invited him to bring in the Congressional Black Caucus to discuss how they could better work together. He called in the Joint Chiefs of Staff to outline what he expected of them and what they might expect of him in defense policy. He went to Capitol Hill and was given the rare Presidential privilege of speaking on the floor of the Senate.

To show that their social occasions would be more open and less formal than Nixon's, the President and Mrs. Ford hosted a glittering dinner dance for Jordan's King Hussein and Queen Alia on a warm summer evening. As the guests danced in the sumptuous East Room, Senator Mark Hatfield and Antoinette Hatfield brushed near Eric Sevareid on the dance floor. "Happy New Year!" Hatfield called to Sevareid. The CBS commentator pondered a moment, nodded wisely, and delivered his opinion: "Happy New Year!"

Ford decided to grant "earned amnesty" to young Americans who had dodged the draft to avoid going to Vietnam. The decision was a clean break with Nixon's attitude, but it appealed to Ford's sense of forgiveness and the national need for reconciliation. "It didn't satisfy everybody," Ford said. "Some thought it was unconscionable to do anything; others thought we didn't go far enough. But I just thought it was the right thing to do."

On the morning of Saturday, August 17, 1974, Ford secluded himself in the Oval Office to choose his Vice President. He had talked with a score of advisers and studied a political chart Harlow had composed to show the merits and weaknesses of the best prospects.

Before he looked over the list, Ford decided the kind of partner he wanted: He should have the ability, experience, and stature to become President. He should be a moderate Republican to balance his own conservative philosophy and record. He must have been elected to high public office. He should be someone recognized as a strong and effective leader in the United States and, if possible, the world. Measuring each prospect against those standards, Ford kept coming back to Nelson Rockefeller.

Ford and Rockefeller had worked together, in party activities, on legislation, and on Rockefeller's Critical Choices Commission. On domestic issues they sometimes differed, but they almost always agreed on defense and foreign policy. Most important of all, Ford believed that Rockefeller would be his strongest possible partner in restoring the strength and credibility of the Presidency.

In an hour Ford made his decision, wrote out a list of nine points to discuss with Rockefeller, and telephoned him.

Rockefeller was vacationing at the picturesque house by the sea he had designed and built on a windswept point near Seal Harbor, Maine. "Nelson," Ford said, "I want you to be the Vice President, and I'll tell you why. I think the country needs you, a person of your stature, both domestically and internationally. I think it will strengthen my Administration at a traumatic time. We have worked together before and I know we can work together very well. And I will give you meaningful assignments; I do not intend that you would just preside over the Senate and go on ceremonial trips. We have tremendous problems, both at home and abroad, and I believe your input, whether in the Cabinet or in the National Security Council, will be invaluable."

Ford methodically went over his notes. He asked about Rockefeller's health and political contributions, and warned him that if he accepted, he must undergo an intense investigation by the FBI and the IRS before confirmation. Ford made it clear that he would handle foreign policy, and wanted Rockefeller to oversee domestic policy. He would assign the political traveling to Rockefeller, but he cautioned him against using the Vice Presidency as a campaign platform for himself. Even though Ford had not yet decided to run in 1976, he told Rockefeller: "I will run, Nelson, and your loyalty is important."

Rockefeller asked for a day to think it over.

In truth, Rockefeller was already thinking it over. He knew that Kissinger, among others, was urging Ford to nominate him. And the ever-present and always influential Mel Laird had called Rockefeller the day before to ask him if he would accept the Vice Presidency if offered.

To Rockefeller, it was not an easy decision. "I never wanted to be vice president of *anything*," Rockefeller was fond of saying. He had known personally every Vice President from Henry Wallace through Ted Agnew, and Rockefeller had often said, "Every one of them was unhappy in the job." But to a man as committed to public service as Rockefeller was, there was but one answer. To one New York City friend he said, "If Jerry Ford wants me to do this, I will go to Washington to help him, and through him, the country."

For twenty-four hours Rockefeller thought it over, then telephoned President Ford and said: "I would be honored to serve."

On the day after President Ford announced the Rockefeller nomination, *The Washington Post* also gave front-page attention to the latest Nixon story: "House Votes 412-3 to Accept Report on Impeachment."

By his resignation Nixon had ended the move to impeach him; but the House Judiciary Committee considered it essential that the evidence of Nixon's crimes be recorded in history. In a 528-page report the Committee detailed the full story of Watergate and Nixon's actions. In the end, the Committee pointed out, Nixon convicted himself: "The President submitted to the Committee . . . transcripts of Presidential conversations, which only confirms the clear and convincing evidence from the beginning, the President knowingly directed the cover-up of the Watergate burglary." In effect, by that vote of 412 to 3, the House of Representatives delivered its final verdict on Nixon: Guilty, on all three Articles of Impeachment.

The ten Republicans who opposed impeachment until they read the June 23 transcript not only voted against Nixon but also issued an artfully caustic statement about the President who lied to them: "Our gratitude for his having by his resignation spared the nation additional agony should not obscure for history our judgment that Richard Nixon, as President, committed certain acts for which he should have been impeached and removed from office."

During his first ten days Ford concluded he had been wrong to keep so many Nixon staff in power, and wrong to think he could manage the White House as he had managed the House Leader's office. His spokes-of-the-wheel system was not working; the open door to six or eight Presidential assistants guaranteed endless discussion and infrequent resolution.

Ford himself observed the open hostility between the Nixon staff and his team: "My own people were saying, 'Everything will be okay as soon as we get rid of these Nixon people.' And the Nixon people were saying, 'We'll have everything the way we want it again as soon as we get rid of these incompetents Ford brought in.'" Ford called Rumsfeld and told him that for the good of the country he had to leave NATO and come back to be his Chief of Staff in fact if not in name. Haig could be dispatched back to the Army with fervent thanks, but dispatched.

Two weeks into his Presidency, Ford was working hard, and sure he could resolve the worst of the problems he inherited. He was getting along well with Congress and the press, and thought he was getting the feel of the economic situation and foreign policy. According to a Gallup Poll, 71 percent of Americans approved of his performance. Sure-handed Hugh Sidey wrote in *Time* that Ford had brought a "transformation" in the White House, "not from mystique but from candor, not from majesty but from humility, not from complexity but from plainness."

Buoyed and confident, Ford decided he was ready to hold a press conference on live television to show his optimism and demonstrate his firm grip on his new job. Through this forum he could talk about the future and sketch his plans to restore national unity.

In preparation, Ford went through a full afternoon practice session the day before with Hartmann, terHorst, Marsh, Miltich, Seidman, and others posing sample questions. He assumed the reporters would zero in on the economy, on the new people he expected to bring on to the White House staff and into the Cabinet. He thought they would want to know about the legislation he planned to send to the Hill, about the Cyprus conflict, the SALT talks, the possibility of war in the Middle East, and his plans to deal with the USSR.

Hartmann, however, warned him he would have to answer questions about Nixon. "Are you going to give him his tapes and papers? Are they Nixon's property? Where are the tapes now?"

Ford was annoyed.

Hartmann continued: "Will you put a stop to all the talk about pardoning Nixon and his Watergate confederates?"

Ford tried an answer: "I have heard no such talk, nor have I authorized any. Mr. Nixon's case is up to the Special Prosecutor and the courts. It would be inappropriate for me to comment while the issues are still before the Courts."

Hartmann and terHorst tested him with other Nixon questions to make sure he knew what to expect, but Ford was vexed at their persistence. "I think you're wasting my time," Ford said.

Leonard Garment, Nixon's longtime friend and still a Special Counsel in the White House, learned of the press conference and wondered whether Ford might be considering an announcement about a Nixon pardon. To try out the idea with the press, Garment mentioned it to John Osborne and Eric Sevareid. Both encouraged Garment and suggested that Nixon should be pardoned. Garment also telephoned former Supreme Court Justice Abe Fortas for his opinion. Fortas agreed that a pardon was appropriate and said a trial of former President Nixon would be a horror.

Garment asked Haig whether he, as Special Counsel, should propose a pardon for Nixon.

"Yes," Haig said. "Time to get something in."

That night Garment drafted a memorandum summarizing the political arguments in favor of a pardon and asked Ray Price to write a Presidential statement to go with it.

By 8:00 A.M. it was ready, and Garment gave it to Buchen for the President, with a copy to Haig. "My belief is that unless the President himself takes action by announcing a pardon today, he will very likely lose control of the situation," Garment wrote. ". . . The national mood of conciliation will diminish; pressures for prosecution from different sources will accumulate; the political costs of intervention will become, or in any event seem, prohibitive; and the whole miserable tragedy will be played out to God knows what ugly and wounding conclusion. . . . For President Ford to act on his own now would be strong and admirable, and would be so perceived once the first reaction from the media passed. There would be a national sigh of relief. . . . The country trusts President Ford and will follow him on this matter at this time."

At 10:30, Garment recalls, Haig telephoned him after meeting with President Ford and the staff members briefing him for the press conference. "It's all set," Haig said. "Don't leave. Hang around."

Garment was relieved. "Clearly," Garment said, "Haig's expectation at that point was that President Ford was going to do it that day."

An hour later Haig called Garment again. "Well, the lawyers have gotta do some lawyering, and it may get gummed up," Haig said.

"Is it on track?" Garment asked.

"It's on track," Haig said.

Buchen read Garment's pardon memo and took it to Ford. "I had been working on some pardon answers for the President, as were other people, because we knew this was going to be a question," Buchen recalls. "I framed my answers to say that it was much too early."

Buchen showed Ford the Garment memo but said, "You don't want to read this memo now, but Garment thinks you ought to say, 'Yes, you're going to pardon him.' He's given some reasons, one, supporting your legal right to do it, and, secondly, the reasons you ought to do it. But I think it's premature, don't you?"

"Yes," Ford said, "I'm going to say we'll just let the matter go on for a while."

Ford never read the Garment memo. He liked and respected Garment and considered him a voice of reason in the Nixon White House. But Ford, by then, had learned not to rely on a Nixon lawyer for advice about anything concerning Nixon.

At Ford's press conference, Helen Thomas, UPI's top White House reporter, put the first question: "Mr. President, aside from the Special Prosecutor's role, do you agree with the bar association that the law applies equally to all men, or do you agree with Governor Rockefeller that former President Nixon should have immunity from prosecution? And specifically, would you use your pardon authority, if necessary?"

Ford reminded the press that he said at his inaugural that he "hoped that our former President, who brought peace to millions, would find it for himself." Rockefeller, he said, reflected the general view of Americans. "I subscribe to that point of view, but let me add, in the last ten days or two weeks, I have asked for prayers for guidance on this very important point. In this situation, I am the final authority. There have been no charges made, there has been no action by the courts, there has been no action by any jury. And until any legal process has been undertaken, I think it is unwise and untimely for me to make any commitment."

Four questions later, a reporter asked: "Are you saying, sir, that the option of a pardon for former President Nixon is still an option that you will consider, depending on what the courts will do?"

"Of course, I make the final decision," Ford said. "And until it gets to me, I make no commitment one way or another. But I do have the right as President of the United States to make that decision."

"And you are not ruling it out?"

"I am not ruling it out. It is an option and a proper option for any President."

Another reporter asked: "Do you feel the Special Prosecutor can in good conscience pursue cases against former top Nixon aides as long as there is the possibility that the former President may not also be pursued in the courts?"

"I think the Special Prosecutor, Mr. Jaworski, has an obligation to take whatever action he sees fit in conformity with his oath of office, and that should include any and all individuals," the President said.

After another question about Watergate and the Ford Administration code of ethics, the reporters gave Ford the opportunity to talk about what he thought important: inflation, "We mean business"; wage and price controls, he was against them; his new economic adviser, "Mr. Greenspan will do an excellent job"; and high oil prices, they must be brought down.

The subject immediately returned to Nixon: "Mr. President, to further pursue Helen's inquiry, have there been any communications between the Special Prosecutor's office and anyone on your staff regarding President Nixon?"

"Not to my knowledge," the President said.

"Mr. President," another reporter began, "you have emphasized here your option of granting a pardon to the former President—"

Ford interrupted: "I intend to."

"You intend to have that option," the reporter said, assuming that was what Ford meant. "If an indictment is brought, would you grant a pardon before any trial took place?"

Visibly irritated, Ford replied: "I said at the outset that until the matter reaches me, I am not going to make any comment during the process of whatever charges are made."

Of twenty-nine questions, fewer than one third related to Nixon; but Ford stepped off the podium seething with anger. Walking back to the Oval Office, Ford said to himself: "God damn it, I am not going to put up with this. Every press conference from now on, regardless of the ground rules, will degenerate into a Q&A on, 'Am I going to pardon Mr. Nixon?'"

As usual, after a Presidential press conference, the staff with access comes in to tell the President what a great job he did. Since this was Ford's first press conference, the flattery flowed. But Butchen warned him his answers on Nixon were inconsistent, and urged him to read the transcript. A few hours later, when Ford saw what he had said, he again became incensed—not only at the repeated questions about Nixon, but also at the contradictions and confusion in his own answers.

Now the press would be hounding him with questions about Nixon. "It would come after Nixon was indicted, which he was going to be," Ford said. "It would come after he was convicted, which he was going to be. It would come after his appeals, probably up to the Supreme Court. It was going to be a neverending process. I said to myself, 'There must be a way for me to get my attention focused on the major problems before us. There must be a way to get the American people's minds off of this terrible experience.'"

Jaworski, in his office a few blocks from the White House, watched Ford's press conference. "I couldn't determine exactly what the President had meant in his replies to the reporters," Jaworski wrote. "I told some of the top members of the staff, however, that I certainly would not ask the grand jury to indict Nixon if President Ford intended to pardon him." But Jaworski thought it would be inappropriate to ask anyone at the White House about Ford's intentions. He decided to wait.

On Friday, August 30, two days after the press conference, Ford brought Buchen, Hartmann, and Marsh into the Oval Office. Haig was already there. Ford swore all four men to secrecy because, he said, he had not made a final decision about the subject he planned to discuss.

Ever since the press conference, Ford said, he had been troubled by the persistence of the press in asking whether Nixon would be prosecuted or pardoned, and by his own muddled answers to their questions. He blamed himself for not having a better grasp of the law on pardons.

Ford paused as he methodically filled and lit his pipe. "I am very much inclined to grant Nixon immunity from further prosecution," Ford said.

The room was so quiet, Hartmann noticed, that the pendulum of the antique clock in the Oval Office "shattered the silence like a burst of machine-gun fire."

Turning to Buchen, Ford said: "Phil, you tell me whether I can do it and how I can do it. Research it as thoroughly and as fast as you can, but be discreet. I want no leaks."

Haig got up to leave, saying it might be inappropriate for him to be there; but Ford told him to stay.

There was dead silence as Ford began to state the reasons for granting Nixon a pardon: "the degrading spectacle of a former President . . . in the prisoner's dock"; the near impossibility of finding an open-minded jury anywhere in the country; the press stories about every step in the legal process that would revive "the whole rotten mess of Watergate." At the end, possibly years ahead, Nixon might be found innocent, Ford said; but if he were to be found guilty, public opinion might persuade the then President to pardon him.

Looking in turn at each of the four men, Ford said: "If eventually, why not now? Why not get it over with and get on with the urgent business of the nation?"

Ford went on to say that his conscience told him a pardon was right, and that he did not want to test public reaction. "My mind is ninety-nine percent made up," he said, "but if anyone in the room has another view, I will welcome it."

"I can't argue with what you feel is right," Marsh said, "but is this the right time?"

"Will there *ever* be a right time?" Ford replied.

Buchen, after thirty years' experience with Ford, could read him well. From the way Ford asked about the authority of a President to grant a pardon, Buchen said, "I could see that he had already made up his mind, and it was my job to go find out *how* he could do it, rather than *whether* he should do it. I knew the questions on the pardon annoyed him greatly, because he wanted to have a press conference about his Presidency. And unfortunately his answers were inconsistent." But he was astonished that Ford seemed ready at that point to pardon Nixon..

"Well," Buchen said, "we ought to get Mr. Nixon to settle his papers at the same time, get him to give them to the United States. As you know, we have physical custody of them, but the Attorney General's opinion is that these papers are his, by right of history. So let's get that settled at the same time. We also ought to get a real statement of contrition when he accepts the pardon."

"Phil, do what you can to get both those things," Ford said. "But for God's sake, don't let either one stand in the way of my granting the pardon. I also want you to get from Jaworski two things—one, the list of offenses for which Nixon is the target, and two, how long after indictment might it be before he could be fairly tried?"

As Ford and Buchen talked, Hartmann—thinking that the pardon would be political suicide—waited for a chance to speak. Looking directly at Ford, Hartmann said: "What everybody believes is that you may pardon Nixon some day, but not right away, and not until there have been further legal steps in the case. You are going to have a firestorm of angry protest."

"Sure, there will be criticism," Ford said. "But it will flare up and die down. If I wait six months, or a year, there will still be a firestorm from the Nixon-haters, as you call them. They wouldn't like it if I waited until he was on his deathbed. But most Americans will understand."

Hartmann suggested he wait until sympathy for Nixon builds, and added: "*Newsweek* says fifty-five percent of the people think further prosecution should be dropped."

Ford said he didn't need any public opinion poll to tell him what was the right thing to do.

Marsh said there would be a bad reaction to the pardon on Capitol Hill; Members would speak publicly against a pardon, even though privately they might be pleased that they would be spared voting on any sense-of-Congress resolution to indict Nixon.

Haig made no comment in the meeting about Ford's pardon proposal. When Ford was briefly distracted by a telephone call, Haig left the room.

Ford closed the meeting by reminding Hartmann, Marsh, and Buchen of the absolute necessity of secrecy until he made his final decision.

After the meeting, Hartmann went alone to the Oval Office to plead with the President: "Don't do it now." Ford told him he had thought about waiting, but decided that since it had to be done, it should be done as soon as possible.

Marsh also went back in to see Ford alone—to make sure that Ford had thought through the inevitable perception of a connection between Haig's August 1 proposal for a pardon for Nixon and Ford's decision, a month later, to grant a pardon. "I wanted the President to see the linkage," Marsh said. "I know that Jerry Ford has a naive streak, and it is there because he trusts people and doesn't see motives that people have. So I felt the obligation to myself to know that the pardon would raise questions of linkage to the meeting in August when Al Haig raised the option of a pardon for Nixon."

In the Oval Office with Ford, Marsh said in his quiet way: "Now, I don't want to make you mad, Mr. President, but I feel an obligation to know myself that you have thought through all aspects of this, including the events of August, and the possibility that at some time the press or someone may learn about those August events and suggest there was some kind of a deal."

The President looked Marsh in the eye, faced directly the man he called "the conscience of my Administration," and said calmly: "Jack, I know exactly what you mean, and what you are talking about. I have thought it through. I have no problem in that regard. I know what people are going to say. But this is the right thing to do."

Marsh was relieved. "I knew when Jerry Ford said that, there wasn't a deal," he said. "I knew in my own heart, in my soul, that Jerry Ford had not made a deal. I could see that Ford had decided that pardoning Nixon was in the national interest, and that he was going to do what was in the national interest whatever the cost to himself."

Ford also talked alone with Haig about the decision. "Al was a factor," Ford said. "You could discuss things back and forth with him. He would be very objective and very perceptive. But Al didn't make a big pitch to me for the pardon of Nixon. He kept saying, 'Sir, it's your decision.'"

Haig did not tell Ford that he was regularly getting word to Nixon on the progress toward a pardon. Despite Ford's demand at his August 30 meeting that all discussions about a pardon be kept secret, Haig had telephoned Ziegler to inform him of Ford's intentions. As Ford and his four advisers continued to discuss terms and timing for the pardon, Haig continued to brief Ziegler, who briefed Nixon.

To make sure that the operation would go smoothly, Buzhardt persuaded Nixon to retain Herbert J. Miller, Jr., a former Assistant Attorney General in the criminal division of the Justice Department, and he persuaded Miller to fly to San Clemente to see Nixon and discuss Ford's plan.

Before he made the final decision to pardon Nixon, Ford asked Kissinger for his reaction. "It is the right thing to do, Mr. President," Kissinger said, but he predicted there would be powerful public reaction against it.

Ford agreed, but said, "Henry, we've got to put this behind us, and get on with all the other things we have to do."

At one point Ford considered talking to two or three friends on Capitol Hill, "but I had three reservations," he said. "One, any such discussion would have almost inevitably leaked. Number two, nobody on the Hill could transpose himself and understand what I was going through in the Oval Office on the economic problem, plus the harassment over the Nixon tapes. Thirdly, I thought my judgment on this matter was as good as, if not better than, any of theirs."

Ford also thought of asking a friendly Democrat to float the idea as a trial balloon. "I decided it was a terrible idea," he said. "I knew the reaction would be bad, and if I had floated it as a possibility, a hell of a lot of people would have jumped all over me, and then it would have been much harder to do. Because people did not understand *then* the absolute necessity of doing it *then*. And the longer it was put off, the worse it would have been."

Ford was never an avid student of American history, but he remembered at the time of the pardon that he had read somewhere how Lincoln, before signing the Emancipation Proclamation, had gone around the Cabinet room, "and everyone was against it. But Lincoln had the only vote that counted. That's how I felt about the pardon. My name was the only one that went on the piece of paper." Ford also remembered the sign that he, as a freshman in the House, had seen on Truman's desk: "The buck stops here."

Ford was well aware that a pardon of Nixon would damage his public standing. "At that time I had not made up my mind to run," he said. "So the decision was made oblivious to any campaign in nineteen hundred and seventy-six." Of more immediate concern to Ford was what the pardon could cost him on Capitol Hill and in popular support—both necessary to governing. But the more Ford thought about letting the Nixon indictment and trial proceed, the more he was convinced that the higher cost would be to keep Nixon and Watergate as the national preoccupation for the balance of his term in office, or longer. For the Ford Presidency and for the country, Ford said, "That was the greatest political disaster I could imagine."

As soon as Buchen was given the assignment to research the President's pardon power and precedents, he went to work. He disciplined himself not to think about the merits of the case. "I was afraid it might prejudice my research," he said. "So I just shut up about whether it should be done or not, and decided I would have to work like hell to get the answers."

To assist him in the research, Buchen recruited Benton Becker, and they worked through the Labor Day weekend. On Tuesday, September 3, Buchen brought in his conclusions to the President. First, he said, Article II of the Constitution stated unequivocally that "The President . . . shall have Power to grant Reprieves and Pardons for Offenses against the United States, except in cases of Impeachment." That power is absolute, Buchen said, and pointed out that a President can pardon a person even before he is indicted. Citing a 1915 case, Buchen said that President Wilson pardoned George Burdick before he was indicted, and the pardon was upheld. In the Burdick case the Supreme Court ruled that "the President has power to pardon for a crime of which the individual has not been convicted and which he does not admit" but added that a pardon "carries an imputation of guilt, acceptance, a confession of it."

In the Burdick case, Buchen had found exactly the precedent that Ford wanted. The next step, Ford decided, was to authorize Buchen to tell Jack Miller, Nixon's lawyer, that a pardon was being considered—but it was not certain.

Again Buchen told Ford that he would like to get an agreement from Nixon on the tapes and documents before the pardon was granted. "If you can, fine," Ford said. "But I don't want to condition the pardon on his making an agreement on the papers and tapes, and I don't want you to insist on any particular terms."

As Ford had directed, Buchen and Becker met with Miller; and Buchen advised Miller that President Ford was considering a pardon for Nixon, but had not yet decided. If he should grant the pardon, Buchen said he felt a statement of contrition by Nixon would be appropriate. Miller said he would do his best but believed that it would be difficult to persuade Nixon to admit any guilt in Watergate. With little difficulty the three lawyers negotiated a plan for Nixon to deed the tapes and papers to the United States, to be stored in a Federal warehouse near San Clemente, in a vault with two keys—one for Nixon, the other held by the General Services Administration. They agreed to submit the plan for the approval of President Ford and former President Nixon.

Ford, upon hearing Buchen's progress report, told Buchen to proceed.

On September 4, 1974, Buchen met with Jaworski at the Jefferson Hotel in downtown Washington. Both lived there, and could meet without attracting press attention.

Jaworski said that President Ford's replies to press conference questions about Nixon left him puzzled. "It sounded like he was saying that any action I might take against Nixon would be futile," Jaworski said. Buchen did not answer Jaworski's implicit question, but said that President Ford wanted to find out from Jaworski what charges might be brought against Nixon, and how long after indictment it might take for Nixon to be assured of a fair trial.

Later that day, Jaworski wrote Buchen that it would be a long time before Nixon could be tried. The unprecedented public condemnation of Nixon in the House impeachment process, the unanimous House Judiciary Committee vote to charge Nixon with obstruction of justice, and the resignation of Nixon had generated such massive pretrial publicity that any trial would require "a delay, before selection of a jury is begun, of a period from nine months to a year, and perhaps even longer," Jaworski said in his letter. Finding an open-minded jury would take still more time, Jaworski wrote, but how much longer "I find difficult to estimate at this time."

In an indictment of Nixon, the major charge was likely to be obstruction of justice in the Watergate cover-up; but there could be others, Jaworski advised Buchen. With his letter Jaworski included a memorandum from his deputy, Henry Ruth, listing ten areas not related to Watergate that were being investigated: Tax deductions for a disallowed gift of pre-Presidential papers, obstruction of justice in the Pentagon Papers trial, concealing FBI records, wiretapping White House aides, and misuse of the IRS and other Federal agencies. However, Ruth wrote of the pending investigations, "None of these matters at the moment rises to the level of our ability to prove even a probable criminal violation by Mr. Nixon."

From the nature of Buchen's request, Jaworski assumed that Ford was considering a pardon; but Jaworski in his letter to Buchen made no recommendation for or against a pardon.

To Ford, Jaworski's letter confirmed what he had surmised, that the indictment and trial of Nixon would go on for years, at least for the balance of his term. The prospect of that long legal process—Nixon indicted, Nixon on trial, Nixon appealing—was the final and decisive element for Ford.

With his mind made up, Ford initiated the steps to grant the pardon. He and Buchen agreed that Becker, who already knew Miller, should go to San Clemente, take Miller with him, and inform Nixon what would be expected of him.

Haig ordered that an Air Force plane be made ready for the Becker-Miller trip. In the Oval Office with Haig and Buchen present, at about 4:30 P.M. Thursday, Ford gave Becker his instructions: Negotiate an agreement on the Nixon tapes and papers if you can, make certain Nixon will accept a pardon if it is offered, and get a statement of contrition if possible. Walking Becker to the door, Ford put his hand on Becker's shoulder and cautioned him: "It's not final, but in all probability, a pardon will be forthcoming. Be very firm out there and tell me what you see."

Becker left for Andrews Air Force Base, where Miller met him. On the flight to California, Becker showed Miller a draft of the pardon that Buchen and he had prepared for Ford to consider. Becker emphasized to Miller that Ford had not yet made a final decision.

As soon as the Air Force plane landed at El Toro Air Force Base, the two lawyers went straight to the Nixon compound at San Clemente. They were met by a hostile Ziegler, who said: "Let's get one thing straight immediately. President Nixon is not issuing any statement whatsoever regarding Watergate, whether Jerry Ford pardons him or not."

Becker turned to leave, and asked how to find the Air Force pilots to take him back to Washington. Miller calmed Becker down, and persuaded him and Ziegler that their mission was too important to permit a breakdown in discussions.

Becker did not realize that Haig had been regularly briefing Ziegler on Ford's highly confidential discussions of the pardon. In an unconscionable breach of faith, Haig had undercut any possibility that Ford could get Nixon to make a statement of contrition in accepting the pardon.

Haig, entrusted with the knowledge of President Ford's strong conviction that the pardon was in the national interest, used that information not to support Ford but to serve Nixon. Before Becker arrived to open negotiations on behalf of Ford, Haig had advised Ziegler that Nixon could expect the pardon on his terms. Haig assured Ziegler that Nixon would be pardoned even if he made no statement of regret for his actions, and even if Nixon refused to give up his tapes and papers.

Neither Becker nor Ford was aware that Nixon, with information from an agent in Ford's most privileged discussions, was negotiating from greater strength. As Ziegler said, "Al Haig and I had discussions relevant to the pardon as Ford moved through the decision and approached the decision."

On Friday, the day after Becker arrived, he, Miller and Ziegler reached a tentative agreement on the tapes and documents. Becker telephoned Buchen, who recommended to President Ford that they accept it. It was signed that day.

In a guarded phone call, Buchen told Becker that President Ford had tentatively scheduled the pardon announcement for Sunday. Ford wanted to do it even earlier, but Buchen said it would take through Saturday to prepare all the necessary legal documents and negotiate a statement from Nixon accepting the pardon.

Becker went back to work with Miller and Ziegler. Ziegler's first draft of a Nixon acceptance blamed Watergate on the White House staff. "No statement would be better than that," Becker told Ziegler. Miller tried a draft. Ziegler came back with a series of drafts, none of which was either a Nixon confession or statement of contrition. All through Friday they went back and forth, with Ziegler often leaving to clear a point or a phrase with Nixon. Late in the afternoon Becker concluded he had worked out the best statement he was going to get.

Remembering Ford's request to report on how Nixon looked, Becker asked to see the former President before he left. Ziegler said no, but Miller persuaded him there was no harm in it.

Becker entered a small, spartan office with a desk flanked by the U.S. and Presidential flags. "My first impression," Becker said, "was unhappily one of freakish grotesqueness. His arms and body were so thin and frail as to project an image of a head size disproportionate to a body. Had I not known otherwise, I would have estimated his age to be eighty-five. The famous Nixon jowls were exaggerated, the face highly wrinkled, the hair disheveled, and the posture and comportment all reminiscent of advanced age. . . . At times he was alert, at times he appeared to drift."

Becker and Nixon discussed briefly the terms for the disposition of the Nixon tapes and records and his access to them.

"Did you ever play football?" Nixon suddenly asked Becker. "How do you think the Redskins will do this year?" Nixon found a President Nixon tie pin and cuff links adorned with the Presidential seal to give to Becker. As they shook hands and said good-bye, Becker thought Nixon was close to tears.

Early Saturday morning, Ford sat alone in the Oval Office to weigh the pros and cons of granting the pardon. Critics, he expected, would say that he was establishing a dual system of justice, and that the lack of a trial would prevent the public from learning the full story of Watergate. Ford was also concerned that Nixon's statement accepting the pardon included no expression of contrition. "I had thought he would be very receptive to the idea of clearing the decks," Ford said, "but he had not been as forthcoming as I had hoped. He didn't admit guilt . . . I was taking one hell of a risk, and he didn't seem to be responsive at all."

The strongest argument for the pardon was that Ford simply believed it was the right thing to do. And, he said, "I was convinced that the sooner I issued the pardon, the better it would be for the country. I decided to make the announcement Sunday morning."

Ford played golf at Burning Tree with Mel Laird that Saturday morning; despite their close and confidential political relationship, Ford did not mention the pardon.

In the afternoon, Ford returned to the Oval Office, and called in the pardon team to review the arrangements for the announcement. This time

Ford included terHorst, his press secretary. Until that point he had deliberately kept terHorst out of the discussions. "We didn't tell Jerry because I knew that if a reporter asked him a question about whether I was considering a pardon, Jerry couldn't tell a lie," Ford said. "By not telling him, I thought I was protecting him and his relations with the press." Even a hint of a possible Nixon pardon, Ford believed, would have generated such public resistance that the pardon would be impossible.

After the highly secret meeting with Ford, terHorst returned to his office and closed the door. "I was stunned by the knowledge that the President was going to do this," he said. TerHorst knew the pardon of Nixon would be a public relations problem of an extraordinary dimension, totally without precedent; and he was miffed that he had not even been consulted about it. He worried that the Attorney General had not been consulted either. "The President just said this is what he was going to do," terHorst said, "and then he asked questions about how we were going to carry it out."

TerHorst spent an hour or so organizing the White House press staff to handle the story about to break, then went home, his illusions about working in the White House further diminished. A week earlier he had confided to Milton Pitts, the White House barber, that he was going to leave the White House as soon as he comfortably could—"the hours are too long, the work too hard, and the stress too much."

After talking to his wife that evening, terHorst decided that he must resign. Sometime after midnight he wrote his letter to the President: "It is with great regret, after long soul-searching, that I must inform you that I cannot in good conscience support your decision to pardon former President Nixon." TerHorst realized that the resignation of the White House press secretary over the pardon would make the situation even more difficult for President Ford, but he felt he had no choice. "I couldn't defend a double standard of justice," terHorst said, "and I didn't intend to spend the rest of my career trying to explain it."

On Sunday, September 8, 1974, Ford rose early and attended the eight o'clock communion service at St. John's Episcopal Church, across Lafayette Square from the White House. "I wanted to go to church and pray for guidance and understanding before making the announcement," he said.

Back at the White House he telephoned Rockefeller, Mansfield and Scott, Albert and Rhodes, and four other Congressional Leaders to tell them in advance what he had decided to do.

Goldwater, on vacation in Newport Beach, California, was awakened to take Ford's call. Since Nixon had not yet been charged of any crime, Goldwater said, "What are you pardoning him of? It doesn't make sense."

"The public," Ford replied, "has the right to know that, in the eyes of the President, Nixon is clear."

"I was stunned at Ford's word," Goldwater said. "This was the same man who had openly admitted that Nixon had deceived the Congress."

Shaking his head in dismay, Goldwater said to Ford: "He may be clear in your eyes, but he's not clear in mine,"

When Ford reached O'Neill, he said: "Tip, I've made up my mind to pardon Nixon. I'm doing it because I think it's right for the country, and because it feels right in my heart. The man is so depressed, and I don't want to see a former president go to jail."

"You're crazy," O'Neill said. "I'm telling you right now, this will cost you the election. I hope it's not part of any deal."

"No, there's no deal."

"Then why the hell are you doing it?"

"Tip, Nixon is a sick man." O'Neill agreed with that; he thought Nixon had been acting strangely long before he resigned. "And Julie keeps calling me because her father is so depressed," Ford added.

"Look," O'Neill said, "I know you're not calling for my advice, but I think it's too soon."

Ford agreed the political reaction would be strong, but said: "Tip, I can't run this office while this [Nixon] business drags on day after day. There are a lot more important things to be spending my time on."

Thirty minutes before he was to go before the television cameras to grant the Nixon pardon, Ford was practicing his delivery when terHorst walked in and interrupted.

"Mr. President, here's a letter of resignation," terHorst said.

Ford stood up. "Jerry," he said, "I think you've made a mistake. I respect your views, and I'm sorry if there was a misunderstanding. I hope you'll reconsider."

"My decision is firm, Mr. President. I've expressed my views in the letter." Ford walked over, shook hands with terHorst, and put his arm around his shoulder. "I am very sorry for this development, Jerry," Ford said. "I hope our friendship will continue."

Ford called Marsh in and gave him terHorst's letter. Marsh immediately talked to terHorst and pleaded with him to delay making his resignation public until at least the next day. TerHorst agreed, then changed his mind—he had already told a reporter—and decided to go ahead with his announcement.

At 11:05 A.M., Ford began speaking from the Oval Office to explain and justify the pardon. He had made the decision, he said, "as soon as I was certain in my own mind and in my own conscience that it is the right thing to do." The fall of Nixon "is an American tragedy [that] could go on and on and on, or someone must write the end to it. I have concluded that only I can do that, and if I can, I must."

Otherwise, Ford said, years may pass "as ugly passions would again be aroused. . . . And the credibility of our free institutions of government would again be challenged at home and abroad. . . . Finally, I feel that Richard Nixon and his loved ones have suffered enough and will continue to suffer, no matter what I do, no matter what we, as a great and good nation, can do together to make his goal of peace come true."

With that Ford read from and then signed Proclamation 4311 granting "a full, free, and absolute pardon unto Richard Nixon for all offenses" that he did commit or may have committed from the noon of his inaugural on January 20, 1969, to the noon of his resignation.

Across America, the reaction to the pardon was outrage. Surprise, shock, and anger—all swept like some contagious fever from the man in the street to the highest councils of public life. Ford's hopes—that people would believe that Nixon had suffered enough and that his decision was in the best interests of the country—were lost in the raging storm of criticism.

Instead of ending the Watergate tragedy, Ford's pardon of Nixon seemed to reopen the wound. Senator Sam Ervin, Chairman of the Senate Watergate Committee, said, "President Ford ought to have allowed the legal processes to take their course, and not issued any pardon to former President Nixon until he had been indicted, tried, and convicted." The American Civil Liberties Union condemned the pardon with a cruel reminder of the past: "If Ford's principle had been the rule in Nuremberg, the Nazi leaders would have been let off and only the people who carried out their schemes would have been tried." Overnight, Ford's favorable rating in the Gallup Poll dropped twenty-two points.

In a thundering editorial, *The New York Times* declared, "This blundering intervention is a body blow to the President's own credibility and to the public's reviving confidence in the integrity of its Government." Columnist Marquis Childs rebuked Ford: "It would be hard to imagine any better way to give new life to the whole Watergate horror." Republican columnist George Will wrote, "The lethal fact is that Mr. Ford has now demonstrated that . . . he doesn't mean what he says." However compassionate Ford's intentions, *The Washington Post* said, the effect of the Nixon pardon is "nothing less than the continuation of a cover-up."

The White House press corps took terHorst's side in his difference with Ford, and commended his statement: "I resigned because I just couldn't remain part of an act that I felt was ethically wrong." Clifton Daniel, Washington Bureau Chief of *The New York Times,* ranked terHorst's resignation as an act of conscience on the high level of Elliot Richardson's when he refused to dismiss Archibald Cox. Rare was the public man willing to support Ford's decision. Senator Hubert Humphrey, on a trip to China when he first heard the news of the pardon, declared: "The pardon is right. It is the only decision President Ford could make."

Out of inexperience, mostly, White House press and other assistants mishandled the follow-up stories to the pardon. Buchen, called to the press room to explain the legal foundation for the pardon, was asked why Nixon had not been required to admit his guilt as a condition of the pardon. "You do not put conditions on an act of mercy," Buchen said.

Ford was dismayed; he had intended to make the point that the pardon was not for Nixon's benefit, but the country's benefit. Yet Ford had departed from the text of his television statement and ad-libbed that the charges against Nixon were "threatening his health."

Acting Press Secretary Jack Hushen said he was authorized to say that Ford was considering pardons for all the Watergate defendants. Hushen was wrong. "I immediately shot that down," Ford said. "I was very upset when I heard that, because there was not a scintilla of truth in it. It aggravated unnecessarily an already difficult situation." But the damage was done: The Senate voted 55-24 for a resolution opposing any other Watergate pardons.

Some of Ford's best Republican friends in Congress could not believe that Jerry Ford would do this to them eight weeks before the election. Minority Leader Rhodes let Ford know that it would cost them a number of seats in the House. "I tried to explain that the national interest overrode any political considerations," Ford said. Rhodes was not mollified.

Special Prosecutor Jaworski said he would not contest the President's authority to pardon Nixon, but he objected to the agreement Becker had negotiated on Nixon's tapes and papers. A Federal judge ruled that all of Nixon's documents must remain under control of President Ford. To close off any chance that Nixon might regain custody, Congress, by an over-whelming vote, passed a law to keep all his Presidential tapes, papers, and gifts under the control of the Federal government.

The vehemence of popular reaction against the Nixon pardon came as an immense shock to Ford. "I thought the public would understand my reasons for the decision, which I tried to explain," he said. "I thought perhaps the public would consider the resignation of a President as sufficient punish-ment, shame, and disgrace. I thought there would be greater understanding, and perhaps forgiveness."

For Ford, the pardon was not only the most damaging and least under-stood decision of his Administration, but, it was also, in his words, "the most difficult of my life, by far." He took the blame himself for the failure of his message to get through to the country, and for underestimating the impact on the public mind.

"I didn't foresee the vehemence," he said. "People said I made it worse, yes; but they said that because they didn't understand the basic reason for granting the pardon. Some did not want to understand it; others may have. But for both groups, somehow I did not make them believe the reasons. We had to close the wound. We had to let the healing that is inherent in the American people take over. But I didn't explain that well enough."

During the furor, Nixon telephoned Ford—who made careful notes of the conversation on a yellow legal pad: "9/17/74—about 10/30 PM. President Nixon called me. Said at outset he would reject pardon if that would help. Sorry he caused me so much trouble. Also discussed foreign policy and the importance of Henry Kissinger. Seemed in reasonably good spirits, but not as strong as usual in his conversation."

Ford, as he listened, thought Nixon's offer to decline the pardon was no more than a gesture, and was sure that anything Nixon might say in public now would only make things worse.

No, Ford told Nixon, it's done.

Ford had decided that Haig must go, but he had not told him so.

After the pardon, Haig was ready to leave. Sixteen months of the struggle to preserve Nixon, and then to preserve the Presidency, had exhausted Haig. And with Ford in the Oval Office, Haig's tour of duty as Acting President was over.

Haig wanted most to go back to the Pentagon. The senior post in the

Army, Chief of Staff, was open after the death of General Creighton Abrams. Haig asked Ford for the job.

Ford said no. Talking with Haig in the Oval Office, Ford pointed out that sending Haig's name up to the Senate for a confirmation hearing would reopen Watergate and reopen the pardon issue. Ford had been specifically warned by Senator John Stennis, the Democratic Chairman of the Senate Armed Services Committee that would consider any Haig appointment in the Pentagon. Haig, Stennis said to a White House aide, could be destroyed if he appeared under oath before his Senate committee.

Ford suggested to Haig that he make him Supreme Allied Commander Europe, a Presidential appointment that would not require Senate confirmation. The command of all NATO military forces was a high responsibility; Ford calculated that it would appeal to Haig's ego and swiftly get him out of the country, out of easy reach of Congressional committees.

Haig accepted. Unfortunately, the news leaked from the White House before the incumbent NATO Commander, General Andrew J. Goodpaster, was informed that he had been replaced. Goodpaster had expected to keep his command for another six months.

On one of Haig's last days in the White House, Jerry Jones, there since the first year of the Nixon Administration, brought Haig a batch of documents to be taken in for the President's signature. Looking up at Jones, Haig said: "You know, Jerry, it's time for me to go. We got Nixon out of here. We got Nixon pardoned. That's a good day's work. I've done all I could do."

Four days after the pardon, Representative Bella Abzug filed a Resolution of Inquiry in the House of Representatives asking that President Ford answer specific questions about the pardon and how it came about. A Resolution of Inquiry is a little-known but powerful Congressional weapon, a right that Congress had exercised for almost two hundred years to obtain specific information about an Executive Department decision.

Abzug's resolution was referred to William Hungate, a folksy Missouri Democrat who headed the House Judiciary Subcommittee on Criminal Justice. Hungate agreed that Abzug's questions were proper, and sent them on to President Ford.

At the White House, the Resolution was routed to Buchen to draft a reply. Buchen wrote, for Ford's signature, a brief letter to Hungate stating that he had already explained the reasons for the pardon, and enclosed a copy of the Proclamation and White House press transcripts. Ford signed the letter, evidently without reading it.

To Hungate and his committee, Ford's reply was almost offensive; even Republicans could not defend Ford's failure to respond to the serious questions posed. Abzug was unrelenting: If the pardon had been granted to prevent an indictment or trial, and if the agreement on the tapes was to conceal evidence, she argued, then Ford might be guilty of abusing power or obstructing justice.

But what Abzug and other Democrats really wanted was an answer to their growing suspicion: Was there a deal between Nixon and Ford for the pardon?

Marsh heard from friends on the Hill about the mishandling of the Resolution of Inquiry and saw the possibility of a serious crisis for President Ford. Marsh talked with Hungate, who agreed to send the White House another letter.

Hungate sent Ford five specific questions about "the time, manner, and circumstances" of the pardon, one of which was: "Had Ford and Haig discussed a pardon of Nixon before he resigned?"

Again the inquiry was given to Buchen to draft a reply. To that critical question about any Haig-Ford discussion of a pardon, Buchen wrote, "No."

Marsh took Buchen's draft and went in alone to see Ford. "Look," Marsh said, "you can't send the letter up to the Hill this way because the answer is wrong."

"Go talk to Phil," Ford said.

In Buchen's office, Marsh said: "Phil, there's something I have to tell you." Then Marsh recounted the story of Haig coming to Vice President Ford with the suggestion that Nixon would resign if Ford would pardon him.

Buchen was dumbfounded: Had his old friend Jerry Ford been part of a deal? "Jack, I guess I ought to resign," Buchen said sadly. "All I have is my integrity. That's all I brought to Washington."

Marsh talked him out of it, in part by explaining how Ford had rejected the pardon deal, and by persuading Buchen of the damage his resignation would inflict on the President.

When Marsh reported back to the President, Ford thought for a moment and said: "You know, Jack, the best thing for me to do is just go up to Capitol Hill, testify, and spell it all out."

Presidents do not testify before Congress—it would be unprecedented—and when Haig, Hartmann, and Buchen learned that Ford intended to do just that, they raised powerful objections. He should just stonewall it; Congress couldn't force him to reply to their questions.

"The nagging news stories and speeches in the House are going to go on and on," Ford said. "I am convinced that the only way I can clear the air and put the issue behind me is to go up and testify."

Buchen continued to argue against Ford's decision to testify on the Hill.

"Look," Ford said, "I've got nothing to hide. I'm going up there."

Ford knew that no statement could be written that would answer all questions from House Members and the press. The only way he would have any chance to convince Congress and the public that there had been no deal with Nixon for a pardon was to go to Capitol Hill, testify, and answer any question any Member might have. Ford realized, far better than his reluctant advisers, the enormity of the risk and possible consequences: His Presidency would depend on his testimony. As a witness, he would be putting the legitimacy of his succession, his personal reputation, and his whole career on the line.

His mind made up, Ford told Marsh to clear the idea with Speaker Albert and Senate Majority Leader Mansfield. Marsh went first to the Speaker's office, taking with him a one-page summary of the points Ford planned to make in his testimony. Albert quickly agreed, telling Marsh: "There is everything to be gained by his coming, nothing to be lost." Albert was certain of the outcome. "I knew this man. I knew it was not in Jerry Ford to make a deal with Nixon."

When Marsh went to the Senate Majority Leader's office, Mansfield puffed on his pipe and listened as Marsh explained Ford's plan to respond to the House inquiry with a personal appearance before a House Committee. There was a long silence before Mansfield answered: "All right, Jack. But tell the President not to make a habit of it."

Marsh talked to Hungate, who readily agreed that Ford was right to come up in person and testify. Together they found Rodino in the House gym, and there the three worked out the ground rules. Ford would not be under oath. There would be one morning session, to adjourn by noon. Questioning would be limited to Members of Hungate's subcommittee and the Chairman and ranking Republican on the full Judiciary Committee.

Rodino, who entered Congress two years after Nixon and had watched him maneuver his way upward, had a theory about what happened. "Nixon, being the kind of manipulator he was, knew that Ford was a feeling, humane, and decent guy, and might have felt that a pardon was something he could count on from Ford," Rodino said. "But Jerry Ford is not the man who would ever make a deal like that. Jerry was like a Boy Scout—the truth is the truth. Any number of people felt there had to be a deal, but they didn't know Jerry Ford."

The Democratic Leaders of the House—Albert, O'Neill, Rodino, Hungate, and others—were all pulling for Ford; they wanted no more talk of another impeachment. Speaker Albert told Marsh: "Nothing is more important to the future of this country than the success of Gerald Ford as President."

The day for Ford's testimony arrived. At 9:30 A.M., October 17, 1974, he and Marsh climbed into a White House limousine for the ride to Capitol Hill. Few words were spoken. Both knew that this Presidential appearance would be a turning point: Ford must deliver a sure and convincing explanation of the pardon of Nixon. If he succeeded, he could meet his responsibilities as President. If he did not—his credibility would be gone, his Presidency disabled, even over.

As he took the witness chair facing the House Judiciary Subcommittee, Ford was ready. For weeks in his Vice Presidential office he had been reviewing in his mind Haig's proposal on August 1 of the pardon, thinking over what had been said and not said. For Ford's prepared statement, Buzhardt and Haig had reconstructed the six options from Buzhardt's notes. Marsh, Hartmann, and Buchen had all worked with Ford to draft his testimony. All had gone over and over the questions he might be asked.

Calm, certain that his decision to grant the pardon was in the national interest, Ford was determined to put his action and his reasoning on the record.

The purpose of the pardon, Ford testified, "was to change our national focus. I wanted to do all I could to shift our attentions from the pursuit of a fallen President to the pursuit of the urgent needs of a rising nation."

Ford said that he decided it was time to end the national division "over whether to indict, bring to trial, and punish a former President, who is already condemned long and deeply in the shame and disgrace brought upon the office that he held. Surely, we are not revengeful people."

Then Ford recounted for the public record what he had done in the critical days before Nixon's resignation:

> He learned from Haig on the afternoon of August 1 that new evidence against Nixon would force him to resign or be impeached. From that moment on, he was preoccupied by the certainty that he would become President. Haig listed the options being considered in the White House, including the sixth—that Nixon could resign and Ford could pardon him. Ford asked about a President's pardon power and Haig replied that White House lawyers advised him that a President did have the

authority to grant a pardon even before any criminal action had been taken against an individual.

At that point, Ford said, he felt it his obligation to determine "what course of action should I recommend that would be in the best interest of the country." He told Haig that he would talk with St. Clair and his wife before he gave Haig an answer on the pardon proposal.

The next day he talked with St. Clair, who confirmed that the new evidence against Nixon would almost certainly be enough to impeach and convict Nixon. St. Clair also disclaimed any role in the pardon proposal. In the afternoon Ford telephoned Haig to say that he would make no recommendation on whether Nixon should resign or not resign, and that their discussion of the pardon the previous day should not be "given any consideration in whatever decision the President might make."

For more than an hour, Ford responded to the Members' questions, none of which brought forth any facts not already on the public record. It was Representative Elizabeth Holtzman of New York who stated aloud the real reason for the hearing: "People question whether or not in fact there was a deal."

"There was no deal, period, under no circumstances," Ford said.

Ford returned to the White House, confident that he had done all that he could ever do to answer the doubts about why he pardoned Nixon. It would never be possible to end suspicion about whether there had been a deal, and Ford knew that. But in his mind there was a crucial difference between what he was *asked* to do to persuade Nixon to resign, and what he *decided* to do a month later. To Ford the distinction was that Haig's proposition of August was to benefit Nixon, and his own decision of September was to benefit the country.

Whatever anyone else might believe, Ford's conscience was clear. He was certain that it had been right to pardon Nixon, and he was equally certain that it was right to go up and show Congress that he had nothing to hide.

After his testimony Ford immediately felt "an unbelievable lifting of a burden." Now he could get on with governing.

Back in the Oval Office, Ford could pause for a moment and see that he was beginning to grow in the Presidency: He was making Executive decisions, not trying to find legislative consensus. He was searching for positive actions to boost the dismal economy, recruiting new and better Cabinet members and staff, planning a summit meeting with Brezhnev in Vladivostok, and setting new goals for himself. With the pardon, and with his public defense of the pardon, he hoped that the American people would see him as what he had long believed himself to be, a political leader with the courage to do what he thought was right, whatever the personal consequences.

With the cheerful buoyancy that was so great a part of him, Ford turned to look ahead with a sort of panglossian optimism that everything would turn out all right now that he told Congress the truth about the pardon. He was sure that things were about to turn up.

Ford was wrong. His troubles were just beginning:

Less than three weeks after Ford testified in defense of the Nixon pardon, he and his party went down to a disastrous defeat in the midterm Congressional elections. The voters handed the Democrats a two-to-one majority in the House and five more votes in the Senate. With more than forty militant new Members in the House and sixty-two Senators, the Democrats began plotting again to seize effective control of the Federal government.

In his first address to Congress, Ford had set out to mobilize Congress and the American people to support their new President; but the election showed a majority of the nation opposed to him. Ford could count on neither Congress nor the people to support his actions.

On top of all that, Ford was coming under attack from within his own party. Republican conservatives in California, Texas, New Hampshire, and other states were openly challenging his policies, his philosophy, and even his competence to serve as President. To the growing numbers of the far right in the party, the rightful heir to the Presidency was not Ford but Governor Ronald Reagan.

A less hardy or experienced politician might have been discouraged by the formidable opposition of the Democrats and some Republicans, by the prospect of being the first President in office to lose a war, by the twin crises of energy and the economy, and by the high cost to his reputation of pardoning a political villain. But Ford had beaten the odds before. He made up his mind to work harder.

21

THE RECORD

Ford was President for 895 days. At the beginning he was such a welcome relief from his predecessor that popular opinion rated him better than he was. Inevitably, as with all new Presidents, his popularity declined as he confronted and dealt with the real world—in his case, an economic recession, energy shortages, the War in Vietnam, crises in the Middle East, and a new and strongly Democratic Congress displaying militant independence. By midpoint in his Presidency, Ford's steadiness in crisis and earnestness of purpose earned him wide respect and a respectable measure of popularity; but this was not enough to bring about his election in 1976 to a full term. After his defeat, Ford slipped from view; and in the public mind he was almost forgotten. In retrospect, Ford's record as President stands like the man himself: solid.

Only a full and separate volume can do justice to the task that Ford confronted in picking up and cleaning up after Watergate and Nixon; but even a summary account can reflect the kind of President he was and the peaks and valleys of his time in the White House.

Character was his greatest asset. Ford had an abundance of character and three other qualities that every modern President needs most: an understanding of how the Federal government works, common sense, and the guts to say "Yes" or "No."

Ford lacked the sense of history that Truman had, and that every President should have. However, as Kissinger said, "He had a great sense of the heartbeat of America. And that's the next best thing. Ford was very much in tune with the country."

Ford came quickly to like the job he had never sought. Up early every morning, as usual, he couldn't wait to get to the Oval Office, hear the latest intelligence reports, get the morning briefing from the Hill, and deal with the problems of the day. Governing was what he liked; he had spent the best years of his life in training for it.

At his big mahogany desk set against the windowed semicircle of his office, Ford was personable, intelligent, and on top of the job. He worked away at his daily tasks with quiet resolution and good-humored intensity. His genial nature was matched with unshakable self-confidence. No man could have more inner security, or a better understanding of his own strengths and weaknesses.

Ford was a practical man; political theory did not interest him much. Nor did grand government schemes. Over a quarter-century he had dealt with Federal programs left over from the New Deal and World War II, and he had heard a thousand new and imaginative solutions to public problems. As President, Ford in effect said: No more new Federal programs; let's look at the ones we already have and see if we can make them work.

Ford was best at what a President spends most of his time doing— reacting to events and circumstances over which he has no control. Every unmanageable problem that humanity confronts anywhere in the world ends up on the White House doorstep. With every crisis, domestic or international, great and small, Ford's first instinct was to listen, to ask questions, to reach out for a diversity of opinion, to hear the facts from those who knew most about the situation. He enjoyed constructive debate. He welcomed a dissenting view so long as it was delivered succinctly and factually. At the end of a discussion he would pause, ask if anyone had anything further to say, and go to the Oval Office. There he would make his decision, without delay, and in writing—he wanted no misunderstanding about his intentions. Once he decided, he didn't worry, or second-guess himself; he moved on to the next task at hand.

As an executive, he was disciplined. He managed his time by planning a tight schedule and sticking to it. His powers of concentration were well developed, and had been since his youth. Whatever the subject, maintaining the triad of nuclear strategy or protecting western sheep from coyotes, he could focus on the matter at hand, and not worry about the last discussion or the next decision. He was always fair, but could be brusque with anyone droning on and wasting his time. By nature he was gregarious, but he also liked to work alone. He often reserved an hour or so to just sit back and think about things.

Presidents are remembered more often for their words than their actions, and Ford was never eloquent. His thoughts and words were plain, direct, everyday; there was no poetry in his native speech or his being. And any suggestion that he articulate soaring goals or a vision for America left him embarrassed.

But Ford knew a good idea when he saw one: In 1975 he proposed the variable-rate mortgage to ease the interest burden on home-buyers, and the press scoffed that it would never happen. He saw the possibilities in electronic data transfer and authorized the Federal regulations for automatic teller machines, even though some of his own aides said no bank would turn over a depositor's money without something in writing. Ford advanced a plan that would have created an American nuclear fuel industry that would fulfill world demand and simultaneously assure greater nuclear safety; but Congress blocked him and thereby opened the world market for nuclear material to less responsible countries. He enthusiastically endorsed a proposal to double the size of the National Park system. Somehow, Ford's ideas never caught on with the public.

Ford did not know how to make himself a popular President. He was so incapable of pretense that he was also bereft of showmanship. Since he had never run for the office he held, he had not developed the skills of public performance, communication, and symbolism that became essential to effective governing in the electronic age. His ease of command and span of knowledge were manifest to all who saw him in person, but not to the citizen outside the Beltway.

In print and on television, Ford lacked verve and élan. He had good personal rapport with reporters, most of whom he genuinely liked; but neither his statements nor his style and personality landed him very often on the front page or nightly news. Try as they did, Ford's press secretaries and public relations experts were not able to portray the quality of the man they knew. Bad luck dogged him as well. After Ford slipped and fell down the rainswept stair of *Air Force One* in Austria, the image of "stumble and bumble," as Betty Ford called it, could never be erased. After that, when he bumped his head on the helicopter door or fell on the ski slope, it revived all the old LBJ stories about Ford's clumsiness.

From his first to last day in the White House, Ford held to the conviction that the first responsibility of every President was to protect America's national security. To Ford that meant simultaneous courses of action: Strengthen alliances, maintain a strong and ready military force, and negotiate with potential adversaries. To assist him, Ford kept two Nixon foreign policy appointees who would excel in any government: Kissinger as Secretary of State, and Scowcroft as Kissinger's Deputy at the National Security Council.

With Kissinger as his coach, Ford held his first summit meeting in Vladivostok with Leonid Brezhnev, the leader of the USSR. Ford and Brezhnev got on well. They began by talking soccer and football, moved on to the serious business of ballistic missiles, and reached an agreement to take another step toward limiting nuclear weapons.

As it turned out, Ford's first summit was more successful than he thought at the time. The structure of arms control was established at Vladivostok; all arms reductions made by his successor presidents followed the outline of the agreement Ford negotiated at Vladivostok.

Long before he became President, Ford had seen that America's most contentious domestic and foreign policy problem was Vietnam. From his first trip to Vietnam twenty years earlier, Ford had been convinced that it was in the United States national interest to use enough of its own military might to prevent the Communists from taking over Southeast Asia. Once he was in the White House, it was all too clear that Vietnam had lost support in Congress and across the land. He knew he must do something about his terrible legacy—a casualty list of more than 50,000 young American men and women killed in Vietnam, and another 200,000 wounded or injured.

"There was a revulsion among the American people against the Vietnam War, the lives lost, the television pictures, the seemingly inconclusive nature of it," Ford said. "The American people are smarter than politicians give them credit for. They saw that our military policy was not going to end that war." In his first months as Commander in Chief, Ford saw the war going badly for the South Vietnamese military forces and government. But he was convinced that pulling out, after the American lives and honor invested there, would tell the world—and particularly the Communist world—that the United States would no longer pay the price to preserve the freedom of an ally.

Just as important, Ford believed that the United States should keep its word to continue economic and military aid to the South Vietnamese; it was part of the commitment Nixon and Kissinger had made to persuade South Vietnam to accept the terms of the Paris peace accords of January 1973. With the North Vietnamese Army openly violating the agreement their leaders had signed, Ford felt it all the more imperative that the United States provide the arms, food, and medicine necessary for South Vietnam to defend itself. But Congress had cut by half the money for weapons, and talked openly of cutting off all support.

Emboldened by Washington's diminishing commitment to South Vietnam, the North Vietnamese opened a new offensive, poured in 300,000 more troops, and seized fourteen provinces in South Vietnam. Quang Tri and Hue were falling; the United States was evacuating all Americans and thousands of Vietnamese from Da Nang. Late in March of 1975, Ford directed General Frederick C. Weyand, the Army Chief of Staff, to fly to Saigon, assess the military situation, and bring back a full report and recommendation.

Ten days later General Weyand returned and reported to Ford that South Vietnam would need, at the minimum, $722 million to arm and equip its troops to defend Saigon, the capital, for enough time to negotiate a political solution to end the war. Without that aid, Weyand said, Saigon and all the rest of South Vietnam would fall to the enemy.

Resolving to try one last time, Ford spoke to a joint session of Congress to ask for the $722 million Weyand proposed to support South Vietnamese military forces and another $250 million for humanitarian and economic aid to the people of South Vietnam. The lives of tens of thousands of South Vietnamese who had worked for the United States and 6,000 Americans still in the country could well depend on aid, Ford said. "We cannot . . . abandon our friends."

Four days later the Senate Foreign Relations Committee came in a body to the Cabinet Room to say no. New York Senator Jacob Javits, a friend of Ford since their days in the House, delivered his interdict to the President: "I will give you large sums for evacuation, but not one nickel for military aid." Javits's words, Ford realized, reflected the will of Congress.

With no other choice, Ford ordered the evacuation of all Americans and as many South Vietnamese as possible. The last U.S. Marine guards were brought out by helicopter, under fire, from the roof of the American Embassy. "It was the saddest hour of my time in the White House, sitting in the Oval Office and watching those last Americans being finally evacuated from Vietnam," Ford said. "To see United States troops kicked out, literally, was a hard thing for a President to swallow, and hard for most Americans to swallow."

On May 12, two weeks after the fall of Saigon, an American merchant ship, the S.S. *Mayaguez,* was seized in international waters six miles off the Cambodian island of Poulo Wai. Ford, informed by Scowcroft at 5:30 A.M., called it "an act of piracy." In no mood to suffer another humiliation of the United States, Ford ordered Defense Secretary James Schlesinger to send a reconnaissance plane to find the *Mayaguez,* to deploy the nearest U.S. carrier force at maximum speed to the area where the *Mayaguez* had been taken, and to position an amphibious force to rescue the crew of forty and retake the ship.

From the first news of the incident, Ford and Kissinger argued in the N.S.C. that the stakes were higher than the seizure of a merchant ship, and reached to the international perception of America's power and will to use that power. "We must show that the United States has not lost its capacity for action," Kissinger said. Schlesinger contended that any military action should be limited to punishment of the Cambodian forces involved.

Ford not only supported Kissinger's stronger course of action; he also decided to personally direct the U.S. response. "The American people expect their President to act—particularly during crises—to restore matters to normal and protect U.S. interests," Ford said. He believed that the humiliating and all too vivid loss of Saigon and Phnom Penh made it "essential for the President to be directly involved."

As the U.S. moved naval forces into position, Ford also told Kissinger to begin immediately through diplomatic channels to try to get the ship and crew back safely.

Since the United States had no direct communication with the government of Cambodia, Ford asked the United Nations and the People's Republic of China to deliver a message demanding that the Cambodian forces release the *Mayaguez* and crew. When Cambodia rejected the message and moved the crew ashore on Koh Tang, another island, Ford was concerned that the crew might be taken to the Cambodian mainland and hidden. "From having lived through the *Pueblo* incident when I was in Congress, I immediately connected the two," Ford said. [In 1968 a North Korean warship fired on and captured the U.S.S. *Pueblo,* an intelligence ship, in international waters. The *Pueblo* was taken into Wonsan and the crew imprisoned.] "The United States had not been able to respond fast enough to prevent the transfer," Ford said, "and as a result, *Pueblo*'s crew had languished in a North Korean prison camp for nearly a year."

Ford ordered Schlesinger to launch a series of naval strikes against airfields and other military targets on the Cambodian mainland and to undertake a Marine helicopter assault to rescue the crew before they could be moved to the mainland. Intense ground fire from 200 Cambodian troops downed two helicopters, but 131 Marines landed on Koh Tang and established a base. As the operation began, a Cambodia radio station broadcast a message that the government was prepared to release the ship, but did not mention the crew. With the airborne assault underway, Marines from the destroyer *Holt* boarded the *Mayaguez* and secured it.

Sometime during the night the Cambodians holding the crew moved them off Koh Tang and onto a small boat. The destroyer *Wilson* intercepted the boat, rescued all the crew of the *Mayaguez,* and took them aboard. With the crew and ship back in American hands, Ford ordered the operation ended and the Marines withdrawn from Koh Tang. But the Cambodian fire was so heavy that another 100 Marines had to go in to cover the withdrawal.

Although the *Mayaguez* and crew of forty were recovered, the cost was high—fifteen U.S. Marines killed, three missing in action, and fifty wounded. In addition, twenty-three Air Force security troops were killed when their helicopter crashed in Thailand in a logistical move to support the operation.

Reviewing the combat reports after the action, Ford learned that Schlesinger did not carry out orders for air strikes against the Cambodian targets. To Ford, it was an unacceptable act of insubordination, and no small element in his decision to dismiss Schlesinger as Secretary of Defense.

Within the United States, reaction to the swift military move by Ford was mixed. To *The New York Times,* Ford's decision was a "domestic and foreign triumph." But anti-military Democrats in the House condemned the action and sponsored a partisan report by the General Accounting Office that said the use of military force had been unnecessary.

Ford believed that his decision was right and the incident fortuitous. "Fate threw an opportunity to us," he said. "It restored American morale, got us back up out of the depths of the defeat in Vietnam, and renewed respect around the world for America."

As President, Ford was always ready to use military force to defend United States interests, but by upbringing and conviction he was a man of peace. The pursuit of peace led him to take part in the 35-nation Helsinki Conference on Security and Cooperation in Europe—against the advice of some of his political advisers. They argued that the USSR would use the summit to sanction its domination of Eastern Europe. But Ford, in exchange for his attendance, had persuaded Brezhnev to discuss reductions in both nuclear arms and in the numbers of Allied and USSR ground forces confronting each other along the Iron Curtain.

Even more important, Ford insisted that the USSR renounce the use of force against its East European satellite countries, and agree to international standards for human rights, self-determination, and the free movement of people and ideas across all borders in Europe. Fifteen years later, after the Berlin Wall came down and the countries of Eastern Europe regained their freedom from Moscow's control, it was clear that the Helsinki Agreements had laid the basis for those changes. "If it can be said that there was one point when the Soviet empire finally began to crack," William G. Hyland, Editor of *Foreign Affairs,* wrote in 1987, "it was at Helsinki."

In the main, Ford had better personal relations with U.S. allies than Nixon had. "Ford always spoke with straightforward sincerity, simplicity, and integrity," British Prime Minister Callaghan said. "Quickly I learnt he meant what he said and would stand by it." But the brevity of his time in the White House prevented Ford from reaching many of his foreign policy goals: He hoped to negotiate and sign a significant treaty limiting strategic arms, reach a peace agreement in the Middle East, establish an accord in Rhodesia, and initiate a series of economic agreements that would simultaneously open markets for U.S. products and provide opportunities for economic growth by allies, adversaries, and developing nations. He wanted to complete the reorganization of U.S. intelligence he initiated. By executive order Ford did establish the principle that the American government would no longer permit any agency to target a leader of a foreign government for assassination; but he also planned to carry out other actions to improve Presidential control and oversight over the C.I.A. and the other intelligence agencies.

In Ford's own view, one of his finest legacies was a nation at peace. When he left office, not a single American in uniform was engaged in battle anywhere in the world.

In conducting foreign affairs, Ford was committed to continuity; he fully supported Nixon's policies and kept Nixon's people. In domestic and economic policy, Ford knew it was time for a change; and he promptly set out to bring about change.

When Ford took office the U.S. economy was in trouble, with inflation at 12 percent annually and interest rates climbing, in part because of fear in the financial community about the instability of the Nixon government.

Upon becoming President, Ford said, "I wanted to project a calmness, and a steady hand. If I tried to be dramatic and failed, I would have made the situation worse." As it turned out, his first effort to deal with the economy made the new President seem inept.

In response to Senate Majority Leader Mansfield and others in Congress, Ford called a "summit" Conference on Inflation to bring together leaders of labor and business, economists, and Members of the House and Senate to discuss the causes of inflation and ways to deal with it. In planning the session, Ford reminded his Cabinet and staff of his strong and long-standing opposition to wage and price controls. The best way to reduce inflation, Ford said, was to cut Federal spending, work with the Federal Reserve Board on "a prudent monetary policy," and arouse public opinion to hold down wage and price increases.

At the summit the nation's leading economists—from John Kenneth Galbraith to Alan Greenspan—declared inflation to be the nation's number one economic problem. As his response, Ford called for a "voluntary citizens program" to be headed by Sylvia Porter, a respected columnist who wrote about business and economics. Every citizen, Ford told a national television audience, can help: "Right now make up a list of ten ways you can save energy and fight inflation."

Two weeks later, Ford reported to Congress on the summit and proposed a ten-point program to deal with inflation. He asked Congress to join him in new legislation to increase domestic oil and gas supplies, to increase capital to expand the economy, to extend unemployment benefits, to stimulate housing construction, to cut Federal spending, and to add a 5 percent surcharge on incomes above $15,000 a year. Finally, pointing to an oversized WIN button in his lapel, Ford called on "every American to join in this massive mobilization" to Whip Inflation Now.

Except for the 100,000 citizens who wrote the White House to enlist in the WIN program, the idea seemed hopelessly impractical, even comic. Within weeks, even Ford lost interest. WIN—buttons and volunteers—disappeared from the White House.

As it had with the pardon of Nixon, Ford's unbounded trust in the innate goodness of the American people led him to assume that they would immediately grasp and support his decision. But Ford learned from the WIN experience. The idea had been almost casually suggested to him. He liked it— the cost would be minimal, the purpose high. So he made it his idea, then saw it fall so flat that it became an embarrassment.

Ford did not again make the mistake of adopting an unexamined idea. After WIN, Ford had his advisers analyze, scrutinize, and debate every major Presidential issue or problem, then come to him with a summary of the pros and cons and individual recommendations from Cabinet and staff involved.

By November of 1974 it was clear that the economists had gotten it all wrong in September. Inflation was not the problem, they said; the problem was unemployment, and the risk of falling into the deepest recession in thirty years. Raising taxes, Greenspan advised Ford, would make things worse.

The issues were complex: Unemployment was at 5.3 percent and headed up. At the same time labor costs in American factories were rising 10 percent yearly and beginning to price U.S. products out of world markets. Corn and wheat crops were poor; consequently, the price of food was going up and U.S. exports down. Federal revenues were dropping and vast new funds were necessary to compensate the growing numbers out of work.

All this was compounded by the energy crisis created after the Arab-Israel War of 1973, with OPEC driving up oil prices that in turn drove up the price of everything else. Oil shortages and costs were damaging the prospering economies of the West and devastating poor nations. As the price of heating oil and gasoline continued to rise in the U.S., shortages and gouging provoked fist fights at the service station and dismay in Washington. With fuel-hungry regions in the Northeast pitted against fuel producing states, and with partisan and factional bickering in Congress, the forces of government were so divided that no solution to the energy crisis seemed possible.

Ford, in an early demonstration of his managerial skills, brought together an extraordinarily versatile and balanced team of advisers to deal with the recession and to plan and execute his economic decisions and policies.

To head his new Economic Policy Board, Ford appointed Treasury Secretary William Simon, a fiscal conservative and successful Wall Street financier. To manage the effort, Ford named William Seidman, an articulate entrepreneur who had political experience and the President's ear. Among the other major players on Ford's team were Arthur Burns, Chairman of the Federal Reserve Board, friend and counselor to Ford for twenty years; Alan Greenspan, Chairman of the Council of Economic Advisers and, in Seidman's view, "a man who had the finest economic bedside manner of any economist ever born"; James Lynn, a brilliant Cleveland lawyer who headed OMB, held strong views, and never hesitated to express them; Paul McEvoy, an economic intellectual and champion of deregulation; and Labor Secretary John Dunlop, a Harvard professor who knew the labor side of politics and economics as well as anyone in the nation. It was the EPB that Ford depended on to counsel him as he moved forward in the most significant initiative of his Presidency.

From the hour he first knew he would become President, Ford saw an opportunity to do something that no President had done since Eisenhower: Make a serious and persistent effort to reduce Federal spending and balance the budget.

As a Congressman, Ford had seen Federal outlays of money go up from $68 billion under Truman, to $92 billion under Eisenhower, to $178 billion under Kennedy and Johnson, to $269 billion shortly after Nixon resigned. Truman had balanced four budgets, Eisenhower three, Nixon one, Kennedy and Johnson none. From Eisenhower through Nixon the Federal debt had gone up from $291 billion to $484 billion.

A central tenet of Ford's beliefs was that a man or a family or the Federal government ought to live within its means. In the House he stood for that principle and voted that principle. As President he knew that it would take years to change the big spending habits of Congress and the Executive departments, but he was determined to start. He foresaw that a spendthrift Congress and a spendthrift Executive would take the Federal government into a monstrous deficit that would cripple U.S. actions at home and abroad—and burden the American people for generations to come.

Ford was not in office long enough to stop the nation's headlong plunge into national debt, but he did show that a President could slow it down. In his first State of the Union address Ford told Congress he would oppose any new Federal spending program. He set forth, in the budget he sent to Congress in January of 1976, a specific and realistic combination of spending reductions and tax increases that would have balanced the budget in three years. Democrats in Congress rejected Ford's proposals, but he still cut spending. Except for unemployment compensation, which went up because of the recession, total Federal outlays in the last Ford budget were lower than in the previous year.

There was no magic to it. Ford was the only President since Eisenhower who had the stomach to stop Congress from spending money, and the knowledge of how to do it. He told the leaders of Congress he would veto excessive spending bills sent to him and he did it—two in his first week in office. "I felt it was the Constitutional mandate for the President of the United States, as *the* person who represented everybody, that this Executive tool had to be used to prevent the Congress from making unwise judgments," Ford said. "The press argued that ours was a negative approach, that I was not reflecting public opinion and that I was destroying my relations with Congress. But I had a deep conviction that the President has to stand up and fight for what he believes is right. And I know of no friend I lost in Congress because I told them they were wrong. The truth is that usually after a veto, Congress came back with more realistic legislation that I could sign."

In all Ford vetoed sixty-six bills. With his ability to forge alliances between Republicans and conservative Democrats in Congress, and the skills of his emissaries to the Hill—Marsh, Max Friedersdorf, and others—Ford sustained fifty-four of his vetoes.

Ford's determination to hold the line on spending brought him into an open confrontation with New York City and provoked the kind of public dispute that Ford usually managed to avoid. In the spring of 1975 Mayor Abraham Beame and New York State Governor Hugh Carey appealed to Ford for a ninety-day credit of $1billion to keep the nation's biggest city from going into bankruptcy. Ford, who had long been familiar with New York's deficit spending habits—expenses were then rising 12 percent yearly, against revenues up only 5 percent yearly—considered the request and turned it down. The city would have to trim its budget, stop granting municipal workers inordinately high wage increases and benefits, and otherwise put its fiscal house in order before he would consider more Federal aid, Ford wrote Mayor Beame. Bluntly, Ford said: "We must stop promising more and more services without knowing how we will cover their costs."

Ford recognized that Governor Carey and Mayor Beame faced enormous political problems in trying to cut spending, but he was adamantly opposed to any Washington help for New York City until the city and state did something to fix their own problem. As New York City tottered on the brink of bankruptcy, Ford decided in October to put on more public pressure. In a speech to the National Press Club in Washington Ford said: "I am prepared to veto any bill that has as its purpose a federal bail-out of New York City." New Yorkers read his message as the New York *Daily News* put it in street vernacular: "Ford to City: Drop Dead."

Soon after, Ford's tough stand worked. Governor Carey and Mayor Beame negotiated with financial experts to impose better controls over the city budget, and came to Washington in November to present a new plan. With that in hand, Ford asked Congress to help the city with short-term loans. In the end, after Ford's conditions were met, he did bail out New York City; and both Governor Carey and Mayor Beame gave Ford credit for rescuing the city from its own profligacy.

Nine months or so after he took over from Nixon, Ford made up his mind to run for a full term as President. Kissinger had stopped Ford from gratuitously putting a term limit on his Presidency; but it was Ford himself who soon after began encouraging press speculation that he would be a candidate.

He liked the job, and thought he was getting better at it. By the end of May, 1975, Vietnam and the *Mayaguez* incident were behind him, and he was making progress toward easing tensions with the USSR. Employment was headed up; inflation and interest rates were going down. He had been looking over the field of likely Republican and Democratic candidates for President, and concluded that not one of them was more qualified than he to be President for the next four years. So he decided to reconsider his pre-confirmation statement that he would not run in 1976. But he had not forgotten his commitment to Betty to retire from politics in January, 1977, so he talked to her about their future. "Whatever you decide," she said, "I am for you."

Betty Ford liked being First Lady and living in the White House. Her sparkle and candor, and her willingness to talk openly of the problems of young people growing up, and about her mastectomy, had lifted her popularity above the President's. The children had adjusted to their new lives, and she was seeing more of her husband than she had when he was a Congressman or Vice President. The whole Ford family agreed that he should run.

At the time, Ford expected no serious opposition to his party nomination. In May a political supporter pleaded with Ford to appoint a campaign manager and get started on organization and planning. "Well," Ford replied, "I believe that if the Republican Party thinks I have done a good job, they will nominate me. And if the people across the country think I have done a good job, they will elect me. So I plan to leave it up to them."

Once again, Ford's overarching optimism and trust in people was about to put his Presidency in jeopardy. "I just never thought Reagan would run against me," Ford said. He could not believe that the author of the Republican "Eleventh Commandment"—"Thou shalt not speak ill of another Republican"—would come after his job in an open attack.

Ford did not know that Nancy Reagan and a band of conservative zealots had convinced Reagan that he, and not an unelected President, was the rightful heir to supremacy in the Republican Party. Nor did Ford realize that Reagan himself had been thinking for years about running for President and had been traveling the country with that thought in mind.

Even after New York's Conservative Senator James Buckley and a score of other prominent Republican conservatives called for an "open Republican Convention," Ford was not concerned.

"The conservatives in the Republican Party were not so much down on Ford as they were up on Reagan," said Stuart Spencer, the master strategist of

Republican Presidential campaigns. According to Spencer, who had managed both of Reagan's campaigns for governor, "Ron was the fair-haired boy, the most articulate communicator I have ever seen in politics, and he captured the imagination of the conservatives and a lot of others."

Spencer was asked to come to the White House to talk to Ford about the threat from Reagan. "Look, this guy's running!" Spencer said to Ford. "Ron has wanted to be President of the United States for any number of years. He feels he was cheated out of his inheritance when Nixon left." At Ford's request, Spencer agreed to come in and help plan and organize his campaign. His first task was to educate Ford and his campaign leaders.

Ford was certainly not naive about Washington politics, but he simply had no grasp of the deadly political combat that every American Presidential campaign had become. Like many politicians who run for President the first time, Ford had no inkling of the time, money, and energy it would take to win the nomination. Nor did he imagine how demeaning it would be. "I had always run pretty much a one-man campaign for Congress where I just worked hard, saw everybody one-on-one, and talked about my record," Ford said. "All of a sudden I found myself in a different ballpark. I just didn't comprehend the vast difference between running in my district and running for President.

"And it burned the hell out of me that the diversion from Reagan caused me to spend an abnormal part of my time trying to round up individual delegates and to raise money. That took me away from what I thought was the way to win the election—being a good President."

Ford did not have a high opinion of Reagan or his governing abilities; from what he knew of Reagan's record in California, Ford did not think he would be a good President. When Reagan telephoned in mid-November of 1975 to say, "I am going to run for President," Ford was disappointed. He knew their fight would leave deep, even permanent, scars in the Republican party; but he made up his mind to win.

At the beginning, the Ford campaign struggled through a series of mistakes. On the premise that he could win the Southern delegates, Ford appointed former Georgia Congressman Howard Callaway to be campaign manager. To appease conservatives, Callaway suggested that Rockefeller would not be on the ticket. Rockefeller protested vigorously to Ford. At first Ford assured Rockefeller that he wanted to keep him. Later, he changed his mind. Rockefeller, as asked, took himself out of the running for Vice President. It was humiliating for a man of such ability and pride as Rockefeller: He was being dumped from a job he had accepted the year before to help the new President. It was humiliating for Ford as well. "It was the biggest political mistake of my life," Ford said. "And it was one of the few cowardly things I did in my life."

Moreover, Callaway's Southern strategy never worked. Southern Republicans were Reagan's most ardent supporters, so Ford had to search elsewhere for delegates. In the first primaries Ford did well; he won New Hampshire, Florida, and Illinois in quick order. He seemed to be going strong until he was upset by Reagan conservatives in North Carolina. Then Reagan won Texas, Alabama, Georgia, and Indiana, and was ahead in delegates for the first time. At that critical point Rockefeller, in a display of loyalty that is not common in American politics, delivered the delegates from New York State. Rockefeller also led other moderate Republican delegates from Eastern states to commit to Ford. Altogether, it was enough to put Ford back in the delegate lead and keep him there until the Convention.

When the Republicans gathered in Kansas City, Ford held his support and on the first ballot won the nomination 1187 to 1070. When Reagan sent word that he did not want to be considered for Vice President, Ford was relieved. After their raw disagreements during the primaries, Ford did not want Reagan on his ticket.

Ford chose Dole for three reasons. He liked and trusted him. Dole was on the short list Reagan recommended. Most important of all, Ford believed that Dole could help in the Midwest and farm states that were essential to any Ford electoral victory.

As he began the general election campaign, Ford was confident but realistic about his chances. His polls, taken just before the Republican convention, showed that he was 34 points behind Jimmy Carter, the Democratic candidate who had swept his party's Convention in New York City.

Spencer and Richard Cheney, who became Ford's Chief of Staff after Rumsfeld was appointed Secretary of Defense, put it plainly to Ford in a personal meeting: "Not enough voters have a strong, positive feeling about the Ford personality and character . . . Because you must come from behind, . . . no strategy can be developed which allows for any substantial error." They reminded Ford that all through the contest for the nomination, the primary results and the polls showed that he had done better by being President and staying in Washington than by traveling around the country to campaign.

The strategy was simple: Show Ford as a responsible and effective President, and raise public doubts about Carter.

Ford took their advice, appeared often in the White House Rose Garden to make a statement for television, and stuck to his job as President. Ford won the first debate; the Gallup Poll showed he had picked up six points and was up to 42 percent, with Carter at 50 percent. But in the second debate, in reply to a foreign policy question, Ford said: "There is no Soviet domination of Eastern Europe." It was a major error; and Ford compounded it when, in response to the follow-up question, he replied specifically that neither Poland, Yugoslavia, nor Rumania was "dominated by the Soviet Union."

Ford meant to say that the United States did not *accept* Soviet control of Eastern Europe, and thought he had said that. When Scowcroft, Cheney, and Spencer tried to get him to clarify his statement, Ford—in a display of the stubbornness he sometimes inflicted on himself—flatly refused to listen. Some three days later, when Ford finally did admit publicly that he had made a mistake, the damage was done. Ford had planned that this debate would show up Carter's inexperience in foreign policy; instead, the news stories were about his own inexplicable blunder.

Ford picked himself up, got back in the game, and moved to within 6 percent of Carter, who was also making mistakes and widening doubts about his capability for the Presidency. Ford was drawing crowds and support, but little enthusiasm. Goldwater, trying his best to stimulate Republican conservatives to work for Ford, found his longtime followers reluctant. Reagan himself did little campaigning for Ford.

In October, with only days to go before the election, bad economic developments struck the Ford campaign. For the second straight month, the Commerce Department reported, the index of leading economic indicators was down. Farm prices had dropped 5 percent in a month, and unemployment was up again.

Ford's momentum was slowed, but the final Gallup Poll showed Ford ahead, 47 percent to 46 percent, and 4 percent undecided. Exhilarated that he had come from so far behind, Ford drove himself forward to the finish, in Pennsylvania, Texas, New York, Ohio, and Michigan, ending his campaign in Grand Rapids so hoarse that he could barely speak.

Through the best and the worst of his 1976 Presidential campaign, Ford never wavered in his belief that somehow he would win the Republican nomination and the election. In the White House family quarters on election night, he sat with close friends grimly watching as Carter took and held a narrow lead. At 3:15 A.M., exhausted, Ford went to bed knowing the odds were against him, but still hoping. Six hours later Ford arrived in the Oval office and Cheney went in alone to say: "Mr. President, we lost."

Ford read through the draft concession statement and then, without hesitation, put in a call to Carter. He asked Cheney to pick up the extension by the couch.

When Carter came on the phone, Ford said, "Governor, my voice is gone, but I want to give you my congratulations. Here's Dick Cheney, he will read you my concession statement."

That done, Ford went out with his family and had Betty read the concession statement for television cameras.

Ford had done his best, but it was not enough. Out of almost 80 million votes cast on Tuesday, November 2, 1976, Carter won 49.9 percent and 297 electoral votes. Ford, with 47.9 percent and 241 electoral votes, lost. It was the closest electoral vote in 60 years.

"I was crestfallen," Ford said. "Betty and I worked very hard to win, and I thought we deserved to win. Considering the mess I inherited, I was convinced that I had done a good job and should have won on the merits. In my judgment the way to win the election was to point out, straightforwardly, factually, the job we had done. That's what I tried to do.

"And it was so close," Ford said. "But, I just accepted it, and decided to go about the business of winding up my Administration and making the transition work."

With his indefatigable optimism, Ford could still find some good in his defeat. He was particularly proud of his family. "I thought Betty did a wonderful job. So did the children. Mike, Jack, Steve, Susan—they all pitched in and gave their maximum efforts. And I was proud of the fact that I came within two points of winning after being thirty-four points behind at the convention. To me, that showed a good campaign."

Even greater than his personal disappointment was Ford's regret that he could not finish the formidable job that history had assigned him. Believing he would win reelection, he had already begun to draft his plans for his full term. He wanted to continue improving relations with the Allies and negotiating with the Soviets to reduce nuclear arms and the risks of a land war in Europe. At Helsinki he had opened a path to freedom and independence for Eastern Europe; he wanted to take that forward. He was sure the American economy would improve under his leadership.

"We had overcome the recession of '74–'75," he said. "Interest rates were down. Inflation was down. The economy was back on the right track. We would have submitted a responsible Federal budget with the goal of gradually reducing the Federal deficit and working down our national debt. I could not promise to balance the budget in four years, but we were headed in the right direction. Had we won, I would have had the reduction of spending and the veto strategy as part of my mandate; and that would make a significant impact on my relations with Congress. No longer could they say I was not an elected President. I would have had greater support for the same restrained fiscal policy that I could carry out in cooperation with Arthur Burns who had the same philosophical view on monetary policy. I was really looking forward to the opportunity."

EPILOGUE

Gerald R. Ford was an ordinary man called to serve America in extraordinary circumstances. In his plain ways and plain speaking, in his forthrightness and genial nature, in his trust in others and their trust in him, Ford was Everyman become President.

Ford's moment in history arrived when the highest powers in Congress were looking for an honest man. They knew exactly where he was; he was one of them. His choice was the act of a Congress that no longer exists, performed by old-time leaders who could swiftly put aside partisan differences to make a momentous decision in the highest traditions of representative government. Congress nominated Ford, confirmed him, forced Nixon out of office, and put Ford in the White House. In retrospect, it all seems part of a grand design.

Ford became President because he was qualified by experience and trusted as a man. He was steady, not brilliant. He was honest. He was reliable. His peers saw in him the qualities of truth and integrity necessary to bring back the legitimacy of the Presidency.

Ford came to the Presidency with the values of his boyhood. "Tell the truth, work hard, and come to dinner on time." So Mother and Dad had taught and lived.

Growing up in a family and community of such virtue had instilled in Ford the qualities of diligence, integrity, and can-do optimism that made college and law school possible. World War II, coupled with young Ford's ingrained sense of duty, had taken him into politics to serve the people of Grand Rapids, who stirred his dreams and gave him his first opportunities to move up in life. In the heady world of Washington, Ford's commitment to duty joined ambition to bear him upward in the House of Representatives. And there the quality of person he showed himself to be led to his appointment with history.

Into the White House Ford brought the habits and maxims that he had always followed: Play the game, play it with all you've got. Play hard, but play by the rules. Teamwork gains the victory. Win if you can; and if you lose, try again. Hard work brings good luck. "On my honor I will do my best . . ."

Unlike his predecessor, Ford was not hated; nor was he as loved as other Presidents have been. He was an earnest workman who did his job, a likable man of the House who brought back comity between Capitol Hill and the White House. "Jerry Ford had the great quality of understanding the difference between an enemy and an adversary," Columnist Jack Germond often said of him. Ford could battle a friend and not lose the friendship; he never bore a grudge. With the wealth of his good nature and a steady hand, Ford restored confidence and moral balance in Washington.

Ford was a better President than candidate for President. He understood how to manage the Federal government, but he never really mastered the media game that Presidential campaigns have become. Nor would he try to fool the voters. He followed a political rule of his own devising: Deliver on your promise, and never promise something you can't deliver.

Ford's greatest single problem in the White House and in the 1976 Presidential campaign was Richard Nixon. For all of Ford's honesty, openness, and integrity, he could never rid himself of the taint of his predecessor who had disgraced himself and the office. Part of it was Ford's own doing: He chose to emphasize continuity rather than change.

After Ford became President, his long friendship with Nixon ended; but it may have broken at the moment when Haig told Ford that Nixon had lied to him and to the country. As President, and after, Ford rarely met or even talked to his predecessor. Forgiving Ford was, but he could never forgive Nixon for lying to him and to the American people. Ford, better than anyone else, could see the scars that Nixon's dishonesty had inflicted on the Presidency and on the body of representative government.

Watergate remains a mystery in many ways. There is no folly in American politics that compares with it. Why Nixon, with his fine-tuned political mind and capacity for manipulation, got involved in the cover-up is a mystery that remains in the depths of Nixon's mind. Most likely the answer lies within the nature of Richard Nixon. As the sage Murray Kempton once wrote of Nixon: "He was . . . so smart about everyone's affairs but his own."

Ford, in his time and in generations to come, may be most often remembered for the pardon of Nixon. It took courage to make that decision, but the far greater test of Ford's character had come a month earlier. When General

Haig proposed, as Nixon's agent, that Ford agree to pardon the President if he resigned, Ford faced a decision that no Vice President and no other man in American history had ever confronted. The plot was unique; but the theme was as old as mankind: Temptation.

There, like a golden apple on a silver platter, was power, position, authority, success, eminence—the primal forces that lure and sustain all those in public life. There, in Ford's grasp if he would accept the terms, was the Presidency.

Certainly, earlier, it had not been the prime ambition of his life. But Speaker he was not to be; instead events made him Vice President. And then, on the afternoon of August 1, 1974, suddenly before this Vice President was the opportunity to say the words that would make him the President of the United States.

Few men in history have ever confronted such a moral and personal dilemma. To make the offer even more tempting, Ford had already concluded in the privacy of his thoughts that the sooner Nixon left office, the better off the country would be. Haig, a man he trusted and respected, confirmed his judgment. For both, the immediate objective was to get Nixon out of office and put the government back on course—and spare the country the ordeal of two public trials of Nixon, first in the House, then in the Senate.

Initially, that immediacy of purpose obscured the danger in the plan. Ford's response was neither swift nor decisive, not yes, not no. Instinct and experience made him pause. Then, with the passage of hours, Ford grasped the enormity of the consequences of the proposal.

In the end Ford walked away from temptation. Ford said no to the deal that would make him President. That decision, as much as anything he did as President, revealed Ford's strength of character, that rock on which he had built his life.

And as it happened, that experience, that momentous occasion when Nixon put the Presidency up for bargain, made Ford's decision to pardon Nixon even more difficult when the time came that it had to be done. Ford knew that Washington holds no secrets for long; the story of Haig's proposal of resignation for a pardon was certain to become known if Ford did grant Nixon the pardon. A pardon in September was certain to raise questions about what had happened behind the closed doors of the White House in August.

Nevertheless, Ford made the decision. He intended, with one sweep of his big arm, to take the Nixon problem off his desk and out of the headlines. His political judgment told him that the pardon of Nixon was right for the country. He was convinced in heart and conscience. Warned by those closest of the personal consequences, Ford still made the decision. He pardoned Richard Nixon.

Throughout his Presidency and thereafter, Ford never wavered in his conviction that he had been right to pardon Nixon when he did, and as he did. "If I made a mistake, and I probably did, it was not having Hartmann or Marsh sit in and listen when Haig came over," Ford said. "But if I, or they, had thrown Haig out of the office, then Nixon might not have resigned. From the country's point of view, that would have been worse."

When Ford decided to grant the pardon, he assumed there would be opposition. But it was his judgment, a month after taking office, that a two-year public trial of former President Nixon in the courts and in the press would have been far more costly to the U.S. economy, to United States leadership in the world, to the confidence Americans had in their political leaders, and to Ford's own chances to be elected to a full term as President. Ford never blamed his failure to win the 1976 election on the pardon. In an election so close, it was obviously a factor. His campaign polls consistently showed that 6 percent of the electorate had not forgiven him for the pardon, and would vote against him for that reason. But he was totally convinced then and afterward that the pardon was necessary to begin healing the nation, even if it had cost him the election. Almost two decades later Ford could say: "My feelings are even stronger today than they were at the time. It was the right thing to do."

Finally, Ford was always philosophical about the suspicion that he became President by bargaining a pardon for a resignation. "I know there are people who want to believe that a deal was made," he said. "I have a clear conscience. I am absolutely certain there was never a deal arranged between Haig and me, or between Nixon and me, or by anybody else."

Watergate and its aftermath not only changed the lives of Nixon and Ford; it changed American politics and government.

The ruin of Richard Nixon came all too close to destroying public trust in the Presidency. For the first time since Harding, Americans were ashamed of their President. A healthy skepticism about politicians has always been a part of Americans' feeling about their leaders; but until 1974, no President was known to be a criminal. Since Nixon, no President has been free from accusations by press and prosecutors that he or his close advisers broke the law for a political end. And none is likely to be.

During the long siege of Nixon during Watergate the power of the President was weakened, and this change in the balance of power in Washington is likely to remain for as long as Watergate is remembered. Congress used the weakness of Nixon to invade Executive power and capture important parts of Presidential authority.

Congress reduced Executive control over Federal spending with the 1974 Budget Act that empowered the House and Senate to increase their control over the national agenda and priorities. Nixon had misgivings about the legislation, but lacked the support to stop it.

Congress invaded the President's Constitutional authority to conduct foreign policy with the War Powers Act. Nixon vetoed the bill, but was overridden. Since that time, every President has found his freedom to act in an emergency hindered. Before the War Powers Act a President would inform the Speaker and the Majority and Minority Leaders of the House and Senate, all of whom could keep a secret. In every foreign policy crisis now, the President must find a score of scattered Senators and Congressmen to explain the emergency, justify his decisions, and hope he can accomplish that in time to respond to the emergency.

Ford was the first President to have to deal with a fractious Congress ingrained with suspicion of the White House. Things had changed radically from the House that he left. The election of 1974 swept aside the House and Senate traditions that respected experience and ensured accountability. Instead, Congress became a loose congregation of independent operators serving parochial interests, local constituencies, and the highest goal—the next election. Congress, always avid for more power, has ended up with more authority than it can handle.

To Ford it was given to be a transitional President, a Constitutional bridge that carried an angry and frightened America back to a measure of accord and confidence in Constitutional government. Looking back on those times, Senator Barry Goldwater observed: "Ford was a good President, not a great President but a good President. He restored honor to the White House, and the country could not ask him to do more, or expect more. History should treat him kindly for that." Edmund Morris, historian and biographer of presidents, said, "Gerald Ford was our most underrated modern President."

As time passes, history may also consider the full measure of the Ford record. He took the country through and out of the worst recession since the Great Depression; he moved the U.S. economy back to growth and prosperity. He put an end to the Vietnam War—albeit a ragged end. With consid-

erable foresight and against heavy opposition from right and left, Ford negotiated and signed the Helsinki Treaty that opened a way for the growth of
democracy in Communist Europe. Ford was the last President to understand
the interdependence of Washington politics and the American economy, and
the last to make a serious effort to break the Congressional habit of governing
on credit. What would happen if the Federal government continued to spend
far beyond its income—Ford's grim fear—turned out to be even worse than
he expected. When President Ford left office, the Federal debt was $644 bil-
lion. Under President Carter, it rose to $909 billion. During President
Reagan's eight years the Federal debt tripled, to become $2,601 billion. When
President Bush left office, he handed President Clinton a Federal debt of
$4,003 billion.

The most significant single accomplishment of Ford was that he restored the
integrity of the Presidency by the example of his own honesty and trustwor-
thiness. Americans could again believe that their President was telling them
the truth. When Ford took office he made one promise: To do his best for
America. He kept that promise.

The abiding truth of the Presidency of Gerald R. Ford is that, in this
splendid American democracy, this one good man could make such a difference.

A P P E N D I X   A

RICHARD NIXON

May 24, 1991

Dear Jim,

As you have no doubt noted I covered the substance of most of your questions in my memoirs, but I welcome the opportunity to elaborate on the reasons for my final decisions.

I believed that there were four major criteria which should be taken into account when a Presidential nominee or a President selects the individual who may be his successor. First and far most important, the Vice Presidential nominee must be one who is fully qualified to serve as President. The second criterion is that the Vice Presidential nominee should be one whose philosophical views while not necessarily identical will be similar to those of the President. This is vitally important because only in this way can a President be sure that his successor will continue his domestic and foreign policies. I am totally opposed to the concept of philosophical ticket balancing. For a conservative to put a liberal on the ticket with him may serve short term political interests but is not in the long term interests of the nation. It invites divisiveness within the Administration and destroys the assurance of continuity once the President leaves office.

The third criterion is loyalty in the broadest sense. The President and Vice President need not be personal friends but they must under no circumstances be personally incompatible. A President would be able to delegate to his Vice President important assignments only if he completely trusted him.

The fourth criterion broadly defined is electability. In the case of my decision this meant confirmability by the Congress. In the case of a Presidential nominee this means that individual he selects must be one who will at best be an asset to the ticket and under no circumstances would be a drag on it.

I believed that every one of the final four met these criteria. One might be stronger in one area and another might be stronger in another area, but overall I was not faced with the dilemma of being forced to choose from unqualified people. For example, Rockefeller and I had been political opponents in three elections. He was far more liberal than I was on domestic policies, but what was important to me was that his foreign policy views were very similar to mine and this was at that time the issue which I considered to be most important.

While Reagan was considered to be more conservative than I was on some social issues, he was one of my strongest supporters on foreign policy. I remember that he was one of the very few national figures who called and offered support after I made the very difficult decision to resume the bombing of North Vietnam after the elections in 1972 in order to convince the North Vietnamese that they had no option except to return to the bargaining table and negotiate a peace agreement.

I had no doubt whatever that Connally measured up to all four criteria in every respect. Ford, however, had a subtle advantage over the others. I had known him longer and better than any of the others. We both served in the House together and we were close personal friends.

In a free-willing private discussion I had with Jerry Ford in 1972, I found that he shared my high opinion of Connally as a potential nominee for 1976. I believed then and now that he would have been an outstanding candidate and would have provided the strong leadership in both domestic and foreign policy that the nation would need after the completion of my second term. For that reason he was my first choice, but as I pointed out in my memoirs it would have been virtually impossible to get him confirmed due to the fact that leading Democrats in Congress shared my view but he would probably be the hardest man to beat if he received the nomination in 1976.

Rockefeller would also have been a very strong candidate, and was by far the best known due to the fact that he had sought the nomination in 1960, 1964, and 1968. Reagan had not yet been tested on the national scene but his proven vote-getting ability in the must-win state of California made him a leading candidate.

Ford met all four of the criteria I had established but was without question the frontrunner when it came to the key qualification of confirmability.

I do not mean to suggest by this that the fact that he was the one who could most easily be confirmed was the primary reason for selecting him. On the other hand, in view of my own weak political position at that time, confirmability had to be a major consideration in my decision.

In retrospect, I think that Connally, Rockefeller and Reagan would have all been outstanding Presidents. But I had to take into consideration the fact that it would have been virtually impossible to get Connally confirmed, and that to select either Rockefeller or Reagan would split the Republican Party down the middle and open the way for a bruising fight for the nomination for President in 1976 which would assure the election of the Democratic nominee.

I do not want to leave the impression which some believe was conveyed in my memoirs that Ford was really a second-choice selection and that confirmability was his only major asset.

Personal factors enter into such a decision. I knew all of the final four personally and had great respect for each one of them, but I had known Jerry Ford longer and better than any of the rest. We had served in Congress together. I had often campaigned for him in his district. In 1962 when ABC invited Alger Hiss to appear on a special entitled, "The Political Obituary of Richard Nixon," Jerry Ford appeared on my behalf. One factor which particularly demonstrated to me that he had outstanding leadership qualifications was the indispensable role he played in getting support for our controversial family assistance program which passed the House but then, unfortunately, was rejected by the Senate.

No one of these incidents was the decisive factor which led to my selection of Jerry Ford for Vice President, but taken together what they added up to was that he was my oldest and closest friend of the four finalists, that he shared my views on domestic as well as foreign policy issues, that he was willing to step up to making tough decisions on unpopular issues, and that he above all could always be counted upon to be a team player. Some of the others among the final four met most of these tests, but Ford's confirmability gave him an edge which the others could not match and was the decisive factor in my final decision—a decision I think was right at the time and have not regretted since that time.

In response to your second question, I made the decision to select Ford at Camp David just before returning to Washington on Friday, October 12, 1973. As was my practice on other major decisions during my Presidency, I was alone at the time and did not consult anyone else before making that decision.

You referred, incidentally, to the conversation that Ford and I had in the EOB two days earlier. As I am sure he will recall, I did not "dangle" the Vice Presidency before him at that time. The meeting gave me an opportunity to assess again his personal qualities and confirmed my previous high regard for him.

I am having a search made at the Archives for notes I probably made as part of my deliberation. I cannot guarantee that we will find them, but in the event they turn up, I will make them available to you for your manuscript.

In response to your fourth question, Sunday, April 29, the day before I announced that Haldeman and Ehrlichman would be leaving the White House staff was the lowest point in my Presidency up to that time. However, at that time I still had an approval rating in the polls of well over 50 percent and did not believe that I would be forced to resign. By the time I selected Ford, my approval rating had sharply declined and while I was still determined to fight as hard as possible to serve out the balance of my term, I felt that as a political realist there was at least a 50 percent chance that Ford might become President.

In response to your fifth question I would say that particularly in view of the negative fallout from the pardon, and the effect of the 1974 and 1975 recession, Jerry Ford did a remarkable job in carrying out the foreign and domestic policies which had been approved so overwhelmingly in the 1972 election. My greatest disappointment, as I'm sure was the case for him, was the fall of Saigon in 1975. But he courageously did everything he could to avoid that disastrous event and I'm sure would agree with me that if the Congress had not withdrawn its support from the South Vietnamese government at a time that the Soviet Union was increasing its support for the North, South Vietnam would have survived as an independent non-Communist country.

He ran a courageous race against great odds for election to the office in his own right in 1976, and it will not surprise your readers to know that I feel the country would have been far better off had he won that very close contest.

Sincerely,

RN

APPENDIX B

GERALD R. FORD

April 22, 1993

Dear Jim:

On August 8th, after being told by President Nixon that he was resigning the Presidency and I would be sworn in the next day, I had very mixed feelings.

I was inwardly deeply saddened that a long time, personal friend, whom I had campaigned for in 1960, 1968 and 1972, and whom I admired greatly as a superb foreign policy Commander in Chief, would resign the Presidency. Betty and I, since early 1949, had had a wonderful relationship with the Nixons. To have such a tragedy happen to good friends was extremely difficult to understand and accept.

On the other hand, it was a tremendous relief to have the festering crisis resolved. For the previous nine months, I had been sitting on a time bomb with a blow up likely to take place at any time as new, damaging evidence kept surfacing. Given my nomination and confirmation to the Vice Presidency, I had repeatedly stated that President Nixon was not guilty of an impeachable offense. This opinion was based on assurances from President Nixon himself and other available information. However, as new information surfaced, my public position on President Nixon's future became more and more tenuous and difficult to justify. Betty and I had never wanted President Nixon to leave the White House until his second term expired in January 1977, but we were not at all comfortable with probable developments for the next 2 1/2 years when there would likely be the impeachment process underway.

The night of August 8th, in our home, was surprisingly uneventful. Betty and I obviously made plans for our trip from our Alexandria, Virginia home to the White House. Both of us had a quiet feeling of confidence that we were prepared to handle our new responsibilities and challenges. After a family meal with Susan and Steve, we retired early. Before sleeping we held hands and offered a prayer using Proverbs 3:5,6, as the theme.

I believe both of us slept well despite the dramatic change in our lives that would take place the next day. This reflected our confidence that we were prepared to do the job. Our 25 1/2 years in Congress, 9 years in a leadership role with frequent White House contacts, gave both of us an excellent background to handle our respective roles.

As we drove into the White House to bid the Nixons good-bye, we reflected on our long and fine relationship with the President, Pat and the two children. We tried to organize what we would say as they boarded the helicopter to leave the White House under these traumatic circumstances.

The Nixon departure was difficult. We strained to say the right words. It wasn't easy. We waved as the helicopter took off for Andrews Air Force Base. We turned and walked into the White House, holding hands. We were joined in our determination to meet our new responsibilities.

Sincerely.

Gerald R. Ford

APPENDIX C

August 11, 1974

Memorandum from Bryce Harlow:

FOR THE PRESIDENT:

An admittedly subjective analysis (attached) of 16 leading "possibles" for Vice President produces five leading candidates: George Bush, Rogers Morton, John Rhodes, Bill Brock and Nelson Rockefeller. Taking them individually:

Bush: Strongest across the board; greatest weakness—regarded as intellectually "light" by many top leaders in the country.

Morton: Also strongest across the board; greatest weaknesses—age and poor health.

Rhodes: Obviously strong in every category; greatest weaknesses—would bring on a divisive leadership fight in House; background in House too similar to the President's; no outreach to political groups not already within the President's orbit.

Brock: Generally strong and especially useful in attractiveness to youth; greatest weaknesses—lack of national stature and Congressional orientation already characteristic of the new Administration.

Rockefeller: Professionally the best qualified, by far, with added strengths of (a) proving President's self-confidence in bringing in a towering Number Two, (b) making available superb manpower resources to staff the new Administration, and (c) broadening the Ford political base. Greatest weaknesses—age, serious conservative irritation (in both Parties), and acute discomfort functioning as Number Two to anyone.

In sum, it would appear that the choice narrows to Bush and Rockefeller. For Party harmony, plainly it should be Bush, but generally this would be construed as a weak and depressingly conventional act, foretelling a Presidential hesitancy to move boldly in face of known controversy. A Rockefeller choice would be hailed by the media normally most hostile to Republicanism, would encourage estranged groups to return to the Party, and would signal that this new President will not be a captive of any political faction. As for 1976, a Ford-Rockefeller ticket should be an extremely formidable combination against any opponents the Democrats should offer.

Therefore, the best choice—Rockefeller.

Total points:

Bush	42	Richardson	34
Morton	40	Holton	34
Rhodes	39	Dunn	34
Brock	38	Reagan	33
Rockefeller	36	Goldwater	33
Scranton	35	Baker	33
Ray	35	Godwin	32
Rumsfeld	34	Laird	29

SCALE 0–5	EXPERIENCE	GEOGRAPHY	G.O.P.	CLEAN IMAGE	SELFLESS SUPPORT OF PRESIDENT
Laird	5	0	3	3	3
Scranton	4	3	2	5	5
Rumsfeld	3	4	3	5	5
Bush	4	5	5	5	5
Richardson	5	4	2	5	4
Morton	5	4	5	5	5
Holton	3	4	3	5	4
Reagan	4	5	4	4	4
Rockefeller	5	5	3	4	3
Ray	3	4	4	5	4
Dunn	3	4	4	5	4
Godwin	4	4	3	5	5
Goldwater	5	4	4	5	4
Baker	4	4	3	5	4
Brock	4	4	5	5	5
Rhodes	4	4	5	5	5

COMPETENCE	NATIONAL STATURE	AGE	BROADEN FORD POLITICAL BASE	RMN FACTOR
5	4	4	3	-1
5	4	3	4	0
4	2	5	3	0
4	4	5	2	3
5	5	4	5	-5
4	4	2	3	3
4	2	5	4	0
5	5	1	1	0
5	5	1	5	0
5	2	5	3	0
4	2	5	3	0
5	2	1	3	0
4	5	1	1	0
4	5	5	4	-5
4	3	5	3	0
5	4	4	3	0

ACKNOWLEDGMENTS

For the idea of writing this book, I am grateful to Hofstra University. In the spring of 1989 Hofstra sponsored a major conference of politicians and academics to examine the Presidency of Gerald R. Ford. For three days on the campus at Hempstead, New York, we looked at the Ford record. Scholars and journalists reviewed Ford's decisions and criticized his mistakes, and Ford's senior staff responded with vigor and candor, trying to remember and explain the way it really was.

From February 1975 to January 1977, I was President Ford's Assistant for Domestic Affairs, so I was invited to take part in the Hofstra discussions. With fascination I also listened to other Presidential advisers describe how Ford came into office; dealt with Vietnam, the Middle East and the Soviet Union; handled Congress; reformed the CIA; campaigned unsuccessfully for a full term; and pardoned former President Nixon. *The pardon:* That was the subject that generated the most spirited debate and drew the largest audiences.

The Hofstra conference on Ford, the seventh in the university's series on presidents, was a significant contribution to the history of the period. But at the end I realized how little was generally known about Ford the man, his public career, and the circumstances of his becoming President.

Here was a story to be told, the story of an honest, little-known citizen from the heartland of the country who took over the White House after the American people came to realize that the President they had elected was a crook.

Fortuitously, at the time of the Hofstra Conference, almost every person who had a part in Ford's public life was still around, available to talk about this man they admired or, in some cases, disdained.

Someone, it seemed to me, should collect and preserve the memories of

Ford—and those closest to him—about the most extraordinary transfer of Presidential power in American history. Someone should tell the story of Ford's early life, how and why he was chosen to be President, and in what ways he succeeded and failed. My experience was such that I could write this story; my interest was such that I decided I should write this book.

Before I began, however, I thought it would be appropriate to see President Ford and find out if he would discuss in detail the events which had changed his life. After sketching my plan for the book, I said: "But Mr. President, my research will turn up mistakes you made, and I hope you will understand that the book may be critical of some things you did."

"Don't be concerned about that," Ford said. "I know more about the mistakes I made than anyone else, and I will tell you what they are, and why they happened."

With that, President Ford directed Frank Mackaman, Director of the Gerald R. Ford Library, to open all his private papers—personal files, family history, college transcripts, military service record—and all his official records as a Congressman, Vice President, and President for my study and use.

In addition, President Ford made available for this book some million and a half words of oral history he recorded privately for his own autobiography, *A Time to Heal.* Like most contemporary politicians, Ford was not a writer but a talker. Like some in public life, Ford could remember practically everything important to him—from his happy boyhood in Grand Rapids to working his way through Michigan and Yale, from action at sea in World War II to his first political campaign, from his first handshake on the House floor with Richard Nixon in 1949 to their last private meeting in the Oval Office a quarter-century later when Nixon finally said he would resign.

Ford's reflections on his life and times were recorded on tape during his first year out of office by Trevor Armbrister, the *Reader's Digest* writer who assisted Ford with *A Time to Heal.* Transcribed, these tapes comprise an extraordinary, first-hand account of this President's forebears, his growing into manhood, his political career, his insights into the five Presidents he served with and came to know, his intriguing relationship with Richard Nixon, and his own time in the White House. As a source of information, and as a starting point for additional research, these Ford transcripts were of incomparable value in putting together this segment of history.

I deeply appreciate all that President Ford personally did to provide me his account of events and his judgments. He opened the record of his life to me. He opened doors for me. In addition, he granted me more than a hundred hours of his time for interviews for this book. No subject was barred; no question went unanswered. He discussed the most sensitive issues of his life and career. He imposed no restriction on how I might use the information, and asked for no right to review what I wrote. He said he would trust me to be accurate about the facts and fair in my judgments. This confidence in his public life and readiness to trust a serious examination of his record is very much a part of the man Gerald Ford is.

For a writer, there could have been no greater measure of cooperation, no greater freedom to tell the story. In my four years of work on this book, no person has been of greater assistance than President Ford himself. I am deeply grateful for his assistance and his trust.

In addition to Ford's openness and good memory, I have drawn heavily from the rich storehouse of information at the Gerald Ford Library. The Ford Library, on the campus of the University of Michigan at Ann Arbor, is a Presidential Library (one of eleven—Hoover through Bush) administered by the National Archives and Records Administration.

When President Ford left office, he and his White House staff filled nine moving vans with decision papers, action memoranda, crisis reports, and other historical documents and shipped them to the National Archives and the future Ford Library. Today this Library could fill as many more vans with the papers it has collected from former officials, organizations, and scholars. Every year, more is being collected and opened. These memoranda, meeting notes, and other papers make a vast and still-forming trove of information that profited me greatly—though I barely tapped the vast volumes of material available. The abundance of this material is there to reward other researchers and scholars interested in the history of post–World War II America.

Director Frank Mackaman, senior Archivist William McNitt, and other members of the Ford Library staff provided greater assistance than can be readily acknowledged. All are professionals who set and achieve high standards for public service. They came up with the facts I needed and added their learning and insights as well. To Frank, Bill, and their associates at the Ford Library, I acknowledge a particular indebtedness.

Ford's friends—all his life he made and kept them—have made an invaluable contribution to this book.

To all his friends who talked with me I am grateful, and particularly to those who worked most closely with Ford during his coming into the Presidency.

John O. Marsh, at the center of events, combined his knowledge of the facts with a great sense of history. For the writing of this book, his counsel was sound, his encouragement indispensable. He was an expert guide through the thicket of events attendant to the last days of Nixon and the first days of Ford. At every major fork in the trail, Marsh could explain what lay down either path.

President Ford has often said, "Jack Marsh was the unsung hero of my Presidency." This book about Ford is a far more complete and accurate account of events because of Marsh.

Robert Hartmann, Philip Buchen, and William Seidman, longtime and loyal friends of Ford, were invaluable sources. Each conveyed to me his vivid memories, his good judgment, and his great knowledge of Ford's strengths and his weaknesses.

Among Ford's colleagues in the House, Melvin Laird, Donald Rumsfeld, Robert Griffin, John Rhodes, and Barber Conable were especially helpful in conveying Ford's qualities as Minority Leader. To understand the transition of power from Nixon to Ford, I relied on interviews with Henry Kissinger, Brent Scowcroft, Alexander Haig, Bill Timmons, and Jerry Jones. Each was an eyewitness to events inside the Nixon White House, and all continued in office into the Ford Administration. I deeply appreciate their assistance in bringing together the happenings of those momentous days.

For the sections of this book about former President Nixon I turned to the Nixon Presidential Materials Staff, also part of the National Archives, and particularly to Scott Parham, Supervisory Archivist of the Nixon papers. The original Nixon tapes and papers are in Arlington, Virginia, where, under a 1974 federal statute, they remain the property of the U.S. Government. But not all the Nixon material is available for study; by a series of legal actions, former President Nixon has prevented outside examination of most of his tapes and many Presidential papers.

The most accurate account of the Watergate cover-up is in the White House tapes that have been released to the public. As Presidential history, these tapes are unique. Step by step, Nixon himself tells the story of the criminal acts that brought him down; and I have drawn heavily from the Nixon tapes for this book.

The first and most detailed outside account of the Watergate break-in and the cover-up was produced by the reporters and editors of *The Washington Post*. By good fortune, I could review the *Post* stories and then discuss the significance of developments with my friend of thirty years, Benjamin Bradlee. These discussions were most important as I reexamined the unfolding of the Watergate disaster. Bradlee, more than anyone else, and the *Post* pursued the Watergate story that led to the Court trials and provoked the Senate hearings that revealed the tapes that ended Nixon's Presidency.

Watergate: Chronology of a Crisis, published by Congressional Quarterly in 1975, is the most concise and comprehensive single document detailing the investigation and prosecution of the break-in and the cover-up. This thousand-page volume covers Watergate from the Senate hearings through the pardon of Nixon; it is an invaluable resource. In addition, I relied on three experienced navigators through the tricky reefs of Watergate. To Senate Watergate co-chairman Howard Baker, minority counsel Fred Thompson, and deputy counsel Howard Liebengood, I owe a great debt. They, more than anyone else, know the complexities of the Watergate crimes and the questions that are still unanswered.

Only two persons important to the Ford story—former President Nixon and former Vice President Agnew—declined to be interviewed for this book. Nevertheless, a mutual friend, Tom Korologos, persuaded Nixon to respond to my written request for his account of how and why he chose Gerald Ford for Vice President. In a letter, President Nixon provided his recollections of that historic decision. The full text of the Nixon letter is included as Appendix A.

For Nixon's own recollections about the long-running Watergate drama I have relied primarily on the first book he wrote after leaving office—*RN: The Memoirs of Richard Nixon.* Although this Nixon book glosses over certain of his actions and omits others, it still illuminates many facets of the Nixon character. In this memoir Nixon not only wrote of his great moments in history, but he also conveyed the dark side of his being. Nixon did so, his editors told me, for two reasons: To make the book credible as history, and to boost sales. Whatever additional purposes Nixon may have had in writing as he did, *RN: The Memoirs of Richard Nixon* is the most revealing Presidential autobiography of this century. A complex man, this Richard Nixon—intelligent, persevering, driven, fearful, with a seismic fault in his character. Never has any U.S. President been so paranoid; never has any paranoid in American public life done more for his country or done more damage to himself and the Presidency.

In response to my request for an interview, Agnew replied: "I have made it a policy to remain silent regarding events that transpired during my political career." In later correspondence, Agnew did confirm information about his early life, and he made available files from the Agnew collection at the University of Maryland; but he would not agree to any discussion.

The best single source of information about the investigation and resignation of Agnew is *A Heartbeat Away,* by two excellent *Washington Post* reporters, Richard Cohen and Jules Witcover. In interviews, Elliot Richardson, George Beall, Mike Dunn, and Haig provided more details of the evidence against Agnew and the race against time to force Agnew's resignation as Vice President before the evidence against Nixon brought about his impeachment as President. For Agnew's side of the story, I have relied on Agnew's own book, *Go Quietly . . . or Else,* and on interviews with his Vice Presidential associates.

The bibliography for this book lists the names of some 190 people who were interviewed. All were generous with their time and memories, and I thank each for his participation. Their knowledge and insights—and in some cases contemporaneous notes—were an enormous asset to me in getting the story right. Where I have made an error, it is my fault, not theirs.

Hal Bruno's dispatches to *Newsweek* covering Nixon's actions in 1973 and 1974 are unexcelled examples of journalistic initiative and sound judgment. R. W. Apple, Jr., shared with me his political judgment as well as a complete record of his political coverage of the 1976 Presidential campaign for *The New York Times.*

For their interest, encouragement, and readiness to help, I am grateful to many more: Penny Circle, Judi Risk, and Lee Simmons, in President Ford's office; Dr. Ray Smock, Historian of the House; Dr. Richard Baker, Historian of the Senate; Jeannie Bowles, Superintendent of the Senate Document Room; Dr. Susan Martin and the staff of the Georgetown University Lauinger Library; Dr. Richard Harms of the Grand Rapids Public Library; Harriet Roll of the Harvard, Illinois, Public Library; Mary Hansen of Portland, Oregon; Rex Scouten, Curator of the White House; David Belin, for his guidance on the Warren Commission and the investigation of the Kennedy assassination; and Paul O'Neill, who understands the way the Federal government works almost as well as President Ford.

The Everett McKinley Dirksen Congressional Leadership Research Center provided a grant to study the relationship between Ford's experience in the House of Representatives and his approach to Executive Office; and I am indebted to Dr. John Kornacki, Executive Director of the Dirksen Center, for that grant and for his generosity in sharing his rich treasure of information about Senator Dirksen.

The Annenberg Washington Program sponsored a 1990 conference on the *Mayaguez* incident, as part of the Annenberg Project on Television and U.S. Foreign Policy. Michael R. Beschloss, Senior Fellow and Director of the

Project, invited me to participate with President Ford and his senior foreign policy advisers in that discussion. It was a candid and revealing discussion, and a most valuable contribution to this book.

Joseph Buzhardt and Mrs. Imogene Buzhardt directed me to Fred Buzhardt's papers at the Strom Thurmond Institute of Government at Clemson University. With the assistance of Institute Archivist James Cross, I found documents that were vital in establishing the close client-lawyer relationship between Nixon and Buzhardt. These papers also revealed the careful legal research Buzhardt had personally undertaken to establish a President's power to pardon.

Four treasured friends from my newsmagazine years encouraged me to undertake this book—Osborn Elliott, Richard Clurman, Lester Bernstein, and Kermit Lansner. Each is an accomplished editor and writer, and over the years I have learned from all. I also benefited from the counsel and guidance of three eminent historians—Michael Beschloss, Edmund Morris, and Richard Norton Smith. Each sets the highest standard in his writing; and each has given me good advice.

I thank my winsome friend, Diana Swoyer, for introducing me to the right literary agent, Peter Matson, of Sterling Lord Literistic; and I thank Matson for finding the right publisher and editors for the book.

For their hospitality as I traveled for interviews with President Ford I am particularly grateful to Bob and Mildred Reveley, in Rancho Mirage, California, and to Terry and Betsy Considine at the Big-4 Ranch in Western Colorado.

I enjoyed working on this book, demanding and difficult though it was. The endless adventure of politics is my favorite subject. Twenty years as a political reporter and another twenty as a practicing politician convinced me that public life is the most challenging of all endeavors. As human drama, politics is unmatched; and so it was with the drama of Nixon's ruin and Ford's rise to power.

Every writer needs a good editor. I was lucky. I had three. At Harper-Collins, Edward Burlingame instructed me in narrative and structure. I learned from Burlingame, and this is a better book because of his tutoring and his careful editing. Subsequently HarperCollins assigned Eamon Dolan to work with me, and I had the benefit of his youthful wisdom and engaging manner. Dolan was particularly helpful in pointing the way to a stronger finish for the book. I am grateful to both and to the editor who contributed the most time and devotion to this book: Scott Cannon, my younger son. I already knew he was a fine writer; but until I asked him to read and offer suggestions on the manuscript, I did not know that he was also an editor. With a sharp pencil, devotion to clarity and brevity, and comments that were often blunt and always constructive, Scott also taught me about writing.

To all of my family I am grateful for their patience and endurance through the four years I spent in researching and writing this book. Both my older son and namesake, James M. Cannon IV, and Scott supported my endeavor and accepted without complaint the loss of our time together. Most of all I thank my wife for understanding and sustaining me in this task I had set for myself. It is to her, Cherie Dawson Cannon, that this book is dedicated with love, gratitude, and respect.

August, 1993
Washington, D.C.

SOURCE NOTES

ABBREVIATIONS

CQ   *Watergate: Chronology of a Crisis,* edited by Mercer Cross and Elder Witt, Congressional Quarterly, Inc., 1975.

CR   Congressional Record.

FD   *The Final Days,* by Bob Woodward and Carl Bernstein, Simon and Schuster, 1976.

GRF/HD   Representative Gerald Ford's House diaries. These documents remain in his personal possession.

GRF/JMC   Interviews of President Ford by the author, 1989–93.

GRFLIB   Gerald R. Ford Library, Ann Arbor, Michigan, a Presidential Library administered by the National Archives and Records Administration.

GRFPP   *Public Papers of the Presidents, Gerald R. Ford, 1974–1977,* Government Printing Office.

GRF/TA   Interviews of President Ford by Trevor Armbrister, 1977–78. (Author's note: Although President Ford granted me access to these transcripts in the Ford Library, they are not yet open for general research.)

Heal   *A Time to Heal,* by Gerald R. Ford, Harper & Row/Reader's Digest, 1979.

HIC   *Inner Circles,* by Alexander M. Haig, Jr., Warner Books, 1992.

NPP   Nixon Presidential Papers. The tapes and papers of former
               President Nixon are located in College Park, Maryland,
               where they are administered by the Nixon Presidential
               Materials Staff, a division of the National Archives and
               Records Administration. By a 1974 statute, President
               Nixon's papers and tapes remain the property of the U.S.
               Government.

NYT   *The New York Times*

PDD   The President's Daily Diary. (For President Ford, at the Ford
               Library in Ann Arbor, Michigan; for President Nixon, at the
               Nixon Presidential Materials office in College Park, Mary-
               land.)

PP   *Palace Politics,* by Robert T. Hartmann, McGraw-Hill, 1980.

RNM   *RN: The Memoirs of Richard Nixon,* Grosset & Dunlap, 1978.

RNPP   *Public Papers of the Presidents, Richard M. Nixon, 1969–1974,*
               Government Printing Office.

VPDS   Vice President's Daily Schedule, available at the Ford Library.

WP   *The Washington Post*

WSJ   *The Wall Street Journal*

PROLOGUE

ix   William McNitt, Archivist of The Gerald Ford Library, pro-
               vided Gerald Ford's schedule for November 7, 1972, from
               Ford Congressional Papers, on file in the Library.

               Three friends of Gerald Ford spent part of this Election Day
               with him—Walter Russell, his campaign manager, Gordon
               Vander Till, who ran Ford's office in the Fifth Michigan

Congressional District, and George terHorst, consultant to the 1972 Ford campaign. Interviews: Russell/JMC Jun 29, 1992; Vander Till/JMC May 19, Jun 29 and Jul 1, 1992; terHorst/JMC Jun 19 and Jul 6, 1992.

Thomas Chase, City Clerk for East Grand Rapids, confirmed the location of Ford's polling place. Chase/JMC Aug 24, 1992.

x   GRF/JMC Sep 1, 1989, and Apr 22, 1992; Betty Ford/JMC Apr 30 and Jul 20, 1990.

NPP: PDD, Nov 7, 1972.

Theodore H. White, *The Making of the President—1972,* pp. 6–14.

RNM, pp. 715–7; David Eisenhower/JMC May 18, 1989.

xi   Videos of election coverage by ABC, CBS, and NBC observed by the author at NPP, then in Alexandria, Va., June 22, 1992, and June 29, 1993.

xi–xii   CBS declaration of Nixon victory, Marty Plissner/JMC Jul 3, 1992.

xii   Election returns, *America Votes, 1972.*

Videos of Nixon-Agnew victory celebration observed by the author at NPP, June 22, 1992, and June 29, 1993.

Spiro T. Agnew, *Go Quietly . . . or Else,* p. 38.

xii–xiii   RNM, p. 717.

xiii–xiv Fords on Election Night: GRF/JMC Sep 1, 1989, and Apr 26, 1990; Betty Ford/JMC Apr 30 and Jul 20, 1990; GRFLIB: GRF/TA.

1. A BOY'S LIFE

1–6   This account of the physical abuse Leslie L. King inflicted on Dorothy Gardner King is taken from copies of court documents in the Ford Library. Marc S. Romanik, chief deputy clerk to the Douglas County District Court, in Omaha, Nebraska, sent these papers to William Casselman, Counsel to Vice President Ford, on April 18, 1974.

These Nebraska court documents chronicle in detail the abusive conduct and dissolute nature of Leslie King. Divorce proceedings began on August 18, 1913, when King charged desertion after Mrs. King escaped from his house with their infant son. Mrs. King filed a counter-suit two weeks later and in December was granted custody, alimony, and child support. But King refused to pay. With bitterness on both sides, the case dragged on in the Nebraska courts for 26 years.

1, 3   For details of the Gardner-King wedding, I have relied on *The Harvard Herald* of September 12, 1912.

1   Sources of additional information: Multnomah Hotel: Historical Summary, Portland Historical Landmarks Commission, May 1981.

1–6   GRF/JMC Apr 24, 25 and Nov 13, 1990; Tom Ford/JMC Feb 27 and Nov 21, 1991; Janet Ford/JMC Feb 27, 1991.

Marjorie King Werner/JMC Oct 12, 1990.

4   Nebraska Department of Health, Division of Vital Statistics, Certificate of Birth for Leslie King, Jr. at 3202 Woolworth Street, Omaha, Douglas County, on July 14, 1913, to Leslie King, wool merchant, and Dorothy Gardner King, housewife.

1–6   William H. McNitt, "The Ancestry of Gerald R. Ford," published by the Ford Library, May 19, 1989.

Inventory of sites associated with President Ford, published by the U.S. Department of the Interior, January 18, 1982.

Report by the Harvard (Ill.) Bicentennial Commission, December, 1976.

Lloyd Shearer, "President Ford's Other Family," *Parade*, September 15, 1974.

Edward L. and Frederick H. Schapsmeier, "President Gerald R. Ford's Roots in Omaha," *Nebraska History*, Summer, 1987.

Frank Santiago, "President Ford's Early Life in Omaha Clouded by Parents' Stormy Marriage," *Omaha World-Herald*, Aug 16, 1974.

"King marriage was stormy," article in the *Sun Newspapers*, August 22, 1974.

6–8   William J. Etten, *A Citizens' History of Grand Rapids, Michigan*, published by A. P. Johnson Company for the Campau Centennial Committee, 1926.

Old Grand Rapids, published by the Grand Rapids Historical Society, 1986.

Michigan History, March/April, 1990.

Richard H. Harms, "George W. Welsh and the Grand Rapids Scrip Labor Program: Government Work Relief before the New Deal," 1990.

Z. Z. Lydens, *The Story of Grand Rapids*, Kreger Publications, 1966.

James Van Vulpen, *On Wings of Progress*, published by Grand Rapids Historical Commission, 1989.

Polk's *Grand Rapids City Directory of 1931*.

8	Arnold Gingrich, *Cast Down the Laurel*, Alfred A. Knopf, 1935.
	William Seidman/JMC Sep 7, 1991.
8–11	GRF/JMC Apr 24, 25, 26, 1990; Tom Ford/JMC Feb 27, 1991; Dick Ford/JMC Jul 2, 1990; James Ford/JMC Jul 2, 1990; Janet Ford/JMC Feb 27, 1991.
11	*Boy Scout Manual,* 1925.
12	Gettings/Armbrister, 1977; GRF/JMC Apr 25, 1990.
12–16	GRF/JMC Apr 25, 1990.
16	Bentley Historical Library, University of Michigan: Letter dated May 11, 1931, from A. W. Krause, Principal of South High School, Grand Rapids, to Harry Kipke, Ann Arbor; letters dated May 15 and May 18, 1931, from Harry G. Kipke to A. W. Krause. Letter dated June 8, 1931, to Harry Kipke from Gerald Ford.
16–17	GRF/JMC Apr 25, 1990.

2. LEARNING

18–21	GRF/JMC Apr 24, 1990, Jul 14, 1992, May 5, 1993, Sep 2, 1993.
	GRFLIB: Transcript of GRF scholastic record, University of Michigan. Letter dated December 10, 1934, from R. E. Hanley, head football coach at Northwestern University, inviting Ford to play in the East-West game in San Francisco January 1, 1935. Letter dated February 11, 1935, from Curly Lambeau, coach of the Green Bay Packers, offering to sign Ford as center for the next football season.
	Ford interview by Claudia Capos, "My years at Michigan made me a better person . . . ," *Michigan Alumnus,* February, 1974.

Robert A. Potter, "A Legacy of Leadership: President Ford and U-M," *Michigan Alumnus,* March/April, 1986.

21–22   GRF/JMC Apr 24–26, 1990.

GRFLIB: Copy of order by John Dalton, Judge of Probate of Kent County, Michigan, changing the name of Leslie King to Gerald Rudolph Ford, Junior, on December 3, 1935.

22–24   John Hersey/JMC Dec 20, 1991; John Nelson/JMC Dec 22, 1991; Robert A. Taft/JMC Dec 20, 1991; William Proxmire/JMC, Dec 20, 1991.

GRF/JMC Apr 24, 1990, and Nov 13, 1990.

24–26   GRF/JMC Nov 13, 1990.

GRFLIB: Ford Vice Presidential Papers, King vs. King, his parents' divorce case.

Letter, undated, from Dorothy Gardner King to Gerald Ford, Jr.

26   GRF/JMC Apr 24, 1990.

GRFLIB: Ford Vice Presidential Papers, Introduction of Vice President Ford to the Yale Law School Club in Washington, D.C., by Myres McDougal, *Parade,* Dec 8, 1974.

26–29   GRF/JMC Apr 24, 1990.

Phyllis Brown/JMC Apr 28, 1990, and Jan 9, 1992.

Dick Ford/JMC Jul 2, 1990.

Philip Buchen, May 20, 1992.

"A New York Girl and Her Yale Boy Friend Spend A Hilarious Holiday on Skis," *Look,* March 12, 1940.

30   GRF/JMC Apr 24, 1990.

31–32   GRF/JMC Nov 13, 1990.

            Yale University School of Law Official Transcript for Gerald
            Rudolph Ford, Jr., copy signed by A. B. Hadley, Registrar, on
            February 23, 1942.

            Yale Law School Class of 1941 graduates, list transmitted by
            Catherine Iino, Director of Public Affairs, Jan 9, 1992.

32–33   Buchen/JMC Apr 2, 1993; GRF/JMC Apr 24, 1990.

            Grand Rapids Public Library and GRFLIB: Interview of Dr.
            Willard Ver Meulen, Jan 26, 1980.

33–39   GRF/JMC Apr 24, 1990, and Sep 2, 1993.

            "History of USS Monterey (CVL 26)," Office of Naval
            Records and History, Ships' Histories Branch, Navy Depart-
            ment, from June 17, 1943, to February, 1946.

            GRFLIB: "The U.S.S. Monterey and the Great Typhoon," an
            undated account of Ford's service on the Monterey during
            World War II.

            U.S. Department of Defense: Complete service record of
            Gerald Rudolph Ford, Jr., including his appointment to the
            U.S. Navy Reserves, transcript of Naval Service, fitness
            reports, ships and stations, medals and awards, from his
            appointment as an ensign on Apr 16, 1942, to his release
            from active duty on Feb 23, 1946.

            GRFLIB: Ford's personal papers relating to his service.

3. THE CHALLENGE

40–41   GRF/JMC Apr 24, 1990; Buchen/JMC Feb 15 and May 20,
            1990.

41–42 GRF/JMC Apr 24, 1990; Brown/JMC Apr 28, 1990, and Jan 9, 1992.

42–44 GRF/JMC Apr 30, 1990; Betty Ford, *The Times of My Life,* pp. 44–49; Betty Ford/JMC Apr 30 and Jul 20, 1990.

44–45 GRF/JMC Apr 30, 1990; Jerald F. terHorst, *Gerald Ford and the Future of the Presidency,* pp. 8–25; Buchen/JMC Feb 15, 1990, and May 20, 1992; William A. Syers, "The Political Beginnings of Gerald R. Ford: Anti-Bossism, Internationalism, and the Congressional Campaign of 1948," *Presidential Studies Quarterly,* Winter, 1990.

45–47 GRF/JMC Apr 20, 1990; Betty Ford/JMC Apr 30 and Jul 20, 1990; Betty Ford, *The Times of My Life,* pp. 16–46.

47–48 Betty Ford/JMC Apr 30 and Jul 20, 1990; Betty Ford, *The Times of My Life,* pp. 47–53; GRF/JMC Apr 20, 1990; Phyllis Brown/JMC Apr 28, 1990, and Jan 9, 1992.

48–50 GRF/JMC Apr 30, 1990; Buchen/JMC Feb 15, 1990, and May 20, 1992; GRFLIB, Fifth District Primary returns in 1948.

50–52 Betty Ford/JMC Apr 30, 1990; Betty Ford, *The Times of My Life,* pp. 58–61; GRF/JMC Apr 30, 1990; GRFLIB, Fifth District General Election returns, 1948.

4. A MAN OF THE HOUSE

53–55 GRF/JMC Apr 25, 1990.

55–56 GRF/HD for 1949; Betty Ford/JMC Apr 30 and Jul 20, 1990; Betty Ford, *The Times of My Life,* pp. 62–69; Ford for 1950.

56–57 GRF/JMC Apr 25, 1990; "The Nation's 10 Outstanding Young Men of 1949," *Future,* February, 1950; Letter dated March 11, 1992, from Jay D. Strother, public relations manager, The United States Junior Chamber of Commerce; GRF/TA.

57–58	GRF/JMC Apr 25, 1990; GRF/TA; Betty Ford/TA.
58–59	Ray Smock/JMC Apr 7, 1992; Donald Kennon and Rebecca Rogers, "The Committee on Ways and Means," *A Bicentennial History 1789–1989;* Garrison Nelson, "Leadership Position-Holding in the United States House of Representatives," *Capitol Studies,* Fall, 1976; GRF/JMC Apr 25, 1990.
59–60	GRF/JMC Apr 25, 1990; Walt Russell/JMC Jun 29, 1992.
60–61	Dwight D. Eisenhower, *Mandate for Change,* pp. 21–22; GRFLIB: Copy of letter dated February 22, 1952, to General Eisenhower from Representative Ford and 18 other members of the House; GRF/JMC Apr 26, 1990; RNM, pp. 101–102.
61–62	GRF/JMC Apr 25, 1990; Laird/JMC Jun 5, 1991.
62–63	GRF/HD, for 1953; GRF/JMC Apr 25, 1990.
63–64	GRF/JMC Apr 25, 1990; Statement by Representative George Mahon to the Senate Rules Committee on November 5, 1973, during hearings on the nomination of Gerald Ford to be Vice President.
65–66	GRF/JMC Apr 25, 1990; Michael R. Beschloss, *Mayday;* Harry Rositzke, *The CIA's Secret Operations.*
66–67	Betty Ford/JMC Apr 30, 1990; GRF/JMC Apr 25, 1990.
67	GRF/TA.
67–68	GRF/JMC Apr 25–27, 1990; *Newsweek,* Feb 15 and Jul 11, 1960.

5. RECOGNITION

69–72	WP, Jan 20, 1961; GRF/JMC Apr 25, 1990; Carl Elliott/JMC May 19, 1993; GRF/Penny Circle May 21, 1993.

70   GRFLIB: Citation by the American Political Science Associa-
                tion in St. Louis, Missouri, on September 8, 1961; HAK/JMC
                Apr 2, 1991.

71–72   Lester S. Jayson, Director, Congressional Research Service,
                "Analysis of the Philosophy and Voting Record of Represen-
                tative Gerald R. Ford, nominee for Vice President of the
                United States," prepared at the direction of the Senate Rules
                Committee, October 25, 1973.

72–73   GRF/HD, 1962; GRF/JMC Apr 26, 1990.

73   GRF/JMC Apr 25, 1990; Donald Rumsfeld/JMC Dec 9,
                1991.

74–75   Betty Ford/JMC; Betty Ford, *The Times of My Life*,
                pp. 120–138.

75–76   GRF/JMC Apr 25, 1990.

76–77   Robert McNamara/JMC, May 20, 1991; GRF/HD, 1963 and
                1964; GRF/JMC Apr 25, 1990; David Belin/JMC Feb 4 and
                Apr 24, 1992; Belin, *November 22, 1963: You Are the Jury*;
                Warren Commission Report, September 27, 1964; James
                Reston, NYT, September 28, 1964.

78   GRF/JMC Apr 25–26, 1990.

78–80   Betty Ford, *The Times of My Life*, pp. 117–128; Michael
                Ford/JMC Feb 8, 1991; GRF/JMC Apr 25–26, 1990.

6. LEADER OF THE OPPOSITION

81–82   Election returns, *America Votes, 1964*; GRF/JMC Apr 25,
                1990; Robert Griffin/JMC Jun 28, 1990; Rumsfeld/JMC Dec
                9, 1991; Betty Ford/JMC Apr 30, 1990.

82–83   GRF/JMC Apr 25, 1990; Laird/JMC Jun 5, 1991; Joseph
                Sterne/JMC Dec 12, 1990; Rumsfeld/JMC Dec 9, 1991.

83–85   Dr. Ray Smock/JMC Apr 7, 1992; Garrison Nelson, "Leader-
             ship Position-Holding in the United States House of Repre-
             sentatives," *Capitol Studies,* Fall, 1976; Donald Kennon and
             Rebecca Rogers, "The Committee on Ways and Means," *A
             Bicentennial History 1789–1989;* Howard Baker/JMC January
             1981; William Hildenbrand/JMC Dec 14, 1989, and Jun 13,
             1990; Senator Mike Mansfield, to a conference sponsored by
             the Dirksen Congressional Center and the United States
             Senate Commission on the Bicentennial, May 17, 1990;
             Howard Greene/JMC Sep 11, 1990, and Jun 10, 1992;
             GRF/JMC Apr 25, 1990.

85–86   *Time,* Sep 14, 1962; GRF/JMC Apr 25, 1990; Burdett Loomis,
             "Everett McKinley Dirksen," *First Among Equals—Out-
             standing Senate Leaders of the Twentieth Century.*

86–87   GRF/TA; GRF/JMC Apr 25, 1990.

87–88   GRF/JMC Apr 25, 1990.

88–89   Betty Ford, *The Times of My Life,* pp. 123–127; Marsh/JMC
             Jun 20, 1991; Betty Ford/JMC Apr 30, 1990.

89–90   Ford Diary for 1965; GRF/JMC Apr 25, 1990; RNM,
             pp. 264–265.

90–91   Laird/JMC Jun 5, 1991; GRF/JMC Apr 25, 1990;
             Hartmann/JMC Mar 2, 1990.

91–92   GRF/JMC Apr 26, 1990; Hartmann/JMC Mar 2, 1990, Jun 19
             and 28, 1991, May 14, 1992.

92–93   GRFLIB: Press clippings, Ford Congressional scrap books;
             GRF/JMC Apr 25, 1990; Election returns, *America Votes 1966.*

93–94   Hartmann/JMC Jun 19 and 28, 1991; GRF/JMC Apr 26, 1990.

94   Janet Ford/JMC Feb 27, 1991; Tom Ford/JMC Feb 27, 1991;
             GRF/JMC Apr 29, 1990; Michael Ford/JMC Feb 8, 1991.

94–95   NYT, Aug 6, 1968; GRF/JMC Apr 26, 1990; Gallup Polls for 1968.

95–96   GRF/JMC Apr 22, 1992.

7. FROM TRIUMPH TO TRAGEDY

97–98   GRF/HD, 1969; GRF/JMC Apr 26, 1990; WP, January, 1969; Author present at Pierre Hotel in November 29 , 1968.

98–100   GRF/JMC Apr 26, 1990; RNM, pp. 414–415; GRF/TA; John Ehrlichman, *Witness to Power,* pp. 197–198; GRF/JMC Apr 27, 1990.

100–101   GRF/TA; PP, pp. 59–72; *Congressional Record* for April 15, 1970; GRF/JMC Apr 27, 1990; John Osborne, *New Republic,* Oct 27, 1973; GRF/JMC Apr 22, 1993.

102   GRF/HD *America Votes 1970.*

102–103   GRF/JMC Apr 26, 1990; Susan Ford/JMC Sep 7, 1991; RNPP; GRF/TA.

103–104   GRF/JMC Apr 27, 1990; Hartmann/JMC Jun 19 and 28, 1991; RNM, pp. 427–428; Ehrlichmann/JMC Sep 27, 1992; John Whitaker/JMC Apr 6, 1992; Whitaker, *Striking a Balance—Environmental and Natural Resources Policy in the Nixon-Ford Years;* Richard E. Thompson, *Revenue Sharing—A New Era in Federalism?;* letter dated February 16, 1991, from former Vice President Agnew to the author; McKeldin Library, University of Maryland, Memorandum of Vice President Agnew's meeting on January 6, 1971, with President Nixon, Governors Nelson Rockefeller, Louie Nunn, and Raymond Shafer "to discuss Revenue Sharing."

104   *Congressional Record* for June 21, 1972.

104–106   GRF/HD, 1972; GRF/JMC Nov 13, 1990; Marsh/JMC Aug 17 and 29, 1989, May 16, Jul 11 and 30, 1990.

106–107	PDD; Neil Sheehan, *A Bright Shining Lie,* pp. 30–33; RNM, pp. 625–626; *The Miami Herald,* June 18, 1972; H. R. Haldeman, *The Ends of Power,* pp. 3–7.
107–108	WP, June 18 and 19, 1972; Carl Bernstein and Bob Woodward, *All the President's Men,* pp. 13–26; Anthony Lukas, *Nightmare,* pp. 202–221; Powell Moore/JMC Apr 3, 1991.
108–109	Ehrlichman, *Witness to Power,* pp. 341–348.
109–110	WP, June 18–20, 1972; Carl Bernstein and Bob Woodward, *All the President's Men,* pp. 13–26.
110–112	RNM, p. 627; H. R. Haldeman, *The Ends of Power,* pp. 8–19; RNM, pp. 630–634.
112–114	John Ehrlichman, *Witness to Power,* p. 79; Charles Colson, *Born Again,* pp. 69–72; Author's conversations with Murray Chotiner 1959–1972; H. R. Haldeman, *The Ends of Power,* pp. 59–61; RNM, pp. 630–631; NPP: Transcript of Nixon meeting with Colson in the EOB 2:20 to 3:30 P.M., June 20, 1972; RNM, pp. 634–635.
114–116	RNM, p. 628; Carl Bernstein and Bob Woodward, *All the President's Men;* H. R. Haldeman, *The Ends of Power;* John Ehrlichman, *Witness to Power;* John Dean, *Blind Ambition;* Anthony Lukas, *Nightmare; Will, The Autobiography of G. Gordon Liddy,* pp. 24, 119–120, 298–306; RNM, pp. 635–639; RNPP: Press conference of June 22, 1972.

8. BETRAYED

117	GRF/HD, 1972; PDD; GRF/JMC Apr 24, 1992; RNM, pp. 639.
118–121	NPP: Transcript of Nixon meetings with Haldeman on June 23, 1972, from 10:04 to 11:39 A.M. in the Oval Office, from 1:04 to 1:13 P.M. in the Oval Office, and from 2:20 to 2:45 P.M. in Room 175 of the EOB.

121–122   GRF/HD, 1972; GRF/JMC Apr 23, 1992; GRF/TA; Hart-
            mann/JMC May 5, 1993; Ford/JMC Nov 13, 1992.

122–123   PDD; RNM, pp. 642–646; NPP: Transcript of Nixon meeting
            with Haldeman and Mitchell on June 30, 1972, in Room 175
            of the EOB from 12:57 to 2:10 P.M.

123–124   RNM, pp. 646–653; Ehrlichman, *Witness to Power,*
            pp. 353–358.

124   RNM, pp. 653–657; Theodore H. White, *The Making of the
            President 1972,* pp. 11.

124–125   RNM, pp. 674–675; PDD; James Reston, Jr., *The Lone Star;*
            RNM, pp. 657–658.

125–126   RNM, pp. 659–663.

126–127   NPP: Video of Republican National Convention of 1972;
            Gallup Poll Aug 20, 1972; Rockefeller/JMC July-August,
            1972; Theodore H. White, *The Making of the President
            1972,* pp. 242 and 326; Gallup Poll, August 30, 1972;
            White, p. 327.

127–128   RNPP: Press Conference of August 29, 1972.

128–130   NYT and WP, September 16, 1972; RNM, pp. 680; transcript
            of Nixon meeting with H. R. Haldeman and John Dean on
            September 15, 1972, from 5:27 to 6:17 P.M. in the Oval
            Office; GRFLIB: Letter dated Sep 28, 1972 from House
            Minority Leader Gerald Ford to Republican members of the
            House Banking Committee; Richard Cook/JMC Mar 22,
            1993; CQ, pp. 5.

130–131   GRF/HD, 1972; GRF/JMC Apr 24, 1992; RNM, pp. 673–674;
            Richard E. Thompson, *Revenue Sharing–A New Era in
            Federalism,* p. 120.

131   GRF/HD, 1972; GRF/TA; GRF/JMC Apr 24, 1992.

| 131–133 | RNM, pp. 708–714; Richard Dougherty, *Goodbye, Mr. Christian,* pp. 119; Theodore White, *The Making of the President 1972,* pp. 327. |

9. THE BURDEN OF GUILT

| 134 | GRF/HD, 1972; GRF/JMC Sep 1, 1989 and Apr 25, 1990; Bill and Peggy Whyte/JMC Feb 26, 1991. |

| 134–136 | H. R. Haldeman, *The Ends of Power,* pp. 162–172; Jerry Jones/JMC Jun 5, 1989; RNM, pp. 744–746, 768–770, 773–779; John Dean, *Blind Ambition,* pp. 152–165. |

| 136–137 | NPP: Haldeman handwritten notes of instructions from Nixon, Nov 14, 1972. |

| 137 | Spiro T. Agnew, *Go Quietly . . . or Else,* pp. 37–40. |

WP, Dec 9, 1972; Transcript of Nixon meeting with Colson January 8, 1973, in the EOB from 4:05 to 5:34 P.M.

| 137–138 | GRF/TA; GRF/JMC Apr 24, 1992; Hartmann/JMC May 14, 1992. |

| 138 | Thomas P. O'Neill, *Man of the House,* p. 242; O'Neill/JMC Jan 24, 1991; Rodino/JMC Sep 28, 1990. |

| 138–139 | RNM, pp. 744–746. |

| 139–140 | John J. Sirica, *To Set the Record Straight;* William Rogers/JMC Jan 11, 1991; *Time* Man of the Year for 1973; Thomas Richichi/JMC Jun 27, 1991; WP, January 16, 1973; RNM, pp. 748–749; CQ, p. xxi. |

| 140–141 | NYT and WP, February 8, 1973; CQ, p. xxii; Senator Howard Baker/JMC Jun 13, 1990. |

(Author's note: Baker was chosen as punishment. Twice he tried to unseat Senator Hugh Scott as Leader of the Senate

Republicans, and twice he lost. Scott calculated that any Republican serving on a committee to investigate a Republican President would be damaged politically. As it happened, the Watergate hearings first brought Senator Baker national recognition.)

141–143   NPP: Transcript of Nixon meeting with John Dean and H. R. Haldeman on March 13, 1973, from 12:42 to 2:00 P.M., in the Oval Office.

143–149   John Dean, *Blind Ambition*, pp. 194–200; NPP: Transcript of Nixon meeting with John Dean and H. R. Haldeman (for the last few minutes) on March 21, 1973, from 10:12 to 11:55 A.M. in the Oval Office.

Ellsberg segment: Anthony Lukas, *Nightmare*, pp. 68–104; CQ, pp. 100–101.

149–150   WP, March 24, 1973; CQ, pp. 9–10.

150–151   RNM, pp. 783–829.

151–152   GRF/TA; GRF/JMC Apr 23, 1992; GRFLIB: UPI report, Apr 14, 1973

152   PDD; RNM, pp. 835–836.

152–153   NYT, April 20, 1973; RNM, pp. 835–840; John Ehrlichman, *Witness to Power*, pp. 385–389; H. R. Haldeman, *The Ends of Power*, pp. 263–287.

153–154   GRF/HD, 1973; GRF/JMC Apr 22, 1992.

154–158   RNM, pp. 845–851; Rogers/JMC Jan 11, 1991; Ray Price/JMC Dec 6, 1990; John Ehrlichman, *Witness to Power*, pp. 389–391; H. R. Haldeman, *The Ends of Power*, pp. 287–296.

158   Elliott Richardson/JMC Mar 3 and 5, 1990; FD, pp. 60–61.

158–159	RNPP, Presidential address on April 30, 1973.
159	WP, May 1, 1973; GRF/JMC Apr 24, 1992.

10. THE REGENCY

160–163	U.S. Weather Bureau records for May 3, 1973; PDD; Garment/JMC Sep 12, 1990; Haig/JMC Nov 6, 1989; RNM, pp. 856–857; H. R. Haldeman, *The Ends of Power*, pp. 299–300.
163–169	Haig/JMC Nov 6, 1989, and Dec 20, 1990; Haig/TA; Haig, *Inner Circles;* Kraemer/JMC May 24, 1991; Kissinger/JMC Apr 2, 1991; *The New York Times Biographical Edition,* May, 1973; Nick Thimmesch, "Chief of Staff," *The Washington Post/Potomac,* Nov 25, 1973; *Current Biography 1973,* pp. 160–162; Lloyd Shearer, "Keep Your Eye On Al," *Parade,* Aug 20, 1972; William Hyland/JMC Sep 14, 1990; Walter Pincus, "Alexander Haig—A Con Man for Europe?" *New Republic,* Oct 5, 1974.
169–171	Haig/JMC Nov 6, 1989, and Dec 20, 1990; Garment/JMC Sep 12 and 24, 1990; H. R. Haldeman, *The Ends of Power,* pp. 299–300; PDD.
171–172	GRF/TA; GRF/JMC Apr 26, 1990; Laird/JMC Jun 5, 1991.
172	NPP, White House press statement, May 10, 1973, and RNM pp. 816 and 823.
172–173	Bradlee/JMC Sep 6, 1990; RNM, pp. 869–871.
173	Elliott Richardson, *The Creative Balance*, pp. 36–47; Richardson/JMC Mar 3 and 5, 1990; Cox testimony to the Senate Judiciary Committee May 21, 1973.
173–174	NPP May 22, 1973; RNM White House press statement pp. 871–873; WSJ, May 23, 1973; CQ, p. 149.

174–175   RNM, pp. 868–875.

175   O'Neill/JMC Jan 24, 1991.

175–176   CQ, pp. 148–150; PDD; RNM, pp. 875–887.

176–177   WP and NYT, Jun 26–28, 1973; CQ, pp. 151–168;
                Baker/JMC Sep 13, 1990.

177–178   Howard Leibengood/JMC Oct 23, 1989; Fred
                Thompson/JMC Jan 25, 1991; Baker/JMC Sep 13, 1990;
                Anthony Lukas, *Nightmare*, pp. 367–382.

178   WP and NYT Jul 14, 1973; RNM pp. 898–901;
                Garment/JMC Sep 12 and 24, 1990; Lukas, *Nightmare*, pp.
                382–389; FD p. 58.

178–179   RNM, pp. 903–904; Lukas, *Nightmare*, pp. 382–389.

179   U.S. Weather Bureau records for July, 1973; CQ,
                pp. 208–212; Lukas, *Nightmare*, pp. 383–389.

179–180   RNM, pp. 909–913; Richardson/JMC Mar 3 and 5, 1990;
                Haig/JMC Nov 6, 1989, and Dec 20, 1990.

11. OUTCAST

181–184   Robert Finch/JMC Jan 24, 1991; Theodore H. White, *The
                Making of the President 1968*, p. 249; letter dated Feb 16,
                x1991, from former Vice President Agnew to the author;
                Richard Cohen and Jules Witcover, *A Heartbeat Away*,
                pp. 16–33; Mike Dunn/JMC Jan 17, 1991; William Safire,
                Before the Fall, p. 323; RNM, pp. 674–675; Spiro T. Agnew,
                Go Quietly . . . or Else, pp. 22–55; Cohen and Witcover, *A
                Heartbeat Away*, pp. 13–15; Russell Baker, "The Biggest Bal-
                timore Loser of All Time," *The New York Times Sunday Mag-
                azine*, Oct 21, 1973; NYT, "A Chronology of Events in
                Agnew Case," Oct 11, 1973.

184–186	George Beall/JMC Mar 12, 1990; Richardson/JMC Mar 3 and 5, 1990; Richardson, *The Creative Balance*, pp. 101–103; Agnew, *Go Quietly . . . or Else*, pp. 50–66; RNM, pp. 816, 912–918, 920, 922–923.
186–188	Richardson/JMC Mar 3 and 5, 1990; Agnew, *Go Quietly . . . or Else*, pp. 95–101.
189–189	Agnew, *Go Quietly . . . or Else*, pp. 101–104.
189	GRF/JMC Apr 23, 1992; Laird/JMC Jun 5, 1991.
189–190	WSJ Aug 7, 1973; Agnew, *Go Quietly . . . or Else*, pp. 107–113; RNM, p. 114.
190	Cohen and Witcover, *A Heartbeat Away*, p. 183.
191	Nelson Rockefeller/JMC August, 1973.
191–192	RNM, pp. 915–918; Agnew, *Go Quietly . . . or Else*, pp. 140–151.
192	Connally/Bruno, September, 1973.
192	RNM, pp. 915–916; GRF/JMC Apr 23, 1992.
192–193	Agnew, *Go Quietly . . . or Else*, pp. 157–171.
193–194	GRF/JMC Apr 23, 1992; O'Neill/JMC Jan 24, 1991; Richardson/JMC Mar 3 and 5, 1990.
194–195	Agnew, *Go Quietly . . . or Else*, pp. 176–180; RNM, pp. 917–920.
195–197	Dunn/JMC Jan 17, 1991; Agnew, *Go Quietly . . . or Else*, pp. 181–192.
197–198	Laird/JMC Jun 5, 1991; Korologos/JMC Sep 26, 1990; Albert/JMC Jul 24, 1990; RNM, pp. 925–926; James Reston, Jr., *Lone Star*, p. 457.

198–199	WP, NYT, Oct 7, 1973; Richardson/JMC Mar 3 and 5, 1990; National Archives: "Exposition of the evidence against Spiro T. Agnew accumulated by the investigation in the office of the United States Attorney for the District of Maryland as of October 10, 1973," presented before Federal Judge Walter E. Hoffman in U.S. District Court, Baltimore, on that date; Richardson, Agnew and Hoffman statements, NYT, October 11, 1973.
199–200	NPP; Archivist Scott Parham/JMC Jul 31, 1992.
200	RNM, pp. 922–923; Agnew, *Go Quietly . . . or Else,* pp. 197–200.

12. THE CHOICE

201–202	GRF/JMC Apr 25 and Nov 13, 1990.
203	Waggoner/JMC Oct 16, 1991; GRF/JMC Apr 24, 1992.
203	PDD; GRF/JMC Apr 24, 1992; RNM, pp. 925–926.
203–205	Stan Kimmitt/JMC Feb 7, 1990; Jun 24 and Jul 10, 1991; Mike Mansfield/JMC May 31, 1991; Albert/JMC Jul 24, 1990; Carl Albert with Danney Goble, *Little Giant.*
205	Laird/JMC Jun 5, 1991.
205–207	PP, pp. 15–20; GRF/JMC Apr 24, 1992; Laird/JMC Jun 5, 1991; Heal, pp. 103–104; Betty Ford/JMC Apr 30 and Jul 20, 1990.
207	Laird/JMC Jun 5, 1991.
	PDD; Heal, p. 104.
207–209	NPP.
209–210	RN letter dated May 24, 1991, to the author, Appendix A; RNM, pp. 925–926.

210–211   PDD; GRF/JMC Apr 24, 1992.

211–212   GRF/JMC Apr 25, 1992; Betty Ford, *The Times of My Life,* pp. 144–148; GRF/TA.

212–213   NPP: Video of President Nixon's announcement of the nomination of Gerald Ford to be Vice President, October 12, 1973; RNPP, "Remarks Announcing Intention to Nominate Gerald R. Ford to be Vice President," October 12, 1973; Thomas P. O'Neill, *Man of the House,* p. 261; James Lynn/JMC Jun 4, 1993.

213–214   GRF/JMC Apr 25, 1992.

13. IMPEACH!

215–217   GRF/JMC Apr 23, 1992; NYT, Oct 14, 1973; CR for Oct 13, 1973; Hartmann/JMC Mar 2, 1990 and Jun 13, 1991; trip by the author to Cedar Springs, Jun 30, 1990; *The Grand Rapids Press,* Oct 14, 1973.

217–219   RNM, pp. 928–931; Buzhardt Papers, Cooper Library, Strom Thurmond Institute, Clemson University; Jones/JMC May 19, 1993.

219–220   Albert/JMC Jul 24, 1990; NYT, Oct 18, 1973; Rodino/JMC Sep 28, 1990.

220–224   RNM, pp. 931–935; Richardson/JMC Mar 3 and 5, 1990; Richardson, *The Creative Balance,* pp. 39–47; NPP: Transcript of Ziegler press conference for Oct 20, 1973; Anthony Lukas, *Nightmare,* pp. 417–441; letter dated Jul 7, 1991, from John Chancellor to the author.

224–225   Timmons/JMC Sep 22, 1992; NPP: Timmons Memorandum to President Nixon, Oct 22, 1973.

225   O'Neill/JMC Jan 24, 1991; WP, Oct 21–22, 1973.

        GRF/JMC Apr 24, 1992; GRF/TA.

225–227   WP, NYT, Oct 21–23, 1973; Albert/JMC Jul 24, 1990;
               GRF/JMC Apr 24, 1992; CR for Oct 23, 1973; Albert, *Little
               Giant,* pp. 362–363.

228   RNM, pp. 935, 943–944; Albert/JMC Jul 24, 1990;
               Rodino/JMC Sep 28, 1990.

14. PASSAGE

229–231   Hartmann/JMC Jun 19 and 28, 1991; Heal, pp. 109–110;
               GRFLIB: "Nomination of Gerald R. Ford to be Vice Presi-
               dent of the United States," *House and Senate Reports, House
               and Senate Hearings, 93rd Congress, 1st Session, 1973.*

232   Howard Cannon/JMC Aug 6, 1991; Rodino/JMC Sep 28,
               1990; GRFLIB: Copy of letter dated Oct 22, 1973, from Ford
               to Senator Howard Cannon, Chairman of the Senate Rules
               Committee.

232–233   Jerry Zeifman/JMC Nov 6, 1991; Rodino/JMC Sep 28, 1990;
               Albert/JMC Jul 24, 1990.

233–249   GRFLIB: Record of Hearings before the Senate Rules Com-
               mittee, Nov 1, 5, 7, and 14, 1973, pp. 1–373.

250–251   GRFLIB: Testimony of Senator Birch Bayh in Hearings before
               the Senate Rules Committee, pp. 144–164. Report of the
               Senate Rules Committee on the Nomination of Gerald R.
               Ford to be Vice President of the United States, pp. 1–110; roll-
               call vote in the Rules Committee on Ford's nomination, p. 97;
               Senate vote on Ford's nomination, CR for Nov 27, 1973.

251   RNM, pp. 943–944; HIC, pp. 437–439; Charles Colson, *Born
               Again,* p. 156; Leon Jaworski, *The Right and the Power,* pp. 1–7.

251–254   RNM, pp. 945–948; Garment/JMC Sep 12 and 24, 1990, Mar
               14, 1991; NPP; Bush/Bruno Nov 9, 1973; WP, Nov 17, 1963;
               CQ, p. 432; Mitchell/Bruno Nov 2, 1973.

254–257   GRFLIB: "Nomination of Gerald R. Ford to be Vice President of the United States," *Hearings before the Committee on the Judiciary, House of Representatives,* November 15, 16, 19, 20, 21, and 26, 1973, pp. 1–729; GRF/JMC Nov 13, 1990; Rodino/JMC Sep 28, 1990; CR for December 6, 1973; Albert/JMC Jul 24, 1990; GRFLIB: Video of Gerald Ford swearing in as Vice President on December 6, 1973.

258   HAK/JMC Apr 2, 1991; Bush/Bruno Dec 7, 1973.

15. THE NARROW PATH

259   GRFLIB: VPDS; GRF/JMC Apr 26–30, 1990; GRF/TA; House Library; NYT, Nov 7, 1973; Susan Ford/JMC Sep 7, 1991.

261   RNM, p. 968; PDD; HIC, p. 449; FD, p. 110; RNM p. 970; Ray Price/JMC Dec 6, 1990.

261–262   CQ; Rodino/JMC Sep 28, 1990.

262   NPP: White House Press Office; CQ.

262–263   NPP; CQ; Mitchell/Bruno, Nov 21, 1973; *The Christian Science Monitor,* Dec 17, 1973; Barry Goldwater, *Goldwater,* p. 338; Goldwater/JMC May 4, 1990.

263–265   GRFLIB: VPDS; Video tapes. WP, Jan 7, 1974; GRF/JMC Apr 26–30, 1990; Hartmann, *Palace Politics,* pp. 81–83; Hartmann/JMC, Jun 19 and 28, 1991; Haig/JMC Nov 6, 1989; Ford/TA.

265   PDD; VPDS; GRF/TA.

265–266   GRF/JMC Apr 24–30, 1990, and Apr 22–25, 1992.

266–268   VPDS; Henry Kissinger/JMC Apr 2, 1991; Brent Scowcroft/JMC Feb 13, 1990, and Aug 13, 1991; GRF/JMC Apr 24–30, 1990; John Rhodes/JMC Dec 4, 1990; Mel Laird/JMC Jun 5, 1991; Hartmann/JMC Jun 19 and 28, 1991; Marsh/JMC Jun 28, 1991.

268–270   U.S. Dept of Defense biographical files; Marsh/JMC Jun 28, 1991; Don Rumsfeld/JMC Dec 9, 1991; Haig/JMC Nov 6, 1989, and Dec 20, 1990; *Richmond Times-Dispatch,* Mar 13, 1967.

270   Hartmann/JMC Jun 19 and 28, 1991; Marsh/JMC May 16, Jul 11 and 30, 1990.

270–271   RNM, 974–975; NPP.

271–272   CQ, p. 568; PDD; NPP; RNM, pp. 989, 992, 993; Rhodes/JMC Dec 4, 1990.

272   NPP; GRF/TA; GRF/JMC Apr 27, 1990.

273–275   Hartmann/JMC Jun 19 and 28, 1991; Marsh/JMC Jun 28, 1991; GRF/JMC Jun 24–30, 1990; VPDS; GRFLIB: Ford Scrapbooks; *London Times,* Mar 17, 1974; NYT, Mar 9 and 17, 1974; NPP; GRF/JMC Apr 22–25, 1992; *New Republic,* Apr 13, 1974.

275–276   NAR/JMC May, 1974; *Newsweek,* Jun 3, 1974; Hugh Morrow/JMC Jun, 1974.

276–277   CQ; Rodino/JMC Sep 28, 1990; Jaworski, *The Right and the Power,* p. 18; NPP; RNM, pp. 1000–1001; Jerry Jones/JMC Aug 31, 1991; FD, p. 203.

277–278   GRFLIB: VPDS; GRF/JMC Apr 24–30, 1990, and Apr 22–25, 1992; GRFLIB: Ford Scrapbooks.

278–280   PDD; Kissinger, *Years of Upheaval,* p. 1124; RNM, p. 1017; CQ; RNM, p. 1019; Waggoner/JMC Oct 16, 1991; RNM, p. 1020; FD, p. 221.

280   Korologos/JMC May 27, 1993.

280–281   CQ; FD p. 262; PDD; GRF/TA; Timmons/JMC Sep 22, 1992; RNM p. 1047; WP, Jul 24, 1974; RNM p. 1050; Haig/JMC Nov 3, 1989; HIC, p. 471.

282   RNM p. 1050; Waggoner/JMC Oct 16, 1991; CQ; WP and
            NYT, Jul 25, 1974; FD p. 264; HIC, p. 472; Lukas, *Nightmare,*
            p. 519; RNM, p. 1052.

282–283   Imogene Buzhardt/JMC, Jan 14, 1993; Buzhardt papers, Spe-
            cial Collections, Robert Muldrow Cooper Library, Strom
            Thurmond Institute, Clemson University; HIC, p. 473;
            RNM, p. 1052; FD, pp. 271–274; WP, Feb 1, 1975: Walter
            Pincus interview of Buzhardt; Pincus/JMC Feb 8, 1993; NPP;
            RNM, pp. 1052–1053.

283–284   VPDS; GRF/JMC Apr 24–30, 1990.

284   Kissinger, *Years of Upheaval,* p. 1196.

            CQ; RNM, pp. 1053–1054.

285   McKee/JMC Aug 9, 1976; HIC, p. 476.

            CQ; WP, Jul 30, 1974.

285–286   Mitchell/Bruno Aug 2, 1974; Garment/JMC Mar 14, 1991.

286–287   PDD; U.S. Secret Service logs; WP, Feb 1, 1975: Walter
            Pincus interview of Buzhardt; Pincus/JMC Jan 8, 1993;
            Haig/TA; Haig/JMC Nov 6, 1989; Buzhardt papers, Special
            Collections, Robert Muldrow Cooper Library, Strom Thur-
            mond Institute, Clemson University; Marsh/JMC Sep 3, Nov
            24, Dec 1, 1992, and Mar 31, 1993.

            (Author's note: In the Nixon Presidential Papers it is noted,
            "as per Nell Yates," that from July 28 to August 6, 1974, no
            log was recorded for President Nixon's meetings and tele-
            phone calls. Only Haig could have ordered or authorized
            Yates to stop keeping the log for this sensitive period. How-
            ever, the Secret Service did keep some records.)

287   RNM, p. 1057; HIC, pp. 476–477; Kissinger, *Years of
            Upheaval,* p. 1198.

288   VPDS; GRF/JMC Apr 26–30, 1990; Heal, p. 123; O'Neill,
            Man of the House, p. 264; O'Neill/JMC Jan 24, 1991; Hart-
            mann/JMC Jun 19 and 28, 1991.

16. PROPOSITION

289–290   HIC, pp. 478–480; RNM, p. 1057.

290–291   VPDS; Heal, pp. 1–3; GRF testimony to the House Judi-
            ciary Subcommittee on Criminal Justice, Oct 17, 1974;
            GRF/TA; GRF/JMC Apr 26–30, 1990; PP, pp. 126–128;
            HIC, p. 480.

291   Buzhardt papers, Cooper Library, Strom Thurmon Insitute,
            Clemson University; WP, Feb 1, 1975, Pincus interview of
            Buzhardt; HIC, p. 481.

291–292   VPDS; PP, p. 128; Hartmann/TA; Hartmann/JMC Jun 19
            and 28, 1991.

292–294   VPDS (Although, Haig's presence was deliberately misiden-
            tified; Hartmann told Ford's secretary to show the visit as
            "Secretary Morton"); Heal, pp. 3–5; GRF/JMC Apr 26–30,
            1990; GRF testimony to the House Judiciary Subcommittee,
            Oct 17, 1974; HIC, pp. 482–483.

            (Author's note: Haig, asked by the author why he proposed
            the pardon deal, replied, "I had no choice. I was told to."
            Haig/JMC Nov 6, 1989.

            Haig wrote in his 1992 book, *Inner Circles,* that he told Ford:
            "Mr. Vice President, the President has made up his mind to
            resign." Ford wrote, some twelve years closer to the event,
            that Haig told him: "I just don't know what the President is
            going to do." Ford testified to Congress, about ten weeks
            after their meeting, that Haig advised him that Nixon had
            not decided to resign, but might do so if offered a pardon.
            The difference is significant.)

294–295	Heal, p. 5; GRF/JMC Apr 24–30, 1990, and Apr 22–25, 1992; Marsh/JMC May 16, Jul 11 and 30, 1990.
295–296	Heal, pp. 6–7; PP, pp. 130–131; Hartmann/JMC Jun 19 and 28, 1991; GRF/JMC Apr 24–30, 1990.
296	PP, p. 132.
296–297	PP, p. 133; Heal, p. 8; GRF/JMC Apr 24–30, 1990.
297	Timmons/JMC Sep 22, 1992.
297–298	Price/JMC Dec 6, 1990.
298	RNM, 1058.
298–299	VPDS; Betty Beale/JMC Sep 1, 1992; GRF/JMC Apr 24–30, 1990; Betty Ford/TA; Betty Ford/JMC Sep 1, 1989, and Apr 30, 1990; GRF/TA; Heal, pp. 8–10.
299–300	Heal, p. 10; GRF/JMC Apr 24–30, 1990.
300	GRF/JMC Apr 24–30, 1990; VPDS; Heal, pp. 10–11.
300–302	Heal, p. 11; GRF/JMC Apr 24–30, 1990; Marsh/JMC May 16, Jul 11 and 30, 1990, Mar 8 and Jun 20, 1991.
302	GRF/JMC Apr 22–25, 1992.
302–303	VPDS; GRF/TA; Heal, pp. 11–12; GRF/JMC Apr 24–30, 1990; Griffin/JMC Jun 28, 1990.
303	VPDS; NYT, (Aug 4, 1974.)
303–304	Wiggins/JMC Nov 12, 1991; RNM, p. 1059.
304–305	Haig/JMC Nov 6, 1989; FD, 337; Griffin/JMC Jun 28, 1990.

305	VPDS; Ford/TA; Ford/JMC Apr 26, 1990; PPS, pp. 136–137.
308	Ford/JMC Nov 13, 1990.
	Mitchell/Bruno Aug 2, 1974.

17. REVERSAL

309	RNM, p. 1061; HIC, p. 487; Prime/JMC Dec 6, 1990.
309–310	VPDS; Hartmann/JMC Jun 19 and 28, 1991; PPS pp. 138–143; Thad Cochran/JMC Jul 29, 1992.
310–311	FD, pp. 348–349 and 352.
311	Griffin/JMC Jun 28, 1990; HIC, p. 489; RNM, p. 1061
	NYT, Aug 4, 1974.
311–312	HIC, pp. 489–491; RNM, pp. 1062–1063.
312	VPDS; Heal, pp. 15–16.
313–314	VPDS; Heal, p. 16; Hartmann/JMC Jun 19 and 28, 1991; Marsh/JMC Mar 8 and Jun 20, 1991.
314	Rhodes/JMC Dec 4, 1990; Timmons/JMC Sep 22, 1992; *Goldwater*, p. 350.
314–315	NPP, Weekly Compilation of Presidential Documents; RNM, p. 1063.
315	Heal, p. 18; Betty Ford/JMC Apr 30, 1990.
315–316	FD, p. 389; Goldwater/JMC May 4, 1990.
316–318	Marsh/JMC Jun 28, 1991; GRF/JMC Apr 26–30, 1990, and Apr 22–25, 1992; Hartmann/JMC Jun 19 and 28, 1991; GRFLIB: Ford notes for the Cabinet meeting August 6, 1974; Kissinger, *Years of Upheaval*, pp. 1203–1205; RNM, p. 1066.

318–320	Heal, pp. 22–23; *Goldwater,* pp. 350–351; GRF/TA; GRF/JMC Apr 26–30, 1990; Hartmann/JMC Jun 19 and 28, 1991.
320	PDD; Timmons/JMC Sep 22, 1992; Korologos/JMC Mar 31, 1993.

18. DELIVERANCE

321–322	RNM, p. 1067; Goldwater/JMC May 4, 1990; Timmons/JMC Sep 22, 1992; GRF/JMC Apr 26–27, 1990; Kissinger/JMC Apr 2, 1991; Price/JMC Dec 6, 1990; RNM, pp. 848, 868, 874, 946, 947, 962, 968, 970, 971, 976, 977, 981, 989, 993, 994, 997, 998, 1005, 1041, 1042, 1044, 1051, 1053, 1054, 1056, 1057, 1058, 1059, 1061, 1062, 1064–1069 (Apr 29, 1973–Aug 6, 1974); CR for August 20, 1974: The House by a vote of 412–3 accepted the House Judiciary Committee Report on Impeachment.
322–323	RNM, pp. 1067–1068.
323	VPDS; GRF/TA; GRF/JMC Apr 26–30, 1990.
323–324	GRF/JMC Apr 26–30, 1990; Buchen/JMC Feb 15 and May 20, 1990, and Nov 2, 1992.
324–326	PP, pp. 153–157; Hartmann/JMC Jun 19 and 28, 1991; VPDS; GRF/JMC Apr 26–30, 1990; Haig/JMC Nov 6, 1989; Marsh/JMC Jun 20 and 28, 1991; Buchen/JMC Feb 15 and May 20, 1990; Heal, p. 26.
326	RNM, pp. 1069–1072.
327	NPP; Timmons/JMC Sep 22, 1992.
327–329	Bull/JMC Mar 5, 1991; Rhodes/JMC Dec 4, 1990; *Goldwater,* pp. 353–355; Goldwater/JMC May 4, 1990.
329	Goldwater/JMC May 4, 1990; Bradlee/JMC Mar 30, 1990.
	Goldwater/JMC May 4, 1990.

329–330	RNM, pp. 1073–1074.
330–331	Chris Vick/JMC Mar 6, 1991; Kissinger, *Years of Upheaval*, p. 1206; RNM, p. 1074.
331	VPDS; GRF/JMC Apr 27, 1990; Marsh/JMC Sep 3, 1992.
	GRF/JMC Apr 27, 1990.
332	RNM, p. 1076; Kissinger, *Years of Upheaval*, p. 1207.
332–335	VPDS; GRF/TA; Heal, pp. 28–30; GRF/JMC Apr 26–30, 1990, and Apr 22–25, 1992.

19. TRANSITION

336–338	GRF/JMC Apr 27, 1990; Heal, p. 30; Marsh, May 16, Jul 11 and 30, 1990; Heal, p. 32; O'Neill/JMC Jan 24, 1991.
338–339	PP, pp. 159–160; Heal, p. 33; GRF/JMC Apr 27 and 29, 1990.
339–340	HIC. pp. 500–501; Leon Jaworski, *The Right and the Power*, Reader's Digest Press, 1976, pp. 217–219.
340	PDD; RNM, pp. 1079–1080.
340–341	GRF/JMC Sep 1, 1989, and Apr 29 and 30, 1990; Betty Ford/JMC Sep 1, 1989; GRF/TA; GRFLIB: NBC video of Ford appearance, Aug 8, 1974; WP, Aug 9, 1974.
341–342	GRF/JMC, Letter of reflections, May 14, 1990, Appendix B.
342	Kissinger, *Years of Upheaval*, p. 1212; RNM, pp. 1084–1085; Lukas, *Nightmare*, p. 566.
342–343	GRF/JMC Apr 29 and 30, 1990; Buchen/JMC Feb 15, 1990, and May 20, 1992; GRFLIB: Buchen Files, Memorandum for the Vice President, Aug 8, 1974; Marsh/JMC May 16, 1990; Rumsfeld/JMC Dec 9, 1991.

343–344	RNM, pp. 1085–1086.

344   RNM, pp. 848–849; Price/JMC Dec 6, 1990; GRFLIB Audiovisual Materials Section, television recording by the White
House Communications Agency.

344–346   GRFLIB Audiovisual Materials Section.

346–347   GRF/JMC Apr 29–30, 1990; GRF/JMC letter, May 14, 1990;
PP, pp. 169–170.

347   Kissinger, *Years of Upheaval,* p. 1214.

(Author's note: The original of Nixon's letter of resignation
is in a vault at the National Archives in Washington, D.C.
McNitt/JMC 6/73. However, an archivist with the Nixon
Presidential Papers in Arlington, Virginia, states there is evidence that Nixon signed other "originals." Where are those
"originals" now? "Ask Sotheby's," the Nixon archivist said.)

347–350   Marsh/JMC Mar 8 and Jun 20, 1991; Friedersdorf/JMC Feb
28, 1992; GRFLIB Audiovisual Materials Section; GRFPP,
p. 1; GRF/JMC Apr 29–30, 1990; Edmund Morris/JMC Jul
12, 1993; Paul/O'Neill/JMC Mar 7, 1990.

350   GRF/JMC Jun 30, 1990.

20. THE LEGACY AND THE PARDON

351   GRFLIB: PDD; GRF/JMC Apr 30, 1990; Albert/JMC Jul 24,
1990; Friedersdorf/JMC Feb 28, 1992; Korologos/JMC Feb 5,
1990.

351–353   PDD; GRFPP, p. 3; Michael Ford/JMC Feb 8, 1991;
Jones/JMC Aug 31, 1991; PP, pp. 174–179; Hartmann/JMC
Jun 19 and 28, 1991; PP, pp. 167–168; Marsh/JMC Jun 28,
1991; GRF/JMC Apr 30, 1990.

353–354   Rumsfeld/JMC Dec 9, 1991.

354   PDD; Seidman/JMC Sep 20, 1990.

354–355   PDD; Kissinger/JMC Apr 2, 1991; GRF/JMC Apr 30, 1990;
                Scowcroft/JMC Aug 13, 1991; GRFLIB: Cable from Ford to
                Brezhnev, Aug 9, 1974 (declassified in 1992).

355–356   GRFLIB: Transcript of White House press conference, Aug
                9, 1974.

356–357   Heal, p. 38; GRF/JMC Apr 22–25, 1992; PP, pp. 177–178;
                Hartmann/JMC Jun 19 and 28, 1991; Rumsfeld/JMC Dec 9,
                1991.

357   PDD; Jones/JMC Aug 31, 1991;GRF/JMC Apr 27, 1990.

357–358   PDD; GRF/JMC Apr 29–30, 1990; Heal, p. 146;
                Kissinger/JMC Apr 2, 1991.

358–359   PDD; Marsh/JMC Jun 20, 1991; Scowcroft/JMC Jul 16, 1992;
                GRFLIB National Security files; *The Jennifer Project* by Clyde
                W. Burleson.

359–360   Becker/JMC Jul 9 and 10, 1991.

360   GRFLIB: Transcript of White House press conference, Aug
                12, 1974; Jones/JMC June 1 and 2, 1992.

360–362   PDD; GRFPP: Address to a Joint Session of Congress, August
                12, 1974; GRF/JMC Apr 22–25, 1992; GRFLIB Audiovisual
                Materials Section; Hedley Donovan, *Roosevelt to Reagan, A
                Reporter's Encounters with Nine Presidents*, p. 134.

362   GRF/JMC Apr 22–25, 1992; CQ, p. 768; Jaworski, *The Right
                and the Power,* p. 219.

362–363   Nixon, *In the Arena,* pp. 19–20; Jaworski, *The Right and the
                Power,* pp. 222–223.

363–365   Jaworski, *The Right and the Power,* pp. 223–238; National

Archives: Documents of the Watergate Special Prosecutor; Henry Ruth/JMC Dec 30, 1992.

365–366   GRF/JMC Apr 22–25, 1992; Marsh/JMC Aug 12, 1991; Rourke/JMC Jan 25, 1991; HIC, 500; CR; NPP: Ronald Ziegler Files; AG Saxbe to President Ford Sep 6, 1974; Becker/JMC Jul 9–10, 1991; CQ, p. 794; PP, p. 246; Jones/JMC Jun 2, 1992.

366–367   PDD; GRF/JMC Apr 22–25, 1992; Mark Hatfield/JMC Jul 31, 1990; GRFPP, pp. 22–28.

367–368   PDD; Harlow/GRF Aug 11, 1974 (Appendix C); GRF/JMC Apr 22–25, 1992; Rockefeller/JMC Aug 19, 1974; letter dated December 2, 1991, from Joseph E. Persico to the author.

368–369   WP, Aug 21, 1974; CR, Aug 20, 1974, House Judiciary Committee Report on Impeachment; CQ, pp. 772, 774–779.

369   GRF/JMC Apr 22–25, 1992.

369–370   GRF/JMC Apr 22–25, 1992; Gallup Poll, Aug 20, 1979; *Time,* Sep 2, 1973; Hartmann/JMC Jun 19 and 28, 1991; Buchen/JMC Feb 2 and May 20, 1992.

370–371   Garment/JMC Sep 12 and 24, 1990, and Mar 14, 1991.

371   Buchen/JMC Feb 2 and May 20, 1992; GRF/JMC Apr 26, 1990.

371–373   GRFPP, pp. 56–66; GRF/JMC Apr 30, 1990.

373   Jaworski, *The Right and the Power,* pp. 240–241.

373–375   Ford/TA; Ford/JMC Apr 30, 1990; PP, pp. 257–261; Hartmann/JMC Jun 19 and 28, 1991; Buchen/TA; Buchen/JMC Feb 15, 1990; Marsh/JMC Jun 20, 1991.

375–376   GRF/JMC Apr 30, 1990; Marsh/JMC May 16, 1990.

376   Buchen/TA; Len Colodny and Robert Gettlin, *Silent Coup,* p. 430; Becker/JMC Jul 9–10, 1991.

376–377   GRF/JMC Apr 30, 1990; Kissinger/JMC Apr 2, 1991.

377–378   Buchen/JMC Feb 15, 1990.

378–379   Buchen/JMC Feb 15, 1990; Jaworski, *The Right and the Power,* pp. 241–242; GRFLIB: Letter from Jaworski to Buchen.

379   GRF/JMC Apr 30, 1990; Becker/JMC Jul 9–10, 1991.

379–380   Becker/JMC Jul 9–10, 1991.

380–381   Becker/JMC Jul 9–10, 1991; Colodny and Gettlin, *Silent Coup,* p. 437; Buchen/JMC Feb 15, 1990.

381–382   GRF/JMC Apr 30, 1990.

382   terHorst/JMC Jan 30, 1993; Friedersdorf/JMC Feb 16, 1993.

382–383   GRFLIB: PDD; GRF/JMC Apr 30, 1990; *Goldwater,* pp. 356–357; O'Neill, *Man of the House,* p. 268.

383–384   Heal, pp. 175–176; Marsh/JMC Jun 20, 1991.

384   GRFLIB Audiovisual Materials Section; GRFPP, pp. 101–104.

384–385   WP, NYT, *Los Angeles Times,* Sep 9, 1974; CQ, pp. 789–795; Friedersdorf/JMC Feb 16, 1993.

385–386   GRFLIB: White House press transcripts, Sep 8, 1974, and thereafter; Rhodes/JMC Dec 4, 1990; CQ, p. 800 and thereafter; Jaworski, *The Right and the Power,* pp. 247–248; CR, Sep 8, 1974, and thereafter.

386   GRF/JMC Apr 30, 1990.

GRFLIB Presidential Handwritting File; GRF/JMC Apr 30, 1990.

386–387   Heal, p. 185; GRF/JMC Apr 22–25, 1992; Goodpaster/JMC Jan 16, 1991; Jones/JMC Aug 31, 1991.

387–388   CR, HR, p. 1367, Sep 16, 1974; CQ, pp. 801–803; Buchen/JMC May 20, 1992; Marsh/JMC Jun 28, 1991.

388–390   Marsh/JMC Jun 28, 1991; Buchen/JMC May 20, 1992; GRF/JMC Apr 30, 1990; Rodino/JMC Sep 28, 1990; Albert/JMC Jul 24, 1990.

390–391   GRFLIB: PDD; GRF/JMC Apr 30, 1990; Library of the U.S. House of Representatives, Report by the House Judiciary Subcommittee on Criminal Justice. Second Session of the Ninety-third Congress, Serial no. 60, for Thursday, Oct 17, 1974, U.S. Government Printing Office.

391–392   GRF/JMC Apr 30, 1990.

392   Paul O'Neill/JMC May 13, 1993; Marsh/JMC Jun 26, 1993; GRF/JMC Apr 16–30, 1990; *America Votes, 1974.*

21. THE RECORD

393–394   Kissinger/JMC Apr 2, 1991.

394–395   Observations by the author; Rex Scouten/JMC May 14, 1993.

395–396   Heal, pp. 213–220; Kissinger/JMC Apr 2, 1991.

396–397   GRF/HD, 1953; GRF/JMC Apr 25, 1990; GRF/TA; Heal, pp. 248–257; GRF/JMC Sep 1, 1989.

398–399   Richard G. Head, Frisco W. Short, and Robert C. McFarlane, *Crisis Resolution: Presidential Decision Making in the Mayaguez and Korean Confrontations*, pp. 101–148; Scowcroft/JMC Feb 13, 1990; GRF/JMC Sep 1, 1989, and Apr 27, 1990; Roy

Rowan, *The Four Days of Mayaguez;* Annenberg Washington Program Conference on the *Mayaguez* Crisis, July 19–20, 1990; Michael Beschloss, editor, *Presidents, Television, and Foreign Crises,* Annenberg Project on Television and U.S. Foreign Policy; William Hyland, *Mortal Rivals,* pp. 113–114; NYT, May 16, 1975; Richard E. Neustadt and Ernest R. May, *Thinking in Time: The Uses of History for Decision Makers,* pp. 58–66.

399–400   Heal, pp. 298–306; Hyland, *Mortal Rivals,* p. 128; GRF/JMC Apr 24, 1992; Marsh/JMC Jun 3, 1993.

400–402   David Gergen, editor, *The Ford Presidency, A Portrait of the First Two Years,* pp. 1–5; Roger Porter, *Presidential Decision Making,* p. 38; GRF/JMC Apr 26, 1990; Heal, p. 125; PP, pp. 296–300; GRFPP for Oct 8, 1974, pp. 228–238; Seidman/JMC May 15, 1993; Seidman, *Full Faith and Credit,* pp. 17–32.

403–404   GRF/JMC Apr 22, 1992; Carol Cox/JMC May 14, 1993; *Budget Baselines, Historical Data, and Alternatives for the Future,* pp. 279–283, 302, 346; GRFLIB: *CQ Almanac for 1976.*

404   GRFLIB: Domestic Council Files—NYC Fiscal Crisis; Charles J. Orlebeke, "Saving New York: The Ford Administration and the New York City Fiscal Crisis," draft of Mar 8, 1989; Bernard J. Firestone and Alexej Ugrinsky, *Gerald R. Ford and the Politics of Post-Watergate America,* volume 1, part viii—The New York City Fiscal Crisis (Hofstra University and Greenwood Press).

404–408   GRF/JMC Apr 26–27, 1990, and Apr 21–22, 1993; Betty Ford/JMC Apr 30 and Jul 20, 1990; Stuart Spencer/JMC Nov 7, 1990; Nelson Rockefeller/JMC Summer, 1975; Cheney/TA; Jules Witcover, *Marathon: The Pursuit of the Presidency 1972–1976,* pp. 33–103, 371–511, 530–656; GRFPP Presidential Campaign Debate of October 6, 1976, pp. 2408–2436; GRF/TA.

408–409	Dick Cheney/JMC Jun 9, 1993.

409–410   *America Votes, 1976*; GRF/JMC Apr 21–22, 1993.

EPILOGUE

412   Germond/JMC May 18, 1993.

Kempton, quoted in *The New Yorker,* March 1, 1993.

414   GRF/JMC Apr 21, 22, 1993.

415   Goldwater/JMC May 4, 1990; Edmund Morris/JMC Jul 12, 1993.

416   Paul O'Neill/JMC Jun 5, 1992: Carol Cox/JMC May 14, 1993; *Budget Baselines, Historical Data, and Alternatives for the Future,* pp. 279–283, 302, 346.

BIBLIOGRAPHY

Agnew, Spiro T. *Go Quietly . . . or Else.* New York: William Morrow and Co., 1980.

Albert, Carl, with Danney Goble. *Little Giant.* Norman, OK: University of Oklahoma Press, 1990.

Ambrose, Stephen E. *Nixon—Ruin and Recovery 1973–1990.* New York: Simon & Schuster, 1991.

Baker, Richard A., and Roger H. Davidson, eds. *First Among Equals—Outstanding Senate Leaders of the Twentieth Century.* Washington: Congressional Quarterly for The Dirksen Congressional Center, 1991.

Barber, James David. *The Presidential Character: Predicting Performance in the White House.* Englewood Cliffs, NJ: Prentice-Hall, 1977.

Belin, David. *November 22, 1963: You are the Jury.* New York: Quadrangle/The New York Times Book Co., 1973.

———. *Final Disclosure, The Full Truth About the Assassination of President Kennedy.* New York: Charles Scribner's Sons, 1988.

Bibby, John F., and Roger Davidson. *On Capitol Hill: Studies in the Legislative Process.* New York: Holt, Rinehart & Winston, 1967.

Breslin, Jimmy. *How the Good Guys Finally Won.* New York: Viking Press, 1975.

Burleson, Clyde W. *The Jennifer Project.* Englewood Cliffs, NJ: Prentice Hall, 1977.

Casserly, John J. *The Ford White House: The Diary of a Speechwriter.* Boulder, CO: Colorado Associated University Press, 1977.

Cohen, Richard, and Jules Witcover. *A Heartbeat Away.* Washington: Washington Post Books, 1974.

Colby, William. *Honorable Men: My Life in the CIA.* New York: Simon & Schuster, 1978.

Colodny, Len, and Robert Gettlin. *Silent Coup*. New York: St. Martin's Press, 1991.

Colson, Charles W. *Born Again*. New York: Bantam, 1976.

Congressional Quarterly, Inc. *President Ford: The Man and His Record*. Washington: Congressional Quarterly, 1974.

Cross, Mercer, and Elder Witt, eds. *Watergate: Chronology of a Crisis*. Washington: Congressional Quarterly, 1975.

Dean, John. *Blind Ambition*. New York: Simon & Schuster, 1976.

Dougherty, Richard. *Goodbye, Mr. Christian*. Garden City, NY: Doubleday & Co., 1973.

Drew, Elizabeth. *Washington Journal—The Events of 1973–1974*. New York: Random House, 1974.

Ehrlichman, John. *Witness to Power*. New York: Simon & Schuster, 1982.

Eisenhower, Julie Nixon. *Pat Nixon, The Untold Story*. New York: Simon & Schuster, 1986.

Feerick, John D. *The Twenty-Fifth Amendment: Its Complete History and Earliest Applications*. New York: Fordham University Press, 1976.

Firestone, Bernard J., and Alexej Ugrinsky. *Gerald R. Ford and the Politics of Post-Watergate America*. Westport, CT: Greenwood Press, 1993.

Ford, Betty, with Chris Chase. *The Times of My Life*. New York: Harper & Row, 1978.

———. *A Glad Awakening*. Garden City, NY: Doubleday & Co., 1987.

Ford, Gerald R. *A Time to Heal*. New York: Harper & Row, 1979.

———. *Selected Speeches*. Arlington, VA: R. W. Beatty, 1973.

———. *Humor and the Presidency*. New York: Arbor House, 1987.

Ford, Gerald R., and John R. Stiles. *Portrait of an Assassin*. New York: Simon & Schuster, 1965.

Gergen, David R., ed. *The Ford Presidency*. Washington: White House Office of Communications, 1976.

Goldwater, Barry M., with Jack Casserly. *Goldwater*. New York: Doubleday & Co., 1988.

Greene, John Robert. *The Limits of Power: The Nixon and Ford Administrations*. Bloomington, IN: Indiana University Press, 1992.

Haig, Alexander M., Jr., with Charles McCarry. *Inner Circles*. New York: Warner Books, 1992.

Haldeman, H. R., with Joseph DiMona. *The Ends of Power*. New York: Times Books, 1978.

Hartmann, Robert T. *Palace Politics*. New York: McGraw-Hill Book Co., 1980.

Head, Richard G., Frisco W. Short, and Robert C. McFarlane. *Crisis Resolution: Presidential Decision Making in the Mayaguez and Korean Confrontations.* Boulder, CO: Westview Press, 1978.

Hersey, John. *The President: A Minute-by-Minute Account of a Week in the Life of Gerald Ford.* New York: Alfred A. Knopf, 1975.

Hyland, William. *Mortal Rivals: Superpower Relations from Nixon to Reagan.* New York: Random House, 1987.

Isaacson, Walter. *Kissinger.* New York: Simon & Schuster, 1992.

Jaworski, Leon. *The Right and the Power.* New York: Reader's Digest Press, 1976.

Kennerly, David Hume. *Shooter.* New York: Newsweek Books, 1979.

Kissinger, Henry. *Years of Upheaval.* Boston: Little, Brown and Co., 1982.

Kutler, Stanley. *The Wars of Watergate.* New York: Alfred A. Knopf, 1990.

Lankevich, George J. *Gerald R. Ford—Chronology—Documents—Bibliographical Aids.* Dobbs Ferry, NY: Oceana Publications, Inc., 1977.

Liddy, G. Gordon. *Will—The Autobiography of G. Gordon Liddy.* New York: St. Martin's Press, 1980.

Lukas, J. Anthony. *Nightmare: The Underside of the Nixon Years.* New York: Viking Press, 1976.

MacDougall, Malcolm D. *We Almost Made It.* New York: Crown Publishers, 1977.

Maresca, John J. *To Helsinki—The Conference on Security and Cooperation in Europe, 1973–1975.* Durham, NC: Duke University Press, 1985.

Mollenhoff, Clark R. *The Man Who Pardoned Nixon.* New York: St. Martin's Press, 1976.

Nader, Ralph. *Gerald R. Ford: Republican Congressman from Michigan.* Washington: Grossman Publishers for the Ralph Nader Congress Project, 1972.

Nessen, Ron. *It Sure Looks Different from the Inside.* New York: Simon & Schuster, 1978.

Nixon, Richard. *RN: The Memoirs of Richard Nixon.* New York: Grosset & Dunlap, 1978.

———. *In the Arena: A Memoir of Victory, Defeat, and Renewal.* New York: Simon & Schuster, 1990.

O'Neill, Thomas P., with William Novak. *Man of the House.* New York: Random House, 1987.

Osborne, John. *White House Watch: The Ford Years.* Washington: New Republic Books, 1977.

Parmet, Herbert S. *Richard Nixon and His America.* Boston: Little, Brown and Co., 1990.

Peabody, Robert L. *Leadership in Congress*. Boston: Little, Brown and Co., 1976.

Persico, Joseph E. *The Imperial Rockefeller: A Biography of Nelson A. Rockefeller*. New York: Simon & Schuster, 1982.

Porter, Roger. *Presidential Decision-Making: The Economic Policy Board*. New York: Cambridge University Press, 1980.

Price, Raymond. *With Nixon*. New York: Viking Press, 1977.

Rather, Dan, and Gary Paul Gates. *The Palace Guard*. New York: Harper & Row, 1974.

Reeves, Richard. *A Ford, Not a Lincoln*. New York: Harcourt Brace Jovanovich, 1975.

Reichley, A. James. *Conservatives in an Age of Change: The Nixon and Ford Administrations*. Washington: Brookings Institution, 1981.

Reston, James, Jr. *The Lone Star: The Life of John Connally*. New York: Harper & Row, 1989.

Rockefeller, Nelson A., Chairman. *Report to the President by the Commission on CIA Activities Within the United States*. Washington: Government Printing Office, 1975.

Rowan, Roy. *The Four Days of Mayaguez*. New York: W. W. Norton & Co., 1975.

Rozell, Mark J. *The Press and the Ford Presidency*. Ann Arbor: University of Michigan Press, 1992.

Richardson, Elliot. *The Creative Balance*. London: Hamish Hamilton Ltd., 1976.

Safire, William. *Before the Fall*. Garden City, NY: Doubleday & Co., 1975.

Schapsmeier, Edward L., and Frederick M. Schapsmeier. *Gerald R. Ford's Date with Destiny: A Political Biography*. New York: Lang, 1989.

Seidman, William L. *Full Faith and Credit*. New York: Times Books, 1993.

Shaffer, Samuel. *On and Off the Floor*. New York: Newsweek Books, 1980.

Shogan, Robert. *The Riddle of Power: Presidential Leadership from Truman to Bush*. New York: Dutton, 1991.

Sidey, Hugh. *Portrait of a President*. New York: Harper & Row, 1975.

Simon, William. *A Time for Truth*. New York: Reader's Digest Press, 1978.

Sirica, John J. *To Set the Record Straight*. New York: Norton, 1979.

Tames, George. *Eye on Washington*. New York: HarperCollins, 1990.

terHorst, Jerald F. *Gerald Ford and the Future of the Presidency*. New York: Third Press, 1974.

Thompson, Kenneth W., ed. *The Ford Presidency, Twenty-two Intimate Perspectives of Gerald R. Ford*. Lanham, MD: University Press of America, 1988.

———. *The Nixon Presidency, Twenty-two Intimate Perspectives of Richard M. Nixon*. Lanham, MD: University Press of America, 1987.

Thompson, Richard E. *Revenue Sharing: A New Era in Federalism?* Washington: Revenue Sharing Advisory Service, 1973.

Turner, Michael. *The Vice President as Policy Maker: Rockefeller in the Ford White House*. Westport, CT: Greenwood Press, 1982.

U.S. Congress. Senate Committee on Rules and Administration. *Nomination of Gerald R. Ford of Michigan to be Vice President of the United States. Hearings and Report*. Washington: Government Printing Office, 1973.

U.S. Congress. House Committee on the Judiciary. *Nomination of Gerald R. Ford to be Vice President of the United States. Hearings*. Washington: Government Printing Office, 1973.

Vestal, Bud. *Jerry Ford Up Close*. New York: Coward, McCann & Geoghegan, 1974.

Weidenfeld, Sheila Rabb. *First Lady's Lady: With the Fords at the White House*. New York: Putnam, 1979.

White, Theodore H. *The Making of the President 1968*. New York: Atheneum Publishers, 1969.

———. *The Making of the President 1972*. New York: Atheneum Publishers, 1973.

———. *Breach of Faith*. New York: Atheneum Publishers, 1975.

Whitaker, John C. *Striking a Balance: Environment and Natural Resources Policy in the Nixon-Ford Years*. Washington and Stanford: American Enterprise Institute and the Hoover Institution on War and Peace, 1976.

Witcover, Jules. *Marathon, The Pursuit of the Presidency, 1972–1976*. New York: Viking Press, 1977.

Woodward, Bob, and Carl Bernstein. *The Final Days*. New York: Simon & Schuster, 1976.

AUTHOR'S INTERVIEWS

Carl Albert

Don Alexander

Marty Allen

R. W. Apple, Jr.

Trevor Armbrister

William Armstrong

Doug Bailey

Howard H. Baker Jr.

Richard Baker

Russell Baker

Bob Barrett

Birch Bayh

Betty Beale

Abraham Beame

George Beall

Benton Becker

David Belin

Doug Bennett

Michael Beschloss

Benjamin Bradlee

Clarence Brown

Lauren Brown

Phyllis Brown

Hal Bruno

Philip Buchen

James Buckley

Larry Buehndorf

Steve Bull

Patrick Butler

Imogene Buzhardt

Joseph Buzhardt

Jack Calkins

James Callaghan

Howard H. Callaway

Holly Cannon

Howard Cannon

Don Carey

Hugh Carey

John Chancellor

Thomas Chase

Dick Cheney

William Clements

Thad Cochran

William Colby

Len Colodny

Barber Conable

Richard Cook

Carol Cox

James Cross

Michael Deaver

Henry Diamond

Howard Dixon

Bob Dole

Mike Dunn

Michael Duval

Lawrence Eagleburger

John Ehrlichman

David Eisenhower

Stuart Eizenstat

Carl Elliott

Richard Fairbanks

John Fawcett

Robert Finch

Hamilton Fish

Betty Ford

Gerald R. Ford

James Ford
Janet Ford
Michael Ford
Richard Ford
Susan Ford
Tom Ford
Max Friedersdorf
Len Garment
Ron Geisler
Jack Germond
Barry Goldwater
Andrew Goodpaster
Howard Greene
Alan Greenspan
Robert Griffin
Alexander Haig
Mary Hansen
Richard Harnes
Robert Hartmann
Mark Hatfield
Richard Hauser
Richard Helms
John Hersey
William Hildenbrand
Judith R. Hope
Joan Howard
George Humphreys
William Hyland
Jerry Jones
Adele James Joyce
Don Kellerman
David Kennerly
Stan Kimmitt
Henry Kissinger
John Kornacki
Tom Korologos
Fritz Kraemer
Melvin Laird
Donna Larsen

Phil Larsen
Paul Laxalt
Mildred Leonard
Edward Levi
Howard Liebengood
Edward Luttwak
James T. Lynn
Ron MacMahan
Steven McConahey
Robert McFarlane
Robert McNamara
Mike Mansfield
John Marsh
David Mathews
Abner Mikva
Charles Minifie
Powell Moore
Hugh Morrow
John Nelson
Rosemary Niehuss
Paul O'Neill
Thomas P. O'Neill
Scott Parham
Richard Parsons
Margaret Pearson
Don Penny
Joseph Persico
Peter Peterson
Walter Pincus
Marty Plissner
Roger Porter
Ray Price
William Proxmire
Arthur Quern
Thomas Rath
James Reichley
James Reston
John Rhodes
Elliot Richardson

James D. Robinson III
Peter Rodino
Peter Rodman
William Rogers
Harriet Roll
Eugene Rossides
Russell Rourke
Roy Rowan
Donald Rumsfeld
Joyce Rumsfeld
Walter Russell
Henry S. Ruth Jr.
Rex Scouten
Brent Scowcroft
John Sears
William Seidman
Richard Norton Smith
Raymond Smock
Theodore Sorensen
Stuart Spencer
Joseph Sterne
Robert A. Taft
George terHorst

Jerald terHorst
Ed Terrell
Fred Thompson
Kenneth Thompson
William Timmons
Gordon VanderTill
Christine Vick
Joe Waggoner
Peter Wallison
C. D. Ward
Marjorie King Werner
F. Clifton White
George White
John Whittaker
Peggy Whyte
William Whyte
Charles Wiggins
Bob Wilson
Don Wilson
Jules Witcover
Allen Woods
Frank Zarb
Jerry Zeifman

UNPUBLISHED SOURCES

Gerald R. Ford Library Oral History: Gerald R. Ford interviews with Trevor Armbrister
    Other interviews by Trevor Armbrister

Howard H. Baker Jr.
James Baker
Bill Baroody
Bob Barrett
Benton Becker
Art Brown
Philip Buchen
Dean Burch
George Bush
James Cannon
James Cavanaugh
Dick Cheney
James Connor
Clem Conger
Robert Dole
Betty Ford
James Ford
Richard Ford
Susan Ford
Max Friedersdorf
Joe Garagiola
David Gergen
Clif Gettings
Barry Goldwater
Charles Goodell
William Greener
Alan Greenspan
Robert Griffin
Alexander Haig

Bryce Harlow
Robert Hartmann
Jerry Jones
David Kennerly
Henry Kissinger
Tom LaBelle
Melvin Laird
Mildred Leonard
Ed Levi
James T. Lynn
John O. Marsh
Charles McVeagh
Paul Miltich
Ron Nessen
Terry O'Donnell
Bob Orben
Paul O'Neill
Elliott Richardson
Nelson Rockefeller
Donald Rumsfeld
John Sawhill
Hugh Scott
Brent Scowcroft
William Seidman
William Simon
Stuart Spencer
Greg Willard
Frank Zarb
Billy Zeoli

Ford diaries 1949 through 1973

AUDIO-VISUAL

Videos:

President Nixon: Announcement of the nomination of Gerald Ford to be Vice President.

Representative Gerald Ford: Testimony before the Senate Rules Committee.

Vice President Ford: Oath of office as Vice President in the House of Representatives.

President Nixon: Resignation speech from the Oval Office.

President Nixon: Farewell to the White House staff in the East Room of the White House.

President Ford: Swearing in and Inaugural Speech in the East Room of the White House.

President Ford: First address to a Joint Session of Congress.

President Ford: First press conference.

President Ford: Second press conference.

Audios:

The Nixon tapes (List attached).

* A Key to Name Abbreviations

SBB	Stephen B. Bull	RGK	Richard G. Kleindeinst
APB	Alexander P. Butterfield	EMK	Egil M. "Bud" Krogh, Jr.
JPC	J. Phil Campbell	JNM	John N. Mitchell
CWC	Charles W. Colson	RAM	Richard A. Moore
JBC	John B. Connally	HEP	Henry E. Petersen
JWD	John W. Dean III	P	The President
JDE	John D. Ehrlichman	DBR	Donald B. Rice
LPG	Louis Patrick Gray III	CGR	Charles G. "Bebe" Rebozo
AMH	Alexander M. Haig, Jr.	WPR	William P. Rogers
HRH	H. R. Haldeman	MS	Manolo Sanchez
CMH	Clifford M. Hardin	GPS	George P. Shultz
TH	Thomas Hart	JCW	John C. Whitaker
EHH	E. Howard Hunt	WHO	White House Operator
HWK	Herbert W. Kalmbach	RMW	Rose Mary Woods
RLZ	Ronald L. Ziegler		

THE NIXON WHITE HOUSE TAPE RECORDINGS

Date	Conv. No.	Time	Participants*	Pages
03/23/71	472-004, 005, 006	10:16–10:19 AM	P, SBB	4
03/23/71	051-001	10:35–11:25 AM	P, CMH, JPC, et al.	
03/23/71	472-021	5:05–5:38 PM	P, CMH, JPC, GPS, JDE, JCW, DBR, JBC	43
04/19/71	482-017,482-018	3:03–3:34 PM	P, JDE, GPS, SBB	33
04/19/71	002-001, 002-002	3:04–3:09 PM	P, RGK (Telcon)	3
04/21/71	485-004	4:18–6:13 PM	P, JNM	4
05/05/71	491-014	9:35–10:15 AM	P, HRH	26
7/06/71	538-015	11:47 AM–12:45 PM	P, JNM, JDE, HRH	15
07/24/71	545-003	12:36–12:48 PM	P, JDE, EMK	6
10/08/71	587-003	10:04–10:46 AM	P, JNM, JDE, SBB	8
10/25/71	601–033	12:35–2:05 PM	P, JDE, SBB, APB	21
03/30/72	697-015	11:50 AM–12:15 PM	P, HRH	22
03/30/72	697-029	1:30–2:30 PM	P, HRH, CWC	42
06/20/72	342-027	2:20–3:30 PM	P, CWC	15
06/23/72	741-002	10:04–11:39 AM	P, HRH, RLZ	38
06/23/72	741-010	1:04–1:13 PM	P, HRH	2
06/23/72	343-036	2:20–2:45 PM	P, HRH, RLZ	13
06/30/72	347–004	12:57–2:10 PM	P, JNM, HRH	2
09/15/72	779-002	5:27–6:17 PM	P, HRH, JWD, SBB	43
09/15/72	779-002	5:27–6:17 PM	P, HRH, JWD	14
11/-/72	000-000	Unknown	CWC, EHH	17
01/04/73	393-013, 014	Unk after 5:15–5:50 PM	P,CWC	17
01/08/73	394-021/395-001	4:05–5:34 PM	P,CWC	15
02/13/73	854-017	9:48–10:52 AM	P,CWC	10
02/14/73	855-010	10:13–10:49 AM	P,CWC,SBB,MS	20
02/14/73	856-004	5:34–6:00 PM	P,JDE	15
02/16/73	858-003	9:08–9:38 AM	P,JDE,LPG	26
02/23/73	862-004	9:35–10:05 AM	P,JDE,SBB	17
02/23/73	862-006	10:08–10:52 AM	P,RGK	32
02/27/73	864-004	3:55–4:20 PM	P,JWD,SBB	21
02/28/73	865-014	9:12–10:23 AM	P,JWD,SBB	43
03/01/73	866-003	9:18–9:46 AM	P,JWD,MS	20

03/08/73	872-001	9:51–9:54 AM	P,JWD	2
03/13/73	878-014	12:42–2:00 PM	P,HRH,JWD,MS	76
03/17/73	882-012	1:25–2:10 PM	P,JWD,HRH	26
03/20/73	884-007	10:47 AM– 12:10 PM	P,HRH	3
03/20/73	885-007	6:00–7:10 PM	P,HRH	26
03/20/73	037-175, 176	7:29–7:43 PM	P,JWD,WHO	17
03/21/73	886-008	10:12–11:55 AM	P,JWD,HRH,SBB	126
03/21/73	421-018	5:20–6:01 PM	P,JWD,HRH,JDE	38
03/21/73	037-204, 205	7:53–8:24 PM	P,CWC,WHO (Telcon)	11
03/22/73	422-020	9:11–10:35 AM	P,HRH	58
03/22/73	422-033	1:57–3:43 PM	P,JWD,JDE,HRH, JNM	106
03/27/73	423-003	11:10 AM– 1:30 PM	P,HRH,JDE,RLZ	84
03/30/73	890-019	12:02–12:18 PM	P,RLZ,JDE	12
04/12/73	044-158	7:31–7:48 PM	P,CWC	17
04/14/73	428-019	8:55–11:31 AM	P,HRH,JDE	95
04/14/73	896-004, 005	1:55–3:55 PM	P,HRH,RLZ,JDE, MS	68
04/14/73	428-028	5:15–6:45 PM	P,HRH,JDE	51
04/14/73	038-034	11:02–11:16 PM	P,HRH	14
04/14/73	038-037	11:22–11:53 PM	P,JDE	25
04/15/73	896-006	10:35–11:15 AM	P,JDE,MS	25
04/15/73	038-042, 043	3:27–3:44 PM	P,HRH,WHO (Telcon)	21
04/16/73	897-003	9:50–9:59 AM	P,HRH,JDE,SBB	15
04/16/73	897-004	10:00–10:40 AM	P,JWD,SBB	55
04/16/73	897-009	10:50–11:04 AM	P,HRH,JDE	11
04/16/73	897-011	12:00–12:31 PM	P,HRH	22
04/16/73	427-005, 006	3:27–4:04 PM	P,JDE,RLZ	20
04/16/73	427-010	4:07–4:35 PM	P,JWD	26
04/17/73	898-006	9:47–9:59 AM	P,HRH,RMW	7
04/17/73	898-012	12:35–2:20 PM	P,HRH,JDE,RLZ	95
04/17/73	898-023/899-001, 899-002	3:50–4:35 PM	P,HRH,JDE,RLZ	28
04/17/73	429-003	5:20–7:14 PM	P,WPR,HRH,JDE, MS	65

04/18/73	900-026	3:05–3:23 PM	P,JDE	17
04/19/73	902-001	9:31–10:12 AM	P,HRH,JDE	27
04/19/73	902-002, 003	10:12–11:07 AM	P,HEP	7
04/19/73	902-009	1:03–1:30 PM	P,JDE	20
04/19/73	429-015	3:45–5:00 PM	P,RAM	69
04/19/73	000-000	[4:50]-? PM	JDE,HWK (Telcon/DB)	11
04/19/73	429-018	5:15–5:45 PM	P,JDE,MB	24
04/19/73	038-125,126	9:37–9:53 PM	P,HRH,WHO (Telcon)	15
04/20/73	903-001	8:15–8:39 AM	P,HRH	15
04/20/73	903-006	11:07–11:23 AM	P,HRH	15
04/20/73	903-019	12:16–12:34 PM	P,HRH,JDE	16
04/25/73	430-004	11:06 AM- 1:55 PM	P,HRH,JDE	114
04/25/73	430-022	4:40–5:30 PM [ie. 5:35 PM]	P,HRH,TH	36
04/25/73	038-150	6:57–7:14 PM	P,HRH(Telcon)	17
04/25/73	038-151	7:17–7:19 PM	P,JDE(Telcon)	3
04/25/73	038-154, 155	7:25–7:39 PM	P,JDE,WHO (Telcon)	13
04/25/73	038-156, 157	7:46–7:53 PM	P,HRH,WHO (Telcon)	3
04/26/73	905-008	8:55–10:24 AM	P,HRH	74
04/26/73	431-009	3:59–9:03 PM	P,HRH,JDE,RLZ, SBB,MS	186
06/04/73	442-001 through -069	Unk bet 10:16 AM and 9:54 PM	P,JWD,SBB, AMH,RLZ,MS	170
06/04/73	039-080,081	10:05–10:20 PM	P,HRH,WHO (Telcon)	19
06/04/73	039-083	10:21–10:22 PM	P,HRH (Telcon)	1

INDEX

Boggs, Lindy, 121, 337
Bork, Robert H., 223, 228, 248
Boter, Peter, 241–42
Boxing, 21, 26
Boy Scouts, 11
Bradlee, Benjamin, 172, 329
Brandon, Henry, 274
Brennan, Peter, 275
Brezhnev, Leonid, 130, 175–76, 222, 279, 333, 355, 396
Brock, Bill, 100, 314, 318–19, 423
Brooke, Ed, 208
Brooks, Jack, 233
Brown, Art, 50
Brown, Garry, 129
Brown, George, 359
Brown, Phyllis, 34, 38, 48
    divorce of, 41–42
    Ford's romance with, 26–32, 41–42, 45
Browne, Robert, 184
Bruce, David, 160
Bruno, Hal, 192, 254, 258, 308
Buchanan, Pat, 152, 208–9, 263, 275, 297, 310–12
Buchanan, Shelley, 312
Buchen, Philip, 32–33, 40, 44–45, 323–26, 336–37, 343, 356, 359, 365–66, 385
    Nixon pardon and, 371, 373–75, 377–80, 387–90
Buckley, James, 208, 271–72, 405
Buckley, William, 137
Budget Act (1974), 415
Bull, Steve, 161, 174–75, 327, 332
Burch, Dean, 314–16
Burdick, George, 377–78
Burger, Warren, 258, 277, 280, 282, 337, 347–48, 361
Burns, Arthur, 266, 334, 354, 402
Bush, George, 203, 207–8, 231, 253, 258, 260, 262, 314, 316, 318, 321, 323, 416, 423
Business, Ford's interest in, 134
Busing for school integration, 246
Butterfield, Alexander, 177–78
Butterfield, Keeney and Amberg, 40–41, 49–50
Buzhardt, Fred, 169–70, 178–79, 186, 191–93, 217–18, 220, 251–54, 262, 277, 282–83, 285–87, 291, 293–94, 298, 300–301, 308, 312, 314, 340, 355, 360, 365–66, 376, 390

Byrd, Harry, 169
Byrd, Robert, 173, 197, 225, 236–38, 245–46, 250
Byrnes, John, 82, 324, 343

Cabinet meeting (August 6, 1974), 315–18
Califano, Joseph, 110, 167
Callaghan, James, 400
Callaway, Howard, 406–7
Cambodia, 88, 398–99
Cameron, Juan, 267
Campau, Louis, 7
Cannon, Clarence, 65
Cannon, Howard, 231–36, 248–49
Cannon, Joseph, 84
Cannon, Lou, 263, 329
Carey, Hugh, 404
Carter, Jimmy, 407–9, 416
Casey, William, 135
Cast Down the Laurel (Gingrich), 8
Castro, Fidel, 112, 120
Caulfield, Jack, 143
Cedar Springs (MI), 216–17
Cederberg, Elford, 202
Central Intelligence Agency (CIA), 65, 101, 196, 285, 358–59, 400
    Watergate and, 107, 118–24, 149, 172–73, 217, 252, 276, 282–83, 312, 316
Chambers, Whittaker, 154–55
Chancellor, John, 102, 224
Chandler, Harry, 91–92
Chapin, Dwight, 132
Cheney, Richard, 354, 407–9
Cheshire, Maxine, 365
Chiang Kai-shek, 63
Childhood of Ford, xiv–xv, 4–6, 8–9
Childs, Marquis, 267, 384–85
Child support, 5–6, 15–16, 24–26
China, 64, 70, 88, 117, 121–22, 130, 132, 165–66, 244, 246, 398
Chotiner, Murray, 155
Chou En-lai, 117, 121–22, 244
Chowder and Marching Society, 54, 57, 68, 324–25
Christian Science Monitor, 262–63
Clinton, Bill, 416
Clower, Dewey, 264
Coaching, 20–23, 26, 31, 33
Cochran, Thad, 310
Colby, William, 359

Colson, Charles W., xiii, 125, 185, 251
  Watergate and, 106, 109, 116, 119,
    124, 126, 129, 135–42, 144–48, 150,
    152–53, 169
Commerce Department, U.S., 408
Committee to Reelect the President
    (CRP; Creep), 105, 107–8, 110, 112,
    118, 131, 143
Communism, containment of, 63–64,
    70–72, 87
Conable, Barber, 208
Conger, Ralph, 12, 20, 23
Congress, U.S., 397, 401, 403–4, 415. *See
    also* House of Representatives, U.S.;
    Senate, U.S.
  election of 1972 and, ix–xii
Congressional Record, 230, 237–38
Conklin, Dave, 19
Connally, John, 76, 106, 124–25, 136–37,
    172, 182–83, 207–9, 251, 285, 418
  election of 1976 and, 211
  Ford's offer to, 153–54, 211
  investigation of Agnew and, 191–92,
    197–98
Conyers, John, Jr., 232, 254–55, 257
Cook, Marlow, 250
Cooper, John Sherman, 75, 205
Cotton, Norris, 319–20
Cox, Archibald, 173–75, 179, 186,
    217–25, 385
  firing of, 217–26, 228, 237, 251
Cox, Ed, 327
Cox, Tricia Nixon, 174, 310–11, 344
Crandall, Bradshaw, 29, 48
Cromer, Lord, 267
Cronkite, Walter, xi–xiii
Cuba, 72, 112, 120, 245
Cuban missile crisis (1962), 73, 167
Curtis, Carl, 320
Curtis, Tom, 83

Dailey, Peter, 127
Daniel, Clifton, 298, 385
Danielson, George, 255–56
Dean, John, Watergate and, 115–16, 118,
    125, 127–29, 135, 141–53, 158–59,
    169, 174–77, 217, 252
Defense Department, U.S., 259–60
Defense spending, 61–62, 87, 122
Democrats (Democratic party), 54, 70,
    99, 103, 135, 219–20, 226, 239,
    271–72, 279, 281, 365, 392, 403. *See

    also specific people*
  conventions of, 124
  election of 1948 and, 45, 51–52
  election of 1960 and, 68–69, 72
  election of 1964 and, 79
  election of 1968 and, 95–96
  election of 1972 and, xi–xiii, 104–16,
    124–27, 130–33, 270
  election of 1976 and, 407–9
  Ford's attack on, 100–101
  Marsh and, 268–70
  Nixon pardon and, 387–88
  Watergate and, 128–30
Democrats for Nixon, 125, 270
Dewey, Thomas E., 51–52, 61, 154–55
Diary of Ford, 72, 76
Dickerson, Nancy, 102
Dirksen, Everett McKinley, 85–86, 95,
    98–99
Dobrynin, Anatoly, 267, 355
Dole, Bob, 83, 110, 277, 407
Donovan, Hedley, 361–62
Dougherty, Richard, 132
Douglas, Helen Gahagan, 59, 112–13
Douglas, William O., 100–101, 238, 256
Drinan, Robert, 232
Dulles, Allen, 65, 75, 77
Dulles, John Foster, 245
Dunlop, John, 402
Dunn, Mike, 182, 195–96
Dutch Christian Reformed Church, 49
Dutch Reformed Church, 49

Eagleton, Thomas, 241
Eastland, James, 204, 280, 320, 363
Economy, U.S., 316–17, 334, 354,
    400–404, 409–10, 414
Economic Policy Board (EPB), 402
Education of Ford, 11–16, 18–21, 26
Egypt, 198
Ehrlichman, John, xi, xiii, 99, 113, 137,
    171, 420
  resignation of, 155–59
  Watergate and, 109, 115, 119–20,
    124–26, 135, 138, 140–41, 143, 146,
    148, 152–53, 155–59, 169, 172, 270,
    291, 339
Eisenhower, David, 327, 344
Eisenhower, Dwight D., 60–61, 67–68,
    72, 139, 245, 403
Eisenhower, Julie Nixon, 174, 310–11,
    326, 342, 344

McKee, Jean, 257
McKee, Pat, 285
McMahan, Ron, 176
McNamara, Robert, 76, 167
Madison, James, 83–84
Magruder, Jeb, Watergate and, 105, 108, 124–26, 144–46, 150
Mahon, George, 64, 267
Malek, Fred, 259, 331
Mann, James, 271
Mansfield, Mike, 84, 109, 171, 203–5, 285, 302, 351, 361–62, 382, 389, 401
Mao Tse-tung, 117
Marines, U.S., 397–99
Markley, Annabel, 134
Markley, Rod, 134
Marriage of Ford, 50–51
Marsh, John O., Jr., 89, 105, 268–70, 292, 294–97, 300–302, 306–7, 309, 313, 316, 325–26, 331–32, 336–37, 347, 352–53, 356, 361, 365–66, 383–84, 404
    Nixon pardon and, 373, 375–76, 388–90
Marsh, Nell Wayland, 268
Martin, Joe, 53–54
Martin, Paul, 331
Martinez, Eugenio, 107, 112, 128, 139–40
Matz, Lester, 183–85, 199
Mayaguez, SS, 398–99
Meany, George, 366
Meeds, Lloyd, 227
"Meet the Press" (television program), 263
Meyer, John C., 288
Miami Herald, 106
Michener, Earl, 54–55
Michigan, University of (Ann Arbor), 16, 19–21
Middendorf, William, 331
Middle East, 198, 220–23, 278–79
Milankowski, John, 56
Miller, Herbert J., Jr., 376
Miller, Jack, 378–80
Mills, Wilbur, 103–4
Miltich, Paul, 267
Mink, Patsy, 227
Mitchell, Don, 208
Mitchell, John, xiii, 99, 127, 135, 183, 185, 308
    resignation of, 123
    Watergate and, 105–6, 108, 110–11,
114–15, 118–19, 123, 125–26, 139–40, 142–44, 146–48, 152–53, 169, 254–55, 285–86, 291
Mitchell, Martha, 99, 105, 123
Moakley, Joseph, 219
Modeling, 28–29, 46
Moley, Raymond, 68
Monterey, USS, 34–38
Moore, Jonathan, 324
Moore, Powell, 108
Morizet, Jacques Kosciusko, 267
Morris, Edmund, 349, 415
Morton, Rogers, 135, 181, 275, 324, 356, 423
Muskie, Edmund, 95–96, 103, 113, 145

Name change, 9, 22
National Advisory Committee on Aeronautics, 67
National Aeronautics and Space Administration (NASA), 67
National Security Council (NSC), 167–68, 196, 355, 358–59, 396
NATO (North Atlantic Treaty Organization), 387
Navy, U.S., 33–39, 61
Nelson, John, 22
Neuman, Frank, 42
Neuman, Peg, 42–43, 47
New Republic, The (magazine), 101, 275
Newsweek (magazine), 68, 275, 308, 375
New York Daily News, 404
New York Times, 77, 140, 144, 152–53, 219, 230–31, 274, 303, 311, 384–85, 399
Nimitz, Chester, 91
Nixon, Donald, 111
Nixon, Hannah Milhous, 155, 346
Nixon, Julie. *See* Eisenhower, Julie Nixon
Nixon, Pat, xiii, 57, 59, 97, 103, 263, 335, 342, 344, 422
Nixon, Richard M., 53, 57, 59–60, 67–69, 78, 89–90, 92, 97–99, 102–8, 110–63, 167–83, 185–213, 216–28, 235–37, 239, 251–66, 269–72, 275–336, 417–22
    election of 1960 and, 67–68
    election of 1968 and, 90, 94–96, 181
    election of 1968 and, 123
    election of 1972 and, x, xiv, 105–8, 110–16, 124–32, 182–83
    Ford's friendship with, 56–57

Haig and, 161–63, 168–71, 173–75,
179, 186, 210–11, 220–23, 251–54,
263, 272, 276, 281–87, 309, 311–12,
315, 322–23, 330, 352–53, 359–60,
362, 365–66, 413
impeachment considered for, 254–56,
258, 261–62, 270–72, 275–79, 281,
283–84, 289–95, 297, 299–300,
303–4, 309–11, 314–17
investigation of Agnew and, 185–200
resignation of, 157, 163, 170, 174,
252–53, 261, 271–72, 283–87,
289–95, 297–99, 304–11, 321–23,
325–27, 329–30, 336, 341–47, 363,
368–69, 414, 421–22
Watergate and, xi, xiii, xiv, 105–8,
110–30, 132–63, 169–80, 194–95,
210, 217–28, 237, 247–48, 251–55,
260–66, 270–72, 276–30, 339–41,
355–56, 362–66, 368–92, 412–15, 421
White House Staff fired by, 135
Nixon, Tricia. *See* Cox, Tricia Nixon
North Atlantic Treaty Organization
(NATO), 56, 122, 245
North Korea, 56, 398
North Vietnam, 88, 93, 126, 183, 397
November Group, 127

O'Brien, Larry, 110–13
Office of Management and Budget
(OMB), 259–66
Old Kent Bank, 231
O'Neill, Paul, 266, 350
O'Neill, Thomas P. (Tip), 138, 175,
193–94, 213, 225, 255, 271, 288,
337–38, 361–62, 383, 390
Osborne, John, 101, 275, 370
Oswald, Lee Harvey, 76–77
Otten, Alan, 331

Palmer, Arnold, 102
Pancoast, Arthur C., 5
Pardons, 283, 286–87, 291, 293–97,
299–301, 305–9, 313, 326–27, 334,
339, 355–56, 370–92, 412–14, 420
reaction to, 382–89
Parvin, Alvin, 100
Patman, Wright, 128–30
Pell, Claiborne, 238, 244–45
Pentagon Papers, 144
Personality of Ford, xiv–xv, 17, 393–95,
411–12

ability to develop allegiances, 41
competitiveness, 10, 12, 28
cunning, 29
good nature and optimism, 12–13, 15,
260–61
honesty and forthrightness, xiv,
10–11, 17
leadership, 11, 209
team player, 15
temper, 9–10, 29
Petersen, Henry, 107–8, 115, 147,
150–51, 187–88, 190–91
Peterson, David, 290
Philadelphia Bulletin, 262
Pitts, Milton, 382
Pond, Ducky, 21
Porter, Herbert, 145
Powell, Adam Clayton, 269
Powell, Clara, 74, 88, 337
Powell, Lewis Franklin, Jr., 282
Press conference (August 28, 1974),
369–73
Price, Ray, 157, 170, 173, 208, 289,
297–98, 309, 312, 322, 370
Proxmire, William, 23
Pueblo incident, 398

Quie, Al, 83, 267, 284, 326
Quonset hut, 49–50

Railsback, Tom, 257
Rangel, Charles, 232, 366
Ray, Bob, 267
Ray, Dixie Lee, 266
Rayburn, Sam, 55, 65–67, 204, 254
Reagan, Nancy, 405
Reagan, Ronald, 94, 108, 127, 207–9,
267, 392, 416, 418
election of 1976 and, 405–8
Rebozo, Bebe, 114, 298, 310–11
Rehnquist, William, 282
Reisner, Bob, 108
Republican Coordinating Committee,
253
Republican National Committee (RNC),
203, 253, 260
Republicans (Republican party), 271–75,
392. *See also specific people*
conventions of, 30, 68, 78, 94–95,
126–27
election of 1948 and, 44–45, 48–52
election of 1950 and, 60–61

election of 1952 and, 155
election of 1960 and, 67–69, 76
election of 1962 and, 72–73
election of 1964 and, 72, 78–81
election of 1966 and, 93
election of 1968 and, 90, 94–96
election of 1968 and, 123, 181
election of 1970 and, 102
election of 1972 and, ix–xiv, 124–32, 182–83
election of 1976 and, 136–37, 154, 211, 404–10
Ford's first involvement with, 30–31
Watergate and, 104–16
Reston, James, 77, 303, 305
Rhodes, John, 85, 92, 267, 272, 277, 284, 304–5, 314, 320, 326–30, 361, 382, 385, 423
Richardson, Elliot, 158–59, 173–74, 179, 385
Cox firing and, 218–23
investigation of Agnew and, 185–88, 190, 193–94, 198–99, 202
resignation of, 220–25
Richmond Times-Dispatch, 269
Ricksen, Phyllis Brown, 27. *See* Brown, Phyllis
Ricksen, Robert, 34
Riegle, Donald, 227
Rockefeller, Nelson, 94, 104, 127, 191, 207–9, 275–76, 334, 362, 371, 382, 406–7, 417–18, 423
as Vice President, 367–68
Rodino, Peter, 138, 193–94, 216, 220, 226–27, 231–33, 254–55, 257, 261–62, 276, 327, 389–90
Rogers, William P., 135, 139, 154–55, 157–58, 160, 205, 207–8
Romney, George, 78
Roosevelt, Franklin D., 30, 32, 311
Rose, Chappie, 153
Rospatch, 231
Rossides, Eugene, 243
Rousselot, John, 208
Royster, Vermont C., 323
Ruby, Jack, 76–77
Ruckleshaus, William, 223–25
Rumsfeld, Donald, 73, 75, 81, 83, 208, 269, 343, 353–54, 356–57, 369
Rumsfeld, Joyce, 353–54
Russell, Richard, 75, 77, 204
Russell, Walter, x

Russo, Joe, 15
Ruth, Henry, 224, 364, 379

St. Clair, Billie, 312
St. Clair, James D., 261–62, 276–77, 280, 282–85, 287, 290, 293, 296–98, 300, 307, 312, 314, 355, 365–66, 391
Salvatori, Henry, 207
Sanchez, Manolo, 342
Sanders, Don, 177–78
Sargent, Francis, 274
"Saturday Night Massacre," 224–28
Saxbe, William, 317–18, 321, 360, 365
Schafer, Raymond, 31
Schlesinger, James, 259–60, 268, 275, 398–400
Schultz, George, 111–12
Scott, Hugh, 104–5, 130, 171, 203, 207, 210–11, 244, 262, 302–5, 314, 320, 327–30, 337, 361, 382
Scowcroft, Brent, 266, 331, 355, 396, 408
Scranton, William, 324, 356
SEATO, 246
Segretti, Donald, 132
Seiberling, John, 232
Seidman, William, 354, 402
Senate, U.S., 52, 61, 67, 130, 197, 224–25, 280, 284–85, 290–92, 300, 302, 314–17, 320–21, 366
Ford investigated by, 233–50
Foreign Relations Committee of, 245, 397
Rules Committee of, 231–51
Selection of Vice President and, 197–98, 203–5, 207–8, 215, 217, 229, 231–51
Senate Watergate Committee (Senate Select Committee on Presidential Campaign Activities), 140–42, 150, 152, 172, 175–79, 237, 252, 261–63
Sevareid, Eric, 102, 126, 366, 370
Shaffer, Sam, 87
Shapp (governor), 210
Shepherd, Harry, 65
Shriver, Sargent, 31
Sidey, Hugh, 369
Silbert, Earl, 139
Simon, William, 402
Sirica, John J., 139–42, 148–50, 217–19, 221, 228, 238, 251, 254, 262, 276, 282, 285, 287, 289–90
Skolnik, Barnet, 184